THE *New* BOOK

OF

MODERN
COMPOSERS

THE *New* BOOK
OF
MODERN
COMPOSERS

Edited by DAVID EWEN

THIRD EDITION, REVISED AND ENLARGED

ALFRED · A · KNOPF : *New York*

(1969)

L. C. catalog card number: 61–15040

THIS IS A BORZOI BOOK,
PUBLISHED BY ALFRED A. KNOPF, INC.

Originally entitled *The Book of Modern Composers*.
Published October 5, 1943. Second Edition, revised and enlarged,
April 1950.
Third Edition, revised, enlarged, reset, and printed from new
plates, October 1961.
Second printing, August 1964
Third printing, July 1967
Fourth printing, November 1969

TO MY BROTHER

Frederic

a belated
but nonetheless heartfelt
expression of gratitude for having been
the first to bring me
to good music

EDITOR'S PREFACE

THOUGH *The Book of Modern Composers* was first published in 1943, and was subsequently revised and updated in 1950 and 1956, the present volume is actually a new book. When editor and publisher discussed the problem of bringing out in 1961 a new edition of this survey of twentieth-century composers, we soon decided that merely bringing the material up to date or modestly enlarging the contents would no longer suffice. What was now needed was a complete overhauling. Critical evaluations written twenty years ago or more no longer proved valid in many instances. A new approach to, and a fresh appraisal of, many twentieth-century composers were now required. In addition, if a proper perspective was to be maintained, it was necessary to reconsider the question of which composers should be selected as the musical spokesmen for our century.

In this volume thirty-two composers have been represented. Four were omitted from the 1950 and 1956 editions to make room for several whom the editor considers for one reason or another of greater significance and of greater interest to music lovers: Samuel Barber, Arthur Honegger, Gian Carlo Menotti, Francis Poulenc, and William Schuman. In the case of the other twentieth-century composers discussed in earlier editions, thirteen in the present volume are treated in new critical essays, fifteen in new personal notes, and half a dozen in either new or greatly expanded artistic statements. In addition, Mr. Slonimsky's introduction on modern music and its techniques has been so greatly expanded and so extensively altered that to all intents and purposes it is a new essay. And, needless to say, the appendixes have similarly been subjected to complete revision. All in all, more than three quarters of the present book consists of new material; only the cream of the crop from earlier editions has been retained.

Except for the fact that the composers now appear in alphabetical order, both the purpose of the volume and its general overall design have not been changed. This being the case, the editor would like to quote from the preface of earlier editions in stating his aims: "This volume, in which the leading composers of different schools are represented, is a cross section of the music of the past fifty years. To present such a cross section with greater truth, the author decided to employ once again a method he utilized some years back: [1] he called upon those critics best qualified by their background, scholarship, and temperament to discuss the different phases of modern music. There has been no dearth of books about modern music. If there is an obvious failing even in the best of these books it is that no writer is sufficiently equipped, or sufficiently free of restricting prejudices, to discuss each different trend of modern musical activity with equal authority. The critic best equipped to write about Schoenberg is not likely to be equally tolerant to Rachmaninoff, and vice versa.

" To give the subject the comprehensiveness of treatment it deserves, the author felt that it was necessary to provide the reader with material other than an authoritative analysis of a composer's work by a prominent critic. He felt that considerable illumination might be thrown on a composer's achievements if, preceding each critical essay, there could also appear a statement by the composer himself on his aims as an artist; whenever such a statement was procurable — either directly from the composer himself, or from printed statements and interviews — it was utilized. The author also believes that, since a composer's music is the integrated expression of his background and personality, some information of a personal nature about the composer himself can be of value. Thus, short biographical sections are included, and together with them . . . an informal portrait of the composer."

[1] *From Bach to Stravinsky*, edited by David Ewen, W. W. Norton, 1933.

CONTENTS

BENJAMIN BRITTEN

MARIO CASTELNUOVO-TEDESCO

CARLOS CHÁVEZ

AARON COPLAND

FREDERICK DELIUS

SIR EDWARD ELGAR

MANUEL DE FALLA

GEORGE GERSHWIN

ROY HARRIS

PAUL HINDEMITH

ARTHUR HONEGGER

BOHUSLAV MARTINU

GIAN CARLO MENOTTI

DARIUS MILHAUD

ILDEBRANDO PIZZETTI

FRANCIS POULENC

SERGE PROKOFIEV

SERGEI RACHMANINOFF

MAURICE RAVEL

ARNOLD SCHOENBERG

WILLIAM SCHUMAN

DMITRI SHOSTAKOVICH

JEAN SIBELIUS

RICHARD STRAUSS

IGOR STRAVINSKY

RALPH VAUGHAN WILLIAMS

HEITOR VILLA-LOBOS

SIR WILLIAM WALTON

THE *New* BOOK

OF

MODERN

COMPOSERS

INTRODUCTION)

MODERN MUSIC:
ITS STYLES, ITS TECHIQUES

Nicolas Slonimsky

MODERN MUSIC is not necessarily new, and new music is not necessarily modern. At any given moment of musical history there exist two opposing waves: the wave of innovation and the wave of simplification. When the wave of innovation is higher, contemporary music becomes new music. When the wave of retrogression prevails, music retraces its steps. But even when the older type of music returns to the crest of the wave, it reappears with frills and embellishments unknown to the generation that created it.

Thus, when classicism came back as a reaction to extreme modernism in the twenties of this century, it was not the classicism of Bach and Mozart, but a new classicism of a new era. Similarly, the neoromanticism of the twentieth century shows a sophistication incompatible with the spirit of the old romanticism.

Neoclassicism employs the classical forms of the prelude, sonata, partita, overture, and symphony, but these forms are invested with new harmonic and melodic content. They are more compact, telescoped into a continuous movement; and the long classical codas are collapsed into a single concluding chord. Neoromanticism retains the principal characteristics of program music with sudden changes of mood, but the subjects portrayed are of modern urban life rather than pastoral idyls or poetic autobiography.

Modern religious music is also modified by a usage that may

be described as neoecclesiastic. The religious feeling is present, but the treatment has features that are decidedly secular.

The essence of classical harmony lies in its diatonic structure. Neoclassicism retains this diatonicism, but extends it to include supernumerary tones, leading to integral diatonicism, or pandiatonicism. Neoromanticism adopts the essential chromatic construction of the nineteenth-century romantic school, but enhances the old usage with an atonal treatment of chromatic tones. The new religious music employs the medieval ecclesiastical modes, but these modes are set in new harmonies or in dissonant counterpoint.

In primitive music, in which rhythm and a nontempered melodic line are the only ingredients, the modern school of composition has found material for the creation of new and complex works. Each style is naturally associated with a certain technique, and is adapted to a definite program. Thus French impressionism was greatly stimulated by the exotic art of the Orient, when native musicians and dancers from Indo-China exhibited their art at the Paris Expositions of 1889 and 1900.

French impressionism thrives on instrumental color. This emphasis on color explains why so little chamber music has been written by impressionist composers, particularly for combinations of homogeneous instruments, such as string quartets. In his only String Quartet, Debussy introduced elements of color by extending and subtilizing the range of dynamics. He intentionally limited the resources of classical development by adopting monothematism, treating the single theme in a variety of rhythmical and instrumental forms.

A curious sidelight of programmatic content in impressionist music is the parodied treatment by Erik Satie. In a piece entitled *Morning Twilight at Noon*, he mocks impressionistic subtlety by brutal literalism, and to the words "the shadow of millennial trees marks 9:17 o'clock," he writes an accompaniment in which the hours are struck in the lowest bass register and the minutes in seventeen quick notes in the treble. When Debussy asked Satie, after a performance of *La Mer*, which of the three movements he liked most, Satie replied: "The first, *From Dawn to Noon*, about a quarter past eleven."

The technique adopted by French impressionism is in conformity with its evocative, exotic subject matter: short expressive themes harmonized by parallel block chords, extreme rarefication of

musical substance, static pedal notes, powerful dynamic accumulations punctuated by sudden outbursts of instrumental color. A
feature in this technique is the integral adoption of the whole-tone
scale, and its concomitant harmony of augmented triads. The
whole-tone scale, of course, is not a new invention. Mozart used
it in a violin cadenza in his *Ein musikalischer Spass*, to make fun
of village musicians incapable of playing their scales correctly.
Schubert employed it in all seriousness in the Adagio of his unfinished C minor Piano Sonata, composed in September, 1828.
Glinka used the whole-tone scale to characterize the malevolent
magician Tchernomor in the opera *Russlan and Ludmilla*. Rossini
wrote a song in 1864 based entirely on the scale in whole tones,
which he described as " Chinese scale."

Liszt was very much interested in the whole-tone scale, and applied it in the score of his *Dante Symphony*. In a letter he suggested
that this scale could be used with great effect as a descending bass
progression with major triads moving in the three upper voices in
contrary motion to the bass. It is interesting that Puccini used precisely this formula in the second act of *Tosca*.

Apparently the whole-tone scale has impressed many composers in many lands as being intrinsically ominous. Herod is characterized in whole tones by Richard Strauss in *Salome*. Rimsky-
Korsakov applies the harmonies of augmented triads and the
melodic steps of the whole-tone scale in the second act of his opera
Le Coq d'or, to describe the desolation of military defeat. In two
Soviet operas — *For Red Petrograd*, by Gladkovsky and Prussak
(1925), and *Battleship Potemkin*, by Tchishko (1937) — the
whole-tone scale serves as the leading motive of the enemy, the
White Guard. In the *Anti-Fascist Symphony*, by Boris Mokrousov,
the Fascists march in whole-tone steps. The blood transfusion from
robots to men in the ballet *Mekhano*, by the Argentinian composer
Juan José Castro, is performed in a whole-tone operation. The English composer Edward Maryon (1867–1954) applied whole-tone
scales in his opera *Werewolf* to depict the wolfish side of the werewolf. Vladimir Rebikov (1866–1920), who claimed priority over
Debussy in the introduction of the whole-tone scale, based an entire piece, *Les Démons s'amusent*, on it. For a century the whole-
tone scale portrayed demons, Fascists, Nazis, and other evil forces.
In film music it has been used to depict Martians and mad scientists.

Only Debussy knew how to use a whole-tone scale as a subtle artistic resource. *Voiles*, the second of his 12 *Préludes* (Book I), is based principally on the whole-tone scale, which is used to suggest the delicate fluttering of boat sails in the wind. The middle section of *Voiles* is built on the pentatonic scale, the most ancient of historically known progressions, common to such unrelated cultures as the American Indian, the Mongolian, and the Celtic. In impressionist music, the pentatonic scale serves to produce an exotic or an archaic effect.

An effective scale used by many composers of different schools is the scale of alternating tones and semitones. Like the whole-tone scale, it is neutral in its structure and so has no tonality. Liszt, Tchaikovsky, and particularly Rimsky-Korsakov made ample use of it. In fact, Russian theorists call it Rimsky-Korsakov's scale. This did not prevent biographers of the Dutch composer Willem Pijper from calling it Pijper's scale. Other composers who believed that they invented it were Felix Petyrek of Vienna (1892–1951) and Ludomir Rogowski (1881–1954) of Poland and Yugoslavia (who called it the Persian scale). Tchaikovsky used the progression of descending whole tones in the bass to characterize the apparition of the old countess in his opera *The Queen of Spades*.

Few German composers were tempted by exotic scales or impressionistic colors. Sigfrid Karg-Elert (he added the second name to offset the unpleasant associations of his real name, Karg, which means miserly) experimented with some impressionistic clichés. The majority of composers in Germany early in this century carried on the Wagnerian tradition, aggrandized to the point of inflation by Richard Strauss. The subject matter of his symphonic poems ranges from deep philosophical concepts, as in *Also sprach Zarathustra*, to personal history, as in his *Domestic Symphony*. Whereas in impressionist music thematic fragments are whims of the moment, appearing out of the colored mist and vanishing into nothingness, in the Straussian musical cosmos every theme is invested with weighty significance, and is metamorphosed rhythmically and melodically in many shapes, using the time-honored devices of augmentation, diminution, and inversion. Elaborate melody guides were published in Germany for the benefit of Strauss enthusiasts so that these thematic transformations could be readily identified. The procedure is, of course, that of the Wagnerian leading motives, but in the works of Strauss they form a much more intricate contrapuntal lattice.

An interesting sidelight on Richard Strauss is provided by the following episode: an obscure Austrian-born composer named Heinrich Noren composed an orchestral theme with variations, *Kaleidoscope*, in which the last variation, inscribed " to a celebrated contemporary," was based on the themes of the hero and his antagonists from *Ein Heldenleben*, Strauss' self-glorifying symphonic poem. When Noren's piece was performed in Dresden on July 1, 1907, Strauss' publishers filed suit for infringement of copyright, but the court ruled against them on the ground that these themes were not recognizable as melodies, but constituted in fact "a conscious negation of melody."

The Wagnerian tide, which had reached its peak in the works of Strauss, subsided when it became obvious that further harmonic inflation and multithematic complication without a radical departure from the tonal principles of nineteenth-century music would make the musical texture opaque and impenetrable. The Wagner-Strauss harmony, with its suspended ninth chords, continual chromatic modulations and six-four chords in a series of interminably protracted cadences, was divested of its glamour. The return to classical simplicity was an instinctive and logical reaction; the clarion call " Back to Bach " was a convenient motto. In Germany, a powerful neoclassical movement arose, supported by Hans Pfitzner (1869–1949), an unsuccessful rival of Richard Strauss, and particularly by Ferruccio Busoni (1866–1924), an enlightened musician of progressive views, who feared that the basic ideals of old music were in danger.

The neoclassical wave was greatly augmented by the stylistic change made by the arbiter of modern musical ideas, Igor Stravinsky. Abandoning his colorful Russian manner, Stravinsky imposed upon himself a regimen of harmonic austerity. Significant of this esthetic departure is Stravinsky's reduction of the luscious score *The Firebird* to a smaller orchestration, in the course of which the gorgeous bird of Russian folklore was deplumed and stripped of its colors. But the statistics of orchestral performances show the stubborn preference among conductors for the original luxuriant firebird.

Stravinsky turned to old composers even for his thematic material; he wrote a suite, *Pulcinella,* on themes of Pergolesi. (As luck would have it, most of the *Pulcinella* materials proved to be not by Pergolesi but by various obscure eighteenth-century composers.) He drew upon Tchaikovsky's melodies for his ballet *Le Baiser de la fée.* To explain his method of artful modernization of the works of the past, Stravinsky declared: " Like a detective, I penetrate the music of this or that composer, and re-create it in my own way."

French neoclassicism differed as much from German neoclassicism as Couperin did from Bach. In old and new Germany, classical forms were receptacles of contrapuntal and fugal ideas; in France, the spirit of elegance and the general preference for harmonic considerations over polyphony led to a more mundane art. Debussy poked gentle fun at the Doctor Gradus ad Parnassum; Ravel evoked a nostalgic scene in his *Pavane pour une infante défunte,* and paid homage to the spirit of classical France in his suite *Le Tombeau de Couperin.*

The revival of classicism had its practical side. The era of huge orchestras and large operatic troupes seemed irretrievably gone at the end of World War I, and composers adopted an economical method of composition in order to secure performances. Music had to serve a purpose or perish. A type of music that became known as *Gebrauchsmusik* arose in Germany, under the influence of Paul Hindemith and others; the various specific forms of this type of composition were *Hausmusik,* or music in the home, and *Spielmusik,* or play music. The ideal that inspired this movement was *Die neue Sachlichkeit,* the new practicality. Soon all Europe was practicing the art of musical economy.

For its technical idiom neoclassicism adopted a type of enriched diatonic writing that this writer chose to call pandiatonicism, a term that eventually found its way into most musical dictionaries. Pandiatonicism establishes functional equality among the seven degrees of the diatonic scale, while the harmonic function of the principal triads remains strong. The concluding tonic chord may be encrusted with diatonic barnacles, but in the pandiatonic technique it has the function of a perfect consonance. The added sixth was a common ingredient of an enriched major triad in American popular music long before the theorists found an explanation for it. In an entertaining booklet, *History, Development and Art of Playing the Boogie-Woogie Style,* by Sharon Pease, we find a fairly accurate definition: " Harmonically this chord will often constitute an in-version of a seventh chord. However, in modern usage it is commonly referred to as a major chord with the added sixth."

Not only the added sixth, but also the added major seventh and major ninth are treated as consonances in popular music as well as in serious works by modern composers. Every note in the diatonic scale can be used in an enriched consonance, except the fourth. This exception is explained by the fact that the fourth of the scale cannot be found in an overtone series, no matter how high we ascend among harmonics, whereas the major ninth, the major seventh, and the major sixth, when placed several octaves above the fundamental tone, constitute respectively the ninth, the fifteenth, and the twenty-seventh overtones. It is important to note that such enriched triads are employable only in major keys, with the major third from the fundamental tone at the foundation.

Melodically, the technique of pandiatonicism allows for a free distribution of the seven diatonic degrees in different registers, forming the leaping melody characteristic of neoclassical composition. Anticipations of such pandiatonic melodies can be found in classical music. An example is a tetrachord descending by ninths in the piano part toward the end of the third movement of Brahms' Third Violin Sonata.

A graphic illustration of modern pandiatonic writing is provided by the *Valse diatonique* from the piano suite 11 *Pezzi infantili*, by Alfredo Casella. The piece is written for white keys only. Tonic subdominant and dominant harmonies are frequently superimposed, resulting in pandiatonic clashes.

When a single tonality, even in its pandiatonic enlargement, became inadequate for modern musical expression, the obvious recourse was to combine different tonalities by direct superimposition, a technique that became known as polytonality. Actually, modern usage limits itself to bitonality — that is, combining not more than two different keys.

The first clear example of bitonal writing is found in Stravinsky's *Petrouchka*, where the C major and F major triads are used in rapid alternation, and also simultaneously, forming a bitonal combination. Darius Milhaud consistently uses the same type of bitonality in his ballet *Le Bœuf sur le toit*.

Much less frequent is the bitonality of two keys separated by a semitone; an example is found in Stravinsky's *Le Sacre du prin-*

temps, where a passage in C major is superimposed on C-sharp major. It is interesting to observe that Stravinsky writes C major as B-sharp major, a scale with twelve sharps, thus implying that no real bitonality exists and that the passage was written in a consistent chromatic scale with a tonal center on C-sharp.

Imitation of natural sounds is a popular device in programmatic music by modern composers. Olivier Messiaen includes in the score of his formidable *Turangalîla Symphonie* a whole array of native Asian instruments to convey the atmosphere of Indian lore that inspired this work. In his *Réveil des oiseaux* for piano and orchestra, the themes purport to represent bird cries as literally as in Beethoven's *Pastoral Symphony,* but Messiaen, voluntarily or instinctively, alters the natural ornithological melodic scheme in the direction of linear dissonances and with the emphasis on atonal intervals, particularly the major seventh and the tritone.

In his symphonic poem *Pines of Rome,* Ottorino Respighi introduced, for the first time in music history, a gramophone recording of a nightingale's song.

Wind and thunder are produced by special instruments in the *Alpine Symphony,* by Richard Strauss. When its performance was announced, a lady who signed her name Aurora Donnerwetter sent a letter to the Berlin musical weekly *Signale für die musikalische Welt,* inquiring whether she should bring an umbrella for protection from the elements. No apprehension was expressed about the effect of the wind machine in the *Antarctic Symphony,* by Vaughan Williams, when it was performed in England in 1953.

The wind machine is a mild contraption compared with the apparatus required in *Auto Accident,* by the American composer Harold G. Davidson (1893–1959), described in the score as follows: " Two glass plates, each resting on a washbowl or crock, to be shattered with a hammer, and the bowls containing the broken glass to be emptied on a hard surface, table, or floor."

When industrial realism was in vogue during the early years of Soviet Russia, Shostakovich included a factory whistle among the instruments of his Second Symphony. Alexander Mossolov introduced a steel sheet, to be shaken longitudinally, in his ballet *Iron Foundry.* Yuli Meitus made use, in his *Dnieprostroy Symphony,* of three tin cans filled with dried peas and tied to a stick. When shaken, the assembly produces a sound not unlike a muffled motor.

The apotheosis of machine music was reached with the production of George Antheil's *Ballet mécanique,* scored for sixteen player pianos, anvils, electric bells, automobile horn, and several airplane propellers, then the very symbol of modernity. Its performance in Carnegie Hall, New York, in 1927, marked an era. A music critic excused himself from rendering an informed opinion on Antheil's work, claiming that the propellers blew away the notes he had made during the performance and that he was too distracted to recall his impressions.

Along with sirens and airplane propellers, strange-sounding and strange-looking instruments of exotic origin, principally from South America, began to make their appearance in the modern orchestra. In the final bars of *Le Sacre du printemps* there is a fleeting solo of the *güiro,* a serrated gourd scraped with a wooden stick. The Cuban *maraca* is included in the score of Prokofiev's cantata *Alexander Nevsky.* Since its subject deals with valorous deeds of a medieval Russian prince, the Cuban instrument is not used for local color, but simply as the purveyor of a new sound.

The subatomic world is the subject of Edgar Varèse's extraordinary *Ionisation,* scored for forty-one instruments of percussion, friction, and sibilation, two fire sirens being in the latter category. The work is beautifully proportioned, with effective antiphonal employment of metallic sonorities (gongs, cymbals, anvils) against drums, wood blocks, scrapers (such as the *güiro*) and shakers (*maracas*). The form is that of a sonata, with clearly outlined sections corresponding to exposition, development, and recapitulation, and concluding with a sonorous coda. Rapid asymmetrical rhythms illustrate the formation of electrified atoms, or ions, while the boom of gongs and the sound of the sirens suggest the liberation of large amounts of radioactive energy. Varèse wrote *Ionisation* in 1931, long before radioactivity became a matter of public concern.

If European composers used the *maraca* and the *güiro* solely for incidental sound effect, Latin-American composers treat their native instruments as important parts of the orchestra. Amadeo Roldán, the Cuban mulatto composer, arrays six sections of percussion instruments in his Afro-Cuban ballet *La Rebambaramba.* Villa-Lobos includes Brazilian percussion instruments in most of his symphonic works. Carlos Chávez has the ancient Mexican instruments *teponaxtle, huehuetl,* and *omichicahuaxtli* in his *Xochipili-Macuilxochitl* (the title refers to the Aztec god of music).

Another resource of new sonorities is the unconventional treatment of standard instruments. Henry Cowell, practicing on an upright piano as a boy, hit upon the idea of playing chords with the fists and forearms. He called the resulting combinations "tone clusters." Cowell had an ancient predecessor, Bernard Viguerie, the composer of *Battle of Marengo,* written to celebrate Napoleon's victory. In it, the sound of the cannon is imitated "by stretching the two hands flat on the three lower octaves, the hands to be kept on the keys until the vibrations are nearly extinct."

John Cage, who studied with Cowell, denatured the piano by placing bolts, screws, coins, and other small objects on the strings. He calls it the "prepared piano."

The growing complexity of rhythmic patterns undermined the stability of metrical structure. The celebrated passage in the finale of Schumann's Piano Concerto that registers in the listener's ear as a stately waltz, while the conductor's beat indicates rapid syncopated time, demonstrates that a uniform metrical time signature had already become inadequate more than a century ago. Modern composers solved the problem by changing time signatures to suit the rhythmic phrase.

In the *Danse sacrale* from *Le Sacre du printemps,* the metrical changes in a rapid tempo reach a point where few conductors can maintain a steady rhythmic pulse. Even more rhythmically involved is the music of Charles Ives. In the second movement of his orchestral suite *Three Places in New England* (composed earlier than *Le Sacre du printemps*), there is an episode representing two village bands playing a march tune simultaneously, but at different speeds, one band going 33⅓ per cent faster than the other. The conductor is here confronted with the necessity of beating three bars of the slower tempo with one hand against four bars of the faster tempo with the other.

In the original manuscript of *Three Places in New England,* Ives used a uniform time signature, $\frac{4}{4}$, with the noncoincident main beats indicated by accents. For the published edition of the score, this writer proposed a polymetric notation, which was accepted by Ives.

Arthur Honegger's celebrated musical locomotive, *Pacific 231*, proceeds within a uniform time signature, $\frac{4}{4}$. The acceleration of the train is effected by the gradual diminution of note values in each bar; the deceleration is produced by augmenting them, until *Pacific 231* comes to a final stop.

The romantic spirit of twentieth-century music found its most eloquent representative in Gustav Mahler, whose symphonies possess a grandeur of design and a depth of expression comparable to the greatest revelations of his predecessors in the Vienna school. Mahler's art is profoundly subjective, not in the autobiographically explicit manner of Richard Strauss, but in a mystical sense of self-doubt, expressed in tortured chromatics, and of pantheistic self-assertion in hymnlike proclamations and unsophisticated folklike melorhythms.

Although Mahler had no contact with impressionism, he was, for different reasons, attracted by Oriental cultures as much as French impressionists were. His great song-symphony *Das Lied von der Erde* is set to texts from Chinese poetry, and the music is built monothematically on a motto of three descending notes of the pentatonic scale, appearing in different rhythmic shapes as if to demonstrate the mystical idea of unity in variety. In his harmonic idiom, Mahler retained basic tonality; only in his last work, the Tenth Symphony, which he left unfinished, did he reach out for atonally organized dissonant harmonies. His state of mind during the composition of this music is reflected in his marginal remarks in the manuscript, culminating in these words: "Madness seizes me . . ."

Akin to Mahler's mystical esthetics was the passionate art of his Russian contemporary, Alexander Scriabin. In quest of transcendental harmonies to express his yearnings, he invented a "mystic chord" consisting of six notes: C, F-sharp, B-flat, E, A, and D. He regarded it as a concord derived from higher overtones of the harmonic series, and made it the foundation of his last symphonic work, *Prometheus: The Poem of Fire*. In his desire to achieve a mystical union of the human senses, Scriabin included in the orchestration a "color keyboard" that was to produce modulating hues in the concert hall to express the changing moods of the music. However, attempts to build such a color keyboard failed because of technical limitations. Scriabin's dream could easily be realized with present-day lighting techniques, but his mystical ideas and even his music itself no longer arouse enthusiasm.

Proceeding from Scriabin's ideas, another Russian composer, Nicolas Obouhov (1892–1954), created a work of enormous dimensions, *Le Livre de vie*, for voices and orchestra. In his mystical ardor, he went so far as to use his own blood for expression marks in the score.

From mystical romanticism a new esthetics emerged, poignantly subjective and inwardly directed. It became known as expressionism. As the word itself implies, it is the converse of impressionism. Whereas impressionist composers observe the passing scene and record their sensations in allusively rich tones, expressionists find their source of inspiration through introspection and exteriorize their inner states in a musical language that is devoid of either literal or allusive imagery. Whereas neoromanticism may be autobiographically revealing, expressionism communicates no more than the hidden content of a psychologically significant dream.

The selection of subject matter in expressionist music is characteristic. Suffering and frustration are the main themes, and the literary sources are often products of nineteenth-century romanticism. The greatest expressionist opera, *Wozzeck*, by Alban Berg, is based on a century-old drama by George Büchner. The finest instrumental creation of expressionist music is Schoenberg's *Pierrot lunaire*, a cycle of " thrice seven poems " by the symbolist writer Albert Giraud, translated into German from the original French. In it Schoenberg makes use of *Sprechstimme*, tonally inflected speech notated on the music staff. Schoenberg was not the first to use *Sprechstimme*. As early as 1897, Engelbert Humperdinck included *Sprechnoten*, that is, spoken notes, in his incidental music to the play *Königskinder*.

Expressionism exteriorizes the subconscious. In order to achieve the subtilization essential for this psychomusical art, extreme delicacy and precision of handling musical materials were necessary. The entire range of tonal and dynamic resources had to be examined and exploited, sounds without definite pitch, the spoken vocal line, unusual instrumental effects. It was therefore only natural that expressionism adopted the technique of integral chromaticism. In this technique, the chromatic scale is broken up and rearranged at angular melodic intervals, with special prominence accorded to the tritone, the *Diabolus in musica* of medieval scholastic science.

Thus arose the language of atonality. Major and minor triads ceased to be the alpha and omega of musical thought. The key signature, the emblem of tonal authority, lost its guiding role in the fluid modulations of chromaticized harmonies.

Long before, there were signs of conflict between the key signature and the ostensible tonality. In Beethoven's Piano Sonata in A major, op. 101, the tonic triad does not appear until the seventy-seventh bar. Brahms, in his *Intermezzo* No. 4 in B-flat major, op. 76, studiously avoids the tonic chord until the penultimate bar. In the works of the Wagnerian school, the key signature became an impediment, for it was almost instantly nullified by a string of accidentals. The key signature was given a *coup de grâce* by Arnold Schoenberg when he organized the inchoate language of atonality into a logical system.

This new organization Schoenberg defined as a " method of composition with twelve tones related only to one another." Essentially it is a twelve-tone version of monothematism, in which the chromatic scale is the matrix of thematic selection, offering 479,001,600 possible " rows " of twelve different notes each. The basic theme, or tone row, or tone series, appears in the forms of melodic inversion, retrograde, and inverted retrograde. These four fundamental shapes of the tone row, including the original one, can be transposed to any chromatic degree, so that the total number of thematic forms is forty-eight. Furthermore, any note in the twelve-tone row can be used in any other register. Descending chromatics can be represented by ascending major ninths; there is in fact an inherent tendency in the melodic formation of twelve-tone music toward large angular intervals.

The tone row is a horizontal progression, but it can also be applied vertically, in counterpoint and harmony. In Schoenberg's *Klavierstück*, op. 33a, the purest example of his twelve-tone method, the tone row is first presented in the form of three dissonant chords of four notes each.

The emancipation of dissonance and the liberation from tonality were Schoenberg's principal aims. In his music and his teaching he actually discriminated against melodic progressions implying tonality, and shunned triadic constructions in harmony, particularly the major triad and its inversions.

Certain corollaries of the twelve-tone technique should be noted: tonality having been abandoned, and key signatures rendered meaningless, the notation is simplified. Total enharmonism is adopted; accidentals are used interchangeably as flats or sharps; E-sharp and C-flat, double sharps and double flats, lose their *raison d'être* and are replaced by their enharmonic equivalents.

It must also be observed that time signatures are retained in atonal and twelve-tone music and that metrical changes are not frequent; rhythmic designs are free, but not necessarily asymmetric; syncopation is rare. It is remarkable that Schoenberg and his disciples adhere to classical forms, even in such details as a repeat of the first section in a dance form or in a sonata.

A hundred years ago John Stuart Mill wrote that he was " seriously tormented by the thought of the exhaustibility of musical combinations. The octave consists only of five tones and two semitones, which can be put together in only a limited number of ways." He need not have worried. The many millions of different tone rows will provide enough thematic material for several hundred years to come.

As with many innovations and discoveries, the method of composing with twelve tones had its numerous forerunners. The underlying esthetic principle is nonrepetition of thematic notes, with a concomitant shift of tonal centers in a highly chromaticized melody.

The opening theme of Liszt's *Faust Symphony* consists of four chromatically adjacent augmented triads in a melodic sequence aggregating to twelve different notes. In the section entitled " Of Science " in the tone poem *Also sprach Zarathustra*, Richard Strauss has an explicit twelve-tone subject. (We must begin with the second note of the theme to account for all twelve notes.) Ardent twelve-tone enthusiasts have found Schoenbergian passages even in Mozart's G minor Symphony, where a progression of ten different notes occurs in chromatically adjacent harmonies of diminished-seventh chords. Needless to say, these examples are nothing more than accidental occurrences inherent in chromatic writing.

A more amusing instance of unintentional twelve-tone writing is a *Hymn to Futurism*, composed in 1917 by old César Cui. His futuristic melody consists of two broken augmented triads at the distance of a tritone, followed by six notes of a descending whole-tone scale, arranged in such a way that all twelve different notes are accounted for. The accompaniment is formed of arpeggios of three chromatically adjacent diminished-seventh chords, also adding up to twelve different notes.

Of real historical importance is the remarkable anticipation of the twelve-tone method in *Tone Road No. 3*, by Charles Ives, written in 1915. Here we find a theme of twelve different notes, which is melodically inverted with complete precision of intervallic equality.

An early theoretical discussion touching on the problems of twelve-tone composition is found in an article by Domenico Alaleona entitled " L'Armonia modernissima," published in 1911 in the *Rivista musicale italiana*. Alaleona introduced the term *dodecafonia* to describe the division of the octave into twelve parts without reference to tonality. The result is, of course, a simple chromatic scale; but the emphasis on the complete independence of each chromatic note from any real or imagined tonal center was a new idea.

The term *dodecafonia* lay dormant for many years, until it reappeared in Italian terminology as *musica dodecafonica*, in French as *musique dodécaphonique*, and in English as *dodecaphony*.

Twelve became a magic number in new music. The Austrian musician Fritz Klein was one of the earliest pioneers of integral dodecaphony. In 1921 he published an orchestral piece entitled *Die Maschine* and captioned " an extonal self-satire." He used the nom de plume Heautontimorumenus, which is the title of a play by Menander adapted by Terence, and means Self-Torturer. Among dodecaphonic ingredients of *Die Maschine* are, besides a twelve-tone theme, a twelve-stroke rhythm, a twelve-interval subject (including the octave and thus containing thirteen notes in all, one of them in duplicate), the pyramid chord, consisting of twelve different intervals from a semitone to an octave, and " the largest chord in music," the *Mutterakkord*, composed of twelve different notes and eleven different intervals, plus an octave as a supernumerary interval.

Fritz Klein's *Mutterakkord* is not, however, the ultimate in twelve-tone architecture, for it has been topped by a *Grossmutterak-kord*, the brain child of the present writer, incorporated as the climactic last chord in his *Thesaurus of Scales and Melodic Patterns*. It contains twelve different notes, and eleven symmetrically invertible intervals, of which the middle interval, a tritone, is the inversion of itself. The total span of the *Grossmutterakkord* is a tritone plus five octaves. It is interesting to note how often the tritone, the *Diabolus in musica* of the medieval theorists, turns up in modern music, as if to suggest that the devil of yore is the god of today. The *Grossmutterakkord* forms the thematic foundation of the "space opera" *Aniara*, by the Swedish composer Karl-Birger Blomdahl, dealing with the nuclear destruction of the planet earth and the emigration to Mars of a handful of survivors.

One of the pioneers of twelve-tone music was Josef Matthias Hauer (1883–1959) of Vienna. As early as 1926 he brought out a treatise specifically named *Zwölftontechnik*. He subsequently challenged Schoenberg's priority, and even had a rubber stamp made that read: "Josef Matthias Hauer, the spiritual protagonist of twelve-tone music, and despite many bad imitators still the only one who knows and understands it."

Schoenberg disposed of such claims of priority in a letter to the present writer dated January 2, 1940: "Although I saw Mr. Klein's twelve-tone composition about 1919, 1920, or 1921, I am not an imitator of him. I wrote a melody for a Scherzo, composed of twelve tones, in 1915, as Webern knows. It was planned as a movement of a symphony, the finale of which was part of what later became *Jakobsleiter*. In my piano pieces, op. 23, I used a technique which I called 'composing with the tones of the basic motif,' and which is certainly a first step toward composing with twelve tones. Besides, you will find that in the first edition of my *Harmonielehre* (1911), there is a description of the new harmonies and their application, which has probably influenced all these men who now want to become my models. At least I know that Hauer used it almost literally in the first edition of his book, and eliminated it later. It states the reasons that led me to this new technique in these words: repetition of a tone produces the danger of lending it the importance of a *Grundton*, which ought to be avoided. I have not much interest in originality, and that is why I never objected to misstatements."

Although dissonant harmony is basic to Schoenberg's ideas, it

is entirely possible to form an integrally tonal dodecaphonic series
containing four mutually exclusive triads, major and minor. Apparently several composers have arrived independently at the solution of this problem of splitting the chromatic scale into four
tonalities. Luigi Dallapiccola made use of four mutually exclusive
triads in his opera *Il Prigioniero*, written in 1944. Rolf Liebermann
of Switzerland used a similar series in his First Symphony. For some
mysterious reason, two of the four mutually exclusive triads must
always be major, and two minor. And there is only one way of
stringing them out in thirds so as to form a chord of the minor
twenty-third. The formula of its construction is simple: take a
tritone down from C (or from any other note); divide this tritone
into three whole tones; build major triads on the upper two notes,
and minor triads on the lower two notes of the whole-tone scale;
finally, spread out the resulting triads in an ascending progression.

Curiously enough, four mutually exclusive triads appear in the
concluding section of Debussy's *Prélude à l'après-midi d'un faune*,
serving as harmonies for a descending chromatic passage. Of course,
there are no dodecaphonic implications in this case.

In order to check the intuitive conclusion that twelve different
notes could be arranged in four mutually exclusive triads only in
pairs of major and minor, the present writer secured the assistance
of Zamir Bavel at the Computing Center of Southern Illinois
University. He obligingly fed the data into a computer, and after
considerable labor the machine ejected some fifty sheets filled with
figures in binary notation, confirming the idea. The computer also
proved that there can be only one chord of linked major and minor
triads, and arranged in thirds, the chord of the minor twenty-third.

The twelve-tone technique permits the incorporation of any
chromatic theme in which no notes are repeated. The B-A-C-H
theme is woven into a twelve-tone string trio by Hanns Eisler, a
disciple of Schoenberg. Alban Berg cleverly inserts the opening
four notes of *Tristan und Isolde* in his *Lyric Suite*. The same
four notes are used, for a vastly different purpose, in the middle
section of *Golliwog's Cakewalk* in Debussy's piano suite, *Children's
Corner*. (The original title is in English; Debussy wrote the suite
for his young daughter, who had an English governess.) The story
is told that Harold Bauer, the pianist, had an argument with
Debussy about Wagner. Bauer was worshipful, Debussy disdainful.
"You cannot laugh at Wagner," said Bauer. "Wait, I will make you

laugh at him," replied Debussy. Some time later he handed to
Bauer the manuscript of *Golliwog's Cakewalk*. Bauer played it
with delight, and only then Debussy told him the secret of his
joke. After the appearance of the Tristan theme (which is marked
"Avec une grande émotion"), there is an antiphonal scherzando,
suggesting a gentle giggle. Debussy had made Bauer laugh at
Wagner.

The rapidity with which dodecaphonic ideas spread throughout
the world was remarkable. Several distinct schools of twelve-tone
composition soon asserted themselves. Schoenberg's principal disciples, Alban Berg and Anton von Webern, themselves became
masters and attracted their own disciples. Alban Berg cultivated
lyric expression, and was less firmly opposed to tonality than was
Schoenberg. The tone row of his Violin Concerto is built on linked
major and minor triads ending in a progression of three whole tones.
Anton von Webern wrote music of pointillistic acuity and thematic
miniaturization. Tone colors and dynamics acquire special significance. Sometimes no instrument is allowed to play more than two
notes of the tone row in succession. This extreme subtilization of
expressive means was the beginning of a new development, serial
composition, in which different intervals, durations of thematic
notes, degrees of intensity, instrumental timbres, become members
of a multidimensional series. The serial principle was anticipated by
Fritz Klein in *Die Maschine,* in a twelve-stroke rhythm and a
twelve-interval theme.

Serial music thus appears to be a generic category of which
dodecaphony is a species. In fact, the Principle of Twelve is not
absolute in serial composition, for there are obviously more than
twelve instrumental timbres and durations. On the other hand,
parameters may be selected that have only a few possible numerical
values. Richard Hoffmann, a pupil of Schoenberg and his last
amanuensis, uses a single reiterated note in five different dynamics,
from fortissimo to pianissimo, as a fugue subject in his *Fantasy and
Fugue*, written in Schoenberg's memory.

Though the order of the notes in a dodecaphonic tone row is
essential, serial composers using a subject of fewer than twelve
notes, or a number of different tone colors, durations, dynamics,
and so on, permutate the members of the series. In the twelve-tone
method, the retrograde movement is the only permutation of the

row, whereas in serial music any grouping of given ingredients is valid.

This higher generalization of dodecaphony did not arrive without previous adumbrations. Schoenberg, Berg, and Webern freely repeated the thematic notes within a tone row, as long as this repetition was but a rhythmic nonthematic procedure. Small fragments of the row also appeared in detached groups, much like thematic fragments of a Bach fugue, which appear in the middle sections before the final return of the subject. Schoenberg's disciples elaborated these usages, so that an individual style is not hampered by the rigidity of the method. The twelve-tone school now numbers among its followers musicians of different origins and stylistic preferences. Among them are such well-known figures as Ernst Krenek and Luigi Dallapiccola. Virtually all European composers born after 1900 have experimented with dodecaphonic or serial techniques, at least as a thematic device. William Walton uses a twelve-tone subject in the finale of his Second Symphony. Benjamin Britten interpolates twelve-tone passages to enhance the chilling atmosphere in his opera *The Turn of the Screw*.

In America, the dodecaphonic fascination has affected composers whose technical procedures are as a rule tonal and nonchromatic. Walter Piston includes a group of twelve different notes as a transitional motive in his ballet *The Incredible Flutist*. Roger Sessions, after many dodecaphonic adumbrations, adopted a fairly orthodox twelve-tone technique in his String Quintet. Aaron Copland uses a series of twelve different notes as a basic theme of his Piano Quartet.

A remarkable testimony to the potency of the dodecaphonic concept is the fact that many established composers of the old generation adopted its basic principles and incorporated subjects consisting of twelve different tones, albeit without integral working out. Béla Bartók has an unambiguous twelve-tone melody, atonal in its intervallic scheme, in the solo part of his Violin Concerto composed in 1938. In his last String Quartets, Ernest Bloch has subjects consisting of twelve different notes, and makes particularly effective use of them in canonic imitation and fugal passages. Frank Martin applies the method of twelve-tone composition in a peculiarly romantic manner, in which the members of the tone row outline an explicit harmonic idea compatible with generic

tonality. Ernst Toch, who for a long time resisted the lure of dodecaphony, eventually wrote a String Quartet specifically designated
as a twelve-tone composition.

The most spectacular conversion to serialism was that of Igor
Stravinsky, whose art, intimately connected with modality and
tonal polyphony, seemed impervious to such penetration. Although
he lived in the same locality as Schoenberg in Los Angeles, the
two great representatives of modern music never met. It was only
after Schoenberg's death that Stravinsky became profoundly interested in the potentialities of twelve-tone music as a theoretical
and practical discipline. His point of departure was the precise
style of Anton von Webern, with serial considerations governing the
selection of tonal, intervallic, and rhythmic units. In his ballet
Agon, written according to the serial principles, Stravinsky specifies the number of dancers — twelve.

Boris Blacher, the China-born German composer of Estonian
parentage, organizes meters and rhythms in an arithmetical series,
such as a simple succession of cardinal numbers, 2, 3, 4, 5, etc., or
a summation series, in which each subsequent number is the sum of
the two preceding numbers, as in the series 2, 3, 5, 8, etc. An
arithmetical row can then be used in retrograde, or permutated in
some other way. An arbitrary unit of note value is selected, say an
eighth note, and the process of actual composition may then commence. Rhythmic figures within assigned meters may also be taken
from the main series. The melody itself may be entirely tonal, and
the resulting impression of a work written according to the principle
of metrical serialization is neoclassical.

Karlheinz Stockhausen of Germany has made an interesting
attempt to connect the tonal series with the metrorhythmic series.
Pitch is determined by the frequency of vibration. The duration of
each individual vibration becomes shorter as the pitch rises. It is
therefore possible to connect mathematically a tone row, expressed
by numbers of frequencies, with a series of durations. In its simplest
form, such a tone rhythm would have long notes in the low register
and short notes in the high register. Curiously enough, this proportion is statistically observed in all classical music. Pedal points are
usually placed in the deep register, and rapid ornamental passages
in the high register. Of course, the direct ratio may be inverted, in
which case notes of long duration will appear in the high register,
and rapid passages be played in the bass. The storm scene from

Beethoven's *Pastoral Symphony* is an example of such an inversion with sustained notes in the high wind instruments and quick figurations in the strings.

The increased role of mathematical formulas in composition imparts a neo-Pythagorean air to mid-twentieth-century music. More and more, numerical combinations are used as indices for thematic intervals, always counted in semitones. Thus the Austrian composer Johann Nepomuk David builds intervallic progressions in his symphonic fantasy *Magische Quadrate* on numbers found in medieval magic squares, in which the sums of numerals in horizontal, vertical, and diagonal directions are equal.

The French composer Pierre Boulez unifies dodecaphonic thematics with rhythm by making duration a function of the position of each note in a twelve-tone row. When the basic row appears in transposition or in retrograde, the rhythmic configuration changes accordingly.

Even more labyrinthine in its integral serialism is the music of Jean Barraqué, in which the various elements of musical composition are closely interrelated as derivatives of a basic mathematical function that governs each work. His *Séquence* for soprano and a group of instruments, in which percussion predominates, created an extraordinary stir in the innermost circle of the French serialists when it was first performed in Paris on March 10, 1956, and the name of Barraqué was added to the living pantheon of ultra-modernism.

The most thoroughgoing attempt to connect the numerical parameters of melodic, temporal, and intervallic elements is made by Ernst Krenek in his *Sestina* for voice and instruments. The German text by the composer follows an intricate form of medieval Provençal poem composed of six-line stanzas (hence the title *Sestina*), and from the varying positions of end words in the succeeding stanzas the composer devises a most ingenious, complex, and yet rigidly logical formula that furnishes the parameters of duration, linear part writing, vertical distribution, and even tempo, all derived from the intervals in the basic tone row.

Parallel to these neo-Pythagorean developments there have been attempts made to analyze old music in terms of serialism, so that simple tonal themes of Bach, Beethoven, and Tchaikovsky are reinterpreted as serial groups, and variations as melodic and rhythmic permutations. But then " numbers " once meant musical periods or groups of notes, as in Drayton's line " In Musick's Numbers my Voice rose and fell."

Intervallic serialism is as old as Bach, who employed different intervals to symbolize joy and anguish, death and resurrection. This esthetic principle finds its modern application in the works of some composers who do not consciously follow a serial idea. Thus Roy Harris tabulates ecclesiastical modes according to the magnitude of the initial intervals of each mode; the larger the intervals, the happier the mood of the mode. The Lydian mode is therefore the most optimistic, and the Locrian mode the darkest.

An esthetic procedure related to intervallic serialism is applied in a uniquely interesting manner by Elliott Carter in his Second String Quartet. Here, each instrument employs a given set of characteristic intervals, used either melodically or in double-stops. The first violin emphasizes minor thirds, perfect fifths, and major ninths; the second violin projects major thirds, minor sixths, and major sevenths; the viola specializes in the augmented fourth and the minor seventh; the cello part is built principally on perfect fourths and major sixths.

Many composers have for centuries made use of letters of the alphabet as a thematic source. Schumann based his *Carnaval* on the theme of four notes spelling the name of the town of Asch in the German musical alphabet, as a sentimental tribute to a lady friend who had dwelt in that town.

Mario Castelnuovo-Tedesco has extended this ancient application into a complete alphabetical system, by assigning the letters of the alphabet to the chromatic scale beginning with A. In this alphabetical system he has written a number of " greeting cards " to friends, taking as a theme their first and last names. In the English alphabet the A above the initial note becomes M, and Z falls on the B-flat two octaves and a minor second above the initial note.

Serial music in all its diversity still limits itself to the tempered scale of twelve chromatic divisions. In quest of more subtle means of expression, a group of Central European composers experimented with a subdivision of the semitone into smaller fractions. Alois Hába of Prague elaborated a theory of such subliminal intervals, developed a special notation for them, composed a number of works for quarter tones, including an opera, and for many years led a seminar on the subject. In Russia, Rimsky-Korsakov's grandson Georgy worked on the practical applications of quarter-tone music. Hans Barth of New York and Ivan Vyshnegradsky of Paris gave concerts on specially constructed quarter-tone pianos.

Ernest Bloch used quarter tones as expressive appoggiaturas in the string parts of his First Piano Quintet. The present writer made an arrangement for strings of an ancient Greek melody from incidental music to Euripides' *Orestes* written in the Greek enharmonic scale. The quarter tones are produced in this arrangement by raising the E string of the violin and the A strings of the viola and cello a quarter tone and letting the rest of the strings play the diatonic degrees of the scale. Occasional quarter-tone progressions suggesting the enharmonic scale were used by Georges Enesco in his opera *Oedipus*.

The most original exponent of microtonal composition is Julián Carrillo of Mexico. His experiments in quarter-tone music go as far back as 1895. He describes his system as *Sonido 13*, that is, Sound 13, lying beyond the twelve chromatic tones. An interesting idea as to the extent of his investigations is given in the introduction to his *El Infinito musical*: " If there is anyone who would like to publish this work, the first chapter will have to present 1,193,232 chords for which it will be necessary to have 14,315 volumes of five hundred pages each." Carrillo's most ambitious achievement is the reduction of Beethoven's symphonies and Bach's forty-eight preludes and fugues to quarter tones, whereby the entire tonal range is cut in half, and the octave is shrunk to a tritone.

With a plethora of mathematical parameters occupying a composer's brain, can there be room for inspiration? In this respect it is pertinent to quote from Schoenberg's letter to this writer commenting on the *Thesaurus of Scales and Melodic Patterns*: " I looked through your whole book, and was very interested to find that you have in all probability organized every possible succession of tones. This is an admirable feat of mental gymnastics. But as a composer I must believe in inspiration rather than in mechanics."

Ernst Krenek has made a challenging observation, that inspiration itself is the result of a number of impulses and impressions statistically accumulated without a conscious participation of the mind, and thus the outcome of an automatic process. He points out that the German word for inspiration, *Einfall,* literally means a falling in — that is, a chance event. This is the most ingenious apologia for the newest of the musical techniques of composition, the "aleatory" method, from the Latin word *alea,* chance.

There are precedents of aleatory applications to musical composition in the classical past. Mozart amused himself as a boy by writing out a dance 176 measures long, with alternative versions for each. The choice is determined by throwing dice. Of course, the substitute measures are set in the same harmonies as the original, and so Mozart's little entertainment is nothing more than a piece in which each measure has a variant.

Modern aleatory music is much grimmer. Nothing is written out in advance. Chance governs the pitch, the duration, the dynamics, and the instrumental timbre. An arbitrary number system is selected to establish a correspondence with these parameters, and the composer goes to work, throwing dice, looking up page numbers at random in a book, or picking out playing cards from a deck.

John Cage, the most uncompromising exponent of the aleatory method, prefers to collect his random numbers from *I-Ching,* an ancient Chinese book of divination, and on his word of honor he never falsifies the data obtained from it.

John Cage's method is even more radical in one of his *Imaginary Landscapes,* scored for twelve radio receivers, which he conducted himself. Twenty-four performers, two for each radio, shift the dials and regulate the degree of loudness. The resulting mixture of musical fragments, soap operas, commercial announcements, and static is of course entirely accidental, and therefore no two performances can be identical. Silences inevitably enter when one of the radios is dialed to a wave length on which nothing is broadcast. Indeed, silences are regarded by Cage as a legitimate means of musical expression — even total silences. In his piano composition entitled *4′33″,* the pianist sits motionless at his instrument for four minutes and thirty-three seconds, and at the expiration of this period of time closes the piano to mark the end. However, in this exploration of zero sonority, Cage was anticipated by Byron Arnold, the author of *Five Incapacitated Preludes for Orchestra.* In a prelude subtitled "Deaf Man," the orchestra goes through the motions of playing, without producing a single sound.

Scheduled noises are not excluded from aleatory scores. When

John Cage sent an invitation to this writer to attend the world première of his *Water Music*, he added: " Unlike Handel's, it really splashes." Indeed, two containers, one empty, and one filled with water, were brought out on the stage, and at a given moment determined by a stop watch, the water was poured from the full container into the empty one with audible effect.

The notation of aleatory compositions usually takes the form of diagrams, in which the basic data are supplied. For instance, a section of John Cage's Piano Concerto is notated by a group of dots, with five intersecting lines drawn at various angles. These lines represent the parameters of pitch, duration, instrumental timbre, and dynamic gradations. The perpendiculars dropped from the dots to the lines give clues to the performer as to actual notes to be played. Deciphering such a score is a skull-breaking enterprise, and great freedom is left to the performer in determining the various parameters. David Tudor, the pianist who has given most of the world premières of works by Cage and other aleatory composers, has become practically a cocomposer.

Morton Feldman, a disciple of John Cage, has evolved his own distinct technique of aleatory writing. His notation usually indicates at least the approximate register (high, medium, low) of each instrumental or vocal part. In his *Intersection for Magnetic Tape*, with reference to the flashing of a green traffic light at a street intersection, he indicates the duration of the entire piece and the number of notes in it, leaving other details to the performer's discretion.

Sylvano Bussotti devised a genre of notation similar to an abstract painting, with a wavy line curving around a music staff. Some notes are actually written out in normal notation, but they serve merely as isolated signposts in an otherwise indefinite program of action.

A method of physical permutation is applied by John Cage when he instructs the pianist to drop the pages of a manuscript on the floor and then pick them up at random and play the piece in this accidental arrangement.

Karlheinz Stockhausen uses the method of visual accidence in one of his works titled *Zeitmasse*, the score of which represents a number of unconnected fragments. The performer is to play any fragment that happens to catch his eye, then any other fragment, and so forth. When he happens to pick out the same fragment twice, the performance is concluded, a logical extension of the principle of cyclic form.

A desire to produce music by scientific means with the aid of mechanical instruments inflamed the imagination of many musicians, but it was only in the twentieth century that mechanically produced music became an important factor. The palm of priority must be given to the Italian futurist Luigi Russolo, the proponent of what he called the *Arte dei rumori*, the Art of Noises, produced by an ensemble of rather primitive noisemaking instruments and described, according to the type of sonority, as crashers, splashers, roarers, snorters, sibilators, and ululators. His noise concerts in Italy and France before World War I were invariably lively affairs, often erupting into riots. The futurists boasted that at one of these concerts eleven members of the audience had to be hospitalized as a result of a fight with the performers.

Joseph Schillinger, who hoped to make a science out of music, described the symphony orchestra as " a heterogeneous aggregation of antiquated tools," and as early as 1918 published an article on " electrification of music." Before his death in 1943, he wrote: " Though there is no universal use of electronic music yet, it is progressing very rapidly. Most of my dream has already come true."

The first electronic instrument was unveiled at the Physico-Technical Institute in Leningrad on August 5, 1920, by the twenty-four-year-old inventor Leon Theremin. He called it Aetherophone, because the sound was generated by the movement of the hand " through the aether." The instrument was later renamed Thereminovox. Theremin's invention was followed by a number of similar generators, the most successful of which was Ondes Musicales constructed by the French radio operator Maurice Martenot. It was equipped with a keyboard capable of producing definite sounds in the tempered scale. At the request of the Hindu poet Rabindranath Tagore, he modified this keyboard so as to produce an approximation of the nontempered intervals peculiar to the Hindu *râgas*.

A great impetus to new sonorous techniques was given by the development of magnetic tape shortly after the end of World War II. Pierre Schaeffer, an engineer of the Radiodiffusion Française, became fascinated by the possibilities of recording on tape various sonorous materials, street noises, snatches of conversations, radio announcements, etc., and then combining them, accelerating or decelerating the recorded fragments, or running them backward. This process he called *Musique concrète*, music based on random sounds of the immediate environment in a sort of concrete counterpoint. For music historians Schaeffer obligingly noted the precise date of his discovery, April 15, 1948.

Musique concrète provides the composer with materials that can be assembled or disassembled and edited by cutting and splicing the tape at will. For utilitarian purposes, such as incidental music in the theater or for the sound track of films, the magnetic tape recorder is ideal. Still, the technique of *Musique concrète* is but a passive recording of undifferentiated and heterogeneous sounds and noises originated without the composer's direct volition. A great step forward was made when it became possible to impress magnetic impulses directly on the tape. For the first time in history, composers had at their disposal an infinitely flexible and versatile medium, capable of producing any given frequency, and encompassing all tonal registers in an uninterrupted continuum. Microtonal music could be at last reproduced with perfect accuracy. Ernst Krenek was the first to avail himself of this opportunity, in his electronic piece in a scale of thirteen notes to an octave.

By combining several sinusoidal sounds devoid of overtones, the new electronic " synthesizers " can imitate faithfully any existing instrumental timbre, and also manufacture hybrid sonorities, an oboe-bassoon, a violin-flute, or a tuba-cello.

With the aid of such electronic music machines, sounds can be metamorphosed beyond recognition. A birdcall can be transformed into a peal of thunder, the noise of a jet plane into a celestial chant; the ugliest rasping sound can be purified into an entrancing melody.

In 1959 the Polish composer Wlodzimierz Kotonski composed an *Étude concrète pour un seul coup de cymbale*. He recorded the sound of a cymbal on tapes, transposed it electronically to eleven different pitches of the chromatic scale, thus forming a twelve-tone row, and assigned to them different durations and dynamic intensities. The ingredients thus obtained were then arranged according to the serial method of composition, and the resulting piece was duly performed at the Fourth International Festival of Contemporary Music in Warsaw.

In 1961 a program of "musical essays in time, space and

sound" was presented in New York City, featuring an overture entitled *Cough Music*, the raw materials of which were originally
gathered at a modern dance recital. The coughs were recorded on
tape, electronically disfigured, accelerated, altered as to pitch, and
otherwise transmogrified, resulting in a fairly effective and rhythmically varied modernistic composition.

Electronic effects instantly became a great boon to composers
of programmatic music. Malevolent forces, which used to be illustrated by such rudimentary devices as whole-tone scales and augmented triads, have now acquired electronic voices. Musical space-
ships can be guided by the tremulous beam of the Thereminovox.
A mad scientist's brain can be attuned to an electronic vibrato, and
the harmony of the spheres can be reproduced with scientific
precision on sinusoidal waves.

Modern electronic techniques introduced a new dimension into
musical performance — stereophony, spatial direction and distribution of instrumental and vocal groups. Trumpets offstage, ensembles
seated on balconies, separately placed antiphonal choirs, all this is
part of the history of musical performance. Modern composers
required even more complex spatial arrangements. In the marginal
notes to his unfinished oratorio *Die Jakobsleiter*, Schoenberg suggests that the sounds of different orchestral groups and choruses on
and off the stage should be channeled through acoustical tubes to
different parts of the concert hall. Returning to this work many
years later, Schoenberg remarks that widely distributed micro-
phones could solve the spatial acoustical problem to his satisfaction.

Charles Ives divides the orchestra into several parts in his
score *The Unanswered Question*; the strings offstage symbolize
the distant listeners who try vainly to answer the perennial question
of existence propounded by the trumpet on the stage.

A further elaboration of the spatial parameter in musical performance is provided in Gunther Schuller's score *Spectra*, in which
the orchestra is divided into seven groups of players by analogy
with the seven colors of the spectrum. The composer gives specific
instructions as to their seating arrangement, which in his view becomes an integral part of the compositional design.

Henry Brant has experimented with the division of the orchestra into several autonomous groups led by different conductors.

. . .

For composers of electronic music the spatial factor assumes a new importance. Serial techniques are extended into Music in Space. Vectorialism, the directional arrangement of stereophonic elements, may soon be added to other serial methods of composi-,tion. It is now possible to speak of a northwest sound or a southeast sound, as members of a vectorial stereophonic series. The principle of nonrepetition of vectorial factors is established by analogy with the dodecaphonic method. The number twelve still preserves its magical significance in electronic music; the loudspeakers in a modern electronic studio in Cologne are constructed in the shape of a dodecahedron.

Resources of composition are further enriched by the use of electronic computing machines. The composer specifies a desired style, classical or modern, the proportion of dissonances and consonances in harmony and counterpoint, the degree of symmetry or asymmetry of rhythmic patterns, and the type of instrumentation. These data are processed by a computer, which prints sheets of paper with figures indicating pitch, duration, etc., which are then translated into musical notation. Lejaren A. Hiller, Jr., and Leonard M. Isaacson of the University of Illinois were the first to produce a piece of computer music, *Illiac Suite for String Quartet* (Illiac stands for Illinois Automatic Computer), performed in Urbana, Illinois, on August 9, 1956.

At the opposite pole to intellectual music inspired by inner mental states and organized according to subjective but logical processes lies an art that derives its materials from folk music.

Since all folk songs, at least in the Western world, are tonally centered, atonal composers reject them as source material. However, polytonal arrangements of folk songs are entirely practical, for the melody remains unaltered, and the dissonant accompaniment in a different key imparts an attractive modernistic flavor. Another method of modernizing folk songs is to distort the melodic elements in such a way that the general intervallic design is still clearly recognizable.

Folklorism is the foundation of all great national schools of composition. Literal quotation from folk songs as an identification tag for a geographical locale is a useful device for programmatic music. Sometimes composers quote original tunes by obscure musicians, under the mistaken impression that they are folk songs. In his symphonic poem *Aus Italien*, Richard Strauss quoted the Neapolitan tune " Funiculi-Funicula," not realizing that it was a popular song by Luigi Denza. In his *Carnaval*, Schumann used the vulgar strains of the *Grossvatertanz* to characterize the Philistines, in the belief that it was an anonymous old dance tune. Actually it was written by Schumann's older contemporary, Karl Gottlieb Hering.

In *Petrouchka*, Stravinsky used a number of popular Russian songs and also a French tune, " Jambe en bois," which he heard played on a hurdy-gurdy in southern France. It turned out to be a published song by a M. Spencer, who promptly asserted his rights. The publishers were compelled to divert a certain portion of Stravinsky's royalties to him.

" Estrellita " is listed in many collections as a Latin-American folk song; but it was written by the Mexican composer Manuel Ponce. At the earnest urging of this writer, Ponce wrote variations on " Estrellita " in the slow movement of his Violin Concerto, in order to reassert his authorship.

The Viennese song " Ach, du lieber Augustin " makes an unexpected appearance in Schoenberg's String Quartet in F Sharp Minor, which was still couched in the tonal framework. The authorship of this song could never be ascertained.

Deliberate quotations from easily identifiable nonfolkloric sources are often resorted to for special purposes. Charles Ives quotes the initial bars of Beethoven's Fifth Symphony in the third movement of his *Concord Sonata* to suggest the atmosphere in the home of the Alcotts, because it was their favorite symphony. In his *Concerto for Orchestra*, Béla Bartók includes a transparent caricature of Shostakovich's *Leningrad Symphony*, which he constantly heard on the radio.

When Villa-Lobos was asked, " What is folklore? " he replied, " I am folklore." By this he meant that the melodies he composed were in every sense as authentically Brazilian as the folk songs of his people. To him, Brazil was present in all music. In his extraordinary instrumental and vocal suites, *Bachianas brasileiras*, his intention was to provide an artistic demonstration that Bach and Brazil were of a kindred spirit, not only because their initial letters were identical, but also because of similarity of musical resources. He even heard Bachian pedal points in the jungle, exemplified by the recurrent high B-flat emitted by the tropical bird arapunga, which appears in one of the *Bachianas*.

The music of Carlos Chávez is imbued with the true spirit of "Mexicanismo" and yet rarely contains explicit quotations from Mexican songs. On the other hand, Aaron Copland makes use of actual Mexican tunes in his tone poem *El Salón México*, subjecting them to melorhythmic metamorphoses that are stimulating to the modern ear without impairing the authenticity of the thematic material.

A remarkable realization of the modern potentialities of eastern European folk music is achieved by Béla Bartók, by emphasizing the natural angularity of intervallic structure and the asymmetry of rhythm. Bartók's collection of piano pieces, *Mikrokosmos* (so called because it is ostensibly intended for small children), includes a great number of Hungarian and Slavic melodies in a variety of settings, from two-part counterpoint in bleak fourths and fifths to strident frictional harmonies. Particularly striking is the vivid piece of programmatic music *From the Diary of a Fly*, a sort of psychoanalytical study of the daily frustrations in the life of a domestic fly, beginning with a buzz in minor seconds and going through a series of polyrhythmic gyrations before subsiding in the end.

Jean Sibelius, whose symphonic music expresses with ultimate fidelity the national consciousness of the Finnish people, accomplished his great national task not by literal quotations, but by transmuting the essential elements of Finnish folk songs into a noble personal language. His only excursion into modernity was a slightly dissonant episode in the Fourth Symphony.

Vaughan Williams, the greatest master of modern English music, professed his admiration for Sibelius, and his symphonic works possess a rhapsodic grandeur that distinguishes the music of the Finnish master. There are also present the characteristic modalities of Russian music, and chordal progressions peculiar to French impressionism. Through all this concourse of crisscrossing influences, Vaughan Williams asserts his own powerful style, unmistakably English in its essence.

Frederick Delius, who lived in England, Germany, and France, absorbed the influences of English folklorism, German romanticism, and French impressionism. These elements are not entirely assimilated in his music, but despite this imperfect fusion Delius succeeded in retaining an important niche among twentieth-century composers.

Grandeur and urbane humor — a dualism characteristic of many English composers of the modern era beginning with Elgar's *Enigma Variations* — are the animating forces of the music of William Walton, whose early *Façade* for narrator and instruments reflects the influence of the sophisticated Parisian grotesque but whose later works are almost Handelian in their stateliness.

Manuel de Falla was the strongest nationalist composer of modern Spain, but his technical applications owe much to the French modernists; in his modal writing there is considerable influence of the Russian school. The point here is that all these elements, easily identifiable out of context, are incorporated by Manuel de Falla with such skillful stylistic absorption that they cease to be alien infusions, and become integral parts of his music.

The works of the four most eminent representatives of Italian modernism, Ottorino Respighi, Alfredo Casella, Gian Francesco Malipiero, and Ildebrando Pizzetti, are all to a certain extent redolent of French impressionism, particularly in the early parts of their careers. Yet all these composers express strong characteristics of a national Italian style; neoarchaic procedures enhance this derivation.

Luigi Dallapiccola is the strongest representative of dodecaphony in modern Italian music, and he combines it with the technical procedures of the Italian baroque. In his vocal works he even applies notational symbolism so that the visual pattern of the notes themselves suggests certain words in the text; thus a reference to a mirror is represented by a mirror canon.

Dodecaphonic devices are also adopted by Goffredo Petrassi, but his style retains the melorhythmic configurations typical of the Italian tradition, and his forms adhere to neoclassicism.

Contrapuntal thinking is the directional force in modern German music as it was in the times of the baroque masters. The strongest representative of this trend is Paul Hindemith. His music has a quality of universality; he regards composition as a craft even more than an art. It is interesting to note that he wrote chamber works for every instrument including the heckelphone. He revives the formal practices of the old contrapuntists in a modern manner. The Prelude and the Postlude in his piano suite *Ludus tonalis* are

reciprocal retrograde inversions; the Prelude can be played by
turning the Postlude upside down, and the Postlude can be similarly
performed from the Prelude. Only accidentals are free, so that when
a page is turned upside down, the sharps and flats should be made
retroactive.

Fusion of styles and techniques is effected in the music of
national composers of many lands. There are strong neoclassical
and impressionistic elements in the works of Bohuslav Martinu, but
his music is nonetheless deeply penetrated with the spirit of Czech
nationalism.

Karol Szymanowski has been called " the modern Chopin," but
his Polonism is a phenomenon of complex consistency; there is a
strong undercurrent of neobaroque counterpoint, with a veneer of
impressionistic colors. Characteristic Polish melorhythms are
clearly in evidence, but are subordinated to the grand lines of his
general style, subjective and somewhat sombre, with a marked affinity to Mahler.

The national Hungarian style of Zoltán Kodály is still rooted
in the nineteenth-century tradition; his harmonies are opulent,
and dissonant combinations frequent, but there is no open break
with the old precepts. In this he differs from Béla Bartók, who made
use of national materials to create a completely new type of folkloric music.

Nationalistic tendencies in modern French music had to assert
themselves in an uncongenial atmosphere of impressionism, with its
wavering tonality and rhythmic vagueness incompatible with the
clarity of French song structure. In various ways, French composers
of the twentieth century combine the spirit of French folkloric elements with the modernistic idioms. Vincent d'Indy was but tan-
gentially concerned with impressionist esthetics, and his works reflect, directly or indirectly, the traditional modes of French folk
songs. The nationalism of Albert Roussel was less explicit; after a
period of impressionist composition, he turned toward neoclassicism
and in this sense became a continuator of the national French
school. The case of Florent Schmitt is interesting because of his
early exploration of dissonant harmonies and polymetric structures
far in advance of his colleagues, then still swimming in a Debussyan sea of subtly colored tones. The strength and complexity of

Florent Schmitt's contrapuntal writing, exceptional among French composers, relates him to German modernism.

It must be recalled that both Debussy and Ravel, the creators of a style that has acquired the indelible label of impressionism, also wrote music in classical forms. Their brilliant and expressive stylizations became a model for neoclassical French music, tinged to a greater or a lesser degree with impressionistic colors. The music of Jacques Ibert exemplifies a blend of impressionistic and neo-classical techniques in a most effective manner. Olivier Messiaen makes use of impressionistic devices only as an adornment of his basically austere music tending toward archaic mystical forms. Jean Françaix cultivates a hedonistic genre of composition as a sort of revival of the old type of French entertainment music. Other French composers of the modern school, abandoning for the nonce their complex techniques, have written instrumental suites and vocal works in this unassuming hedonistic manner, among them Darius Milhaud.

So many composers from eastern Europe, Spain, and South America made Paris their home that a singular phenomenon of expatriate national music with a French accent developed. Such is the music of Alexandre Tansman, whose stylizations of Polish melodies preserve the balance between artless folklore and French sophistication. The Spanish composers Manuel Infante and Federico Mompou, who spent most of their lives in Paris, produced music that was both authentically Spanish and typically Parisian. Joaquín Turina was also exposed to modern French influences during his sojourn in Paris, but his music represents a more direct and more literal treatment of Spanish melorhythms.

Georges Enesco, the most prominent Rumanian composer of modern times, spent most of his life in Paris, and his *Rumanian Rhapsodies* and other works of native inspiration reflect a Gallic elegance of manner. However, he never ventured into outspoken modernity.

Sophisticated folklorism is the natural successor to the patriotically and racially inspired national schools of the nineteenth century. Modern harmonic treatment, with its frequent recessions into the archaic past, is actually more compatible with the spirit of primitive music than are the smooth four-part arrangements in the German academic manner. The primitivism of *Le Sacre du prin-*

temps and of Prokofiev's *Scythian Suite* conveys the musical image of pagan Russia much more powerfully than the conventional stylizations.

In national schools of composition on the threshold of entering the world of modern music, there are signs of emancipation from German academic usages. The German-educated Icelandic composer Jón Leifs retains some Germanic traits in his *Icelandic Overture*, but its melorhythmic design is peculiar to the dissonant diaphony of ancient Icelandic chants. Yoritsune Matsudaira subjects the pentatonic melodies of Japanese court dances to a treatment in the serial technique, in dissonant counterpoint. The Chinese-American composer Chou Wen-chung builds musical images of pointillistic acuity in an economical but colorful style in his tone poems such as *And the Fallen Petals* and *All in the Spring Wind*, drawing on ancient ceremonial chants for his thematic materials.

In every epoch there are survivors of the previous schools of composition who are willing to experiment with new ideas. Leoš Janáček lived long enough to be affected by novel harmonic and coloristic resources. Similar stylistic innovations distinguish the last works of the neoromantic Danish composer Carl Nielsen.

Alexander Gretchaninov, who died in New York at the age of ninety-one, and whose music originated in the deepest recesses of old Russia, was attracted by impressionistic harmonies and made use of them in some of his piano pieces. Reinhold Glière wrote music saturated with the spirit of Russian nationalism, but he was not averse to idioms from the vocabulary of modern French music.

Glazunov lived to witness the universal spread of modern music, which he regarded as an ugly intrusion. Rachmaninoff showed some interest in modern techniques, but his own style never swerved from the once-chosen path of dramatic lyricism.

Another figure from the Russian past, Nikolai Medtner, the originator of a new romantically inspired form, the wordless fairy tale for piano solo, remained hostile to modernism to the end of his life.

Nikolai Miaskovsky, of Medtner's generation, holds the unique distinction of having written twenty-seven symphonies, a number that would be only average for an eighteenth-century composer but is probably a record in modern times. Miaskovsky experienced the influence of impressionism, but his style rests upon romantic traditions. His attempts to write folkloric music were unsuccessful. Rachmaninoff, Glazunov, and Medtner left Russia after the Revolution and died abroad. Miaskovsky remained in Russia.

The fate of Nikolai Rosslavetz, the first Russian composer to write atonal music, was tragic, for he could not find a point of contact with Soviet reality. He died in obscurity during World War II.

Stravinsky left Russia before World War I, never to return. Prokofiev lived abroad for a number of years after the Revolution, but eventually went back. In Russia he immediately faced the problem of cleansing his cosmopolitan style of modernistic impurities and of reasserting his national consciousness. His music of the Soviet period lost some of its former aggressive power, but never lost its gaiety, as demonstrated by his musical fairy tale, *Peter and the Wolf*, written for the Children's Theater in Moscow.

The conflict between cosmopolitan modernism and folkloristic nationalism in Soviet music is dramatically illustrated by the creative evolution of Dmitri Shostakovich. His early music reveals considerable preoccupation with modernistic devices; his greatest talent seemed to lie in satire and burlesque. These elements never disappeared from his music, but they became incidental to the lyric and dramatic expression. The turning point in his career was the opera *Lady Macbeth of Mtsensk*, which was officially denounced as an unworthy product of cosmopolitan formalism and decadent naturalism. To counteract these undesirable qualities, Soviet spokesmen established the concept of Socialist Realism, described in the charter of the Union of Soviet Composers as follows: " Soviet composers must pay attention principally to the victorious progressive foundations of contemporary reality, to all that is heroic, bright, and beautiful, all that distinguishes the spiritual world of Soviet man. This must be incarnated in musical images full of beauty and life-asserting power. Socialist Realism demands intransigent struggle against antinational modernistic tendencies characteristic of the decay and corruption of contemporary bourgeois art, against obeisance and servility to modern bourgeois culture."

The diversity of individual styles among Soviet composers is nonetheless considerable. Dmitri Kabalevsky writes music that bears the imprint of modernity within the framework of classically established forms. Tikhon Khrennikov composes in an effective neoromantic manner. A similar romantic spirit animates the works of Nikolai Rakov. Lev Knipper succeeded so well in bringing together symphonic and popular idioms that the choral ending of one of his symphonies was adopted as a Red Army song.

Aram Khatchaturian writes symphonies, concertos, and ballets rooted in Armenian melos, with a harmonic accouterment that is decidedly of the twentieth century. The melorhythms of Azerbaijan are effectively used in the works of Fikret Amirov. Otar Taktakishvili of Georgia cultivates an expressive melorhythmic style peculiar to Caucasian folk songs with their quasi-Oriental inflections.

In contrast to the emphatic musical nationalism of Europe, American composers are not concerned with the calculated formulation of a national style. Charles Ives, whose works are profoundly American, was a great individualist who worked apart from the main current of American music. Roy Harris, who eloquently professes his faith in the musical destiny of America, assiduously cultivates classical forms.

The Americanism of Aaron Copland is far from literal, even in works of such specific designation as *Lincoln Portrait, Appalachian Spring,* and *Billy the Kid.* The contrapuntal and harmonic organization of American melorhythmic materials is distinctly recognizable as part of Copland's personal idiom, so that these works are not stylistically divergent from the rest of his music composed according to purely structural considerations.

William Schuman employs American tunes in his works of explicit programmatic content, and has even written an opera on the subject of baseball; but his main stylistic strength lies in the expressive application of highly advanced harmonic and contrapuntal techniques.

Howard Hanson proclaims himself an ardent believer in romanticism as a natural human attitude toward music, but his romanticism is of a general Nordic type without specific references to American song materials.

The music of Samuel Barber is marked by a nostalgic lyricism and passionate rhapsodism of great subjective power. Barber is certainly not a folkloric composer, and yet there is a clear American imprint in his intensely concentrated style.

David Diamond writes music of extreme emotional tension, revealed in a quasi-atonal melodic style and spasmodic rhythms; but he can also compose pieces in an almost serene classical mood.

A practical type of American modernism is demonstrated in the works of Paul Creston, with a strong tonal foundation and asymmetric rhythmic pulse. Norman Dello Joio leans toward classical forms in his instrumental compositions, but knows how to impart a sense of passion in his choral and dramatic music.

Randall Thompson excels in vocal composition, often to texts from American sources, set in universally acceptable harmonies. Douglas Moore is quite direct in his approach to folkloric subjects; his sophisticated stylizations, with ironic overtones, enhance the lyrical and dramatic qualities of his materials.

Walter Piston has declared that music written in America is American music and should not be equated with a narrowly limited folkloric composition; his symphonies and chamber works contain syncopated passages in an expressively American manner, but only as parts of classically designed and logically developed forms. Folkloric considerations are completely absent from the esthetic credo of Roger Sessions, who composes music of architectonic balances and contrasts, in which the sole criterion is intrinsic validity.

A romantic spirit animates the music of Gardner Read, but his romanticism is expressed in techniques of cumulative complexity.

Constructive and aggressive modernism is the essence of the music of Wallingford Riegger; his Americanism can only be inferred from certain melorhythmic inflections.

Intricacy of melorhythmic design reaches extraordinary proportions in the instrumental works of Elliott Carter, where every element is assigned a special function in the general scheme. A similarly involved style is cultivated by Vincent Persichetti, whose expressive means are equally effective in neobaroque counterpoint.

The *Zeitgeist*, the spirit of the times, does not pass over America without a musical response. Leonard Bernstein's panoramic work for piano and orchestra, *The Age of Anxiety*, portrays the agitation of modern life with singular power. A versatile modern genius, Bernstein has written music of social significance for the mass audiences; his *West Side Story* is a work of unprecedented originality in the popular theater.

Of all American composers, Elie Siegmeister makes the most explicit use of authentic folk songs, many of which he gathered during his folkloric excursions, presenting them as symphonic materials in an undistorted classical manner.

Morton Gould's American " symphonettes " reflect the re-

gional spirit of the country in a brilliant light style on the border
line of popular music. Beyond the pale separating American music
of earnest endeavor from the mass product of a commercial type are
found various programmatic suites by Ferde Grofé, depicting
scenes and sites of the United States in a literal but picturesque
manner.

One of the most important and fertile developments of popular
American music is jazz. It is at once a style, a technique, and an
improvisatory art. The word itself is probably onomatopoeic; the
fanciful etymologies suggested for its origin have no more validity
than the belief that the word " hurricane " is derived from the notion that one should hurry and hold onto a cane during high winds,
or that irredentists are erring dentists. The first mention of the word
" jazz " in print occurred in the theatrical trade magazine *Variety*
on October 27, 1916. Jazz bands became popular in New York in
1917; after the Armistice, jazz was exported to Paris. The jazz era
had begun.

Objectively speaking, jazz is a form of composition in binary
song form, arranged in rigidly symmetrical periods in $\frac{4}{4}$ time. The
standard length of a jazz tune is thirty-two bars. The heart of
jazz is syncopation, with the main beat strongly marked in the bass.

The typical instrumentation of early jazz bands consisted of
the banjo, cornet, clarinet, trombone, upright piano, and double
bass. The banjo, a relic from an earlier type of syncopated music
called ragtime, soon disappeared from jazz bands; the cornet was
replaced by the trumpet, and the saxophone was co-opted as a principal solo instrument.

An overwhelming majority of jazz tunes are in major keys,
with a lowered seventh furnishing a characteristic " blue note."
When a jazz player refers to a C seventh chord, he means a blue
seventh chord with a B-flat. It may be said therefore that the blue
jazz scale is the mixolydian mode. When the third of the scale is
also lowered, the result is the Dorian mode. But the melodic turns
and intervallic usages of jazz tunes are of course totally different in
their functions from the old ecclesiastical modes.

The harmonic treatment of jazz has a modern ring. Plagal
cadences predominate, with the subdominant chord fortified by a
blue seventh. When authentic cadences are applied at all, they

take the form of the dominant ninth chord followed by the tonic seventh without the blue note. In the piano part, common major triads are pandiatonically enriched. Chromatic progressions of consecutive major ninth chords, the clichés of impressionistic harmonization, are favorites of jazz pianists. Changes of key are effected by unprepared modulations, most frequently a major third upward. Thus a jazz tune in C major is apt to have an E major variant.

The antecedents of jazz as a melorhythmic form can be traced to the Negro spirituals; as an art of improvisation, jazz blossomed in New Orleans; but as a type of composition, it flourished first in the cosmopolitan streets of New York City, along Tin Pan Alley. Jewish composers from immigrant families were particularly adept in catching the lilt of syncopated jazz; but the tunes manufactured by them have the inflections of old-world ballads. Wistful ditties in minor keys annexed the rhythmic syncopation of ragtime and jazz, creating a potent hybrid form that became the foundation of the highly successful American musical comedy. With the appearance of the phonograph, American jazz tunes flooded the world and influenced popular music everywhere.

Jazz music became a folk art. It is a law of history that with the formation of a new medium of popular expression, a poet of great gifts appears and converts it into a new artistic language. Such a musical poet was George Gershwin. His *Rhapsody in Blue* was the first large piano composition based on jazz rhythms. His *Porgy and Bess* was the first opera integrally built on Negro jazz. Gershwin's songs embody polyrhythmic combinations of great interest. The rhythmic formula of his tune "I Got Rhythm," unassumingly encompassed in $\frac{4}{4}$ time, represents a succession of changing meters, consisting of one bar of $\frac{2}{16}$, four bars of $\frac{3}{16}$, two bars of $\frac{2}{16}$, four bars of $\frac{3}{16}$, and a bar of $\frac{2}{16}$. His "Fascinating Rhythm" represents overlapping meters of $\frac{7}{8}$, $\frac{8}{8}$, and $\frac{3}{4}$. The remarkable thing is that this rhythmic complexity does not in the least impair the popular appeal of Gershwin's songs.

George Gershwin created symphonic jazz, working from simple popular tunes toward higher forms. His contemporary Aaron Copland (like Gershwin, a native of Brooklyn) approached jazz from the symphonic side of the art, incorporating its melorhythms in his so-called Jazz Piano Concerto.

European composers discovered jazz as a fresh and spontaneous folk art and, at a point of musical evolution when modernism was in danger of sterility, found it immensely attractive. Ravel, Milhaud, Honegger, and other French composers made use of jazz. Ernst Krenek wrote a satirical opera, *Jonny spielt auf*, in which a Negro jazz player conquers the world with his irresistible art and in the finale sits on top of the terrestrial globe.

With the advent of the Nazi regime, jazz was declared to be a Negro-Jewish product, racially corrupt and esthetically inadmissible. A booklet issued for the Düsseldorf Exposition of Degenerate Art in 1938 had on its cover the picture of a Negro playing the saxophone and wearing the Star of David.

In the Soviet Union there was opposition to jazz as a by-product of capitalist decay, "the music of the fat men," as Gorky phrased it. The attitude was changed as jazz found defenders among Soviet musicians and was finally accepted as a type of folk music. The *Encyclopedic Musical Dictionary* published in Moscow in 1959 defines jazz as "a kind of entertainment music, predominantly in dance forms." The Soviet definition further discriminates between improvisatory jazz inspired by Negro songs and commercial jazz "cultivated in capitalist countries and their dependencies by means of radio, phonograph, motion pictures, and sheet music." This commercial jazz "generated a quantity of standardized songs and dances of banal and decadent nature."

While the generic form of jazz music has persisted through nearly half a century of its existence, several jazz techniques have developed. Of these, boogiewoogie has great vitality. The chief characteristic of boogiewoogie is the *ostinato* figure in the bass, suggesting the form of a *chaconne* or a *passacaglia*, with the constant rhythmic flow in eighth notes, the rhythm alluded to in the title of the popular song *Beat Me, Daddy, Eight to the Bar*. There followed a transitory rhythmic jazz style known first as rebop, then bebop, and finally simply bop, marked by a heterogeneous application of all sorts of idioms and derivations, from primitive Afro-Cuban rhythms to pseudo-modernistic melodic and harmonic devices. So-called progressive jazz proceeded further toward a meeting with cultivated modern music, adopting string instruments, and borrowing already obsolescent materials, such as the whole-tone scale, from the old vocabulary of European music.

Jazz has invaded even ecclesiastical music. Geoffrey Beaumont, vicar and warden of the Trinity College Mission in Cambridge, England, has written a *Twentieth-Century Folk Mass* in an outspoken jazz style, bristling with syncopation, and arranged in typical jazz harmonies. "The Jazz Mass," as it has been nicknamed, was first performed at St. Luke's Church, Chesterton, Cambridge, on Sunday, November 16, 1952, and has since been given in many other churches in England and America.

In the 1950's a new type of music called rock 'n' roll became extremely popular. Structurally it is a jazzed-up country ballad with a monotonously repetitive melody against an unvarying metrical beat. The electric guitar in the hands of the singer replaces the old-fashioned banjo.

The hypnotic power of syncopated American music is very great. Young audiences at jazz concerts, not only in America but also in Europe, are often so carried away by the music as to break the barriers of civilization in uncontrollable frenzy. Not even the greatest virtuosos aroused comparable ecstasies. At the 1960 Jazz Festival in Newport, Rhode Island, a mob of rock-'n'-roll enthusiasts staged a riot in the streets that completely overwhelmed the defenses of municipal authorities.

Changes of fashion and growth of sophistication are responsible for the decline of some picturesque clichés of modern music. The whole-tone scale, a favorite resource of impressionistic exoticism, became completely obsolete. But it was reborn, rather surprisingly, in twelve-tone music, since two mutually exclusive whole-tone scales add up to all twelve chromatic notes.

The pentatonic scale served honorably to illustrate Indian life in the works of MacDowell, and Japanese life in Puccini's *Madama Butterfly*, before it fell into desuetude; but, like the whole-tone scale, it reasserted itself in dodecaphonic writing, as a grouping complementary to the diatonic scale.

Diminished-seventh chords, which furnished dramatic effects in old Italian operas, particularly when used in chromatically rising and sinking progressions, vanished from the active harmonic vocabulary early in the century. A similar fate befell the once-popular augmented triads and the Wagnerian-Debussyan major ninth chords.

Despite the great variety of idioms and techniques in modern music, certain stylistic features are common to nearly all schools, impressionistic, neoclassical, expressionistic, and even electronic. These are: thematic brevity, asymmetric rhythms, compactness of major forms, compression of cadences, avoidance of sequences, and virtual abandonment of formal development.

Medieval treatises on musical theory often began with the words " Brevitate moderni gaudent " — the moderns rejoice in brevity. This applies perfectly to the moderns of the twentieth century as well. Thematic phrases are short in the works of impressionist and expressionist composers. In the neoclassical type of composition, the themes grow longer, but asymmetrical rhythms produce an effect of fragmentation. There are exceptions. Roy Harris, who cultivates asymmetrical rhythms, builds musical phrases of great length. In his Fifth Symphony, one thematic statement represents a continuous melorhythmic line 118 measures long.

Sequential progressions, whether tonal or modulatory, are avoided by modern composers as automatic procedures tending to weaken the musical line. And since sequences are commonly used in the development section in classical music, modern composers are likely to condense formal development or even to eliminate it altogether. The variation forms continue to be widely used, however, but in modern works they become refractions, polarizations, and asymmetric projections of the original thematic material.

Long rhetorical cadences of classical and romantic music are relics of an irretrievable past. The repetition of the final tonal chord, the earmark of classical overtures and symphonies, is now regarded as an unnecessary redundancy. The final chord is apt to be unprepared and abrupt; a striking example is the ending of Prokofiev's March from the opera Love for Three Oranges. However, endings on a dissonant chord are relatively rare. Even atonal composers prefer to conclude their works with a noncommittal unison. An overwhelming majority of pieces in a neoclassical style end on loud major triads, quite often in the simplest key of C.

The longest single instrumental work of the modern era is Opus clavicembalisticum, for piano solo, by Kaikhosru Sorabji,

British-born composer of Parsi and Spanish origin. It contains a *passacaglia* with eighty-one variations. The contrapuntal and rhythmic idiom is of enormous complexity, and the melodic material has reference to Indian modes.

The shortest piece of modern music is the fourth of the *Five Pieces for Orchestra*, by Anton von Webern; it measures only six and one-third bars in $\frac{3}{4}$ time and lasts nineteen seconds, according to the metronomic timing.

In the field of opera, the modern trend toward compactness is particularly pronounced. Grand opera is virtually a forgotten art. Survivors of the nineteenth century continued to write operas in the old grandiloquent style, but the new generation turned to chamber opera, requiring a few soloists, a small chorus, and a reduced orchestra. One of the few significant grand operas of modern times is Samuel Barber's *Vanessa*.

Benjamin Britten and Gian-Carlo Menotti are the most successful representatives of modern music drama. Britten inclines toward naturalism and expressionism, and selects subjects of somber drama, as in *Peter Grimes, The Rape of Lucretia*, and *Billy Budd*. Although his harmonic idiom is dissonant and polytonal, simple triadic progressions are common.

Menotti is a true heir to the Italian realistic school, and he succeeds in creating a distinctive personal style of great dramatic power. He writes his own librettos in English, selecting contemporary subjects of emotional impact, as in *The Medium*, the story of a fraudulent spiritualist who falls victim to her own deception, and in *The Consul*, portraying the agonizing tragedy of people fleeing political terror. Menotti is omnivorous in his harmonic and melodic style; there are elements from many sources, and it is Menotti's ability to blend these materials that elevates his operas to a level of artistry.

Tragedy and satire possess the imagination of opera composers in the modern era. Social and political disillusionment in Germany found its outlet in satirical topical stage works produced there after the end of World War I. In his *Dreigroschenoper*, Kurt Weill castigated the social injustice and moral decay of the contemporary world. In France, Darius Milhaud and Francis Poulenc wrote short operas and ballets in which euphoric exultation alternates with depression and resignation. The atonally distorted, polytonally harmonized Polka from Shostakovich's ballet *The Age of Gold* was staged in a Russian production as a satire on a current disarmament conference. In America, Marc Blitzstein wrote short operas of social consciousness, in a style approaching that of Weill. He also made a highly idiomatic American version of Bertolt Brecht's libretto to Weill's *Dreigroschenoper* (*The Threepenny Opera*).

A folkloristic genre misleadingly called " folk opera " (in the sense of a work in a folk manner) became popular among American composers, along with the " ballad opera." Douglas Moore composed a stage piece designated as a " soap opera," with reference to the lowly radio serials usually sponsored by manufacturers of soap.

The mythological and historical subjects that inspired opera composers of the past have not lost their attraction in modern times. Orpheus, Persephone, Antigone, Orestes, Iphigenia, and Medea still stride the operatic stage, singing atonally of their anguish and sorrow.

Old opera composers treated historical subjects as melodrama, calculated to produce a maximum effect on the stage. Modern composers prefer a symbolic interpretation. Darius Milhaud's opera *Christophe Colomb* is a pageant in which the chorus comments on the fate of Columbus in the manner of the Greek theater; numerous dramatic techniques are applied, including that of the motion picture, the first such use in an opera.

Hindemith's concept of historical opera is sociophilosophical, touching on the problems of an individual asserting himself in a hostile environment. In *Mathis der Maler*, a sixteenth-century German painter withdraws from the civil strife and turmoil around him to pursue his creative work. In *Die Harmonie der Welt*, the true harmony of the spheres is divined by Kepler and astronomical truth prevails over obscurantism.

Remarkably few operas written in a distinctly modern idiom attain popular acceptance. Even such an epoch-making masterpiece as *Pelléas et Mélisande* is rarely heard. Alban Berg's *Wozzeck*, one of the most forceful creations of music drama, still remains outside the repertory of large opera houses. Among the operas of Richard Strauss, *Der Rosenkavalier* is much more popular than the starkly modernistic *Salome* and *Elektra*.

· · ·

No clear demarcation line divides modern opera from oratorio. Stravinsky's *Oedipus Rex* can be performed either on the stage or in concert form. The score is written in a neoarchaic manner, and the Latin text seems to emphasize the detachment of the work from contemporary forms. It signalizes the reversion to medieval and Renaissance mystery plays, as perceived by a highly cultivated modern mind.

Ecclesiastical subjects appear in many stage works by modern composers. Modern Biblical operas, oratorios, and cantatas may abound in dissonance, but the religious spirit that animates them is unmistakable. Stravinsky's *Symphony of Psalms* possesses all the magnificence of old religious works. Honegger's dramatic psalm *Le Roi David* is imbued with reverence. His stage oratorio *Jeanne d'Arc au bûcher* is a dramatic interpretation of the martyrdom of the French heroine, with the full application of dissonant techniques, and realistic effects such as the howling of the hounds illustrated by a rising glissando on the electronic Ondes Musicales.

On the other hand, Ildebrando Pizzetti's *Assassinio nella cattedrale*, based on T. S. Eliot's poetic drama dealing with the murder of St. Thomas à Becket, renounces all advanced harmonic and contrapuntal procedures and returns to the symbolic manner of old mystery plays.

Vaughan Williams revives the theatrical religious allegory in *The Pilgrim's Progress*, which he designates as " a morality."

The title of Virgil Thomson's opera *Four Saints in Three Acts* (there are actually more than a dozen saints, and the number of acts is four) suggests a religious subject, but the opera is in reality a sophisticated setting, in aggressively simple harmonies, of one of Gertrude Stein's ineffable plays.

A remarkable stylization of archaic elements is achieved by Carl Orff in his *Carmina Burana* for soloists, chorus, and orchestra, to Latin and German texts of medieval student songs found in the monastery of Benediktbeuren in Bavaria. Mock solemnity alternates with unrestrained jollification; the harmonies are barely touched with dissonance, and yet the effect is decidedly novel.

Musical descriptions of historical events usually borrow their subjects from a fairly remote past, but the process is accelerated in modern times. Kurt Weill wrote a radio cantata on Lindbergh's flight immediately after that epoch-making event. Schoenberg's cantata *A Survivor from Warsaw* reflects the tragedy of the Warsaw ghetto. It is a work of stark realism, incorporating in its text the shouted orders of Nazi executioners and a prayer in Hebrew of the victims.

In the "scenic action" *Intolleranza 1960* by the Venetian composer Luigi Nono, dedicated to Schoenberg, refugees are tortured to the accompaniment of dissonant twelve-tone counterpoint. An atom bomb explodes in a park named Dummyland sending a dodecaphonic cloud to the skies with electronic sound stereophonically concentrated on the audience. When it was first performed at the Venice Festival of Contemporary Music in 1961, it created a sensation. But there was also organized hostility. Mimeographed copies of an anti-dodecaphonic manifesto signed "Ordine Nuovo" were showered upon the public from the balconies. The document is interesting. It proclaims: "The only thing that is absent from this festival is music itself. We refuse to admit that this agglomeration of sounds and dissonances called dodecaphony contains a minimum of musical essence. It lacks the concept of hierarchy, the fulcrum about which revolve the values that make traditional music an eternal art. Dodecaphony is but an arrangement of notes contrasting with one another, a demonstration of what happens when democracy is carried into the realm of music."

Several Soviet operas dealing with events of World War II were produced in Russia even before that war ended. Prokofiev's opera *The Story of a Real Man* is based on an actual case of a Soviet flyer who lost both legs in air combat, but returned to active air service.

Outside Soviet Russia, *The Death of Rasputin*, by the Russian émigré Nicolas Nabokov, produced in 1958, describes events that took place in 1916.

As a protest against the conventional type of opera, whether old or modern, Boris Blacher resolved to dispense with libretto altogether and leave the action, the music, and the dialogue free. In his "abstract operas" there is no plot, and the continuity is indicated solely by a succession of emotional states: Fear, Love No. 1, Panic, Love No. 2, and so on.

Modern ballet music is marked by a diversity of styles and techniques similar to that of modern opera. The decisive change from the classical ballet was effected by the Ballet Russe of Serge Diaghilev, the Russian impresario who never gave performances in his

native land, but concentrated his activities in France. He produced
the epoch-making ballets by Stravinsky, *Petrouchka* and *Le Sacre
du printemps*, in which the dancers were compelled to follow the
constantly changing meters and asymmetrical rhythms totally different from conventional choreography. Debussy and Ravel, Manuel de Falla and Prokofiev, Poulenc, Auric, and Milhaud wrote ballet music for Diaghilev. The style established by these scores indelibly influenced ballet music everywhere.

The subject matter of modern ballets ranges widely from neo-
primitivism, as in *Le Sacre du printemps*, to hedonistic urban folklorism, practiced particularly by Paris composers. Mythological subjects are treated in modern ballets, as they are in modern opera, in
the light of psychological abstraction, with atonal melodies and
asymmetric rhythms expressing the angular movements and sur-
realistic postures of the dancers on the stage.

The Dutch composer Henk Badings wrote an electronic ballet,
Cain and Abel, in which the ancient Biblical drama of fratricide is
illustrated with the aid of a sinusoidal wave generator capable of
producing mathematically pure harmonics in a non-tempered
scale, a multivibrator which can vary the relative intensity of upper
harmonics at will and thus secure a constant change of tone color,
a reverberation machine producing overlapping echoes, a modu-
lator that amplifies the differential tones generating eerie shadow
chords beneath the principal harmonic tones, a noise filter allowing
to select desirable frequencies from the mass of so-called " white
noise " covering the entire audible range, and an optical siren,
which transforms light beams into tone-color melodies.

Composition for films has not kept up with modern techniques.
Schoenberg's *Accompaniment to a Cinematographic Scene* was
written for an imaginary film. Stravinsky and Hindemith never
wrote film music. Georges Auric has written some witty music for
French films. Commercial Hollywood studios employ composers
who have specialized in a type of promiscuous music manufacture
in which pseudo-modernistic effects are superimposed upon the
most obvious clichés. Only experimental cinema has produced some
original film music.

Radio became an important outlet for modern composers.
State-supported stations in Europe and commercial stations in
America commissioned works of all descriptions, including operas.
One of the earliest radio operas was *The Old Maid and the Thief*,

by Menotti. *Green Mansions,* by Louis Gruenberg, was also written for a radio broadcast. Dallapiccola's opera *Il Prigioniero* was commissioned by the Turin Radio. Radio Geneva commissioned Frank Martin to write a Christmas oratorio, *Le Mystère de la Nativité,* and after its successful presentation it was produced as an opera at the Salzburg Festival in the summer of 1960.

With the advent of television, it became possible to produce full-fledged operas in a mass medium, without sacrificing the visual aspect. *The Taming of the Shrew,* by Vittorio Giannini, was televised in color in 1954; a fairy-tale opera, *Griffelkin,* by Lukas Foss, was presented in 1955. The most successful television opera of all was *Amahl and the Night Visitors,* by Menotti, first broadcast on Christmas Eve, 1951, and repeated annually.

Modern ballet has also been presented on television, in Europe and America. Perforce all such productions of opera and ballet on television must be short; television cannot replace the stage.

No technique of composition is pure and self-consistent. There are deviations from the strict precepts of the twelve-tone method in Schoenberg's own works. Styles and techniques overlap, creating idioms in which modern and conventional elements are freely intermingled. Syncretism, an incongruous combination of conflicting elements, gradually evolves into practical eclecticism, until the foundation is laid for a new unified style. But even deliberate inconsistencies of style can serve an artistic purpose. Varèse interpolates two bars of C-major chords in his otherwise dissonant score *Arcana* in order to create an unexpected contrast. Ravel's *Bolero* is a tour de force of tonal uniformity, maintaining the key of C throughout, but at the very end there is a sudden brief digression into E major, before returning to the final C. The music of Charles Ives demonstrates that seemingly incompatible elements of style can be integrated with telling effect.

Despite this rich diversity of styles and idioms, it is possible to draw a clear line of demarcation between traditional and modern music. Before the year 1900, every composition, and each self-contained section within it, had to end on a sound comprising not more than three different notes set in perfect harmony, i.e., a major or a minor triad. Furthermore, the last chord had to be based on the same tonic as the principal key of the entire work. In his song *Wenn,* written in 1897, Richard Strauss had the whimsical notion of violating this rule by concluding in a key a semitone higher than the designated principal tonality. After this heterotonal coda, he inserted a sly footnote: " Vocalists who may wish to perform this song before the end of the nineteenth century are advised by the composer to transpose the last seven bars a semitone lower so as to end the composition in the same key in which it began."

In the twentieth century, with incredible suddenness, composers stopped treating dissonances as unstable entities requiring eventual resolution into a certified consonance, and let them stand on their own. Treated as independent and self-supporting entities, dissonant harmonies acquired an equilibrium, like a gyroscope, spinning, but stable.

Dissonances became emancipated, and modern music became a historical fact.

As never before in the long history of music, composers now have at their disposal unlimited resources of sonority. Theoretically it is not beyond the bounds of possibility that fugues and other forms of a definite pattern can be manufactured by digital computers. The role of the composer under such circumstances would be reduced to that of a prime mover who gives only the initial impulse, a supreme judge who selects the most perfect theme and the most fitting development from numerous musical fragments made available to him by automatic permutation.

Will all this liberate the composer from the chores of invention? Even the most scientific-minded adherents of ultramodern methods among composers hesitate to abdicate their functions.

If historical parallels are of any validity, the next phase of music in the third quarter of the twentieth century will be a new romanticism with the subjective reference enormously enhanced, and the prodigious capacities of electronic music subjugated to the wishes and the whims of a composer who will strive, as composers have always done, to say something in music that has never been said before.

(SAMUEL BARBER)

1910-

BIOGRAPHY

SAMUEL BARBER was born in West Chester, Pennsylvania, on March 9, 1910. He started composition when he was seven, and by the time he was twelve he was playing the organ at church services. He received his musical training mainly with Isabelle Vengerova and Rosario Scalero at the Curtis Institute, which he had entered in 1924. In 1928 a violin sonata won the Bearns Prize, and in 1932 his *Overture to the School for Scandal* became his first orchestral work to be performed. Between 1935 and 1937 he traveled throughout Europe as a recipient of two Pulitzer Traveling Scholarships and the American Prix de Rome. In 1937 he became the first American composer to be represented at the Salzburg Festival, with a performance of his *Symphony in One Movement*. The première of two other orchestral works in 1938 — by the NBC Symphony under Toscanini — brought him additional recognition: *Adagio for Strings* and *Essay No. 1*. After serving in the Air Force during World War II, he received a Guggenheim Fellowship and the New York Music Critics Circle Award for his Cello Concerto in 1947 and in 1959 he received an honorary doctorate from Harvard. He was awarded the Pulitzer Prize in music for the opera *Vanessa* in 1958, for the Piano Concerto in 1963. In 1966, his opera *Antony and Cleopatra* opened the new Metropolitan Opera House in the Lincoln Center for the Performing Arts.

PERSONAL NOTE

Nathan Broder

BARBER works slowly. He attaches great importance to his thematic
material, and the search for the right themes is often painful and
long drawn out, with many discarded along the way. When he is
engaged in such a search he is usually in a bad temper and wanders
about, silent and melancholy. He has been seen sitting in a train,
drawing staves and writing notes in the air with his fingers and
erasing them with a sweep of the hand. When he was working on
the Piano Sonata he left his dentist's office and walked around for
hours, oblivious of the wad of cotton in his mouth, discovering it
only when he had to eat. Once satisfactory themes are found, his
mood changes immediately to one of gaiety and exhilaration.

The traits he exhibited as a boy and young man have not altered in the course of the years. He is still withdrawn and rather
cold, though urbane, when with people he does not know well, but a
spring of humor occasionally bubbles to the surface. This humor
can take a caustic turn: when he was introduced to a new American
ambassador in Rome, Barber told him how glad he was to meet at
last an ambassador fond of music. " Aren't most ambassadors interested in music? " asked the diplomat. " Oh, no," said Barber.
" In fact, if more governments loved music we should have no need
for ambassadors at all." Sometimes, however, his wit becomes
acidulous and gains him no friends. But when he is with intimates,
his humor ripples merrily along. Such business transactions as he
must concern himself with are annoying chores, belonging to a remote and uninteresting sphere and to be disposed of as quickly as
possible. Even his choice of amusements is rather circumscribed.
He cannot, for example, endure card games and has no instinct for
games of any sort. Once, when he and Menotti were stranded in
Italy with insufficient money to return to the United States, Menotti took him to a gambling casino and persuaded him to risk his
few remaining dollars on roulette. Barber forgot to take his win-
nings off the table and, since the same number kept coming up,
won $600. He has never gambled since.

An excellent pianist when he is in practice, he is incapable of any other type of manual dexterity. " I hate," he once wrote to Jeanne Behrend, " to ask any musician to make a package — it always takes *me* an entire morning." He is constantly losing things and cannot fry an egg or operate a phonograph. " Sam is the only soldier in the United States Army who never learned how to take a gun apart and put it together again," Menotti has said. On the other hand, Barber's household and life in general are highly organized, whereas Menotti's are completely disorganized. Menotti has made it a point to cause Barber to miss trains and ships " in order to make Sam relax," but this method of treatment has not been very successful.

Barber has always been fond of walking in the country. He reads a great deal. One of his favorite authors is Stendhal, whom he admires for his combination of classic clarity and passion. Others whom he has studied through the years are Dante, Goethe, Joyce, Proust, and Melville. Barber first became acquainted with Melville through reading an Italian translation of *Moby Dick*, and he has had it in the back of his mind ever since to write a work — perhaps an oratorio — based on that novel. Until Menotti wrote *Vanessa* for him, Barber searched for many years for a suitable libretto for an opera. He discussed opera projects with Thornton Wilder, Stephen Spender, and Dylan Thomas, among others. Once Edward Johnson, manager of the Metropolitan Opera Company, and Edward Ziegler, his assistant, offered Barber $5000 to write an opera. There was one string attached — the composer had to work with a librettist already chosen by the Metropolitan. When Barber discovered that he would not have complete freedom in the choice of a libretto, he declined the offer.

His taste in other matters is in general unusually discerning. It has enabled him to acquire works of art by men who later became famous. He is a perceptive traveler, sensitive to the idiosyncrasies of the peoples of various countries. He is also something of a gourmet, with a special predilection for soups. " I would like," he once said, " to be buried with a sprinkling of croutons over my coffin."

BARBER

Nathan Broder

To THOSE who are familiar with the work of American composers produced from about 1930 on, one of its most fascinating aspects is its variety. Every type of idiom that has made a place for itself in the world of serious music in this country, and some that are still struggling to do so, have their adherents among our creative musicians. As was to be expected, critics and historians have found it convenient to lump all these men into a few groups and to label each group. Allotted to the class of " neoromantics," and regarded as one of its most outstanding representatives, is Samuel Barber.

Now, pigeonholing of this sort often results in oversimplification; and labeling Barber's music neoromantic, though helpful in describing his earlier works, disregards significant elements in his later and more important products. Traditional procedures are characteristic of all of Barber's music up to about 1939. After that time, however, they begin to be mingled with or replaced by methods that can only have arisen in the musical climate of our time. This change and growth in style reveals itself in the melodic structure of his music, in its harmonic and contrapuntal texture, and in its rhythm.

The melodic structure in the earlier music is largely governed by its tonality. A typical line may be lyrical in character, with a certain simple freshness, despite its traditional shape, or it may be dramatic and expansive, characterized by broad leaps. In the later music the lyric type of line tends to become more chromatic and the dramatic type, while retaining the broad leaps, is contracted into a short theme, jagged and biting. Here tonality is no longer the principal determining factor; instead, certain intervals dominate the melodic structure.

Even in his earliest works, each of which is based on a single tonal center, there is a constant oscillation between major and minor. Sometimes the identity of the tonal center itself is subtly veiled by the shifting harmonies: e.g., " With Rue My Heart Is Laden " (1928), " Rain Has Fallen " (1936), String Quartet (1936). On the other hand, Barber did not hesitate to use the simplest means when they would serve his purpose. Thus the effectiveness of " Let Down the Bars, O Death " (1936) is enhanced by a few expressive discords in a sensitive, strictly chordal texture wholly in G minor; and the questioning conclusion he sought for the *Essay No. 1* (1937) was achieved merely by ending on the unsupported dominant tone.

After about 1939, in keeping with the general change in Barber's style that began to take place at that time, the harmonic texture grows more dissonant; and, though most of the works are still based on a tonal center, devices new to Barber's music are introduced. " Anthony O Daly " (1940), a keening plaint, is entirely constructed above or below the tone E, which is sounded in all but four of the eighty-six measures. Polyharmony appears, not only to point up the end of a surrealist text as in " The Queen's Face on the Summery Coin," or to color a passage in boogiewoogie style as in the first of the *Excursions* (1944), or to recall a violent murder as in *Medea* (1946), but to intensify the emotional power of an " abstract " work as in the Second Symphony (1944). In *Medea* tonality as a means of unification is frequently abandoned, and its place is taken by an interval. The whole work grows out of the interval of the second (or its expansion, a ninth, or inversion, a seventh), which determines the chief thematic material and delineates important structural points. Several of the movements, for example, begin with a ninth. The interval of a second is similarly important in the Second Symphony and the *Capricorn Concerto* (1944). In the tender and nostalgic *Knoxville: Summer of 1915* (1947) Barber returns to traditional key relationships (though not to traditional harmonic textures), the work as a whole being based on an oscillation between F-sharp minor and A major. Yet even here seconds and ninths combine to intensify a climactic passage. And in the Piano Sonata (1949) tonality is partly abandoned while Barber explores the expressive possibilities of the twelve-tone style of writing.

At the Curtis Institute Scalero laid more emphasis upon counterpoint than any other element of composition, and prescribed innumerable exercises, insisting upon vital and meaningful writing in all parts. The beneficial results of this intensive training are apparent throughout Barber's output. His music is seldom static; and even where the harmonies are ambiguous, the contrapuntal texture is alive. He does not often employ the old polyphonic principles, like those of the passacaglia and fugue, that have been enthusiastically revived by many of his colleagues; but when he does, it is to good effect. Here, too, we find evidence of the change that Barber's style has undergone. The Passacaglia in the First Symphony (1936) may be said to stem from Bach by way of Brahms. The polytonal fugue in the *Essay No. 2* (1942) is closer to our times. But the fugue in the Piano Sonata, the kind of *ostinato* treatment accorded the principal subject in the finale of the Second Symphony, the *ostinato* that accompanies the strange second theme of the Cello Concerto (1945), the *ostinato* figure in *Medea's Dance of Vengeance* (1956), and the canon in the last act of *Vanessa* (1957) are wholly contemporary in spirit and origin.

The rhythms are varied and active and free from mannerisms. Even in his earliest songs (e.g., " With Rue My Heart Is Laden ") the vocal line is often fluid and carefully suited to the rhythms of the words, with frequent changes of meter where necessary. Much of the melancholy charm of a song like " The Secrets of the Old " (1938) arises from its supple rhythm. In the instrumental music the rhythms range from the solemn, even stride of quarter notes in the *Adagio for Strings* (1936) to the most volatile and capricious irregularities. The later music has a general tendency to avoid the obvious, and this tendency is clearly shown in the choice of rhythms. Even when writing a simple folklike tune, as in the third *Excursion*, Barber achieves a piquant, casual effect by unusual rhythmic organization.

Barber's feeling for form is very strong, and it is in this respect that his music shows the closest ties with the past. The large works are firmly rooted in the principles of sonata construction. Yet even here one seldom (except perhaps in the earliest pieces) has the impression of a slavish reliance upon well-tested models; instead, all sorts of changes are rung on the traditional procedures, and the resulting structures usually seem the logical ones for imaginative and well-integrated treatment of the material. A favorite method is to build a whole movement out of material presented in its introduction: e.g., the first movement of the Serenade for String Quartet (1929) and the first movement of the *Capricorn Concerto*. The entire First Symphony, which, although performed without pause, falls into the usual four sections, grows out of three themes, all introduced in the opening section. The Scherzo is derived from the first, the Andante is based on the second, and the Passacaglia com-

bines the first and third. The second section of the String Quartet
ends with an abbreviated recapituation of the first, but this final
portion starts in B-flat minor and only gradually modulates to the
home key. The two *Essays* are especially interesting illustrations of
Barber's gift for gaining satisfying conclusions by employing, in altered form, material used early in the same work. In *Essay No. 2* the
subject of the fugue is derived partly from the opening theme and
partly from a figure accompanying that theme in the timpani, the
figure having been first foreshadowed in the lower strings; and the
whole final peroration (thirty-four measures) is spun out of a four-
chord motif that had first appeared in the brass against the second
theme in the strings. The form of the vocal works is of course
largely governed by that of the text, but the choice of the text is
sometimes determined by the unusual formal possibilities it offers.
We have seen, for example, how " Anthony O Daly " is unified by
the constant reiteration of one tone. *A Stopwatch and an Ordnance
Map* (1940), with its double refrain, falls into the following musical
and poetic pattern:

p   A stopwatch and an ordnance map.
    At five a man falls . . . (eight measures)

  p   All under the olive trees.

f   A stopwatch and an ordnance map.
    He stayed faithfully . . . (fourteen and a half
    measures)

  p   All under the olive trees.

ff   A stopwatch and an ordnance map.
    And the bones are fixed . . . (twenty-four meas-
    ures)

  pp   All under the olive trees.

Barber's orchestration is tasteful, restrained, and varied. He
has a keen ear for instrumental colors, and, in keeping with the
fundamentally poetic character of his music, his colors are never
neutral, never, except, perhaps, in the *Capricorn Concerto*, chosen
for their own sake alone, but always with the aim of enhancing
the music's expressiveness. In the earliest works he relied on more
or less traditional combinations, but he soon developed an ability
to exploit in fresh ways the idiomatic capacities of the individual
instruments of the normal symphony orchestra.

. . .

Lyricism is not a prominent quality in the significant American music of the 1930's. That decade is marked by a search for style, a working-out of personal idioms. It is the period bounded, in Roy Harris, by the First Symphony (*Symphony: 1933*) and the Viola Quintet; in Aaron Copland, by the *Piano Variations* and the Piano Sonata; in William Schuman, by the earliest published work (*Four Canonic Choruses*) and the Third String Quartet. The ferment of such a time produced important and exciting works, but it was not conducive to the calm contemplation of beauty for its own sake. Barber, primarily a lyric poet, remained aloof from the swirling currents in which many of his colleagues were immersed. His visions were not of the sort that required the forging of an individual idiom; they could be best expressed in an existing and well-known tongue. (Hence the widespread and abiding popularity of such a work as the *Adagio for Strings*, the expressive content of which does not have to hurdle any stylistic obstacles to reach the average audience.)

At the first performance of the Second Symphony (1944) some listeners showed distrustful surprise at what they regarded as a sudden change in Barber's style. Careful study of his works shows that the change is basically little more than a natural technical enrichment, the first extensive evidence of which appears in the Violin Concerto (1939). Here an almost willfully cultivated Mendelssohnian simplicity is suddenly interrupted by a presto *perpetuum mobile* full of irregular rhythms and quite un-Mendelssohnian dissonances. It is as if the composer had suddenly lost patience with certain self-imposed stylistic restrictions. With this change of style, which was foreshadowed here and there in earlier works, there now began a transitional period, in which sometimes the older elements predominate, as in the song " Nocturne " (1940), and sometimes the newer, as in *Essay No. 2*. The older traits scarcely appear at all, and the newer ones are intensified, in the Second Symphony; but lyricism returns, in a new garb, in the Cello Concerto, where it is evoked by the nature of the solo instrument, and in large portions of *Vanessa*. In all of these works Barber has employed his new technical gains in an attempt to fuse an essentially lyric spirit with an awakened awareness of the restlessness and discordance of our times. There have been occasional wanderings into bypaths — the *Excursions* for piano, the only instance of Barber treating American folk idioms, and the *Capricorn Concerto,* in which he experiments with rhythms and colors in the Stravinskyan manner. The style resulting from the fusion of old and new elements is seen at perhaps its best in the taut, intense, and deeply felt music of *Medea's Meditation and Dance of Vengeance*, the Piano Sonata, the *Prayers of Kierkegaard* (1954), and parts of *Vanessa*. This is the goal toward which Barber was feeling his way in the transitional compositions.

His work, as a whole, is like a living organism with a clearly stamped individuality, enriching itself as it grows. And this organism mirrors the qualities of the man — his dedication to art, the elegance and refinement of his taste, his unswerving adherence to the highest standards, his constant search for new means of creating beauty, a search guided by a sense of discrimination and a power of self-criticism that prevent him from being stampeded into adopting novel techniques merely because they are novel and widely used.

$\big($ BÉLA BARTÓK $\big)$

1881 - 1945

BIOGRAPHY

BÉLA BARTÓK was born in Nagyszentmiklós, Hungary, on March 25, 1881. He began to study the piano at an early age and soon disclosed such exceptional talent that he appeared in a public concert when he was ten, and composed several piano pieces of unusual brilliance. In 1893 he began systematic study of music with Laszlo Erkel in Bratislava. Some time later, he became a friend of another Hungarian musician, Ernst von Dohnányi (four years his senior), who influenced the younger boy strongly. When Bartók finished his elementary studies, he enrolled in the Royal Academy of Budapest, where he studied under Thomán and Koessler from 1899 to 1903.

For a few years after leaving the Academy, Bartók filled a variety of positions, including those of pianist, arranger, and teacher, without too much financial gain. One of his early works, the symphonic poem *Kossuth*, was performed in Budapest in 1904. In 1907 Bartók became an instructor at the Royal Academy.

In 1905 Bartók became interested in Hungarian folk music. This folk music was far different from the meretricious and sentimental gypsy songs that Europe had long accepted as authentically Hungarian; it was more virile, passionate, and barbaric. Between 1905 and 1914 Bartók divided his time between his activities as teacher and composer with intensive travels to every corner of Hungary in search of long-forgotten folk tunes and dances. In this endeavor he was soon joined by another brilliant Hungarian musician, Zoltan Kodály. Together, they collected more than six thousand examples of native Hungarian music.

Bartók's preoccupation with Hungarian folk music inevitably influenced his own creative work. Like the Hungarian folk song, his own music became severe and harsh and passionate. It was many years before Bartók received recognition; performances of his early works invariably inspired great antagonism and misunderstanding. Not until 1917 did Bartók taste success for the first time. The première of his ballet *The Wooden Prince* was warmly received in Budapest. Increasing fame came to him with an opera, *Duke Bluebeard's Castle*, a pantomime, *The Miraculous Mandarin*, a *Dance Suite* for orchestra, and the Second String Quartet.

Bartók traveled throughout Europe as a pianist in performances of his own works. In 1927–8 he toured the United States. He returned to America shortly after the outbreak of World War II, to live here the remaining years of his life. In this country, Bartók composed several major works, in a refined, simplified, and subjective style, which are considered among his greatest. He died in New York City on September 26, 1945.

PERSONAL NOTE

Ernö Balogh

FROM his third visit to the United States, Bartók never returned to Budapest. His remains, in a triple coffin, are buried in a cemetery on the outskirts of the city of New York. This New York represented much of what he sought to avoid all his life: noise, rush, many people and buildings, heavy traffic on the street with its accompanying exhaust fumes, commerce and commercialism, tidal waves of opportunities for the practical-minded in any field, an Eldorado for the opportunist. He knew this New York, this America, from his earlier visits. The dictatorships that surrounded him in Europe, which he hated — no matter from which side they blew their poisonous pollutions — compelled him to find refuge here.

Gradually his situation shaped to conditions under which he

created his last four works in the last years of his life. These works, as good as any of his earlier best, prove that in spite of being rooted deeply in the European tradition he could create just as well on American soil. If conditions of health and finances permitted, he could create anywhere. He could work under the shadows of the Adirondacks in New York State and also in the small, crowded apartment of famous but furiously noisy Fifty-seventh Street in New York, in which he composed with fertility but feverishly (in more than one meaning of the latter word), until he had to be taken to the hospital, a few blocks away on the same street, where he died a week later.

The last years of Bartók in New York can be divided into two periods: the first, from his arrival in October, 1940, until the spring of 1943; the second, from May, 1943, until his death.

During that first period, when his sickness nearly triumphed over the delicate and fragile frame of the man who carried such an indomitable soul and flaming spirit, he tried to earn a living from concerts, lectures, and the royalties on his compositions, although he was disturbed and sometimes alarmed by the lurking illness that finally destroyed him. The only productive work at this time was done on his folklore collections. He considered that his most important form of activity, more important than composing. He felt that very few people were trained to preserve the rapidly disappearing and irreplaceable treasures of folk songs and was dedicated to this mission. During these first two and a half years he was nostalgic for his home and European environment and wished in vain to hear his compositions performed.

When Bartók's health and finances reached their lowest ebb, the American Society of Composers, Authors and Publishers (ASCAP) took over the Bartók case. From that day until his death all necessary bills were paid by ASCAP without his ever even seeing a single bill, and ASCAP also paid for the funeral. No exact figures exist, but it is estimated that ASCAP spent at least $16,000 for expenses directly connected with his illness.

The most significant symptom of his sickness was a persistent fluctuating fever and constant weakness. By spring, 1944, it was evident that it was leukemia. The doctors were able to control this with medication and blood transfusions. He spent his last days in the hospital, mostly in pain and in a half coma, then slipped into a full coma and gradually burned away until death came shortly after 11 A.M. on September 26, 1945.

The day he was taken to the hospital he planned to continue his composing. During that last summer he worked in the only way he knew: from sunrise to sunset. And he loved it. This way of working, without interruption, was characteristic of the man. His *Concerto for Orchestra* was done in this continuous way.

The tragedy of Bartók was not only the lifelong struggle with poor health and constantly recurring financial difficulties, but also the neglect of his works, the ridicule of the press, and the lack of response of the audience on those rare occasions when he heard his works performed.

This man, whose music had elemental sweep, barbaric rhythms, and penetrating force, never weighed more than 116 pounds and sometimes as little as eighty-seven. His slow, even, measured walk was characteristic of his personality. When he came out on the Carnegie Hall stage, with delicate steps, to receive the ovation at the American première of his Violin Concerto, one New York newspaper said that he looked like a botany professor from a girls' college.

But the small and fragile body was endowed with an iron will and an uncompromising character. Although he spoke deliberately, with a soft voice, he could say a great deal without using an unnecessary or unimportant word. This mild-mannered composer refused to utter a word he did not believe. He was eminently correct in his attitude toward others and expected the same in return. But he was never as severe with others as he was with himself.

He had blue eyes, which revealed a sharp, keen mind. He was interested in everything: science, foreign countries, unusual foods, literature, languages, and, especially, philology. He was, in fact, more interested in things than in people. This knowledge of fields other than music was not superficial; he penetrated deeply into a subject and had a strong passion for accuracy. His crystal-clear mind was quick to see the humorous side of a situation, and his life was simple and modest.

He not only never had luxury but even resented the thought of it. He refused to ask favors or to accept help. His pride and integrity showed the same strength that his music radiated. It was not easy to help him, as he did not want charity.

It was part of the "Bartók tragedy" that not until immediately after his death did his popularity spread to every part of the world. On the other hand, fate did smile at Bartók in his last two years. He enjoyed, finally, the applause of the widest public and not only of the selected audiences of the various small societies of contemporary music. He had the pleasure of being wanted and commissioned by such outstanding artists as Serge Koussevitzky, William Primrose, Bartlett and Robertson, Yehudi Menuhin, Benny Goodman, and Joseph Szigeti.

The last time I saw him was when I bid him farewell in New York in June, 1945, before he went to the country with his wife. He looked well and was in best spirits. His wife remarked, as they both took me to the elevator, "Now, there is really no reason for Béla to complain; his health is good, he has composing to do in a place he loves and where he can be undisturbed." Bartók smilingly added, "Yes, I think everything is all right now. But how will my health be in the future?" The elevator arrived, and we wished each other a pleasant summer and looked forward to seeing each other in September. I never saw him again.

THE COMPOSER SPEAKS

Béla Bartók [1]

SPEAKING roughly, the period from 1910 was not revolutionary at all. In art that is not possible. In art there are only slow or fast progressions. It is essentially evolution, not revolution.

I myself, I believe, have developed in a consistent manner and in one direction, except perhaps from 1926, when my work became more contrapuntal and also simpler on the whole. A greater stress of tonality is also characteristic of this time. Before that, from about 1918 to 1924, my work was more radical and more homophonic.

With maturity, it seems to me, comes the wish to economize — to be simpler. Yes, this may account for similar trends in the

[1] This statement appeared in an interview with Friede F. Rothe in the *Etude*.

music of the other composers of my generation. Maturity is the period when one finds the just measure, the middle course that best expresses his own musical personality. The young composer is inclined to give everything he has at once. If I could write my First Quartet again, I would not write it the same way, naturally. Today I see in it some superfluous material and some resemblance to Wagner. My Fifth Quartet is a more individual work. As for the composer's individual style — there is no explaining it other than that it must come from himself.

The musical language of a " national composer " must be as natural to him as his native tongue. The musical education in countries of younger cultures works completely against this. What is a natural enough phenomenon, the use of older and established but nevertheless foreign material for teaching, creates the real difficulty in the development of an intrinsically native style and expression.

Hungary, for example, did not have a real national art music until recently. This could not be otherwise, since she was occupied for more than three hundred years by foreign peoples — first by the Turks and then by the Austrians. Political instability and cultural upheaval do not make the best soil for artistic expression, and for Hungary this became possible only at the beginning of the last century. We might say that Hungarian music began with Liszt. His life, however, was not favorable to a real national expression; he did not even speak Hungarian.

This same trend, the desire to create a national art, is operating in the smallest countries today. Or one should say " was," since World War II retarded all such efforts for a long time. Considering that there are so many small countries, and so few outstanding composers — there are only about ten or fifteen in one century — it is quite impossible for them all to crop forth with great national music. Yet, in the end, it is always the composer with strength, purpose, and individuality who puts his country on the map, and not the other way around.

The appropriate use of folk-song material, the basis for national music, is not limited to the sporadic introduction or imitation of old melodies, or to the arbitrary thematic use of them in works of foreign or international tendencies. It is rather a matter of absorbing the means of musical expression hidden in them, just as the most subtle possibilities of any language may be assimilated.

It is necessary for the composer to command this musical language
so completely that it becomes the natural expression of his musical ideas.

BARTÓK

Hugo Leichtentritt

MY first acquaintance with Béla Bartók dates back to 1906 or 1907
in Berlin. One day my friend, the young Hungarian composer Erwin Lendvai (one of the few pupils of Puccini), paid me a visit,
bringing with him a shy and modest-looking, slim youth, whom he
introduced as his friend and fellow student, Béla Bartók of Budapest. They had both been pupils in composition of Hans Koessler
at the Budapest Royal Academy. Lendvai had often spoken to me
with admiration of the scholarly and artistic teaching of Koessler. For that reason I was from the very start interested in young
Bartók and expected great things of him even before I had seen
or heard a note of his music. Bartók likewise must have had an
exaggerated notion of my importance as a critic, even though at the
time I was a beginner like my visitor. He showed marked signs
of respect for me, but after a few polite introductory phrases we
both settled down to business in earnest. He seated himself at the
timeworn miniature piano (a grand piano was beyond my reach
at the time), picked out from his bag a number of manuscripts,
and began to play. I do not, after such a long lapse of time, recol-
lect what works he played. Only one item impressed itself so vividly
on my mind that I seem to hear it in my imagination even now:
a set of little piano pieces with the oddest harmony that had ever
come to my notice. It was not the extravagant Wagnerian chromaticism — the last word in advanced harmony in those years —
nor was it akin to the refined *clair-obscur* impressionistic harmony
of Debussy, at that time very little known in Germany. It gave the
impression not of a polished refinement but, on the contrary, of a
primitive, rustic, strong, instinctive feeling for colorful sound. In a
word, the first brief acquaintance with Bartók's music revealed in

a few minutes, even so many years ago, Bartók's basic national trait, stemming from his native Hungarian soil. Everyone in those days had quite a definite notion of Hungarian music, derived from Liszt's *Hungarian Rhapsodies* and Brahms' *Hungarian Dances*. Yet this Bartók Hungarian music was different from these well-known models. Only much later did we learn that Bartók and a school of modern folklorists made a decided distinction between the music of the Hungarian gypsies, which Liszt and Brahms presented in an artistic arrangement, and the rustic music of the indigenous Hungarian peasants, the aboriginal Magyar folk music never before artistically exploited. This was what young Bartók was after, and as he grew older and matured he sought and found a methodical access to this extremely interesting and in many ways fascinating music of the Hungarian plains and mountains. In its melodies, its rhythms, scales, and sentiment, this Hungarian music differs basically from Germanic music. It is a part of Balkan music, which has been really explored only in the twentieth century. Rumanian, Bulgarian, Serbian, Albanian music, even Greek music, has more or less affinity to the Magyar folk music. They all gravitate toward the Oriental Asiatic rather than toward the Western European music.

Bartók's great achievement and his importance for the art of music consist in the exploration of this southeastern music, and in his artistically distinguished treatment of this novel material. He has enriched musical idiom by new effects and devices of rhythm, melody, color, and harmony. Additionally, he has expressed in his music a temperament, a sentiment of a new kind, differing from both the Germanic and the Slavic emotional type. Evidently it was Bartók's aim to achieve with this Hungarian music something similar to what Mussorgsky and Tchaikovsky had so successfully done with Russian music, Chopin so uniquely with Polish music, and Smetana and Dvořák for the cause of Bohemian music. They all had, so to speak, translated a provincial dialect into the internationally understood language of modern music without losing, in this process of adaptation and transformation, those distinctive national traits on which the charm and impressiveness of their music is largely dependent.

Whether the musical world will finally accord Bartók a rank equal to Chopin, Smetana, and Mussorgsky is a question that only the future can answer. Before the tribunal of history the case of

Bartók has so far been investigated fragmentarily. For a musician of his great and international reputation Bartók's lifework is far too little known. He shares this fate with Arnold Schoenberg, whose music, like that of Bartók, is practically unknown to the great mass of the music-loving public. But who is bold enough to predict or to deny that the music of these two little-performed composers may or may not in the future rank higher than the productions of Stravinsky and Hindemith, both extremely fortunate in obtaining ready and frequent performances of each new work?

For these reasons it seems prudent to reserve a final judgment of the permanent value of Bartók's music. Will the future place Bartók in the class of the great creative composers or that of the great authorities on folklore? He is, I believe, sure of a high rank in either one or the other of these categories, possibly even in both.

Besides being vitally interested in the musical folklore of southeastern Europe, Bartók is also a musician of radically modern stamp, rivaling the most advanced composers of our age in his attempts to extend the technical possibilities of the art and finding an expression of the tendencies, emotionally and stylistically, that dominate our age and give it its distinctive and unique note. From this double center of gravity can be deduced the formula describing the nature of Bartók's music in utmost brevity: to a folklore material discovered mainly by himself, he applies all the resources of the most advanced modern technique of composition. Though in one half of this program he is a companion of Schoenberg, in the other half he is most radically opposed to him, as Schoenberg uses only an abstract, artificially constructed melodic material, and is not interested in popular tunes and folk dances. In Bartók's music, however, folk-song and -dance material are the main melodic sources, and even in the few works that one might properly call "abstract" or absolute music he cannot disassociate himself from the peculiar Hungarian melodic turns and characteristic rhythms.

This short essay does not pretend to review all or even the principal works of Bartók. All it can do is to select from the considerable mass of Bartók's music a few especially characteristic works for closer inspection. Glancing over a list of his earlier published compositions, one is struck by the preponderance of small forms over large. There are no symphonies, only a few works in the sonata form, but many single dances and songs and suites. It is very difficult in this country to find anywhere a complete collection of Bartók's works. A great part of this music is written to Hungarian words, a language known only to very few foreigners. The theatrical output of Bartók has, moreover, hardly been performed outside of Hungary (with the exception of a small number of German performances). It is a hopeless task to give in words an appropriate idea of a complicated modern operatic work written in a language one cannot understand, accessible (if at all) only in a piano score, and, moreover, never heard by the reviewer in actual performance.

The present writer has witnessed only one of Bartók's dramatic works, performed in Berlin in 1929 — the opera *Duke Bluebeard's Castle* (1911). This new version of the frequently treated Bluebeard legend has high poetic and musical, but questionable dramatic, values. I quote from a review written by me in a German newspaper in 1929: " The value of the libretto written by Béla Balázs lies not in a stirring dramatic action, but in the poetic essence of the ballad originally written for declamation. The opera public can hardly be expected to trace the profound meaning of the poem behind its visible symbols, as the theatrical impression contributes very little to an easy understanding of this symbolic poetry. It is thus hardly possible to ensure this ' opera-act ' a really theatrical impression, but just as little can one dispense with a visible theatrical frame by performing the work in concert. This very regrettable vagueness makes the work really homeless: it is fit neither for the stage nor for the concert hall. In itself the valuable, quite original, music abounds in fascinating and glowing orchestral colors, and excels in the convincing expression of psychic emotions. It is a pity that so admirable a score has been made really useless."

Perhaps it is best to approach Bartók through *Mikrokosmos* (1926–37). This work is a collection of 153 progressive piano pieces, a sort of Gradus ad Parnassum of modern music in general and of the Bartók idiom in particular. Many of the tiny pieces may seem musically insignificant, but they all have a decided instructive and technical value, from the pianistic angle. A master who is fully acquainted with all the intricacies of modern piano technique and the last developments of harmony and rhythm has here skillfully reduced each principle by itself to simple formulas, and by working in an interesting and vital manner on these isolated formulas he impresses them forcefully and agreeably on the receptive mind of the student. Some of the contrapuntally more involved little exercises seem like Bach inventions translated into the modern idiom. Other pieces invite a comparison with Czerny's études; still others seem to glance retrospectively at the nimble and spirited Scarlatti sonatas or at Chopin mazurkas. Yet despite all these evident and probably intentional similarities, every single piece, even the smallest five-finger exercise, has the unmistakable Bartók stamp. The student here learns easily through ear and through his fingers the complexities of modernistic, polytonal harmony, long before he is able to understand intellectually their involved and not yet clearly formulated theory. This method is similar to learning geometry by the inspection of figures rather than by mathematical reasoning.

Best known of all Bartók works are a number of smaller piano pieces. Many pianists are familiar with the quaint *Piano Suite* (1916), the picturesque *Rumanian Folk Dances* (1909), the *Hungarian Peasant Songs* (1915). The *Allegro barbaro* (1911) has perhaps become best known. This piece is, in its harsh and crude sound, its savage fury, typical of Bartók's predilection for the primitive, even barbaric, as opposed to the prevalent esthetic superrefinement and aristocratic intellectualism. In these respects the *Allegro barbaro* does not, however, go so far as the Second Violin Sonata (1922).

What is Bartók's conception of the problems of rhythm and melody? His rhythm has hardly any relation to jazz. It is derived from Eastern folk music immensely rich in complex rhythms that have been smoothly refined in the polished art music of Central Europe. The *Dance Suite* for orchestra (1923), which was played by almost all the major symphony orchestras before World War II, abounds in striking and subtle rhythmic effects. Even the ordinary $\frac{4}{4}$ time yields in Bartók's hands surprising effects. The *ostinato* rhythms so frequent in Russian music are a regular component of Bartók's music. How cleverly he turns the ordinary monotony of these *ostinato* figures into quite surprising and charming impressions can be easily shown in the pages of the *Dance Suite*. Another favorite rhythmic device consists in maintaining strictly a rhythmical formula in the left hand without any change, whereas the right hand at the same time takes many liberties in accents and in time. Thus a subtle art of rhythmic counterpoint is brought to a high perfection, and an irregular play of accents in one hand sets off the regular accents in the other.

The unconventional type of Bartók's melody, especially in his later instrumental music, is certainly an obstacle to popular success of his austere and sometimes almost savage practice of the art. For most listeners melody is generally obtained from singing. These melodic vocal tunes occur often in Bartók's arrangements of folk songs. In his instrumental compositions, however, his melodic type has its origin often in the fantastic improvisations of the Hungarian and Rumanian rustic players and shepherds. Everybody today knows the "Shepherd's Song" in Wagner's *Tristan und Isolde*, the classic example of this improvised shepherd's music. Compared to the music of the Oriental and semi-Oriental Balkan rustic virtuosos, however, the "Shepherd's Song" is quite simple and unpretentious. Here we perceive an extremely complicated, fantastic, and exuberant melody, full of strange arabesques, rapid runs, ecstatic trills, dynamic contrasts, irregular structure, sudden changes of time, of slow and fast tempo, with pathetic accents, brimful of emotional outbursts. The usual method of notation hardly gives an adequate idea of how these rhapsodic fantasies should be performed. To catch the spirit of this music and to give it the genuine flavor, one must have imbibed it since childhood in its homeland.

It is this type of melody that makes the Second Violin Sonata and the later string quartets so difficult to understand for most listeners. Without exaggeration it may be stated that in point of melodic complexity this Bartók "theme," with its equally subtle piano accompaniment, hardly finds its equal in the entire literature of music.

Lastly, a class of highly problematic Bartók works demands attention. All through the history of music, a few works in almost every century stand apart as experimental curiosities, as abnormal products outside of the main vital current. Bartók, too, has contributed a few works to this literature of strange abnormalities. The Second Sonata for Violin and Piano is one of the most complicated and enigmatic compositions in existence. Though it may be possible for a penetrating analysis to "explain" intellectually the structural qualities of its form, the nature of its melody and harmony, yet the ear of most listeners refuses to be convinced by the actual sound of this really unpleasant work. Practically no one knew what this strange music was trying to express. Bartók has in this work, and in some of his later string quartets, shown a predilection for what I would call "bitter" sound. Evidently, this tendency is to

counteract the "sweet" sound prevailing in much of the eight-
eenth- and nineteenth-century music, especially the sugary sentimentality of most popular pieces. In my opinion, however, he goes
decidedly too far in this reaction, and often substitutes extremely
harsh and artificially constructed sound complexes for the more
natural and agreeable sounds. Withal, the quartets contain extraordinary things. There is, for example, a Lento in the Third Quartet
(1927) that manifestly bears the stamp of a great artist. Olin
Downes, in his review in *The New York Times*, described the nature of this piece so fittingly that I quote his words: " The Lento,
beginning with mysterious sustained dissonances, dropped like a
veil of color through which the song of the cellos is presently heard,
is of a mystical beauty.

Some of Bartók's last works show a return to greater simplicity
and to a more orthodox traditional manner of writing. A good sample of this simpler, more popular style is the *Divertimento*, string
for orchestra (1940). It is an adaptation of the eighteenth-century
concerto grosso to the modern idiom. The dialogue between solo
and *tutti* dominates all three movements. Here is a work at the
same time complicated and primitive, modern and traditional, artistic and popular, strange and natural. It is complicated in rhythm
and harmony, popular and natural in its melody, full of refinement
in color, yet almost naïve in its sentiment. To combine all these
great contrasts and to shape them into something coherent, vital,
and striking, yet easy to grasp, is a most difficult problem, to be
solved only by an eminent creative artist. In spite of its peculiarities, this score is easily grasped by the great public; yet it also fas-
cinates the fastidious critic with its ingenious complications, which
might elude the ordinary listener.

The works of his last ten years encircle the formal problem of
the concerto. The Violin Concerto (1938), the *Concerto for Orchestra* (1943), the Third Piano Concerto (1945), and the unfinished Viola Concerto are stations on the road to Bartók's last,
purest, and most concentrated style. More or less they all show a
tendency to a more popular, acoustically more agreeable manner
(abandoning his former extravagant and dissonant harmony). A
return to tonality, blended with short stretches of tonally dissolved
harmony, acting as a powerful spine in the tonally clear expanses,
is now evident. These last works are a very personal interpretation
of that neoclassical style dominating the last decades.

(ALBAN BERG)

1885 - 1935

BIOGRAPHY

ALBAN BERG was born in Vienna on February 9, 1885. For a long time music was only a hobby for him. In 1905 he became an Austrian government official. Not until 1907 did he decide to devote himself seriously to music. He resigned his government position, went to Berlin, and there became a pupil of Arnold Schoenberg. Between 1910 and 1914 Berg composed the *Peter Altenberg Lieder* (*Five Songs for Orchestra*), *Four Pieces for Clarinet*, and *Three Orchestral Pieces*, which revealed strongly the influence of Schoenberg. During World War I, Berg served in the Austrian Army. After the war he turned to the composition of *Wozzeck* — an opera that was to make him world-famous. When, in 1925, the world première of the opera took place in Berlin under the baton of Erich Kleiber, it created a profound impression (one critic went so far as to say that this performance was " the most striking musical event in the history of opera since *Pelléas et Mélisande* "). Performances followed in many leading opera houses of Europe. In 1931 Leopold Stokowski introduced it to American audiences through performances in Philadelphia and New York.

Berg wrote a second opera, *Lulu*, which he did not live to complete and which was introduced in its unfinished state in Zürich on June 2, 1937. Berg's last composition was a remarkable violin concerto. From the atonality of his earlier works, Berg progressed to the twelve-tone tecnhique, which he endowed with rich lyrical invention, romantic ardor, and dramatic pulse. Berg died in Vienna on December 24, 1935.

PERSONAL NOTE

Paul A. Pisk

PORTRAITS of Alban Berg, revealing the proportionate symmetry of his features and his tall, lean figure, bear a striking resemblance to those of Oscar Wilde. Even Berg's way of parting his hair, and his manner of dress, resembled those of the poet.

Alban Berg was not fond of the hectic life of the metropolis. Yet he could tolerate it, even master it. Stories are told how he charmed singers and musicians performing his works. His gentle, sympathetic attitude, sometimes marked by sarcastic humor, was always in evidence. But the composer was truly in his element in the Alpine lake district of Carinthia, where he spent a part of every year. In his earlier years he lived at the Berghof, a family estate near the Ossiach Lake; later on, he made his home in his little cabin Waldhaus near the Wörther Lake. In this vicinity were beautiful mountains and two lovely villages.

In Vienna, Berg made his quarters in a quiet street of a suburb, where he could always look at the green gardens and avoid the disturbance of the noise and dust of the city. In this house he kept his remarkable musical and literary library. Surrounded by the tender care and understanding of his beloved wife, Helene, he did his creative and critical work.

Neither narrow-minded nor fanatic, he held in kind esteem many composers who otherwise were banned from the Schoenberg inner circle. In the selection of his personal friends he was fastidious; a friend could always count on him completely. Besides his fellow students, the Schoenberg disciples Anton von Webern, Erwin Stein, and Friedrich Polnauer, his intimate circle included Mrs. Gustav Mahler (the widow of the composer) and her family.

Berg owned a little Ford, his only recreation after strenuous work. His health was very unstable. A love affair at the age of eighteen, followed by an attempted suicide, disturbed his mental and physical equilibrium. At twenty-three he suffered a first attack of bronchial asthma, from which he never completely recovered. He visited hospitals and sanatoria intermittently. He tried to overcome his physical handicap by drinking great quantities of tea in order to stimulate himself; he was also excessively fond of good wine and food.

It is tragic to realize that lack of money was indirectly responsible for his last, and fatal, illness. On my way to the Venice Music Festival of 1934, I visited him in his country home. He complained that he suffered from severe toothaches, and he did not have the funds to consult a dentist. A year later, doctors said that his fatal illness, furunculosis with ensuing blood poisoning, may have been caused by defective teeth.

Only a few days before his death he was still able to attend rehearsals and the performance of his *Lulu Suite*, symphonic excerpts from his last, uncompleted opera. In spite of his suffering, which he bore with heroism, he found kind words for the orchestra, the conductor, and the soloist. He patiently corrected mistakes. After the successful concert there was a celebration, which Berg attended. But his personal friends knew that he was a very sick man. He consumed huge amounts of aspirin to mitigate his pain. The next day he was brought to the hospital, which he was destined never to leave alive.

Berg's pleasant and gentle way of expressing himself was only the surface of his personality. Behind his good humor and light wit lay a profound philosophical mind as well as a creative imagination. He inclined toward mysticism. He believed in the symbolism of numbers and was at home in the study of comparative religion.

Nobody could ever forget his ability to analyze music and bring out every hidden structural detail as well as its emotional background. His students profited immensely from his ability to put his own mental standards aside completely while showing them what was wrong or lacking in their submitted compositions. He never forced them to adopt his own style of expression. For this reason, he was able to number among his students many independent individualities.

THE COMPOSER SPEAKS

Alban Berg [1]

I NEVER, even in my dreams, contemplated a reform of the opera through the composition of W*ozzeck.* Just as little did I intend that the work, when completed, should serve as a model either for myself or for other composers. Nor did I expect or assume that it would establish a " school."

Aside from a desire to create good music, to fill out — so to speak — the intellectual content of Büchner's immortal play, to translate his poetic idiom into a musical one, I intended, at the moment when I decided to compose the opera, nothing more than to bring to the theater that which by right belongs to the theater. I wanted to create music at every moment conscious of its responsibility to drama — yes, even more, drawing from within itself those elements necessary for the transposition of drama into reality — an achievement that demands of the composer the resolution of all essential tasks of stage direction. This was to be done without violating the autonomy of the music, without interference by extramusical elements.

That this occurred through the adoption of the older musical forms (which was regarded as one of the most important of my alleged operatic reforms) was of course self-evident. In some respects, their absorption into the realm of the opera — to so great an extent — might appear novel. But it does not constitute a service. I must, therefore, decidedly reject the assertion that I have through these innovations introduced a reform of the opera.

Since, in explaining my work in this way, I have no desire to depreciate my work — which others, who do not know it so well, can do so much better — I shall reveal what I believe to be my exclusive contribution: no matter how well one may be acquainted with the musical forms to be found in this opera, with its stringent and logical construction, with the artistic skill exhibited in its details, I demand that from the moment the curtain rises till the moment it falls no one in the audience be conscious of this diver-

[1] This statement is from an article by the composer in *Anbruch.*

sity of fugues, inventions, suite forms, and sonata forms, variations, and *passacaglias* — no one, I repeat, be filled with anything
but the *idea* of the opera, which far transcends the individual for-
tunes of *Wozzeck*.

And in this, I believe, I have been successful.

BERG

Paul A. Pisk

ALBAN BERG is often called the romanticist of the Schoenberg
school. His work is considered a bridge between the work of Richard Wagner and impressionism on one side and, on the other, the
radical tendencies in structure and emotional expression found in
the works of the younger composers of the modern school.

His belief in emphasizing specific kinds of emotions was purely
romantic. His music functioned as a link because he did not refuse
to use passages of a more or less recognizable tonality even after
having adopted the technique of the twelve-tone system. Berg's
music is more accessible to the general audience than Schoenberg's, in spite of the complexity of its intellectual structure. It may
be that the dramatic element — the text or the spoken word —
often helped to make it more comprehensible.

Before Berg met Schoenberg, who was the decisive influence
in his career, he was most strongly influenced by those composers
who dominated Vienna in the last decade of the nineteenth century. The work of Brahms stood in monumental splendor, the last
pillar of classicism. Berg's works never failed to show the constructive principles and the minute brainwork characteristic of Brahms'
masterpieces. Then there was Anton Bruckner, who endeavored to
transplant the elements of Wagnerian harmony, orchestration, and
motif technique to the realm of the symphony. Finally, there were
the compositions of Gustav Mahler, which revealed the influence
of both Brahms and Bruckner, yet were more progressive in orchestration and polyphony.

French impressionism, with its dissolution of the functional relations between chords and with its emphasis on tone color, was yet another root from which Berg's style stemmed.

Looking over his comparatively few, but all-important, compositions, we find the definite tendency of growth and maturing away from these influences. His start, however, was overshadowed by the composers mentioned above. Later he was strongly impressed by Schoenberg. But gradually, in the last two decades of his life, his unique personality came more and more to full bloom.

After several preliminary vocal and instrumental compositions, which are partly unpublished, partly lost, Berg wrote *Seven Early Songs* (about 1907). These songs, in their first edition, show clear signs of romanticism, reminding one sometimes of the melodic lines of Schumann and Wagner, sometimes of certain whole-tone progressions of Debussy and the younger Schoenberg. Their directness and intensity, their mastery of form, deeply affect the listener. Twenty years after they were written, Berg adorned them with a most unique orchestral accompaniment. By blending various sound groups and applying rich instrumental experience he changed entirely the type and emotional quality of these songs. His orchestral sound was then definitely opposed to the romantic, so that a new, dematerialized sound was created. Though the songs were not yet fully independent, they form an integral part of Berg's work.

The Piano Sonata, op. 1 (1908), maintains strong connections with the past. The *Tristan*-chromatic can be easily recognized in it; also, in some elements, Schoenberg's *Kammersymphonie*. The single movement reveals close-knitted construction of motifs and themes that are skillfully varied. The accompaniment is strictly developed from the thematic material, the links being formed by part-motifs. The dramatic character of the whole work is somewhat softened in the more melodic lyric development section.

The String Quartet (1910), in which Berg continues his gradual emancipation from tonality, is held together by the strictest economy of material. In its second movement we even find premonitions of twelve-tone construction, but without surrender of the symphonic form. The harmonies are derived from contrapuntal lines, as clashes of the independent voices. The melodic material, mostly dramatic in its character, is very concise. The scheme of the sonata form in the first movement, and of the rondo in the second, is not touched. Throughout the whole work the development of the short motifs, their parts and beginnings, can be followed. Therefore there is no need for extended development sections.

Five songs with orchestral accompaniment, set to postcard inscriptions by the Viennese poet Peter Altenberg, bear the opus number 4 (1912). Two of them were performed in 1913 at the Large Hall of the Musikverein in Vienna. A scandal followed; the booing and hissing reverberated for a long time in Berg's life. The score calls for a large symphony apparatus: three choirs of woodwinds, four horns, three trumpets, four trombones, plenty of percussion, harp and piano, plus the usual strings. The songs — from eleven to fifty-five bars in length — are only sketches for later vocal compositions, dramatic snapshots, so to speak, never lyric songs in the common sense. Berg introduced here an entirely new orchestral hue, with exotic instrumental combinations: flutter-tongue, tremolos, etc.

Four Pieces for Clarinet and Piano (1913) is the first of Berg's compositions dedicated to Schoenberg. These pieces are extremely progressive, seeking only expression in their aphoristic brevity. We find hardly any thematic material, no repetitions or sequences, only free variations. The structure of the whole set of miniatures is, however, sonatalike: Allegro, Adagio, Scherzo, and Finale, with an embryonic rondo idea.

His next work, the *Three Orchestral Pieces* (1914), belongs among his more important compositions. There are three numbers: Prelude, Round Dance (*Reigen*), and March. They all show the composer using new contrapuntal devices and creative tone color. There is no double of voices in the orchestra any longer, no filler-in material in the conventional sense; only genuine color-producing individual voices. Every instrument is handled in a very subjective manner, every note of a chord given to another instrument. Most intense direction for dynamics helps to create entirely new shades.

The last consequences of the late romantic period are reached here. Berg is about to sever himself from all stylistic and psychological ties with Gustav Mahler, which had existed up to that time. Especially remarkable is the second piece, a stylized waltz, which Berg called an orchestral study for his *Wozzeck*. In its introduction all themes, later used separately, appear together, combined and outlined in a masterly fashion. The March is Berg's most complicated score. We find here not the usual three-part formal structure, but strophic sections with changing combinations and development of cell motifs, treated like the twelve-tone rows in the later works, and using inversions and retrograde forms.

Berg was thirty-six when he finished *Wozzeck* (1921), the first of his dramatic compositions and the work that brought him fame not only all over Europe but in the United States as well. In 1914 he saw a performance of the dramatic fragment *Wozzeck*, by the romantic German poet Georg Büchner. Berg immediately felt the power of this drama. He adopted its loose twenty-five scenes for his musical purpose, compressing them into fifteen scenes and three acts. Berg subdivided this drama into three parts: Exposition, Denouement, and Catastrophe. This gives the opera the three-part structure of A–B–A. In the first act Berg finds adequate musical forms of absolute music with which to describe his characters: suite, rhapsody, military march, cradle song, *passacaglia*, and a rondolike *andante affettuoso*. The second act as a whole is a symphony in five movements: sonata, fantasia and fugue, largo, scherzo, and *rondo martiale*. Here the tragedy is developed. The Catastrophe, in which Wozzeck commits the murder and atones for it through suicide, is musically cast into five inventions: on a theme, on a tone, on a rhythm, on a key (the famous orchestral interlude in D minor, summarizing the entire tragedy), and on a persistent motion (*perpetuum mobile*).

The composer worked six years on his opera, from 1914 until 1920, finishing the orchestral score in 1921. He created the first extensive musical drama free from the bonds of tonality. *Wozzeck* appeared so difficult that nobody thought it would be possible to perform it in its entirety. A few selections (three pieces) were played at the music festival in Frankfurt in 1924. Their success was so great that the Berlin State Opera decided to give the work a complete performance in 1925. It has since been performed in other European theaters, as well as in Philadelphia and New York (in 1931) under the baton of Leopold Stokowski.

Between *Wozzeck* and Berg's second and last opera, *Lulu*, we find two works of more intimate character, in the field of chamber music: the *Chamber Concerto*, for violin, piano, and thirteen woodwinds (1925), and the *Lyric Suite*, for string quartet (1926).

The *Chamber Concerto* was written as a gift for Schoenberg's fiftieth birthday. In a letter in which Berg dedicated his work to

Schoenberg (a letter full of analytic and philosophic thoughts) he revealed many structural details of the concerto. One remark in Berg's dedicatory letter betrays the fact that he still clung to romantic tendencies. He stated that it seemed easier to talk about the formal aspects of the work than about its intimate emotions; but he tried to make his music full of expression, speaking of friendship, devotion, a world of human relationships, music after all not being mathematics alone. Berg attempted to prove this not only in this work, but in the *Lyric Suite* as well.

In the *Lyric Suite*, one of Berg's best-known and most widely performed works, he uses for the first time the twelve-tone technique of Schoenberg. The general character of the quartet is expressed in the title. We do not find here the gigantic polyphony of the *Chamber Concerto*, but rather an expansive homophony with an emotional tendency toward the darker ranges of human feeling — despair and depression. Two quotations, one from Wagner's *Tristan*, the other from Zemlinsky's *Lyric Symphony*, give clear indications of these feelings.

The *Lyric Suite* proved so successful that the composer arranged its three middle movements for string orchestra, to comply with the demand for more frequent performances.

Immediately after having completed the *Lyric Suite*, Berg searched for a libretto for a new opera. He found it in Wedekind's tragedies of sex, *Earth's Spirit* and *Pandora's Box*, both dealing with the strange life and fate of Lulu, prototype of the indomitable female soul.

In this opera Berg tried to achieve highest musical unity by deriving all his material from a single twelve-tone row. It would be too complicated to show here how all motifs and themes, characterizing the people in this opera, are derived from this one set. Willi Reich has done this, in an interesting study of *Lulu* in the *Musical Quarterly*.

Five separate parts of the opera, called symphony pieces — partly instrumental interludes, or songs, or fragments of other various sections — were combined by the composer into the so-called *Lulu Suite*. This work, first performed in Europe in 1934, was the last of Berg's compositions the composer was destined to hear.

In order to give some idea of the general principles employed by Berg in this opera, I should like to quote a portion of a letter written by him in which he outlined his ideas:

" In contradistinction to *Wozzeck*, where the character and the completeness of the many short scenes necessitated the use of self-contained character pieces in the variety of musical forms, even those of pure instrumental music, *Lulu* called forth a preference for vocal forms, like arias, duets, trios, and ensembles up to twelve voices. . . . I thought to make each scene, each act, complete in itself."

Berg was able to finish only two acts of *Lulu* in complete score, and a third of the final act. The rest he had outlined in *particelle*, that is, all vocal parts and all instrumental accompaniments, with exact indications of the instruments on three to four staffs. There is a definite possibility of completing the opera with the use of the composer's specific directions. However, when the first scenic production was staged in Zürich in 1937, after the death of the composer, the producers were content to offer only the authentic work in its incomplete state.

The American violinist Louis Krasner suggested to Berg that he write a violin concerto. The death of Berg's dear friend Manon Gropius supplied Berg with the emotional impetus. The Violin Concerto (1935) was dedicated to " the memory of an angel " — a requiem, tragically enough, not only for a dead friend but for the composer himself, who did not live to hear it.

The Concerto is in two movements, the first describing the young girl herself, and the second depicting her tragic death and final deliverance. After a short introduction, a graceful andante in ternary form opens the concerto, followed by an allegretto that utilizes one of those melodies which are characteristic of the folk song of the peasants in the Alps. It speaks for Berg's highly developed artistry that he could derive even such a melody from the twelve-tone system. The second movement, allegro, expresses the tragedy. It is freely written, in three parts, decidedly rhythmical, and powerful in its emotional expression. A pedal point speaks of death, and the beautiful Bach chorale *It Is Enough* is introduced. In the closing section the folk song recurs, cemented by the *cantus firmus* of the chorale: the human soul has found eternal rest and salvation. The Violin Concerto had its first performance in Barcelona, Spain, in 1936, and made a profound impression. Subsequently, Mr. Krasner performed it extensively in the United States.

Berg's creative output stands definitely at the end, and at the same time at the beginning, of an era in music history. Through his music, later generations will find the path to a new harmony and to that musical language which is most apt for the expression of the emotions of the twentieth century.

(ERNEST BLOCH)

1880 - 1959

BIOGRAPHY

ERNEST BLOCH was born in Geneva, Switzerland, on July 24, 1880. His love for music, revealing itself when he was still a child, made it possible for him to overcome the wishes of his parents to make him a businessman. In his fourteenth year Bloch studied composition with Jaques-Dalcroze and Rey. Three years after this he was a pupil of Ysaÿe and Rasse in Brussels. There followed a few years of further study in Germany with Knorr and Thuille.

In 1901 Bloch composed his first major work, a symphony. Discouraged by his inability to procure a performance for the work, he suddenly decided to return to Geneva and enter the business establishment of his father. For the next few years he devoted himself conscientiously to his father's shop. Composition, however, was not neglected. During the late hours of night Bloch worked on his music, creating several significant works, including an opera, *Macbeth*. This opera was introduced at the Paris Opéra-Comique in 1910, attracting the attention of Romain Rolland, who then became Bloch's first stanch admirer.

In 1916 Bloch visited the United States, as a conductor of the Maud Allan troupe. The company went into bankruptcy, leaving Bloch stranded in this country without financial resources. A few distinguished musicians, hearing of his plight, worked to bring him to the attention of the American music public. Their efforts resulted in several important performances of Bloch's works, including that of his First String Quartet by the Flonzaleys, the *Trois Poèmes juifs* by the Boston Symphony Orchestra, and an entire program of his major works by the Society of Friends of Music in New York. When, in 1919, Bloch won the thousand-dollar Elizabeth Sprague Coolidge Award for his Suite for Viola and Orchestra, his fame in this country was further solidified.

In 1920 Bloch was appointed director of the Cleveland Institute of Music. He remained in this post for five years, then became director of the San Francisco Conservatory of Music. In 1927 his *America* won a three-thousand-dollar award offered by *Musical America* for an outstanding American symphonic work, receiving the unanimous vote of the judges. This composition was introduced simultaneously by several of the leading symphony orchestras of America. In 1931 an endowment enabled Bloch to retire to Switzerland, there to devote himself exclusively to composition. For several years Bloch remained in Europe, residing in Switzerland, Italy, and France. In 1934 he returned for a visit to America, at which time he conducted the first performance of his *Sacred Service* in New York.

During the last years of his life, Bloch lived in Agate Beach, Oregon. Though seriously ill most of the time, and usually in pain, he proved unusually prolific, producing many major works. In 1954 he was the first composer selected by the New York Music Critics Circle for awards for compositions in two different categories: for orchestra, with the *Concerto grosso* No. 2, and in chamber music, for the Third String Quartet. Bloch died in Portland, Oregon, on July 15, 1959.

PERSONAL NOTE

Suzanne Bloch

THIS can only be a superficial sketch of Father. To describe him fully would require endless chapters. So complex a personality presents many different pictures, which cannot be adequately described in a few pages.

When I look back at the storms and lulls, tragedies and comedies, within our family circle, one of his qualities stands out particularly: Father lived each of our lives intensely and expected us to share his own life with equal intensity. He always confided in us. Sometimes we were too young to understand the full implications of his disclosures. At other times, when we *did* understand, they proved to be disturbing experiences to us.

Each of us children went through a period of being " the only one who understands " him. This brought with it a great responsibility. Father's heart was always full. His likes, dislikes, enthusiasms, letdowns, went to such extremes that they overflowed. His capacity for joy, suffering, anger, and affection was immense. Whoever was there to share it received the full measure of it. It was an avalanche of feelings that overwhelmed the one who came into contact with it. When the lull came and one emerged into the commonplace everyday life of plain mortals, one carried away an incredible impression.

During our childhood he filled our lives with wonderful experiences. We had music day and night. We still remember those marvelous evenings when, from our beds, we could listen to the sounds of *Schelomo, Macbeth,* the *Psalms.* This music was to us a deep, intimate language connected with the mysterious shadows and lights that only children can understand.

Father also gave us our profound love of nature, our capacity to find in it peace, courage, and comfort. He taught us mushroom lore, and up to this day our eyes are so trained that whenever we are in the open our eyes instinctively search for chanterelles or boletuses.

When Father was deeply impressed by a book, he had to share his reactions with each one of us. In the past, a scene like the following was enacted over and over again in our home. Picture a quiet Sunday afternoon. Mother is sewing or reading in her room. The three children are busy with homework or blissfully wasting time. From the parlor comes a series of sounds: a cough, a laugh, either good-humored or sardonic; a loud " Ha! " Suddenly a call: " Marguerite, *les enfants,* come here for a minute! " In a short while, the Bloch family is gathered, listening to a dramatic reading from Flaubert, Walt Whitman, Shakespeare, or Clarence Day.

We had a severe dose of Freud at one time. Many years later it was Havelock Ellis. Father's literary choice of the moment was known among us as " The Book." His enthusiasm for people was similar. One day, after he came home elated over another mar-

velous person he had met, my sister said calmly: " Another one."
Father roared with laughter. The saying became a refrain in the
family.

Though he was never a tyrant with us, his strong views could
not help influencing us. There was a time when our friends complained that we children began all our sentences with: " Father
said." Frankly, to this day, some of our opinions have a strong
Bloch tinge, even though individually we have reacted to many
things differently from the way he did.

As we grew up and went through all the silly and miserable
phases of adolescence, Father became irritated at and intolerant of
the ideas we brought home. He suffered whenever he saw outside
influences change us. He would then explode at anything we had
to say. We became strangers. Events in his emotional life did not
help to bring us any closer. He suffered unnecessarily to notice in
us what is normal in all growing children. Though he always held
free theories about his life, he showed himself to be conservative
about his children's actions. But when he tried to prevent us from
making mistakes, and failed to do so, he never indulged in " I told
you so " at the fulfillment of his prophecies.

Many years ago, the worst he had foreseen about a decision
I had made against his will had taken place. We met in New York.
I was crushed, but defiant. We had a long talk, and tears were shed.
Then he took me out to lunch, bought me the very best cigarettes.
Finally, he took me into a bookshop to get me Nietzsche's *Thus
Spake Zarathustra* for comfort!

Having a firm theory that children should not be forced to
study music, he did nothing about finding out whether any of us
were gifted. Perhaps he left the responsibility to Mother, who, in
turn, expected him to take the initiative. Thus, it was not until I
was nine — and then thanks to a Geneva schoolmaster — that
I began to take music lessons. Father was then away in America.
Upon his return, the discovery of my music study filled him with
joy. At once he began to give me a thorough training in *solfège*,
for which I am eternally grateful. Later on came rudiments of harmony and counterpoint. He explained everything to me very rapidly, taking gift and intelligence for granted.

I remember the lessons, which were never very regular. They
often lasted two hours. I emerged from them dazed from the pipe
smoke and concentration. I can see Father's long upward-curving

finger sliding over the page, rapidly pointing to passages of importance, or catching the consecutive fifths or octaves I had overlooked. Most of the work was done away from the piano, with the
result that I learned to *hear* and to compose without being a
slave to the keyboard.

Concerts were a treat. We would sit in a gallery at Carnegie
Hall. Father's pet trick was to tell me what wind or reed instrument was playing, then, later, whispering suddenly to me: " *Quel
instrument?* "

Thanks to Father's theory that certain esthetic experiences are
more valuable than routined study, he permitted me to sing under
him when he conducted a small *a cappella* chorus. I often sang
soprano, or alto, and even amused him when I suggested helping
out the tenors, who were few in number. We never realized then
how valuable this contact with Josquin Després, Orlando di Lasso,
etc., would be for my later work!

After an evening of motets and madrigals, we would trudge
home by subway, refreshed by an ice cream, a weary but blissfully
happy pair. Such experiences enriched our lives, and it is with
gratitude that we recall them. He gave us so much. His first thought
was for the family. One must realize that this was not an ordinary
father. This was a creative artist who had written many great works;
who had all reasons to think and live for himself; who, tormented
and torn, was often tempted to break away from bonds. Yet never
did he shake off his responsibilities. For this he always had my
sympathy and my admiration.

THE COMPOSER SPEAKS

Ernest Bloch [1]

MUSIC consists, for the greatest part, of the incomparable legacy
left to us by the great masters. When we study their lives and their
works, people like Palestrina, Bach, Beethoven, and Wagner appear

[1] This statement was prepared by the composer for this book from various
earlier writings.

to us not only as marvelous musicians, but also as tremendous human personalities. Their message, comparable to that of Homer and Shakespeare in literature, surpasses infinitely what we commonly conceive as music, the world of sounds. The meaning behind, the spirit of the message, transports us into another world, and makes us think, feel, live differently. It is not because they were great masters of the notes only, but because they were great men first. They expressed their vision through music.

The works of Bach, for example, in spite of their overwhelming technique and amazing perfection and beauty, sprang forth from something deeper and higher than music itself — his conception of life. It is impossible to disassociate the music of Beethoven from the greatness of the man Beethoven. Thus, too, Richard Wagner is infinitely more than a musician or even an artist.

When art is conceived in this way and becomes an expression of a philosophy of life, it is no longer a luxury, a fad, or a cult of big names of virtuosos. Questions of the personalities of interpreters, which seem to play such an important part in the artistic discussions of our day, disappear. It is a storm that carries one away, unites all men in a unit of solidarity, shakes them to the bottom of their souls, waking them to the greatest problems of their common destiny.

Bach, Beethoven, and Wagner never had any idea of amusing or diverting. They had a message to deliver to humanity through words and sounds. That is all that preoccupied them. When the public is wearied of the childish harmonic, instrumental, and rhythmic games with which our generation seems mostly concerned, the message of these great masters will still shine in all its glory, because, being purely human, it is eternal.

Spiritual values can never die. The universal idea must prevail. This crucial idea has permeated all my life and most of my works, from the first C-sharp minor symphony to my *Sacred Service* — my ultimate faith and belief in the unity of man, in spite of real racial values and dissimilarities. My faith is in justice — even delayed — on earth, in the right of each man to live his life decently and usefully and giving to the community what he can give, according to his gifts, his forces. This is the great idea of our great prophets, and also, in many ways, the ideal of prophets of other races, like Confucius, Buddha, Christ.

BLOCH

David Ewen

SOMETHING of the ecstasy of the Hebraic prophet molded the artistic career of Ernest Bloch. No Biblical Jeremiah consecrated himself to the pronouncement of prophetic truths with more passionate idealism and self-abnegation than Bloch to the composition of music. To Bloch, the creation of music in general — and Hebrew music in particular — was a sacrosanct mission. It has been recorded that as a child Bloch wrote upon a slip of paper a vow that he would devote his life to music. This slip of paper he placed under a mound of rocks over which he burned a ritual fire. Bloch's career, thus launched, assumed in his eyes the aspect of religious consecration. And a consecration it remained throughout his life.

Few composers of any day were so unswervingly true to themselves and to the artistic principles they adopted in early manhood as was Bloch. Like the ancient Hebraic prophet, he was always sublimely sure of himself, always intoxicated with the self-assurance that the truth rested with him, fully convinced of the significance of his artistic mission. To Bloch, as to the Biblical prophet, love for and faith in humanity were essential parts of his *Weltanschauung*. Bloch's music, therefore, was a conscious attempt to uplift man, to reveal to him new conceptions of beauty and truth.

The Hebrew prophet comes to mind in speaking of Bloch's deep-rooted mysticism. Bloch was not a religious man in the formal and accepted sense of the term; nor was he so racially chauvinistic as his Hebraic music might suggest. His religion was, rather, a world religion, and his God a spiritual Being for all men. It was the spiritual and poetic qualities of religion that appealed so sensitively to him.

It is these qualities of the Biblical prophet in Bloch that compelled him in several decades of artistic self-expression to cling tenaciously to those ideals and standards he adopted in his youth. And it is these qualities that brought to all of his music a nobility of conception, a profundity of expression, almost an otherworldliness, that are Bloch's most distinguishing traits as a composer.

Bloch's creative career reveals three distinct periods. The first of these, spanning the years from 1901 to 1915, produced his Symphony in C-sharp minor (1901), the opera *Macbeth* (1909), the *Poèmes d'automne* (1906) for voice and orchestra, and the two symphonic sketches entitled *Hiver–Printemps* (1905). In these early works, the style that is today recognizable as Bloch's is already manifest in embryo. That barbaric ferocity and passion, savage in their intensity, fill this early music with an enormous vitality and energy; the fully developed melodic lines and the free use of the rhythmic elements are already clearly apparent. Moreover, there are evident certain Hebraic qualities — the use of Oriental intervals and of vivid harmonic colors. And already one can discern in this music the high idealism and nobility of a great heart that speak so unmistakably in Bloch's later works.

In or about 1915, Bloch's style underwent a definite change. It was at this time that he became imbued with the ideal to create a Hebrew music that would give expression to his race. Truth to tell, the development of Bloch's music from the first period of the Symphony in C-sharp minor to the Hebraic period was not quite so sudden as many critics have been tempted to suspect. The careful ear can discern many qualities in Bloch's early works that are Hebraic. One need but note the elegiac sadness in portions of this symphony and the almost Chassidic mysticism of the fugue of the last movement, the religious fervor of the *Poèmes d'automne*, the Oriental flavor of Bloch's harmonizations, and the Semitic intervals in his melodic line to realize that Bloch evidently felt the Hebrew spirit keenly from the very first and attempted, however gropingly, to transfer it into his music. It was not until a little more than ten years after the Symphony in C-sharp minor, however, that Bloch openly acknowledged himself to be a Jewish composer. " Racial consciousness is absolutely necessary in music, even though nationalism is not," he announced as his new esthetic creed. " I am a Jew. I aspire to write Jewish music not for the sake of self-advertisement, but because it is the only way in which I can produce music of vitality — if I can do such a thing at all." At another time, in explaining his Jewish music, Bloch wrote: " It is not my purpose or my desire to attempt a ' reconstruction ' of Jewish music, or to base my work on melodies more or less authen-

tic. I am not an archeologist. I hold that it is of first importance
to write good, authentic music — *my own music*. It is the Jewish
soul that interests me, the complex, glowing, agitated soul that I
feel vibrating throughout the Bible . . . the freshness and naïveté
of the Patriarchs, the violence of the prophetic books; the Jew's
savage love of justice; the despair of the ecclesiastes; the sorrow
and the immensity of the Book of Job; the sensuality of the Song
of Songs. All this is in us, all this is in me, and it is the better
part of me. It is all this that I endeavor to hear in myself, and
to translate into my music; the sacred emotions of the race that
slumber far down in our soul."

With such works as the *Two Psalms* (137 and 114) for soprano and orchestra (1914), *Trois Poèmes juifs* (1913) for orchestra, composed in memory of his father, and *Psalm 22* (1914)
for baritone and orchestra, Bloch definitely discovered his race and
associated himself with it. By the close of the year 1916, Bloch
was to travel even deeper into the Hebraic world he had recently
begun to explore, with the completion of such works as *Schelomo*
(1916), for cello and orchestra, a portrait in tone of a great Biblical
Jew, and *Israel Symphony* (1916), the proud and exultant af-
firmation of his race.

It is this Hebrew period that produced many of Bloch's most
famous works. While I, personally, do not accept all of this music
with the unqualified enthusiasm of some critics, I cannot deny
that, at its best, it speaks with sublime vocabulary. Bloch's music
often has a profound depth, an enormous vision, an inspiring eloquence, and a contagious enthusiasm. Its tremendous vitality is
irresistible; and we seem, in this music, to catch a new glimpse at
the soul of beauty. However, it is my personal feeling that both the
Israel Symphony and *Schelomo* (always with the exception of
sporadic superb pages) are too self-conscious. Certain elements of
Hebrew music — the Oriental color, the ritual trumpets, the augmented second intervals in the melody — have been superimposed
on the music and are not integral and inevitable parts of it. Both
of these works fail to convince as Hebrew documents. They are at
their best when the Hebrew message is less strongly emphasized.
It is almost as though, freed from the constraining necessity of composing music essentially Hebrew in technique, Bloch could give his
inspiration free rein, and it was able to soar and expand.

In his third period, Bloch is less the Hebrew musician and

more the composer for all races and creeds. While certain Hebraic mannerisms still cling to him — and while, in specific works, the subject matter is essentially of Hebrew origin — it is not of one race that Bloch speaks but of all mankind. Even his *Sacred Service* (1933), designed for use in the Jewish synagogue, was intended by him to be infinitely more than a ritual service for his race; he hoped to create a monumental Song of Faith for all humanity. " Though intensely Jewish in roots," is Bloch's own explanation, " the message seems to me above all a gift of Israel to the whole of mankind. It symbolizes for me far more than a Jewish service, but, in its great simplicity and variety, it embodies a philosophy acceptable to all men."

It is in this third, and crowning, period of Bloch's creative evolution that he produced those works that represent the fullest and ripest expression of his genius: the First *Concerto grosso* (1925), the First Piano Quintet (1924), the *Sacred Service* (1933), A *Voice in the Wilderness* (1936), and the Violin Concerto (1937). During this period he also composed works less striking in character than those enumerated above, including: *Quartet Pieces* (1924), *America* (1926), and *Helvetia* (1928). In most of these works, Bloch seems to have digressed sharply from his Hebraic path. The discerning critic will realize, however, that the digression is not quite so marked as might first be suspected. The First Piano Quintet, the First *Concerto grosso*, and *America* may not be Hebrew compositions; but who can doubt that they are the creations of a Jew? One critic has well pointed out that the Indians of *America* dance with Chassidic feet; in the same vein it might be said that the Indian thematic material from the first movement of the Violin Concerto is sung by a Jewish voice. Bloch may have deserted Hebrew music, but Hebrew music has refused to part with him. As a matter of fact, the First Piano Quintet is, in my opinion, the most successful of his attempts to give expression to his race. It is a profoundly religious document. Its religion does not consist in artificial exteriors, but rather in the religion of philosophers. Through its expressive harmonies Spinoza trumpets his intellectual love of God; the meditative mysticism of Chassidic folklore seems to speak in the placid counterpoint. The religion of the quintet purifies and exalts; it shows us more clearly than any other of Bloch's music the true soul of the Hebrew religion.

In *America* and in *Helvetia*, Bloch pays tribute to his two countries. If both these works are disappointing it is only because the composer does not seem to feel the spirit of his countries so intimately as he does that of his race. Unquestionably there are moments of heroic grandeur, power, and majesty in *America*. But both *America* and *Helvetia* lack conviction. In *America* the anthem that Bloch fashioned for the close is not a culminating paean of praise that one had the right to expect from a work of such proportions; it is a trite and rather effete melody such as might have been penned by a schoolboy.

However, with *A Voice in the Wilderness* and *Sacred Service*, Bloch is once again the master speaking a high-minded language of Hebraic origin but designed for humanity. The *Sacred Service* was composed in a passion inspired by the fear then haunting Bloch that he was on the verge of death. He had been ill for more than a year, and the conviction was strong within him that his *Sacred Service* was to be his last work. That Bloch should be obsessed with thoughts of death at the time he was constructing a monumental religious work was an enormously significant fact. There are certain artists who suddenly acquire a new vision, a new insight often profound and otherworldly, as though they had caught a glimpse of the eternal, when they believe themselves to be at the threshold of death. Beethoven composed his last quartets under such stress; Mozart, his *Requiem*; Wagner, *Parsifal*. Bloch, too, was similarly affected. There are pages in the *Sacred Service* that seem to peer into another world and to catch glimpses of the infinite.

In this work " the sacred emotion of the race that slumbers far down in our soul " has been given eloquent expression. It is a work compounded of tenderness and passion, power and humility. It has visions of unearthly beauty (the passage for alto and viola, " And These Words Which I Command," for example) that lay upon the spirit of the listener an angelic serenity that uplifts and ennobles. There are passages, on the other hand, that an honest critic cannot accept, such as the closing orchestral portion of the first part, and the *Yimloch* chorus, which brings the second part to an end — bombast and pomp, for the most part. Yet acknowledging these defects and lamenting them, the *Sacred Service* remains a work of outstanding importance. Listen to the awe and grandeur of the *Shema*, following immediately after the heart-moving poignancy of the *Veohavto*; listen to the superb majesty of

Tzur Yisroel; listen to the terrifying mystery of the *Kodosh* — listen to these passages and you will hear a music springing from inspiration, a music born out of pain and stress and ascending toward a new world.

Bloch's next important work, *A Voice in the Wilderness,* for orchestra and cello obbligato, is a better integrated work than the *Sacred Service.* If it never voices the note of sublimity achieved by the *Sacred Service* in its best pages, it is a more coherent artistic conception, never relinquishing its high plane of mysticism and beauty, never yielding to a banal thought. Like the best of Bloch's music — the First Piano Quintet and the *Sacred Service* — it is not Hebraic through the adoption of technical devices; it is Hebraic in its spirit of idealism and resignation, in its prevalent mood of introspection and poetry, in its moving pathos and stirring drama, in the incandescent spirituality with which it is aflame. It is written with conciseness and inevitable logic.

Spirituality, intensity, and inexorable logic characterize and make significant several of Bloch's last works, notably the String Quartets Nos. 2, 3, and 4 (1946, 1951, 1953), the Second *Concerto grosso* (1952), the Symphony in E-flat (1955), and the Second Piano Quintet (1957). Each is an unqualified masterwork. Each represents the master at the height of his creative powers. Each provides eloquent testimony that up to his last day Bloch was one of the most strongly gifted and imaginative composers of our time, ever conscious of his artistic destiny, ever progressing unfalteringly toward his artistic goal.

(BENJAMIN BRITTEN)

1913 -

BIOGRAPHY

BENJAMIN BRITTEN was born in Lowestoft, Suffolk, England, on November 22, 1913. From earliest childhood he revealed extraordinary musical talent: he began composing when he was five, completed his first string quartet in his ninth year, and by the time he was sixteen had produced a symphony, ten piano sonatas, a half dozen quartets, and numerous songs. In 1934 Britten published a *Simple Symphony* that incorporated material from pieces he had written between the ages of nine and fourteen.

His academic study took place at Gresham's School, Holt, in Norfolk. At the same time, he studied the piano, and took lessons in theory from Frank Bridge, who was a profound influence in his development. Between 1930 and 1934, Britten attended the Royal College of Music, studying composition with John Ireland, and piano with Arthur Benjamin and Harold Samuel. He was only twenty-one when he first attracted public attention, with the *Fantasy Quartet*, for oboe and strings, successfully introduced at the International Society for Contemporary Music Festival in Florence in 1934.

In the summer of 1939, Britten came to the United States, remaining until 1942 and in those years writing several major works, the *Sinfonia da Requiem* and his first opera, *Paul Bunyan*, both introduced in New York in 1941. After returning to England, Britten completed his opera *Peter Grimes* on a commission from the Koussevitzky Foundation. Its success first in London and then in many of the world's music centers placed him among England's major creative figures, a position he subsequently solidified with later operas. During the coronation festivities in 1953 he was created a Companion of Honor. In 1964 he received the first Aspen (Colorado) Award, and in 1965, the Order of Merit.

PERSONAL NOTE

Eric Walter White

BRITTEN is first and foremost a professional musician. Composer, pianist, viola player, research scholar, and musical editor — in the course of his career he has been engaged in multifarious activities connected with music, and if he has carried them out successfully and well, it is because he has taken the trouble to acquire the necessary technique. In his broadcast talk " The Composer and the Listener " in 1946 he said: " Obviously it is no use having a technique unless you have the ideas to use this technique; but there is, unfortunately, a tendency in many quarters today to believe that brilliance of technique is a danger rather than a help. This is sheer nonsense. There has never been a composer worth his salt who has not had supreme technique. I'll go further than that and say that in the work of your supreme artist you can't separate inspiration from technique. I'd like anyone to tell me where Mozart's inspiration ends and technique begins."

For technical reasons, among others, he is always prepared to work to order. He does not believe in allowing his talents to rust. As an artist, he wants to serve the community and has shown himself ready to accept commissions of every kind. He finds virtue in serving all sorts of different persons and believes that even " hack work will not hurt an artist's integrity, provided he does his best work with every commission."

To have as many new ideas as he has and to work as hard as he does argues not only extraordinary fertility and fluency but also great sensitivity. If an artist lacks feeling, he loses much of the impetus toward expression. Britten shows himself sensitive in many ways — particularly to cruelty and suffering. Many of his operas contain (or imply) scenes of almost sadistic cruelty, and they inevitably lead to episodes of warm compassion and pity. This intense sympathy with the victims of oppression probably lies at the basis of his pacifism; and Hans Keller has made the interesting suggestion that " by dint of character, musical history, and environment, he has become a *musical pacifist* too."

There are many aspects of Britten's character that could be pursued if one felt inclined. His sense of humor (or should one say his sense of proportion?); his brisk fancy and ambivalent imagination; his fondness for children. He remembers with pleasure his own youth in East Anglia — fetes and obstacle races, bicycle rides, tennis tournaments, bathing parties, making friends and making music — and projects himself without difficulty into the minds and hearts of young people today. That is why he writes such good music about children and for them to listen to and play.

Suffolk is his home county. He was born there, and he lives there today. Some of his operas are set there — *Peter Grimes, Albert Herring*, and *The Little Sweep*. It was therefore a fine compliment when in the summer of 1951 he was made an Honorary Freeman of the Borough of Lowestoft. On that occasion he took the opportunity of confirming his allegiance to that part of England. In his speech of thanks he said: " Suffolk, the birthplace and inspiration of Constable and Gainsborough, the loveliest of English painters; the home of Crabbe, the most English of poets; Suffolk, with its rolling, intimate countryside; its heavenly Gothic churches, big and small; its marshes, with those wild sea birds; its grand ports and its little fishing villages. I am firmly rooted in this glorious country. And I proved this to myself when I once tried to live somewhere else."

THE COMPOSER SPEAKS

Benjamin Britten [1]

FOR most of my life I have lived closely in touch with the sea. My parents' house in Lowestoft directly faced the sea, and my life as a child was colored by the fierce storms that sometimes drove ships onto our coast and ate away whole stretches of the neighboring cliffs. In writing *Peter Grimes*, I wanted to express my awareness of the perpetual struggle of men and women whose livelihood depends on the sea — difficult though it is to treat such a universal subject in theatrical form.

I am especially interested in the general architectural and formal problems of opera, and decided to reject the Wagnerian theory of " permanent melody " for the classical practice of separate numbers that crystallize and hold the emotion of a dramatic situation at chosen moments. One of my chief aims is to try to restore to the musical setting of the English language a brilliance, freedom, and vitality that have been curiously rare since the death of Purcell. In the past hundred years, English writing for the voice has been dominated by strict subservience to logical speech rhythms, despite the fact that accentuation according to sense often contradicts the accentuation demanded by emotional content. Good recitative should transform the natural intonations and rhythms of everyday speech into memorable musical phrases (as with Purcell), but in more stylized music the composer should not deliberately avoid unnatural stresses if the prosody of the poem and the emotional situation demand them, nor be afraid of a high-minded treatment of words, which may need prolongation far beyond their common speech length, or a speed of delivery that would be impossible in conversation.

The scarcity of modern British operas is due to the limited opportunities that are offered for their performance. Theater managers will not present original works without a reasonable hope of recovering their costs of production; composers and writers cannot thrive

---

[1] The above statement, an extract from the Introduction to the Sadler's Wells libretto of *Peter Grimes*, was selected by Mr. Britten for this book.

without the experience of seeing their operas adequately staged and sung; the conservatism of audiences hinders experimental departures from the accepted repertory.

BRITTEN

Eric Walter White

MUSIC was an early love of Britten's. He started to compose when he was five; piano lessons began two years later, and viola lessons when he was ten or eleven. Before leaving his preparatory school at the age of fourteen, he had more than one hundred opus numbers to his credit, including six string quartets, twelve piano sonatas, dozens of songs, sonatas for violin, sonatas for viola and cello, suites, waltzes, rondos, fantasies, variations, a tone poem entitled *Chaos and Cosmos,* a symphony for gigantic orchestra including eight horns, and an oratorio entitled *Samuel.* Of this phenomenal juvenile output, nothing has been published except a few excerpts from early piano pieces and songs that were used as the basis of the *Simple Symphony* (1925, revised 1934) for string orchestra.

The first public performance of any of his works was given in London at a Macnaghton-Lemare concert of new music on December 12, 1932, while he was still a student at the Royal College of Music. The works included in the program were a *Fantasy* for string quintet (unpublished) and three two-part songs for female voices to words by Walter de la Mare. His reputation as a composer grew rapidly after he left the college in 1934. A set of choral variations for unaccompanied choir entitled A *Boy Was Born* was broadcast by the BBC early in 1934. The same year his *Fantasy Quartet,* for oboe, violin, viola, and cello (1932), was included in the program of the International Society for Contemporary Music at Florence; and this marked the beginning of his reputation abroad. About the same time he joined the G.P.O. Film Unit and during the four years 1935–9 wrote incidental music for sixteen documentary films made by that unit and two documentary films and a feature film made by other companies. In 1939 he visited Canada and the United States for three years and on his return to England settled down in his native East Anglia.

None of Britten's instrumental compositions fits into the accepted category of the instrumental symphony; but several of them are of real symphonic stature. One of his earliest works, the *Sinfonietta* (1932), a chamber symphony for ten instruments, employs a symphonic layout with considerable cleverness. The *Simple Symphony*, though written in four movements with carefully contrasted thematic material, seems to be nearer a suite than a symphony. The *Sinfonia da Requiem* (written in 1940 in memory of his parents) has a program that is explicit in its title. Although the three movements (" Lacrymosa," " Dies irae," " Requiem aeternam ") are strongly contrasted, they are all in the same key, and some of the musical material appears in more than one of the movements. It is characteristic of Britten's bias toward vocal music that the greatest of his symphonies should be a choral rather than an instrumental symphony — the *Spring Symphony* (1949). In planning a symphony that would deal with "the progress of winter to spring and the reawakening of the earth and life," he chose a dozen English poems, which he grouped in molecular fashion to form the four main movements, and showed great virtuosity in setting this heterogeneous material in a unified musical idiom and giving the work the specific gravity of a symphony.

There are three important concertos: the Piano Concerto in D (1938), the Violin Concerto in D minor (1939), and the *Diversions on a Theme*, for piano (left hand) and orchestra (1940). In each of these, the composer subsequently had second thoughts and carried out a number of revisions. In 1946 an Impromptu was substituted for the Recitative and Aria that originally formed the third movement of the Piano Concerto; minor changes were made in the Violin Concerto in 1950; and the *Diversions*, which had been written for the one-armed Viennese pianist, Paul Wittgenstein, was revised in 1951, one of the original eleven variations being omitted.

Britten has always been attracted by variations as a musical form; and two of his greatest successes in this field have been the *Variations on a Theme of Frank Bridge* (1937) and *The Young Person's Guide to the Orchestra* (1946). The *Variations on a Theme of Frank Bridge* was specially written for the Boyd Neel String Orchestra for the Salzburg Festival of 1937. *The Young Person's Guide* was planned as a set of variations and a fugue on a theme from Purcell's incidental music to *Abdelazar* and is intended to show off every department and instrument of the orchestra in turn. Both works have proved very popular not only in the concert hall, but also in the theater, where at various times their scores have been used as accompaniment for at least six different ballets.

His chamber music includes two string quartets (1941 and 1945). *Lacrymae* (1950), reflections on a song of Dowland for viola and piano, is another fine example of his talent for varying a theme. The *Six Metamorphoses after Ovid* (1951), for oboe solo, forms an outstandingly successful suite for an unaccompanied wind instrument and is particularly effective when played in the open air.

Throughout his career, Britten has shown a special feeling for the voice and has poured forth in profusion songs, song cycles, part songs, and every kind of choral work and cantata. The choice of words to set — whether English, French, Italian, German, or Latin — has always been a matter of serious importance to him, for he realizes that syllables, words, phrases, and sentences can serve as a vital part of a musical structure and enjoys trying to reconcile the meaning that lies behind the literal façade with the musical idea behind the notational façade.

Britten has always been a reader of discrimination and a lover of English poetry. At first he chose existing texts for his songs and cantatas; but *Our Hunting Fathers* (1936), a symphonic cycle for high voice and orchestra, was the first of his works with a specially written text. On this occasion, his friend, the poet W. H. Auden, chose as his theme man's relations to animals and wrote an original prologue and epilogue of his own to frame three poems he had selected to illustrate animals in their various roles of pests, pets, and prey. This collaboration prospered. Shortly afterward, Britten selected five of Auden's poems and set them as a song cycle for high voice and piano called *On This Island* (1937). Auden collaborated with Randall Swingler to provide the text for *Ballad of Heroes* (1939), a work for high voice, chorus, and orchestra intended to honor the men of the British Battalion of the International Brigade who had fallen in the Spanish Civil War. And on Britten's voyage back from America in the spring of 1942, he set a specially written text of Auden's, the *Hymn to St. Cecilia*, for mixed voices unaccompanied, which proved to be one of his simplest, loveliest, and most moving works.

Britten's friendship with the tenor Peter Pears has been responsible for a number of his most successful vocal works. These include numerous song cycles. The *Seven Sonnets of Michelangelo* (1940), in the original Italian, the *Holy Sonnets of John Donne* (1945), *Winter Words* (1953), with lyrics by Thomas Hardy, and *Six Hölderlin Fragments* (1958), in the original German, are for tenor and piano. *Songs from the Chinese* (1958) are for tenor and guitar. In addition to *Our Hunting Fathers*, there are three orchestral song cycles — the setting of some of Rimbaud's poems from *Les Illuminations* (1939), in the original French, a small anthology of English poems illustrating various facets of night entitled *Serenade* (1943), and another anthology exploring the recesses of sleep entitled *Nocturne* (1958).

To be distinguished from these song cycles are the canticles, in which the composer takes a more extended text and deals with it as a single musical entity rather than a cycle or suite of different songs. The first canticle (1947) is a setting of a poem by Francis Quarles for tenor and piano; the second (1952), for alto, tenor, and piano, is the scene of Abraham and Isaac from the Chester Miracle Play and is set with recitative separating passages of arioso; the third (1954) is a setting for tenor, horn, and piano of Edith Sitwell's poem " Still Falls the Rain."

There are also numerous motets, anthems, and cantatas, including *A Ceremony of Carols* (1942), *Rejoice in the Lamb* (1943), to words by Christopher Smart, *Saint Nicolas* (1948), to a specially written text by Eric Crozier, and the *Missa brevis* in D (1959). For the five hundredth anniversary of Basel University he composed a setting of extracts from the Latin text of the University Charter called *Cantata academica* (1960), which is replete with ingenious musical devices.

Britten's predilection for vocal music would not necessarily have led him to opera unless he also had a natural feeling for the stage and the dramatic potentialities of music. His interest was quickened by the incidental music he wrote for films in his early years, which led to commissions for incidental music for plays and radio-feature programs as well. His first operatic experiment was a choral operetta, *Paul Bunyan* (1941), with libretto by Auden; but this was not a success when produced at Columbia University, New York. His real chance came with *Peter Grimes* (1945), which was commissioned by the Koussevitzky Music Foundation and produced at Sadler's Wells Theater, London, on June 7, 1945. Its impact was decisive. It was an immediate artistic and popular success, not only in England but also abroad, for in the course of the next few years it was produced in nearly twenty countries in different parts of the world.

After this, it was natural that he should continue to exploit the operatic vein. Partly because of personal preference and partly because of operatic conditions in England he decided to write some of his subsequent operas — e.g., *The Rape of Lucretia* (1946), *Albert Herring* (1947), and *The Turn of the Screw* (1954) — for a small chamber-music combination, i.e., a group of solo singers and an instrumental ensemble of about a dozen soloists.

Britten has also shown great virtuosity in the way he tackles problems of operatic structure. Like Verdi in his last two operas, he moves rapidly and easily between the various degrees of intensity needed for recitative, airs, arioso passages, and concerted ensembles; and his operas tend to be most satisfactory when the musical flow is continuous within the acts, sometimes with the assistance of interludes joining the different scenes. *Peter Grimes, The Rape of Lucretia, The Turn of the Screw*, and *A Midsummer Night's Dream* (1960) are specially successful examples of this gift for formal organization. The sixteen scenes into which the two acts of *The Turn of the Screw* are divided combine the salient formal features of the variations and the cycle in a particularly brilliant way. A looser and possibly less successful musical organization is to be found in *Gloriana* (written for the coronation of 1953), in which each of the eight individual scenes is a self-contained tableau.

In his operas as in his other compositions, Britten's style is eclectic, his idiom modal; and his musical metrics often echo the familiar structure of English prosody. This should make it comparatively easy for the public to appreciate his operas, were it not for the fact that frequently some kind of dichotomy seems to occur. An example of this can be seen in his choice of characters with split or imperfectly integrated personalities. Peter Grimes is a case in point — also the eponymous hero of the comic opera *Albert Herring*, and Captain Vere and Claggart in *Billy Budd* (1951). A favorite device is the combination, not necessarily the reconciliation, of two completely different musical streams; and in this connection he frequently uses enharmony.

Psychological problems appeal to him as operatic subjects — the psychopath earns his sympathy and understanding; manifestations of violence and cruelty arouse his deep compassion; the theme of maltreated youth is almost obsessional. In *Peter Grimes*, the fisherman's sadistic outbursts against the boy apprentice form the mainspring of the tragedy; and the boy's situation is made all the more poignant because the part is mute and his feelings can only be expressed indirectly. There is a similar problem in the children's opera *The Little Sweep* (1949), where the boy hero is also exploited and maltreated by his master; but on this occasion the ending is a happy one. In *Billy Budd* the novice's flogging is an essential element in the action and produces a feeling of intense compassion that pervades the whole work. The dominant theme of *The Turn of the Screw* is that of innocence betrayed.

In this last opera, the composer has no difficulty in conducting the action on three different levels: a normal level on which the adults live and communicate with each other; an abnormal level on which the adults become aware of the ghosts but fail to establish communication with them; and a supernatural level on which the ghosts communicate with the children in a secret understanding that leads inevitably to corruption. In *A Midsummer Night's Dream* he shows a similar ability to deal with the three different groups of characters — the fairies, the lovers, and the mechanicals — preserving their musical identity, while subordinating their development to the plan of the opera as a musical whole.

(MARIO CASTELNUOVO-TEDESCO)

1895-1968

BIOGRAPHY

ARIO CASTELNUOVO-TEDESCO was born in Florence, Italy, on April 3, 1895. He studied music at the Cherubini Institute of Music in Florence, later becoming a pupil of Ildebrando Pizzetti, who influenced him greatly. When he was fifteen years old he wrote a talented work for the piano, *Cielo di settembre* (later orchestrated by him). In 1920 he composed his first major work, a setting of three verses by St. Francis of Assisi, *Fioretti*. Five years after this, his opera *La Mandragola* won the Italian Prize and was given its first performance in Venice in 1926. In 1930 one of Castelnuovo's works was performed in the United States for the first time when Arturo Toscanini directed the *Symphonic Variations*. During the next few years other major works were introduced in America under the direction of Toscanini, and in performances by Heifetz, Piatigorsky, and others. In 1939 Castelnuovo-Tedesco left Italy for America, establishing his home first in Larchmont, New York, then in Los Angeles. In the same year, he personally introduced his Second Piano Concerto with the New York Philharmonic Orchestra. He has since been active in Beverly Hills as a teacher of composition and as the creator of several scores for motion pictures. He has also produced many major concert works, including several scenic oratorios, and a few works that are American in subject and background. In 1958 his opera *The Merchant of Venice* received first prize in an international competition sponsored by La Scala in Milan; it was successfully introduced at the Florence May Music Festival in the summer of 1961.

PERSONAL NOTE

Walter Arlen

THE street is quiet. Tall trees shade it and keep it cool. The hasty pace and fashionable garishness of three bustling boulevards nearby seem far away and unreal as Mario Castelnuovo-Tedesco greets you upon entering his modest but comfortable home in Beverly Hills. His slightly bent figure, his gaze from behind thick-lensed spectacles, make him look like a medieval scholar, surrounded as he is by innumerable manuscripts, ancestral miniatures, and memorabilia.

There are photographs from another era and another land on the grand piano. A large painting by his architect-son Lorenzo and a draft for a telegram in Gabriele D'Annunzio's boldly oversized handwriting, framed over a desk piled high with correspondence, are the room's only eye-catching accents.

But all is dominated by a great window extending from floor to ceiling. Its light floods this study and its most important object: an inconspicuous simple drafting table on whose sloping top the maestro composes.

He composes constantly, in ink, without piano, and, if for orchestra, directly into score. What has been finished is neatly recorded, with dates and opus numbers, in two small books with florid covers.

There is a third book. Its cover matches the others. Its title is " Hollywood." Its contents record a chapter of activities that Castelnuovo-Tedesco likes to keep strictly separate. He speaks of it with the same gentle amusement and disarmingly charming sarcasm he is wont to bestow upon compositions by some esteemed colleagues whose musical paths he deems in error.

Not that he deems his associations with Hollywood in error. This unassuming man of quiet culture, who has ghostwritten for, taught, and advised practically every screen composer and jazz musician of the motion-picture capital, has not hesitated to accept credit for musical scores of films involving some of Hollywood's most glamorous personalities. He simply wishes to distinguish between two aspects of his life — one dedicated to the conception and

creation of grand operas, concertos, cantatas, chamber works, choruses, and songs; the other occupied with background music timed
with split-second precision to fit the dictates of a world as far removed from the Bible and Shakespeare, as Florence and Tuscany
are from Hollywood and Vine. But the Book of Hollywood was
written, even if all that may survive is a sheaf of anecdotes incorporated in the composer's autobiography.

Castelnuovo-Tedesco composes swiftly and easily. Neither
musical nor personal struggles — and he has had his share of both
— seem to ruffle him. His pervasive, astute intelligence and his
penetrating sense of humor are his sharpest, indeed his only, weap-
ons. They have helped him face all situations. Hence his serene, almost constant, smile, and his kindly, almost fatherly bearing toward
everyone save the stupid. Thus, aided by the gracious ministrations
of his wife Clara, with whom he shares an avid literary appetite
and countless other humanistic interests, Castelnuovo-Tedesco proceeds peacefully from one life cycle to another.

Cycles in his life, he feels, are many. Florence is revisited
cyclically. On a musical scale, there is of course his early preoccupation with Shakespeare. It has yielded periodic results in overtures to twelve of the plays, settings of numerous sonnets, and
operas. The memory of two huge puppets in his mother's drawing
room was the eventual stimulant for the marionette opera *Aucassin
et Nicolette*. His Jewish background led him again and again to
the Bible as a source of inspiration. And the first play the five-year-
old boy saw, Vittorio Alfieri's *Saul*, to which his father took him
to witness the farewell performance of the great Tommaso Salvini,
was in 1960 turned into an opera as op. 191. Finally, who is not
familiar with the lifelong fascination the Spanish idiom and the
guitar hold for him? Since the *Coplas* of 1915 there has been a
recurring tide of Spanish music, with or without guitar. The latest
wave, signed as usual simply " Mario," has beached *Platero and I*
(twenty-eight poems, for narrator and guitar, from Juan Ramón
Jiménez' book) and *Twenty-Four Caprices after Goya*.

And so the cycle goes on.

THE COMPOSER SPEAKS

Mario Castelnuovo-Tedesco [1]

I AM asked to speak of my aims as a composer, but I really have very little to tell. In my artistic life, I have had only one ideal: to write good music without prejudices of any kind. Writing music has always been a need for me ever since I was a child, from the time I was nine years old and my mother began to teach me to play the piano. It seemed to me that everything could be expressed or translated into music: the landscapes I saw, the books I read, the pictures and statues I admired. As I grew up, I learned that the things that can be expressed musically are not quite so numerous, and I strived to be inspired by what was in me rather than what was outside of me. My principal sources of inspiration have been: my home place (Florence and Tuscany), the Bible, and Shakespeare.

Even though as a young man, like all Italians, I wrote operas, I did not have too much faith in that medium for a long time. I have a predilection on the other hand for instrumental forms. Among symphonic forms I prefer, outside of the overture, that of the concerto for solo instrument and orchestra because it seems to me to express, much better than the symphony can, the dualism between the creative individual and the surrounding collectivity. My favorite among instruments is the piano, my own instrument and my confidant. One of my ambitions has always been to wed my music with the purest and highest poetry in the form of the song for voice and piano. So great is my passion for this form of art that I once wrote, and I repeat it here, that if there is any composer I envy it is Franz Schubert for his *Lieder*.

As far as theories are concerned, I do not believe in theories. I have never believed in modernism, or in neoclassicism, or in any other isms. I believe that music is a form of language capable of progress and renewal (and I myself believe that I have a feeling for the contemporary and, therefore, am sufficiently modern). Yet music should not discard what was contributed by preceding generations. Every means of expression can be useful and just, if it is

---

[1] This statement was written by the composer expressly for this book.

used at the opportune moment (through inner necessity rather than through caprice or fashion). The simplest means are generally the best. I believe that my personality was formed to a decided degree quite early, but what I have sought to do, during my artistic evolution, has been to express myself with means always simpler and more direct, in a language always clearer and more precise.

I have always believed in God, in the family, and in the country. I have been living far from my own native land. I hope to be able to give to the great country that has given me a haven, to America, the best of my life and my art, just as I gave them for more than thirty years, in full and absolute conscientiousness, to my own country.

CASTELNUOVO-TEDESCO

Roland von Weber

ALT WIEN (1923), with its famous fox-trot last movement, has become, to the American public's ear, as much the audible symbol of Mario Castelnuovo-Tedesco as has the popular *Bolero* become that of Maurice Ravel, or the *Rhapsody in Blue* the symbol of George Gershwin; and perhaps as aptly. Certainly it shows many of Castelnuovo's musicianly traits: its form is simple, clear, deft; its melody is as Tuscan (and as Byzantine) as the work-song improvisations — *stornelli* — of the farmers in the Tuscan fields and vineyards; its romantic charm is undeniably his, as is the skill with which its dramatic "Fox Trot Tragico" — the composer's first venture into the American idiom — is used to heighten the lyric effectiveness of the other movements. Lastly, *Alt Wien* shows a pianism adroit and masterly beyond that of any other Italian composer of this century. Yet all of these characteristics are better shown in more important works; and left unshown is the greater expression of Castelnuovo's art, the song.

On examining the hundreds of pages of manuscripts, published and unpublished, from Castelnuovo's pen, one essential quality comes to the ear and eye: the unity of expression in one whom I am tempted to call " the Italian Brahms." From his youthful piano works and songs (1910–18) through the stage works and concertos of the thirties, and in his present mature compositions, there is one unchanging art, a true musical integrity. Here are no problems, no experimentalism, no intellectualism, no disjointed modernism, no reassembled chords, and no theories to be explained, but a clear, direct expression that has matured by deepening itself and subtiliz-ing its techniques. So it was with Brahms: the mature Brahms of the Fourth Symphony and the last piano compositions had not altered his expression from the early sonatas for the piano; there had en-tered a maturing process, far more than a development or an evolution through experimentation or the search to find himself; it is *audibly* the same Brahms. Castelnuovo is audibly himself, and himself alone, from his beginnings as a composer. Again like Brahms, there are songs along the way, a richness of treasure that threatens often to outweigh the greater works among which they are to be found. As in Brahms' music, there is extraordinary variety in the songs, in the overtures and concertos, in the chamber music; but the lyric intensity, the melodic patterns, the shaping of the forms, the direct power through direct speech, show the unmistak-able signature of the man.

The music of Castelnuovo has been shaped, conditioned, given background by certain unavoidable factors:

1. His Tuscan — more exactly, his Florentine — birth and cul-ture. Those who know the hills of Tuscany, its trees, its skies, its seasons, its proverbial culture, find in this music its pure expression, and, in the songs and stage works, hear the texts of its greatest poets from Dante to Poliziano, from Machiavelli to Palazzeschi and Redi.

2. His study of English, which brought him to an early and profound knowledge of Shakespeare — witness the thirty-three songs (1921–5) and the piano *Epithalamium*; the three duets (1937); the concert overtures: *Taming of the Shrew* (1930), *Mer-chant of Venice* and *Twelfth Night* (1933), *Julius Caesar* and *Win-ter's Tale* (1934), *A Midsummer Night's Dream* and *King John* (1940), *Antony and Cleopatra* and *Coriolanus* (1947); and the op-eras *All's Well That Ends Well* (1956) and *The Merchant of Ven-ice* (1958). To a study of English and American poetry are owing the songs with excellently chosen texts by Milton, Byron, Scott,

Shelley, Elizabeth Barrett Browning, D. H. Lawrence, Walt Whitman, Edna St. Vincent Millay, Arthur Guiterman — a full seventy songs.

3. His friends — and his mother. To the latter's preference for French as a language are owing the songs with texts by poets loved in his youth: Joachim du Bellay, Olivier de Magny, Rabelais, the romantic de Musset, the moderns Proust, Gide, and Valéry, and, lastly, his choice of *Aucassin et Nicolette* (1938) for a chamber opera, considered by many his finest work. To his friends is owing the exploration at first hand of the extended technical possibilities of certain solo instruments, in the concertos written expressly for their use. Heifetz is responsible for the violin concertos; Piatigorsky for the Cello Concerto; Segovia for the two Guitar Concertos.

4. Two "atavistic" tendencies: a love for Spain and a capacity to write authentic Spanish music, attributable to the Spanish origins of his family more than four centuries ago; and a strong pull toward the ritual melodies of his church. The Spanish influence is strongest in the early *Coplas* (1915), eleven short songs on Spanish popular poems, the most excellent of his youthful work; in the powerful Ballades, *Romances viejos* (1933 and 1935), and in the eloquent *Romancero gitano* (1953), for guitar and small orchestra, on poems of García Lorca. To the ritual-chant influences are owing those major works for the piano, *The King David Dances* (1925), the most serious and extended of them all, the *Three Chorals on Hebrew Melodies* (1926); the majestic violin concerto, *The Prophets*, dedicated to Heifetz (1931); the *Sacred Service* (1943), as well as several Biblical "Scenic oratorios" that can be staged or presented in concert versions, *The Book of Ruth* (1948), *The Book of Jonah* (1951), and *The Song of Songs* (1955).

There is one other influence of which it is necessary to speak: Ildebrando Pizzetti. Castelnuovo's voluntary apprenticeship to Pizzetti (though he was already a fully equipped musician before he went to his well-loved master) was the outcome of a natural affinity, a kinship of mind and spirit rather than a question of submission of pupil to teacher. The influence of the "greatest Italian among composers" on Castelnuovo's work has proved to be scant, indeed, though both pursued similar ideas, one of them — the only important one in this case — being the restoration of the declamatory line (*recitativo*) to the reasonable norms of Italian speech melody. Even here, where Pizzetti (true to a "cause" and a "prob-

lem ") abandons song melody almost entirely for the accompaniment, winding the voice declamation around this trellising, Castelnuovo reinforces the song melody by urging the voice to the same
phrases.

All composers obviously have their preferences for certain
forms and for certain instruments. Bach was essentially the organist
above all; Beethoven, the pianist; Brahms, neglecting the symphonic form until he had grown to maturity, never slighted his
piano or the voice. Castelnuovo follows Brahms in that he, too, has
so far neglected the symphony, keeping to the overture and the
concerto as orchestral forms, and preferred above all the voice and
his own instrument, the piano. Castelnuovo's pianism deserves a
special word. In a world that jumped from the feats of Szymanowski
to the defeats of contemporary " Scarlattianism," Castelnuovo has
written half a hundred or more piano compositions so completely
pianistic as to appear neoromantic. But after listening to pianistic
" nudism " for a decade (Stravinsky, Casella, Hindemith in various
works), what a relief it is to find again piano music, elegant, rich,
ravishing in the full strength of its resonant resources! From the
early *Cipressi* (1920) to the striking Sonata (1928) there is no end
to the diapason of piano tone. *La Sirenetta e il pesce turchino*
(1920) and its companion *Vitalba e Biancospino* (1921), the previously mentioned *King David Dances* (1925) and the Sonata
(1928), the two piano concertos (1927 and 1937) and the Hollywood works of the 1940's show the same undiminishing and unimpaired piano mastery.

The stage works of Castelnuovo are deeply imbued with the
full spirit of the composer. The earliest, *La Mandragola* (1920–3),
is without doubt one of the most brilliant comedies that have
graced the Italian operatic stage since Verdi's *Falstaff*. A musical
setting of the wittiest and bawdiest drama of the golden age of the
Renaissance, the opera is Florentine to the end of Machiavelli's
diabolical teeth and the composer's honey-and-vinegared pen.

Bacco in Toscana (1925–6), based on Redi's well-known
poem, is a Tuscan folk opera, redolent of Tuscan fields at vintage,
heaped with peasant choruses, saturated with the wine of good
Tuscan melody. It is a smaller work than the *Mandragola*, but fresh
as new wine.

Aucassin et Nicolette (1938), written for solo voice, a small
orchestra, and marionettes, and as yet in manuscript, remains to me

the composer's masterwork. Restricted in means, it finds redoubled efficacy in expression; and the composer's affection for the text, together with the biographical fact that he began its composition after a period of depression and ill health, have led to a prodigality of invention and swiftness of expression that overcome all resistance. That the delicacy of the score has not led to preciosity but to keener, stronger simplicity is a tribute to the mature and purely musical nature of the composer. The sly humor, the declamation, the set arias, the deft characterization, set this French work quite on a pedestal.

Castelnuovo-Tedesco's last two operas are both to texts by Shakespeare: *All's Well That Ends Well* (1956) and *The Merchant of Venice* (1958).

As an American, it awakened admiration in me a decade ago to find in this friendly musician an immediate and certain response to what was American, in the unique sense that Walt Whitman is American, that good jazz is American, that Coca-Cola and mint juleps are American. That Castelnuovo-Tedesco, Tuscan, could take Whitman's " In Louisiana I Saw a Live-Oak Growing " and unerringly surround it with a setting as French and Spanish as any Creole, touch it with a cloven-footed jazz rhythm that lent it authentic magic, was uncanny. A flair for American rhythm had marked the fox trot in *Alt Wien*, was the motivation for the " blues " Ballade of the Piano Sonata, as of several smaller piano pieces before 1930. When the ten-song Whitman cycle, *Leaves of Grass*, for voice and piano, was written (1936) — serious, plain, fine music, male music for masculine poetry — it became apparent that this jazz syncopation had not been (as it was often with other European composers) a jeer at American " culture," but was the evidence of a straightforward absorption of atmosphere, effectively and honestly used. From 1936, when " Louisiana " was written, American civilization has had a hold on Castelnuovo. Soon after he had come to live here, some of his work became colored by American impressions, most notably *Stars* (a musical description of four motion-picture favorites) and *Nocturne in Hollywood,* both for piano and both written in 1940–1; the songs of Millay and Guiterman; *An American Rhapsody* (1943); *Humoresques on Foster's Themes* (1943); and the *Indian Songs and Dances,* for orchestra (1943).

(CARLOS CHÁVEZ)

1899 -

BIOGRAPHY

CARLOS CHÁVEZ was born in Mexico City on June 13, 1899. After some lessons in piano, mainly with Manuel Ponce, he went to France in 1922, coming into contact with its musical life. After this European trip, he stayed for several years in New York, further enriching his musical experiences. Back in Mexico, he turned to teaching as a profession, but devoted most of his time to composition.

Chávez was soon to become a dominant musical figure in Mexico. In 1928 he founded the Orquesta Sinfónica, which he conducted from its inception. From 1928 through 1934 he was the director of the National Conservatory in Mexico City. He also filled the post of head of the Department of Fine Arts until 1953. In these offices, Chávez has been the greatest single force in the reorganization of the musical life of Mexico. Chávez also made monumental contributions to the cultural life of Mexico by traveling into secluded corners of his country and unearthing extraordinary examples of native Mexican folk music. In 1938 he received a Guggenheim Fellowship.

Chávez has been active as a conductor in the United States, directing most of our major symphony orchestras, usually in performances of his own music. He was visiting professor of music at Harvard in 1958–9; his lectures were published in the book *Musical Thoughts* (1960). He has been decorated by France, Belgium, Sweden, and Mexico, and in 1960 was elected a member of the American Academy and National Institute of Arts and Letters.

PERSONAL NOTE

Nicolas Slonimsky

THE most striking quality in Carlos Chávez in personal meetings is self-possession. North Americans have a mythical image of their Southern neighbors as highly excitable people whose actions are dictated by sudden outbursts of passion, political, artistic, or amatory, and whose genius is unrestrained by method. Either Chávez is not a typical Latin American or our ideas about his people are mistaken.

For some reason Chávez is believed by some to be of Indian extraction, but this happens to be incorrect. If there is any Indian blood in him, Chávez says, it may be in the third or fourth generation on his mother's side; he traces his paternal ancestry far back to the early Spanish settlers in Mexico.

Solidly built, full of muscular energy, with curly but not unruly hair, and flashing eyes, Chávez is a man of the world. He is gregarious, is gallant with the ladies, and observes the tradition of kissing their hands. He is a gourmet; his favorite dish is the Montezuma pie made of tortillas, and he gladly passes his special recipe for it to friends. He likes wine in moderation.

Chávez enjoys conversation on any conceivable subject — politics, art, literature, as well as music — and on each subject he entertains very strong opinions. In professional life, he is extremely candid in expressing his likes and dislikes. When a friend does something he regards as wrong, he says so bluntly. When a former antagonist joins a cause that Chávez himself supports, he becomes an ally, and the former enmity is instantly forgotten.

It is no secret to anyone conversant with the artistic situation in Mexico that Chávez wields great power there. But he never uses this power to advance egotistical projects. His egotism is reserved for his ideals in Mexican national music. Almost single-handedly, he reconstructed the obsolete pedagogical methods at the National Conservatory of Music, of which he was director for many years. He organized and conducted the finest symphony orchestra Mexico ever had. As chief of the Department of Fine Arts of the Secretariat of Education, he promoted concert life and encouraged young Mexican artists and composers. These are accomplishments that required not only talent for organization but also energy to overcome bureaucratic inertia, and skill of political maneuvering. With all these preoccupations, he never interrupted his principal lines of activity, composing and conducting.

Chávez is culturally at home in the United States, where he appeared many times as guest conductor. In 1959 he was engaged as the Charles Eliot Norton lecturer at Harvard University, a signal honor. He wrote his lectures himself, in English, and delivered them with remarkable fluency, with a pronounced but not unpleasing Spanish accent. He expounded his ideas on musical esthetics with the same vigor of conviction that animates his practical work as composer, conductor, and educator.

His self-possession is particularly in evidence at his rehearsals with American orchestras. He is always punctilious in keeping the schedule; he approaches the task with the sole intention of achieving the best possible results. His beat is clear and precise; he does not indulge in verbal explanations of the music; he is businesslike. These are qualities that American orchestra musicians appreciate as much as, or even more than, conducting talent, and Chávez is regularly re-engaged. Only once in a while does he depart from American concert customs, as, for instance, when he decides to change the order of the program at the last minute, and announces the fact viva voce to the audience.

My meetings with Chávez — in Mexico, in New York, in Boston — were scattered over the years. I met him for the first time in New York when he was still in his twenties, but even then he impressed me by the firmness of his purpose. He never affected modesty, and seemed to realize the worth of his music; but he never sought favors, and never used circuitous ways to promote his career. Since his compositions were objectively of a high caliber, and since his conducting talent was obviously professional and effective, he did not have to wait long to achieve recognition.

With artistic success came a degree of prosperity. In addition to his earnings in Mexico, guest conducting engagements paid well in the United States. And his Harvard lectures brought him a small fortune, for according to the stipulations of the Charles Eliot Norton Fund, its lecturers receive fees that should be no less than those paid to any speaker at any American university, and that means in excess of three thousand dollars a lecture.

THE COMPOSER SPEAKS

Carlos Chávez[1]

NOTHING is wholly new. Each thing, however new it appears, had many antecedents. It is often said that Bach was the father of music in the literal sense of the word. By this is meant that this great master gave life to something that did not exist. Many people believe this — some because of naïveté, others because of lack of information or attention. Bach would not have been Bach if Vivaldi, Buxtehude, and Luther had not lived before him. Luther, Buxtehude, and Vivaldi made the appearance of a Bach inevitable.

We nevertheless find in the constant evolution of music certain eras in which it has been possible to synthesize with great success conquests made in various subsidiary branches of the main trunk. Bach, for example, took advantage of the instrumental and theoretical advance reached in his own epoch with the clavichord, the pipe organ, and temperament. In such epochs evolution has proceeded so rapidly as not to allow time to consider antecedents, and we therefore have an impression of spontaneously generated novelties. We should, then, keep this in mind when thinking of a new music, and not expect sudden revelations, disconnected from the past and from the general conditions of the present.

I speak of the possibility of a new music because these are at present in sight, realizations both innumerable and varied, and because new forms of art correspond to new physical means and new sociological circumstances. We are not, then, dealing with the art of a more or less distant future, but of the present in which we live. The artist should belong to his time, and has but one means of doing so: by steeping himself in history in order to extract from it the experience of past generations, and by knowing his own world

[1] This statement is from Carlos Chávez' book *Toward a New Music*.

with all its developments and resources, so that he may be able to interpret its own fundamental necessities.

After having glanced at the new instruments that today are within our reach, we might have some doubt of the possibility of an artist, in order to produce his new creations, dominating such complicated apparatus as the sound film, for example, in all its detail. But let us note that the composer has always been capable of managing his mechanical instruments. If Chopin had not managed the piano as perfectly as he did, he would not have produced the marvelous piano music we all know and admire. In the same way, the composers who will make a true musical drama of the cinema will be those who know how to manage its various instrumentalities as perfectly as Chopin dominated the piano.

Every instrument develops a related instrumental aptitude in the individual. The exercise of the function makes it become instinctive, and in this way it will come about that the new instruments will be at our command, as useful and natural as our voice and hands. If we look at the problem implied for the composer in conceiving a complex filmed music drama, we find that it is, in different manner and degree, the same problem presented in the case of an opera or a symphony: that of familiarizing himself with the instrumental means. In a classic symphony, each musical part is decided in relation to the instrumental possibility. The part played by the violin fits that instrument, and is inappropriate for the tuba. This propriety of music in relation to the instrument that produces it is what a musician means when he talks about a violinistic, unviolinistic, pianistic, or unpianistic passage.

A composer who knew only the mechanism of the violin would be unable to write for orchestra or opera. It may seem too difficult, this achieving of an understanding of very varied and complex mechanisms, but intellect and practice make it possible. In the particular case of the cinema, the new " apprenticeship " will not begin while musicians continue making only adaptations. The musical adaptations for cinematographic films are not more or less satisfactory than any other adaptation. Every adaptation implies the use of a thing originally conceived for another purpose. The music of *Tristan* fits that opera better than any other.

The dreadful salads of sections of classic works, sentimental melodies, and popular songs that are generally confected to accompany films prove nothing but the inability of producers to conceive original cinematographic works with their own music. The same thing happened in the seventeenth and eighteenth centuries, when the famous *pasticcio* music for operas was made, pasting the " favorite " airs of the period together without rhyme or reason.

The apprenticeship is slow. New art forms are not made in a day. The function of the true composer for the cinema is not that of superimposing music on the scenes to the order of the director of the production. He should have a conception of the cinematographic work as a whole, and of music's fulfilling an integral function within it. So that the artist may be capable of such conceptions, he must have a profound understanding of the potentialities of all the cinematographic instruments.

Correlatively, the new physical media of art are valid only when they prove their effective ability to serve the expression of new forms of art, or new ideas and feelings. The composers of the present need large fields of experimentation in which to develop new instrumental aptitudes. It is very natural that, for the moment, no hints of new productions are at hand, since the artists are far from the instruments, while the only ones who know them are the engineers. Piano music would never have existed if the instrument had not come into the hands of artists. Only providing composers and artists with the means of knowing and familiarizing themselves with the new media will pave the way toward the birth of new art forms.

CHÁVEZ

Miriam Gideon

" I BELIEVE only in the present."

" Nothing is wholly new."

" Each work of art is a particular case of solving the always complex problem of human expression."

These three statements by Carlos Chávez reveal various aspects of the man and his work, attitudes that in the long view fall into place within a totality.

A Mexican, and descendant of men of science and letters, Chávez displays the skill and erudition as well as the preoccupation with indigenous Mexican elements that his ancestry has no doubt in some measure determined.

His early works reflect the influences to be expected in a young composer educated on European musical traditions. They show withal a sure and sensitive handling of ideas that are valid but not yet strongly individual. Among these early compositions are the First Symphony (1919), First String Quartet (1921), and the following, also written in 1921: First Sonata, *Páginas sencillas*, 4 *Estudios*, and 4 *Valses*, all for the piano, as well as the songs *Cantos mexicanos* and 4 *Poemas*. These show a firm command of material as yet not expressive of the fully developed composer.

A first visit to Europe in 1922 served to disenchant the young composer with the musical mores of the Old World and to prepare the way for his coming of age. His next creative period was an excursion into abstraction, suggested more by the titles than by the contents of the works, as in the songs 3 *Exágonos* (1923) and *Polígonos* for piano (1923). In the latter work, a slow, curving, yet energetic melodic line bursts into a jagged outline; unisons and octaves expand into seconds and ninths and dissolve back again; bland consonances become astringent dissonances; there is a profusion of diatonic passages, not necessarily thematic; sudden reiteration of motives; intricate, often violent, rhythmic patterns; many sequences. These traits are present in other works of the same period and have persisted in later works as well. The Sonatina for piano (1924) shows some of them and, at the same time, the romanticism of his earlier pieces. The dynamic indications are significant for later works as well: "la stessa intensità per tutte le voci," "sempre rigorosamente in tempo." One feels a juxtaposition of, if not a conflict between, the spontaneous and the intellectualized.

Other piano pieces of this period share many of these characteristics: *36* (1925), *Solo, Blues, and Fox* (1928), *Paisaje* (1930), *Unidad* (1930), and the Third Piano Sonata (1928). The sonata was dedicated to Aaron Copland, who finds it "too personal for ready understanding, too taut, highly condensed for popular consumption." In these works there are sudden changes from modal and diatonic thematic ideas to widely leaping lines and a highly complex, urgent rhythmic organization. The 10 *Preludes* (1937), though written somewhat later, are similar and are in fact "white note " pieces, with accidentals appearing seldom and systematically. These compositions have evoked in some critics the spirit of the composer's native country. Herbert Weinstock, for example, feels that the 10 *Preludes*, *36*, and the Third Piano Sonata suggest " the unsensuous harshness of Mexico's highland landscapes . . . magnificent and spacious plateaus of craggy distances, where stolid people wring a livelihood from a forbidding nature."

The compositions of the next years established Chávez' position as an outstanding composer of Latin America and a significant figure for the world at large. Here he speaks with unmistakable accents of his own: a fusion of native and personal idiom. Many external factors played a part in this growth: the outbreak of the Mexican Revolution in 1910 and its continuation well into the 1930's stimulated his concern for the plight of the Mexican peasant. In 1921 he was commissioned by the Secretary of Education to write a ballet, *El Fuego nuevo* (*The New Fire*), which first brought him into prominence as a modern Mexican composer, employing as it does native percussion instruments and a somewhat advanced musical language. Another ballet followed in 1926, *Los Cuatro Soles* (*The Four Suns*), based on an ancient Mexican legend. Then came *HP* (*Horsepower*), in 1927, a ballet that represents, according to the composer, the relation between the North and the Tropics, a " symphony of the sounds around us." The last movement involves native dances: local color is created not only by the melodies and rhythms of the " Huapango " and " Sandunga," but also by the use of native instruments along with the full orchestra. The composer states that native material was not the constructive basis for the work, but was used because it happened to coincide with his own form of self-expression — a statement borne out rather dramatically by the close, where melodic motives of the dances are transformed, slowed down, and harmonized with the gravity of a baroque ending.

The appointment of Chávez to various important positions in the cultural and political life of his country inspired him to discover and disseminate its indigenous treasures as well as to assimilate them. In 1928 he became conductor of the Orquesta Sinfónica of Mexico and elevated that group to an orchestra of fully professional status. The same year he became director of the National Conservatory and in 1933 chief of Fine Arts of the Secretariat of Public Education. In the latter capacity he instigated and directed

research into the music and instruments of the Mexican Indian
before the Cortesian conquest — that is, of the Mayas, Aztecs, and
Toltecs — carrying this interest not only into his own creative
work, but into the teaching procedures of the Conservatory and
public schools. In 1933 he organized the Orquesta Mexicana, composed of ancient instruments of pre-Cortesian tribes.

Many works of this period are bound up with his public functions. *Llamadas* (*Calls*), 1934, a "Proletarian Symphony" for
chorus and orchestra, was performed by public demand at the dedication of the Palace of Fine Arts, after it had become familiar to
choruses of school children and amateurs in its original shorter
version. Another work for chorus and orchestra has strong Mexican
features — *Tierra mojada* (*Humid Soil*), written in 1932. *El sol*
(*Corrido of the Sun*), 1934, also for chorus and orchestra, is based
on an original Mexican *corrido*, set to an apostrophe to the sun,
which deals equally with rich and poor. Here one feels the assimila-
tion of folk material into a strong personal utterance; there are contrasts of forceful unison singing with blocks of dissonance, and lyric
passages for women's voices or full chorus in parallel thirds in the
typical fashion of the Mariachi band. Other works for chorus, written a few years later, but using folk material directly are *La Paloma
azul* (*The Blue Dove*), 1940, a setting of a well-known Spanish
song, with sensitive, mild dissonances characterizing the music in a
somewhat stylized way; *Arbol que te sequeste* (*Tree of Sorrow*),
1942, an unaccompanied setting of a folk song that, though brief, is
an exquisite realization of its poetic and folk values — fragile dissonances, *ostinato* rhythms, an extended pedal, and truncated vocal
lines evoking a tender and distant melancholy. In the *Obertura
republicana* (1935), Chávez exalts the popular music of his country, basing the work on three Mexican songs. All are presented with
exaggerated features — the essence rather than the total reality:
"Zacates," a march with high excited brass above a typical martial
bass; "Club Verde," a waltz, now sentimental, now coquettish,
sailing above a stereotyped waltz accompaniment; this idyl is interrupted by a drum roll that introduces a revolutionary war song,
"La Adelita," harmonized by the ever-present parallel thirds. The
composer's attitude toward this work is vehement, perhaps even
tongue-in-cheek; he remarks that this, the national music of Mexico of the nineteenth century, deserves symphonic treatment as
much as do minuets or colonial Masses. Even the title "over-

ture " is selected, he says, " not because of its formalistic meaning, but because it sounds well."

The two works by which Chávez is best known are the *Sinfonía de Antígona* and the *Sinfonía India*. The former was written in 1932 as incidental music to a stage performance in Mexico City of Jean Cocteau's version of the *Antigone* of Sophocles. Reorchestrated and adapted as a symphony in one movement, it is intended to portray by its intense melancholy Antigone's exaltation and rebellion, her heroism and martyrdom. Chávez secures this partly by instrumental color: the work is scored for an augmented wind section, darkened by heckelphone, alto flute, and eight horns, as well as for a large percussion section including Indian drum. Obsession pervades throughout. It is felt in the gravitation of many passages to a single tone, B, to which point many of the climaxes are directed, and in the use of a three-note motive, chromatically descending: F-sharp, F, E, into which much of the thematic material dissolves. Motives built on the descent of a larger interval (usually a fourth or a third) to a second lend a sense of desolation. Harmonies are built on fourths and fifths, thirds being avoided, according to the composer, as out of character with the Greek musical system. The work stands as a stunning achievement of stark nobility with a minimum of means.

The *Sinfonía India* was completed in New York in 1936 and broadcast in a world première by the Columbia Symphony Orchestra, the composer conducting. Here Chávez draws on three Mexican-Indian tribes — the Seris, Yaquis, and Huicholes — using melodies that are major in feeling and triadic in construction. Three lively sections frame two quieter ones based on the Yaquis melody, which dominates the work by its poignant beauty and greater melodic continuity. A skillful transformation of themes takes place by means of dramatically planned reiteration and setting in bare octaves, fourths, and fifths, with an occasional adroit countermelody. The sonority of primitive Indian instruments, including rattling strings and rasping stick, is preserved throughout. The work shows a masterful control of folk material within a strong individual statement.

Continuing his interest in pre-Cortesian instruments, Chávez wrote a number of compositions — among them, *Xochipili-Macuilxochitl* (the Aztec god of love and music), 1940 — for primitive Indian instruments. *Xochipili* was performed the same year at the Museum of Modern Art in New York by a special group of Mexican performers. The *Toccata,* for percussion instruments (1942), received its première in Mexico City in 1947. Imagination and craft produce here a fascinating interchange of effects within a clearly felt structure. The first movement is confined to drums, the timpani tuned in perfect and augmented fourths. The second movement moves into an ethereal world of bells, chimes, gongs, xylophone, and glockenspiel, the last weaving delicate motivic threads through the gently insistent texture of the other instruments. The third movement returns in the main to instruments without definite pitch; intensification through tempo acceleration and reiteration provides a satisfying conclusion. The *Toccata* is a kind of apotheosis of percussion sonorities of the Mexican Indian, as is the *Sinfonía India* of melodic material.

Since the composition of these strongly colored Mexican works, Chávez' music has gradually become more subjective. Among his more extended works is the Concerto for Piano and Orchestra (1940), first performed by the New York Philharmonic Orchestra in 1942. Here the composer travels a considerable distance harmonically and thematically — as, for example, in the first movement, where extremes are most apparent in the alternation of the soft dissonances of the opening, with its modal themes and almost impressionist harmony, and the steely dissonances of succeeding passages. The second movement has an unusual play of sonorities between low sustained piano and harp and shows the composer's characteristic skill in handling seeming contradictions — for example, a melodic line that combines folklike simplicity and introspective complexity and a tonality that shifts between clear and ambiguous definition. Many critics have considered this work Chávez' most important up to that period and a significant one for Latin-American music in general.

In 1943 Chávez was commissioned by the Elizabeth Sprague Coolidge Foundation to write music for a ballet for Martha Graham, which the dancer presented as *Dark Meadow.* The orchestral suite *Daughter of Colchis* is drawn from this ballet, retaining what was to have been the original title and concept: Medea and her land of origin, Colchis; the conflict in Woman, embodied in Medea, in whom the malevolent is at war with the tender and loving. In its evocation of Greek tragedy the work suggests the *Sinfonía de Antígona* — its austerity, economy, and eloquence. The musical vo-

cabulary, too, is similar: modal and exposed lines, harmonic reserve, few sharply defined rhythmic patterns.

During the next few years Chávez wrote a number of chamber
works — among them, the Third String Quartet (1944); choral
works, including the *Canto a la tierra* (*Song to the Earth*) of 1945;
the piano compositions *Fuga* (1948) and *3 Etudes* (1950); and the
Concerto for Violin and Orchestra (1950).

Chávez subsequently composed three symphonies. The Third
Symphony (1951) was commissioned by Clare Boothe Luce and
won the Caro de Boesi prize at the first Caracas Festival in 1954,
when it was introduced by the New York Philharmonic Orchestra
under the composer's direction, and made a forceful impression
with its "craggy strength." Like many of Chávez' more recent
works, this symphony is built of freer and more personal stuff: wide,
dissonant melodic intervals, jagged chord blocks, layers of diatonic
movement. The Scherzo is a fugue, with a brittle, syncopated subject. The work abounds in characteristic *ostinati*, reiteration, and
urgency of rhythmic patterns, but emotion is less palpable, and the
horizon is wider.

The Fourth Symphony (1952) was commissioned and introduced by the Louisville Orchestra, the composer conducting. Some
of Chávez' attitudes toward music find expression in this work,
which he later named *Sinfonía romántica*. He believes tonality to
be "essential," the absence of it "tiresome." In the Fourth Symphony an underlying sense of key is felt clearly, though often
obliquely. A main theme is referred to in each movement, as in
the cyclic romantic symphony of the nineteenth century. The slow
movement stands out — an incredibly long line unfolding constantly in the violins, a long-breathed, unbroken surge of intense
lyricism. Faster and almost equally relentless is the final *vivo*, where
feverish excitement is tinged with the ominous color of a bass
drum. Chávez achieves in this symphony an immediacy less usually
found in his recent works. His mark is indubitably there, however,
in the diatonicism, often remote, the insistent elements of melodic
and rhythmic repetition, the violent dramatic contrasts. One feels a
similarity to the contemporary Russian school in the unashamed
romantic sweep, the martial drumbeats, the frenetic excitement, the
tantalizing sense of slipping over the edge of tonal security.

A more sharply defined personal idiom is present in the Fifth
Symphony, for strings (1953), commissioned by the Koussevitzky

Music Foundation. A reconciliation of apparent contradictions takes place throughout this work: the constant expansion of the baroque side by side with the symmetry of classic recapitulation; sharp dissonance and clear consonance; complex textures and bare ones; continuousness of line and obsessive reiterations. The slow movement is the peak of the work — original and expressive, suggesting now the ferocity of a Bartók, now the ecstatic and morbid atmosphere of the Berg Violin Concerto, but the totality is unique. There are many unusual sonorities, and a remarkable passage at the close of the movement where harmonics for all strings suggest the high flutes of the Mexican Indian, and the orchestral fabric gives a sensation of distant, rhythmic breathing.

Since the completion of the last three symphonies, Chávez has written his first opera, *El Amor propiciado* (*Love Propitiated*). Commissioned by the Rockefeller Foundation and Lincoln Kirstein, it received its first performance as *Panfilo and Lauretta* in May, 1957, at the Brander Matthews Theater of Columbia University. The libretto, by Chester Kallman, is based on Boccaccio's *Decameron;* the setting, a villa in Tuscany in the fourteenth century to which the leading characters have retreated to escape the plague. Four plays are improvised as diversions: " Cupid and Psyche," " The Raising of Lazarus," " Mary Magdalene," and " The Fall of Man." In these, the actual characters of the opera live out their real desires, and preserve their musical identity as well by characteristic melodic styles. In an atmosphere of imminent death and decay (" Deny the grave and you deny the womb "), the indirectness and symbolism of the language (" When half my heart is earthenware, how can it learn to lie? ") and the plots within a plot make for a work of extreme complexity, difficult to project as a musical work for the stage, yet compelling in imagination and dimension. There is a striking array of appropriate styles and textures: from the many-faceted closing chorus of Act I, in which the principals, Venus, Cupid, and Psyche, sing of their fate against a bleak and dissonant funeral chant in Latin; through contrasting arias (Panfilo's grim portrayal in acrid dissonances of the plague-devastated city; the aria of the rejected and exploited Elissa, with its wide, chromatic leaps; Venus' final aria, " Look on Love with No Disguise," in softly curving lines above a romantic triadic harmony); to the transparency of the final chorus, " Time, That Closes Every Eye," with its concluding section in E major.

In *Invención*, for piano (1958), Chávez arrives at a kind of summit of self-revelation. All of his writing for this instrument seems in a sense to deal particularly with his stated " always complex problem of self-expression " rather more directly than do his works for other media, in which literary, dramatic, national preoccupations are involved. The piano pieces, however, cut across the apprenticeship of the early 1920's, the experimentalism of the latter part of that decade and the 1930's, and up to the present time eschew more external forces, whether they be ethnomusicology, neoclassicism with its greater accessibility, or the margins of dodecaphonism. In the *Invención* Chávez reaches into his private world. An imposing one-movement work lasting twenty minutes, it is staggeringly difficult of execution, relentlessly lavish in ideas, extreme in emotional range, defying as always consistency and reveling in contradiction. Though his other works give us, perhaps, a more rounded picture of the composer, the *Invención* epitomizes in many ways his inner aspects.

Viewed as a whole, then, this commanding figure in Latin-American music shows himself to be a creative spirit of iron self-belief, widely ranging affinities, and ever-expanding reaches of expression.

(AARON COPLAND)

1900 -

BIOGRAPHY

AARON COPLAND was born in Brooklyn, New York, on
November 14, 1900. He began to study music in his thirteenth year,
becoming a piano pupil of Victor Wittgenstein and Clarence Ad-
ler. He soon coupled his study of the piano with harmony lessons
with Rubin Goldmark. In 1921 Copland went to Paris, where he
became the first enrolled student of composition at the Fontaine-
bleau School of Music, studying for three years with Nadia Boulanger. When he returned to America in 1924 he was awarded a
Guggenheim Fellowship, enabling him to spend two additional
years in Europe.

Copland first attracted attention in America in 1925 when his
Symphony for Organ and Orchestra (later rescored without organ
and retitled First Symphony) was performed in Boston and New
York. His *Music for the Theater*, written in a jazz idiom, brought
him additional fame when, in 1927, it was selected to represent the
United States in the festival of the International Society for Contemporary Music held at Frankfurt. In 1930 his *Dance Symphony*
won a five-thousand-dollar award of the RCA Victor Company for
an outstanding symphonic work by an American.

Copland has been one of the leading forces for spreading propaganda for, and arranging concerts of, modern American music. He
has been chairman of the board of directors of the League of Composers, founder of the Copland-Sessions Concerts in New York, director of the American Festivals of Contemporary Music at Yaddo,
and organizer of the American Composers' Alliance. He has been a

participant in the Koussevitzky Music Foundation, the Composers Forum, and the United States Section of the International Society for Contemporary Music. He has written frequently for leading journals, is the author of several books on music, and has lectured at the New School for Social Research, in New York, and at Harvard University.

As a composer, Copland has been the recipient of numerous awards and honors, including the Pulitzer Prize for *Appalachian Spring* and the Boston Symphony Award for his Third Symphony. In 1956 he received an honorary doctorate from Princeton University, and in 1964 the Presidential Medal of Honor.

In the fall of 1941 Copland made an extensive tour of South America as pianist and conductor and in 1960 appeared as conductor in the Soviet Union. He has also made numerous appearances in Israel and in several European countries. Between 1940 and 1965 he headed the composition department at the Berkshire Music Center at Tanglewood.

PERSONAL NOTE

Israel Citkowitz

ALL in all, Aaron Copland is a most elusive personality to portray. One could no sooner describe a particular quality than its opposite would appear to counter it. In a less well-balanced personality these contradictions would create conflict and division. Copland can balance them, and, far from canceling out, these opposites complement each other and work together like well-meshed gears. One could head his biography with the title " The Practical Poet," and that would indicate Copland's faculty of teaming opposites. A poet he is — any one of his scores, whether intended for the concert stage, the movies, or a child's study period at the piano, displays his imaginative powers. And as for his practicality, one need only plot a curve around some of the peripheral points in his career to recognize that only a person with an immense gift for practical organization could cover such a range without serious damage to his creative energies. In this easy faculty for twining varied strands of activity into a smooth whole Copland seems less like the hard-driving executive of our day than like some Continental figure of the eighteenth or nineteenth century. There is a Gallic touch in Copland's perfect self-possession that brings him into spiritual kinship with those elegant literary figures in French history who could range the continent of Europe in the service of their state, secure in every language and custom, and yet secure in their personal resources and creativity.

What the French would describe as *disponible* — that is, the quality of a suspended and disengaged force ready to crystallize into any desired form — characterizes Copland's attitude of mind. The artistic counterpart of this quality of *disponibilité* is of course manifest in the success with which he has operated in so many genres. It is this quality of mind that enables Copland to engage himself in his varied pursuits with the utmost ease and economy. But this quality is interesting not only for its pragmatic results. The high-powered executive who keeps a brace of secretaries busy is surely no spiritual phenomenon to marvel at. What is extraordinary is to find in a composer this faculty of displacing and moving the focus of his activities. The violent drive of creative energies does not make for easy displacement. In the nineteenth century, Baudelaire's giant albatross, king of the azure, but clumsy and infirm on the ground, was a symbol for the poet. To Copland this psychology of the nineteenth-century artist is completely foreign. The dramatic tensions between life and art that these artists generate are not for him. He moves between various levels of activity with an air of balanced detachment that is at once the irritation and the envy of his more perfervid colleagues.

Amid the after-concert gatherings of composers that Copland relishes he sits with an air of serene impartiality that makes everyone else seem like a youthful barbarian. Yet with this goes an ingenuousness and a wit almost childlike in their effect — just as a child's detachment from the turmoil and preoccupations of its elders can point up their foibles with devastating clarity. But Copland's detachment does not bespeak a lack of sympathy for his fellow artists. It is very characteristic of him that no sooner had his own career been launched than he was already engaged in furthering the careers of others, many of whom have since attained international prominence. When one considers that one of the occupational hazards of composing today is an insular tightness in the composer himself, a sheer inability to transcend the limits of the composer's own interests and self-interest, Copland's insistence in the uncovering of new talent is an extraordinary phenomenon. It is not that he stands alone in manifesting a constant interest in the music of others, but that the sources of this vital interest are not bound up with the mainsprings of his own ego. It is the outcome of a truly disinterested and objective personality.

The objective composer has of course been widely trumpeted today. The nineteenth-century romantic has been repudiated again and again. The curious aspect of this oft-proclaimed *neue Sachlichkeit*, the new objectivity, is that it involves almost entirely modes and techniques of musical composition, while the composers themselves display the same emotional patterns as the most violent romantic of the nineteenth century. Copland on the other hand is in the paradoxical position of displaying what might be called a romantic temperament and coloring in his music, while psychologically the emotional pattern of the romantic artist is completely remote to him. One could easily transpose a figure like Aaron Copland's against a classical background. In a peruke his face would take on a resemblance to Haydn's. In a period of secure religious beliefs he could satisfy his own strong urge for the centrality and communion of social beings. His practicality, that of the artisan and not of the notary, would fit naturally into the general scheme.

Others in our day have staked out their claims in a grander manner, but Copland by a slow unassuming process of accretion has developed to an imposing stature. At the present, in the very mid-point of his career he is an arresting figure, unique in his combination of qualities, and still *disponible*, still ready to crystallize the forces at his disposal into some new pattern. If, as some Frenchman put it, beneath every appearance of vainglory lurks a modest ego, very dependent for its nourishment on outward acclaim, then one can only say of Copland that his simple, unassuming, and urbane manner must carry behind it an enormous self-possession and dignity.

THE COMPOSER SPEAKS

Aaron Copland [1]

IN THE art of music, creation and interpretation are indissolubly linked, more so than in any of the other arts, with the possible exception of dancing. Both these activities — creation and interpretation — demand an imaginative mind — that is self-evident. Both bring into play creative energies that are sometimes alike, sometimes dissimilar. By coupling them together it may be possible to illuminate their relationship and their interraction upon the other.

Like most creative artists, I have from time to time cogitated on the mysterious nature of creativity. Is there anything new to be said about the creative act — anything really new, I mean? I rather doubt it. The idea of creative man goes back so far in time, so many cogent things have been written and said — acute observations, poetic reflections, and philosophic ponderings — that one despairs of bringing to the subject anything more than a private view of an immense terrain.

Still, the serious composer who thinks about his art will sooner or later have occasion to ask himself: why is it so important to my own psyche that I compose music? What makes it seem so absolutely necessary, so that every other daily activity, by comparison, is of lesser significance? And why is the creative impulse never satisfied; why must one always begin anew? To the first question — the need to create — the answer is always the same — self-expression; the basic need to make evident one's deepest feelings about life. But why is the job never done? Why must one always begin again? The reason for the compulsion to renewed creativity, it seems to me, is that each added work brings with it an element of self-discovery. I must create in order to know myself, and since self-knowledge is a never-ending search, each new work is only a part answer to the question " Who am I? " and brings with it the need to go on to other and different part answers. Because of this, each artist's work is supremely important — at least to himself. But why does the art-

---

[1] Mr. Copland's statement comes from *Music and the Imagination*, a book comprising his Charles Eliot Norton lectures at Harvard.

ist presume to think, and why do other men encourage him to think, that the creation of one more work of art is of more than merely private import? That is because each new and significant work of art is a unique formulation of experience; an experience that would be utterly lost if it were not captured and set down by the artist. No other artist will ever make that particular formulation in exactly that way. And just as the individual creator discovers himself through his creation, so the world at large knows itself through its artists, discovers the very nature of its Being through the creation of its artists.

Jacques Maritain has summarized this idea of the necessity and uniqueness of the work of art in these terms: it is the artist's condition, he says, " to seize obscurely his own being with a knowledge that will not come to anything save in being creative, and which will not be conceptualized save in a work made by his own hands." Thus the creator finds himself in a precarious position because, first, the involuntary nature of creation makes the moment of engendering an art work uncertain, and then, once conceived, there comes the fear that the conception may not be brought to fruition. This gives a dramatic aspect to the composer's situation. On the one hand the need for self-expression is ever-present, but on the other hand, he cannot, by an act of will, produce the work of art. It must be entirely spontaneous, or if not spontaneous, then cajoled, induced, gradually perceived — so that each day's work may spell failure or triumph. No wonder many creative artists have been reputed to have had unstable characters.

Up to this point, the situation of the musical interpreter is not so very different from that of the creator. He is simply the intermediary that brings the composer's work to life — a kind of midwife to the composition. He partakes of the same dedication of purpose, the same sense of self-discovery through each performance, the same conviction that something unique is lost, possibly, when his own understanding of a work of art is lost. He even partakes of the involuntary nature of creation, for we know that he cannot at will turn on the wellsprings of his creativity so that each performance may be of equal value. Quite the contrary, each time he steps out upon the concert platform we wish him luck, for he shares something of the creator's uncertain powers of projection. Thus we see that interpretation, even though it may rightfully be thought of as an auxiliary art, does share elements of creativity with the mind that forms the work of art.

But now let us consider the essential way in which creation and interpretation are radically different. The interpretative mind can exercise itself on a given object; it cannot itself supply that object. The making of something out of nothing is the special province of the creative mind. The composer is a kind of magician; out of the recesses of his thought he produces, or finds himself in possession of, the generative idea. Although I say " the recesses of his thought," in actuality the source of the germinal idea is the one phase in creation that resists rational explanation. All we know is that the moment of possession is the moment of inspiration; or to use Coleridge's phrase, the moment when the creator is in " a more than usual state of emotion." Whence it comes, or in what manner it comes, or how long its duration, one can never foretell. Inspiration may be a form of superconsciousness, or perhaps of subconsciousness — I wouldn't know; but I am sure that it is the antithesis of self-consciousness. The inspired moment may sometimes be described as a kind of hallucinatory state of mind: one half of the personality emotes and dictates while the other half listens and notates. The half that listens had better look the other way, had better simulate a half attention only, for the half that dictates is easily disgruntled and avenges itself for too close inspection by fading entirely away.

That describes, of course, only one kind of inspiration. Another kind involves the personality as a whole, or, rather, loses sight of it completely, in a spontaneous expression of emotional release. By that I mean the creative impulse takes possession in a way that blots out in greater or lesser degree consciousness of the familiar sort. Both these types of inspiration — if one can call them types — are generally of brief duration and of exhausting effect. They are the rarer kind, the kind we wait for every day. The less divine afflatus that makes it possible for us to compose each day — to induce inspiration, as it were — is a species of creative intuition in which the critical faculty is much more involved. . . . Long works need intuitiveness of that sort, for it is generally the shorter ones that are entirely the result of spontaneous creativity.

Mere length in music is central to the composer's problem. To write a three-minute piece is not difficult; a main section, a contrasting section, and a return to the first part is the usual solution. But anything that lasts beyond three minutes may cause trouble. In treating so amorphous a material as music the composer is confronted with this principal problem: how to extend successfully the seminal ideas and how to shape the whole so that it adds up to a rounded experience. Here, too, inspiration of a kind is needed. No textbook rules can be applied, for the simple reason that these generative ideas are themselves live things and demand their individual treatment. I have sometimes wondered whether this problem of the successful shaping of musical form was not connected in some way with the strange fact that musical history names no women in its roster of great composers. There have been great women musical interpreters, but thus far — I emphasize, *thus far* — no examples of women composers of the first rank. This is a touchy subject, no doubt, but leaving aside the obscure and various reasons for the historical fact, it appears to indicate that the conception and shaping of abstract ideas in extended forms marks a clear boundary between the creative mind and the interpretative mind.

In all that I have been saying about creative thinking there is implied the strongly imaginative quality of the artist's mentality. I stress this now because there has been a tendency in recent times to put the emphasis rather on the artist as craftsman, with much talk of the composer's technique. The artist-craftsman of the past is held up to us as the model to be emulated. There is a possible source of confusion here: amidst all the talk of the craftsmanlike approach we must always remember that a work of art is not a pair of shoes. It may very well be useful like a pair of shoes, but it takes its source from a quite different sphere of mental activity. Roger Sessions understood this when he wrote recently: "The composer's technique is, on the lowest level, his mastery of the musical language. . . . On a somewhat higher level . . . it becomes identical with his musical thought, and it is problematical in terms of substance rather than merely of execution. On this level it is no longer accurate to speak of craftsmanship. The composer is no longer simply a craftsman; he has become a musical thinker, a creator of values — values which are primarily esthetic, hence psychological, but hence, as an inevitable consequence, ultimately of the deepest human importance."

It is curious that this concern with craftsmanship should have affected an art that has developed no successful large-scale primitive practitioners, in the sense that there are accepted primitive painters. Music boasts no Henri Rousseau, no Grandma Moses. Naïveté doesn't work in music. To write any sort of usable piece presumes a minimum kind of professionalism. Mussorgsky and Satie are the closest we have come in recent times to a primitive composer, and the mere mention of their names makes the idea rather absurd.

No, I suspect that the stress placed upon the composer as craftsman, especially in teacher-pupil relationships, comes from a basic mistrust of making private esthetic judgments. There is the fear of being wrong, plus the insecurity of not being able to *prove* that one is right, even to oneself. As a result an attitude is encouraged of avoiding the whole messy business of esthetic evaluation, putting one's attention on workmanship and craft instead, for there we deal in solid values. But that attitude, to my mind, side-steps the whole question of the composer's own need for critical awareness and for making esthetic judgments at the moment of creation. As I see it, this ability is part of his craft, and the lack of it has weakened, when it hasn't entirely eliminated, many potentially fine works.

The creative mind, in its day-to-day functioning, must be a critical mind. The ideal would be not merely to be aware, but to be "aware of our awareness," as Professor I. A. Richards has put it. In music this self-critical appraisal of the composer's own mind guiding the composition to its inevitable termination is particularly difficult of application, for music is an emotional and comparatively intangible substance. Composers, especially young composers, are not always clear as to the role criticism plays at the instant of creation. They don't seem to be fully aware that each time one note is followed by another note, or one chord by another chord, a decision has been made. They seem even less aware of the psychological and emotional connotations of their music. Instead they appear to be mainly concerned with the purely formal rightness of a general scheme, with a particular care for the note-for-note logic of thematic relationships. In other words, they are partially aware but not fully aware, and not sufficiently cognizant of those factors which have a controlling influence on the success or failure of the composition as a whole. A full and equal appraisal of every smallest contributing factor with an understanding of the controlling and most essential elements in the piece, without allowing this to cramp one's freedom of creative inventiveness — being, as it were, inside and outside the work at the same time; that is how I envisage the "awareness of one's awareness." Beethoven's genius was once attributed by Schubert to what he termed his "superb coolness under the fire of creative fantasy." What a wonderful way to describe the creative mind functioning at its highest potential!

It is one of the curiosities of the critical creative mind that although it is very much alive to the component parts of the finished work it cannot know everything that the work may mean to others. There is an unconscious part in each work — an element that André Gide called *la part de Dieu*. I have often felt familiar, and yet again unfamiliar, with a new work of mine as it was being rehearsed for the first time — as if both the players and I myself had to accustom ourselves to its strangeness. The late Paul Rosenfeld once wrote that he saw the steel frames of skyscrapers in my *Piano Variations*. I like to think that the characterization was apt, but I must confess that the notion of skyscrapers was not at all in my mind when I was composing the *Variations*. In similar fashion an English critic, Wilfrid Mellers, has found in the final movement of my Piano Sonata "a quintessential musical expression of the idea of immobility." "The music runs down like a clock," Mellers writes, "and dissolves away into eternity." That is probably a very apt description also, although I would hardly have thought of it myself. Composers often tell you that they don't read criticisms of their works. As you see, I am an exception. I admit to a curiosity about the slightest cue as to the meaning of a piece of mine — a meaning, that is, other than the one I know I have put there.

Quite apart from my own curiosity, there is always the question of how successfully one is communicating with an audience. A composer who cannot in advance calculate to some extent the effect of his piece on the listening public is in for some rude awakenings. Whether or not he ought to take this effect upon an audience into account at the time of composing is another matter. Here again composers vary widely in their attitude. But whatever they tell you, I think it is safe to assume that although a conscious desire for communication may not be in the forefront of their minds, every move toward logic and coherence in composing is in fact a move toward communication. It is only a slight step when a composer tries for coherence in terms of a particular audience. This idea of music directed to a particular public is usually a bit shocking to the music lover. It doesn't matter how many times we tell the familiar story of

Bach writing each week for the honest burghers of Leipzig, or Mozart's relations with the courtly musical patrons of his day; audiences still prefer to think of the musical creator as a man closeted with his idea, unsullied by the rough-and-tumble of the world around him. Whether or not contemporary composers think about this matter of communication with their audience, they haven't been signally successful at it.

COPLAND

Marion Bauer

In his book *What to Listen for in Music,* Aaron Copland gives a clue to his own aims, character, and achievements as man and artist: " Every artist's work is, of course, an expression of himself, but none so direct as that of the creative musician. He gives us, without relation to exterior ' events,' the quintessential part of himself — that part which embodies the fullest and deepest expression of himself as a man and of his experience as a fellow being.

" . . . When you listen to a composer's creation you are listening to a man, to a particular individual, with his own special personality. . . . Whatever personality a composer may have is expressed within the framework of his own period. It is the inter-reaction of personality and period that results in the formation of a composer's style."

An examination of Copland's music definitely reveals the effect of his own personality and the influence of the time and the environment in which he works.

The thoroughness and conservativeness of his early musical training gave him the kind of technical security and foundation indispensable to the serious composer. His exposure to the Parisian musical life, to study with Nadia Boulanger, to the intoxication of hearing music by Stravinsky and the French composers of the early twenties, had a definite effect on the molding of his style. The fact that jazz at that time had taken the European composers by storm gave him material that he as an American, born and brought up in the first wave of its popularity, knew better than they how to handle.

Other factors in Copland's development show traits that stem from his Russian-Jewish heritage. The quality of his melodic line frequently is Hebraic, but he seldom consciously seeks out Jewish folk melodies. His trio *Vitebsk* is one of the exceptions.

The works in large form, written either in the Paris years or under their influence, include a Symphony for Organ and Orchestra (1924); *Grohg*, a one-act ballet (1925); *Music for the Theater* (1925), a suite for small orchestra; and Concerto for Piano and Orchestra (1926). The ballet, never presented as such, reached the public in an excerpt called *Cortège macabre* and, in still another guise, as the *Dance Symphony*, which received the RCA Victor Company Award in 1930. The Symphony for Organ and Orchestra, which served to introduce Copland to the American public in 1925, was later revised and rescored as his First Symphony. One of the best known of his early scores, *Music for the Theater*, for chamber orchestra, was composed in 1925 at the MacDowell Colony in Peterboro, New Hampshire, as a commission from the League of Composers. The Concerto for Piano and Orchestra dates from 1926. In the last two, *Music for the Theater* and the concerto, the jazz element is strongly in evidence, although Copland afterward turned away from its conscious use.

From this group of compositions, a very definite and original musical personality emerges: a clear, logical thinker; a richly endowed musicality; a brilliant craftsman; a nonsentimentalist; a man of high-strung, nervous vitality, one who works with directness, fearlessness, honesty, supreme concentration, and with little superfluous detail, development, or decoration. The complexity of this early style and the frequent harshness of his dissonance show Copland reflecting the characteristics of the age. The changes that took place in general in composing styles and formulas in the 1930's have manifested themselves in particular in his music. So from complexity he has turned to a conscious and definite simplification; from harmonic harshness to a gentler, more amiable procedure. But the older style was no more nor less a musical portrait of Copland than is the later style a picture of the composer of *El Salón México* (1936), the ballets *Hear Ye! Hear Ye!* (1934) and *Billy the Kid* (1938), *An Outdoor Overture* (1938), *The Second Hurricane* (1937), and the incidental music for films.

Contrasting nostalgic and orgiastic moods dominate the music

of his first period. Nostalgia looks out from the pages of the Introduction and the Andante Moderato of the *Dance Symphony*, the
Prelude of the First Symphony, and for a few measures the opening
of the Finale, from the Interlude and Epilogue of the *Music for the
Theater*; and occasional glimpses are found in the softer passages of
the Piano Concerto. One discovers the gentler Copland also in some
of the short works, such as his youthful song *As It Fell upon a Day*
(1923), on an early seventeenth-century poem, for soprano, with
flute and clarinet accompaniment; the lovely *a cappella* setting of
Edwin Arlington Robinson's *The House on the Hill* (1925), for
women's voices; the first of the *Two Pieces* for string orchestra
(1928); and his "Song" on a lyric by E. E. Cummings in the
Cos Cob Song Volume. This mood is sometimes pastoral, sometimes Hebraic, and occasionally "blues" in character.

The wild, boisterous mood swishes its tail and rears its head
very frequently in the Piano Concerto; also in the "Dance" and
"Burlesque" of *Music for the Theater*, the Scherzo of the Symphony, the Allegro Vivo of the *Dance Symphony*, and in the three-
part chorus for women's voices, *An Immorality* (1925), on a text by
Ezra Pound. Curiously enough, however, Copland always holds the
mood in leash by means of his intellectual and technical mastery.
The youthful exuberance that seemed unbridled in the first hearing
of the Piano Concerto is an effect rather than a cause. It is the result
of his extraordinary rhythmical sense, the brilliancy of his orchestration, and the pungency of his polytonal effects. For his dissonance
is achieved through polytonality and not atonality. In other words,
Schoenberg's inventions have made less of an impression on Copland than have Stravinsky and Milhaud methods. His own use of
polyrhythms, although derived from jazz, is original and exciting.

In his handling of rhythm, Copland is completely American.
The vitality of his rhythmic patterns in practically every composition infuses his work with life. Multirhythms (that is, swift changes
of meter), a contrapuntal web of rhythms (polyrhythms), a reckless, fearless bravado, an ironic wit, all are offshoots of his inherent
response to a fundamental rhythmic urge.

As one sees in Debussy the effect of impressionistic painting,
so one might claim the influence of the abstractionists on Copland's
music as evinced in his use, melodically, of angles, lines, and planes.
Soft contours, long and involved developments, pastel harmonies,
are conspicuous by their absence. His style involves sharply defined

motifs, reiteration of short figures and of bits of thematic material, an uncompromising harmonic starkness without prettifying, planes resulting from melodic and instrumental juxtapositions, frequently a percussive, staccato, dry piano tone such as one finds in the concerto, *Piano Variations* (1930), and the trio *Vitebsk: Study on a Jewish Melody* (1929).

At least, such were the characteristics of the earlier style, to which he has added new and interesting ingredients. Owing no doubt to the versatility of his nature, he has been a human barometer and has registered in his own terms the sociological and artistic changes that have taken place in the last decade.

When Copland returned to America after his sojourn in Europe, he gave time and attention to the problems and possibilities of the music of his native land. He discovered a new American audience, one created by the motion pictures and the radio, another among the younger generation. The latter, he found, were temperamentally more prepared for the newer idioms than the old concert-goers of fixed tastes and prejudices. He realized that this new audience was having a retroactive influence on the rising generation of composers, an influence that was showing itself in a symptomatic simplification of musical language and idiom. No composer trained in the earlier and complex idioms has responded more whole-heartedly to the change than has Copland himself. Not only has it affected the character of his own output, but he has shown a generous, constructive spirit in his interest in and encouragement of young American composers, individually and through the organizations with which he has been connected. In the Copland-Sessions Concerts and the American Festivals of Contemporary Music at Yaddo, Saratoga Springs, of which he was a founder, many works by Americans were programmed. Copland has actively participated in fostering the new spirit in those concerts of the League of Composers devoted to the presentation of works by young Americans. He was founder of the American Composers' Alliance and its first president.

Copland's new style reached the public in the spring of 1937 by way of his two-act " play-opera," *The Second Hurricane*, which was given at the Neighborhood Playhouse, New York, with children of the Henry Street Settlement Music School participating. The whole was planned for amateur performance: children's chorus, grownups' chorus, two adult and six child soloists, and an orchestra of twenty pieces. Copland knew how to control his technique and musical thought so as best to interpret the simple and fresh language of the libretto by Edwin Denby. He understands the adolescent mind and character well enough to have written effectively and successfully for high-school age, with great economy of means and expert setting of the words. Paul Rosenfeld wrote prophetically: " In fact, this revealing little play-opera may be very influential on the future of American music: as a work representative of a new tendency to simplicity without sacrifice of either musical expressiveness or of musical quality."

A radio commission from the Columbia Broadcasting System, announced as A Saga of the Prairie (a title chosen from many sent in to the station after the performance of Music for Radio in July, 1937), shows the same straightforward melodies, colorful harmonization, and effective orchestration as The Second Hurricane. It is a work of softer curves and more amiable effects than are to be found in Copland's earlier style. He again displayed appreciation of youthful psychology in his Outdoor Overture, written for and performed by the orchestra of the High School of Music and Art. He wrote a fresh, spontaneous score in which the melodic patterns, rhythmic vitality, orchestration in tonal strata, are characteristic and thoroughly disciplined.

One of the most popular, as well as important, of his later orchestral scores is El Salón México, inspired by the memory of his first visit to Mexico in 1932, and performed there by Carlos Chávez in 1937. The work is based on popular melodies, the type that Copland heard in a dance hall in Mexico City. " In that ' hot spot ' one felt, in a very natural and unaffected way, a close contact with the people," he said. " It wasn't the music I heard, but the spirit that I felt there which attracted me. Something of that spirit is what I hope to have put into my music."

And in the spirit of El Salón México, Copland's earlier and later styles are blended in the use of the more obvious and simple popular and folk material and in the verve and skillful handling of the syncopated dance rhythms, and of the brilliant, appropriate orchestration. Here is music that is more gay than ironic, more friendly than repellent, more consonant than dissonant, although dissonance is by no means lacking.

After El Salón came the ballet Billy the Kid (1938), written for the Ballet Caravan. Clever, commonplace when necessary, simple, jazzy, and full of vitality, it reveals the versatile Copland in a pleasing and successful role. His ballet *Hear Ye! Hear Ye!* drew from Colin McPhee the statement (*Modern Music*, March–April, 1936) that " one cannot rest without alluding to its vitality, exhilaration, and pungent orchestration, particularly in the jazz parts. Not the least of Copland's many gifts is the ability to write the most exciting jazz I know, a jazz whose nervous energy could only be felt by a New Yorker, and by one who was thoroughly aware of his city's night life from Minsky's Burlesque to Harlem."

These characteristics of " vitality, exhilaration, and pungent orchestration " are present in every work, from the least to the greatest. They are found not only in the works already discussed but also in his *Symphonic Ode* (1929), written on commission for the fiftieth anniversary of the Boston Symphony Orchestra and played in 1932, and in his *Quiet City* 1939), for trumpet, English horn, and strings, which was programmed by Serge Koussevitzky in 1941 at the Berkshire Symphonic Festival. This work was called " a small and perfect piece, essentially the reflection of a distinguished and important personality," by a young critic (Robert Ward, *Modern Music*, March–April, 1941). " Its long rising line of emotional intensity reaches a climax of great poignancy and then subsides again to the mood of the opening."

This brings to mind an important element in Copland's workmanship — his extraordinary feeling for musical form. He might be a musical construction engineer in the way he plans and builds. Often he practices great economy as, for example, in his setting of E. E. Cummings' " Song," in which the design of the entire accompaniment is contained in the first measure. Also, in the working out of the four-note angular motif in his *Piano Variations* he has modeled with a keen sense for design. This same feeling for rhythmic and harmonic pattern is apparent in the trio *Vitebsk*, in which he juxtaposes major and minor triads so as to approximate a quartertone effect on the piano. He also uses actual quarter tones on the violin and the cello.

Paul Rosenfeld states picturesquely, in *An Hour with American Music*, that " the great interest of his music remains the architectural one, the interest of the independent, projected, self-sufficient object. And in their structurality, their faithfulness to the line of strength, his tonal edifices resemble nothing so much as steel cranes, bridges, and the frames of skyscrapers before the masons smear them with their stonework."

Subsequent major works in characteristic style include the Piano Sonata (world première in Buenos Aires, October, 1941, during Copland's musical tour of South America); *Lincoln Portrait*, for narrator and orchestra, commissioned and played by André Kostelanetz on May 14, 1942; the ballet *Rodeo*, commissioned by the Ballet Russe de Monte Carlo, and presented in New York, October 16, 1942; *Danzón cubano*, composed for two pianos, to celebrate the twentieth anniversary of the League of Composers, played in December, 1942, and later orchestrated and performed in Baltimore under the direction of Reginald Stewart in February, 1946, a recipient of the New York Music Critics Circle Award in 1947; *Appalachian Spring*, a ballet that earned the composer the Pulitzer Prize in music, written for Martha Graham on a commission by the Elizabeth Sprague Coolidge Foundation, and first presented at the Library of Congress, Washington, D.C., on October 30, 1944; the Third Symphony, commissioned by the Koussevitzky Music Foundation, and given its première in Boston, October 16, 1946; the quartet for piano and strings, introduced at the Coolidge Festival in Washington, D.C., October 29, 1950; and an opera, *The Tender Land*, presented by the New York City Opera on April 1, 1954.

Copland has had his share in the comparatively new field of American documentary and Hollywood films, and he has fitted his style to the requirements remarkably well. *The City*, an excellent documentary film on housing, was shown at the New York World's Fair in 1939. His first Hollywood collaboration was in John Steinbeck's *Of Mice and Men*. Next followed *Our Town*, to Thornton Wilder's play, in 1940; later came the scores for *North Star*, *The Red Pony*, and *The Heiress*. In documentaries he also completed music for *The Cummington Story*.

In *Appalachian Spring* and the Third Symphony one finds the apotheosis of what might be called Copland's American style. In the ballet he quotes folk tunes, but in the symphony the lyric line is strongly Early American, an Americanism that is definitely converted and absorbed from his conscious studies of folk song and hymnody.

(FREDERICK DELIUS)

1862 - 1934

BIOGRAPHY

FREDERICK DELIUS was born in Bradford, England, on January 29, 1862. His father, a prosperous wool merchant, planned a business career for him. After Delius had spent two years in Manchester, in the business establishment of a relative, he sought an avenue for escape. He broached the idea to his father that he go to America to work in an orange grove. His father acquiesced. In 1884 Delius came to Florida to superintend an orange plantation his father had bought for him. Delius did not devote himself too assiduously to his work as planter. Instead, he turned wholeheartedly to musical pursuits, studying the piano, harmony, and counterpoint. Finally he abandoned the pretense of business altogether. He went to Danville, Virginia, to become a teacher of music, then worked as an organist in New York. His savings enabled him to go to Leipzig to study at the Conservatory with Sitt, Jadassohn, and Reinecke.

In 1888 Delius settled in a country home in Grez-sur-Loing, France, where he was to stay for the remainder of his life. During the next forty years he composed a series of masterpieces in which his style became fully crystallized: the opera *A Village Romeo and Juliet*, the choral *A Mass of Life*, and the series of tone pictures for orchestra including *Brigg Fair*, *In a Summer Garden*, *Summer Night on the River*, and *On Hearing the First Cuckoo in Spring*.

It was in Germany that Delius first achieved recognition as a composer, through a series of performances of his works between 1904 and 1907. In England, his fame was to come much more slowly, largely achieved through the missionary work of the conductor Sir Thomas Beecham.

After the war Delius became a victim of paralysis. Three years after this, he became totally blind. Despite his suffering, Delius did not abandon composition. Enlisting the services of a disciple, Eric Fenby, who had come to live with him, Delius dictated his last works, note by note.

On June 10, 1934, Delius died at his home in Grez-sur-Loing. His body was transferred to southern England and buried in Limpsfield to the accompaniment of Delius music performed in a nearby church under the direction of Sir Thomas Beecham.

PERSONAL NOTE

Eric Fenby

THE MUSICIAN Delius was greater than the man. He lives for us now in his music, and not by reason of his outstanding qualities as a man. What was extraordinary in the man as I knew him was not so much that which was inherent in his nature, but that which was largely the fruit of his unbelief and the secluded life he found it necessary to lead in order to perfect his art; namely, his intellectual isolation, his inhuman aloofness, his penetrating truthfulness, wholly indifferent thereby whether he hurt people or not, his utter contempt for the " crowd," and his all-embracing self-sufficiency. To these were added his colossal egotism, his dreadful selfishness, his splendid generosity (particularly to those of his old friends who had fallen on hard times), his equal indifference to money and honors, his exceptional refinement, and his noble triumph over an almost total physical incapacitation.

That he was a true artist if ever there was one, none can deny. Everything and everyone was subservient to the chief business of his life — his music. That was the only thing that mattered. The rest could go.

It must not be imagined that Delius had always been the country dreamer that the music of his maturity would suggest. There had been a wild and reckless youth spent in the great cities of the world, with much traveling over half the earth, and many love affairs, and one, the affair of his life, which had come to nothing. There had been no inclination to settle down in the country now that his studies in Leipzig were completed. On the contrary, he loved the Paris of those days, and the gay and picturesque Scandinavian students there who were so vital to his happiness. The men liked him; the women adored him. But there were moments when he felt he must get away from the market place. . . .

His continual appearance of serenity — a serenity I always likened to the serenity of a lion as it sits gazing nonchalantly at one at the zoo — and his silence, ominous and full of awful possibilities, underlined his occasional remarks to a degree that had to be seen and heard to be believed.

There was no nonsense about him; nor would he tolerate it in others, and if he was bored he showed it plainly. Even when dining with his friends, if the conversation was not equal to the good food, and the good wine, for which his table was renowned, I have heard him suddenly say to his man, with the unmistakable accent of a Yorkshireman: " Begin to read! " And his guests have had to sit in silence for the rest of the meal.

Woe betide anyone whom he found to be a liar and a cheat! That person was never forgiven. I have seen Delius take an instant dislike to his man for no other reason than that he felt sure the fellow was not filling his glass to the brim. He knew the number of mouthfuls in a glass.

As I watched his servants feeding him, dressing him, and carrying him hither and thither, the thought struck me more than once how horrible it was that with his lively contempt for ordinary men Delius should be so pathetically dependent on ordinary men. Nor would he stop for a moment for a chat with the kindly villagers whom we frequently met in the evenings on our way up the street, or returning from their work in the fields.

" If anybody comes up to us when we're out, take no notice. Keep going! " were his orders when I first went to Grez. Never did I see him unbend.

No workman was ever allowed to pass near him as he sat in the garden, and if the electrician called unexpectedly to examine the radio, he was not admitted till Delius had been carried away or they had put a screen around him. He remained an autocrat to the very end.

The sympathetic view to take is that he never understood the ordinary man because, so far as I can make out, he had never known the ordinary man. I used to tell him that if he had ever talked to the ordinary man, as he pottered about in the little greenhouse, of his allotment on his half-day holiday, he would have found him a delightful fellow.

The fascinating Northern dialect of a Grieg, the aristocratic utterance of a Chopin, he preferred to the common language of a Bach, a Beethoven, or a Sibelius. Being a man of excess, he exaggerated what in others was unessential. It had been so all his life. If he must smoke, then he must smoke all day long; if he was to have spinach, then spinach it had to be almost every meal; if it was to be beautiful harmony, well, then beautiful harmony it had to be all the time. There were no half measures with Delius. In a man of less force and refinement such chromatic excess would have been positively harmful, as it was in Spohr, who lacked the strength and sweep of a Delius.

Refinement was a religion to Delius. I cannot recall a single instance of ever hearing him make a vulgar remark. He was as intolerant of bad manners as he was of ignorance.

That was the man as I knew him, hard, stern, proud, cynical, godless, completely self-absorbed — the man Frederick Delius.

THE COMPOSER SPEAKS

Frederick Delius[1]

IT IS a great mistake for young composers to study too much. People with a little talent nearly always kill it by too much learning. Learning kills instinct. It is just as dangerous as too much reflection.

You can't teach a young musician to compose any more than you can teach a delicate plant how to grow, but you can guide him a lit-

[1] These statements come from *Delius as I Knew Him*, by Eric Fenby.

tle by putting a stick in here and a stick in there. Composition as taught in our academies is a farce. Where are the composers they produce? Those who do manage to survive this systematic and idiotic teaching either write all alike, so that you can say that this lot belongs to this institution, this lot to that, or they give us the flat beer of their teachers, but watered down. In all probability those who are most aware of this depressing state of things are teachers themselves. How can music ever be a mere intellectual speculation or a series of curious combinations of sound that can be classified like the articles in a grocer's shop? Music is an outburst of the soul. It is addressed and should appeal instantly to the soul of the listener. It is not experimental analysis like chemistry. Never believe the saying that one must hear music many times to appreciate it. It is utter nonsense; the last resort of the incompetent. And another thing: the amateur musician is better without a knowledge of the science of music. When you see a lovely rose you treasure it as it is; you don't pull it to pieces to appreciate its beauty and find out where its delicious perfume comes from. So it should be with music.

It is fatal with most of the critics if a composer has found it necessary to reject German forms and refuse to mold his thought into standardized patterns. One can't define form in so many words, but if I was asked I should say that it was nothing more than imparting spiritual unity to one's thought. It is contained in the thought itself, not applied as something that already exists. Look at Walt Whitman. Whitman spent his whole life writing *Leaves of Grass*. It is his individual contribution to art. Nobody else could have written it. So with my own work.

There is evidently something wrong with musicians who can suddenly change their entire outlook and experiment in a tonal ugliness. Is the present tendency perhaps due to lack of imagination, lack of emotion? Is it perhaps the outcome of our hasty mode of life, or a striving after publicity, arrivism, sensationalism, or self-advertisement? Is it an equivalent of fashion? It is difficult to tell. But I feel certain that no outward influences, no set principles or theories, can give birth to beautiful music.

DELIUS

Bernard van Dieren

Everyone who knew Delius personally loved him. I have never heard an anecdote told about him that did not illuminate anew this one undoubted fact. At times the telling might reveal the slightest tinge of critical acidity, to remind one of Delius' own bluff outspokenness. But it is remarkable that with whatever tendentiousness a story about him was told, it invariably left the impression that here was a man of whom someone might disapprove, whom yet no one could hate. Delius, in spite of the many difficulties he had to contend with, never was embittered, and never encountered bitter antagonisms. One has heard musicians call Sibelius vulgar. One has heard of others who detested Busoni, or who could not bear to have Strauss named. I have seen people turn pale at the mere mention of Mahler.

With Delius, such disparaging and such violent feelings did not occur. There was sufficient personality in his work, and he had enough genius to rouse envy. Still, in many respects he held a place apart. There was something irresistibly affecting and touching about everything he wrote. The most refractory traditionalist or the grimmest antimodernist could not summon the harsh feelings their principles demanded for really powerful denunciation of Delius' esthetic sins.

Some of his German critics used to describe him as an iconoclast. They said he was uncompromising, ruthless, and inclined to be sacrilegious. " Delius," someone said to Mahler, " has no respect for the great composers. He does not care whether a work is written by Bach or by a conservatory student." " Delius is right," replied Mahler, who regarded such wholeheartedness and such admirable frankness about old music as excellent examples for younger men who had heard quite enough of the respect due to the Great Masters.

But Delius was not reckless in his judgments. He had a very precise notion of the value of belief derived from a venerable tradition. In an interview shortly after the war he declared his emphatic disapproval of the fashionable contempt for established masters as preached by the Diaghilev clique. He strongly insisted on the need for reverence in the artist's attitude toward his art. He may have held radical philosophical doctrines, but they were aristocratically pagan. There was nothing of the morose sans-culotte in him. He never felt any vocation for the barricades and for battles for the proletarian's right to a bowler hat. Suburban heroism was as uninteresting to him as the intrigues of amorous duchesses, the two poles between which the imagination of many of the bold thinkers of his early days turned. More than anything, however, he loathed the determined facetiousness of the French Russians and the Russian Frenchmen who, in his later days, had the ear of the wide-awake modernity hunters and the highbrow-mongering snobs. " As if a man walked into church without trousers " was one of the phrases his indignation inspired.

On the other hand, he was, and remained to the end of his life, cheerily unrepentant in his rejection of studied formality. No hoary tradition impressed him by its long history, and no technical proficiency filled him with submissive awe. Academic correctness alone seemed to him as futile as the legendary dinner jacket of the public schoolboy on safari among the savages. No white man's burden ever troubled him. His conceptions of *noblesse oblige* were of a different order altogether.

He looked for the appeal of simple humanity in every composer's language. If it failed there, the other qualities counted for nothing. In his fervor for this one thing, he perhaps overstepped his usual line of pleasant common sense now and then. He was liable to underrate the value of achievements that cannot rouse our emotions. Intellectual appeal by itself seemed to him an unworthy object. Any musical utterance that addressed the intellect more than accidentally would irritate him very soon. Therefore he found it far from easy to believe that a genuine musician could be moved by organic perfection unless it was unreservedly put to the service of lyrical expression. He distrusted the artistic honesty as well as the esthetic susceptibility of those who professed to feel otherwise.

Technical devices and constructive ideals for which he had no personal use appeared to him factitious. He readily detected pedantry of purpose and aridity of imagination behind the desire for their employment. He could say to one of his disciples: " My dear fellow, there is nothing in counterpoint. I have done all that stuff myself. You may take it from me that it leads nowhere." When he described his conservatory exercises, he candidly believed that he had experimented with the idiom of Bach and found it ineffective. Apparently he did not reflect that he had only examined a few primitive rules of grammar, and that this did not yet amount to any very useful attempt to discover what ingredients might be abstracted from them that could prove of value to his own musical speech.

Delius, throughout his career, had a very shrewd perception of his limitations. Although, possibly, he might have made a more liberal use of the ready-shaped formulas of music, nothing could better demonstrate the reliability of his artistic instinct than his avoidance of them. He never overreached himself as so many lesser composers continually do. He may be said to have attempted too little: he could not be said to have ever attempted too much. If he deprecated the use of conventional contrapuntal technique in conversation, his object mostly was to warn an immature artist against the blind worship of cerebral profundity.

Where his own work was concerned, Delius knew exactly what he wanted, and he rarely failed to convey the essence of his message. Toward the end of his life, amidst protracted suffering borne with unfailing self-command and philosophic detachment, his musical ecstasy lost some of its incandescence. When every bar was no longer so intensely felt as in the music of his full manhood and his greatest artistic maturity, he may even have descended to the application of mechanical devices for the completion of a basic design. Here, by the submission to one weakness, he revealed another. He had never learned how to achieve the appearance of successful artistic performance when inspiration was flagging. He had never needed to cultivate that kind of technique, and where he had recourse to it, a certain lack of versatility in the range of his resources became evident. But if he had been able to mask the absence of the old emotional depth he would no longer have been the same unified personality. He had made us too certain of what we might expect of him.

In every one of his works we see the whole man. Within its limits his weaknesses are charms.

One of the most stupid criticisms of Delius was that he remained all his life an amateur. From the narrowest professional angle there may be perceived a glimmer of truth in the saying. But only negatively. Only because he loved music, and because he loved composing music with a most unprofessional affection.

Exclusive professionals felt doubtful about a composer who did not " move " amongst them, who held no appointments, who never sat as an examiner and played no instrument. To them, in short, he was a somewhat distant figure living in seclusion in a foreign land in more than one sense. It is probably true that Delius would not have passed any set examination. The same is indubitably true of many an examining professor. Delius at least never tried to examine others. But he could do things that very few of those who pride themselves on their professional *savoir-faire* could approach. So far from being a fumbler, as in their polished imbecility a few wiseacres have decreed, he was a virtuoso. He was a virtuoso who knew hesitations, but a virtuoso none the less. He solved with sovereign ease problems for which no conservatory can prepare a man and for which no indications are to be found in any textbook.

The subtlety of his perception in orchestral timbres was as astonishing as the assurance with which he applied it. He relieved the simplest orchestral texture by master strokes of unexpected color. He added original tints to the most familiar combinations. To a glaring chorus of brass he knew how to give a softly glowing shade of deep browns and purples. And to the brutally sharp-edged screeches of the woodwind he could lend a silvery profile that made it more dazzling while toning down the obtrusive angularities.

These are the high peaks of his achievement. It is foolish to denigrate the technical mastery of a man who can perform such feats.

A conductor told me that a certain passage for the violoncellos in *Appalachia* (1902) sounded marvelously witty, although it was " all wrong for the instrument." He did not seem to think it possible that Delius might have brought off an effect at which he had been aiming. He probably did not realize that such things do not at the right moment fall into the right place by accident. The infatuation of devout professionals can reach a depth and extent where they become blinded to the most obvious evidence. When they see a composer walk through lanes that they themselves have never trod and that are not marked on their maps, they refuse to believe that he can know where he is going.

When every possible criticism is made and met, when every possible praise has been reviewed, together with the contradiction it has received in other quarters, there remains the certificate that Delius was one of the most remarkable figures in the history of music. In the narrower frame of our own time, he was without question one of the three or four composers of such pronounced individual merit that they will be personally remembered. Among these again he is the one whose characteristics run least danger of becoming dissolved in the stylistic commonplace by which our period may be one day identified. It is unthinkable that at some future date any work of Delius could be described as just " typically twentieth century." It is highly probable, on the contrary, that later generations will, even as many of us do today, at once recognize a couple of bars as pure Delius.

It is relatively easy to copy a Delius piece, especially on a small scale. But that is just because copying alone is feasible. It is out of the question that anyone should work successfully on similar lines.

A composer's vaunted technique might be compared in considerable part to that of the eighteenth-century purveyor of poetry for all occasions. The composer, too, must have the fitting turn of phrase available for every emergency. The high-class tool bag of the poet contained a select range of guaranteed and finely tempered classical allusions. The composer also has several sizes of threaded screwline ready on all thicknesses of melodic bolts to take every harmonic nut, and vice versa. With such an outfit one rises to the fantastic heights of a plumber who should dispense with a mate.

Delius dispensed with the whole bag of tricks. All plumber-composers were convinced this could only mean that he did not know what use to make of the approved tools. It did not occur to them that he might do a better job with those he had designed for himself.

There cannot be many scores in existence that are so full of skillful ingenuity and dexterity of craftsmanship, combined with such felicity of invention, as Delius' A *Village Romeo and Juliet* (1901). The average musicmaker, when he looks at this strangely quiet work that burns with such white heat at the center, sees little else than a bewildering number of lost opportunities. He cannot believe that they could have been deliberately missed by a man who would be able to exploit them at all. At a hundred points there occur situations that, musically and dramatically, simply seem to clamor for the effective application of some standard expedients. But Delius, instead of writing the many pages that the barest routine could dictate to almost any composer, insists on making a fresh effort every time. He condenses the whole of his exquisite musical sensibility in a few brief phrases that owe nothing to the helpful formulas that, like so many faithful dogs, almost beg to be taken out for the occasion.

Delius, when he obeyed his intuition, found it easier to be

original. Quite conceivably he would have found it difficult to do the obvious thing. But he did the better thing every time.

Can a composer hope to attain a higher degree of technical perfection? What could be more desirable than that he should be able to appear most convincing and most complete in his every utterance, just there where he follows the line of least resistance? An imposing exhibition of abstract knowledge might hold our interest. But it does that because it recalls to our mind the earlier successful exploitations of a similar procedure. It does not touch us directly, as a few heartfelt notes of Delius can do.

Every situation and every inflection in the course of its exposure squeezes music out of Delius' heart. He is not concerned with that particular dramatic development of the theme which procures a maximum effect with a minimum of effort. His sole object is to communicate the intensity of his musical emotion at any given moment. The reactions of his entire being transformed every sentiment into tones, melodic curves, and orchestral colors. Whether at the same time these conformed to some principle or other was frankly a matter of complete indifference to him. Should they do so, all the better; should they not, none the worse.

He did not subscribe to any doctrine of symphonic or operatic righteousness. If ever he developed theories he kept them to himself. Those he discussed were obviously improvised. The trend of an argument might lead him into contradictions or into vaguely extravagant assertions. But this was just because he need never bother his head about theories and their logical application. One thing mattered to him, and that was that he knew no uncertainties when he was at work. He listened to the music in him, and it sufficed. He could trust it. He had the wisdom that science can only destroy.

He did not attempt to prove a system by experiment. He did not try reasoned conclusions with one opera after another. He knew only one way — his way. The relative crudity of Margot-la-Rouge (1902) and the mildly decadent refinement of Fennimore and Gerda (1910) are two forms of discharge of the same obligation. Yet always identical. Delius pays in specie. Unlike those dramatists who pay one part in kind, one part in small change, and the rest in sight drafts and very long-term bills, Delius gave good red gold all the time. It matters little, then, if he gave gold dust and nuggets first, hallmarked brass and minted coin afterward.

But for this solvency he had to suffer. Such protracted integrity was too good to be believed in. He never troubled to find extraneous means of telling the world about it. He did not advertise how much he had already given and how much more he proposed to do, or in what forms. It satisfied him to know that he had been reliable, and lavish even to the bounds of generosity. He no more attempted to draw attention to his achievement than to his theories, if he ever postulated any. He was no more a *raisonneur* than a demagogue.

He was resolute in his convictions, but they were his own concern. His public had only to deal with his finished works, and he had in fact no desire for other contacts with them.

If one has to state briefly what is most remarkable in Delius, wherein lies the distinction that obviously separates him from all others, a few points may at once be singled out as suitable for aphoristic statement. For all his intensely individual views and sensations, Delius never becomes morbidly subjective. He never had to fight the temptations of the grandiose and of the superb gesture that would present intimate personal experience in terms of universality. This saved him from the fate of the self-analyzing, self-absorbed poet, who asks us to see world tragedies in the collision of his private troubles and joys. He found the basic material for his music in those of his sensations which have an appeal for all. He sagaciously selected, and discarded the rest. We call such material objective since it deals with matters that all human beings meet in their own lives. But we also call objective all that the whole of humanity can experience when it is summed up in one man's work. But Delius was not a Shakespeare, and he is the more admirable for his understanding of the character of his own genius. He was at no time in danger of the other, almost worse, fate of the so-called objective composer — that is, the one who expects us to recognize all the troubles and all the joys of the world as only a few facets of the blinding shine that reflects the cosmic upheavals of his vast soul.

Delius' art is so completely satisfactory because while being definitely circumscribed it is so justly balanced. His music never undertakes to convey anything that does not belong to the adventures of every sensitive human spirit. To all that he touched he gave a new meaning, a new color, a new outline, a new loveliness, and a new poignancy. Music is greater, richer, and deeper for what he gave to it.

(SIR EDWARD ELGAR)

1857 - 1934

BIOGRAPHY

SIR EDWARD WILLIAM ELGAR was born in Broadheath, near Worcester, on June 2, 1857. In his sixteenth year he went to London to enter a solicitor's office. After three years he decided to abandon law for music. Returning to his home, he immersed himself in musical occupations, studying theory and several instruments by himself. In 1879 he returned to London to study the violin with Adolf Pollitzer. After five lessons he was convinced that a virtuoso career was not for him. He returned to Worcester to conduct a glee club and serve as bandmaster. After a short holiday in Germany, he became organist of St. George's Cathedral.

In 1889 Elgar married Caroline Alice Roberts. It was her influence that brought him to a career as composer. In 1891 he settled in Malvern and, having deserted all other musical occupations, turned to composition. Two years later *The Black Knight*, a choral work, was performed in Worcester. This was followed by other choral compositions, performed with moderate success. Elgar's first important works were the *Enigma Variations* for orchestra and his choral masterpiece, *The Dream of Gerontius*.

For the next dozen years, up to the outbreak of World War I, Elgar produced a series of works that placed him in the vanguard of modern English composers. These works included the *Introduction and Allegro* for strings, a symphony, a violin concerto, and the orchestral *Falstaff*. During World War I, Elgar served as a special constable in the Hampstead Division, then in the Hampstead Volunteer Reserve.

Elgar was knighted in 1904, received the Order of Merit in 1911, was appointed Master of the King's Musick in 1924, and in 1931 was given the highest honor that the Crown could confer on a musician, that of baronetcy.

Elgar visited the United States in 1905 and 1907, when he received honorary degrees from Yale and the University of Pennsylvania.

He died in Worcester, England, on February 23, 1934.

PERSONAL NOTE

William H. Reed

ELGAR was intensely fond of the country. Like William Morris, he was in love with the earth. He seemed to me to know every inch of Worcestershire (his own country), Herefordshire, the Malverns, Gloucestershire, and the Severn and Wye Rivers. He never tired of talking of them, exploring and re-exploring them if only to see again all the things he knew to be there; and his great joy was to have a kindred spirit with him to share in these pleasures, and to see his own joy reflected in the face of another. Side by side with this went his great love for humanity, especially the village folk and those in the humbler walks of life. Position or station was nothing to him in his dealings with his fellow creatures; but the things they said and did were for him of inexhaustible and abiding interest. He gave me the impression that he could remember without the slightest effort everything that anyone had said or done within his experience, with the date and every detail complete. This is of course impossible; but, if only I could remember a tenth of what I gleaned from listening to his conversation on our many jaunts in a two-seater car through the highways and byways of Worcestershire, I should be an extraordinarily well-informed man. . . .

One of his amusements at one time was throwing the boomerang. When we were tired of our musical jobs we used to go to one of his beloved spots and practice with the boomerang, watching its peculiar flight and constantly striving to acquire the necessary skill to bring it back to our feet at the end of it. . . .

Another diversion . . . was The Ark. This was the name given to an outhouse, at his home in Hereford, which had been converted into a laboratory — the inside furnished with shelves and a bench and innumerable bottles, retorts, Bunsen burners, test tubes, and all the paraphernalia of an analytical chemist. Here Elgar would retire and ease the burden of his destiny as a composer by pretending to be a chemist. . . .

He was like a child in many respects; and although when I suggested any frivolous amusement or did anything boyish he would rebuke me with: " Oh, Billy, when, if ever, will you grow up," he was very much the same himself. One of the Gloucester Festivals occurred when the " Beaver " craze was in vogue. He made me play this game with him, the rule being that, if we met a man with a beard, the one who cried " Beaver! " first scored one, except when it was a *red* beard, when he scored three. We actually set out through the streets of Gloucestershire, our scores mounting, and Sir Edward's excitement culminating when he spotted two red beards approaching, and got in his " Beaver " each time before I had even seen them. . . .

Some of his reactions from music into the more commonplace were more unexpected. For instance, one of his refuges from the tyranny of his genius was the turf. Part of his enjoyment of this, I feel sure, was derived from the queer names of the horses and the jargon of the race track. But he made a study of it as he did of everything he took up, and mastered the whole betting sufficiently to convince me that he could have set up as a fully qualified bookie if he had been driven to it. Every morning at breakfast his newspaper was opened at the sports page, and the lists and tipsters' fancies reviewed. It was all Greek to me; but I had only to wait until he had completed his list of possible selections for the " three o'clock " or the " four o'clock " or whatever it was at Cheltenham, or Folkestone, or elsewhere. Then he would say: " Now, Billy, what about a horse for today? " and would read out his lists of names at a great rate. When he came to one called Semiquaver, I cut in with " half a crown on Semiquaver: that will be sure to go fast." He agreed quite seriously and put something on himself. No one was more surprised than I was when later in the day we found that it had won.

Sir Edward was a member of the Worcester Race Club and so could go to the enclosure at the Worcester Races. I went with him once or twice and found as much entertainment in watching *him* in this strange and, to me, new environment as in the racing.

I don't know how he got on financially, whether he won or lost. He was always reserved and mysterious in these matters; but I gathered from things he said from time to time that he managed to lose no more than he could afford for the fun of the sport. . . .

Elgar's tastes in music were all-embracing: he liked nearly all music that had tune, rhythm, or color. He loved some of Bach's music, but by no means all; and he had no great affection for the Elizabethan composers. Byrd, he pronounced insipid except for a few works. He liked Purcell, but would not join in the furor about Tudor music that arose amongst a certain set of young composers. He would not rave about folk tunes. I don't think he ever made use of one in his own works. He held that the business of a composer is to compose, not to copy. . . .

He loved all the old music that he had loved as a boy. Elgar's boyish pleasure in Suppé did not in the least interfere with his relish for Stravinsky; and the fun he got out of *L'Oiseau de feu* or *Petrouchka* never put Mendelssohn, Gounod, Grieg, and Schumann out of court. He loved Schumann and would discuss his symphonies at great length. The music entranced him; but he felt the weakness of the orchestration. He often surmised how certain other composers with a gift for orchestration would have scored this or that passage — what Wagner would have done with it, or Berlioz, or Richard Strauss; and I knew by the light in his eyes that he had a complete picture of it in his head, and knew very well what he himself would have done with it. But he felt strongly that the personality of the composer should not be overshadowed by anyone else attempting to " improve " upon the original.

He spoke very little of the works of his contemporary composers, especially of the younger school. He liked some of them in a mild sort of way, but none of them gave him such thrills as he derived from the classics or the Handel oratorios.

ELGAR

Basil Maine

TRIBUTES have been paid in every shape and form to the life and work of Sir Edward Elgar. It is but natural that many of these tributes should refer to Elgar's full and complete life; but, with the fragments of his unfinished symphony in mind, musicians will ever remember his death as a calamity. The otherwise admirable appreciation that appeared in *The Times* contained one misleading sentence: "It may be said with certainty, however, that the Third Symphony will not now be forthcoming. We shall never know what was the music which he found lying all about him in this strange and disjointed world, so different from that of his youth. Perhaps the effort to piece it together into a consistent whole was too much for him." The last words imply that Elgar's creative power had weakened toward the end. That, I am sure, was not the case. When the symphony was first commissioned by the BBC, Elgar made good progress in his work upon it. The oppressive heat waves brought the first interruption. He fell back upon Torquemada's crossword puzzles as being the nearest approach to the difficulties of symphonic construction. Nothing easier than those monstrous Sabbath Day problems was sufficient to occupy his leisure, unless to foretell a future happening upon a racecourse be deemed a simpler matter. When the heat had passed, there came the Hereford Meeting of the Three Choirs and the rehearsing and conducting that he always willingly undertook at festival time. Soon after came the blow. Only then was coherent musical thought, especially symphonic thought, made impossible, although, even during that last painful illness, he refused to let go the idea of his symphony.

In the summer of 1933, I was staying with Sir Edward Elgar at his home in Worcester and I had good reason to believe that the new work was growing fast. He was full of it. On one occasion he brought out several sheets of manuscript, sat down at the pianoforte, and, playing, reconstructed what was already existing of the symphony. He warned me that I should get no proper idea of its sound if I listened to it as pianoforte music, and I recalled with what scorn

he used to refer to the mere " keyboard composer." As he played the
themes of the first movement and their development, and described
the instrumentation, he appeared to be regarding the music as something not of his own creation — something he had discovered by
chance and now must tend like a watchful gardener for the promise
of flowering it held. It was always so with him. " It is my idea," he
once confessed, " that music is in the air all around us, and that, at
any given time, you just take as much as you want." That confession helps us to understand the contempt he had for the kind of
composer who could never create except in a house filled with
stained-glass windows (or with lilies or Wedgwood china or incense
or any other atmospheric thing). The keyboard mind and the
stained-glass-window mind — in music, I think, Elgar had no
stronger aversions. There was another almost as strong — the mind
that delights in frightfulness. He could never be accused of lacking
interest in younger composers. The postwar history of the Three
Choir Festival reveals that he took great pains to further the claims
of the oncoming men; but never indiscriminately. Not long ago I
heard from him some first-rate invective after the performance of a
young man's concerto. I will not go too far in my disclosure, but the
fact that the solo part was for a stringed instrument doubtless accounted for his wrath, for the string family was nearest his heart, as
all who know the *Introduction and Allegro* will admit.

Elgar took his music from the air. A mystery though that must
appear to ordinary people, let us allow that he did so. But a further
mystery confronts us, one that is suggested in the passage from *The
Times* that I have already quoted. What kind of music was he
finding in the air that lately had been so full of harsh conflict?
Would the baneful influence have made any fundamental change
in his symphonic expression? I can only answer that certain harmonic passages in the unfinished symphony seemed to me to be a
fresh revelation of Elgar's mind. That they were not born of theory
it is hardly necessary for me to assert, for no theory was ever the
forerunner of any of Elgar's major compositions. Nor could those
passages be in any way linked up with the feverishly cerebral experiments of the " new music." As I heard them they were simply a
reminder of the fact that Elgar had always been a pioneer in harmonic invention. Did we not know it as soon as we heard the Prelude to *The Dream of Gerontius* (1900) and those startling chords
that punctuate the pleadings of the Angel of the Agony? How much

the younger British composers owe to his enriching of harmonic resources (to that alone) is not always fully recognized. And it is my
belief that the creative force in him was continually developing,
even if there had been no striking manifestation of it since the death
of his wife. In what I heard of that last great adventure, the Third
Symphony, I thought I saw the glimmering of new light breaking
through his harmonic imagery. Something was there, I vow, that
had never before been expressed in quite the same way.

It was during a visit to him in the nursing home that I first
realized that, except through a miracle, the symphony could never
come into being. Yet on that ocasion I was not altogether unhappy,
for, in spite of great pain, his spirit was almost cheerful. Soon after I
had entered his room he began to describe a piece of country he himself had discovered and had shown to a few privileged friends. " You
won't find it in any guidebook," he said. " Those fellows who write
as guides to the English countryside don't know the real England.
I'll take you to this place when I'm well again." Then for about
twenty minutes he gave me a lucid account of the secret place. It was
part of the Teme Valley, and some of it, he hinted, had found its
way into one of his compositions. I have recalled that occasion here
to remind myself how often the English scene has found its way
into Elgar's music. In the Pianoforte Quintet (1918), it is there;
and in the String Quartet (1918), and the Sonata for Violin and
Pianoforte (1918), in the symphonies, in *Falstaff* (1913), in the
Violoncello Concerto (1919). In the slow movement of the Violin
Concerto (1910) it is there again, transcended in a way that is entirely Elgar's own and yet in spirit is comparable to the *Pastoral
Symphony* of Vaughan Williams and to much of Delius.

Edward Elgar's understanding of English life and character
was as great as his love for the English landscape. People and incidents were the unfailing inspiration of a musical train of thought.
I am not thinking so much of *Froissart* (1890) — where, in the
clarinet's little song, the voice was unmistakably heard almost for
the first time — of *King Olaf* (1896) — there it was again, clearly
ringing, in Olaf's bold approach to Sigrid — of *Caractacus* (1898),
of the *Enigma Variations* (1899), or even of *Cockaigne* (1901)
— not so much of these as of the symphonic compositions. In the
First Symphony (1908) the greatness of an era is eloquently proclaimed. The farewell to that greatness is the Second Symphony
(1910), with its episodes of splendor, ecstasy, foreboding, spiritual

conflict, grief, and resignation. In the Violoncello Concerto we are mourning for departed greatness. As much as any other music, Elgar's symphonic creations must be set against a background of life if they are to be wholly comprehended. The Englishry of Elgar's music is an inescapable quality.

This, however, is not to say that Elgar was merely a national composer in the sense that Grieg and Smetana are. It is often overlooked that almost all those who frankly recognized the worth of Elgar's first big works and gave him practical encouragement were men of foreign birth and extraction. Richter is one of the first names that come to mind, and with it a letter that the composer wrote, thanking him for a sympathetic and masterly performance of *Cockaigne* at Liverpool. Richter's playing of the overture had the effect of making Elgar dissatisfied with his own music, and he added: " I hope the symphony I am trying to write will answer to these higher ideals, and if I find I am more satisfied with it than with my present compositions I shall hope to be allowed to dedicate it to my honored friend, Hans Richter." Next to Richter we think of Richard Strauss. After the success of *Gerontius* at the Lower Rhine Festival it was Strauss' tribute to our master composer that called the English public to attention. Then there were Jaeger (who, in the Nimrod section of the *Enigma Variations*, inspired one of the finest memorials in music), Julius Buths, Rodewald, and Frank Schuster.

At that time England's little world of music was unprepared for Elgar's coming. There was too sharp a division between institutional and noninstitutional groups. Even at the Norfolk and Norwich Festival of 1899 Elgar's repute was by no means commensurate with his achievement. That this was first acknowledged by foreign musicians is surely sufficient to show that Elgar was in the main stream of European music; for no foreigner, least of all a German, could have been expected at the beginning of the century to praise or even to be aware of any music that was unrelated to the holy German dynasty. But even this virtue can be turned against an artist by his detractors, for he can be too closely related; and they begin to hunt for " influences." They can be easily discovered in Elgar, of course, as in other great composers who have used the traditional forms, but often they have been wrongly interpreted. Do we think of disqualifying Schubert or Mahler or Sibelius or Busoni, or, indeed, any neoclassical composer, because he has been influenced by Beethoven? Then there is Wagner. Critics have fallen into the too-easy

habit of detecting Wagner's footsteps in the work of every composer
who had the misfortune to enter the field just after him. As if those
footsteps could have been silenced! They are to be heard in *Gerontius;* that is natural enough. But have we not heard too much of that
oratorio being a protraction of *Parsifal,* and too little of its pioneer-
ing harmonic thought? And the detectives have sometimes been
wide of the mark. Elgar told me last winter that they were quite
wrong in finding that the device of thematic diminution in *Cockaigne* had come from *Meistersinger,* and then showed me the passage by which it *had* been suggested. With whom had he served as
apprentice this time? Not with Wagner, but with Delibes! The work
was *Sylvia.*

Hardly less ubiquitous than Wagner's influence is that of
Brahms. At the time Elgar was entering his phase of symphonic
thought he had accepted a professorship at Birmingham University
and had taken Brahms' symphonies as the subject of his lectures.
When his own symphonies and concertos appeared there was, therefore, room for busy speculation. The differences between composers,
however, are important. Compare the general enunciations, for example. Brahms works from bare, sometimes lean, statements toward complexity, while Elgar opens with a profusion of ideas and
then moves toward their reconciliation. The galvanic beginnings of
Elgar's symphonies tend to bewilder him on first acquaintance, so
many threads is he required to take up immediately and pursue. To
become familiar with the thematic features as such is a simple matter, for Elgar never fails to give them point and character both in
the melodic outline and in the equally important harmony; but
familiarity with the treatment of the features, with the organic
processes, demands a degree and a kind of attention that must
needs lift the listener out of his ordinariness.

To insist too much upon the later influences in Elgar's career
and to forget those of his boyhood is to approach his art from a
wrong angle. During his most impressionable years there came his
way the music of Karl Philipp Emanuel Bach and of those almost
forgotten composers Schobert and Koželuch; and among the influences of adolescence can be counted Tudor church music, Mozart's and Haydn's Masses, Meyerbeer, the operas of a traveling
company's repertory, together with Shakespeare and Voltaire. Then,
as always in his development, such experiences were assimilated only
to give his individuality a keener edge; for, since those early instances

which have been cited above, no composer's voice has been so immediately recognizable as Elgar's. There is, moreover, no insularity in his art. The liberal distribution of tastes and attractions during youth was evidence of his mind's range. Not that his music is unconditioned by national environment. In that respect he is in the company of Beethoven, Brahms, and Sibelius. But, like these, he is nationalist by grace, not by adoption of folk song. Melodies that were once folk music but are no longer — these he eschews, especially in compositions that are deliberately patriotic in motive. Instead, we find him writing melodies of his own, one of which became a folk song in his own lifetime. If folk song means anything at all, it is that once upon a time it was popular song. But let a composer of our own age write such a melody, and see how the folk-song enthusiasts knit their brows! " Land of Hope and Glory " and Sibelius' tune in *Finlandia* are regarded as crimes that the authors must expiate. So confused and contradictory are our judgments!

We have mentioned a few of the more common disparagements. They appear even more insignificant when we think of Elgar's stature as a symphonic writer. He stands with the greatest. To say that the symphonies, concertos, overtures, and *Falstaff* are the intense co-ordination of emotional experience is not to reduce their attainment. Nor need we fear to admit that each carries a program of some kind. There is Beethoven's example. In the *Pastoral* he took liberties, and even if we think that it is therefore so much the weaker as a symphony, there is still the *Choral Symphony*. To all who think of symphonic form as being a vessel divinely set apart to hold only pure music, that work is the final rebuke. Was the symphony made for man, or man for the symphony? We know that it was made for Elgar no less than for Bruckner, Brahms, and Tchaikovsky before him and for Vaughan Williams and Arnold Bax after him. Elgar's name shines among these and others because of his peculiar genius for orchestral writing, which, incidentally, helped to raise the standard of playing in England. Elgar was loved by English orchestral players. The memory of early days when he was a humble bandsman filled him with sympathetic appreciation of their work. He was one of them. Unsparingly he devoted himself to making his music understood by them. They have proved themselves worthy. English orchestras do indeed know their Elgar, know the idiom of his phrase, the curve of his eloquence, the secret of bowing his ecstatic melody and of breathing his rich harmony. Not only was

Elgar the first composer to bring England to the front rank as a producer of instrumental music; he also helped to lay the foundations
upon which we have built at least two of the best orchestras in Europe. We are entitled to think as highly of our present-day composers. There is good reason to believe that no finer music than
theirs is being written in any other country. If that belief prove
true, historians of the future will see in Elgar's major works the
flowing of the main stream from Germany to England.

That the stream flows deep and wide in English as in German
environment is witnessed by *Falstaff*. And this work can also be
cited as an answer to those who, perhaps with *Caractacus* in mind,
assert that Elgar missed the better part of his vocation in refusing
to write an opera. It is true that with a more amenable libretto
Caractacus might well have been Elgar's opera. As it stands, the
Eigen-Orben episodes are unconvincing. These lovers are merely
conventional appendages to a theme that, because of its inherent
nobility, had no need of such an attachment. But, even if Elgar had
met with a good enough libretto to persuade him to write an opera
on this or another theme, we may be sure that his development
would still have been along symphonic lines. He had opportunities
to enter the opera field. At one time Ricordi wanted to commission
three operas from his pen. His answer was that his knowledge of
Italian was too small and that nobody wanted to hear an opera in
the English language. A request from Covent Garden found him
equally diffident.

We need not take the reasons for his refusal too seriously. The
real reason was that there was a stronger pull in another direction.
Elgar's was always a symphonic way of thinking. The spontaneity
and nervous energy of his most characteristic music would have been
impeded by the imposition of nonmusical conditions. Of course it
can be argued that such conditions are, in fact, imposed by an oratorio or cantata text, and it is true that there are passages in Elgar's
oratorios and cantatas where the purely musical part of his mind,
with its continual aspiration toward the larger freedom of symphonic
thought, appears to be fretting under the burden of the text. But the
conditions of cantata and oratorio are more or less amenable to
music's demands, and Elgar relieved the tension by making use of
the leitmotiv method; and, as in Wagner's use of the method, the
themes, since they are musical ideas and not merely labels or visiting cards, serve for generation as well as association. Opera's condi-

tions are less tractable. Wagner solved the problem of uniting drama and a symphonic style by becoming his own librettist. That was his only possible way. So could he subject the design of his dramas to the exigencies of symphonic thought. Elgar, not attracted by the idea of writing his own librettos, turned to Shakespeare. But there are no opera librettos in Shakespeare's works. (The uncommon skill of a Boïto is wanted if Shakespearian proportions are to be reduced for opera's purpose and the essence of the drama retained.) Avoiding the pitfalls into which some other English composers have fallen, Elgar renounced the text altogether and conceived the character, life, and death of Falstaff in the form of a symphonic study. In this he was able to let loose the fullness of his individuality and imaginative force, and succeeded in capturing a quality that by analogy can be called Shakespearian.

The symphonic nature of Elgar's *Falstaff* cannot be too much emphasized. The music's behavior is guided by an inner logic of its own rather than by a series of scenes and events. (Yet the agreement between the inner logic and development of the drama is no less marked here than in Alban Berg's *Wozzeck*.) The general plan of the work can be regarded as a combination of suite and symphony. The first movement of the A-flat Symphony is an example of Elgar's use of a theme group instead of a first subject. The same predilection is to be observed in the opening episode of *Falstaff*, which is in effect a " first movement " developed from the opposition of a threefold theme group and, as second subject, the Prince Henry motif. The tavern scene and the exploit at Gadshill together introduce the scherzo element. After so much breathless activity the music, no less than Sir John himself, is now in need of rest. The quiet regularity of a gavotte measure lulls him to sleep to dream of his boyhood. The next episode (Allegro) is a combination of march and song; and, after the Gloucestershire Interlude, the underlying rhythm of which is that of the Gigue (remembered in tranquillity), there comes a finale of true symphonic splendor based on a transformation of earlier themes.

On the other hand, those who prefer to stress the continuity of *Falstaff* will find that its plan has much in common with rondo form. True, the features do not appear so clearly as in Strauss' *Till Eulenspiegel*, but the recurrence of the main Falstaff theme (with or without one of the subsidiary themes) leaves the general impression of a rondo, if allowance is made for the latitude of the intervening adventures. But whether it is regarded as a continuous texture or as a succession of movements, whether it is judged according to its general plan or according to the generative power of its themes, it is the symphonic nature of this study that provides its distinctive quality.

However wide a view we take of the range of music written for a modern orchestra, *Falstaff* will appear as one of the peaks. With that attainment in mind we can but wonder what heights Elgar would have reached in the Ben Jonson opera he was planning and had partly written. Even after hearing passages from this work, I still found there was room to speculate as to the nature of the whole conception. Which would have been preponderant, the symphonic or the dramatic element? Of one thing we may be certain: that opera would have been so much the greater achievement for the vantage ground gained in *Falstaff*.

(MANUEL DE FALLA)

1876 - 1946

BIOGRAPHY

MANUEL DE FALLA was born in Cádiz, Spain, on November 23, 1876. His mother gave him his first piano lessons, after which he was taught by Galluzo, Odero, and Broca. He was then sent to the Madrid Conservatory, where he was profoundly influenced by two teachers, the composer Felipe Pedrell and the pianist José Tragó. It was Pedrell who turned the young student to native Spanish music. When Falla completed his studies at the Conservatory, he turned to serious composition, producing in 1905 his famous lyric drama *La Vida breve*, which won first prize in a competition for national opera conducted by the Real Academia de Bellas Artes. Two years after this, Falla visited Paris, and was so intoxicated by its musical life that he remained there seven years. He studied French music and came into personal contact with many leading French composers, including Claude Debussy.

In 1914 Falla returned to Spain, at which time his *La Vida breve* received its first Spanish performance. During the next few years Falla traveled extensively throughout Andalusia, finally settling in Granada. In 1915 he composed the music for the ballet, *El Amor brujo*, performed for the first time that year in Madrid. He also completed that year an outstanding work for piano and orchestra, *Noches en los jardines de España* (*Nights in the Gardens of Spain*). With these two works, Falla was definitely recognized as the leading composer of his country.

As a result of a commission by Diaghilev, Falla composed *El Sombrero de tres picos* (*The Three-Cornered Hat*), which became one of the most striking successes of the Ballet Russe, after being introduced in London in 1919. Falla subsequently composed several works of extraordinary character, including a puppet show, *El Retablo de Maese Pedro*, and a concerto for harpsichord.

During the Civil War in Spain, Falla allied himself with the Franco forces, because he saw in the Franco nationalist movement a check to the antireligious activities that had been taking place throughout Spain. In 1938 Falla was appointed president of the Institute of Spain. Disillusionment with the Franco government sent him out of Spain in 1939 to Argentina. He settled in Alta Gracia, in the province of Córdoba, near the city of Córdoba, and there he died on November 14, 1946.

PERSONAL NOTE

Lincoln Kirstein

THE countryside around Córdoba, Argentina, is strongly reminiscent of Granada, the composer's native home. He lived the last years of his life with his sister at the Villa del Lago, about thirty-seven kilometers from Córdoba. It was a small home set halfway up a hill.

Falla had long been very sick. He had had bronchial trouble and had swallowed a pin, the infection from which had further irritated his throat. Then he had bitten his tongue, talking very energetically at table, even though his doctors forbade him to be active or indeed to talk much.

Falla was terrified of pneumonia. He had a big Spanish table to work at, which had a kind of skirt around it and under which he used to keep a brazier. But a local *aficionado* of his music had subsequently given him an electric stove.

The Fallas had no money at all. They managed to scrape by with great difficulty on the proceeds of concerts that he gave once or twice a year in Buenos Aires. Of course, practically all his available working time was spent on attempting to complete *La Atlántida*, a great oratorio upon which he had been working for almost a decade. But Falla had little opportunity to work. He had no piano. It was not clear whether he could not afford one, whether the house was too small to take one, whether he was too proud to accept one, or indeed whether he had one he did not like to play on. On one occasion, one of his local admirers had offered to take him to the nearby town of Carlos Paz, where there was a hotel in which there was a good piano. Falla decided to make the effort to go. But the trip was dusty and noisy. The room in the hotel was drafty and full of echoes. It made him too nervous ever to go again. Kind friends offered to take him to Mass. But he only felt able to fulfill the obligatory offices.

People were always trying to commission works. From England, from Spain, and from the United States there were continual offers. Choral groups in Barcelona and Palma de Mallorca wanted works. But he was too easily upset to try something new. He hated noise so much that he moved from Carlos Paz a kilometer and a half to Villa del Lago because he imagined it was quieter. Yet both places were so deathly still that his sister was constantly terrified at night. In their tiny house, in which there was nothing but a few pieces of furniture, the windows were heavily barred and all the doors were doubly locked. People were obviously not encouraged to come to see them. As for his sister, she said wistfully that she never left the house because Falla might want something. She couldn't even go out to buy clothes. Those she wore she had bought in Spain.

Don Manuel was a tiny man with large eyes burned deep into his bald skull. His head was very fine, with a fringe of iron-gray hair like a low tonsure. His skin was waxen brown. He carried a cane like a soldier, forcing service out of it. His mouth was very narrow. He stood at the table to talk, resting his large hands on it. His features were elongated as if by a combination of spiritual discipline and disease. He had the fanatic, suppressed, asceticism of St. Francis as imagined by El Greco.

He spoke first in a very formal Spanish, then in a perfect classic French, in a beautiful voice, very energetically, although his doctor had forbidden him to talk. He spoke of his illness. He had been very sick, the world as a whole was sick and so unsettled that even if God permitted his body health to work, his mind and heart would not be in it. If he could have four consecutive weeks of peace he could finish *La Atlántida,* because he composed music and thought of music all the time, but there were too many interruptions when he actually started to put it down. He wished to return to Spain, where he could really work and where he had many friends. He carefully reiterated that he was permitted by the present Spanish government to return. This he could do, although many of his friends were now exiles and had lost their citizenship.

Falla seemed continuously frightened, suffering from a real guilt or fear. He was preoccupied with his health, but this other thing was something different. Perhaps it was memories of the Civil War, the terrible compromises and decisions that had to be made or could not be made. He was sicker than he knew.

THE COMPOSER SPEAKS

Manuel de Falla [1]

THE excellence of natural Andalusian music is revealed by the fact that it is the only music continuously and abundantly used by foreign composers, and though the songs and dances of other nations have been equally utilized in universal music, this use is almost always reduced to the simple application of their characteristic rhythms.

Certainly many of these rhythmic forms have given rise to works of the highest artistic quality, as have some old European dances (gigues, sarabands, gavottes, minuets), but in addition to the fact that these are few in number, each separate nation is represented by, at most, a couple of examples of these purely rhythmic forms, to the exclusion, in the majority of cases, of the rest of their constituent elements.

Our natural music, on the contrary, has not only been the source of inspiration for many of the most illustrious modern foreign composers, but has served to enrich their means of musical expression, revealing to them certain great musical values systematically disregarded by the composers of the so-called classic period. And

[1] This artistic statement comes from the composer's book, *Escritos* (1947), and is published with the permission of Pantheon Books Inc., from whose *Composers on Music*, edited by Sam Morgenstern, New York, 1956, this excerpt is taken.

that is the reason that the moderns (who call those authors modern who date from after the middle of last century) did not limit themselves to taking one element only from our music, but all, absolutely all elements that go to form it, always provided they lent themselves to the tempered scale and the usual notation.

This influence to which we refer is the one directly exercised by popular Andalusian song, the backbone of which is represented by *cante jondo*.

The name *cante jondo* is applied to a group of Andalusian songs, of which we believe the genuine prototype to be the so-called *siguiriya gitana*, from which proceed others, still preserved by the people, like the *polos, martinetes,* and *soleares*, which retain marked qualities distinguishing them within the large group formed by the songs commonly called flamenco.

This last term should only be strictly applied to the modern group, which includes the songs called *malagueñas, granadinas, rondeñas* (this last an offshoot of the previous two), *sevillanas, peteneras,* etc., which cannot be considered other than an outgrowth of the ones cited in the preceding paragraph.

Once we admit that the *siguiriya* is the typical song of the *cante jondo* group . . . we must admit that this Andalusian song is perhaps the only European song that preserves in all its purity — in both structure and style — the highest qualities inherent in the primitive songs of the Orient. . . .

Let no one think that the *siguiriya* and its derivatives are simply songs transplanted from the Orient to the Occident. Here we have, on the contrary, a grafting, or better, a sharing of origins, which was certainly not revealed at a single given moment, but which follows the accumulation of folk history evolved in our peninsula. And that is the reason why the song peculiar to Andalusia, though it coincided in its essential elements with that of peoples geographically remote from ours, maintains an intimate character, so peculiar to itself, so national that it cannot be confused with any other.

FALLA

Gilbert Chase

THE STORY of Manuel de Falla's art is that of an unceasing quest for the musical soul of Spain. And as he drew nearer and nearer to the eternal essence of Spain, he drew further and further away from the public that acclaimed his earlier works. This is not because Falla had adopted a willfully hermetic attitude, but simply because the public had refused to follow him along a path that to him appeared not only necessary but inevitable. The explanation of this situation is not far to seek.

For the world at large, Spanish music is still terra incognita. The so-called " Spanish idiom " in music, immediately recognizable everywhere, consists mainly of the late-nineteenth-century conventionalizations of certain Andalusian flamenco songs and dances, plus variations on the jota of Aragón. The most mediocre musician, Spanish or foreign, can be assured of instant success by injecting either of these ingredients into any of his compositions. Outside of the flamenco and the jota, there is little of Spanish music that comes within the pale of the average person's interest or knowledge.

It is only now beginning to dawn upon a very few people that Spanish music is not all castanets and tambourines and guitars, jotas, *sevillanas*, and " *Olés!* " A handful of alert intellectuals have discovered that Spain is an important musical nation with a rich tradition going back to the Middle Ages and achieving a splendid florescence in the Renaissance. Though there was some deterioration after the seventeenth century, the vital spark was always kept alive by an exceptional musician here and there, until Felipe Pedrell took up the torch and with his indefatigable energy made it burn brightly for the present generation of composers. Pedrell made known the neglected masterpieces of Spain's musical past and the rich heritage of her living folk music. He enunciated the principle that from this twofold tradition, artistic and popular, the vital creations of modern Spanish music should spring.

In the early years of the present century, when Manuel de Falla was a struggling young musician in Madrid — struggling not only

materially, but also esthetically, to find himself as an artist — he had
the good fortune to become a pupil of Pedrell for several years. It
was also a stroke of fortune for Pedrell, because in this young musician he had found the only artist in all Spain with the will, the vision, the genius, and the knowledge to carry his doctrine of enlightened nationalism to its ultimate conclusion. Pedrell was the word;
Falla was the deed.

But Falla was no mere blind, unreasoning follower of Pedrell, or
of anyone else. He carried his studies of old Spanish music, and his
investigations of Spain's musical folklore, even further than Pedrell
had done. He accepted in principle Pedrell's doctrine of folk music
as a creative source, but he refused to interpret this as involving a
systematic exploitation of actual folk themes. He was more concerned with the spirit than with the letter of folk music. When the
people themselves vary their folk songs with an infinity of changes,
why should the composer attempt to reproduce literally any particular version? The essence of these songs is to be found in the characteristic rhythms, modalities, and melodic intervals that determine
their musical structure, and it is upon these basic elements that the
composer should build. He should not seek tunes, but ways of musical thinking.

In seeking to determine the antecedents of Falla's art, a third
influence should be mentioned: that of the zarzuela. Originating in
the seventeenth century as a play in which music and dancing alter-
nated with spoken dialogue, the zarzuela was revived in the nineteenth century with the same features but with a more popular character. The zarzuela composers utilized popular songs and dances in
their scores, treating them without much artistic distinction, but
with a certain attractive verve. The most gifted of the nineteenth-
century zarzuela composers was Francisco Asenjo Barbieri, from
whom Falla derived no small degree of stimulation. In fact, Falla's
music stems fundamentally from a fusion of the idealistic nationalism of Pedrell with the realistic " popularism " of Barbieri.

Falla's first and only opera, La Vida breve, which launched him
on his career as a composer by winning a national prize in 1905,
owes more to the best tradition of the zarzuela than to any pseudo-
Wagnerian conception of lyric drama as expounded by Pedrell. La
Vida breve, with its slight plot and lack of dramatic substance, owes
its vitality to the songs and dances in popular style, and these in turn
belong to the tradition of the zarzuela. Of course, Falla worked on a

much higher artistic level, and showed a much greater technical
command of orchestration, as well as a profounder penetration of
the folk element, than any of his predecessors or contemporaries in
the field of the zarzuela. Even though it fails to be a great, or even a
thoroughly effective, opera, *La Vida breve* set a higher artistic standard for the Spanish lyric theater than any hitherto achieved, and it
remains an unsurpassed model as regards the use of Andalusian folk
idioms in the lyric drama.

Turning to more immediate influences in Falla's formative period, his seven-year sojourn in Paris (1907–14) is of paramount importance. It was there, chiefly under the informal tutelage of Dukas
and Debussy, that Falla acquired the splendid orchestral technique
that was to give him a unique and commanding position among
modern Spanish composers. His best-known contemporaries, Albéniz and Granados, made their greatest impression with piano
pieces. With Falla, Spanish music achieved authentic and effective
orchestral utterance for the first time. It is true that in Paris he met
Albéniz and that the latter's influence is apparent in the *Four Spanish Pieces* for piano published in 1909. But the first full revelation of
Falla's powers came with the " symphonic impressions for piano
and orchestra " entitled *Nights in the Gardens of Spain,* composed
from 1909 to 1915.

In the three movements of this work ("In the Generalife,"
"Distant Dance," "In the Gardens of the Sierra de Córdoba"),
Falla achieves a consummate synthesis of "the Andalusian idiom"
in symphonic music. Esthetically and technically, its genealogy
may be traced from *El Albaicín* of Albéniz and the orchestra of the
French impressionists. But the fundamental originality of the work
is evident not only in the technical transformation that these elements undergo in Falla's hands, but also in the quality of intense
personal emotion that permeates the music. Hitherto the Andalusian idiom had been exploited chiefly for its colorful and picturesque effects, regarded always as something exotic. Here Falla,
without sacrificing any of the vivid sensuous power inherent in the
idiom, makes of it something poignantly poetic, intensely evocative,
charged with profound emotional overtones, mysteriously tragic,
unfathomably moving. This is Andalusian music written *from
within.* Not a single folk tune anywhere, but everywhere the palpi-
tating spirit, the warmth, and the fatalism of Andalusia.

In his next work, the ballet *El Amor brujo* (1915), Falla

turned to the gypsy aspect of Andalusian folklore. This story of a beautiful gypsy girl from Granada who is pursued by the specter of her dead lover, arising continually between her and the man whom she now loves, provided Falla with a perfect subject for the blending of the supernatural and the realistic. The score includes a vocal part, a solo for contralto in which the characteristic traits of *cante jondo* — the " deep song " of Andalusia — with its strange amalgamation of Byzantine-Arabic-Hebraic-gypsy elements, are used to create a background of brooding fatalism, against which the final triumph of happy love is all the more overwhelming. Each of the brief musical scenes of which the work consists is a perfect evocation of some particular mood or emotion, ranging from fearful terror to tender ecstasy. In the famous *Ritual Fire Dance*, to exorcise the evil spirits, is concentrated all the sheer primitive force of repetitive rhythm inherent in the Andalusian-gypsy dance, which stems from immemorial incantations of ancestral tribes. And here, again, there is not a single folk tune. The whole composition is tremendously realistic, but this is a realism that is creative, not merely reproductive.

When we look back upon Falla's compositions of this period, it seems as though he were bent upon exhausting every possible phase of the Andalusian background in music. Only the humoristic aspect now remained to be touched, and this he embodied in his next ballet, *El Sombrero de tres picos* (1919), which in its revised form became a bright jewel of the Diaghilev repertoire. This ballet is based on the story of the same title by Alarcón, but this in turn is drawn from popular sources. Throughout Andalusia there are numerous versions of folk ballads telling the story of *The Corregidor and the Miller's Wife* (which was the original title of Falla's ballet). In this sparkling and witty composition, Falla permits himself to quote a few folk tunes, but only incidentally, as passing allusions. The principal dances, such as the miller's farruca and his wife's fandango, and the final jota, are original creations based on popular rhythms. The influence of the guitar — Spain's national instrument, which Falla holds in the highest esteem — is apparent in the instrumentation of this score.

In the same year that Diaghilev produced *El Sombrero de tres picos* in London, Falla composed his *Fantasía bética* for piano (1919), which marks a turning point in his artistic career. Provincia Baetica was the ancient Roman name for Andalusia, hence this

work is in effect an " Andalusian Rhapsody," but it is utterly remote
from any conventional conception of what that term might denote.
The prevailing Phrygian mode, the sinuous *cante jondo* type of
melody with a guitarlike accompaniment, characteristic dance
rhythms such as those of the *sevillanas* — these and other features
of the Andalusian idiom are embodied in this composition, yet the
total effect is not recognizably " Spanish " to the average hearer. Its
Hispanism reveals itself only upon careful analysis. The technical
difficulty of the work, the complex ornamentation, the superposition
of tonalities — all these factors tend to subordinate the local folk
elements to a more abstract musical development.

In the *Fantasía bética* it is clear that Falla is determined to
take leave, musically, of Andalusia. It is a final summing up of all
that he had to say on that subject, a musical valedictory. In five
major works he had brought the Andalusian idiom to its maximum
potentiality of artistic expression, so that there was no alternative
save to repeat himself or seek new ground. Not being the sort of
artist who repeats himself, Falla chose the latter course.

As an Andalusian by birth and background, it was natural that
Falla should have drawn so much of his musical inspiration from
Andalusia. But as an artist profoundly conscious of the spiritual
substance of Spain, and as a scholar equally aware of Spain's glorious musical heritage, it was also natural that he should eventually
gravitate toward Castile, which is the spiritual and historical core of
Spain. This gravitation toward Castile is evinced in his puppet
opera, *El Retablo de Maese Pedro* (1919), based on an episode from
Don Quixote, written originally for the private theater of the Prin-
cesse de Polignac in Paris. It recounts how the Knight of La Mancha
and his Squire were entertained in the courtyard of an inn by
Maese Pedro with his puppet show, enacting the story of Don Gay-
feros and the beautiful Melisendra (based on an old Spanish ballad). There are two sets of puppets, the larger representing the characters in Cervantes' novel, the smaller those in Maese Pedro's show.
The vocal parts are " dubbed " by singers in the orchestra pit; or the
large puppets may be replaced by singers, with or without masks. In
any case, the *mise en scène* is extremely complicated, and this is
probably the chief reason why the work is not more often performed.

In this chamber opera, scored for a small orchestra (including
harpsichord), Falla has endeavored to create, without rigid archaism
but with a profound historical sense, a musical atmosphere corre-

sponding exactly to the time and spirit of Cervantes' novel. Out-
wardly, the entire musical structure is simple and direct to the point
of naïveté; but actually there is a subtlety and sophistication of
means that reflects the psychological complexity of the Quixotic
episode, the confusion between the " real " and the " unreal " reaching its climax in the Knight's furious onslaught upon the puppet
Moors when they are about to overtake Melisendra and her de-
liverer. Don Quixote then delivers an eloquent peroration in praise
of knighthood, bringing the work to a close.

This work is considered less " Spanish " than Falla's preceding compositions by people who have no knowledge of the traditional Spanish sources upon which he drew. Actual folk material is
employed very sparingly (there are allusions to an old Catalan
Christmas song near the end), but in its rhythms and harmonies
(often modal), in its melodic contours and in the instrumental writing, the composition evokes the musical art of Spain's " Golden
Age." The melody for the words " Traveler, traveler, posting to
Paris," is absolutely in the style of the old *romances* (ballads), including the characteristic triple time, and so is the slow melody that
accompanies Melisendra's reverie in scene two.

The importance given to the harpsichord in this score, and certain rhythmic features of the writing (especially in the opening
" symphony "), clearly foreshadow the style of Falla's next major
composition, the Concerto, for harpsichord (or piano), flute, oboe,
clarinet, violin, and cello (1923–6). This work, in fact, may be considered a more " abstract " and concentrated expression of the musical values inherent in *El Retablo*. It is a very brief work, in three
movements (Allegro, Lento, Vivace), and magnificent effects of
sonority are obtained with the utmost economy of means. In the
slow movement, which this writer considers the most original, the
most beautiful, and the most Spanish of all Falla's musical utter-
ances, the impression of vastness — as though one were in the interior of some great cathedral — conveyed by the sweeping arpeggios of the harpsichord and the ingenious spacing of the solo instruments is truly overwhelming.

In the first movement of the Concerto, Falla uses the theme
of a delightful sixteenth-century song by Juan Vázquez, " De los
alamos vengo, madre," which undoubtedly had its original inspiration in popular sources. So naturally is this blended with the other
themes, and with the general texture of the composition, that its

presence seems to have escaped the attention of most commentators. The last movement, with its characteristic alternations of $\frac{3}{4}$
and $\frac{6}{8}$ time, sparkles with a very Scarlattian — and very Spanish —
rhythmic vivacity. The Harpsichord Concerto marks the culmination of Falla's Hispanism. Never has the eternal essence of Spain
been so nakedly embodied in music. It is Manuel de Falla's masterpiece.

(GEORGE GERSHWIN)

1898 - 1937

BIOGRAPHY

GEORGE GERSHWIN was born in Brooklyn, New York, on September 26, 1898, and lived most of his childhood and boyhood in New York's East Side. He studied the piano with Charles Hambitzer, and harmony, counterpoint, theory, and orchestration with Edward Kilenyi. When he was sixteen he was employed as staff pianist by the music-publishing house of Remick in Tin-Pan Alley. He remained at Remick's for three years, and by the end of that time he had a few popular tunes to his credit. His first song hit, "Swanee," and his first Broadway musical-comedy score, La, La, Lucille, both came in 1919. In his twentieth year Gershwin was commissioned to prepare the score for George White's Scandals, an assignment he continued for the next four editions of that revue.

He was already one of the most successful men in the song business when, late in 1923, Paul Whiteman commissioned him to write a large work in the jazz idiom for an all-American music concert he was planning. The work Gershwin wrote for Whiteman was the Rhapsody in Blue. Its performance at Aeolian Hall, New York, on February 12, 1924, made Gershwin one of the most successful composers in America. From public performances and the sale of phonograph records and sheet music, it brought the composer a fortune. When the screen acquired a voice, the score was filmed for a mammoth musical-comedy production. When radio came to prominence, the slow section of the Rhapsody became Paul Whiteman's identifying theme song.

Following the composition of the Rhapsody in Blue, Gershwin

divided his time between popular and serious music. In the popular field he produced a series of successful musical comedies climaxed in 1931 by the Pulitzer Prize satire, *Of Thee I Sing!*, the first musical production ever to receive that award. In a serious vein he wrote a piano concerto, the tone poem *An American in Paris*, a second rhapsody, a set of jazz preludes for piano, the *Cuban Overture*, *Variations on I Got Rhythm*, and the folk opera, *Porgy and Bess*.

In the last years of his life, Gershwin wrote several scores for the talking pictures. He died suddenly in Hollywood, California, on July 11, 1937, following an unsuccessful operation on the brain. After his death, his reputation as one of America's most significant composers became virtually world-wide, with a several-year world tour of *Porgy and Bess* by an American company, and frequent all-Gershwin concerts in the capitals of Europe and the Near East. His screen biography, *Rhapsody in Blue*, was released in 1945. Another motion picture, utilizing his music — *An American in Paris*, in 1951 — became the second musical production to receive the Academy Award as the best picture of the year. *Porgy and Bess* was adapted into a highly successful motion picture, in a Samuel Goldwyn production, in 1959.

PERSONAL NOTE

David Ewen

GERSHWIN was a human dynamo. He rarely walked on the street or the golf course — he had to run. He rarely walked slowly up a flight of stairs, but leaped a few steps at a time. He had more vitality when sick than others did in the full flush of health. He was a man of irrepressible enthusiasms, a man who had an extraordinary zest for living and for enjoying. He loved games of all kinds, and had the capacity for making everything he indulged in a kind of game. When he found a new diversion, he went after it with incomparable intensity and passion. When it was golf (his game was in the eighties), he played it every free moment he could find, and golf dominated his conversation and thinking all the time. Then it was something else: backgammon, croquet, ping-pong, photography, fishing, swimming, horseback riding, roulette. Generally he preferred pastimes that taxed his muscles. He was physically powerful, with the build of an athlete and muscles that knew the discipline of exercise. Besides participating in various sports, he was methodical about doing setting-up exercises at regular intervals. He liked baseball a great deal, but rarely played it, for fear of hurting his hands. Once while watching Harry Ruby, the song writer, play ball, he remarked sadly, " I couldn't afford to take a chance on my hands the way you do. But then your hands don't matter so much." It took a little time for Ruby to realize that Gershwin really meant no slur on his ability as a pianist but was solely preoccupied with thoughts about himself. Later on Ruby confessed, " He was, of course, right." In baseball, Gershwin satisfied himself by being a spectator, as he did in boxing and wrestling, both of which he loved.

His fine muscular co-ordination, which made him such a splendid pianist (and frequently without practicing) and so good an athlete, also made him an excellent dancer. He used feet, body, and hands with the limpid grace of a trained performer. He sometimes gave strikingly effective imitations of Fred Astaire, even in some of his more adroit steps; and during the rehearsals of his musical comedy *Lady Be Good*, Gershwin gave Astaire a valuable suggestion for an exit step for " Fascinating Rhythm." His gift at mimicry was also apparent at other times. Highly visual, with a detective's keen eye for detail, he would come home from a party and give remarkable imitations of the gestures, vocal inflections, and little personal idiosyncrasies of somebody interesting with whom he had met and talked.

Gershwin never put on attitudes or poses for effect, never assumed grandeur with those less famous than he, nor ever tried to pretend he was more than he was when he mingled with the rich or the powerful. In all of his social contacts, as in his business dealings, he was direct, straightforward, and unassuming. He never required the services of a business representative, never had his own press agent, and never kept a lawyer on a retainer. When he had good cause to sue, he usually refused to do so (the exception was when Florenz Ziegfeld refused to pay him royalties for *Show Girl*), preferring a financial loss to an ugly squabble in court. He never used friendships to promote anything he wrote; it was always his friends who sought him out for his music. While he enjoyed beautiful surroundings and comfort, he avoided ostentation of all kind. He had no expensive jewelry; except for a secondhand Mercedes-Benz in 1927, he never owned a foreign car or a yacht; he never entertained in a baronial manner. His one indulgence in swank was his beautiful living quarters in New York, a seventeenth-floor penthouse on Riverside Drive for many years and after that an elegant apartment on East Seventy-second Street.

His music was the be-all and end-all of his existence. He loved to write it, play it, talk about it all the time. He was proud of it when he felt it was good, and did not hesitate to say so. He was in love with his music, and he had a lover's expansiveness in extolling the many attractions of his beloved. He talked about himself or his works with an objectivity that made it seem as if he were talking about somebody else. He sometimes alluded to George Gershwin in the third person, as if Gershwin already belonged to the ages and he were only one of many admirers. This kind of detachment led him to make many ingenuous remarks and responses that have often been quoted to point up his amusing tendency toward self-adulation. When a friend came to him after an all-Gershwin concert to tell him, with breathless enthusiasm, that it was "wonderful," Gershwin asked in all simplicity: "Just wonderful — is that *all?*" He would describe a musical giant like Manuel de Falla as a "Spanish Gershwin." When a hotel manager once called to report a complaint that he was playing the piano too loudly and at too late an hour, he remarked: "Maybe they don't know that *Gershwin* was playing?" From his mother's virtues he singled out one for special admiration: "She is so modest about *me*."

The peculiar thing about his egocentricity was that it was never objectionable, and nobody ever resented it. There was such an air of childlike innocence and ingenuousness and quiet self-assurance about him that people were actually won over to his exuberance and enthusiasms. Besides, he had a wonderful gentleness that completely compensated for his self-centered nature. He liked people, was kind and generous to them, and was rarely heard to say anything cruel or malicious about anybody.

To say that Gershwin was egocentric, however, is to give only one side of a complex personality; it is essential to put that egocentricity in proper perspective.

If he was excited about his own music, he was also enthusiastic about the good music of other popular composers. Gershwin not only often played the music of others with genuine zest and delight but was always ready to provide composers with whatever help they might need. Vernon Duke, Hoagy Carmichael, Arthur Schwartz, Harold Arlen, and Vincent Youmans are only a few of the many who were first lifted to recognition through Gershwin. When Arnold Schoenberg arrived in America in 1933, Gershwin established a fund so that some young composer might study with the master at the Malkin Conservatory of Music. " Even at the time of his death," once wrote George Antheil, " I personally know of four American white hopes whom George was supporting."

One other factor, besides his generosity and enthusiasm for rival composers, must be taken into account in the discussion of Gershwin's egocentricity. He was also capable of humility and self-depreciation. He might be the proud parent boasting of an offspring's commendable traits; but, like many a proud parent, he was also painfully conscious of his offspring's shortcomings, and sometimes to a greater degree than were his critics. There were many times when he tended to magnify the shortcomings of his technique out of all proportion to their importance. " There is so much I have to learn," was a lament he often voiced. He admired conservatory-trained musicians out of all proportion to their significance. He was usually in awe of composers with complex and abstruse techniques, and in their presence he often became as self-conscious as a schoolboy — he who could move with such poise and aplomb among the great of the financial and social world. When composers like Stravinsky, Ravel, or Schoenberg praised him to his face he became as flustered as if he had been the perpetrator of a fraud.

Though he had a lifelong weakness for beautiful women and had been many times in love, Gershwin never married. It seemed as if his complete absorption in his music and his career made it impossible for him to give himself to a woman in the way a successful marriage demands, and he knew it. Women found it impossible to penetrate the concrete wall of his creative ego. Once, hearing that a girl in whom he was particularly interested had suddenly married somebody else, he remarked to his brother Ira: " I'd be terribly heartbroken if I weren't so damned busy." This reaction is both typical and significant. He never really gave himself so completely to any woman that losing her left a vacuum in his life. Some of the girls he loved complained that he seemed incapable of real sentiment or tenderness; most of the time with them he was so wrapped up in himself and his thoughts that he was only vaguely conscious of their presence. Gershwin often plagued his friends with questions as to whether or not it was wise for an artist to marry; whether marriage did not put a serious impediment in the way of an artist practicing his art. But he was not really seeking an answer and often did not wait for one. He was only looking for an excuse to avoid a permanent relationship.

THE COMPOSER SPEAKS

George Gershwin [1]

THE great music of the past in other countries has always been built on folk music. This is the strongest source of musical fecundity. America is no exception among the countries. The best music being written today is music that comes from folk sources. It is not always recognized that America has folk music; yet it really has not only one but many different folk musics. It is a vast land, and different sorts of folk music have sprung up in different parts, all having validity, and all being a possible foundation for development into an art music. For this reason, I believe that it is possible for a number of distinctive styles to develop in America, all legitimately born of folk song from different localities. Jazz, ragtime, Negro spirituals and blues, Southern mountain songs, country fiddling, and cowboy songs can all be employed in the creation of American art music, and are actually used by many composers today. These composers are certain to produce something worth while if they have the innate feeling and talent to develop the rich material offered to them. There are also other composers who can be classed as legitimately American who do not make use of folk music as a base, but who have personally, working in America, developed highly individual styles and methods. Their new-found materials should be called American, just as an invention is called American if it is made by an American.

Jazz I regard as an American folk music; not the only one, but a

---

[1] This statement is from two essays by the composer that appeared in the books *American Composers on American Music*, edited by Henry Cowell, and *Revolt in the Arts*, edited by Oliver M. Saylor.

very powerful one that is probably in the blood and feeling of the American people more than any other style of folk music. I believe that it can be made the basis of serious symphonic works of lasting value, in the hands of a composer with talent for both jazz and symphonic music.

It is difficult to determine what enduring values, esthetically, jazz has contributed, because " jazz " is a word that has been used for at least five or six different types of music. It is really a conglomeration of many things. It has a little bit of ragtime, the blues, classicism, and spirituals. Basically, it is a matter of rhythm. After rhythm in importance come intervals, music intervals that are peculiar to the rhythm. After all, there is nothing new in music. I maintained years ago that there is very little difference in the music of different nations. There is just that little individual touch. One country may prefer a peculiar rhythm or a note like the seventh. This it stresses, and it becomes identified with that nation. In America, this preferred rhythm is called jazz. Jazz is music; it uses the same notes that Bach used. When jazz is played in another nation, it is called American. When it is played in another country, it sounds false. Jazz is the result of the energy stored up in America. It is a very energetic kind of music, noisy, boisterous, and even vulgar. One thing is certain. Jazz has contributed an enduring value to America in the sense that it has expressed ourselves. It is an original American achievement that will endure, not as jazz perhaps, and will leave its mark on future music in one form or another. The only kinds of music that endure are those which possess form in the universal sense and folk music. All else dies. But unquestionably folk songs are being written and have been written that contain enduring elements of jazz. To be sure, that is only an element; it is not the whole. An entire composition written in jazz could not live.

GERSHWIN

David Ewen

ONE of the most impressive and singularly significant facts about Gershwin is the way he progressed toward a single goal from his

boyhood on. He sought from the very first to achieve artistic validity
as a composer through popular music. It is surely significant that he
should have sensed, and become convinced of, the destiny of American popular music at a time when it was in its unkempt infancy;
when it was regarded by all serious musicians with the distaste of an
impatient adult for an irresponsible child. In discussing ragtime or
Irving Berlin's songs with his first important teacher, Charles
Hambitzer, Gershwin said: " This is American music. This is the
way an American should write. This is the kind of music I want to
write." He was only sixteen years old then, but already he was convinced that a serious composer could produce important art by
bringing to popular music the harmonic, rhythmic, and contrapuntal resources of serious music. And he felt that the use of large musical forms for popular idioms could provide a creative artist with a
broad avenue for self-expression.

His North Star, then, was the mission to write popular music
with the techniques and approaches of serious music, and serious
music with the techniques and approaches of popular music. As an
apprentice in Tin-Pan Alley, writing his first popular songs, he also
wrote *Rialto Ripples* (with Will Donaldson), a first effort to transfer a jazz style to piano writing. And as the mature creator of a
three-act opera, almost twenty years later, he was still writing popular songs.

If he kept on writing popular music after becoming celebrated
with more serious efforts, it was not only for the money it brought
him; on several occasions he proved his willingness to brush aside a
fortune in contracts when his conscience demanded that he turn to
serious projects. He wrote popular music because it brought him
profound artistic satisfaction. He brought to it all the skill, high
principle, and artistry of which he was capable. As he worked on his
best songs, he subjected them to continual revision, refinement, and
editing in his pursuit of the *mot juste*. The popular song was one
facet of his art, and an important one; the larger works were another. He needed both media to give complete expression to his
artistic personality.

It was, to be sure, with his serious compositions that he won an
honored place among the foremost composers of the twentieth century. The first of these was a one-act Negro opera, originally entitled
Blue Monday, which was heard only for a single night in *George
White's Scandals of 1922*. (Feeling that the opera was too depress-

ing for a Broadway revue, George White had it removed from the
production immediately after the opening-night performance.) The
libretto, by Buddy De Sylva, was not very impressive. If one were
not certain of De Sylva's seriousness of purpose, a suspicion might
arise that he was here ribbing opera librettos in general. And
Gershwin's music was not strong enough to carry the load of a feeble
book. Inexperienced as he was in dramatic writing, he produced not
an integrated opera but a series of popular songs connected by jazz-
like recitatives. Some of the songs are appealing: the " Blue Monday
Blues "; the aria " Has Anybody Seen My Joe "; and the spiritual
" I'm Going to See My Mother." There was a successful attempt to
use jazz for humorous effects, as in the entrance of the customers in
the saloon. But all this material was not well integrated into the
dramatic context, and it appears to have been no more than grafted
upon the score to provide interest. The music lacked atmospheric or
dramatic interest, while the recitatives were stilted and stiffly contrived.

Blue Monday, renamed 135th Street, has on several occasions
been revived since 1922, including a television production on the
" Omnibus " program in 1953. It cannot be said that rehearings
have brought a new perspective. In 1953, as in 1922, 135th Street
was a work of an apprentice.

But with his very next concert work, Gershwin took a giant leap
forward — and made history. The composition was the Rhapsody in
Blue (1924), written on commission from Paul Whiteman for
Whiteman's concert of American popular music at Aeolian Hall,
New York, on February 12, 1924. It was the Rhapsody in Blue that
gave Whiteman's concert its significance, transforming the Whiteman experiment of presenting a popular-music concert in a serious-
music concert auditorium from an idle curiosity to an artistic event
of the first magnitude. The Rhapsody in Blue gave status to jazz as a
medium for serious artistic expression; it carried Gershwin to world
fame and wealth. On stage, on screen, on records, over the radio, in
the concert hall, in the ballet theater, the Rhapsody has achieved a
popularity equaled by few serious works of music before or since. In
the concert hall it has outstripped any other single contemporary
work for frequency of performance. It has entered the repertory of
every major American symphony orchestra and has been directed by
the foremost conductors of this generation.

The form of the Rhapsody in Blue came from the Hungarian

Liszt; the main slow section was derived from the Russian Tchaikov-sky; and the harmony sometimes suggests the French Debussy or the Polish Chopin. Yet, like the melting pot that is America, the *Rhapsody* fused the various foreign elements into a personality wholly American. The *Rhapsody* is American music in its youth, brashness, restlessness, optimism. It is also Gershwin in the freshness of its rhythmic and melodic ideas, in its vitality and muscular energy, and in its unerring instinct for effect.

The opening measures reveal Gershwin's instinct for effect — the yawp of the clarinet. After a low trill, the clarinet begins a seventeen-note ascent; halfway up there is a pause, and then the clarinet resumes its upward flight with a portamento. Then it reaches out for the first theme. Once stated, the jaunty opening theme yields immediately to a transition section in the winds that carries a suggestion of the second main theme. This brisk second theme — finally stated in the piano — further conveys the feeling of reckless abandon established by the opening clarinet passage. This second theme appears and reappears in the orchestra and is the basis of an extended coda for the piano. The piano then leads with a few ascending chords toward the principal section of the work: the rhapsodic slow movement for strings, which has become one of the most frequently quoted and best-known excerpts in serious American music. The full orchestra takes up the song. Then a quick recollection of its opening phrase in fast tempo invokes the final section. After a climactic pronouncement of the opening clarinet theme by full orchestra, the piano wistfully recalls the second theme. The *Rhapsody* ends abruptly with a brief and dramatic coda.

The *Rhapsody in Blue* is by no means a consistent or integrated masterwork. Some of the things its severest critics have condemned in it are the weak spots. The form is diffuse; the thematic subjects are at times developed awkwardly and without inventiveness; there are lapses in inspiration where repetitions of familiar ideas or ineffectual transitions of scales and chord passages try to fill the gap; there is some naïveté and some amateurishness in the harmonic construction. But the basic melodic and rhythmic material is so fresh and good, and is presented with such verve and spontaneity, that the work as a whole never loses its ability to excite the listener.

The success of the *Rhapsody in Blue* led Walter Damrosch and the New York Symphony Society to commission Gershwin to write a piano concerto. The Concerto in F (1925) is a much more

astute and much more musical work than the *Rhapsody in Blue*.
The form has less tendency to ramble before arriving at the convenient stopping-off point of a new salient thought; there is less reliance on convenient passage work to fill in gaps. Most of the time
Gershwin seems to know where he is heading, and he proceeds toward the new idea with the sure gait of one who knows the lay of
the land.

There is greater richness and variety of thought in the Concerto
than in the *Rhapsody*. What we have in the Concerto is not only
just one or two good melodies, as was the case with the earlier work,
but a gushing of wonderful ideas, refreshing in their contrasting
idioms and moods. And, unlike the *Rhapsody*, where a new inviting
subject comes almost as a surprise to the composer, most of the
ideas in the Concerto are permitted to evolve and develop naturally
out of the musical texture. The Concerto is interesting not only for
its thematic subjects, but also in the way the material is presented,
extended, enlarged, combined, and transformed.

The gamut of moods, feelings, and atmosphere is much more
elastic in the Concerto. In the larger work we get some of the abandon, wit, satire, and nostalgia of the *Rhapsody*; but to all this is
added something equally vital: the shimmering poetic beauty of
the second movement, in which jazz is made to plumb new artistic
depths.

The tone poem *An American in Paris* (1928) was Gershwin's
first attempt at programmatic writing: a musical portrait of an
American, strolling along the boulevards, attracted by the sights and
sounds of Paris, but nonetheless nostalgic for home. The tone poem
opens with a walking theme in strings and oboe — not the stately
gait of that other famous walking theme, in Mussorgsky's *Pictures
at an Exhibition*, but light and gay. The music is then punctuated
with angry taxi horns to suggest the madcap Parisian traffic. A mu-
sic-hall tune follows in the trombone. As the American continues
his walk, a second walking theme appears, more vigorous than the
first, in the clarinet. A solo violin represents a transition to the wail-
ing blues melody in muted trumpet. This is succeeded by a Charleston melody for two trumpets. When the blues then returns it is no
longer a lament, but robust and joyous.

Gershwin's first title for his *Second Rhapsody* (1931) was
Rhapsody in Rivets. The idea of " rivets " appears in the opening
measures: an incisive rhythmic subject for solo piano that bears a

family resemblance to the first principal subject of the *Rhapsody in Blue*. The rivet theme is assumed by the full orchestra, which then embarks upon a rhumbalike melody of its own. Both subjects receive detailed development. A transitory passage in solo piano leads to the broad-flowing blues melody that is the heart of the composition. It appears in the string choir, is taken over by the brass, and then receives extensive elaboration by both the solo piano and the orchestra. The two earlier themes are recalled and embellished before the rhapsody comes to a vigorous close in both piano and orchestra.

With the *Cuban Overture* (1932) Gershwin revealed an increasing technical dexterity in the use of rhythm, just as in the *Variations on I Got Rhythm*, for piano and orchestra (1934), he demonstrated new powers in the art of variation. The *Cuban Overture* is in three sections. A provocative rhythm, partly rhumba, partly habanera, opens the work. The first theme, of Cuban identity, makes its appearance in the strings. A three-part contrapuntal episode then leads to the second theme, which is soon combined contrapuntally with fragments of the first theme. A solo-clarinet cadenza leads to the middle section, which is mostly a gradually developed canon in a melancholy vein. This canon is in two voices and is unusual in that (unlike traditional canons) it has a harmonic background. After a climax is built out of the *ostinato* theme of the canon, the finale makes its appearance in a strettolike manner. The composition ends with a dynamic and exciting rhumba in which native Cuban instruments of percussion are used.

The *Variations on I Got Rhythm* had for its point of departure one of Gershwin's hit songs, "I Got Rhythm," which Ethel Merman introduced so dynamically in the musical comedy *Girl Crazy* (1930). The work opens with a four-note ascending phrase from the first measure of the "I Got Rhythm" chorus given by the solo clarinet. The theme is passed on to solo piano, then to full orchestra. At last the solo piano presents the song (chorus only) in its entirety. The variations that follow reveal Gershwin's remarkable progress in the science of developing and altering a stated theme. He changes not only its basic structure, melodically and rhythmically, but also its mood and feeling. The first variation is a release of animal energy; in the second, the theme suddenly becomes a melancholy dirge. In other variations the melody grows muscular and aggressive; or it is as festive as a New Orleans Mardi Gras, with the orchestration a veritable pyrotechnical display of fireworks and the piano a glittering cascade of whirling figures; or it is a poignant and deep-throated blues melody.

Each of Gershwin's serious works from *135th Street* on was an advance from its predecessor in technical assurance, know-how, musical articulateness, subtlety of style, and mastery in the use of popular elements, though not necessarily in sheer inspiration. His folk opera *Porgy and Bess* (1935) was his last serious work, and his greatest one from both the technical and artistic points of view. Here he was finally the fully mature composer, sure of himself and of his direction.

It is the folk element rather than the outpouring of unforgettable songs and duets that is the strong suit of *Porgy and Bess*. Like another great national opera — Mussorgsky's *Boris Godunov* — the chief protagonist is no single character, not Porgy or Bess in the Gershwin opera nor the Tsar Boris in Mussorgsky's. Mussorgsky's masterwork is first and foremost a mighty drama of Russian society. Gershwin's opera is an epic of Negroes, mostly a picture of the lower depths of Negro life. The tragic love of Porgy and Bess in Catfish Row, in Charleston, South Carolina, is incidental to the humor and pathos, the emotional turbulence, the psychological and social maladjustments, the naïveté and childlike terror, the violence and tenderness of the much-abused Negro in a Southern city.

To portray this people in all the varied facets of its personality, Gershwin made extensive use of musical materials basic to the Negro people. His recitatives are molded after the inflections of Negro speech. His songs are grounded either in Negro folk music or in those American popular idioms which sprang out of Negro backgrounds. His street cries simulate those of Negro vendors in Charleston. His choral pages are deeply rooted in spirituals and " shouts."

So completely did Gershwin assimilate and absorb all the elements of Negro song and dance into his own writing that, without quoting a single line from outside sources, he was able to produce a musical art basically Negro in physiognomy and spirit, basically expressive of the heart and soul of an entire race. The transmutation of Negro musical idioms and styles into a powerful and moving art was one indication of Gershwin's growth as a composer. Another was his new ability in tone painting, in translating into musical terms many different moods and backgrounds. The opening Prelude, with its brilliant picture of the helter-skelter and turmoil of life in Catfish Row is in marked contrast to the eloquent portrait of a serene Catfish Row early at dawn in the Prelude to Act II, Scene 3. The dramatic writing in the Kittiwah scene, in the hurricane music, and in the scene in Serena's room during the storm is balanced by the tender lyricism of his love music.

But it is in the many subtle details of his writing that Gershwin proves most conclusively his new-found mastery as a composer for the serious stage and his formidable development as a creative artist. One cannot fail to note how he uses vocal glissandi to heighten the tragedy of the wake scene; how he interpolates the ejaculation " huh " into the work song " It Take a Long Pull to Get There " to suggest the physical effort of rowing a boat; how dramatically telling is the juxtaposition of the spoken dialogue of the detective with the answers sung in the trio in Act III, Scene 2; how the use of the spoken dialogue for the white folk and sung recitatives for the Negro provides subtle contrast between the races; how he continually alternates chords and *ostinato* rhythmic patterns to keep the play moving; how skillfully he either gives warning of a later song or subsequently refers to it with an orchestral recollection; how he breaks up the accents in " My Man's Gone Now " to intensify the pathos (not unlike the way Beethoven did in the closing measures of the funeral march of the *Eroica*); and how effective is the use of the broken monotone in the closing lines of " A Woman Is a Sometime Thing." If one notices these details, the shattering impact of the whole becomes understandable.

Writing Negro music so strongly flavored with folk ingredients was certainly the logical goal for Gershwin. The man who wrote *Porgy and Bess* grew out of the boy who had acquired a vivid and unforgettable musical experience from hearing a Negro jazz band in Harlem; out of the young man whose first effort to outgrow the limitations of a song was to write a one-act Negro opera; out of the successful composer whose best writing was in the Negro idioms of the blues and ragtime; the white man who could compete successfully with Negroes in their competitive " shouts " during Gershwin's visit to Charleston. But *Porgy and Bess* was Gershwin's inevitable achievement for still another reason: it represents, at last, the meeting point for the two divergent paths he had all his life been pursuing — those of serious and popular music. The serious musician is found at his best in the musically distinguished tone speech, in the powerful antiphonal choruses, in the expressive dissonances and chromaticisms, in the brilliant orchestration, in the effective atmospheric writing, in the skillful use of counterpoint in the duets and particularly in the last-scene trio. The popular composer emerges in the jazz background of several choruses like that in Act II, Scene 1, " Woman to Lady "; in the two songs of Sportin' Life, " It Ain't Necessarily So " and " There's a Boat That's Leavin' Soon for New York "; and in Crown's sacrilegious blues ditty, " A Red-Headed Woman Makes a Choochoo Jump Its Track." Yet there is no feeling of contradiction, no sense of incongruity, in this mingling of the serious and the popular, for the popular is as basic to Gershwin's design as the serious, with its own specific artistic function.

Gershwin had the courage and stamina of genius to cut new paths for music, and to make these paths broad highways upon which many others would follow his lead. His significance as a pioneer can hardly be overestimated; in *Makers of the Modern World*, Louis Untermeyer considers Gershwin to be one of the four most important composers to shape musical trends in the past century (the other three being Wagner, Debussy, and Stravinsky). When Gershwin started in popular music, a trained musician was a *rara avis* in Tin-Pan Alley. Men such as Jerome Kern or Victor Herbert, both well equipped by training, were phenomena not usually encountered in the song industry. But not even Kern or Herbert brought to their popular writing the wealth of inventiveness, imagination, daring, and complexity of means we find in Gershwin. In an area where entertainment-appeal was the primary, if not the exclusive, goal, Gershwin bravely introduced artistic considerations. More than any other single person he made it possible for later popular composers like Kurt Weill, Richard Rodgers, Vernon Duke, and Leonard Bernstein to write the kind of popular music they did and to find a large audience receptive to it.

It was also Gershwin who convinced serious musicians throughout the world of the value of using American popular idioms in classical music. He was not the first to do so. Before the *Rhapsody in Blue*, Stravinsky had written *Ragtime*, for piano, and Milhaud *La Création du monde*, a ballet in jazz style; and before them there had been the tentative efforts of Debussy and Satie to employ American popular styles. But this music had little or no impact on the musical thought of our time. It was regarded by the intelligentsia as a spicy exotic dish to pique the jaded musical appetite. It was Gershwin who brought full acceptance to our popular styles, techniques, and materials in the world of serious music. After the *Rhapsody in Blue* — and largely because of it — came the deluge: Krenek's *Jonny spielt auf*, Hindemith's *Neues vom Tage*, Kurt Weill's *Mahagonny*, Ravel's " Blues " Sonata and the *Concerto for the Left Hand*, Constant Lambert's *Rio Grande*, Aaron Copland's Concerto for Piano and Orchestra, and John Alden Carpenter's ballet, *Skyscrapers*.

One more point: Gershwin helped create and establish an American musical art that no longer aped the speech of Europe and that could have been produced nowhere but in this country. In this tendency, our music has taken a giant leap forward since the 1920's. Many of our gifted composers are producing music deeply rooted in American backgrounds, psychology, experiences, and culture; and it is for this reason, above all others, that American music is now regarded with respect in foreign capitals. Today we are beginning to recognize — perhaps for the first time — what a role George Gershwin played in bringing about this development.

(ROY HARRIS)

1898 -

BIOGRAPHY

ROY HARRIS was born in a log cabin in Lincoln County, Oklahoma, on February 12, 1898. While he was still a boy, his family migrated to California, building a farm in the San Gabriel Valley. When he was eighteen, Harris acquired a farm of his own. One year after this, he joined the Army as a private. When the war ended, Harris returned to California and, abandoning farming, registered in the Southern Branch of the University of California as a student of harmony. To earn his living during this period of study he drove a truck for a dairy.

His harmony class at the university convinced him that he wished to become a trained musician. He approached the well-known California composer, Arthur Farwell, and asked to become a private pupil. Harris worked with Farwell for two years. Harris' first composition, an *Andante* for strings, written under the watchful eye of his teacher, was selected from a mass of manuscripts submitted to the New York Philharmonic Orchestra. It was presented by the Philharmonic at the Lewisohn Stadium in the summer of 1926.

In 1926 he went to France to study with Nadia Boulanger and was enabled to remain there for two additional years as a result of a Guggenheim Fellowship. In Paris he composed his first major work, the Concerto for Piano, Clarinet, and String Quartet, which was introduced in Paris and praised by the French critics.

Sickness brought him back to the United States in 1929. His rise to fame as a composer was meteoric. In 1931 he was virtually unknown; yet less than a half dozen years later he was the most frequently performed serious American composer. Most of his major works of this period were recorded by the leading phonograph companies, and he was the recipient of innumerable commissions for special works. In 1935 a poll conducted by the New York Philharmonic among radio listeners placed him in first position among American composers. To this position he was re-elected the following year by another national vote, this time conducted by the phonograph-record department of *Scribner's Magazine*. When the Pro-Arte Quartet presented a cross section of chamber music of the past hundred years at the Chicago Century of Progress Exposition, it included only one work as the contribution of the twentieth century — Harris' Second String Quartet. And, in 1939, the Roth Quartet selected Harris' Third String Quartet to represent American chamber music at the International Conference of Musicologists in New York.

In 1930 Harris was awarded a Creative Fellowship by the Pasadena Music and Arts Association. Since then he has been head of the composition department of the Westminster Choir School in Princeton, New Jersey, and composer in residence at several distinguished institutions, including Cornell University, Colorado College, Utah State College, George Peabody College for Teachers, and Indiana University. In 1960 Harris became director of the International Institute of Music, a division of the Inter-American University, in Puerto Rico. In 1961 he joined the music faculty of the University of California in Los Angeles. Sweden decorated him with its Military Order in 1965.

During World War II, he served as chief of the Music Division of the OWI. In 1958 he was sent by the United States State Department as a cultural ambassador to the Soviet Union, where he became the first American to conduct his own symphony with a Russian orchestra.

PERSONAL NOTE

Johana Harris

MOST people think of my husband as a good-natured, easygoing Westerner. And so he is. But he is many other people as well. To

me he is a child — always eager — always ready to believe in everyone, always expecting miracles to happen, always being hurt and
enraged by the social and economic injustices that he sees and feels
everywhere he goes. And yet he is an unquenchable optimist who
loves beauty in every phase of living.

In his creative life he is a priest and devil rolled into one bundle
of uncompromising drive. In his creative state his mind works in a
strange way. Words mean only sound syllables to him. It is impossible to carry on a rational word discussion with him. He may
not answer — or even hear sentences addressed to him — or he
may make nonsense rhythm sequences or rhyme a long chain of
unrelated words. At such times he should never go amongst strangers
or to conventional concerts, which depress him terribly with their
worn-out idioms.

As a husband, friend, teacher, he is loyal and generous — I
must say a spendthrift of his time and energy and talents.

He is a child who will never grow old. Each new idea, situation,
person, book, event, is a new adventure. His maturity is to be found
in the craftsmanship and concentration of his creative life.

Before we were married, Roy warned me that composers should
not be counted on to make good husbands. He argued that composers search for the good life, and the good life does not mean
property and money in the bank; it means, rather, living wherever
the cultural climate is favorable to composers.

A quarter of a century of married life has certainly proved his
conviction to be true.

There was once a popular song, " Don't Fence Me In." This
pretty well describes the prime basic law that governs my husband's life.

Our large family of five children has lived well wherever we
wandered, and I am certain there could be no more devoted husband
and father than this strange quixotic man. And yet, he has not given
in one inch on his ideals about music, people, or society.

Perhaps his greatest strength is his unlimited capacity to
absorb disappointments without being destroyed by them.

God help any woman married to a composer if she is not
devoted to music and its creation.

THE COMPOSER SPEAKS

Roy Harris [1]

I FINALLY decided to choose music as a lifework because it was the only language I found to be constant. I made my choice late in life. I was twenty-eight years old. Prior to this I had studied a good deal of philosophy and sociology and economics. I had also studied a good deal of literature and read all the plays that I could acquire. Always I came to the same dead-end conclusion: that the word language was so relative and depended so utterly on the experience of those to whom it was addressed that I found no basic a priori values upon which to build. For a while I was sorely tempted to go into a deep study of philology to see if I could find basic roots of all the languages as related to the development of human institutions, but I feared that my life would be too short to undertake this study.

Meanwhile I became more and more absorbed in music. I discovered to my satisfaction and delight that music had some a priori values, that week after week a certain given melody retained its same values, that a certain progression of chords always aroused in me the same reaction. And so music became for me a sort of vessel in which to gather permanent values of life upon which I could depend and with which I could build my own world around me. When finally I was privileged to devote my whole time and energy to music, I found out very quickly that the values that were most understandable and satisfying to me were those which were achieved in the high periods of classic expression.

Since that time I find the large contrapuntal forms much more exciting and more satisfying. I have become increasingly convinced that music is a fluid architecture of sound and that all the elements of music — melody, harmony, counterpoint, dynamics, orchestration — must be co-ordinated into a swift-moving form that fulfills itself from the root idea to its complete flowering in organic ornamentation. My convictions have been confirmed by the study of

[1] This statement was written by the composer expressly for this book.

such masters as Josquin Després, Orlando di Lasso, Palestrina, Vittoria, Bach, Mozart, and, less consistently, Beethoven. Nature has also confirmed my conviction about what music should be. Nature surrounds us constantly with the most beautiful examples of classic craftsmanship. We ourselves could not live and enjoy life if we did not embody that wonderful co-ordination of craftsmanship which makes us a functioning organism.

I believe that music has been steadily running downhill since Beethoven, because orchestral color has been exploited at the expense of all the other elements of music. This sort of romantic attitude has governed man for more than two hundred years and has brought us to such a sorry pass. We have constantly exploited personal ambition at the expense of the body politic. So the romanticists have done in music. It really is an attitude of supreme egoism wherein the individual assumes a *summum bonum* of all wisdom and beneficence in his own self. One generation is not long enough for man to become wise; and so we have suffered greatly in losing the wisdom of tradition. And so the romantic composer who thinks that he can in one lifetime offset the sum total of all the highest and best that all other composers in all times and periods preceding him have sifted out through experience is condemned to produce an unbalanced and immature expression.

In the last two decades the music world seems to be splintering into more extreme groups with more violent dialectics. The post-Beethoven historical trough in which we find ourselves has descended even deeper than I had anticipated. I had thought we had hit rock-bottom with Stravinsky's *Le Sacre du printemps* and Schoenberg's *Pierrot lunaire*, both historically significant works; but with the advent of the *Musique concrète* and the tape-assembly mosaics and all the other experiments in escapism from musical tradition, we still suffer from the postwar and presentiment of prewar psychoses that are leading creative music deeper and deeper into the wilderness of creative bewilderment. All this, of course, is a violent esthetic reaction to our time period and, as such, certainly historically legitimate.

I personally believe that this is a powerful antidote against the excesses of romanticism, and as such is of course a concentrate of romanticism. I also am convinced that if humanity arrives at a workable solution of international peace, we will have a great new period of growth in the humanities; and that music will again find a proper balance of indigenous melody, harmony, counterpoint, form, and orchestration that will be generated out of the exciting and challenging activity that humanity will experience in building a new world.

HARRIS

John Krueger

I REMEMBER disliking the music of Roy Harris. This memory is vivid and contains a touch of chagrin: I had been guilty of rejecting something because I could not understand it. Today it is my opinion that Harris' music is a vital contribution in this century to the accumulation of musical thought. Perhaps it is even more important than this.

We may assume one or two things to be true in observing the history of music. Either the development of music since Bach's time has been the " main stream " of musical evolution, or it has been a tangent to that main stream. If we assume the latter to be the case, Harris may well be an extremely important composer historically.

It is possible to consider the romantic era, as does Harris, as a detour in the development of the art. During this delightful and very popular detour we experience new expressive resources in melody, and orchestration becomes a surging torrent of power and fascinating color. Unfortunately, however, great counterpoint almost disappears, rhythmic complexities and refinements do not equal those of Renaissance music, and harmony becomes absorbed and minimized into a sameness of sound in which chords lose much of their individuality. During that time, musical form advanced little. It just became longer in service to the modern orchestra. The highly praised sonata-allegro form is in reality a very loose adaptation of the ternary form to accommodate two melodic ideas, and the symphony is an adaptation and philosophical development of the suite.

Although there were, of course, great contributions during this era, parts of our heritage became lost to us for a time. The evolution of music before the eighteenth century was concerned with refining the power of the art to influence and change the listener. In the Greek pre-Christian period, for example, the Doctrine of the Ethos resulted in warnings against certain modes because they would have an effect upon the civilization subjected to them. The Roman Catholic Church repeatedly removed from its music the interval of the tritone and the Locrian mode because they represented evil. We wonder at the economy of means with which Gregorian chant heightens the sense of awe and reverence in a church congregation. We thrill at a multiplicity of expression in Bach counterpoint, each melodic line gaining expressive power from its relation to the other lines. Perhaps most of all in the romantic period we miss the sense of pride in craftsmanship that became partially replaced by calculated devices aimed at creating a supposedly more personal emotional emphasis.

I would attribute to Roy Harris the role of bringing us back to what I believe is the main stream of musical evolution, and the salvaging of the most important contributions of our predecessors as he so does. He is fulfilling this historical regeneration by an enthusiastic examination and revaluation of the basic materials and principles of creative music. This ability to analyze and judge the materials and techniques of music is the basis of the Harris idiom and style.

It is in harmony that we find the greatest gap between Harris and his contemporaries. He has organized vertical sound that speaks in an entirely new way. It is no longer sufficient that harmonies be consonant or dissonant. Within these categories harmony becomes a spectrum of color — emotional values — bright or dark, warm or cold, happy or sad — capable of a large range of expression.

Starting with the *Cumberland Concerto* (1951) Harris began to experiment with compound-triadic harmonies or twelve-tone rows. This led to studies in compound organum harmonies, poly-faux-bourdon harmonies, and mixtures of both — which he is now using. Yet this very complex harmonic palette is clear, architectural, and meaningful. This use of harmonic color is quite similar to the use of color spectrum by van Gogh and Gauguin — a whole movement may contain a large variety of the same kind of harmonic color. For instance, *Abraham Lincoln Walks at Midnight*, a chamber cantata for mezzo-soprano, is in mood a very dark and very sad work, yet the harmonic color is luminous in its darkness. " Give Me the Splendid Silent Sun," the first movement of the Eighth Symphony (1960), is brilliant with very bright polychords until the Whitman poem modulates to the sorrows of war, where the harmonic texture changes to extremely dark and savage, but clear, colors. These are startling departures from the traditional techniques of harmony.

Harris has often been accused by laymen of writing atonally. This is, of course, not the case. A sense of tonality is always present. At times several tonalities are concurrently present. He is not, however, restricted by a major-minor scale system. Instead, his tonalities flow over modes that shift from bright to dark to amplify the emotionality of the melody. Harmonies are not related by key. (This is where listeners may find difficulty in following his ideas.) This gives greater freedom of choice of a harmony. Control of harmonic choice is through voice leading and the selection of just the right sound to identify an emotion. This means of organization is surely as logical as the traditional method.

Certainly in his melodies the Harris trade-mark is immediately distinguishable. His melodies are often based on American folk music, not necessarily from the standpoint of the thematic material, but in the sense that his melodic thinking seems to be governed by the same emotional nature that caused our ancestors to sing as they did. If he uses a folk song for a theme, he generally does not quote it literally, but by the use of quasi-sequence makes it more effectively expressive. At times the folk song is almost unrecognizable, but the essence of it is still present. His melodies are sophisticated, but they communicate emotions that are direct and forceful. They are usually quite stern, although occasionally we find a humor and a rollicking rejoicing that remind us of the farmer of the Western plains. Paul Rosenfeld said he was reminded of Brueghel's painting.

The Harris melody is apt to be long, self-generating, and polytonal, and very distinctively personal. There are great broad lines of sound, primarily conjunct, with a regularity of pulse from which stems a feeling of strength and confidence. " He has a natural gift for the melodic line, and his melodies are in some uncanny way reflective of the American scene without being literal quotations," wrote Nicolas Slonimsky in The Christian Science Monitor. " It is as though he would restore melody to its old place at the fountainhead of symphonic music," said H. T. Parker in the *Boston Evening Transcript*, "but a newly found melody of these times, of his own, of his America."

His melodic style is inseparable from his rhythmic organization. He uses an evolving rhythmic sequence structure. The rhythmic sequence, however, does not coincide with phrase length. This device results in a constant freshness while unity is solidly maintained. The use of rhythmic sequence as it appears in Harris' music is reminiscent of the isorhythmic of Machaut in the *ars nova* period of the fourteenth century.

In his orchestration, Roy Harris uses extreme ranges of the instruments for the sake of their specific tone qualities. He has also integrated much of the bizarre combinations of instruments of the jazz band. There is a quality of orchestration that is uniquely Harris. The masses of sound seem often to be one behind the other, as we might see a picture montage. The conductor must then be concerned not only with balance, but also with the amount of projection of the various instruments. In the Third Symphony (1937), for example, the woodwinds weave a band of counterpoint, the brasses punch through this like great shafts of metal, while the strings create a more diffused wall of sound in the background, and the timpani come into prominence and recede again.

It is impossible to discuss Harris' music without touching on counterpoint. This is an integral part of his style, and is interdependent on his harmony. Harris maintains and teaches to his students that counterpoint is the weaving of melody through a harmonic texture that is complementary to the melos of the melody. He does not believe that a composer can write counterpoint well until he can write melody and harmony as a technical reflex to his subjective impulse. The end result of his contrapuntal craft is a texture that flows so naturally that it seems effortless to write and to hear. (How else could one have written the eleven-part counterpoint in the second section of the Third Symphony, or the canons and fugues of the Third String Quartet, 1938?)

While the quality of sincerity, which is strong in Harris' music, stems largely from the discipline of his melody, harmony, and rhythm, it seems, also, to derive from his form. His form is classic, self-generating, and usually monothematic. To Gustave Reese in *Grove's Dictionary of Music and Musicians* " Harris is a straightout classicist . . . but, it must be urged, such a classicist as only the present world-scene could produce." At the completion of a work we feel that we have been presented with an emotional experience, often shown in many facets, over an expanse of time. We are not conscious of development sections as his material grows naturally with the vigor of its own life. From this organic development comes the great sweep that characterizes his style and seems so symbolic of our nation. " I think," once said Serge Koussevitzky, " that nobody has captured in music the essence of American life — its vitality, its greatness, its strength — so well as Roy Harris."

He uses a device of anticipating and foreshadowing a new treatment of material, as well as recalling, in little side remarks, the preceding ideas. The sections of a work seem, because of this device, to flow into one another, so we are hardly aware of a change. The Third Symphony, for example, presents to us a symphonic exposition of the evolution of Occidental music. It moves from homophony through organum, faux-bourdon, the Renaissance counterpoint, and on to contemporary sounds in as natural a manner as did history itself evolve.

There is an overwhelming intuitive logic in Harris' sense of proportion and timing. Although his music does not seem to be architectural in the academic sense, it gives the assurance that its structure is carefully crafted. There is a critical balance in the construction that makes it possible for an incorrect performance to destroy this proportion. Thus, a work may " not quite end " in one performance and work with great finality in another. If we are distracted while listening to a work, we may miss an idea necessary to the culmination of it. This music demands vital listening, and its rewards are invigorating.

There is another quality in the music of Roy Harris. This is almost indefinable. We hear it in the music of Bach and Beethoven. I hear it in Harris. For lack of a more complete term I would call it the " touch of a master." There is a certain confidence and daring in the melodic turns, almost an arrogance in the selection of a sound, and a grandeur to the sweep of a form. As you study his music you know instinctively that the man is fully aware of his Time: that he has absorbed its joys and its sadness and its searching spirit. You understand also that the man is aware that he is destined to express his Time through his music, and that he has accepted this responsibility.

(PAUL HINDEMITH)

1895 - 1963

BIOGRAPHY

AUL HINDEMITH was born in Hanau, Germany, on November 16, 1895. Because his father objected to a musical career for him, Paul Hindemith ran away from home in his eleventh year, earning his living by playing the violin in dance orchestras, motion-picture houses, and cafés. At the same time, he entered the Hoch Conservatory in Frankfurt, where his teachers included Arnold Mendelssohn and Bernhard Sekles.

In 1915 he became concertmaster of the orchestra of the Frankfurt Opera, becoming its conductor in 1923. During these years he founded and played in the famous Amar String Quartet, which toured Germany in programs of modern chamber music. Hindemith also achieved fame as a composer: for three consecutive years, between 1921 and 1923, major works of his were featured on the programs of the Donaueschingen Festival in Baden-Baden. He was also performed in Salzburg.

His style as a composer can be said to have become crystallized with a concerto for piano and twelve solo instruments (*Kammermusik*), introduced in 1925 at a festival of modern music in Venice. One year later his opera *Cardillac* — successfully presented at the Dresden Opera under Fritz Busch — focused the attention of the entire music world upon him. *Cardillac* was followed in 1929 by the provocative jazz opera, *Neues vom Tage*. After that, Hindemith wrote another opera — his masterwork, *Mathis der Maler* — together with numerous compositions for chamber-music groups and for orchestra, and a great variety of smaller functional pieces for radio, movies, pianola, and schools that have been grouped by critics under the classification of *Gebrauchsmusik* ("workaday music ") — a term invented for Hindemith.

From 1927 to 1935 Hindemith taught a master class in composition at the Berlin Hochschule für Musik. In 1934 he became a storm center in Nazi Germany when the Kulturkammer condemned his music as antagonistic to the spirit of the " new Germany " and decreed that he did not meet the specifications of a true Aryan composer.

In 1935 Hindemith left Germany and came to Turkey, where he was commissioned by the government to reorganize its musical life. In the spring of 1937, on an invitation from the Elizabeth Sprague Coolidge Foundation, Hindemith visited the United States for the first time. Soon after that he settled permanently in this country, joining the music faculty of Yale University in 1940 and becoming an American citizen in 1946. In 1949 he returned to Germany for the first time since World War II, to receive a hero's welcome. Four years later he went to live in Zürich, Switzerland, where he became a member of the faculty at its university. He also began making numerous appearances throughout Europe as a guest conductor. In 1954 he received the Sibelius Award of $35,000 conferred each year on an outstanding personality in the world of music. In 1963 he received a $52,000 Balzan Award. He died in Frankfurt on December 28, 1963.

PERSONAL NOTE

H. H. Stuckenschmidt

A SHORT, pudgy man, with delicately formed limbs and friendly blue eyes, stands in the center of a group of young people. He is speaking to them of the mystery of musical inspiration. " Don't put too much stock in the gift of God," he says. " Being an artist means work. The easygoing person will never have inspiration. Get up early in the morning, set the body in motion with a few gymnastic exercises, and then the spirit will begin to move within you. Only, don't imagine that you are geniuses! "

Thus spoke Paul Hindemith — the accent of his speech South German, a somewhat broad Frankfurt dialect.

Throughout, Hindemith has always manifested a strong peda- gogic impulse, a will to transmit his own craft and knowledge to others. He is a born teacher. In 1927 Franz Schreker brought him to the Hochschule für Musik in Berlin as professor. Hindemith began settling down. With his wife — the former Gertrude Rotten- berg, a native of Frankfurt, and daughter of the director of the Frankfurt Opera — he then occupied an elegant dwelling in the western section of Berlin. In summer, they would go South and often wander through the South German and Swiss countryside, spending nights in rustic inns.

Hindemith has had only scanty formal education. However, during the Berlin years, he began to widen and deepen his knowl- edge. He became a self-taught scholar: he acquired foreign lan- guages, studied history, concerned himself methodically with music theory. In the thirties he was insatiable in his hunger for knowledge, especially of the humanities. He immersed himself in the civili- zation of the past, although he was very much of and in this world. The man who perused the folios of the Berlin State Library in the morning, or debated with Johannes Wolf concerning Gregorian music, would the same day be busy on a cabaret piece, *Neues vom Tage*, in collaboration with Marzellus Schiffer, in the frivolous style of Offenbach! The man who would play ancient cornets at the Hochschule would also be at work developing in conjunction with his pupil Oscar Sala and the engineer Friedrich Trautwein the first practical and usable electronic musical instrument, the Trau- tonium!

Once I visited Hindemith unannounced. I could scarcely get into his apartment. For Hindemith was at his favorite occupation — working with toy trains. Tracks were laid on rugs and floors; trains rumbled from kitchen into bathroom, and beneath doors into the bedroom. At such times, it was forbidden to speak about music. Hindemith crawled on all fours, set up sidings, oiled the wheels of tiny sleepers, repaired complicated switches.

At that time he had an ambition to play all instruments. He played the horn and trumpet; worked on the oboe and clarinet; learned the knack of blowing on the flute and breathing at the same time; strummed somewhat dryly on the piano, and in private even attempted to sing. . . . Always he was interested in the practical, the craft element of life. Passionately he would saw and plane lumber into small tables and chairs. But from all these hobbies, he would return to his favorite viola, of which he was then a master — celebrated, as soloist of the Furtwängler concerts in Berlin, Vienna, and other musical centers.

He read a great deal, but only literary works, which were most congenial to his universalistic hunger for culture. When Fascism and the Nazis came to power in Germany, he immersed himself almost exclusively in the study of art history, Latin texts, Gregorian chant, and the Renaissance music of the Netherlands.

In 1935 he left for Ankara, but soon moved to Prague. Occasionally we met in the latter city, in Vienna, and in 1938 in Zürich during the rehearsals and première of *Mathis der Maler*. He had become more serious; the turn of events in Germany, which oppressed us all, had estranged him from his fatherland. I gained the impression at that time that he had discovered strong religious attachments, which have since stamped themselves on his works. The Hanau scapegrace, the imp of the Donaueschingen years, always ready for a practical joke and a grotesque improvisation, had turned into a mature, serious master.

In 1949 I once more met the Hindemiths in the United States. I was invited to their lovely home in New Haven, where Hindemith was active as professor at Yale University. His telephone conversations were conducted in almost perfect American-English, though the accent was an unforgettable Frankfurtese. At table we spoke of Germany, whose intellectual and moral state Hindemith regarded with great skepticism. He appeared then occupied with all sorts of mystical and philosophical problems, concerning which he spoke only very casually. Externally, he had changed little — only a small double chin and a few neck creases pointed to a mounting corpulence.

In the 1950's Hindemith returned to Europe, but not to Germany. He settled in Switzerland. He was the recipient of many honors in recognition of his great learning and genius and of his profoundly serious musical achievements. He has received numerous honorary doctorates; he became professor at the University of Zürich; he delivered festival addresses on Bach and other masters. In his books he has been concerned with various problems of music. The text of his opera *Harmonie der Welt* stamps him as a considerable thinker who sees the great cosmic relationships symbolically reflected in harmony.

In the forty years of his creative activity, Hindemith has traversed an impressive course. In spite of his preoccupation with metaphysical and philosophical problems, he has remained a foe of all abstraction. And just as his *Unterweisung im Tonsatz* takes as its starting point the reality of overtones, so the ear has remained for him the first and last court of appeals in musical matters. The making of music — not the speculative transcending of its limits — that is his testament.

THE COMPOSER SPEAKS

Paul Hindemith [1]

Music is mostly looked on as a means of enjoyment, and most composers are concerned solely with providing material to satisfy the listener's desires. On such means of enjoyment enormous sums of money are expended, and those who produce them are allowed freedoms — dictatorial power, the arbitrary right of disposing of the labor of others solely for the exhibition of uncontrolled phantoms of sound — with which our social order (or disorder) is otherwise too generous.

" Sensational," too, is a word that has no meaning on these levels of work. Of course, nothing is easier to write than sensational things. Any incompetent can have his successes as a composer today, if he but understands how to distract the attention of his listeners from musical problems and shift it over to some other path — most commonly, nowadays, the path of politics or nationalism. But even in the purely musical domain there are sufficient possibilities for sensationalism. Cannot one write unheard-of (and to date literally unheard) harmonies? Melodies so full of genius that no one can sing them, play them, or understand them?

---

[1] This statement comes from the Introductory Remarks to the new version of *Das Marienleben*, translated by Arthur Mendel.

Sounds that rattle, tinkle, crackle, and clatter beyond anything hitherto known?

Are there not methods of composition compared with which the secrets of Hermes Trismegistus seem no more problematical than the telephone book? In a word: cannot one be vastly modern (or *contemporary*, for those who don't like the old-fashioned term)?

(Isn't it refreshing to see attacks mounted against "modernity"? For many the grapes are sour — they rejoice at every blow that the neologists receive. But should not the unswerving modernists, on the other hand, now and then come to the realization that nothing is more wearisome or more futile than the most antiquated of all manias: the rage to be modern?)

There are indeed periods in the history of music in which an *ars nova* must shake off artistic habits that have grown stale, in order to permit any healthy development to continue. But we have been experiencing such an *ars nova* continuously since the death of Beethoven — an *ars nova* that, to be sure, has found its satisfaction in a search for externals. "Let's do something new!" That was easy to say in the days when the new consisted of Bayreuth tubas, giant orchestras, and syntheses of the arts. But this "new," after a thousand variations, has grown empty, while the ancient striving for the spiritual deepening of music is as new as ever. With all the appreciation that one may reasonably bring to technical innovations, since they should make our work easier, we should nevertheless minimize the word "new" in the term "new art" and emphasize rather the word "art."

Such an attitude influences the form a composition takes, down to the last note. The primary elements of composition (rhythm, melody, and harmony) are then no longer placed one upon another like building blocks, but rather each element is determined by the vision of the complete work, and in each the labor of composition proceeds from the large to the small, from the general to the particular, from the skeleton to the body, from the continuous to the discrete.

Meter is no longer allowed to place everything else under its yoke, but is relegated to its proper sphere, and basic rhythmic forms of greater extension, resting on irregular proportions, are preferred as the source material in the field of temporal relations.

Melody then does not remain confined to the explicit interval steps from each tone to the next, but is laid out in advance over longer periods, and then subdivided.

Individual harmonies are then considered important only to the extent that they take their assigned places in the working out of the superior harmonic principle — that of tonality.

The accompanying constructive factors of dynamics, tone color, agogics, and so on are placed entirely at the service of the co-ordinated co-operation of the primary elements.

A listener who is willing to follow along this path will undoubtedly feel something of the spirit of this way of working. He will not seek only for the confirmation of preconceived opinions, for stylistic tricks, or for a purely superficial emotional satisfaction.

HINDEMITH

Norman Del Mar

THE gradual emergence of Hindemith as one of the undisputed, and even venerable, figureheads of contemporary music is a comparatively recent development in musical history. The cause and effect of the time element in the rise of this indefatigable master is of a significance not always fully realized. Yet it bears directly upon his outlook, stylistic evolution, and eventually upon the particular niche he has carved out for himself in the world of music.

Paul Hindemith was born in 1895 — that is to say, thirteen years after the birth of Stravinsky, fourteen after that of Bartók, and no less than twenty-one after that of Schoenberg, to cite the three key figures of his generation whose influences on the course of twentieth-century music have been parallel in importance, if widely divergent in direction. This disparity of age becomes immediately relevant on consideration of the progress of music during the years surrounding World War I.

For this was the period of extravagant experiment, when the great warhorses were being produced on the largest scale in the spirit of *fin-de-siècle* superromanticism, and often with the de-

liberate intention of shaking the foundations of conservative tradition. During these years, each of the younger exponents of advanced
techniques followed the example of the already established Strauss
in his *Salome* and *Elektra* and precipitated toward each his *ne
plus ultra* in his own particular direction, whether it was *Le Sacre
du printemps, Erwartung,* or *The Miraculous Mandarin.* Each in
turn then passed through phases of violent reaction that formed
part of a general movement in postwar music.

This period of revolutionary excesses and abrupt *volte-faces*
was entirely missed by Hindemith. At its eruption no more than a
student, he was toward its decline still only beginning to cultivate,
simultaneously with his first engagements as executant (later to
prove so vital to his artistic stature), his newly acquired technique
in contrapuntal ingenuity and other branches of original composition. In this he was at first influenced to a considerable extent
by the scholastic tradition still exerted so powerfully on the conservative background of German music by Reger and his admirers.

It was in fact during the passing of this era that the first flood
of original work poured from Hindemith's pen, including the three
startling one-act operas and the first great spate of chamber music.
Several of the works contained in this mass of writings are of
particular importance for the way in which they show for the first
time so many features of Hindemith's later manner. The splendid
Viola Sonata (one of the six sonatas for various instruments bun-
dled together under op. 11, 1922), for instance, already conceals
the cynic and the humorist within its still fundamentally romantic
nature. Its form, too, is immensely ingenious and accomplished in
the way the finale roughly interrupts the Theme and Variations
that constitute the middle movement, only itself frequently to be
interrupted by further and increasingly grotesque variations. In
addition, the use of folk songlike material, the freely irregular
bar lengths, and the block-chord formations are all early instances
of devices that remained for a long time important landmarks in
his technical equipment, even though his mental outlook was to
pass through radical changes.

For, with the universal postwar reaction fully set in, it was
hard for the young composer to evade the psychological influences
that this had brought in its train, and from which few composers
throughout the world escaped altogether. In the utterly disillusioned
and unsettled society of the 1920's artists of all kinds, not only in

music, found that they had lost the ability to take themselves or
their emotions seriously. Introspection and any philosophizing
tainted with *Weltschmerz* seemed to belong wholly to the past,
whilst in its place came indulgence in the ridiculous and in all
forms of satire. Nothing is more characteristic of this aspect of
the prevailing mood than the texts chosen by composers, such as
Milhaud's *Catalogue of Agricultural Implements,* set to music
complete with prices, or Stravinsky's *Mavra,* with its exploitation
of the newly arisen servant shortage. The keynote is a resolution
on the part of the composer to avoid at all costs showing his heart
even under his shirt — let alone on his sleeve, as had been so predominantly the tendency so very few years earlier.

A second trend characteristic of postwar psychology was toward the equally unemotional neoclassic movement so often attributed exclusively to Stravinsky but to which the other great
figures also contributed in their own way. . . .

In addition, one more practical feature of the music of this
period came as a natural outcome of the radically altered economic
conditions. In place of the huge trappings of the Mahlerian orchestral and choral forces, many composers took pride in limiting themselves to tiny groups of sometimes oddly miscellaneous performers.

Fascinating, even laudable, as this reversal may have been, it
scarcely provided the atmosphere in which a new master could
create an international reputation on account of the epoch-making
impact of his work. Unperceptive and ill-humored as it proved, Cecil
Gray's description of Hindemith in 1924 as a " sandbank in the
wide ocean of notes in musical Germany " can today raise a smile
of understanding. After all, if by comparison with the excesses of
his older colleagues Hindemith's *enfant-terrible* period seemed tame
and of merely ephemeral importance, this mattered not at all to the
enthusiastic young composer who poured out music of all kinds in
fabulous quantities, the true evaluation of which has only gradually
become possible in retrospect. In fact, each of these new stylistic
trends, and, above all, the increasingly workaday attitude of composers to their craft, happened to fit in admirably with the lively
humor and unself-pitying, inventive spirit of Hindemith, who
embraced them all eagerly as ideal vehicles for the development
of his natural form of self-expression.

The first of these tendencies, the cynical evasion of romantic
or personal emotion and the liberal use of the grotesque, made its

first wholly uncompromising appearance in Hindemith's work in such pieces as the *Kammermusik No. 1*, op. 24, no. 1 (1922), with its incredible outer movements and its stipulation that all performers be invisible to the public! Professor Tovey, who always had a soft spot for Hindemith, although it is clear that he knew only one side of the composer at the time, wrote amusingly about this work and its creator: "Hindemith's music, even in his earlier works, will sound strange to many listeners. It is a severely disciplined art and rests upon massive and extensive theoretical foundations. . . . The listener must not expect too much help from an analysis. The most experienced score-reader would be little the wiser if I gave quotations from the opening movement, *sehr schnell und wild*. It is a short movement alternating between a shrill bickering motive in a treble region around F-sharp, and deeper pentatonic objurgations around and about C on the fourth string of the violins. It ends with a universal glissando and bump."

The Finale centers around a fox trot by Wilm Wilm, which Hindemith mischievously accompanies by scale passages simultaneously on all twelve degrees of the octave. The movement is entitled " 1921 " and, like a similarly dated piano piece of the same period, reflects the Pagliaccilike " laugh for very misery " philosophy so prevalent in Germany at that time.

As for the one-act operas already referred to above, their attitude to life is apparent in the very titles: *Mörder* (*Murder*), *Hoffnung der Frauen* (*Hope of Women*), and *Das Nusch-Nuschi* (1921). The last is a superb piece of riotous tomfoolery intended for performances by Burmese marionettes. There is scarcely a serious moment from first note to last. The quotation of the " King Mark " music from *Tristan*, as the emperor discovers that his favorite general has seduced all four of his wives, merely provides the *coup d'état* for a score bristling with satirical effects of every kind, from a chorus by a couple of dressed-up monkeys to an extremely high falsetto part for the chief eunuch. The *Nusch-Nuschi* itself turns out to be half gigantic rat and half alligator. This charming apparition supports the smiling figure of Kamadeva, the god of desire, who sings a short duet with a *cor anglais* before vanishing into thin air to the accompaniment of a trombone solo.

But this form of artistic mockery is perhaps epitomized in the three-act opera *Neues vom Tage* (1929). Here all the traditional operatic " numbers " are reversed. In place of a love duet, there is a hate duet, with husband and wife throwing the breakfast things at each other. Instead of a Wedding March, we have a Divorce Ensemble, and the big conventional *scena* of every Act II consists here of the notorious scene with the heroine (in the revised version, the hero) sitting naked in her bath, surrounded by, amongst others, the co-respondent, the hotel manager, and his entire gesticulating staff. The music to this magnificent burlesque is set for an utterly unconventional semichamber orchestra, the use of which contains one happy idea after another. It is apparent on every page that Hindemith is enjoying himself hugely.

It is, however, the neoclassic movement that ultimately had the more important impact on Hindemith and became increasingly in evidence in the easy fluency of his style. The purely formal pieces naturally reflect most clearly this aspect of his early work, although the ruthlessness of his counterpoints and their aggressive cumulative effect gave him at one time the reputation of a confirmed atonalist, this view being supported by even so wise a scholar as Professor Scholes. Though this was actually incorrect, the illusion was certainly given at times by the way in which Hindemith threw himself into the general rejection of romantic euphony, despite his persistent mannerism of weighing anchors of block tonality at intervals during the stretches of harmonically starved part writing.

But although he later admitted, in an extended Preface to be discussed in due course, that the counterpoint of this time " left the satisfactory logical sound of the whole in the care of heaven," this was by no means always true. This apparently atonal style was only one of the many devices in which Hindemith experimented in his ardent interest in every form of technical skill. Polytonality, composition based on unconventional intervals such as fourths and sevenths instead of thirds and sixths, use of unexploited modes and scales in whole or part, everything was grist to his mill. The works of this period frequently have no signatures of time or key, his assumption of tonal and rhythmic elasticity being complete and undemonstrative. The ingenuity of his derivatives or elaborations of all the classical forms fills one with delight, while his inspiration is usually at hand to prevent his skill from deteriorating into mere note spinning.

Nor was his preoccupation with technical resources confined to those of composition. The possibilities of tonal color and executive agility fascinated him equally and seem at times to have provided him with the main stimulus to compose. In this he was, of course, splendidly provided for by the current interest, born of economic necessity, in small and varied groups of performers. This last of the postwar trends, discussed above, Hindemith pursued to its bitter end. The variations of the ensembles required for even his larger works of this period are innumerable, with only one exception: the standard symphony orchestra appears scarcely at all for purposes of accompaniment and not once on its own until the Concerto for Orchestra, op. 38 (1925)! Even this is an isolated work, seven years passing before the next of its kind appeared, the *Philharmonic Concerto* (1932). As can well be imagined, the results of this fascination with medium as such are sheer joy to perform. Indeed, this emphasis on musicmaking is crucial to the understanding of this first main period of Hindemith's development.

From here to *Gebrauchsmusik* is obviously the closest possible step. Today Hindemith rejects the label (literally, " utility music," if one can overlook the misleading wartime connotation of the word) with impatience. But the provision of *Spielmusik* — that is, music written to be played or sung in the home by the music lover, as opposed to its specific creation as an art form — had logical precedence in musical history. Hindemith wrote quantities of this kind of music, ranging from *Five Easy Finger Pieces for Piano* and *Educational Work for Violin Ensembles in First Position* (four grades) to the more advanced type of *Music to Play for Strings, Flutes, and Oboes* and the *Cantata for Children's Choir, Solo, Speaker, Strings, Wind, and Percussion*, which latter forms part of a *Plöner Musiktag.*

Unfortunately, symptomatic as the movement was of the present-day composer's constant concern over the broad schism between his work and the general music public, it was based on a misconception of the causes and nature of the decline in amateur musicmaking in a mechanical world. As a result, it never caught on to any extent and faded away, having achieved little more than yet another outlet for the apparently inexhaustible flow of Hindemith's musicmaking.

As the twenties gave way to the thirties, a desire for important artistic utterance once more arose, and Hindemith readily fell in with the new spirit, none the worse for having marked time during an experimental phase.

It would, however, be entirely false to imply that up to this time Hindemith had produced nothing of more than academic or curiosity value. The fine Third String Quartet, with its magical, haunting slow movement, and the profoundly inspired song cycle, *Das Marienleben*, of which more will be said later, both date from as early as 1922. One need only remind oneself of such masterpieces as these to realize that behind the façade of humorous cynicism and the refugelike role of carpenter-musician, as it were, lay a true and serious artist who was maturing fast and was constantly, if quietly, proving that, far from being a local " sandbank," he would soon be an international figure to be reckoned with.

Hindemith had in 1931 suddenly abandoned the classification of his works by opus numbers after the attainment of his half century (though many works of similar nature are grouped together under a single opus number, thus making the true score rather higher!). This might suggest that the relative merits of worthy and quantity had begun to weigh more and more heavily upon the prolific composer, until in self-conscious awareness of his already mountainous output he determined to set aside so convenient, yet implicating, a yardstick.

This maturing period culminated in a number of works similar in conception and execution to those of earlier years, but now more consistently serious in the thought that lay behind the easy, if still dry and acrid, contrapuntal style. The Second String Trio (1934) contains something akin to the spirituality of the posthumous Beethoven quartets. The high-minded intention of the oratorio *Das Unaufhörliche* (1931) is self-evident and most impressive, though the layout of the work is unexpectedly conventional. Even the still numerous examples of the typical genre of the first period, now described as *Konzertmusik* for assorted combinations, are all on an increasingly high level of integrity. When the social structure of internal Germany was rocked to its foundations by the Nazis, the mature musician was ripe for an artistic comment that the world could not ignore.

The opera *Mathis der Maler* (1934) remains even today the outstanding landmark in Hindemith's entire career. The libretto was the composer's own and shows a depth of philosophic thought wholly unprecedented in his previous work. It expounds in historical guise the ever-living problem of the function of the artist at times of national stress. Should the artist remain aloof from the turmoil

raging around him, perhaps at most expressing through the agony
of his search for unattainable truth and beauty the troubles and tor-
ments of his miserably unsettled age? Or should he, from pity and
humanitarianism, enter blindly into a conflict the implications of
which he cannot fully understand, the course of which he cannot
hope to alter? As Hindemith, in the guise of Mathis, his medieval
painter-hero (a figure, incidentally, taken from life), asks himself:
" Have you fulfilled what God required of you? Is what you create
and portray enough? Are you only of use to yourself? " Set at the
time of the Peasants' Revolt, in scenes of bitter violence, the action
plunges the wretched painter into perplexing mazes of power politics, in which he wallows hopelessly. His heart-searchings are brilliantly transformed in the Sixth Tableau into a symbolic struggle of
the Temptation of St. Anthony as depicted in one of the actual
paintings of the real Matthias Grünewald. The device is clearly
born of Wagner's use of the writings of the real Hans Sachs, yet it
never fails to impress, not only by its scholarship but by its aptness
and sincerity. The overriding problem remains at last an inevitable
enigma, Mathis returning tired and discouraged to his beloved work,
having caused more harm than good by his interference in a problem many times too big for him. Nevertheless, the opera leaves one
convinced that the author by no means absolves the artist from a
share in the common responsibility.

The implicit reference to current events was obvious enough for
Hindemith to incur the disfavor of his country's new rulers, though
in their Philistine detestation of any *avant-garde* artistic movement
they had already labeled him a " cultural Bolshevik." As a result,
the work was banned, thus indirectly serving Hindemith's purpose
better than a blind eye would have done.

Yet even Furtwängler's famous act of defiance to the Nazis with
respect to *Mathis,* and the consequent notoriety of composer and
opera, would not have had such a far-reaching artistic effect had
not the music itself also shown a generosity of spirit and an accessibility of style far in advance of even the greatest of the earlier pieces.
At one stroke Hindemith attained full international status as one of
the outstanding composers of the century.

The Symphony that Hindemith built out of extracts from
Mathis quickly became a standard work in the concert repertoire,
and it might well have been hoped that the newly acknowledged
master would now concentrate on cementing the link he held at last

with the wider music-loving public. But this prospect was interfered with by yet another of Hindemith's activities.

Already in 1927 the erstwhile *enfant terrible* had assumed the role of *maître*, and this teaching connection had ever since continued to grow in importance alongside the unceasing creative work. With *Mathis* behind him, Hindemith turned his attention to crystallizing into formulas the principles and techniques that had hitherto unconsciously stood him in such good stead. In 1937 he published the first volume of the great textbook, *Unterweisung im Tonsatz* (rather too freely rendered by *The Craft of Musical Composition* in the American edition, although the translator apologizes for this in a footnote). A later volume and other textbooks have since followed at regular intervals up to the present day. In these Hindemith exposes in unique detail his workshop both of composition and musical instruction, analyzing everything down to the smallest tool. *Unterweisung im Tonsatz* is a truly astonishing work, which has been justly compared in importance with the theoretical writings of Rameau. For, in the first chapters, Hindemith goes right back to the fundamentals of music, suggesting logical revisions in the tuning of the tempered scale. From this beginning he evolves, by radically slow degrees, a system of musical construction and analysis based entirely on acoustical principles. His researches delve into the mathematical origin of tonal color and the scientific relationships of each note of the chromatic scale derived from combination tones. Here he was palpably working in direct opposition to what he regarded as the unnatural tonal anarchy of the Schoenberg school, even though in the conclusion to the first volume he subjects one of Schoenberg's later piano pieces to analysis according to his, Hindemith's, own constructional concepts. A valuable précis on Hindemith's methods and intentions is given by Mosco Carner in his *Study of 20th Century Harmony*. Moreover, as Carner quite rightly says, " modern composers are given a means by which to control and plan in a very deliberate manner the choice of chords and the harmonic disposition of a work." As a vehicle for teaching and as a vade mecum for the apprentice composer, such a volume of scientifically evolved dogma, it is clear, is beyond price. But it is somewhat doubtful whether the cold-water influence of the master professor upon the white-hot inspiration of the master composer in the person of the same man can ever be beneficial. For creative style needs to retain a generous, if

not undisciplined, degree of fluidity to meet the often wayward requirements of genius. It is not hard to assess the reputations as
composers of the great theorists of the world through the centuries,
beginning perhaps with Fux himself, who is listed as the author of
over four hundred compositions! Indeed, in the case of at least two
modern masters taken at random, Dukas and Dohnányi, their assumption of professorships led to the total drying up of their creative originality and effort, at one time so striking in both cases.

The effect on Hindemith was indeed perceptible, though it is
largely a matter of contention as to how damaging it has been. For
throughout this extended period of technical consolidation, Hindemith continued to produce works amongst which were isolated but
regular masterpieces, such as *Symphonic Dances* (1937) and the
ballet *Nobilissima Visione* (1938), the whimsy and spontaneity
of which were unimpaired by the rigidity of his avowed system.
The ballet music in particular has, in keeping with its title, a degree
of nobility quite unique in Hindemith's work, and it is very well
that he brought it within the range of the concert program by selecting from it a well-balanced and soberly contrasted suite of movements. The action centers around the life of St. Francis of Assisi,
and Hindemith's music describes the meditative fervor and asceticism with consummate understanding. The cadence figure in the
second section of the first movement, describing the mystical wedding of the saint with Poverty, is extraordinarily affecting in its
simplicity. But it is the wonderful closing *passacaglia,* headed in the
original with the Latin words " Incipiunt laudes creaturarum," that
represents the culminating point of Hindemith's classical style.

Nevertheless, the tendency toward dryness and uniformity of
color in his fundamentally unemotional style did become accentuated at this time. If the personal idiom of the later works is more
cultivated, the unfailing variety of invention in the course of a work
is no longer so fascinating. His concentration on the color of melodic and chordal progressions turned him away from his earlier
enthusiasm for dabbling in the broader colors of exotic instrumental
combinations. Above all, in his teaching he discouraged his students
from experimenting with instrumental color, an incredible dic-
tum from the composer of the *Kammermusik* and *Konzertmusik*
series! It was only the quality of the musical line that mattered,
just as Brahms used to circulate the opinion that he cared little on
what instrument his music should be performed, although anyone

who has heard Brahms' wind-instrument chamber music played entirely on strings cannot fail to doubt that composer's sincerity in this matter!

Hindemith's sonatas, dashed off easily for, in turn, every instrument of the orchestra, typify this period, which reached its climax with the famous *Ludus tonalis* for piano solo (1942). This vast undertaking represents Hindemith's *ne plus ultra* along his newly chosen scholastic path and corresponds roughly with Schoenberg's Suite, op. 29, for piano, clarinets, and strings, as being the most uncompromising embodiment of his theoretical principles. The fact that despite its severity it immediately reached an unusually wide audience can no doubt be attributed in part to its high level of artistry throughout. But history shows that this does not always follow, as no doubt it should, and at least half the credit for its ready universal acceptance must go to the circumstance that it was in perfect accordance with the contemporary spirit of wide classical sympathies that were an odd characteristic of artistic taste during World War II.

Hindemith subtitled the work "Studies in Counterpoint, Tonal Organization, and Piano Playing." As far as the last category goes, this is no more applicable in *Ludus* than in any other of Hindemith's piano works, and in any case the difficulties in his pianistic style have always been less on technical than musical grounds. These are, of course, quite another matter, and from this point of view the work deserves the closest attention.

It consists of a set of twelve fugues interspersed by Interludes and enclosed within a Prelude and Postlude. The fugues, all in three parts without exception, are arranged in order of key, corresponding with Hindemith's basic scheme of tonal relationships as laid out in *Unterweisung im Tonsatz*. The Interludes serve both to modulate from one fugue to another and to provide opportunities for as many varieites of style, mood, and form as possible within the over-all scheme of the work. As regards the Prelude and Postlude, they have attracted more attention than any other section, owing to the brilliantly successful device that the latter is the exact mirror inversion of the former. All in all, it is clear that, as Mátyás Seiber says, the work is planned as a kind of latter-day *Well-Tempered Clavier* and *Art of the Fugue*, a dangerous and courageous undertaking, for it courts inevitable comparisons — not work for work; that would be naïve; the question arises rather over the validity of any possible view of Hindemith as occupying an equivalent position in the present century to that occupied by Bach in his. In this it would be important to bear in mind not merely the ultimate value of the works, but the functional circumstances in which they were created. The parallel is by no means exact; the claim happily not made. But the haunting analogy cannot wholly be forgotten by the critical mind in its approach to an otherwise masterly product of scholarship.

Despite the success of *Ludus tonalis*, the professional view of Hindemith's position that it naturally enhanced scarcely improved the universality of his prestige, which had always inclined toward esteem rather than popularity. With the abandonment of his earlier policy of avoiding the use of normal forces, the standard popular orchestral forms were now open to him, and in fact the last number of years had seen the appearance of such, once unthinkably conventional, pieces as a true violin concerto, cello concerto, symphony, theme and variations. This policy he now continued with the *Symphonic Metamorphosis of Themes by Weber* (1943), an overture, *Cupid and Psyche* (1943), and a Piano Concerto (1946). The first of these is an undeniably attractive work (despite the provoking liberty taken with the *Turandot* theme!); nevertheless, in view of the now firmly set medium of expression he had during this period resolved upon, with its predominantly dry harmonic flavor, thickness of texture, and uniformity of orchestral color, this attempt at deliberately feeding the standard concert repertoire was only moderately successful.

In 1946 Hindemith celebrated the end of World War II with a requiem, *When Lilacs Last in the Dooryard Bloom'd*, which showed an entirely new depth and spirituality. Dedicated " For Those We Love," it is a setting of the peom by Walt Whitman. Hindemith had been constantly in America since 1940, but it is impossible to detect any American influence in his general style or outlook. His discovery of the work of this great American poet seemed, however, at this awesome moment in the world's history to open wide momentarily the sympathetic reaction of Hindemith's genius. The sad intensity of the instrumental prelude, built throughout on an organ point; the great central fugue; the poignant hymn, " For Those We Love," set as a duet for the two solo singers, followed by the choral " Death Carol "; the magnificent stately introduction and March with its use of parade drum and army bugle, so beloved of Whitman; and the heart-rending Finale; all are the work of a deeply inspired tone poet and architect.

Once again, however, this proved an isolated work of its kind, Hindemith's restless spirit moving off at a tangent. His next important production was an entirely revised version of his early song cycle, *Das Marienleben*, settings of the fabulously beautiful poems of Rainer Maria Rilke based on the life of the Virgin. These songs, originally composed in 1922, had understandably always been close to the composer's heart, and already in 1939 he had returned to them and recast four for voice and orchestra, settings of exquisite taste and sensitivity. The newly revised version of the whole cycle had been announced as " in preparation " ever since 1941, but the work had proceeded gradually and with immense care. When it finally emerged in 1948 it proved to carry with it a lengthy manifesto describing in detail its *raison d'être* and, with the composer's customary thoroughness, comparing the relative merits of the two versions. This manifesto is, of course, extremely revealing of Hindemith's changed attitude to his stylistic trends of the 1920's. But many of the hotheaded and hence less carefully practical results were inseparable from so violently reactionary a period, and much as one may agree in principle with an older and wiser composer's indictments, a feeling of concern that he may spoil something of the initial spark is aroused when it becomes clear that he intends to revise on a large scale the work of his youth.

The new version of *Das Marienleben* is indeed radical, some of the songs being not merely revised but entirely rewritten, while only a single song remains wholly untouched. For example, in the introductory remarks he says of the third song, " The Annunciation of Mary ": " The old version, judged by the severest standards, could in no way stand up to serious examination. It is accordingly replaced by quite a new setting. This attempts a peaceful sonority in direct contrast with the disturbing harmonic and tonal restlessness of the old song. . . . In place of the intensely penetrating repetition of individual motifs, separated by rests, we now have long-drawn-out lines of melody." This quest for continuity, for smoothness of sonority and line, is one of the main features of Hindemith's changed attitude to his art. Yet in the maintaining of variety and interest, the dramatic impact of the central recitativelike middle section of this song was not without its effect. Moreover, the use of terse figures built up through repetition, which now evokes such severe censure, was a welcome change of *modus operandi* after the habitually even-flowing style of also the young Hindemith.

Nevertheless, most of the revisions are unquestionably beneficial. The raising of the *tessitura*, if once again at the expense of variation of color, removed from the vocal line the strain of unfair competition with the intricate piano part and other unpractical effects born of inexperience. This elimination of the necessity of forcing the lower voice also has the desirable result of placing the cycle within the range of a far greater number of sopranos. Again, Hindemith says with noteworthy humility: " Should the composer notice that the singer continues to stumble at the same places even after zealous and thorough application, then he must ask himself whether his work is really worth such fruitless strain."

Practical considerations of balance are also in strong evidence in the redrafting of some of the songs. In deciding to retain the *fugato* that formed the basis of the ninth song, " Of the Marriage at Cana," Hindemith realized that its violence and business obscured the clarity of the all-important vocal line. He accordingly gave the *fugato* its head in a tremendous piano introduction, using it thereafter only with the greatest discretion as an accompaniment. This had the effect of doubling the length of the song, and this new stature, together with the immensely impressive introduction, makes of the piece " the dynamic climax of the complete plan," as Hindemith puts it. Here we reach a further crucial guiding principle constantly before the composer during his work of revision. This is nothing less than a double graph of dynamic and expressive intensity as drawn by the succession of songs in their new form. " The old version," he writes, " was essentially a row of songs held together by the text and by the continuity of its action but beyond that following no general plan of over-all consumption. . . . Wise distribution of power, calculated placing of the points of greatest and least intensity — all this was unknown to the composer of the old version. Like all else of which he knew no better, he left it to his musical instinct."

Despite the justice in all this, perhaps the professor in correcting the results of his own impetuosity, as he would those of any of his pupils, underrates the value of instinct. The proverb " first thoughts are best " often has real validity in artistic matters, and in many places the burning virility and direct sincerity of the original work have faded to a comfortable glow of accomplished writing.

Hindemith now embarked on a series of works featuring wind instruments, beginning with a Clarinet Concerto (1947). To this burst of specialized activity belongs also the Concerto for Horn and Small Orchestra (1950), with its utterly unorthodox last movement. This consists itself of a series of smaller movements . . . the outer ones being the slowest, so that the entire concerto ends in effect with the dying notes of its slow movement. The center . . . is in two parts; the first is a short rapid movement, whereas the second is an extended recitative above which stands a short poem marked Declamation. This proves upon examination to fit to the notes of the solo horn's recitative line, which it comments upon in poetical analogies.

Such a conception gives rise to uncertainty as to the correct procedure in performance, but clearly springs from a return to Hindemith's youthful delight in playing with coloristic and formal devices. This seems, moreover, to have revived yet again the freshness of his invention, for in the midst of these works there appeared in 1950 a Sinfonietta that can only be described as " vintage." In addition, he seems at this time to have been drawn to other works of his first period, making in his nostalgia revised versions of several of them. Even his occasional pieces are amusingly reminiscent of earlier days, such as the Canticle of Hope, written for the UNESCO convention of 1953, the material for which contains parts for two orchestras of indeterminate size and song sheets for the audience!

One of Hindemith's works of importance suggests that he may have reached one more turning point in his output. The symphony Die Harmonie der Welt (1951) is an enormous work of great complexity, derived from an opera of the same name. The subject matter may well be the most elaborate Hindemith has yet tackled. It concerns the life of Johann Kepler, the seventeenth-century astronomer and philosopher who overstepped the boundaries of true scientific calculation and attempted to corelate the mathematical laws of the universe with the modes of music. The concept of the Music of the Spheres is one of the oldest in the history of philosophy, and Hindemith derived the titles to the movements of his symphony from a sixth-century Roman author who is believed to have been himself propounding ancient Greek theories. These titles, " Musica Instrumentalis," " Musica humana," " Musica mundana," are of course highly evocative to a musician of Hindemith's inventive capacity, and the results are full of startling flights of imaginative fancy, while the virtuosity required from all departments of the orchestra is of a wholly new order in Hindemith's work.

The relationship of this symphony to its parent opera naturally recalls that of *Mathis*, and it may well prove that Hindemith has reached a climax in his work comparable with that earlier pinnacle. His fertility appears to be as inexhaustible as ever, while his indomitable spirit is once again ready to dare new and formidable problems of style and texture. One may reasonably look forward to a new period of creative activity that will link up and pursue the more enduring elements in each of the remarkable phases of his exceptionally full career. Above all does one await with eagerness the appearance of further enduring masterworks with that inevitable quality yet varying character which prove that the fine artist has the stature and personality of a great man. Whatever may transpire, however, his position and influence as classicist, theorist, and master, with that so endearing love of his subject, are assured for all time.

(ARTHUR HONEGGER)

1892 - 1955

BIOGRAPHY

ARTHUR HONEGGER was born in Le Havre, France, of Swiss parentage, on March 10, 1892. After studying the violin in Paris with Lucien Capet, and taking courses in music at the Zürich Conservatory, he attended the Paris Conservatory, where he was a pupil of Widor and Vincent d'Indy. In 1916 some of his songs were performed in Paris, and two years later there took place in that city an all-Honegger concert. His name first gained prominence in 1920, when it was joined with those of five other young Frenchmen in a school labeled by Henri Collet " Les Six," a group that included Milhaud and Poulenc. Honegger's reputation became firmly established soon thereafter with such provocative works as *Pacific 231*, for orchestra, and the oratorio *Le Roi David*.

Honegger paid his first visit to the United States in 1929. He returned in 1947 to conduct a master class at the Berkshire Music Center in Tanglewood but was prevented from fulfilling this assignment owing to poor health. During World War II he was engaged in Paris in the resistance movement, but creative work was not abandoned. Both during and after the war he wrote some of his most significant works, including several widely performed symphonies. He died in Paris on November 27, 1955.

PERSONAL NOTE

Everett Helm

NOT only was Arthur Honegger a highly gifted composer; he was also one of the most pleasant and charming of men. The gentleness of his demeanor was matched by a quiet but ready wit. There was no vanity in his character, nor was he touched by those feelings of personal ambition or professional jealousy which all too often mar the tempers of composers. He was a generous colleague, happy at the success of his friends and interested in their works, while modestly belittling the success of his own. " As to my success," he wrote in 1950, " I attribute it to the fact that my career began in a climate entirely opposed to ours — after the Armstice of 1918. . . . We young composers found all the doors open."

" The Six " — of which Honegger, Milhaud, and Poulenc were the most illustrious members, and which represented in the 1920's the most radical trends in French music — did, indeed, enjoy a particularly happy situation; yet Honegger's forthrightness in admitting this fact is noteworthy. Speaking of that time, he says in his autobiographical book, *I Am a Composer* (*Je suis compositeur*): " We thought that another war was impossible, that the world would move toward science, art, and beauty." In his last years, Honegger was of quite the contrary opinion. His statements in *I Am a Composer* are pessimistic to a degree. " I believe that we are living the last instants of our civilization; these last instants are necessarily painful. . . . Social progress regiments each individual into a concentration-camp kind of life. It makes the existence of an independent being almost impossible. . . . What can possibly be left over for the arts and for music? Do you really believe that a creator of spiritual values, who is the prototype of individualism, still has the possibility to survive, to dedicate himself to his art, to write music? "

Honegger's was essentially a romantic nature. He describes himself as a " double national." Born in Le Havre of Swiss parents, he spent most of his life in France. In his youth he came under the influence of Richard Strauss and Reger, then of Debussy and Fauré.

Later Stravinsky, Schoenberg, and Milhaud played a part in molding his style.

Pacific 231 and a similar experimental work, *Rugby*, lie quite outside Honegger's main creative stream. He was in his heart not a " bright young modern " but a thoroughly earnest and serious composer, touched by a strong vein of mysticism. In *Jeanne d'Arc au bûcher* and the apocalyptic *Symphonie liturgique* Honegger gives voice to the hopes and fears that plagued his complicated nature — a strong religious feeling on the one hand and a pessimistic realism on the other.

The nobility and tragic greatness of Honegger's thought during his latter years find cryptic expression in two sentences that he wrote toward the end of his life. " One must confront with a clear eye, as one confronts death, the end of our musical culture, which will precede by only a little the end of our culture in general. Afterward, one may console himself with the thought that from the rubble of this culture a new one will arise."

THE COMPOSER SPEAKS

Arthur Honegger [1]

COMPOSITION is not a profession. It is a mania — a sweet folly. Composition is the most mysterious of all the arts . . . a great part of my work stands outside my own volition. A good composer finds the golden mean between prose and poetry, between craftsmanship and inspiration.

I reserve the title of composer for those whose aim is not to cater to the public's taste in everyday enjoyment but, first and foremost, to create a work of art, to express some thought, some emotions, to crystallize their attitude to esthetic or purely human problems. They wish to earn a place in the history of music as worthy

[1] The above statement comes partly from Honegger's book *Je suis compositeur* (1951) and partly from a lecture delivered by Honegger at the International Conference of Artists, in Venice, in September, 1952.

successors to the great masters of the past. A man with such an ambition is an idealist, which nowadays means a harmless type of
lunatic.

The distinguishing characteristic of the composer is that he is a
man whose whole effort and overriding concern is to produce a com-
modity for which there is no demand. He may be compared to a
manufacturer of old-fashioned bowler hats, button shoes, or " mystery " corsets. We all know how heartily the present-day public despises these objects that, in the recent past, were the hallmark of
elegance. In music, and this is where my comparison breaks down,
the public wants only what was written a hundred years ago. It regards the art of music as consisting in the performance of classical
and romantic works, with the possible addition of a few more modern compositions that have waited an appreciable time in outer
darkness. The modern composer is a kind of gate-crasher forcing his
way into a party to which he has not been invited.

We are thus faced with the fact that music must be a hundred
years old or, at least, have reached a sufficiently respectable age to
ensure that the majority of listeners will, I do not say " understand "
it, for that word is meaningless in connection with music, but at
any rate listen to and enjoy it.

In my opinion, what has estranged the music lover from the
contemporary composer is the latter's rather childish pretentious-
ness in expressing himself in a deliberately complicated form. As
sight reading is already none too easy, there is no need to add to its
difficulty. It is, however, far harder to find a clear than ultrasubtle
form of expression, and all too often the composer yields to the
temptation of writing in a style that appalls the performer. He
lightly imagines he is showing transcendent skill by changes in time,
torrents of notes and chords piled up like a skyscraper. Mere child-
ishness! Today every stage in the production of music costs a
fortune. It is a foolish offense to waste time and money by such
writing, which no longer impresses the simple but is a sure sign of
incompetence.

There is no denying that the effort needed to bring a new work
before the public is out of all proportion to the number that are of
any real value. Under a kind but misguided policy, all too many
mediocre works get performed once, thus giving a certain rash satisfaction to one person and doing disservice to the general interests of
young composers.

HONEGGER

Norman Demuth

IN THE years 1954–5 French music suffered three losses in the deaths of Claude Delvincourt, the director of the Paris Conservatory, Guy Ropartz, last surviving pupil of César Franck, and Arthur Honegger. Thus three generations of French composers followed each other in quick succession. Delvincourt's music did not penetrate other than French concert halls to any striking degree, and although Ropartz was a well-known European figure at the beginning of the century, he had faded into the background in France by reason of his age, although he continued to compose until the last few years of his life. Honegger, on the other hand, was a household name all over the world.

Vincent d'Indy was once asked whither he thought music would progress. His reply was that it would go in the direction indicated by the next composer of genius. Pressed for a name, he looked significantly at Arthur Honegger, who was a member of his conducting class.

Honegger's association with the group " Les Six " and the circumstances surrounding the institution of the group have been discussed in many places. There was never any question of a mutual style or a mutual approach to esthetics, and each member pursued his own individual path. Georges Auric and Germaine Tailleferre became slick and fashionable; Francis Poulenc kept within the confines of the salon; Louis Durey soon severed his connection with the group and retired to the country " to write a page a day." Darius Milhaud cried, " À bas Wagner "; Honegger cried, " Vive Wagner!," but did not in any way try to ape that composer.

While Milhaud regarded " symphony " in terms of " sound for orchestra " and eschewed everything except plain statement, Honegger thought otherwise, and with the exception of some short pieces written between 1916 and 1920 he concerned himself with producing symphonic and dramatic works on a large scale. Honegger, unlike Milhaud, was no iconoclast. He was always the most serious of the group, even in his earlier days, and never had Milhaud's astonishing fecundity. Swiss by parentage, he studied for the most part in Paris at the Conservatory under such typically French teachers as André Gédalge, Charles-Marie Widor, and Vincent d'Indy. Having thus absorbed French culture at the source, he cannot be considered anything but a French composer. His music has no Swiss affiliations; it is fundamentally French, but does not in any way resemble the Fauré-Debussy type of Gallicism. He was never to be considered a member of " L'École de Paris," which consists of foreigners resident in Paris whose training was undergone elsewhere but who became assimilated into the current of French musical activities.

Honegger suffered for many years from the reputation of *Pacific 231* (1923), an early *jeu d'esprit* that attracted attention by reason of its novelty but, considered as a work of symphonic proportions and impulse, has everything to commend it. Associated with this work, and at the other end of the scale, was the *Pastorale d'été* (1920), a short symphonic poem in simple ternary form for chamber orchestra whose scope immediately made it approachable. These two works detracted from such things as *Horace victorieux* (1921) — a mime symphony — *Chant de joie* (1923), and the First Symphony (1930). But nothing stood in the way of the dramatic oratorio *Le Roi David* (1921), which established Honegger as an outstanding figure and which gave Vincent d'Indy his clue to the future. This comparatively early work, which still never fails to move and impress, showed Honegger at home with the small orchestra on a big canvas, and he succeeded in making his limited forces sound like a full orchestra.

Honegger wrote his First Symphony in honor of the Boston Symphony, as did Roussel write his Third Symphony and Stravinsky his *Symphony of Psalms*. The work is rather acidulated and, in spite of the swaggering context, repels instead of attracts. It is worth noting that performances are few and far between. The Second and Third Symphonies were written in France and Switzerland respectively.

The Second Symphony, for string orchestra (1941), is music of spiritual discomfort. Not only did Honegger's age prevent him from taking an active part in World War II — he was forty-nine when he wrote it — but his Swiss nationality forced him to remain neutral, and he saw all his French contacts fall to pieces. Even the quicker movements have an air of solemnity about them, and the atmos-

phere is elegiac. In the Finale the first violin is in F-sharp major and
the rest of the strings are in the minor. Only the first-violin part
has a key signature. A Chorale played on a trumpet, doubled by the
first violin, sends out a message of hope, but in spite of its compound duple time Honegger contrives to make its vital rhythm
sound mournful, as if it were a kind of dance of death.

The Third Symphony, *Symphonie liturgique* (1946), is in three
movements for ordinarily full orchestra plus piano. The movements
are headed " Dies irae," " De profundis clamavi," and " Dona nobis
pacem " respectively. It was a further reaction to war conditions, but
the issue was then no longer in doubt. Honegger was obviously
looking forward to the future, but some regard it as a form of
requiem.

No liturgical themes are used. The title arose from the three
psalms that have their place in the Liturgy. It is a work that has
emotional contact with the several textual headings. For this reason
it is comforting to find that the liturgical melody for the " Dies
irae " is neither distorted not maltreated. The second and third
movements conclude with a flute line that solves the misery implied
by the text. The third is ominous in the same way that Beethoven
was ominous in the *Missa solemnis*. Honegger is no more optimistic
that mankind will find its solution by itself and suggests that the
message of peace will not be received or accepted. The concluding
section is redolent in feeling of Debussy's *The Martrydom of St.
Sebastian*, and the mood is resignation.

The rest of this movement is a solemn, relentless march that
might have been written by Berlioz — indeed, the opening rhythm
is, quite accidentally, the same as that in the *Marche au supplice*.
There is enormous power in this music. The long strong theme is
Berliozian in quality, and the effect is almost overwhelming. I am
not at all sure that Honegger's admiration for Beethoven did not
play a certain part in this symphony's conception. Its continuity is
superbly maintained, and the long slow movement is genuinely inspired.

The *Symphonie liturgique* is one of the monuments in
twentieth-century music.

The Fourth Symphony, *Deliciae basilienses* (1946) was composed for the twentieth anniversary of the Basel Chamber Orchestra, which is conducted by Paul Sacher. It was written in the style
of orchestral chamber music, the piano having an important and

individual role. This is restrained Honegger, so restrained that
when it was performed in London one critic remarked that it was
feeble. Compared with what one usually expects from Honegger,
this may be an accurate assessment, for gentleness and tenderness, to say nothing of delicacy, are qualities unexpected in his
music. Of the three very delightful movements, the first shows the
scholarly restraint and adherence to form of the Schola Cantorum
and Vincent d'Indy — Honegger proved that with modifications
the traditional frameworks were still of value. In the second movement Honegger deliberately wrote music in the spirit of the baroque
age. This is apparent in the very decorative countersubject to the
main material. A long trumpet tune is suggestive of the trumpet
melody on the organ, known as the " cornett " stop. During the
movement, the theme " Z'Basel an mim Rhy " (Franz Abt) is introduced, and the music represents an interpretation of the baroque
spirit heard in twentieth-century ears.

The Finale is more modern, and there is little hint at pastiche.
It ends quietly, another feature that surprised the critic in question
(he could not have heard the *Liturgique*). It suggests that the early
strength and power had sobered down, and vitality differently directed. As long as the listener does not expect " traditional "
Honegger, he should find this work perfectly delightful.

The Fifth Symphony, *Di tre re* (1950), was written for the
Koussevitzky Music Foundation and dedicated to the memory of
Natalie Koussevitzky. It is more interesting than inspiring, but in
spite of its being cyclic throughout, the derivations, processes, and
quotations are not paramount. What little slow movement there is
intrudes upon the delicate scherzolike second movement. Here is a
surprising reflection of the Franck Symphony in reverse, for one
can refer to the " slow movement " of that work, even though it is
marked Allegretto (and usually played mournfully Adagio). The
texture is slender, another unusual quality, but it, again, ends
quietly. Honegger's powers of invention are seen here at their most
refined and mature moment, but I do not detect quite the same impulse, and the work sounds as if it gave its composer a unique kind
of pleasure in its composition. It is interesting — and attractive —
for its abstract esthetics. The ear is never rudely disturbed, even in
the more explosive moments, and there is a great deal to charm the
listener. Honegger was nearing the end of his too-short life. He may
have found relaxation in the interplay of fragments. If so, there is no

sign of it as being the end and not the means. There is no Beethoven or Berlioz in this work.

It should be noted that the transposing instruments are printed
with their real sounds. This is an annoying habit and, although supposed to be a short cut to score reading, actually makes this exercise
more difficult.

Although Honegger wrote several ballets, he was never commissioned by Diaghilev to compose one. Honegger could never have
been sufficiently ephemeral or superficial for Diaghilev's requirements, but elsewhere in the theater he was as great as in the concert
hall. Of his fourteen dramatic scores of all sizes, *Antigone* (1927),
Jeanne d'Arc au bûcher (1935), together with the charming *Nicolas de Flue* (1939) — and of course *Le Roi David* — are works that
will rank among the hierarchy in the panorama of dramatic music.

In the same way that Roussel revived the old opera-ballet in
Pâdmâvatî, Honegger revived the medieval *mystère* in *Jeanne
d'Arc au bûcher*. The *mystère* consists of a combination of music,
poetry, dancing, mime, and spoken dialogue in prose. As far as I can
ascertain, Honegger's is never given its proper title but is advertised
as a " dramatic oratorio," an ambiguous description that precludes
any dramatic impulse in the music — what could be more dramatic
music than that of the *St. Matthew Passion*? Yet its proper place is
in a sacred building and not in the theater. Concert performances of
Jeanne d'Arc au bûcher reveal the dramatic qualities of both text
and music. In the theater it is one of the most impressive spectacles
in the lyric repertory, seconded by Delvincourt's *Lucifer*. Honegger
confirmed his descent from Berlioz in this work. It reaches the pin-
nacles of greatness and will surely constitute a landmark in the
history of music. The other such work — *La Danse des morts*
(1938) — does not convince me, personally, but I know that many
others rank it as high as *Jeanne d'Arc au bûcher*.

In the course of a great many verbal and written tributes to his
memory, it was stated more than once that Honegger " broke away "
from " Les Six " and gradually became Teutonized. Nothing could
be further from the truth, save in one respect, namely, that he
thought on a symphonic plane. In the last century and during the
early part of the present one it was fashionable to say of any French
composer who thought in terms of line rather than sound, who
scored boldly and solidly, that he was " Germanic " and " Wagnerian." All the Franckistes were so blamed, as also was Paul Dukas

(who was never one of the Franck circle), mainly because at a climax near the end of *La Péri* he used a formula common to Wagner for two or three bars. Honegger has been thus stigmatized, and there are several French composers still living who, in turn, may well bear the stigmata: Chailley, Jolivet, Messiaen, Dutilleux, Barraud, Loucheur, among others. These assessors are incapable of viewing French music as truly French unless it is slim and slender, sensuous and wilting, but never " strong." The influence otherwise is not Wagner. It is Berlioz. Honegger's pedigree traces from Berlioz through Franck to Vincent d'Indy and emerges with its own strongly marked individuality. A certain harmonic astringency can align him with Roussel. All this is as evident in his chamber music as in his dramatic and symphonic music — in the latter case, the *Symphonie liturgique* particularly.

Honegger composed a great deal of music, but he was by no means prolific. In his book *I Am a Composer,* he showed that ideas never came easily to him, although once they had entered his head he experienced little difficulty in dealing with them. There is all the evidence of an immense amount of trouble having been taken over even the smallest piece, and there is never any feeling of strain or striving toward the ultimate goal. The music moves forward easily and resolutely. The ear is not conscious of the cerebral symphonic derivations.

Honegger proved himself to be the composer of his generation — if one who has studied the greater part of his output very carefully may be allowed to prophesy. This cannot be determined for some years, probably between twenty and thirty. Like Ravel, he may be taken for granted and enter the repertory in the ordinary course of things. Performance will always be an " occasion " rather than an " event "; the former should always signal performance of the world's great music.

Every great composer is so in his own light, his own right, and in his own manner. It is possible to speak of " great French, English, American, Scandinavian, and so forth, composers," meaning that their greatness is restricted to their own cultures. Honegger joins the great ones of the world because he is universal.

(BOHUSLAV MARTINU)

1890 - 1959

BIOGRAPHY

BOHUSLAV MARTINU was born in Polička, in Bohemia, on December 8, 1890. He showed signs of musical talent early, appearing as violinist in public concerts in his eighth year. When he was sixteen he entered the Conservatory of Prague, specializing in the study of the violin. When his studies were completed he joined the Czech Philharmonic as violinist. He held this post for ten years. In composition he was mostly self-taught, having written music since boyhood. In 1922 his ballet *Istar* was introduced at the National Theater in Prague. This was followed two years later by a second ballet, *Who Is the Mightiest?*

In 1922–23 Martinu attended the composition class of Josef Suk. He never completed this course. A sudden decision brought him to Paris in 1923, where he became a pupil of Albert Roussel. Until 1940 Paris remained his home; its musical life had a great influence on his creative evolution. In 1932 a String Quartet, awarded first prize by the Elizabeth Sprague Coolidge Foundation, brought him into prominence in America. He also won other awards, including the Czech State Prize and the Smetana Prize.

In 1941 Martinu came to the United States to find a new home. In this country he created some of his most significant music, including several symphonies (of which the Sixth achieved international recognition), concertos, and various other orchestral and chamber-music works. For five years he was a member of the music faculty of Princeton University. In 1946 he was appointed professor of composition at the National Conservatory in Prague. After that he lived intermittently in Prague, New York, and Switzerland, but in 1952 he became an American citizen. He died in Liestal, near Basel, Switzerland, on August 28, 1959.

PERSONAL NOTE

Miloš Šafránek

IN THE winter of 1934 I once sat with Martinu at a rehearsal of the opera *The Miracle of Our Lady* in Prague. I saw before me a man changed almost beyond recognition. In everyday life Martinu gave the impression of being shy, polite, indulgent toward the weaknesses of his fellow men; but at the rehearsal he was exactly the opposite. He felt that his intentions regarding the opera were misunderstood, and his criticism was relentless to the point of fury. Finally, his expressions became so violent that it was found necessary, in order to avoid a scene, to drop the curtain. The reason for Martinu's anger did not lie in the misinterpretation of details of his work. It was caused by the diametrical opposition between his own conception and that of the stage director, who in the composer's absence had allowed the actors to interpret *The Miracle of Our Lady* as a conventional stereotyped opera, with all the stage theatrical mannerisms that this implies. . . .

In these outbursts of justified anger I found the true characteristics of Martinu's personality, his deep convictions, and his artistic greatness of stature. Martinu imagines " intensely and comprehensively," as Shelley expressed it in his *Defence of Poetry*; and his imagination is " the great instrument of moral good, the organ of the mortal nature of man." He lay aside his own individuality, divesting himself of all personal uncertainty; and by putting himself in the place of others, in the widest sense, came into the open and reached a definite impressional expression of artistic truth, emotionally as well as rationally. In *The Miracle of Our Lady* Martinu did not portray his personal problems, but those of mankind in general — the moral, intellectual, and emotional values common to all. He was firmly opposed to anything that might separate him from the common man. Everything that the egotism of the artist might bring forward to set himself above his fellow creatures — that is not " along the line of an unselfish devotion to the best " — was foreign to him. Martinu's greatest realities lay in the values created by relationships; he agreed with modern philosophy that " no part of the living world can be known by itself alone." He was intensely conscious of all the changes of the present times, believing that we are, in the words of Professor Ralph Tyler Flewelling, only on " the threshold to yet greater truths of a rational world."

And yet in spite of this quality of impersonal detachment, Martinu's work is a full expression of himself. No external mandate, no material difficulties — of which he had more than his share — was ever able to divert him from his chosen path and artistic goal. He was not lacking in depth or substance, although, because his work is without those superficial effects and meaningless climaxes which to certain critics imply these qualities, he was sometimes held to be so.

Martinu's own opinion was that his music could best be regarded from the point of view of light. The shadows are created by the angles at which the light is projected in order to produce light. It is not necessary to create darkness in order to produce light; quite the contrary. And for Martinu light signified life — " the total push and pressure of the cosmos," as William James has expressed it. To him it did not include isolationalism, analysis of the ego, renunciation, self-pity, or the baring of a deep inaccessible soul. It was energy, strength, pure joy, even humor; and, above all, it was faith and conviction. Martinu was in every way a positive man, and his work a living organism. He possessed what Goethe called " die exacte Phantasie," and was firmly in opposition to all Faustism, skepticism, and irony — in a word, to the entire " superman " complex. The " Demon of the Absolute," which for so long haunted romantic music, did not exist for him.

Martinu was firmly convinced that mankind was approaching a new era; and this is anticipated in his work. He believed that this new era — just as after the crusades — would be happier, more poetic, and more chivalrous; that it would bring the true brotherhood of man. He also felt that after the present crisis the arts would rise in all their grandeur, purity, and beauty. In the cause of this new art — this music for man — Bohuslav Martinu was one of the humblest and most faithful of workers.

THE COMPOSER SPEAKS

Bohuslav Martinu [1]

I THINK I am better at writing music than in writing about it. I do not like placing the creative process under a microscope, to explain a work, to look at the molecules (so to speak) instead of examining the body as a whole. So far as I am concerned, a work should live by itself, and not as a result of analyses. I do not think that it is necessary for the public to enter the laboratory, where it understands nothing, and where the artist himself sometimes needs to reflect a long time in order to grasp the meaning of things.

I think the greatest danger facing contemporary music is that it seeks, through analyses and explanations, to justify itself; it seems afraid of not appearing sufficiently " contemporary " or " modern." All this can only end in creating a mental attitude that is not at all favorable to the composer in giving free play to his ideas. It can only restrain him from expressing himself fully, completely, and honestly.

We play continually with the words " modern " and " contemporary," and by doing so we complicate for ourselves the creative process, which is, in itself, quite mysterious and complicated. To chase after novelty, at any price, is obviously not a good system. It has nothing whatsoever to do with the desire to seek new musical expression. New musical expression should arise from the subject matter, should be the result of a composer's personality and experiences; it should not be the result of unusual technical means. Technical means are the artist's private business. The technique comes out of the work itself; not the work from the technique. Music is not a question of calculation. The creative impulse is identical with the wish to live, to feel alive.

In a difficult world of social upheavals, of political chaos, it is more necessary than ever not to obscure our artistic purpose. We should keep our ideals clear, our convictions firm, and maintain the artistic faith that represents and speaks for our life and work. The composer should concern himself with this, and not with a useless play with words.

[1] This statement was written by the composer expressly for this book.

MARTINU

Paul Nettl

Two major trends of modern Czech music have been represented by the work of Czechoslovakia's two leading twentieth-century composers. One of these composers, Bohuslav Martinu, was the spokesman for the international group, because of his alliance with French music. The other composer, Jaromir Weinberger, was the voice for the equally popular native trend.

In 1923 Martinu suddenly decided to go to Paris, which then became his second home. Paris had a decided influence on the creative work of the young musician. Yet, truth to tell, Martinu had already betrayed some Gallic influences in his composition even before his departure to France. Such French characteristics as ease, delicacy, economic use of orchestral means of expression, a measure of rationalistic approach, and, above all, an almost curt rejection of all kinds of sentimentalisms are to be found in many of his early compositions. Martinu had always considered that elements of Western musical culture were an integral part of the Czech national musical style. In fact, it cannot be disputed that the Czechs have had as many tendencies in common with the French as with the German. The naïvely spontaneous, creative quality of a Smetana, Dvořák, and Janáček is more akin to Western conceptions of artistic culture than to the analyzing, abstract, and philosophical concepts of the Germans, though there is an interplay of both forces in the art of the Czechs.

In the first quarter of the twentieth century there existed in Czechoslovakia, side by side with the cult of Smetana, a strong Germanophile tendency inspired by the examples of Bruckner, Mahler, and Richard Strauss. Against this, Martinu took up the cudgels from the very beginning of his career, believing that pure tone is essential in music. Debussy, therefore, became the ideal, the paragon of Martinu's musical ambitions. To this influence, and to that of Mozart, he allotted places of first importance. In the early days of his French period, French impressionism so colored his thinking that he chose exotic themes (Chinese texts) and exotic keys (as, for example, in his Oriental ballet, *Istar*). A second subject that interested him was the collective experience of humanity, the movement of man in masses. As early as in 1918, in the *Czech Rhapsody*, he had tried to express the uprising of his countrymen. And when, in 1927, Lindbergh's flight across the ocean caused a wave of enthusiasm among the French, Martinu was inspired by the movement, psychology, and tumultuous vitality of the crowd to write the orchestral work *La Bagarre* (1927). The same forces moved him to write *Half Time*, which was composed on the occasion of the football games between the French and the Czech teams, in France, in 1918. In the same group belong *The Miracle of Our Lady* (1933), the *Mass at Camp* (written for the Czech soldiers in France in 1940), and the *Double Concerto* (1938).

Martinu was a lonely soul, preoccupied with the problems of his art, the core of which is the union of form and content. He was always designated a " French " composer by those Czech musicologists and esthetes who used this term derogatorily to imply that he lacked " deeper meaning." This whole period was for him the most difficult and trying of his artistic life. He could not help feeling that the current Czech creations, so different from his own, put him in the wrong light. His own consciousness, his tone, his technique, so removed from the abstractions of the German *Tiefsinn*, placed him in another camp. He felt that there surely must be something wrong at home, in the music of his native land. This classification by his countrymen brought him many unhappy hours, because he felt that his own music sprang from the pure and free spirit of his own Czech people; because he knew that he had always been a true Czech and remained so even in Paris, where, at last, he had found the universal accents of his musical language.

It is not difficult to guess the feelings of young Martinu when he first arrived in Paris. He discovered that his so-called " French " style had really no blood relationship with what was considered " French " in Paris, and he was reinforced in his determination to remain a native Czech. Though he was greatly impressed by the French " Six," by Stravinsky, and by the Russian ballet, the typical manifestations of musical life in Paris did not appear sufficiently serious-minded for his taste. He was particularly disappointed in the loose artistic discipline prevailing in musical circles, especially the choice of themes by composers, which occasionally overstepped the limits of the permitted and appeared to him unworthy of artistic treatment.

All these factors, as well as the difficult struggle for very existence, weighed heavily upon him. This was a period of deep depression. No musician in Paris, with the exception of Stravinsky, made
any impression on him. Martinu felt that there was much in common between himself and the talented Russian, but he knew that
his own path, which he had to follow hesitatingly and instinctively,
lay elsewhere. His own impressionist language, his homophonic approach, was not altered; his distrust of the current polyphonic treat-
ments persisted. He composed comparatively little.

His gradual acclimatization to life in Paris finds expression in
his composition *Half Time*. This "football symphony," as it is
sometimes called, is a symphony of rhythm. The material is reduced
to short motifs, and is put on paper with short, accentuated strokes.
I still recall what a whirlwind of astonishment, admiration, and
disgust this work aroused when it was performed for the first time at
the Prague Festival of the International Society for Contemporary
Music in 1925. In this work there is, as it were, a concentration, a
summing up of Martinu's whole impressionist past. We may consider it not only the highest point but also the closing word of his
development in this direction.

The composition *La Bagarre* was performed for the first time by
Serge Koussevitzky in New York in 1928. One year later there followed the *Military Symphony*, the title of which was changed to
Allegro symphonique when it was performed in Paris. The accented
lines of *Half Time* have vanished. Their place is taken by a new lyric
mode that does not yield in perfection of form to Martinu's former
rhythmic beat. Again there is a change in the working method of
the composer — a new turn, this time toward polyphonic treatment.
Together with this, there is a reduction of the orchestra, occurring
for the first time in the opera *Juliette* (1938).

In this connection, his lyric works should be mentioned: *Serenade* (1930), *Partita* (1931), and *Inventions* (1934), which constitute an interesting combination of baroque and impressionist
style. Polyphonic treatment and subtlety of tonal invention are by
no means incompatible, especially when the combination is effected by a temperament such as Martinu's. The First Piano Concerto (1925), which served to introduce Martinu to Paris, belongs
in this category.

After *Half Time*, Martinu began to return to Czech folklore.
He saw a new ideal in the Czech drama, the theater rooted in the

life of the people. He sought to produce music that was simple, without technical problems, like the folk songs of the Czechs. To fulfill this plan, he conceived a definite scheme, desiring to train and educate a whole retinue of coworkers (stage managers, conductors, directors of the ballet, etc.) who were to continue his work in the field of the drama. According to his theory, Czech opera had heretofore confined itself to certain definite and restricted themes, treating either rustic life or heroic-historical subjects. His aim was to introduce into Czech operatic literature new themes and sources, above all the rich material of Czech folklore, the countless poetic Czech legends, folk games, children's games, miracle plays, and the themes of the strolling players at the country fairs.

The first contribution to this field is his popular ballet *Špaliček* (1931), written in the style of a variety show, with rapid change of scenes and many colorful portrayals of Czech life, with the text drawn from Czech folk tales. *The Miracle of Our Lady* embodies his theory of opera, different from that of Wagner. This musical medieval miracle play consists of three parts, each independent of both the others. One of these, "Mariken of Nimwegen," is based on a text by Henri Ghéon; another, "The Birth of Our Lord," stems from an old folk-legend; the third, "Sister Pascalina," is also derived from a popular text. In this opera, the chorus, like that of the classic tragedy, has the function of commenting upon the action, of serving as "narrator." To these musical dramas of Martinu we must also add the ballet *The Theater Behind the Tower* (1935), a kind of Czech *commedia dell' arte*, with a Czech Harlequin and Columbine, and a series of folk songs. All the texts were written by the composer himself.

We should not forget to mention two radio operas, *The Voice of the Forest* (1935) and the *Comedy on a Bridge* (1936), which were primarily intended for performance by an ensemble of amateur actors and singers, like the *Schulopern* known to German students. Finally, we have his first grand opera, *Juliette* (1938), with a text by Georges Neveux. Actually, Martinu here abandons the local and the folklore field and creates a great symphonic drama.

Perhaps this is the appropriate moment in which to explain something of Martinu's artistic procedure and method of work. His dominating principle was to attain, above all, clear thematic development and a transparency of melodic line on a foundation of absolute music. He never sought for effect, but aimed to impress by simple, almost primitive, means. All the single elements of his musical form (polyphonic treatment, harmony, and tone color) were made subordinate to the organic flow of the whole work. For this last reason, we find in his work a deep understanding of clear construction and form, organic unity of the whole. The melodic line is chaste and pure, concentrated in form, removed from all romantic and sentimental discursiveness and chatter. The theme never appears in its complete form at the beginning, as it does in the work of the classic composers who vary it with tonal variations and imitations; with Martinu, it takes its final form gradually, as the whole phrase is rounded out and developed. The theme thus grows into a unified whole, becomes an image of the psychic growth. For this reason, Martinu makes no use of subsidiary or accessory themes. This feeling for rhythmic variety and architectural composition is certainly one of the inheritances of Czech musical culture. Martinu's ability to handle the orchestra reveals his long apprenticeship with the Czech Philharmonic Orchestra. We find in his work no vague, nebulous writing; the tone is always decided, transparent, and clear. Sometimes we find surprising tone effects. Equally admirable is his sense of workmanship and style: his chamber music is never orchestral in form, nor is his dramatic music merely symphonic in treatment.

Though romantic music may have enriched our musical culture by bringing to it emotion and sentiment, it was, nevertheless, bound up with the introduction of nonmusical elements into music. One of the consequences has been the confusion of genre, as the French call it, and a frequent discrepancy between intention and execution. This characteristic is best seen in the symphonic works of Mahler. Even the primitive idea of impressionistic musical writing, which was intrinsically far removed from tonal exaggeration, is turned by Mahler into empty illustrative writing, often becoming merely chaotic, nihilistic noise. By carefully observing this abuse, without prejudice, Martinu arrived at a new form of expression, first in his chamber music (*Ricercari, Double Concerto,* and *Concerto grosso*), then in his opera *Juliette.* His style is concentrated, following only the tenets laid down by his deeply musical nature, naïve, natural, spontaneous, and primitive.

Diametrically opposed to the principles of Wagner, Martinu confined his effects to the simplest means. Putting aside all Wagnerian dynamics, dramatics, and musical prophesying, he aimed at an autonomous musical development of themes. Let the stage be the stage, and (unlike Wagner) let it beware of trying to reach into the world of the spectator! No leitmotivs, no attempt at creative illustrative themes; only purely musical architecture! He was able to fit his text to his purposes, so that every element of the theater — gesture, facial expression, etc. — was one with the music. Martinu's diction in his operas was not dramatic recitative, but a kind of melos poetry, which is grounded exclusively in the musical line. The orchestra was merely accompaniment, never there for its own sake, approaching the ideal orchestra sought by Mozart. Martinu intended above all to arrive at an immediate and direct impression through purely musical means.

In *Juliette, Double Concerto, Ricercari* (1938), *Concerto grosso* (1938), and the First Symphony (1942), Martinu reached new heights in the expression of lyricism. His " mourning melody " is especially audible in his *Double Concerto*, written during the tragic fate of his people following the Munich Pact of 1938. It is, in fact, an elegy, which strikes the heart of the hearer deeply — a cry of despair. Lyrical song of the most expressive kind is also found in his Concerto for Violin and Orchestra (1943) and in the pastoral Second Symphony (1943).

With Stravinsky, Krenek, Hindemith, and other modern composers, Martinu shared the interest in baroque and classical musical forms, as seen in his *Toccata e due canzoni* (1946), among other works. In his youth he became acquainted with the *Sinfonia concertante* of Haydn. While in Princeton, in 1948, he discovered the score of that symphony, which so fascinated him that he wrote his own *Sinfonia concertante*, for four solo instruments, strings, and piano. According to his statement, he composed the work in order to intimate the optimism and happiness reflected in Haydn's compositions. Martinu's archaic tendencies are stressed further in his Concerto for Harpsichord and Chamber Orchestra (1935), and the *Concerto da camera*, for violin, strings, and timpani (1941). Other major works from his later years are his Sixth Symphony, *Fantaisies symphoniques* (1955), his opera *The Marriage*, based on Gogol, and performed by the NBC Television Opera Company in 1953, and *What Men Live By*, after Tolstoy (1953). In 1956 he dedicated to Rafael Kubelík his tone poem *The Frescoes of Piero della Francesca*. His operas *La Locandiera*, after Goldoni (1954), *Greek Passion*, after Nikos Kazantzakes (1956), and *Ariane*, after G. Neveux

(1958), should also be mentioned. This international trend did not prevent him from lingering on memories of his childhood, as seen by his *Variations on a Slovaenian Theme* (1958) and numerous Czech and Polish dances. In the last of these he even surpasses Dvořák and Smetana in a somewhat stylized realism when imitating the sounds of a rural accordion playing popular dance music.

It has been the function of the Czech musician to bring to foreign countries that which is characteristically Czech in him. This has been the case since the eighteenth century. From that time on, the Czechs have worked abroad and have made their impress on the world of music. Among these exponents of a universal music we find Stamitz, Richter, Tomaschek, Smetana, Dvořák, and Janáček. Martinu, too, began as a national musician, but passing over and above it he reached international fame and significance. By his career he proved that he was a compatriot of Comenius and Masaryk, the philosophers who rose above their narrow nationalist phase to a universally valid and significant humanism.

(GIAN CARLO MENOTTI)

1911 -

BIOGRAPHY

GIAN CARLO MENOTTI was born in Cadegliano, Italy, on July 7, 1911. After attending the Milan Conservatory for three years, he came to the United States in 1928, where he established permanent residence. As a student at the Curtis Institute in Philadelphia he completed a one-act comic opera, *Amelia Goes to the Ball*, which was successfully performed in Philadelphia and New York in 1937 by members of the Curtis Institute under Fritz Reiner and in 1938 was given at the Metropolitan Opera in New York. Here, as in all later operas, he was his own librettist. (In 1957 he provided Samuel Barber with a libretto for his Pulitzer Prize-winning opera, *Vanessa*.) Menotti achieved outstanding acclaim for *The Medium* in 1946. Two subsequent operas received the Pulitzer Prize in music: *The Consul* in 1950 and *The Saint of Bleecker Street* in 1955. Another of his operas, *Amahl and the Night Visitors*, written for television in 1951, has been many times performed over television as a Christmas presentation. In 1958, Menotti initiated an annual summer festival of the arts, "The Festival of the Two Worlds," in Spoleto, Italy. After its introduction at the Opéra-Comique, Paris, on October 22, 1963, Menotti's comic opera *The Last Savage*, to his own libretto, was staged by the Metropolitan Opera, New York, on January 23, 1964.

PERSONAL NOTE

Winthrop Sargeant

GIAN CARLO MENOTTI is a handsome, rather rangy Americanized Italian who fits none of the accepted formulas of the Broadway success story. He is not interested in Hollywood offers. He has already worked in Hollywood and doesn't think much of it. He isn't particularly interested in money. " For me money is a poison," he has said. " I don't want it. Let them drown in it. I will drown in something else."

To people who like to think that Menotti has demonstrated that Broadway rather than the Metropolitan is the place for modern opera, he is a disappointment. He doesn't think very highly of the Metropolitan's methods, but he doesn't think much of Broadway either. " Broadway," he affirms with great enthusiasm, " supports some of the worst atrocities that have ever been seen. . . . The theater is thought of as entertainment, not as art. It is time that we boycott that form of theater." In fact, Gian Carlo Menotti seems to have a scunner against the very idea of success. When favorable reviews started coming in after the opening of *The Consul,* he cut short the overjoyed comments of his backers. " Now," he cautioned solemnly, " is the time for humility." Later he explained, " Artists must be very stubborn. What defeats the artist in America today is his willingness to compromise in order to achieve success."

Aside from his rather formidable ideas about art and commercialism, Gian Carlo Menotti is a polished yet boyish and quietly exuberant individual with a poet's absent-mindedness, a fiction writer's irreverence for fact, and an insatiable curiosity about people. His conversation is apt to consist entirely of superlatives. When he is questioned about his own life, these superlatives are apt to expand into complete fantasies, which he solemnly insists are as true as gospel. He loves horror stories, magicians, and spiritual mediums. He once hired the hypnotist Polgar, whom he met at a party of Greta Garbo's, to hypnotize him and was sincerely pained when the hypnotism failed to work. A deeply preoccupied driver, he has collided with numerous roadside warning lights while piloting his car

to and from Manhattan. He once absent-mindedly described his
height on an immigration questionnaire as 11 feet 5 instead of 5
feet 11. He speaks English with an Italian accent, writes it with the
elegance of a professional man of letters, and believes it to be the
ideal language for opera. He is also an occasional and hopelessly
incompetent devotee of tennis, which he plays with what he likes to
regard as typically Anglo-Saxon enthusiasm. He is a prodigious and
inaccurate gossip, with an obsessive interest in the private lives of
others. One of his close associates recounts how, on an ocean voyage, Menotti spent hours listening through the wall of his stateroom
to a fight between a couple in the next cabin. He has on occasion
been surprised surreptitiously reading the diaries and private letters
of his acquaintances, the surprise seeming to cause him no embarrassment whatever.

Menotti shares a neat, ultramodern, and fancifully furnished
house at Mount Kisco with the well-known American composer
Samuel Barber and a poet, Robert Horan. There he spends most of
his spare time in spirited conversation and such harmless pursuits
as bird feeding and the contemplation of a fine collection of modern
paintings and Italian folk sculptures. The house contains a radio, a
phonograph, a wire recorder, none of which works. It also contains
Menotti's mascot, a near-life-size marionette of a medieval warrior
in full armor called Orlando. The studio where he works is a small,
cramped room just large enough to hold himself and a grand piano.

Menotti sees few of his fellow musicians, and often expresses
his distaste for the esoteric technical fads that are the rage of high-
brow " modern music " circles. What he particularly doesn't like is
what he describes as " chicness," the tendency of modern composers
to overlook sentiment and insist on being smartly and dissonantly in
tune with the latest musical vogues. " Sophistication per se," he
maintains, " is the antithesis of music. Music can express only fundamental, immediate emotion." When he is accused of writing sentimental music he sticks unabashedly to his position. " Well, all
right," he exclaims. " Why not be sentimental sometimes? "

Actually, what more austere and high-brow composers refer to
as his sentimentality is one of the human qualities that cause Menotti's operas to stand out as little masterpieces in their field.

THE COMPOSER SPEAKS

Gian Carlo Menotti [1]

OPERA is the very basis of theater. In all civilizations, people sang their dramas before they spoke them. I am convinced that the prose theater is an offspring of these earlier musicodramatic forms and not vice versa. The need for music accompanying dramatic action is still so strongly felt that in our most popular dramatic form, the cinema, background music is used to underline even the most prosaic and realistic situations.

It is unfair to accuse opera of being an old-fashioned and ungainly dramatic form. Actually, what people put forth as examples is largely the operatic output of the nineteenth century. Considering the length of time that has gone by since then, it is quite amazing what life there still is in those old pieces. How many plays of that same period have survived this test as well? Wouldn't most of us prefer hearing a Verdi opera to sitting through a Victor Hugo play? I may even venture to say that many of the so-called " great plays " of this century will be forgotten when dear old *Traviata* is still holding the boards. All of this cannot be explained away simply by condemning as foolish or gullible millions of music lovers.

To criticize a theater piece as too theatrical is as senseless as to criticize a piece of music for being too musical. There is only one kind of bad theater: when the author's imagination steps outside the very area of illusion he has created. But as long as the dramatic creates within that area, almost no action on the stage is too violent or implausible. As a matter of fact, the skill of the dramatist is almost measurable by his ability to make even the most daring and unpredictable seem inevitable. After all, what could be more theatrical than the last entrance of Oedipus or the death of Hamlet or the insanity of Oswald in *Ghosts*?

The important thing is that behind these apparent excesses of

[1] These paragraphs appeared in an article by Menotti in *The New York Times Magazine*.

action, the author is able to maintain that significant symbolism which is the very essence of dramatic illusion. In the words of Goethe: " When all is said and done, nothing suits the theater except what also makes a symbolic appeal to the eyes. A significant action suggesting a more significant one." Modern dramatists are much too timid about " theater," and such timidity is fatal to an opera composer, for music intensifies feeling so quickly that, unless a situation is symbolically strong enough to bear this intensity, it becomes ludicrous by contrast.

Nothing in the theater can be as exciting as the amazing quickness with which music can express a situation or describe a mood. Whereas, in the prose theater, it often requires many words to establish a single effect, in an opera one note on the horn will illuminate the audience. It is this very power of music to express feelings so much more quickly than words that make librettos, when read out of the musical context, appear rather brutal and unconvincing.

There is no such thing as a good or bad libretto per se. A good libretto is nothing but one that inspires a composer to write good music. *Götterdämmerung* would have been a bad libretto indeed for Puccini, and I can imagine nothing more disastrous than Wagner deciding to set *Madama Butterfly* to music.

Too many people think that only exotic subjects from the past are suitable for an opera. That is nothing but a romantic inheritance from the last century. Just as modern poets have been moved to examine and interpret the uniquely contemporary life, there is no reason why the composer should not do the same. That is not to say that modern opera must have a contemporary subject. As Lorca, Eliot, or Dylan Thomas have found inspiration in sources as varied as folklore, remote historical events, or newspaper headlines, so should the composer permit himself that same freedom.

One may ask why, if opera is a valid and vital form, it hasn't stimulated more successful contemporary contributions to the theater. Most modern composers blame their failures on the librettos, but I am afraid that the fault more often lies with the music. Opera is, after all, essentially music, and such is the ennobling or transfiguring power of music that we have numerous examples of what safely could be labeled awkward plays transformed into inspiring operas. We have, however, no single example of a successful opera whose main strength is the libretto. I have often been accused of writing good librettos and mediocre music, but I maintain that my librettos become alive or illuminated only through my music. Let anyone read one of my texts divorced from its musical setting to discover the truth of what I say. My operas are either good or bad; but if their librettos seem alive or powerful in performance, then the music must share this distinction.

One of the reasons for the failure of so much contemporary opera is that its music lacks immediacy of communication. Theater music must make its point and communicate its emotion at the same moment the action develops. It cannot wait to be understood until after the curtain comes down. Mozart understood this, and there is a noticeable difference in immediacy between some of his symphonic or chamber-music styles on the one hand and his operatic style on the other. Many contemporary composers seem to fear clarity and directness, perhaps because they are afraid of becoming obvious. To quote Goethe: " We must not disdain what is immediately visible and sensuous. Otherwise we shall be sailing without ballast."

MENOTTI

Robert Sabin

WHATEVER Gian Carlo Menotti's permanent place in the history of opera may turn out to be, there is no question about the tremendous impact that his brilliant and versatile talent has had upon the contemporary musical theater. If not one of the fixed stars, he will at least have figured as a dazzling comet. For a quarter of a century he has turned out a series of works that have invariably proved to be dynamic living theater, whatever their musical and dramatic failings.

Although he is unquestionably an eclectic composer, Menotti has always given an original twist to his borrowings, and he has constantly experimented with new ideas in the theater. At the very beginning of his career, we find the influence of Italian *opera buffa* especially strong, with Wolf-Ferrari as a major source of inspiration. Then, Menotti turns toward *verismo* (as did Wolf-Ferrari), and we find him choosing themes from contemporary life and infusing the sensationalism of his material with an undertone of political and social reality. Unlike Puccini, who has obviously been very dear to him, as well as a model in many ways, Menotti has not shied away from realism, but has mingled it freely with the fantastically imaginative strain that invariably breaks out in his operas.

Thus, we have a curiously diverse musical personality — a skillful and witty comedian who nonetheless writes grim and horrible tragedies; an heir to the past who does not hesitate to satirize his beloved masters; a realistic social commentator who bursts out into the most fantastic impossibilities; a musical traditionalist who commits hair-raising musical heresies without the flicker of an eyelash.

Small wonder that Menotti himself has supervised and directed the productions of most of his operas and that they have, more often than not, been given in theaters as musical dramas rather than in the grand-opera houses of the world. Nor should we be surprised that *The Medium* proved to be a vastly better motion picture than the film adaptations of Puccini, Verdi, and other operatic masters of the past.

The Menotti who burst upon the American scene in 1937 with the production of *Amelia Goes to the Ball* was obviously a young man who had a fresh lyric talent but whose feet were firmly planted on the ground of operatic tradition. This work, which reached the stage of the Metropolitan Opera on March 3, 1938, after its production by the Curtis Institute at the Academy of Music in Philadelphia and on Broadway, has since been given by the New York City Opera. It has invariably charmed its audiences, and it must be admitted that Menotti has never surpassed its spontaneity and verve. The milieu — Milan, 1900 — had a nostalgic attraction for the composer, who had played the piano as a boy in the salons of the wealthy Milanese. The libretto, which he wrote himself (as he always has), revealed a genuine literary gift as well as a sprightly dramatic invention. (Menotti's original Italian was expertly adapted in English by George Meade.) And the score bubbled over with melodic bonbons and harmonic conceits. It boasted a romanza for each of the leading characters, effective duets and trios, and an uproarious finale with chorus. True, the materials would not bear too close inspection as to durable quality and originality of invention, but no one cared, so delightful was the *brio* of this youthful comedy.

The " Americanization " of Menotti was apparent in *The Old Maid and the Thief* (1939), his second venture into the realm of *opera buffa*. In this hour-long comedy, which showed how " a virtuous woman made a thief of an honest man," the terseness, the homeliness, and the breezy freedom of the music and libretto are typically American. The setting is no longer Milan but an American village; the types are no longer European, but unmistakably American. Menotti has already become a master of easy, flowing recitative, interspersed with solos and ensembles. True, the actual music of this bright and somewhat brittle comedy shows little or no trace of the American musical vernacular, but this was perfectly understandable in a young composer whose head was still full of European music, although he was rapidly forming and ripening his own style.

A new Menotti was revealed in *The Island God*, a poetically symbolistic and grandiose tragic opera that was produced by the Metropolitan Opera in 1942. Also one hour in length, with one act and three scenes with musical interludes, it was the antithesis of his previous work in all respects. The heavy orchestration with resounding brass was influenced by late Puccini, as were the large-scale solos and duets. The musical dialogue at the opening of the opera and elsewhere showed that he had lost none of his flair for this type of writing, but *The Island God* was obviously a gesture toward grand opera, although a stylized and personalized one. As in *Amelia Goes to the Ball*, Menotti composed his music to his own Italian libretto, which proved readily adaptable to singable English, this time in a version by Fleming McLiesh. The trouble was that *The Island God* was neither fish nor flesh, and Menotti simply could not summon a sufficient intensity and grandeur of lyric expression to make a lasting impression in so ambitious a vein.

But the lessons he learned in this venture were not wasted, for he hit upon a new style, wholly his own and completely integrated, in his next work, *The Medium* (1946). From its ominous, crashing opening chords to its horrifying ending, this music drama never faltered or lost its grip upon the audience. There were no disturbing " set pieces " or passages of conventional filler. Everything flowed naturally into everything else, and the peaks of lyrical expression were reached through dramatic development. And Menotti, the master of theatrical illusion, came into his own in this lurid and somehow convincing story of a woman caught in the coils of the superstitious belief she was using to exploit others.

All of the elements that constitute Menotti's major contribution to the contemporary musical theater are found at their best in *The Medium:* a naturalistic and musically adept handling of recitative, which blends imperceptibly into heightened melodic expression; a small orchestra employed with such consummate skill that one feels no need for the impact of the gigantic grand-opera ensemble; a fully rounded dramatic treatment in which all minor characters are clearly and lovingly delineated; melodic ideas of a more or less traditional character transformed by freely dissonant harmonic treatment and bizarre orchestral color; an intimacy of style and atmosphere more like the theater than the opera house, but always translated into musical terms.

The Telephone (1947), Menotti's next work, was an occasional piece, but nonetheless full of wit and a satirical allusiveness. Far more sophisticated than *The Old Maid and the Thief*, it thumbs its nose at traditional opera while showing at the same time an affectionate dependence. It is light and frothy but not trivial.

From this persiflage Menotti turned to the grimmest realism and tragedy in *The Consul* (1950), his most ambitious and his most uneven work up to this time. Although it revealed little creative musical growth, this powerful indictment of political persecution positively seared audiences with its superbly contrived dramatic suspense and musical coloration.

Certain dangerous flaws in Menotti's style appear all too clearly. For one thing, he begins to grow careless about the insertion of solos and ensembles, which jar us and do not blend with the surrounding texture of the work. Thus the conventional trio for Magda, John, and the Mother in Act I, Scene 1, is a severe letdown from the swift, staccato action that surrounds it. Much solider and more convincing music would be needed for contrast here. And the ensembles in Act I, Scene 2, and Act III, Scene 2, are bits of musical stucco where we need steely strength. Nor does the profound seriousness of the theme make it possible to get away with a shameless tear-jerker like the Grandmother's song to the dying baby: " Won't you smile for Granny? "

And Menotti's wild and unbridled imagination leads him into

introducing fantastic episodes that clash violently with the realistic human purpose of the rest of the work. Cleverly limned as is the character of Nika Magadoff, the professional magician, he wreaks a great deal of harm to this drama. And such passages as that in which Magda pulls her head out of the gas oven to listen to a cheap marching song outrage our sense of dramatic rightness and musical conviction.

But, with all its weaknesses on its head, *The Consul* remains a masterly bit of modern theater. If the set pieces are weak and out of style, the recitative is magnificently handled and the orchestral background is tremendously effective. Menotti's tricky but successful modulations serve him well; he uses harmony as an integral part of his expressive technique as a dramatist. And such moments as Magda's heroic denunciation of the cruelty of man to man are great theater, even though they are not great music.

The Protean Menotti takes us into another new world in his next work, *Amahl and the Night Visitors* (1951). Here we find little trace of the feverish tension of the preceding tragedy, although he characteristically introduces into this touching and lyrical narrative of the Three Wise Men on their way to Bethlehem a dramatic episode of supposed theft and protective mother love. In the airs and dances of the shepherds as well as in Amahl's music, we are charmed by an unforced, if sophisticated, lyricism. And, again characteristically, Menotti has drawn upon a wealth of childhood memories and keen observations of human eccentricity in his musical portraits of the royal pilgrims. Composed for television, this work is especially notable for its clever adaptation to the medium. It maintains a lively visual line of development while avoiding any unduly static musical episodes. Yet one never has the sense of abruptness or spottiness.

The major faults and virtues of *The Consul* recur in *The Saint of Bleecker Street* (1954). This fantastic composite of styles and idioms, held together by the sheer force of the composer's imagination, has a stunning theatrical impact. The music, often tawdry but always enormously skillful, leans heavily on Mascagni and Puccini — and not the best. But only Menotti could have contrived to blend the raw realism and religious mystery of the libretto into a fabric that holds, dramatically, from beginning to end.

After a rather stiff opening, hampered by a sugar-coated religiosity in the choruses and other passages, Menotti reaches his full stride in Annina's tremendous scene in which she receives the stigmata — a genuine tour de force. At the opposite end of the emotional pole, Desideria's luscious aria in Act II combines the sensuous smoothness of Duparc with the dramatic punch of Mascagni. Once again, Menotti has trouble with set pieces. The duet of Michele and Desideria takes us straight back to conventional opera, and Maria Corona's tragicomic ditty in the subway scene is completely out of context. But the final scene is deeply moving, as the dying Annina takes the veil.

In *Maria Golovin* (1958) Menotti avoids the harsh, almost brutal violence of his writing in *The Consul* and *The Saint of Bleecker Street,* while retaining a typically melodramatic and sentimental plot. The score is a patchwork of borrowings from previous works of his own as well as from various masters from Puccini to Debussy, but it has a new refinement of texture and delicacy of color. And it is unmistakably Menotti, for all its eclecticism. Once again, in the extremely amusing dialogue of Dr. Zuckertanz on the arts, we find one of those interpolated numbers which the composer loves to inject into a foreign context. In the blind boy, Donato, we encounter one of those physical handicaps which Menotti uses so cleverly to heighten pathos. And the contrast between the Mother, Maria, and the sluttish, jealous Agata represents a familiar formula. But although the ingredients are the same, this master of musical cuisine always knows how to whip up a new dish with a fresh recipe.

Menotti has now perfected his dramatic and musical technique to the point where he can do pretty much as he pleases in the theater. But the great question mark remains as far as the actual quality of his music and the durability of his dramatic ideas are concerned. Has he been too versatile, too clever, too adaptable to theatrical conditions? Time will tell. But one thing is certain: he has enlarged the theatrical vocabulary of his time and he has inspired a whole school of young opera composers. This in itself is a major achievement.

(DARIUS MILHAUD)

1892 -

BIOGRAPHY

DARIUS MILHAUD was born in Aix-en-Provence, France, on September 4, 1892. In 1909 he entered the Paris Conservatory, where for the next few years he was a pupil of Gédalge, Widor, Dukas, and Vincent d'Indy, among others. He won prizes for counterpoint, fugue, and composition. In 1917 he became an attaché to Paul Claudel at the French Legation in Rio de Janeiro, where he wrote several works for the stage to texts by Claudel and compositions influenced by the popular idioms of Latin America. After returning to France, he first became widely known in 1920 when, in a newspaper article, Henri Collet linked his name with those of five young French composers (Auric, Durey, Poulenc, Honegger, and Tailleferre) and baptized the group " The French Six," or " Les Six." In 1922, Milhaud visited the United States, making appearances as lecturer and as pianist and conductor in performances of his works. With a prolific output of major works in all possible forms and media — some in a popular idiom, others in an ultramodern style — Milhaud rapidly assumed a dominant position in French music, until, with the death of Ravel, he was generally conceded to be France's foremost composer.

In 1940, Milhaud settled for several years in America, serving as a member of the faculty of Mills College in California. Though stricken by a crippling arthritis, which made locomotion both difficult and painful, Milhaud continued making guest appearances as conductor, conducting while seated. After the end of World War II he began to divide the year between his activities in Paris, where he became professor at the Conservatory, and the United States.

PERSONAL NOTE

Robert Lawrence

DARIUS MILHAUD is a formidable man. On first meeting, you have the sensation of running up against a wall of granite, such are the reserve and feeling of strength that his massive size and crowning shock of black hair engender. Later this opening manner may give way to real warmth tinged with an attractive irony. But Milhaud's dignity is the common denominator of the composer and of his music.

He hates insincerity in any form, sparing no one if he suspects an interested motive or an opinion that runs contrary to inbred feeling. It used to be said that at Mills College, in Oakland, California, where he taught for half a dozen years, Milhaud did not hesitate to be short with renowned visitors from the East, while extending at the same time the most courtly treatment to young students. The keynote to the man's character is his love of youth and of freshness in art and in life; his aversion to the static and pretentious. And as a crystallization of this attitude has come the latest phase in Milhaud's career — that of educator. His present reputation in this country is based as much upon the vitality he has brought into teaching as upon his music.

My own introduction to Milhaud took place years ago in Vichy. Those were the days before Franco-German collaborationists had taken over a delightful spa. The only hint of what was to come lay in Jeunesse Française posters, violent in tone, displayed in the windows of empty shops. And we all drank tea at the golf club across the river Allier with Richard Strauss, who was visiting the resort.

The late Albert Roussel was there, too, along with Jacques Ibert, Kurt Atterberg, Peder Gram, and other noted musicians, attending an international congress of composers. As Milhaud and his smart-looking blonde wife, Madeleine, sat at the tea table near the stream, which was honeycombed with fish nets, they spoke of the United States, of their travels here, and of their intimacy with the English language.

When next I saw them — aside from brief glimpses at New York's Lewisohn Stadium and Carnegie Hall — they were in residence at Oakland's Mills College in a charming little house on the hill. That was in the summer of 1941. For those who are unfamiliar with the surroundings of San Francisco, Oakland is the local Brooklyn, without the charm or traditions of Manhattan's neighboring borough. Yet Mills College is a cultural oasis there and fosters a definite intellectual life.

Again the occasion of our meeting was a meal — lunch, this time. In the serenity of the Milhaud household — a serenity that had been achieved only at the cost of a harrowing and heartbreaking flight from France — the Milhauds entertained three young American composers, their son Daniel (who at the age of twelve proved to be a roaring bass-baritone), and myself. The talk turned to composition and the growth of American talent. And I saw that the whole direction of Milhaud's career had turned from one of free play to an active and stimulating contact with students. He was now a powerful force, aside from his own achievements in the field of creative music, in our universities. And he, along with a few others, was doing much to remove the drabness and monotony that often attach themselves, with justice, to the phrase " music education."

THE COMPOSER SPEAKS

Darius Milhaud [1]

THE MOST difficult thing in music is still to write a melody of several bars that can be self-sufficient. That is the secret of music. Although the technique should be as perfected as possible, that is a lesser essential. Anybody can acquire a brilliant technique. The important thing is the vital element — the melody — which should be easily retained, hummed, and whistled on the street. Without this fundamental element, all the technique in the world can only be a dead letter.

A composer should be acquainted with all of music; above all,

[1] This statement was written by the composer expressly for this book.

he should love all music that is worthy of being loved. Beyond this, a young musician should not permit himself to be shut within the prison of any one system. He should develop the wealth of his fantasy and of his imagination, and constantly strive to renew his means of expression.

He should learn to familiarize himself with the secrets of every technique. Diatonic expression may lead one primarily into the polytonal domain, but it should not exclude the study of atonal chromaticism. What I cannot tolerate is the slavish adherence to any one system. Why should one limit his means of expression? It is not easy, in the first place, to express oneself. All the different stages through which musical technique has passed should enrich our present musical idiom. When one speaks of tonality, bitonality, polytonality, atonality, or neoclassicism, all this seems to me to be an elementary and almost useless division of music into compartments. We should make use of everything at our disposal that can help a work to present itself as fully and as completely as possible. We should open our windows wide on an unlimited musical horizon.

I have never been able to understand the establishment of different categories in music: classical music and modern music; serious music and light music. It is most unjust. There is only *music*, and one can find it in a café melody or an operetta tune as well as in a symphony, an opera, or a work of chamber music.

Overlengthy developments and useless repetitions are to be avoided. We should strive to maintain exact proportions in every work. Sobriety and simplicity are the best counselors of any composer. A solid and logical construction is indispensable. I am left helpless in the presence of rhapsodic works devoid of structure or overladen with endless developments of unnecessary complexity.

But each work calls for its own special style. A quartet is not written in the same way that a ballet is, or a film score like a sonata. The composer must adapt his tendencies, and remember that a ballet must be danced to, and must be subject to choreographic necessity; also that a film must move a wide and varied public at the same time that it preserves the pure expression of the composer. The composition of an opera or a quartet demands the same love as a score for the theater, in which the dramatic necessity limits the composer, and where often a gripping atmosphere has to be created within a few bars.

I have no esthetic rules, or philosophy, or theories. I love to write music. I always do it with pleasure, otherwise I just do not write it. I have always made it my business to accept musical jobs of every kind. Naturally, there are certain types of work that I prefer; but a composer should do everything with application, with all the resources of contemporary technique at his disposal. He can then hope that, after a life of hard work, he will see some works survive, works in which the melodic line has impressed itself indelibly on the memory; for melody alone — the only living element in music — permits a work to survive.

MILHAUD

Norman Demuth

Milhaud's opus numbers hover about the four-hundred mark. Before this wealth (the irreverent might call it this plethora) of music, the commentator can be forgiven for being dismayed. No one except Milhaud himself can claim with truth to know it all.

However, many of these opus numbers represent music that is small and ephemeral: film and theater scores, songs, piano pieces, and so forth. Milhaud labels everything with an opus number. Opening Georges Beck's *Catalogue chronologique complet* at random discloses that this policy can extend from an enormous opera, *Les Euménides*, op. 41 (1917–22), to a small *Poème de Corneille* for voice and piano, op. 178 (1937); from the Fifth Symphony, op. 322 (1953), to " Chat," op. 356 (1956), the last a small song to Jean Cocteau's words. It would appear, therefore, that opus numbers can be deceptive.

Milhaud has always been prolific and has been gifted with undiminishing facility. There is nothing wrong here, since there is nothing slick, apart from some youthful indiscretions. I see few signs of fluency, however. Ideas obviously come easily to him, and it is for the individual to separate the wheat from the chaff according to his own personal taste and judgment. I do not know how much Milhaud tears up — a weekly examination of composers' wastebaskets would be illuminating and enlightening.

A close study of Milhaud's catalogue reveals that his purely orchestral works are comparatively few, compared with the number written for soloists with orchestra. All his concertos have been composed with a specific soloist in view, and their value varies. I am unable to say if it was Yvonne Astruc or Spring that impelled the idea of the charming *Concertino de printemps*, op. 135 (1934); there have since been the *Concertino d'automne*, op. 309 (1950), for two pianos and eight instruments, *Concertino d'été*, op. 311 (1951), for viola and chamber orchestra, and *Concerto d'hiver*, op. 327 (1953), for trombone and strings. Nor can I say if it was Stell Andersen or nostalgia for Provence that impelled him to write the equally charming *Fantaisie pastorale*, op. 188 (1938). I have no doubt, however, that these works would have been written in any case because the poetry of the four seasons would in all probability have given Milhaud the initial urge.

On the other hand, there seems to be a certain attraction to Hindemithian *Gebrauchsmusik* in those works which have no avowed or apparent romantically objective background, and Milhaud appears to have succumbed to the wiles of performers and written music that otherwise might well not have been composed. This is not to suggest that Milhaud's works pour along a conveyor belt or that there is a factory for their production; it is here that he displays his powers of craftsmanship, powers that sometimes do not come up to the required standards of artistry. For example, I can see little justification for the First Violin Concerto, op. 93 (1927), save that it should show off the technical prowess of Mme Sitter-Sapin. The first and third movements are devoid of musicality and consist mainly of explosive rhythms of an interesting, but in no sense musical, kind, the third being emptier of ideas than the first; and the second reflecting its composer's South American sojourn (for its tune is subtle and insidious), strongly redolent of a high-class Rio café.

I doubt very much if he would have written a Concerto for Marimba-Vibraphone, op. 278 (1947), had the idea not been put into his head by Jack Connor, but I am very surprised that he has never written one for Ondes Martenot.

Commissions and requests have often come his way, but, by and large, Milhaud's works, particularly his large operas, have been written because he is a *compositeur malgré lui*. Sometimes the two impulses have coincided. Regarding "symphony" in its fullest sense as a climax to a career or at least an enterprise to be post-poned until full maturity, Milhaud determined not to write a full-scale one until he was fifty years old. However, he commenced and terminated his First Symphony three years in advance of this anniversary, and it coincided with a request for a work of substance from the Chicago Symphony Orchestra.

Milhaud was the iconoclast of " Les Six " and was not taken altogether seriously during the 1920's. It was the less serious side of his musicality that was first revealed outside France, while inside his country the outlook of the group as a whole led to a bad kind of *snobisme*. Too many manifestoes were issued. Too many idols were knocked down. Too often the watchword was " à bas." The " smart " ballets of Serge Diaghilev, to which Milhaud contrib-uted *Le Train bleu*, op. 84 (1924), were taken so seriously that they came to be regarded as the standard seriously impelled works of their generation instead of what they were, simply jolly, slightly mad, entertainments. Essentials and a return to simplicity became the war cry. " Symphony " as such was to be abolished, and the genre was to return to mere statement of " sound " for a number of instru-ments. No more symphonic developments or processes — " À bas d'Indy! " — hence the *Petites Symphonies*, opp. 43, 49, 74, 75, 79 (1917, 1918, 1921, 1923). No more impressionism, for French music was to be taken out of the hothouse — " À bas Debussy, Dukas! " But Romanticism remained, for Milhaud's First and Sec-ond *Petites Symphonies* bore the subtitles *Le Printemps* and *Pas-torale* respectively, and the Third, *Sérénade*. Further, the Second Violin Sonata, op. 40 (1917), could boast a beautiful bucolic first movement and a gloriously imagined second, the third being redo-lent of the French countryside and peasantry.

Why go to poetry for words to set to music? Milhaud found them in catalogues: *Machines agricoles*, op. 56 (1919), and *Cata-logue de fleurs*, op. 60 (1920). The latter was not so original as all that, as Jean-Philippe Rameau had said that he felt himself capable of setting a similar price list with the greatest of ease. As for the return to simplicity — did not Jean-Jacques Rousseau preach that gospel in the eighteenth century?

In retrospect, all this seems very small fry to have upset the musical esthetics of an entire culture, and one doubts if it would have been so universally effective had not Stravinsky been active in Paris at that time and formed a kind of unofficial background for revolution; but it served its purpose, since it gave tradition and convention a severe shaking. So far as Milhaud was concerned, it aroused his interest in the timbres obtainable with small instrumental forces. This interest touched a novel plane with the three *opéras-minutes: L'Enlèvement d'Europe*, op. 94 (1927), *L'Abandon d'Ariane*, op. 98 (1927), and *La Délivrance de Thésée*, op. 99 (1927), wherein he put his policy of using single orchestral soloists into practice.

It is only right to point out that while this group was effective and extremely vocal, a very great number of younger and older French composers did not subscribe to its principles, their music being in every way just as " up to date," if not so fashionable: Delvincourt, Roussel, Rivier, Jolivet, and so forth.

Unfortunately, all this activity drew away from the really serious side of Milhaud, and most people were unaware of the fine original thought that was underlying the popular high jinks. The rhythms he brought back from Brazil had a certain fascination, but seemed out of place in the concert hall, and when the Symphonic Suite from the music to Claudel's *Protée*, op. 57 (1919), was played at a Concert Colonne concert under Gabriel Pierné, the scenes equaled those which witnessed the production of *Le Sacre du printemps*. The gentle sway of the *Saudades do Brasil*, op. 67 (1920–1), for piano, however, had a different effect. But were there not a great many " wrong notes " in them?

Milhaud's early friendship with Claudel influenced his whole musical life. Milhaud wrote the incidental music for Claudel's translation of the *Oresteia* of Aeschylus. The first part, *Agamemnon*, op. 14 (1913–14), is rhetorical in style, and the music is mainly declamatory. There is hardly any free lyricism, and this *Dialogue de Clytemnestre et du Chœur*, of which it consists, is in the style of *recitativo stromentato espressivo*. In addition to a full instrumental force, a chorus is used orchestrally. The work forms a most original *scena*.

Part II, *Les Choëphores*, op. 24 (1915), is a more serious proposition, and here can be found the first step toward a consistent use of polytonality. This section consists of seven movements, and the whole makes a satisfactory work in itself. The chorus is used orchestrally and vocalizes accompanimentally. The most notable feature is the use of spoken verbal rhythms, mostly delivered with great force. This is very effective and maintains dramatic continuity where dialogue spoken in the ordinary way would intrude upon the musical context. It concludes with a whispered " Où? Où? Où? " Nothing like this had ever been devised before, and it is interesting to note that it was composed while Milhaud was still in Widor's class at the Paris Conservatory.

Neither of these scores was written with actual stage production in view. Claudel's translation needed music, and Milhaud supplied the need, irrespective of its ultimate use.

Part III, *Les Euménides*, op. 41 (1917–22), sees the polytonal manner in its most complete form. This is a work of the highest magnitude and importance – and, it could be added, difficulty. The " battery " is used with great individuality, while the speech rhythms give a dramatic intensity impossible to imagine. With its massive columns of thirds, its consistency and extreme clarity, this work is one of the monuments of the twentieth century, but, alas, its resources make its appearances few and far between. It bears out what I have said, that Milhaud is a *compositeur malgré lui*, for it must have been written for the pure joy of so doing.

Milhaud's other large-scale operas proved him to be a dramatic composer of great power and ability – indeed, I would go so far as to say that it is in this world that he reigns supreme today. For one who initially preached the gospel of compression, it is quite surprising to follow his progress. The climax so far has been *Bolivar*, op. 236 (1943), which kept the audience in the Paris Opéra for some hours and earned its composer twenty-seven curtain calls at its première on May 12, 1950. Yet Milhaud derives from no one. It would be possible to see him in the descent from Meyerbeer and Wagner, not, let me hasten to add, in any musical sense, but in the approach to spectacular and symphonic opera. I can find little suggestion of any descent from Berlioz except, perhaps, in a general way relating to his use of the " battery." Milhaud himself would " give the whole of Wagner for one page of Berlioz," as was reported in *Entretiens avec Claude Rostand*.

It is impossible to divide Milhaud's output into so many " periods " unless we detach the early fashionable works, which, of course, are too dated, although they would include *La Création du monde*, op. 81a (1923), which did much to establish Milhaud in a world sense.

Milhaud composed eighteen string quartets; Nos. 14 and 15,

op. 291 (1948–49), comprising two such works, may be played simultaneously as an octet or separately as two distinct quartets. This is not altogether original, since Antonín Reicha (1770–1836) wrote a similarly divisible work. Milhaud's two quartets are well contrasted between themselves, but as separate entities each has its own consistency. In this genre Milhaud adopted a rather cold abstract approach, and the music is more interesting for its contrapuntal writing than for its esthetic appeal. Now and again there is a certain triviality in the counterpoint that makes a clear dividing line between Nos. 1 to 9 (1912–35) and Nos. 10 to 18 (1940–50).

Urban and sophisticated though Milhaud's earlier works may have been, he has always been at heart a Provençale, and some of his finest works have been written in the garden of his house, L'Enclos, in Aix. Like the *Suite provençale*, op. 152a (1936), the First Symphony, op. 210 (1939) — only twenty-two years separate this big work from the first *Petite Symphonie* — is redolent of the scenes and people round him. The movements are headed " Pastoral," " Très vif," " Très modéré," and " Final," the spirit of the first movement pervading the whole work. When World War II broke out in 1939, Milhaud was creatively paralyzed, and it was not until his arrival at Mills College in California that he began to recover his morale. There the influence of his surroundings, his ability to settle anywhere (thanks to a much betraveled life), and his contact with American composers and students encouraged him to continue thinking along big lines. His sense of patriotism made him try to vie with his hosts. The enormous resources that he found at his disposal gave him added hope and purpose, one of the most significant revelations being the composition of the Second Symphony, op. 247 (1944). Here the spirit is nostalgia, but the final movement, " Alléluia," suggests that by this time America had healed his sorrow.

Liberation began to be something realizable in French hearts, and in 1946 Milhaud was commissioned by the French Radio to compose a *Te Deum*. This was not enough for him. The *Te Deum* must be the climax to a great paean of thanksgiving, following a wordless choral *Pastoral*. Thus the Third Symphony, op. 271 (1946), took shape, and it traveled back to France for performance in 1947. This is the most directly personal and most deeply felt of his first four symphonies. The whole of Occupied France seems to be covered in it. This may be due to the impulse given by the text of the *Te Deum*, which emerges with nobility and grandeur. It is here that Milhaud disproves the theory that he has neither the ability nor the inclination to move his listeners.

In 1947 the Minister of Education commissioned a symphony to commemorate the 1848 Revolution, in further pursuance of the idea of liberation. The Fourth Symphony, op. 281 (1947), was composed on board ship on the Pacific and Atlantic oceans while returning from San Francisco to France. The movements are headed " L'Insurrection," " Aux Morts de la République," " Les Joies paisibles de la liberté retrouvée," and " Commémoration 1948." All this is not to be taken literally. The French have long since recovered from the political tyrannies of the eighteenth and nineteenth centuries, and this particular revolution is synonymous with liberation in general. It is idealistic in conception.

The first movement reflects a rising of the Provençale peasantry and a march upon the capital. It is suggested by a drum-and-cymbal rhythm and by certain piccolo tunes such as a village piper would play on the march. The strings underline these ordinary tunes in polyphony, giving them a significance of their own. The music gains force as it proceeds and in due course becomes expressive and pictorial. It is crude music underlining crude situations. There may be more skill than musical inspiration, but it is very vivid.

The second movement is a soliloquy, not a grim funeral march. Its chamber-music atmosphere and keen sense of tone contrast make it particularly poignant. There are no signs of folk music or modality, and the dead are the Dead of France, both rural and urban.

The happiness of liberation is manifest in the diatonic and triadic scherzo, which is never bombastic or revengeful.

The fourth movement logically consolidates the centenary in very much the same language as the first, but the period is 1947 and no reference is made to the songs of the original marchers. It is slapdash music, but well shaped.

There were to be no more symphonies until 1953, when Milhaud wrote his Fifth, op. 332. Milhaud did not share Honegger's reticence and his respect for " the Fifth," a respect that prevented him from using this numerical classification. Milhaud also showed no hesitancy in passing " the Ninth," for in 1960 he composed his Tenth Symphony, op. 382, the Ninth, op. 380, being finished a year earlier. Nos. 5 to 8 were composed at Mills College, where Milhaud went each year as a member of its music faculty; clearly the American milieu is conducive to his ideas, which spread over a wide canvas. The Fifth Symphony was commissioned by the Italian Radio; the Seventh, op. 344 (1955), by the Belgian Radio. The Sixth Symphony, op. 343 (1955), commemorates the seventy-fifth anniversary of the Boston Symphony Orchestra, while the Eighth, op. 362 (1957), is dedicated to the University of California in Berkeley.

Of this second set, I, personally, prefer the Eighth, which seems to me to differ in approach from the others and to be more highly contrasted. There are moments of extreme delicacy and charm, and the music always moves symphonically forward. However, one sometimes feels that the impulse is somewhat perfunctory and one result of routine thinking.

Perhaps Milhaud is most successful when there is an extra-musical approach to the symphony. He regards the genre as less formal but more fundamentally polyphonic than did Honegger. Form per se hardly concerns him, and he is more concerned with the interplay of themes, adding an apt new idea as it enters his head, than with their development. The music is spontaneous. If Milhaud is inclined to bang the orchestra about in his louder moments, the quieter ones are invariably impressive, and the texture is as clear as chamber music. All these works occupy an honorable niche in symphonic music for their individuality and originality.

In between there are lighter-weight symphonic scores like the *Symphoniette*, for strings, op. 363 (1957), and the *Symphonie concertante*, for trumpet, bassoon, double bassoon, and chamber orchestra, op. 376 (1959), together with concertos and various smaller works, all very much in the chamber-music spirit.

Meanwhile, Milhaud composed a large-scale opera, *David*, op. 320 (1952), for the King David Festival in Jerusalem in 1954. Unlike Honegger's *Le Roi David*, this is not an oratorio, "dramatic" or otherwise, but an opera on the scale of *Bolivar*. Milhaud himself regards this as one of his finest and most significant works.

If it is not possible to classify Milhaud's music into "periods," as I have suggested, it is possible to remark the ever-increasing contrapuntal bases of his works as his catalogue progresses. This is most notable in the works written after his first arrival at Mills College, when the style became, in general, less poetic and increasingly abstract. It would not be wrong to divide his output in terms of "art" and "craft," the former denoting those works which seemingly were impelled from within, regardless of any performers, and those written "to order" without very much overt impulse save to make music. In the latter case, the counterpoint often follows much the same pattern and does not bear the mark of necessitous composition. In the case of the chamber music, the quartets and quintets are more interesting to play than to listen to and may be said therefore to have succeeded, since this genre was intended primarily for performance and not for listening. It is curious to note, however, that there is only one String Trio thus far, op. 274 (1947), and no piano trio, and it is equally curious that no such ensembles have ever come his way.

It would not be wrong to consider that Milhaud has over-written himself, and one wonders to what opus numbers his would mount had he been blessed with normal good health, for there have been long stretches of time when illness prevented him from working or even from reading. This is as may be, but I cannot think of any other composer whose catalogue is of such consistent interest. If not every opus number represents a masterpiece (and some are very insignificant), there is in nearly every case something to interest and often to delight. Generally speaking, Milhaud is never a dull composer. However, his fecundity is probably his worst enemy. With so much from which to choose, where is the performer to start? What shall be omitted? What is good and therefore worth playing? What is not very good, but is worth playing from the point of view of the executant? What is not worth playing at all — and who shall judge? This is one reason why performances are so often restricted to the established works of Milhaud and so little interest is shown in the others.

In a world torn by dodecaphonism and cerebrality, and dragged this way and that, Milhaud pursues his own path, unaffected by musical polemics and fashions. His music is as uncompromising as any of that written by the youngest wild tyro, is still debatable, still fascinating. It can be heard at its best in the large-scale operas. As I have said, *Les Euménides* is one of the monuments of the twentieth century, with *Le Sacre du printemps*, Schoenberg's *Variations for Orchestra*, Honegger's *Jeanne d'Arc au bûcher*, and Messiaen's *Turangalîla*.

(ILDEBRANDO PIZZETTI)

1880-1968

BIOGRAPHY

ILDEBRANDO PIZZETTI was born in Parma on September 20, 1880, the son of a piano teacher. Pizzetti entered the Conservatory of his native city in his fifteenth year, where he proved his talent by composing two operas that showed great promise. He was graduated in 1901 with a diploma in composition. For a short time he held the post of conductor, then turned to teaching. From 1907 until 1909 he was on the staff of the Parma Conservatory. He then became professor of theory and composition at the Institute of Florence, rising to the post of director in 1917. Subsequently, Pizzetti became director of the Milan Conservatory. In 1936 he taught composition at the St. Cecilia Conservatory in Rome, and from 1948 to 1951 was its director. In his numerous posts as teacher and director, Pizzetti has influenced an entire generation of rising Italian composers.

Soon after his graduation from the Parma Conservatory, Pizzetti composed an opera, which he entered in a competition conducted by an Italian publishing house. His disappointment in not winning an award turned him, for a while, from opera to chamber and symphonic music. Gabriele d'Annunzio brought him back to the theater by providing him with *Fedra*, the text of which was based on the Greek tragedy. It took Pizzetti three years to compose the score to the opera. In 1915 it was introduced at La Scala. *Fedra* was followed by *Debora e Jaele*, which took six years to compose, and which, after its première at La Scala in 1922, placed Pizzetti in the vanguard of Italian composers. Since then, Pizzetti has composed many other notable works for the theater as well as distinguished orchestral and chamber music. In 1930 he visited the United States, and in 1931 Buenos Aires to conduct *Fra Gherardo*. Since 1960 he has been president of the Italian Society of Composers and Authors.

PERSONAL NOTE

Guido M. Gatti

SINCE the death in 1920 of his first wife, Maria Stradivari — loyal and courageous companion in the most difficult years of his career — Pizzetti has never ceased to dress in dark clothes: striped trousers and velvet jacket bordered with silk. A tribute to the memory of the mother of his children, Maria Teresa and Bruno, the black suit (or, exceptionally, gray during the hot season) means also fidelity to those ethical and esthetic principles upon which the musician modeled his life. Just as he has not changed the color of his clothes so he has not modified at any time the standards of his conduct as a man and as an artist. To those who tell him that all these objectives are not suited to the experimental fever of the present time, he replies that fashion does not interest him at all and that he would never do what he does not feel: and he adds that, in any case, if one proposes to change one's ways one must change them in essence, from within, rather than from without as so many do today.

This loyalty to the sentiments from which his personality was formed is reflected also in the inanimate objects that surround him in his house. If there is a change in either the size or the decoration of the apartments successively inhabited by Pizzetti in Florence (from Via Spontini to Ponte alle Mosse to Via de' Serragli), in Milan, and in Rome, the room in which he works, and to which he draws the few friends whose company he loves, seems to have remained always the same, owing to the furniture, the piano, the books, and the ornaments arranged on the furniture; the collection of " good things in the worst taste " that clutters the large table; the marble paperweight, the erasers, the box of tobacco in the form of a tree trunk, the writing pad of frayed leather, the pipes with their accessories, and on the piano the photograph of Verdi, in its plush frame, presented him by an old conductor who was Verdi's friend. As for the " upright " piano, it is still the same one on which *Fedra* was composed, a little old piano of doubtful German origin, with its fine candles, which Pizzetti lights when the first shadows no longer permit him to decipher the notes of the score. Gifts of more valuable instruments have been made to him, which he has either refused or placed outside his " sanctum." Only to the humble companion of his first artistic confessions does he know how to confide his thoughts; to reject it would seem to him an act of black ingratitude, such as would not win him the indulgence of the higher spirits and would even favor the influence of the evil eye. Pizzetti really is superstitious, and is not ashamed to say so, holding himself to be in the best company of the foremost artists of every time and place. Never would Pizzetti commence a new work on a Tuesday, nor would he mark a page of one of his scores with the number " 17 ": after " 16 " comes " 16 + 1." And his signed scores are often adorned with four-leaf clovers he has found and picked during his meditative walks.

Pizzetti always replies to letters, even if they reach him when he is completely engrossed in composition. He replies personally, and with a good old pen with holder and nib (the typewriter is completely unknown to him), and with a clear and careful calligraphy; and his signature, with the spirals that surround the name as in an inscription, is consistent with his tastes. It is a real signature (not a scrawl or the suggestion of a signature), such as we see in the pages of old legal acts of the last century. As for the text, each letter has considered form and dimensions, even if it does not contain esthetic observations or ideas. His language makes use of expressions that recall the speech of Florence, the city that, through his having lived there so many years, he loves as a second mother city. And indeed it cannot be said that the climate and scenery of Tuscany have not contributed at least as much as those of Emilia, where he spent his childhood, to the nature of his creative imagination.

When Pizzetti is working, usually in the morning hours, he does not like to be disturbed: no one can enter his studio except the cat. I have seen many cats in Pizzetti's house, of every breed and color: tabbies, Siamese, Angoras, Persians. The Siamese cat,

Celina, has presided, from the top of a piece of furniture, at the composition of the works of the most recent years, and a fat male cat of fine Persian breed answering to the name of Safid (which in Persian means simply " white ") is today the master's darling and of those close to him. When Pizzetti interrupts his work, he takes Safid in his arms and strokes and fondles him like a father, or even a loving grandfather. Pizzetti is a grandfather twice over: of Nicoletta, the daughter of Maria Teresa, and of Uliva, born to Ippolito, the son of his second marriage. And he does not like to be parted from his family. He has never undertaken a long journey without being accompanied by a member of his family. His second wife, Signora Riri, is always at his side wherever he goes in connection with his work: to conduct his compositions, to hold meetings, to preside at competitions.

Pizzetti prefers the country to the city, the poets and writers of the past to those of the present, fruit and vegetables to all other food, the pipe to the cigar or cigarette. To relax and rest he chooses the cinema rather than the theater, and his favorite films are comedies. Unable to say witty things or make a play on words, he laughs like a boy on a holiday when he is told amusing stories. And he never reads the criticisms of the daily papers on his works the day after a performance. Some member of the family puts them together, and he will read them, if ever, when the echo of the applause accorded him by the public has died away.

THE COMPOSER SPEAKS

Ildebrando Pizzetti [1]

THE lyrical elements in the operas written between 1700 and 1800 were so fatal and led to so many absurdities because they were introduced not for the sake of the drama but for the sake of the singers. Hence the arbitrary agglomeration of " pieces of music " to favor the first soprano or leading tenor or basso profundo. The musicians who composed these operas asked of the librettists not

---

[1] From an essay about opera by Ildebrando Pizzetti in *Musical Quarterly*.

a dramatic poem but a series of song texts. The audiences that listened to them did not seek a reason for these arias, but were pleased enough if they were well sung. The melodrama of 1700 to 1800 was a hedonistic means to a social end. Its dramatic short-comings were overlooked for the sake of the pleasures it offered. Nor did occasional " reforms " touch the real kernel of the evil.

What do we understand by melody? What are its functions in dramatic music? There was a time when some people declared that there was no melody in the music of Beethoven; and in 1858 critics wrote that there was no melody in Verdi's *Rigoletto*. Is melody a simple succession of sounds? Certainly not, or it would be something purely mechanical. Melody is emotion translated into musical sounds. Nor does the translation require an elaborate vocal line, so long as it rings true. . . .

Dramatic music should express life in action — conflicts of matter and mind, of instincts and aspirations, of egoism and moral duty; and lyrical music should express the transcendence, the over-coming of these conflicts. There is no music other than these two types, not even outside the music for the stage. There is no true or great art that is not the expression of a conflict and its resolution, of a drama in which individuals, or sentiments, or ideas are evolved, and its catharsis. Symphonic music obeys the same laws, even though it be without words; it must have dramatic life to be music at all, that is, it must have a content born of conflict, lest it be a mere juggling with sound and noise.

PIZZETTI

Guido M. Gatti

AT the eighty years he attained in 1960, Ildebrando Pizzetti worked without respite: from day to day there mounted on his table in his beautiful house in the Via Panama in Rome the sheets of the score of his new opera, *Lo Stivale d'argento*. He rests, one might say, in working: in about sixty years of activity he has never passed a day without writing a note or at least without the thought

of such writing. The list of his output confirms that. For the theater, eleven dramas from *Fedra* (1909–12) to *L'Assassinio nella
cattedrale* (1958), in addition to a great deal of incidental music
for plays, some involving great effort, as that for D'Annunzio's
La Pisanella (1913) and the *Agamemnon* of Aeschylus (1930); for
the concert hall numerous symphonic compositions of broad scope,
including *Concerto dell' estate* (1928), *Rondò veneziano* (1929),
the Symphony (1940), and the Violin Concerto (1944); yet again,
chamber music such as the Sonata for Violin and Piano (1919),
a classic in the violin repertory, and the two string quartets (1906,
1933); the highly regarded compositions for chorus, and the songs,
considered among the most successful products of his imagination;
and many other things. But if, in each page that he releases for
print, there is always the inscription of his poetic personality as an
artist, in addition to that of the gravity and discipline of his creative
achievement, one may assert that in the history of the music of
this century Pizzetti will be entitled to a prominent place above all
as a musical dramatist, as originator of a drama for which he has
invented a particular language of its own of extreme versatility and
coherence.

His passion for the theater goes back to the years of his early
youth, even of his adolescence. One should not forget that he was
born in Parma and lived there the first thirty years of his life, and
that Parma is the place where the melodrama has always had its
most passionate disciples and connoisseurs, a subject for the most
fiery discussions, for the most profound disputes in home and
piazza. The spiritual soil of the region of Emilia made throughout
the nineteenth century a conspicuous contribution to the opera
life of the nation, in addition to having produced such famous
artists as Giuseppe Verdi among composers and Arturo Toscanini
among interpreters. The young Pizzetti always turned to Verdi as
an incomparable master of art and life. As a pupil at the Parma
Conservatory, Pizzetti was able to visit Verdi's villa of Sant' Agata
— immersed in the fascinating plain of the Po between the glittering
waters and long rows of poplars and the willows shimmering in the
wind — and it became the sanctuary of his dreams and his aspirations. There are traces of deep affinity between these two musicians that go beyond stylistic and dramatic influences, appearing
also on the plane of morality and artistic tradition. Ways of life
and art combine to present in Pizzetti a certain type of romantic

artist of which today he remains perhaps the sole representative
in Italy. Pizzetti detests abstract art and those tricks of art which do
not originate in the heart of man, which are solely preoccupied
with form, putting all effort into the resolving of technical problems;
and at the same time he finds useless, unworthy of consideration,
music that does not contain in its essence a message to man, does
not say a word of wisdom or sympathy. (Speaking in 1925 to the
pupils of the Milan Conservatory, of which he was at the time
director, he said: " He who professes art without loving it, without
believing in it as in a most high form of religion, is as a priest who
would say Mass without believing in the sacrament of the Eucha-
rist.") Verdi " went into a complete frenzy " — the words are his
— when he heard people speak of a music that entertains, and
Pizzetti would not react differently if one were to speak to him of
being amused in listening to a theatrical opera. Verdi believed in
the passions of his characters and would not have written a page
without compassion or conviction: the imagination of Verdi was
nourished by fundamental and simple sentiments, which can be
comprehended by all, of every place and time. Pizzetti has also
loved his characters, has sought to understand them, to justify in
them those actions which conflict with law and social convention.
From one work to the next, the human inquiry is more searching,
the analysis deeper, the theme more concentrated, so that one may
say — without, let us feel, diminishing the importance of the work
— that he may be considered the creator of a *single* (in the broad
sense) character, and that in his dramas he imposes a uniformity
of sentiment and ideology so concentrated as to exclude the possibility of the action's resting on subsidiary episodes and facts.

Such a unity of dramatic concept has its reflection in language, to which Pizzetti has always remained faithful. If we review
the musical events of the last fifty years, one asks how a musician
may pass through all the esthetic and expressive vicissitudes we have
experienced without being tempted by the insidious call of the
sirens on all sides and of all aspects. Perseverance in dramatic expression, manifest in its basic features even in the youthful *Fedra*,
has been recognized in him even by those critics who are averse to
it. Pizzetti is perhaps the only composer of our time in whose works
one cannot distinguish phases or successive styles.

Of minute stature, Pizzetti nevertheless possesses the un-
conquerable strength of will to overcome the many adversities

against which he had to struggle in the first half of his career. To assess them, it is enough to think of the Italian musical situation in the first thirty years of the present century — of the absolute predominance in Italy of the realistic melodrama both in the public taste and in the preferences of the directors of opera companies, and of the uncontested fame of musicians like Puccini, Mascagni, and Giordano. *Fedra*, the opera on which Pizzetti had worked with an indefatigable passion for three years, sacrificing everything to it, had a long wait for production, notwithstanding the flattering introduction by D'Annunzio, admirer of the young musician and his librettist. Finally presented at La Scala on the eve of Italy's entrance into World War I, it was so coldly received that no other theater attempted to undertake it. Many years passed after that distant 1915 before the name of Pizzetti re-emerged on the Placards of a lyric season with a new opera: in 1922, at La Scala, with the memorable performance that Arturo Toscanini gave to Pizzetti's second opera, *Debora e Jaele,* followed six years after that, under the same direction, by *Fra Gherardo.* But the years of obscure waiting did not affect, even superficially, the faith of the musician in " his " drama. Alien to sophistication and shy of ceremony, Pizzetti lived, in the period of his maturity, a modest life divided among creative activity, the family to which he is deeply attached, and the teaching that he carried on until a few years ago — teaching that, it is not necessary to add, does not seek to impose upon the nature of the young, or urge them to imitate, the creative style of the teacher. Proud of his work and modest at the same time in the presence of genius, Pizzetti wishes to be considered today in the correct perspective of recent history: a master of the Italian musical generation flourishing in the last thirty years, after having contributed in the early years to the revival of musical taste and culture through the publication since 1909 of critical essays on the work of the Italian musicians of the nineteenth century, from Bellini to Verdi, and on the more significant contemporary composers.

(FRANCIS POULENC)

1899-1963

BIOGRAPHY

FRANCIS POULENC was born in Paris on January 7, 1899. After studying the piano with Ricardo Viñes and composition with Charles Koechlin, he allied himself with a group of young progressive French composers known as the Societé de Nouveaux Jeunes. As one of them he wrote and published in 1917 the *Rapsodie nègre*, for voice and orchestra. Recognition came to him, in 1920, when his name was joined with those of five other young French composers (including Milhaud and Honegger), who became collectively known as "The French Six" or "Les Six." During the 1920's and early 1930's Poulenc produced several noteworthy compositions in the economical, and at times witty, style of the new French school, the most notable of these being the Concerto in D minor, for two pianos and orchestra, and the *Concert champêtre*, for harpsichord and orchestra. He also distinguished himself as a composer of songs. Just before the outbreak of World War II, his style gained in emotional and spiritual content. He created a succession of major works — climaxed by his opera *Les Dialogues des Carmélites*, introduced at La Scala on January 26, 1957 — which placed him in the front rank of twentieth-century composers. Poulenc paid his first visit to the United States in 1948-9, when he toured the country in joint recitals with the baritone Pierre Bernac. He died in Paris on January 30, 1963.

PERSONAL NOTE

Henri Hell

Colette has drawn a portrait of Poulenc, " the cherished child of our age," at his country home in Noizay, near Amboise, at the time of the *Animaux modèles* (1942). " Fortune has favored him ever since *Les Biches*. . . . At the time of his first successes he was so young that he was believed to be affected, so brilliant that he was considered superficial, and he was looked upon as a fop. Such praises, suggesting some distinguished dignitary, were in fact addressed to a big countrified fellow, bony and jovial. I don't want to upset him; I want only to recall him in the way I best knew him. Up a chalky hill, Poulenc lives in a big airy house with vineyards all around, and there he makes his wine, and drinks it. Even his sparkling orchestration has roots in the richness of the soil. You see immediately that water is not his favorite beverage. With that strong, sensitive nose of his and the changes of expression that flash through his eyes, he is both trusting and wary, easy for his friends to get on with, a poet of the soil."

A great-grandfather was a gardener at Nogent-sur-Marne during the First Empire. Hence, perhaps, his love of flowers and the geometrically laid-out garden at Noizay, with boxwood hedges surrounding two little obelisks. Since this has been his country home over a period of thirty years, the legend has been created of Poulenc as a composer from Touraine inspired by the Loire. This is far from the truth: neither the work nor the man derives from this region.

Nor, in fact, is he the musician of the soil of Colette's portrait. The country means nothing to him; which is surely why, without distraction, he has been so productive at Noizay, turning to creative account memories of the paradise of Monte Carlo and the *bals musettes* of Norgent-sur-Marne. His Parisian haunts have been the old quarters of Le Marais and the Île Saint-Louis, the Faubourg Saint-Antoine and the coarse costermonger market of Les Halles. Regular visits were made in his youth to some of the lower music halls and café concerts near the Place de la République, where he gave rein to a genuine passion for the popular singers of the day, Jeanne Bloch (whose repertory included *Prostitution* and *Vierge flétrie*, which he had hoped might inspire an opera) and the renowned Maurice Chevalier. These visits were often made in the company of an old school friend, a champion boxer, and their girl friends, a shoe-stitcher and a feather-dresser. A reflection of this period was the song " Toréador," on words of Jean Cocteau.

Religious leanings [are found in] visits to the ancient Sanctuary of Rocamadour, and in the choral works from the Mass onward. St. Francis of Assisi and St. Anthony of Padua are the saints with whom the composer of the *Carmelites* has affinities. On the score of the opera is the inscription: " God preserve me from the drearier saintly figures of history." The ascetic features of Catholicism are unknown to him.

Discussions of his work have shown that sources of Poulenc's musical inspiration are frequently to be sought in painting and poetry. Much of his work would indicate an abundant and easy flow of inspiration, though in fact some of his most natural music has been painfully hammered out, set aside, and revised. Aware of his limitations, he has not readily accepted commissions, among them the request from William Primrose for a Viola Concerto.

" Music should humbly seek to please " was the hedonistic motto of Debussy. Throughout the long history of French music, indeed in many of the most engaging features of French civilization, the potent pleasure-seeking principle has been the root force; and as the seductive art of Poulenc makes its way into the heart it is clear enough that this principle is alive still in the musical soul of his country.

THE COMPOSER SPEAKS

Francis Poulenc [1]

THERE is a duality in myself as well as in my music. My father was a devout Catholic, and it was from him that I had inherited

[1] The above statements come from interviews, with John Gruen in *Musical America* and with Olin Downes in *The New York Times*.

my religious inspiration. In fact, I had a great uncle, the Abbé Joseph Poulenc, who was the curé of Ivry-sur-Seine, so that a strong religious tradition is firmly tied to my work. It was from my mother, on the other hand, that I inherited my great love for music; she was a delightful pianist with excellent musical taste. I recall being completely enthralled when she played Schubert, Mozart, Chopin, and Schumann. I was also much inspired by some of the lesser composers in my mother's repertoire, such as Massenet, Grieg, and Anton Rubinstein. I am certain that it was my mother who inspired me to write my *mauvaise musique*. It was also my mother's part of the family that kept abreast of the entire artistic world; my uncle Papoum introduced me to my love for the theater, and it was from him I learned about Réjane, Sarah Bernhardt, and the like.

Let us have a truce to composing by theory, doctrine, and rule! Above all, let not a composer seek to be in the mode. If you are not à la mode today, you may not be out of the mode tomorrow.

There is only one law for the composer, and that is to be himself, to ape no one, to find out by experience in writing what he really thinks and feels.

It is the alpha and omega of the creative artist. It is his only title to recognition or such measure of reputation as he achieves. And his only protection against destruction.

POULENC

Edward Lockspeiser

THERE are few composers presenting today such a definite and unmistakable profile as Francis Poulenc. His art is in the best sense the art of a natural composer. Abstract theories are unknown to him, nor has he any use for the coldly calculated mathematics of music. Instinct is his guide — a purely musical instinct. His individuality was at once declared in the earliest of his works, and gradually a world of his own has been marked out and described.

He first came before the public when he was eighteen with the

Rapsodie nègre (1917). Browsing in a Paris bookshop, Poulenc came upon a volume of verse quaintly entitled *Les Poésies de Makoko Kangourou.* These poems, supposedly written by a Negro from Liberia, were a deliberate hoax. Negro art was the fashion of the day and, unconcerned with their authenticity, Poulenc maliciously decided to set the bogus poem " Honoloulou." The youthful charm of the work, its musical instrumentation and streak of genuine humor, made an immediate impact. It was a roaring success, and overnight the career of the eighteen-year-old composer was launched.

From then on Poulenc's output has been continuous and abundant. It may be divided into several categories: the numerous songs, of which there are well over a hundred; the piano works; the chamber-music works; the religious works; the ballets and the operas.

The earliest of the songs is the cycle *Le Bestiaire* (1919), on humorous poems portraying animals by Guillaume Apollinaire. The accompaniment is for flute, clarinet, bassoon and string quartet. Of the same year is another ironic cycle, *Cocardes,* on poems by Jean Cocteau, the promoter and spokesman of " Les Six," of which Poulenc was a member. Six years later he chose Ronsard as his poet for a set of five songs, and the following year he wrote the *Chansons gaillardes.* These, on anonymous seventeenth-century poems, ring a tauntingly seductive note with praise of wine, women, and song, shot through with racy allusions. In 1931 he wrote further sets of songs on poems of Apollinaire, and another on poems of Max Jacob. In the Apollinaire songs he establishes the borderline between irony, in all its degrees, and a full-blooded lyricism. The settings of Jacob are amusing caricatures and are often broadly comical.

In 1934 Poulenc gave the first of his historical recitals with Pierre Bernac, and this association greatly fructified the composer's art as a song writer. Poulenc himself went so far as to declare that he learned the art of song writing by accompanying Bernac in the songs of Schubert, Schumann, Fauré, Debussy, and Ravel. In 1935 he dedicated to Bernac the *Cinq Poèmes,* the first of the songs on poems of Paul Éluard, sung by Bernac at their first public recital in Paris, in 1935, at the École Normale. In 1937 his setting of another group of Éluard's poems, *Tel jour telle nuit,* was proclaimed at its first performance to be a French counterpart of the song cycles of Schumann. Poulenc's temperament was ideally suited to the lyrical qualities of Éluard's poetry, so vibrant in emotional warmth, so lucid in imagery. The cycle of nine songs is here a form complete in itself. Music is somehow made to uncover unsuspected overtones and associations in poetry, and in such a way that the ideal of the poet and the musician become one.

Another cycle of Apollinaire poems is *Banalités* (1940). "Hôtel," the second in this cycle, is built around a lazy, sweet tune, a mere two pages of lyrical melody perfectly brought off. An entirely different problem was presented by the poem "Sanglots," exposing the misery in the hearts of all men. The setting is in every way worthy of the poem. The remarkable modulations in the piano accompaniment, which somehow reveal the inner pulsation of the poem, and the sensitive co-ordination of vocal and poetic inflections establish a unity of poetry and music reaching far beyond the idea of a simple "setting."

In 1951 another Éluard song cycle was written, *La Fraîcheur et le feu*, which must be placed in the front rank of the vocal works. The writing is extremely subtle, and the inspiration wonderfully distilled. "Unis la fraîcheur et le feu," says the poem — "brought together in freshness and fire" — which is in fact a true description of the music that illuminates it. The cycle is dedicated to Stravinsky, in homage to whom there is a quotation from his piano *Serenade*.

Everyone knows the *Mouvements perpétuels* for piano, written in 1918 and performed by Poulenc's piano teacher, Ricardo Viñes, the next year at one of a series of concerts in Paris called *Lyre et Palette*. The qualities of these three short pieces are self-evident. Spontaneous and most attractively melodious, they display, in the manner of Erik Satie, a genre of the eighteenth-century harpsichord composers, tastefully spiced with twentieth-century notions of dissonance. In 1928 Poulenc produced two *Novelettes*, the second of which is a mischievous little rhythmic essay revealing yet another aspect of the composer's gift for an expression in music of banter and dry wit. *Pastourelle* (1927) is widely known in a piano arrangement, but it was originally conceived for orchestra as a contribution to the children's ballet, *L'Éventail de Jeanne*. In the same year he wrote the *Pastorale, Toccata,* and *Hymne* in the form of a piano suite. The brilliance of the *Toccata* has been admirably conveyed by Horowitz, while the *Hymne* contrives to mate stylistic elements of Chopin and Stravinsky. The twelve *Improvisations* completed in 1941 contain some of Poulenc's best piano music. The twelfth of this set is a " Homage to Schubert," the eleventh recalls Schumann, the sixth Prokofiev, and the fourth Chopin. But something original is created as the styles of these admired composers are evoked. Not overconcerned with structural problems, these are true improvisations, several of them being particularly appealing.

This is the place to consider the incidental music for *Babar the Elephant*. In 1945 Poulenc wrote the incidental music for this story for the amusement of his cousin's children. The story, in one of the delightfully illustrated " Babar " books of Jean de Brunhoff, is well known. The score is for narrator and piano. Each of the episodes is described by the spoken voice, the music being purely descriptive. Each section is a piano piece, complete in itself, in the form of a " Lullaby," a " Rêverie," a " Galop," a " Nocturne," and so on. This is a pointed and charming score, containing some of the best pages of the composer's piano music, and is a counterpart in Poulenc's work of Schumann's *Kinderscenen* or Debussy's *Children's Corner*.

The first of Poulenc's concertos is the *Concert champêtre* (1927–28), for harpsichord. This, with the earlier harpsichord concerto by Falla, is one of the most remarkable of the modern works for this instrument. An allegiance to the older harpsichord composers is immediately apparent. The work is conceived as a homage to the composer's musical ancestors but not as a pastiche of their works. Poulenc's distinctive features invariably emerge in much the same way as the features of Ravel are firmly stamped on *Le Tombeau de Couperin*. In the same way Poulenc wrote the *Aubade* (1929), originally conceived for a solo dancer, pianist, and chamber orchestra of eighteen. This characteristic French work is conceived in the *style galant* of the opera-ballets of Rameau. It is a true *divertissement*, subtle in the interplay of sentiments.

The Piano Concerto of 1949 was commissioned by the Boston Symphony Orchestra. Its form is simple to follow: two contrasted themes are the mainstay of the opening movement; the second movement is a typical Andante; and the final rondeau, using a popular American song is a tongue-in-cheek skit. The piano is not brought into prominence as in the traditional romantic concertos, nor are the themes developed in the conventional manner. It is a concerto of tunes rather than of themes — which is one of its merits.

One of the most popular of the chamber works is the Trio for piano, oboe, and bassoon (1926). Poulenc had set himself the unusual problem of combining the percussive piano with two wind instruments. Pictorially, one is sometimes reminded of a chase, sometimes of a dialogue. Normally, however, the main musical discourse is entrusted to the piano, while the bassoon is relegated to the role of a discreet commentator and the oboe is allowed to intensify the more lyrical flights. The very heart of Poulenc is in this adroit little work. The Sextet for piano, flute, oboe, clarinet, bassoon, and horn dates from 1932, but was rewritten in 1940. It consists of two lively outer movements and, as the central panel, a charming *divertimento*. The form of the first movement is somewhat incoherent, but the admirable writing for the wind instruments is always in character.

A large section of Poulenc's work consists of a series of religious choral works. The Black Virgin at the Sanctuary of Rocamadour and also a veneration for St. Anthony of Padua were the external origins of his religious inspiration. Yet the simple fervor that emanates from these intensely lyrical works has also a more intimate and homely appeal. Sometimes, it is true, the pure-of-heart composer crosses the religious boundary in the spirit of the juggler performing his tricks before the Virgin of Notre-Dame. But more often, in the *Litanies* (1936) and particularly in the *Stabat Mater* (1950), a remarkable and telling simplicity comes into Catholic religious music again. In 1937 Poulenc wrote one of his major works, the Mass in G major, for mixed *a cappella* choir, which he dedicated to his father. The purity of these serene pages was inspired by the composer's almost human conception of God. At the opposite extreme from the flamboyant religious music of the nineteenth century, this beautiful Mass, suggesting the unadorned architecture of a Romanesque church, requires nothing but an unaccompanied choir to make its telling effects of fervor and simplicity. In the *Stabat Mater* each of the twelve sections establishes a contrasting mood so that together they encircle a whole range of religious experience, from sorrow and grace to drama and majesty. Though saved from any kind of baroque excess, the writing is noticeably more ornate than in the Mass.

Poulenc's first major work was the ballet *Les Biches*, produced by the Diaghilev company in 1924. With its ironic and slightly rakish twists, its traditional elegance of musical thought, this delightful work goes straight to the point, its one aim being to bring delight. It is graceful, but it does not sink to a level of inspidity or mere prettiness. An irresistible gaiety emanates from this unconstrained ballet score in which there is more of the composer's inner self than might at first appear. Occasionally, the sensitive composer hides behind his mask — and his music in these moments is flooded with some sort of heartfelt melancholy. Poulenc's second ballet, *Les Animaux modèles*, based on a set of fables of La Fontaine, was given in Paris in 1942 and contains some severe, moving pages of remarkable dignity and restraint.

The first of Poulenc's three operas, *Les Mamelles de Tirésias* (1944), is based on a racy and wholly Parisian farce by Guillaume Apollinaire dealing with the change of sex in one of the characters. In the tradition of Chabrier's *Le Roi malgré lui*, of which it has the same rumbustiousness, and Ravel's *L'Heure espagnole*, of which it has the same perception and wit, Poulenc's score provides the crazy skit with some of the finest music he has written. Twelve years separate *Les Mamelles de Tirésias* from the completion of *Dialogues des Carmélites* (1956), given at La Scala in 1957 and subsequently in many countries and also on television. The libretto is the story of thirteen nuns of the Carmelite convent at Compiègne who were condemned to the guillotine during the French Revolution. The vocal writing is distinguished by a skillful merging of recitatives and lyrical episodes. Interest is primarily maintained in the voices, and the principal roles are cast for recognized types of operatic voices. The Revolution itself is no more than a remote background, totally excluded from the Carmelite convent and from the devout otherworldly souls of the sisters. The touching musical portrait of Sister Constance, the moving scene between Blanche and the Mother Superior, and the agonizing scene of the Mother Superior's death are examples of the extent to which Poulenc was able to identify himself with elusive spiritual drama.

In *La Voix humaine* (1959), Poulenc returned to Jean Cocteau the poet with whom he had been so closely associated in his youth. This is a one-act opera for a single character. One has to be kept in a state of tiptoe excitement if a tour de force of this kind is not to appear manufactured. I think it is right to say that Poulenc's curtain raiser comes off most successfully. More than this, it is extremely entertaining. It is not an opera that demands any kind of penetrating explanation or analysis. Like Cocteau's play, on which it is based, it immediately makes its full impact on its own merit. A brilliant idea brilliantly carried off, this little opera holds you almost at the tension of the Grand Guignol.

(SERGE PROKOFIEV)

1891 - 1953

BIOGRAPHY

SERGE PROKOFIEV was born in the district of Ekaterino-slav, in southern Russia, on April 23, 1891. His mother gave him piano lessons when he was a child. Before long, he began to compose, and wrote an opera at the age of nine. Taneiev saw some of his piano pieces and was sufficiently impressed to advise serious study with Glière. Prokofiev's first contact with formal instruction in composition brought immediate results. After a few months of study he wrote a symphony, two small operas, two piano sonatas, and a violin sonata. In 1904 he enrolled as a student in the St. Petersburg Conservatory. There he studied composition with Liadov, orchestration with Rimsky-Korsakov, and conducting with Tcherepnin. He also studied piano with Anna Essipova. During his student days he composed prolifically, and several of his piano pieces were published. In 1914 Prokofiev was graduated from the Conservatory with three diplomas and the Anton Rubinstein Prize for piano playing; he performed his First Piano Concerto at the commencement exercises.

During World War I he wrote several of his most important works, among them the *Scythian Suite* for orchestra, the *Classical Symphony*, and the First Violin Concerto. In the spring of 1918 he left Russia and by way of Siberia and Japan arrived in America for the first time. He gave concerts of his own piano works in New York and elsewhere, and wrote the opera *The Love for Three Oranges* for the Chicago Opera Company. He subsequently settled in Paris, where he wrote several ballets for Diaghilev. Koussevitzky performed his symphonic works and became his Paris publisher at the

Éditions Russes. In the meantime Prokofiev continued to appear as pianist in his own compositions. He made several tours of the United States as guest conductor and pianist, the last in 1938.

In December, 1933, Prokofiev returned to Russia and settled in Moscow as a Soviet citizen. Some of his most successful works were written during his Soviet period, including the Fifth Symphony, the musical fairy tale, *Peter and the Wolf*, the ballet *Romeo and Juliet*, and the opera *War and Peace*. But despite his great prestige he was not spared official censure. His name was conspicuously included in the Resolution of the Central Committee of the Communist Party of February 10, 1948, which vigorously denounced the leading Soviet composers for their "formalistic" tendencies. To these charges Prokofiev offered a mild rebuttal.

Prokofiev died suddenly of cerebral hemorrhage in his apartment in Moscow in the late afternoon of March 5, 1953, the day on which Stalin died a few hours later. The news of Prokofiev's death was not made public for several days, and most foreign dispatches misdated it March 4, an error that found its way into several reference books. Soviet composers in a whole assembly paid tribute to Prokofiev's coffin, laid in state in the Central House of the Composers' Union in Moscow. In 1957, Prokofiev was posthumously awarded the Lenin Prize.

PERSONAL NOTE

Nicolas Slonimsky

IT sometimes happens that a composer's personality — his physical appearance, his psychological make-up, his social attitudes — corresponds so perfectly to his art that the music and the man become natural counterparts of each other. The music of Serge Prokofiev was his best portrait.

Prokofiev was tall, prematurely balding, with long legs, long arms, and long fingers that seemed prehensile at the keyboard. His bodily movements were angular and quick, his gestures abrupt. He had a voice that cut through the air without being loud, and a brusque manner of speech, often laden with sarcasm. He totally ignored social amenities, but he had many devoted friends to whom he was loyal.

These physical, psychological, and social characteristics are reflected in his music, with its tremendous kinetic energy, short and almost abrupt thematic statements, and a spirit of irreverence toward established traditions. But there is also in Prokofiev's music a spirit of lyricism, all the more profound because lyric passages occur in contrast to typically boisterous episodes. He regarded this lyric element as very important and resented being classified merely as a brilliant composer of witty modernistic works. Commenting on an article I had written about him, Prokofiev said, in a letter from Paris dated May 28, 1931: " I like your article, but I regret that you passed in silence my latest period, which I regard as the most significant. Besides, it presents the best conciliation of the conflicting elements in my former phases. Incidentally, there is no ' absolute preponderance ' of $\frac{4}{4}$ time in my music, for which you hit me in your article."

It was not a mere coincidence that Prokofiev's favorite recreation was chess. He was in fact the best chess player among composers since Philidor, and he ranked in Russia just below the grandmaster level. The basic qualities of a good chess player — planning, logic, precision — were also qualities that he demanded from himself, and from other composers. He detested musical untidiness, but was full of admiration for technical skill and discipline in performance as well as in composition.

I recall a characteristic episode, when I sat next to Prokofiev at the Paris debut of Dimitri Mitropoulos in 1932. Mitropoulos included in his program Prokofiev's Third Piano Concerto, playing it himself and conducting the orchestra from the keyboard. Prokofiev watched the spectacle — such duplication of functions was a novelty then — with unconcealed amazement. " This is a regular circus stunt," he whispered, " I could never do anything like that! "

Prokofiev enjoyed finding minor faults with composers whose importance he never challenged. He once told me he had found forty-eight errors on the very first page of the proofs of Stravinsky's *Symphony of Psalms*, which was being published by Koussevitzky's Éditions Russes. Prokofiev's own work, a revised version of his early *Sinfonietta*, was being processed at the time in a four-hand piano arrangement, and I volunteered to check the proofs, even though Prokofiev assured me that he was the best proofreader of his own music. To my delight I found a glaring error, a bass clef instead of the treble clef. Prokofiev congratulated me on my achievement, which impressed him much more than my repeated attempts to please him by my articles.

Prokofiev had a healthy appreciation of his own craftsmanship in composition. Once, after a performance of his *Scythian Suite* by an American orchestra, he turned to a young friend, a Russian composer who had a work performed on the same program, and who had recurrent trouble with his orchestration, and observed: " See how *I* could orchestrate at the age of twenty-three! "

Like all composers of genius, Prokofiev was often unfair to others whose style of composition was completely alien to him. Nor did he cultivate veneration for his own former idols. When Koussevitzky planned a performance of Scriabin's *Divine Poem* at one of his Paris concerts, Prokofiev — who had gone through a Scriabin phase himself — told him that Scriabin's score needed sprucing up to save it from debacle. " Bass-drum rolls here and there might help," he suggested. Koussevitzky became angry at such blasphemy, and Prokofiev changed the subject.

Prokofiev began his career as a rebel against tradition, but he ended by establishing a tradition of his own. There are few Soviet composers who have not experienced Prokofiev's influence, but the unique combination of kinetic energy, gaiety, and lyric poetry that constitutes the essence of Prokofiev's art could only be reproduced by the miracle of Prokofiev's physical resurrection, for his music was the natural product of his living personality.

THE COMPOSER SPEAKS

Serge Prokofiev [1]

I STRIVE for greater simplicity and more melody. Of course I have used dissonance in my time, but there has been too much disso-

---

[1] The first part of this statement is from an interview with Olin Downes in *The New York Times*; the second, from *Sovietskaya Musica* (April, 1941).

nance. Bach used dissonance as good salt for his music. Others applied pepper, seasoned the dishes more and more highly, till all healthy appetites were sick and until the music was nothing but pepper. I think society has had enough of that. We want a simpler and more melodic style for music, a simpler, less complicated emotional state, and dissonance once again relegated to its proper place as one element in music, contingent principally upon the meeting of the melodic lines. Stravinsky once told me that he dreamed of a style so simple and pure that it should consist only of two melodies.

As a matter of fact, counterpoint, no matter how melodic and clear it is, can go only a certain distance when it comes to tonal combinations. You may say as much as you like of the human ear and the capacity for adapting itself to more and more complicated music. I do not discover that the ear's capacities increase so rapidly or enormously. Three melodies remain about the limit that the average ear can grasp and follow at one time. This can be done when the melodies are clearly sounded, and contrasted in pitch and tone color. For a short time the ear may perceive and assimilate the effect of four different parts, but this will not be long continued if the four parts, or melodies, are of equal importance. Listening to a four- or five- or even six-part fugue, the ear is conscious possibly of the presence of all the voices, but it only perceives and follows precisely the most important of the melodies being sounded. The other parts fill in, enrich the musical background and harmony, but they become as blurred lines of the picture. They are not clearly recorded in the listener's consciousness as separate melodic strands in the tonal fabric. This being true, it behooves the composer to realize that in the polyphonic as well as in the structural sense he must keep within certain bounds.

Who can go further in combining melodies in a wholly intelligible and sonorous manner than Wagner in the peroration of the *Meistersinger* Prelude? There we have two principal melodies, the one on the top, the other at the bottom, of the orchestra, with the third motif, rather than the melody, in the center, and a running figure of less importance. The ear accommodates all of this, but it could hardly hold more.

Music, in other words, has definitely reached and passed the greatest degree of discord and of complexity that it is practicable for it to attain. I do not speak, of course, of using many instruments for the purpose of harmonic and instrumental color. That is another matter, although even in this field it is becoming apparent that sheer quantity of instruments does not necessarily make for sonority or increased variety of orchestral tone. I think we have gone as far as we are likely to go in the direction of size, or dissonance, or complexity in music.

Therefore, I think the desire that I and many of my fellow composers feel, to attain a more simple and melodic expression, is the inevitable direction for the musical art of the future. The question enters, of course, what is melody? Thirty years ago, Wagner's *Götterdämmerung* was considered to be an opera without melody. Today very few people would deny that the score, whatever its shortcomings or disadvantages, is replete with melody.

What people usually accept as a melody is that musical phrase which above all is not new as to intervals, rhythm, or style. Thus Puccini is a composer considered especially melodic — that is, his themes fall into the category of intervals and chords to which the human ear has long been accustomed, and which it is in the habit of accepting. But it is obvious that with the passage of years the recipe for melody changes.

However these questions are considered, it is obvious that there is an immense desire to win back to simplicity, to reach again, as it were, a clear spot in the forest and chart the course of music anew. And here is a striking thing, though significant of just what if anything each must judge for himself: there is a return to classic forms that I feel very much myself. As regards opera, I sense the need for some freshening of ideas and alterations of form, even though the question of form is here particularly debatable, owing to the fact that the form of the opera must be determined essentially by the form of the dramatic subject. But in the field of instrumental or symphonic music I do not feel the same need. In that field I am well content with the forms already perfected. I want nothing better, nothing more flexible or more complete, than the sonata form, which contains everything necessary to my structural purpose.

The principal lines that I followed in my creative work are these: the first is classical. . . . It assumes a neoclassical aspect in the sonatas and concertos, or imitates the classical style of the eighteenth century as in the Gavottes, the *Classical Symphony*, and, in some respects, the *Sinfonietta*.

The second is innovation, the inception of which I trace to my meeting with Taneiev, when he taunted me for my "elementary harmony." At first this innovation consisted in the search for an individual harmonic language, but later was transformed into a desire to find a medium for the expression of a strong emotion as in the *Scythian Suite*, the Symphony No. 2, etc. . . . This innovating strain has affected not only the harmonic idiom, but also melodic inflection, orchestration, and stage technique.

The third is the element of the toccata, or motor element, probably influenced by Schumann's *Toccata*, which impressed me greatly at one time. This element is probably the least important.

The fourth element is lyrical. It appears at first as lyric meditation, sometimes unconnected with melodies . . . but sometimes is found in long melodic phrases, as in the opening of the First Violin Concerto. . . . This lyric strain has for long remained in obscurity, or, if it was noticed at all, then only in retrospection. And since my lyricism has for a long time been denied appreciation, it has grown but slowly. But at later stages I paid more and more attention to lyrical expression.

I should like to limit myself to these four elements, and to regard the fifth element, that of the grotesque, which some critics try to foist on me, as merely a variation of the other characteristics. In application to my music, I should like to replace the word grotesque by "scherzoness," or by three words, giving its gradations: "jest," "laughter," "mockery."

PROKOFIEV

Nicolas Slonimsky

PROKOFIEV belonged to the middle generation of twentieth-century Russian composers, standing between those who, like Glière and Vassilenko, made their reputation before the Revolution and composers like Shostakovich, whose formative years were spent under the Soviet regime. The prerevolutionary composers had to be "naturalized" as Soviet musicians, but Prokofiev's music needed only slight adjustments to satisfy the requirements of "Socialist Realism," the Soviet slogan for an artistic reflection in music of the new reality of life.

The evolutionary catalogue of Prokofiev's works shows an extraordinary constancy of purpose. There are no sudden changes of style from one work to the next, no false neoclassicism, no excursions into the extreme practices of modernism. He never abandoned tonality as the mainstay of his musical language; his symphonies and concertos bear explicit indications of key, C major being his favorite. He was definitely " consonant " with the spirit of the Russian Revolution; his rhythmic energy corresponded to the kinetic ideals of the times; he was a musical optimist.

Yet Prokofiev was a cosmopolite. He lived many years in the West, and was a familiar figure in Paris and New York. He was one of the star composers for Diaghilev's Ballet Russe, an enterprise that was regarded by Soviet spokesmen as a falsification of true Russian art. For one of his ballets, *Le Pas d'acier* (1924), Prokofiev chose a Soviet subject, the march of steel industry after the Revolution. In the atmosphere of Western opposition to Soviet Russia, the production was a shocking surprise, and Diaghilev was upbraided by his capitalistic supporters and some newspaper writers for staging a " Bolshevik " spectacle. On the other hand, *Le Pas d'acier* was criticized in the Soviet press as a grotesque and improper representation of a very important subject. Several other works by Prokofiev were rejected by Soviet spokesmen for similar reasons, but this reaction did not affect the Soviet appreciation of Prokofiev's music as intrinsically progressive and ideologically acceptable. In 1927, when Prokofiev made a prolonged concert tour in Russia as a pianist, he received an enthusiastic welcome.

Although the separation between the Russian *émigrés* in Paris and elsewhere and the Soviet citizens was at the time total and unbridgeable, Prokofiev was exempt from restrictions on either side. In fact, he held two passports, the so-called Nansen passport for stateless individuals and refugees and the Soviet passport, which enabled him to travel without legal difficulties in Europe and in the Soviet Union. Soon he made his final choice, and in December, 1933, settled in Moscow, without abandoning, however, his annual visits to the West.

Some stylistic alterations accompanied Prokofiev's change of status from a Russian Westerner to a Soviet citizen. Particularly in his music for the theater, he veered away from constructivist practices, typical of European stage music of the time, toward a less abstract art which may be described as romantic realism, rooted in the concrete imagery of life. Distilling the three principal ingredients of his music, dynamism, lyricism, and sarcasm, Prokofiev formed a style with less sarcasm than in his earliest works, while enhancing the lyric power and leaving his youthful dynamism undiminished.

Prokofiev's creative biography began at a very early age, perhaps earlier than Mozart's. He composed an *Indian Galop* when he was five years old, and at the age of nine he completed an opera, *The Giant*, in three acts and six tableaux, to his own libretto. It was written in piano score, in ink; the vocal line followed the melody of the right hand. At the age of twelve he wrote a complete opera, *Feast During the Plague*, after Pushkin. At that time he was taking lessons from Glière, to whom he dedicated his First Symphony, written at the age of eleven.

By the time Prokofiev reached adolescence, he had accumulated a respectable list of works. Like Mozart and Schubert, Prokofiev was in the habit of dating his compositions; about a hundred piano pieces written between 1899 and 1907 are still preserved in the original manuscripts. After that he began to mark the opus number. Opus 1 was a piano sonata. His last opus number, 137, was also a piano sonata.

In the St. Petersburg Conservatory, which he entered in 1904, he soon asserted his individuality as a composer, much to the distress of his composition teacher, Liadov, who sarcastically asked Prokofiev if he would not be better off studying with some such modernist as Debussy or Richard Strauss. Although Prokofiev carried the grand prize as a pianist and played his First Piano Concerto as a graduation work, he was not regarded as an outstanding talent in composition. Rimsky-Korsakov noted down his opinion of Prokofiev at an examination: "Gifted but immature. Worked very little. Progress insignificant."

In St. Petersburg, young Prokofiev quickly acquired notoriety as an *enfant terrible* of music. He played his piano pieces, full of modernistic devices, at concerts given by the *avant-garde*. There was little respect at these gatherings for pedantic rules: *esprit* and *élan* counted more than counterpoint. Prokofiev had dutifully passed his examinations in the fugue, but once out of the classroom he relinquished strict fugal writing. His interest carried him far beyond scholastic preoccupations. There is no counterpoint for counter-point's sake in Prokofiev's symphonies and chamber music, but the independence of polyphonic writing, the skill in canonic imitation, the freedom of the melodic line, all testify to the excellence of his academic training.

Prokofiev's first work of major importance was the *Scythian Suite* for orchestra, which he wrote shortly after his graduation in 1914. The music is descriptive of the sun worship in pagan Russia, and Prokofiev drew a tone picture of great power; the Finale with its sustained brass sonorities actually conjures up the image of the blazing sun. Prokofiev's teacher Liadov was also attracted by subjects from pagan Russia, but he presented them in an evocative manner of nineteenth-century Russian nationalism. Prokofiev's *Scythian Suite* signalized a complete break with the conventional Russianism, as did Stravinsky's *The Rite of Spring*, the subtitle of which is " Scenes of Pagan Russia."

The antagonism of many professional musicians toward Prokofiev's aggressive modernism and professed disrespect for established tradition led to a scandal. Leonid Sabaneiev, an estimable Moscow writer and himself a composer, published a devastating review of the *Scythian Suite*, which was announced for performance in Moscow on Christmas Eve, 1916. He described it as cacophony that no person with a sensitive auditory organ can endure, and concluded the review by stating: " The composer himself conducted the work with barbaric abandon." Sabaneiev made the fatal error of not attending the concert, which had been canceled at the last moment owing to the exigencies of wartime. Since Prokofiev was in possession of the manuscript, and there were no copies, the hapless critic could not even claim visual acquaintance with the score, and Prokofiev had the great satisfaction of publishing the pertinent facts in the Moscow musical press.

Still in Russia, Prokofiev wrote one of his most popular works, the *Classical Symphony* (1917). The form, the thematic development, the orchestration, are entirely in the classical tradition, with not a dissonance remaining unresolved. There is no spurious stylization, no mockery of the time-honored form; every melodic turn, every rhythmical inflection, every harmonic progression, all point to Prokofiev's typical idiom, with its gentle humor, dynamic pulse, and lyric poetry. In the Gavotte, the deceptive modulations into unexpected keys sound as though Prokofiev was thumbing his nose at tradition, but not even the most pedantic conservatory professor could find here any breach of harmony rules.

The *Classical Symphony* was composed in the year of the Russian Revolution. In the same year Prokofiev wrote a work completely different in style and inspiration, the cantata *Seven, They Are Seven*, to a ritual text from an ancient Sumerian legend. Scored for a large orchestra, chorus, and tenor solo, it is one of Prokofiev's most "leftist" works, abounding in unrestrained dissonance. As in the *Scythian Suite*, ancient rites receive here an ultramodern treatment.

Between ultramodern primitivism and twentieth-century classicism, Prokofiev found a style that suited him most. His harmonic idiom was established in the framework of tonality with modal inflections. Chromaticism, particularly in its post-Wagnerian aspects, remained alien to Prokofiev. Except in his early works, Prokofiev was never tempted by impressionistic tone painting, preferring literal pictorialism, often with an ironic twist. In his ballets, the action is illustrated by clearly projected musical images. And yet, the musical materials are sufficiently rich to be used independently of the stage; his ballet suites for symphony orchestra are extremely effective. Prokofiev's Fourth Symphony (1930) is based entirely on the themes from the ballet *The Prodigal Son*, but it must be admitted that neither represents Prokofiev at his best.

Prokofiev's ironic art is in evidence in his earliest piano pieces — *Sarcasms* (1914) and *Visions fugitives* (1917) — and in the *Humorous Scherzo* for four bassoons (1912). His ballet *Chout* (the title is the French transliteration of the Russian word for buffoon), produced by Diaghilev in Paris on May 17, 1921, is animated by the same spirit of grotesquerie. The best work in the genre is his *opera buffa The Love for Three Oranges*, which Prokofiev conducted with the Chicago Opera Company on December 30, 1921. The famous March in this opera is a perfect example of consistent modern stylization; it is almost entirely in triadic harmony, but the succession of these triads is so free that tonality hangs in suspense in every bar. Its abrupt ending on the chord of C major is unique in the history of cadences.

In his piano concertos, Prokofiev created a new type of virtuoso style, occupying the intermediate position between the classical form and the modern application of piano sonorities treated as an integral part of the orchestra. The percussive quality in rapid rhythmic passages is emphasized while the traditional chordal harmonies and arpeggios are sparingly used.

A similarly economic virtuoso technique is applied in Prokofiev's two violin concertos, in which the decorative element is subordinated to the purely musical content. Prokofiev also wrote two concertos for cello and orchestra.

Curiously enough, Prokofiev's works written in a deliberately folkloric manner are ineffective. He paid tribute to this genre in his *Russian Overture* (1936) and in his symphonic suite with soloists and chorus entitled *Songs of Our Days* (1937). Still less successful were Prokofiev's attempts to write music for state occasions. In 1937 he composed a cantata on the twentieth anniversary of the Soviet Revolution, to texts from Marx, Lenin, and Stalin, scored for a double chorus, symphony orchestra, military band, and an ensemble of accordions. It was never performed, and the work remained in manuscript. In 1939 Prokofiev wrote a cantata for Stalin's sixtieth birthday, using texts in seven languages from popular poems of seven nations of the Soviet Union. Prokofiev's last work of this type was a secular oratorio, *On Guard for Peace* (1950), to texts voicing the Soviet political line of the time.

Prokofiev's inability to compose to order was surely not a sign of declining creative powers. He wrote great music for the film *Alexander Nevsky* (1938), glorifying the historic Russian hero who defeated the Teutonic Knights in the thirteenth century. It was performed in concert form shortly before the outbreak of World War II, and the historic parallel between the medieval German invaders and the Nazis was pointedly brought out. The work was praised in the Soviet press and enjoyed considerable success outside Russia as well.

After the Nazi invasion of Russia in 1941, Prokofiev responded to the patriotic impulse with a symphonic suite entitled simply *1941*. A much more moving work was his *Ballad of a Boy Who Remained Unknown* (1943), the true story of a young Soviet guerrilla fighter who destroyed an enemy staff car, sacrificing his own life. In 1945 Prokofiev wrote the *Ode to the End of the War*, scored for an unusual ensemble, including four pianos, eight harps, sixteen double basses, brass and percussion, but omitting violins, violas, and cellos. The work was sharply criticized in the Soviet press as a reversion to Prokofiev's "Western" and experimental type of composition.

Humor and satire remain Prokofiev's peculiar gifts. The film music to *Lieutenant Kije* (1934), well known in the form of a symphonic suite, is an example of this lighter side of Prokofiev's creative genius. The story deals with a bureaucratic error that created the name of a nonexistent lieutenant out of two verbal particles in an official czarist document; Prokofiev treats it with gentle irony, and not without nostalgia, when the mythical Kije is allowed to die in order to save the bumbling officials from further embarrassment.

Perhaps the most perfect work among Prokofiev's lyrically humorous inspirations is the symphonic fairy tale, *Peter and the Wolf*, written for the Children's Theater in Moscow in 1936, with a text by Prokofiev himself. Each character in the story is portrayed by a different instrument, the young Red Pioneer Peter by a romantically adventurous theme of the strings, his grouchy grandfather by the bassoon, the bird by a flute, the duck by an oboe, the cat by a clarinet in the low register, and the wolf by chords of three horns. In fact, Prokofiev had a didactic purpose in writing the score, to acquaint young children with the sounds of orchestral instruments. But as often happens in music history, works of modest intent, executed with perfection, become minor masterpieces. *Peter and the Wolf* is an example.

Much more ambitious was Prokofiev's ballet *Romeo and Juliet* (1935). Prokofiev needed courage to select a subject that Russian music lovers associated with Tchaikovsky's famous overture-fantasy, but he dared and succeeded. *Romeo and Juliet* became a repertory ballet in the Bolshoi Theater, and its popularity increased with the years. Prokofiev was almost as successful with his next ballet, *Cinderella*, staged at the Bolshoi Theater on November 21, 1945.

His opera *Simeon Kotko*, on the subject of the civil war in the Ukraine, was produced in Moscow on June 23, 1940, but had an indifferent reception. In 1940 Prokofiev completed a "lyrico-comic" opera, *The Convent Wedding*, after Sheridan's play *The Duenna*; it was not performed until the end of the war.

Prokofiev's major operatic undertaking was *War and Peace*, after Tolstoy, which he planned as a real grand opera. He began its composition in 1941. As in his cantata *Alexander Nevsky*, the parallel between the historic past and the Nazi attack was made clear. The opera was brought out in concert form in Moscow on October 16, 1944, but the result was not quite satisfactory. Prokofiev withdrew the score for revisions, and worked on it for several years, completing the orchestration of the final version a few weeks before his death.

Despite the incredible difficulties of the war, with the German armies occupying almost half of European Russia before the turn of the tide, Prokofiev continued to compose with amazing energy. Even his stock of music paper gave out and had to be replenished from abroad after an appeal was made by his American friends.

On January 13, 1945, Prokofiev conducted in Moscow the first performance of his Fifth Symphony. It received great acclaim in the Soviet press, and the verdict was similar when it was brought out in America. The score possesses the best qualities and none of the faults of Prokofiev's music. The melodic writing is imbued with lyric poetry; the national Russian character is revealed in the broad diatonic structure and pulsating rhythms; the rich modulating harmonies remain remarkably transparent, and the orchestration is supremely effective.

Prokofiev wrote two more symphonies. The Sixth, performed in Leningrad on October 11, 1947, failed to match the excellence of its inspired predecessor; the Soviet critics found in it a return to modernistic formalism. But Prokofiev's Seventh Symphony, his last, aroused a unanimous chorus of praise after its initial performance in Moscow on October 11, 1952; it was described as a Symphony of Youth; indeed, its lyricism and its gaiety possess an unassuming youthful quality not found in such explicit terms among Prokofiev's works since the *Classical Symphony*. But the reaction of most European and American music critics to this work was totally different; it was taken as a sign of Prokofiev's surrender to the demands of the Soviet ideology of simplification. Nonetheless, the Seventh Symphony proved extremely popular abroad as well as in Russia.

This success came during a harrowing period in Prokofiev's creative work. His name was included among " formalistic " composers in the Resolution of the Central Committee of the Communist Party on February 10, 1948. Like other Soviet composers mentioned in this document, Prokofiev was expected to offer an explanation of his position in this matter. Accordingly, he addressed a letter to the Union of Soviet Composers, admitting that " elements of formalism " penetrated his music through " an infection caught from contact with Western ideas." But he vigorously protested that he " never questioned the importance of melody," and pledged his determination to avoid formalistic practices in an opera he was then composing. This opera was *Tale of a Real Man* (1948), describing the true exploit of a heroic Soviet pilot who lost both legs in combat but returned to service. It was, therefore, a great shock to Prokofiev when, after a trial performance of the opera in December, 1948, it was condemned in vicious terms as an unworthy treatment of the subject and false to the spirit of Soviet ideals.

On October 8, 1960, Prokofiev's opera was produced at the Bolshoi Theater in Moscow. In a warmly laudatory review, *Pravda* commented on the " melodic generosity of the music, the songful quality of the arias and the epically powerful characterization of the hero." The hero himself, Alexey Petrovich Maresyev, attended the performance, embraced and kissed the interpreter of the part (in Prokofiev's libretto he appears simply as Alexey, without the last name), and said: " Prokofiev's opera brought back to me the unforgettable days of the Great Patriotic War."

Prokofiev's health showed alarming symptoms in 1949, when he suffered a stroke. However, he was not incapacitated, and was hard at work a few hours before his death, which came suddenly, on March 5, 1953, at six in the afternoon.

(SERGEI RACHMANINOFF)

1873 - 1943

BIOGRAPHY

SERGEI RACHMANINOFF was born in Oneg, in the government of Novgorod, Russia, on April 1, 1873. He was extraordinarily precocious in music. But he confessed that, at first, his indolence prevented him for cultivating music fully. As a student at the St. Petersburg Conservatory he was able to keep stride with his fellow pupils more through his native gifts than through application to study. Zverev aroused the boy's love for music and awakened his ambition. The teacher induced Rachmaninoff to enter the Moscow Conservatory, where Rachmaninoff became a brilliant student. In 1892 he won the gold medal for composition for his one-act opera, *Aleko*. By his twentieth year Rachmaninoff had produced his famous *Prelude* in C-sharp minor, which took the world of music by storm. By his twenty-fourth year he was recognized as outstanding at the piano, with the baton, and in composition.

His career did not proceed without complications. The first performances of his First Symphony (in Moscow) and the First Piano Concerto (in London) were failures. Rachmaninoff succumbed to a despair from which he could not free himself for several years. He became obsessed with psychopathic fears that he was a failure, without talent; there were times when he was almost in complete stupor. Fortunately, a cure was effected through the power of auto-suggestion. With new heart and spirit, Rachmaninoff returned to creative work and found that ideas came copiously. He wrote his Second Piano Concerto and dedicated it to the physician who had cured him.

The Second Piano Concerto in 1901 marked Rachmaninoff's return to success; to this day it is still his most popular work. He re-entered the concert field, and shortly after the turn of the new century received recognition throughout Europe as one of the supreme interpreters of piano literature and in Moscow as an outstanding conductor. He also resumed composition. In 1907 he completed two major works for orchestra, his Second Symphony and the tone poem *The Isle of the Dead*.

In 1909 Rachmaninoff visited the United States for the first time, introducing himself as pianist, composer, and conductor. He revisited America in 1917, this time arriving as an exile from Russia, seeking a new home. In November, 1939, the thirtieth anniversary of his first American appearance was commemorated in New York and Philadelphia with a cycle of three concerts in which Rachmaninoff appeared with the Philadelphia Orchestra in the triple role of conductor, pianist, and composer. He died at his home in Beverly Hills, California, on March 28, 1943.

PERSONAL NOTE

David Ewen

RACHMANINOFF was essentially a sad and lonely man. He was an exile from his country for many years, and he never quite adjusted himself to the strange setting of a foreign land, however hospitably it may have received him. Formerly, he had two homes, one in New York, the other in the beautiful setting of the Swiss Alps. The war robbed him of one of these homes, but, to speak more accurately, he was a man without any home whatsoever, and was so ever since he left Russia. Away from his native land he felt himself in utter isolation. Only those who knew Rachmaninoff well realized his loneliness, a loneliness that no mere crowded drawing room of friends could satisfactorily dispel. To catch a glimpse of him during one of his frequent solitary walks along Riverside Drive or in Beverly Hills — his long supple frame bent slightly, as if under a weight; his slim, lined face contracted — was to appreciate the extent of his solitude. He confessed his homesickness openly.

His daily life was methodical, and he tried to vary his habits as little as possible even when on tour. After breakfast he practiced for about an hour, then attended to his correspondence and appointments. Lunchtime arrived at one, and was followed by a short nap. Then came another period of practice. Dinner was at six. The food was usually simple and consisted of famous Russian dishes. If Rachmaninoff had a concert to give, he arrived at the hall with meticulous punctuality. If the evening was free, he read, or enjoyed conversation with a few personal friends. Composition he reserved for the summers, when he was freed from the tyranny of concert engagements; then he worked on his music from early morning to night. He was always making sketches, however, jotting down ideas and themes as they occurred to him.

THE COMPOSER SPEAKS

Sergei Rachmaninoff [1]

I AM not a composer who produces works to the formulas of preconceived theories. Music, I have always felt, should be the expression of a composer's complex personality; it should not be arrived at cerebrally, tailor-made to fit certain specifications. A composer's music should express the country of his birth, his love affairs, his religion, the books that have influenced him, the pictures he loves. It should be the product of the sum total of a composer's experiences.

I do not have much heartfelt sympathy with music that is experimental, your so-called "modern music." Yet, though I myself could not learn to write or love such music, I can respect the artistic aims of the composer if he arrives at his so-called modern idiom after an intensive period of preparation. Too much radical music is sheer sham, because the composer has set about revolutionizing the laws of music before he has even mastered them himself. There is a famous Russian painter by the name of Vrubel who paints mod-

[1] Sergei Rachmaninoff dictated this artistic statement to the editor for the purpose of this book.

ernistic canvases. But, before he strove toward a new and radical expression, he mastered the old rules and achieved a formidable technique.

In my own composition, I am greatly helped if I have in mind a book I have recently read, or a beautiful picture, or a poem. Sometimes I keep in mind a definite story, which I try to convert into tones without ever disclosing the source of my inspiration, for I am not writing program music. This is particularly true when I write one of my shorter pieces for the piano. A short piece has always given me much more pain, and has presented to me many more problems, than a symphony or a concerto. Somehow, in writing for the orchestra, the variety of colors provided by the instruments bring me so many different ideas and effects; but when I write a small piece for the piano, I am at the mercy of my thematic idea, which must be presented concisely and without digression.

I am a Russian composer, and the land of my birth has inevitably influenced my temperament and outlook. My music is the product of my temperament, and so it is Russian music; I never consciously attempt to write Russian music, or any other kind of music, for that matter. I have been strongly influenced by Tchaikovsky and Rimsky-Korsakov; but I have never consciously imitated anybody. I try to make my music speak simply and directly that which is in my heart at the time I am composing. If there is love there, or bitterness, or sadness, or religion, these moods become part of my music, and it becomes either beautiful or bitter or sad or religious. For composing music is as much a part of my living as breathing and eating. I compose music because I must give expression to my feelings, just as I talk because I must give utterance to my thoughts.

RACHMANINOFF

Richard Anthony Leonard

THROUGHOUT his life, Rachmaninoff had an acute sense of his own limitations, always proceeding cautiously, whether as a composer, conductor, or pianist. Thus he remained always a conservative. During his lifetime the entire art of music moved through an astonishing metamorphosis. In the year of his birth Wagner was completing *Die Götterdämmerung,* and when he died Stravinsky was approaching his Symphony in Three Movements. Of the esthetic light-years that lay between these works one could find no hint in Rachmaninoff's music. From first to last it remained in the nineteenth-century romantic tradition. It remained, too, a typical product of a conservative Russian eclecticism.

Rachmaninoff was one of the most brilliant students ever to attend the Moscow Conservatory. In 1891, in his eighteenth year, he won highest honors for piano playing; and in 1892 he was awarded the gold medal of honor for composition, graduating a year ahead of his class. Part of his task for the final examination was the composition of a short opera. In a few weeks Rachmaninoff wrote his one-act opera, *Aleko,* based on Pushkin's poem *The Gypsies;* and the following year it was produced with considerable success in Moscow. Meanwhile, the young man had also impressed Moscow audiences as a piano virtuoso. Thus, at the age of twenty, he was already one of the most promising figures in Russian music circles.

It was at this moment that Rachmaninoff had the remarkable fortune to compose the most famous piano piece of modern times — the C-sharp minor *Prelude.* The popularity of this work, which began with a performance by Siloti in London, spread to every corner of the music world.

Success went straight to the composer's head. But he was to learn the lesson of humility in the cruelest possible way for a young artist. For several years he had been working on his First Symphony, in D minor, and in 1897 came its première under brilliant auspices when Glazunov conducted it in St. Petersburg. To the amazement of the young composer, the first performance was a fiasco. The orchestra played execrably, and Glazunov conducted so badly that it was believed he was drunk. Rachmaninoff finally fled from the hall. Later the St. Petersburg critics took delight in mangling the work of a young Moscow hopeful. Wrote Cui: " If there were a Conservatory in hell, Rachmaninoff would get first prize for his Symphony, so devilish are the discords he places before us."

Rachmaninoff was shocked almost to the point of insanity. Several other disappointments, including a broken love affair, seem to have struck him at the same moment. Whatever the real cause

of the crisis, Rachmaninoff was never again the same man. To the
end of his life he suffered from melancholia and from doubts about
his own talents.

Fortunately . . . the composer's family persuaded him to consult . . . Dr. Nikolai Dahl, who was experimenting with autosug-
gestion and hypnotism. Every day for three months, Rachmaninoff
sat in a darkened room while Dr. Dahl repeated again and again the
words: " You will begin to write your concerto. You will work with
great facility. The concerto will be of excellent quality."

The effect was magical. Rachmaninoff set to work and in the
summer and early autumn of 1900 he completed the slow movement
and finale of his Second Piano Concerto, in C minor. These he
played at a concert in Moscow under Siloti with immense success;
and the following spring he composed the first movement. Dr. Dahl
had spoken not only with singular persuasion but with prophecy,
for the C minor Concerto is one of Rachmaninoff's best works and
one of the most successful pieces of its kind in Russian piano literature.

After Dr. Dahl, the composer owed his greatest debt to Tchaikovsky. The C minor Piano Concerto is a child of the celebrated
B-flat minor, with similar flower-laden and highly scented melodies,
and a technical display almost as theatrical. The piece resembles a
romantic costume drama of the late nineteenth century, with a leading role that is an actor's dream. The pianist, like the actor, enjoys all
the choice scenes designed for melancholy brooding, impassioned
love-making, furious conflict, and final triumph. The lights play
constantly upon all the facets of his heroic conduct and all his
changes of costume.

Whatever else Dr. Dahl had done for Rachmaninoff, in the
C minor Concerto he certainly had set free the young composer's
lyric gifts. The melodies are among Rachmaninoff's most effective,
and they are set forth with a fine variety in the Tchaikovsky manner.
Whether they are proclaimed boldly in octaves, embroidered with
piano tracery, sweetly sung by solo woodwinds, embedded in the
soft velvet of the strings, or shouted by the full orchestra and solo
instrument — always the melodies are given preferred treatment.

Late in 1906 Rachmaninoff took his family to Dresden, where
he remained for the better part of three years. This was one of the
most fortunate decisions of his life, for in the German city he found
both the intellectual stimulus and the isolation he needed for crea-

tive work. The Dresden period yielded a number of large-scale works, the Second Symphony (1907), the tone poem *The Isle of the Dead* (1907), the First Piano Sonata (1907), and the Third Piano Concerto (1909).

The Second Symphony, in E minor, was originally a mammoth work running an hour in performance. The composer later sanctioned various cuts, which are generally observed today. The piece shows Rachmaninoff's rapid rise to mastery of technique. Themes are manipulated and integrated with ingenuity; contrapuntal skills are present everywhere; the use of the instruments is brilliant. The composer relied strongly on what he must now have realized was his most precious asset — the richly mellow, long-flowing themes that he could stretch into a kind of endless melody. Yet the symphony misses fire. It is still too long and it lacks variety. The symphony's chief fault, besides its now old-fashioned style, is the familiar one of size without significant content.

The tone poem *The Isle of the Dead* bears the subtitle, " To a Picture by A. Böcklin." Arnold Böcklin (1827–1901) was a Swiss painter who achieved a considerable academic fame in his day and an enormous popular success with this picture. A volcanic island north of the Gulf of Naples became under the painter's brush a romantic vision of nature's receiving vault for the dead — whitened cliffs, shrouding cypress trees, a lifeless sea, and a boat approaching with a cargo of death.

For this sepulchral scene Rachmaninoff wrote some of his most characteristic music. He evoked perfectly the chill landscape and the funereal mood. His piece has a solemn dignity, conveyed with the composer's unusual feeling for the darker orchestral colors. Effective allusion is made to the notes of the " Dies irae," which were to haunt Rachmaninoff all the days of his life. If the piece suffers, it is from excessive length, being too long a meditation on a single gloomy theme. The picture, moreover, no longer enriches the music. Böcklin's canvas has become little more than a chromo that most listeners to Rachmaninoff's tone poem would prefer to forget.

The Isle of the Dead shows clearly that with Rachmaninoff's residence in Dresden a familiar pattern had begun to form itself once more. The powerful influences of the West were crowding in upon the consciousness of this Russian artist. In Germany he also experienced for the first time the mighty ground swell of the Wagnerian music dramas. Thus *The Isle of the Dead* mixed Rachmaninoff with Tchaikovsky and Wagner — long lyric phrases, impassioned climaxes, melting harmonies, all in the familiar mood of Russian melancholy.

The Third Piano Concerto, in D minor, was the last of Rachmaninoff's larger Dresden works. It represented a climax in his career, for many years would pass before he would again create anything for the piano of comparable power. The concerto is also a monument to the composer's own mastery of the instrument. It is one of the most difficult pieces of its kind, and in the concert hall he met its challenge with thrilling command of every technical resource.

The Third Piano Concerto has been called " a fitting epilogue to the era of the romantic piano concerto," and indeed it practically brings to an end the concerto of the Lisztian type, that which blends primarily the lyric with the theatrical. Sonorous and impassioned, it generates emotional excitement in a series of waves. The piece also shows the composer's development as a craftsman. It is long and intricate, but it hangs together.

Rachmaninoff's importance as a composer for the piano is magnified when viewed in the special field of Russian music. With his contemporary Scriabin, he practically created a literature of Russian piano music, which heretofore had contained only a few isolated specimens of value. It does not detract from Rachmaninoff's achievement to point out that the nationalist flavor of his work varies greatly and that often all trace of Russianness is lost.

Rachmaninoff's piano style stemmed directly from the romantic masters of the West, especially Chopin and Liszt, with occasional passing reference to Schumann and even Brahms. It is interesting to note that the Russian composer must have observed, but almost totally disregarded, Debussy's revolutionary treatment of the piano. Instead, he concentrated on the Chopin-Liszt framework of singing melodies and rich sonorities, decorated with elaborate technical embellishments. Though the formula was old, he yet contrived to use it with individuality.

The best of Rachmaninoff's piano art is epitomized in his *Preludes*. Following Chopin, he wrote twenty-four essays in this form, one in each of the major and minor keys. The famous C-sharp minor began the set and was composed in 1892; then came the ten *Preludes* of op. 23, composed in 1903; and finally the thirteen *Preludes* of op. 32, composed in 1910 following the fertile Dresden period.

In miniature these pieces trace the growth of Rachmaninoff as an artist. The C-sharp minor *Prelude* is a brilliant flash of talent; though hackneyed almost to oblivion, it is still a remarkable success for a young man not yet out of his teens. In the ten *Preludes*, op. 23, Rachmaninoff has matured, but is still strongly under the influence of Chopin. The moods are impassioned, declamatory, meditative, or dreamy; the harmonies shift with vivid chromatic colors; lovely melodies ride above waves of arpeggios or from a welter of swirling figurations. All is beautifully pianistic, perfectly written for the instrument. The melodies have not the distinction of Chopin's; they resemble more often Tchaikovsky's. But they have, too, the peculiar touch of Rachmaninoff himself, especially in their ability to extend at great length without loss of motion.

In the final thirteen *Preludes* of op. 32, Rachmaninoff reached a climax. Imaginative, varied, often daring, these pieces represent one of his chief contributions to the piano music of his age. A few of them (e.g., the serenely beautiful G major) are restrained and express a reserved sentiment, but most of the others are powerfully built, full of declamations and dramas, demanding prodigious technical skill and a bravura style.

The fifteen *Études-Tableaux* were composed in two sets — six in op. 33 (1911) and nine in op. 39 (1917). The title was intended to indicate that each piece grew from the composer's contemplation of some picture. The various canvases were never fully identified, but most of them are said to be by Böcklin. The lack of knowledge is not vital, for in Rachmaninoff's pieces the étude far outweighs the picture interest. The pieces are closely related to the final set of *Preludes*, being massive in style and difficulty. Musically they do not quite attain the interest of the finer *Preludes*.

It almost goes without saying that as a composer of songs Rachmaninoff remained firmly in the romantic tradition and that the realism of Mussorgsky left no impression on him. He was again a son of Tchaikovsky, and his songs breathe only the romantic airs. Most of them are hymns of passionate longing, or desire, or lovely landscapes.

Rachmaninoff's approach to the song was similar in many respects to Schumann's. He was primarily a pianist, and the accompaniment in his songs is seldom a mere prop or a means of underlining the vocal line. By going along on a contrapuntal track of its own, the piano collaborates with the voice in stating the poetic thought. In Rachmaninoff's earlier songs the piano parts are

often overwhelmingly dramatic or even flamboyant; but in the more
mature pieces they are far more laconic, spare, and subtly under-
stated.

When the Revolution finally descended upon Russia in 1917 Rachmaninoff tried to remain aloof, as he had so often in times of crisis.
He cared little for politics; but as the storm broke, piling up into
wreckage a rotted, thousand-year-old social structure, he soon
realized what was to follow. " Almost from the beginning of the
Revolution," he said later, " I realized that it was mishandled."

Late in 1917, Rachmaninoff tried to concentrate on the task of
a fourth piano concerto, but his increasing fear for his wife and
children made his life intolerable. Then came a sudden deliverance.
He received an offer for a concert tour of Scandinavia. The composer was able to secure a passport for himself and his family, but
he could give no hint of his real plans. He left his home in Moscow,
carrying a small suitcase with a few personal belongings; everything
else that he and his wife owned, including many of his manuscripts,
he abandoned.

For almost a decade after the beginning of his exile Rachmaninoff the composer remained silent. Then in the summer of 1926, in
France, he finished his Fourth Piano Concerto, in G minor. Those
who were present at its première performance in 1927, remember
the chill of disappointment. This Concerto seemed like a pale
ghost of its clanging and colorful predecessors. The slow movement
presented a problem: its first theme had a disconcerting resemblance
to the nursery tune, " Three Blind Mice." The entire piece seemed
to be a reworking of old ideas.

There was to be one magnificent revival of the composer's
creative vigor, and it came in the summer of 1934. At his Lake
Lucerne home he wrote his *Rhapsody on a Theme of Paganini*, for
piano and orchestra. The *Rhapsody* is a series of twenty-four variations. The theme itself was already famous as a vehicle for variations, having been used by Paganini himself, Liszt, and Brahms.
The Russian composer's work is concertolike in size, brilliance, and
difficulty; from deceptively simple beginnings it grows steadily more
complex and ingenious with the pianist exhibiting one diamond
after another in his blazing virtuoso's crown.

An enormous span of almost thirty years separated Rachmaninoff's Second Symphony from his Third, in A minor. The latter

work was composed in Switzerland in the summers of 1935 and 1936 and was first performed by Stokowski and the Philadelphia Orchestra on November 6, 1939. " It was played wonderfully," wrote Rachmaninoff to a friend, adding ruefully that " the reception by the public and the critics was . . . sour." The symphony has not yet been able to reverse this early decision. Even less interesting were the *Symphonic Dances*, for orchestra (1940–41). After that, Rachmaninoff composed no more.

Like Tchaikovsky's music, Rachmaninoff's has attracted the admiration of the general public and the hostility of many critics. It is true that his music has much more of emotional and intellectual substance; it often seems extravagantly sentimental, almost too poetical and sweet for this age of steel and blood. It was written in an idiom of the past, always an easier method than to write in the ingenious, daring, and intricate idiom of the future, where the standards are not yet established and the boundaries are not fixed. Thus Rachmaninoff's music seems old-fashioned, even soft, especially when compared with the art of such hardy adventurers as Stravinsky, Prokofiev, Schoenberg, or Bartók. We know now that Rachmaninoff was a troubled, sensitive man for whom the time was out of joint. He longed to live in an age and in a century that had vanished into the past. For all its softness, however, and its anachronistic sentiments, his best music has vitality. It continues to live. Most of its strength came from the composer's lyric gift, on which he leaned heavily. When this natural outpouring of melodic ideas failed him, he had the good sense to stop composing.

It might be said of Rachmaninoff that he was a typical Russian composer because he seemed able to write on two planes — as a nationalist who could project much of the spirit of his country, and as an eclectic who had assimilated widely from Western music. His achievement in the field of piano music was considerable. His *Preludes, Études-Tableaux*, concertos, and the *Paganini Variations* make up a solid body of fine music, no less worthy of respect because it is related to the nineteenth rather than the twentieth century. Rachmaninoff must share some honors with his contemporary Scriabin, whose art was bolder and more experimental; but there can be little doubt whose music is more durable.

(MAURICE RAVEL)

1875 - 1937

BIOGRAPHY

MAURICE JOSEPH RAVEL was born in the French-Basque town of Ciboure on March 7, 1875. He entered the Paris Conservatory in 1889 and in 1897 became a composition pupil of Gabriel Fauré, who exerted a profound influence upon him.

In 1901 Ravel composed a cantata, *Myrrha*, which won the second Prix de Rome. In 1902 his first important piano pieces, *Jeux d'eau* and *Pavane pour une Infante défunte*, were introduced by Ricardo Viñes; in 1904 his Quartet in F major, introduced in Paris, made a striking impression.

In 1907 Ravel became the object of controversy when his *Histoires naturelles* was introduced in Paris. This work inspired denunciations of leading critics, who called Ravel an imitator of Debussy. A few critics, however, were much more discerning. Headed by M. D. Calvocoressi, these writers pointed out features in Ravel's works that were completely different from those of Debussy and demonstrated how Ravel's music was in spirit and texture directly antithetical to that of Debussy.

From this controversy Ravel emerged victorious when, during the next three years, he produced a series of remarkable works in which his personality was firmly established: the orchestral *Rapsodie espagnole*, the *Mother Goose* suite for four hands, and the sparkling one-act opera, *L'Heure espagnole*. In 1910 Diaghilev commissioned Ravel to prepare a ballet on the theme of Daphnis and Chloë. It was introduced with great success on June 8, 1912.

During World War I, Ravel served in the French Army as

motorist in the Ambulance Corps. When he returned from the battlefront after the war he bought a villa in Montfort l'Amaury, where he lived up to the end of his life, composing such famous works as *La Valse*, *L'Enfant et les sortilèges*, and *Bolero*. During 1930 and 1931, Ravel devoted himself to the composition of a work that he felt to be his fullest expression as a creative artist — the Concerto in G for Piano and Orchestra. Ravel's last works were a Concerto for Left Hand and a cycle of three songs entitled *Don Quichotte à Dulcinée*.

Maurice Ravel died on December 28, 1937, following an unsuccessful operation on the brain.

PERSONAL NOTE

Madeleine Goss

IN his personal life, Maurice Ravel was precise in every detail. Small, both in stature and in build, his slender figure was always dressed in the latest and most irreproachable style. No effort was too great for him to make in achieving the effect he sought, whether this was a matter of matching ties, socks, and handkerchiefs to a certain suit or of working out the intricate detail of a composition.

As a whole, his life was colorless, almost devoid of so-called " human interest "; no violent emotions or overwhelming passions clouded the clear mirror that reflected his art. He was a channel through which music flowed, controlled and guided by his superlative craftsmanship, but unrestricted by the self-limited vision of those who live too intensely personal lives.

Ravel had a strongly detached nature. His attitude toward his own music was as impersonal as if it had been the work of another. He could seldom be persuaded to listen to his own compositions. At concerts he would escape to the corridors for a " cigarette libératrice." He was indifferent to success, and the idea of a " career " never occurred to him. The greater the public's acclaim, the more resolutely he clung to simplicity. He made music because he had to ("comme un pommier fait ses pommes"), never with a thought of advancing himself or of making money. He was completely unbusinesslike — did not even want pupils to pay for their lessons — and made barely enough from his compositions and concerts to live in comfortable but modest style.

As host of Le Belvédère, Ravel was gracious and entertaining. He greeted his friends quietly, but the engaging frankness of smile and the sparkle of his black eyes spoke more eloquently than the words of welcome that he found himself unable to express. All leading musicians of the day found their way at one time or another to the "doll's house" at the top of the hill in Montfort l'Amaury. There were gay parties with hours of music and endless discussion. Toward the close of the day, Ravel would usually suggest a walk through the forest to the village of Rambouillet — "pour prendre un petit verre."

As a storyteller, Maurice Ravel (sometimes called "Rara" by his friends) was clever and amusing; he expressed himself well, with simple elegance and a certain dramatic ability. Everything he did, even to the relating of anecdotes, was influenced by his desire for perfection. He had an unusual gift for imitation, and could reproduce the calls of birds and animals in a singularly realistic way. If someone paid him a compliment he would try to conceal his pleasure and embarrassment by turning aside with a humorous bird or animal cry. . . .

With Debussy he had a common trait in his passion for cats. Ravel's innate reserve and shyness left him only when he was with children or animals. A Siamese family shared his quarters at Le Belvédère for several years and were his chief delight and amusement. The inscrutable natures of these animals, with their unusual intelligence and curious devotion, reminded him, he said, of the Basque temperament. He not only understood cats — he could talk their language.

Many touching tributes have been paid to the memory of Maurice Ravel, including a number of biographies. A short biography by Grasset includes the following tribute: "Maurice Ravel was one of the noblest personifications of the French soul. Elegant in his simplicity, disdainful of appearances . . . faithful in his friendships, indulgent to ingratitude, capable of all delicacy and also of all audacity . . . he inspired the beginning of this century with his radiance."

THE COMPOSER SPEAKS

Maurice Ravel [1]

I AM not a " modern composer " in the strictest sense of the term, because my music, far from being " revolution," is rather " evolution." Although I have always been open-minded to new ideas in music (one of my violin sonatas contains a " blues " movement), I have never attempted in it to overthrow the accepted rules of harmony and composition. On the contrary, I have always drawn liberally from the masters for my inspiration (I have never ceased studying Mozart!), and my music, for the most part, is built upon the traditions of the past and is an outgrowth of it. I am not a " modern composer " with a flair for writing radical harmonies and disjointed counterpoint, because I have never been a slave to any one style of composition. Nor have I ever allied myself with any particular school of music. I have always felt that a composer should put on paper what he feels and how he feels it — irrespective of what the current style of composition may be. Great music, I have always felt, must always come from the heart. Any music created by technique and brains alone is not worth the paper it is written on.

This has always been my argument against the so-called " modern music " of the younger rebel composers. Their music has been a product of their minds and not of their hearts. First they created elaborate theories, and then they composed music to satisfy those theories. They built up beautiful reasons why the music of our time must be cut and dried, why it must be mathematical and intellectual (as an expression of a machine age). Then they went ahead and composed that type of music to justify their reasons. That is why I have never taken the works of these experimental composers too seriously. I have always looked upon it as an intellectual pose, an affected gesture. And great music has never been the result of a pose.

And how can you reduce music to a logical syllogism or to a mathematical formula? If you do, music loses its noblest attribute, as an expression of human emotions. Music, I feel, must always be

[1] This statement is from an interview with David Ewen in *The Etude.*

emotional first, and intellectual second. That is why, in composing, I have never been tempted by the radical style of the young and very interesting composers. I agree that there is some fascination to their music; I agree, too, that it does contain power and a considerable amount of originality. But their music has no heart and no feeling. We react to it intellectually, not emotionally. And so, although as experiments there may be something to say in defense of all this music, it is, in my opinion, an artistic failure.

Then, besides being cerebral, " modern music " is, for the most part, very ugly. And music, I insist, must be in spite of everything be beautiful. I do not understand the arguments of those composers who tell me that the music of our time must be ugly because it gives expression to an ugly age. Why does an ugly age need expression? And what is left to music if it is denuded of beauty? What mission has it, then, as art? No. Theories are all very fine. But a composer should not compose his music to theories. He should create musical beauty directly from his heart, and he should feel intensely what he is composing.

RAVEL

Guido Pannain

RAVEL's musical personality is outlined against a misty background that wavers between sentiment and buffoonery, between humor and self-abandon. Some have imagined that they saw therein traces of a Spanish temperament. The idea is false. The facts of his Pyrenean ancestry, of the recurrence of the Spanish rhythms in his music from the *Habanera* (1895) to *L'Heure espagnole* (1907), do not make him less of a Frenchman at heart. Actually he is far more French than Debussy, who, notwithstanding the limitations of his lyrical horizon, is a poet unrivaled in depicting shadows and rainbow reflections — a lyrical pantheist in whom sound becomes at once the thought and the artistic object. He is filled with living, breathing exaltation by the vision of nature — the nature of a symbolist.

Ravel, on the other hand, is always in control of his talents.
His emotion remains neatly defined in lyrical contours. Although
at times it may seem literary or artificial, transient or unsubstantial,
his musical world is impregnated with the emotional element. Here
and there one is even reminded of Chabrier, Massenet, or Puccini.
Yet though the emotional content of his work is involved, its form
is crystal-clear. In Debussy, Pelléas and Mélisande are two phantoms, the passing shadows of a dream. But Ravel's characters have
true life, though they dwell in the land of fable; though they exist
solely in a name — the mere images of a sigh or a smile, as in the
Pavane pour une Infante défunte (1899). Their life is as real as
that of their creator. . . .

Ravel is an artistic dandy; he throws over the most elementary
musical statements a colored veil that the physical senses cannot
analyze but that delights the mind from the richness of the literary
associations it unites to the musical. The composer is the spiritual
heir to the last half century's poetic feeling in France, and at the
same time he is a connoisseur of contemporary life, of that Parisian
quality of richness and evanescence in thought which, in the words
of Marinetti, " after having collected and brought to perfection in
its person all the graces and subtleties, the achievements of artistic
thought, from sheer perversity splits its colossal head by banging
it against the walls of the unattainable." The thin odor of literary
associations and the distorted flavor of ordinary life are combined
into those distilled harmonies, those miniature melodies. It is the
music of the literary *bourgeoisie* whose roots lie in the refined
debauchery of Baudelaire, which became petrified in the heart of
Mallarmé, where the affections had been replaced by the ultra-
refined sense of harmony. But Ravel is able precisely to build from
these cold splinters a living jewel, to contemplate it with smiles
and sighs, with an emotion that is not false, and that needs, if he
is to maintain his integrity of spirit, to be hidden by being rarefied.
In the full noonday of his music there lurks a shadow, in every
melody there lies the whisper of hidden feeling, in every harmony
the smile that has no touch of cheap irony, but only the faint echo
of malice. It is the irony and the lightheartedness of a wise child,
delighted by the vast spectacle of the natural world, happy in the
fresh interest that everything holds for him, from the passing flight
of a bird to the nearby quivering of a green leaf.

This is the true Ravel, the Ravel who has been so inappropriately labeled a satirist. The key to his outlook rests in the flux of mental states, reproducing and renewing themselves endlessly, yet retaining a certain unity of vision. Compare the sadness of *Le Gibet* with the pert satire of *L'Heure espagnole;* the ecstasy of *Soupir* with the lightness of *Shéhérazade* (1903); the morbid voluptuousness of *Surgi de la croupe et du bond* and the popular sparkle of *Tzigane* (1924) with the malicious reticence of the blues in *L'Enfant et les sortilèges* (1924–25). Ravel's essentially subjective lyricism can be recognized clearly, not only in those works of his which are best from the musical standpoint, but also when he fails to maintain a balance between technical form and the flight of his imagination. The sustained lyrical quality of his works such as the *Pavane pour une Infante défunte,* the first and second movements of the Quartet (1902–03), the Sonatina for Piano (1903–05), the first movement and *passacaglia* of the Trio (1914), the series of *Miroirs* (1905) and *Gaspard de la nuit* (1908), the *Valses nobles et sentimentales* (1911), the *Mother Goose* suite (1908), and the episode of the Princess in *L'Enfant et les sortilèges* is undeniable.

The fundamental element in Ravel's music is fed, yet not nourished, by elaboration of themes, and is swollen by exaggerated " pianistic " technique. It radiates a harmonic color that destroys the true romantic emphasis, and necessitates an incoherent, noisy stylism. When, however, Ravel's pianistic qualities do not degenerate into mere professional bravura, they become a manifestation of true musicianship. Frequently it has happened that his musical ideas have had their first expression through the pianoforte medium, from the Sonatina to the *Mother Goose* suite, originally a duet for piano; from the *Valses nobles et sentimentales* to *Le Tombeau de Couperin* (1914–17). The *Valses nobles et sentimentales* is a thing of delight — but that ennervating and emasculate delight which is so prevalent in the art of Ravel. The sensual and the romantic intertwine in changes from light to darkness, from veils of obscure harmonies to bursts of song. The first *valse,* cheerful and introductory in its nature, seems to throw open the door upon a world of voluptuous dreams, in which the old romantic *Walzer,* although living again in that form which the moderns have despised, sounds nevertheless convincingly contemporary. The musician is exploring, by the light of modern culture, the beau monde of a forgotten and less subtle age.

A romantic spirit, too, informs many episodes of the ballet *Daphnis et Chloé* (1909–12). Here there is a close-knit laconic expression upon which its creator has shed the almost overpowering light of his fancy. Yet, nevertheless, the artist has remained entangled with another problem — the problem of music in the theater.

Music, in the art of the ballet, can only be understood through the attitude of the Greeks, for whom sound and gesture were but different expressions of a single sentiment. Today gesture is a detached expression that becomes sentiment — the spirit of the dance — only on condition that it is spiritually interwoven with the rhythm; and when the music accompanies without penetrating it, the plastic form (which has no essential difference from the spoken drama) can only be expressed as a stationary frieze. In *Daphnis et Chloé* Ravel unhappily remains in a condition of complete dramatic palsy. The reverse is the case in the *Mother Goose* suite, which is not a musical subject drawn from the dramatic action, but action born in terms of music, so much so as to make visual scenery unnecessary. In *Daphnis et Cholé* he succumbs to that difficulty which overcomes so many musicians in the theater — of harmonizing an economy of action with an economy of musical expression. The true musician, the musician transcending the limits of the theater, is there, true enough; but wavering between the harmonic ultrarefinements of the real Ravel and an unexpected Wagnerian imitation, he seems at the beginning of the third part to be torn in half. Confronted by a dramatic action too indefinite to absorb into itself the music, he has merely created a musical score that is too derivative to have life for its own sake. The true musical expression is concentrated in the dance episodes, which realize a magical lyrical emotion in the solemn sensuality of the sacred dance, in the many-colored splendors of the general dance, and in a hundred finished details through which shine the alluring smile of the purest Ravelian coquetry.

In the sonata form, Ravel has written a Quartet, a Sonatina for Piano, a Trio for Violin, Cello, and Piano, and two sonatas, one for violin and cello (1920–22), the other for violin and piano (1927). To this category belongs also the *Introduction and Allegro*, for harp and small orchestra, a work that, although bearing the date of 1906, is little more than a promising juvenile composition.

The Piano Sonatina is Ravel's masterpiece. Here he has attained to the ideal balance between the form that hampers him like a foregone conclusion and his own individualistic melodic expression. In the actual musical quality of the Sonatina the same Ravel as elsewhere can be seen; but the true miracle of this miniature jewel lies in the perfection of the ensemble, that harmony between the part and the whole which is at once the cross and the reward of all artistic creation.

The Quartet has many virtues, but it lags behind the harmonious and well-knit Sonatina. In detail full of melodious freshness and solid, well-placed harmonies, it remains regarded as an entity unequal and fragmentary. It lacks the great virtue of the Sonatina — the fusion of the part in the whole. Out of the four movements, one is superfluous; and this superfluous section (and herein lies the real fault) is not isolated, but is distributed throughout the last three. The first movement, however, is a model of musical balance, in every way worthy of the composer of the *Mother Goose* suite.

Similarly, the Trio, beginning in an atmosphere that is purely musical in its conception, during the succeeding movements describes an artistic parabola. Of the four movements the only successful ones are the first and third: the first with its plastic development shows the echo of Grieg; the third is a finished *passacaglia*. The second and fourth are complete failures.

Nor can the Sonata for Violin and Cello be ranked amongst his good works, as compared with the Sonata for Violin and Piano, which in the first movement shows Ravel finding himself again. The other two movements of the Sonata are not on the same level as the first, although the second (significantly entitled a " Blues ") recalls the wit and vivacity of the first. The last movement, " Perpetuum Mobile," is a bravura piece for the violin that, as the title suggests, never rests from its phosphorescent sparkles, while the piano decorates them with light chromaticisms.

A point of considerable interest in Ravel is the relation between instrumental and vocal music. Ravel is an etcher in writing for the voice. His line is an arabesque of sound. He achieves perfect articulation of the word, and unites it in some cases to sounds that are intrinsically part of the harmonic structure, and then the outcome is pure song; or, alternatively, he contrives to strike a mean between song and recitative. Recitative is a form that may be defined as recitation in song, and owes its effect to both music and speech. Ravel's recitative lives; not because it is a declamation that is sung, or a song existing in declamation, but because it is part of a musical whole.

Although its logical existence essence is limited by the word, it achieves the importance of a counterpoint in respect to the instrumental part — a counterpoint that is a declamation. The notes are no longer an interpretation of the word; the word rather becomes a comment on the notes that have already acquired in themselves the sense of the words. A most striking example is found in the setting of Paul Verlaine's " Sur l'herbe," which is spiritually akin to the *Valses*. One might go so far as to say that this is not a lyrical piece for song and pianoforte, but one for pianoforte with vocal accompaniment. And the same applies — though less cogently — to *Placet futile*.

We can now understand those *Histoires naturelles* which made such a stir in 1907. The controversies and discussions aroused were natural, for Ravel had set real prose to music, and made the inhabitants of a zoological garden the objects of lyrical effusion. But even these unusual characters made evident his bizarre talent. For the picture he gives us is perfect. Everything in it becomes music — though Ravel does not intend to draw these animals as they are, but to fashion them in keeping with his means and resources. The outward impression of the image melts in the movement of harmonies; everything reflects the ardor of its creator, and lean prose becomes lyricism.

Maurice Ravel's two best-known works for the theater are *L'Heure espagnole* and *L'Enfant et les sortilèges*. Nohain's *L'Heure espagnole* is what, in modern slang, would be called a *pochade*. The key to its action, which takes place in the shop of an old watchmaker, is to be found in the disparity of age that makes inevitable a clash of physical needs between him and his wife. Torn between the rival advances of a poet and a banker, the woman ends up by giving herself to a strong-armed muleteer. The tale is coarse and scarcely witty, and it lingers over various scabrous details. The essential thing is that the action boils down to a kind of pattern formed by the pendulum swing of the watchmaker's great clocks. This happens in fact to such an extent that it becomes symbolic of the clock

case in which the woman has carried into her bedroom first the one,
then the other of her sham lovers — and the farce ends in monotony. We see only a woman surrounded by four idiots — one of
whom actually carries off the prize. But the music depicts neither
the imbecility nor the sensuality of the characters. It is merely a
commentary, a running accompaniment to this *pochade* in very
poor taste. However, it is indisputable that the beauty of some of
the detail is permanent and lasting; the rapid dialogue, full of
doubles ententes, adapted to the music with a mastery of language
always fluent and plastic, is one of the best examples of recitativo.

In *L'Enfant et les sortilèges*, by Colette, the action is poetry
in motion and realized to the full in music. The hero is a child —
the inevitable child of the fairy tales — a rascal, a vandal, passionate
and hasty. But, as if by enchantment, Truth comes to life around
him, and while it demonstrates by the light of lyrical beauty what
is the life he desires, it is a living reproach to him. Truth is a dream,
but what else can it be to a poet? The sorcerers of this opera, in
in which the inner key to Ravel's art is given once again, are really
the symbol of external things; the poltroons who refuse shelter to
the devastating child, dancing their confused minuet of conflicting
harmonies; the clock that, with its querulous tragicomic sorrow,
mourns the lost life, and makes the most of its sorrow, in the manner
of a lover in Puccini; and the fire, personified by a tiny soprano,
who throws off a little rondo full of bravura and life, behind which
lies the cinder with which the flame struggles vainly. The scene is
the twilight time; a hint of moonlight steals into the room. A child
is frightened, but from the pages of the book, which he had thrown
away, come distant voices of shepherds and shepherdesses; a cheerful retinue of tambourines and flageolets. The pastoral scene takes
shape, charming and gentle, graceful and modest. Then the delightful procession vanishes. But now one of the pages of the book
flutters open and there is revealed — first a languid white hand, a
head of purest gold, then the princess herself; the adorable princess
of the legends, misty as the vision of a dream. The child recognizes
the figure: it is she! — the princess conjured up by dreams from the
white cradle — and the melody that accompanies her comes from
the deepest wells of the heart, the clearest, the sanest, and the most
purely vocal of all Ravel's melodies, human and living in its appeal,
whose rise and fall is that of the human passions and the human
breath. The voice of the princess is contrapuntally interwoven with

the delicate instrumental texture, and her musical image becomes a human soul.

The next scene is the garden, filled with equivocal breezes, where the music of the frogs blends with that of the owl; where birds whistle and dragonflies buzz to slow waltz rhythms to the counterpoint of the nightingale. It is the dragonfly that the callous child had already transfixed with a pin; he knows the dancing animals — but in a moment of fright he gives a cry of " Mother! " And then the beasts fall upon him, teasing him, biting and stinging, then scratching. But in the scuffle a small squirrel is hurt, and falls near the child. It is the moral of the tale, the end of the tale; for the small infant is filled with pity for the beasts; he tries to help the little wounded animal, and the action redeems him; he becomes worthy of the help of the mother on whom he cried.

In the garden scene it seems that the creative power of the music is on the wane. This kind of botanical and zoological pantheism is reproductive rather than creative, in so much as the imitative sounds are not always susceptible of translation into music. One might say that the first cry of the bat was a warning signal, that the last part of this fine work was degenerating with the increasing loquacity of the animals. Nevertheless, the action concludes with a happy thought, and the musician winds up the fable with a charming madrigal, in an atmosphere of redemption, sung by all this little brute creation.

In thirty years of musical activity Maurice Ravel was never false to his nature. Neither the follies of expressionism, nor the noisy objectivity of the postwar phase, nor the vagaries of industrious and industrial charlatanism could persuade him to adopt fashionable poses. And, above all, he never yielded to that opportunism to which so many musicians, many of them talented, have bent the knee; men who in their first youth were ardent rebels; who weakened and gave way to the desire for easy and worldly success.

(ARNOLD SCHOENBERG)

1874 - 1951

BIOGRAPHY

ARNOLD SCHOENBERG was born in Vienna on September 13, 1874. He was a pupil of Alexander von Zemlinsky, whose influence on the young man was profound. Under Zemlinsky's guidance, Schoenberg composed the first of his works to achieve public performance: a string quartet, introduced in 1897 by the Wiener Tonkünstler Verein, and a set of songs, which appeared soon after this on a concert program of Professor Gärtner. The most important of his early works came in 1899, *Verklärte Nacht*, for string sextet (later rescored for string orchestra). The *Gurre-Lieder*, begun during this period, was not completed until thirteen years later.

In 1901 Schoenberg married Zemlinsky's sister. His style of composition was now undergoing radical change. He was evolving a new style that reacted against the Wagnerian romanticism of his earlier works and was revolutionary in its flagrant use of atonality. The first works to show the new direction were two string quartets and a *Kammersymphonie*. In 1924 he finally established a system of composition that employed twelve arbitrarily selected tones, a system with which he had been experimenting for a number of years. This "twelve-tone system" resulted in such works as the Suite for Piano, op. 25 (1921), the *Klavierstück*, op. 33a (1928), the Violin Concerto (1936), and the Piano Concerto (1942).

Because of his unorthodox approaches in both his atonal and twelve-tone compositions, Schoenberg was for many years an object for scorn and ridicule at the hands of critics and audiences who refused to understand his artistic aims. However, there was a small group of pupils who studied under him and who were inspired to write in a similar idiom. These — including Alban Berg, Erwin Stein, Anton von Webern, and Egon Wellesz — valiantly fought his battle. They helped organize the Verein für musikalische Privataufführungen in Vienna, after World War I, to introduce the music of Schoenberg and his school to Viennese music audiences.

When Hitler rose to power in Germany, Schoenberg sensed that the menace of Fascism would spread throughout Europe. He therefore voluntarily expatriated himself in 1933 and set up a temporary home in Paris, where, as a gesture against Nazism, he reassumed his Jewish faith, which he had abandoned in 1921. Late in 1933 he came to the United States and soon thereafter settled in Los Angeles, California, where he joined the music faculty of the University of Southern California and, after that, of the University of California at Los Angeles. In 1941 he became an American citizen, and in 1947 he received the Award of Merit from the National Institute of Arts and Letters. His seventieth and seventy-fifth birthdays, in 1944 and 1949, were celebrated in this country with commemorative performances of his major works. Schoenberg died in Los Angeles on July 13, 1951.

PERSONAL NOTE

Dika Newlin

"This book I have learned from my pupils," wrote Schoenberg in the preface of his *Harmonielehre* (1911). These paradoxical words characterize an attitude to which the composer was to remain faithful all his life — namely, a devotion not only to the idea of teaching but to the close relationship between teacher and pupil. Thus he was able to win many loyal disciples, who often became not merely his pupils in a formal sense but his true friends.

It is from the viewpoint gained in three years of study with Schoenberg in Los Angeles (1938–41) that I write these words about the composer's personality. Can one write about this personality as distinguished from the music? Hardly, for in Schoenberg personality and means of expression were so intimately fused that it has always seemed to me difficult to understand one without knowledge of the other. Therefore, these few details gleaned from many notes made during the time of my studies with Schoenberg should not be understood as merely gossipy reportage, but may, on the other hand, serve to illuminate many features of his music that might otherwise be incompletely understood.

A class or lesson with Schoenberg was — like listening to one of his compositions — always an adventure. When the little man with the massive head came briskly into the room you never knew what was going to occur in the next hour. We always hoped for one of his " good " days, for, when he was in an excellent mood, the class was not only intellectually stimulating but also thoroughly entertaining. Not that it was ever a relaxing experience to present your compositions to Schoenberg! As he himself did not play the piano (except enthusiastically and badly with one finger when he was carried away by the piano four-hand rendition of one or another of his favorite classical quartets, which he could no longer resist joining in) the pupil had to play his or her own composition before the class, or, if this was impossible, one of Schoenberg's young assistants would present the work. After such a performance, suspense would reign as — sometimes for as long as ten minutes — Schoenberg would stalk back and forth, shaking his head lugubriously. Then, judgment would be pronounced. The epithets used might range from " a leetle poor " to " razzer correct " (the latter was high praise!), but often more drastic comparisons were employed. After the performance of one student's string quartet, a long silence was eventually broken by the sentence: " Zees is an octet! " " Hmm? " " I said, zees is an octet." " How so, then? " " You need four men to play, four men to turn the pages. Iss no posies [pauses, rests] in zees piece! " (Schoenberg, in his later period an avowed apostle of the importance of achieving a transparent musical texture through the judicious use of rests, always liked to say in this connection, " Posies are never bad! ") Trenchant words never failed him in the case of graver musical misdemeanors. " Put it in ze vaste box! " was a favorite piece of advice. One girl tried to excuse a sloppy piece of work by explaining that she had written it in a restaurant during the lunch hour. After profound consideration, Schoenberg offered this suggestion: " Try anuzzer restaurant." Another young lady's all-too-lightly conceived minuet was written off with the words, " Monumentally trivial." Although a lack of seriousness in a student's works was always deplored by Schoenberg, an excess of pathos or of " souped-up " romanticism was equally detested by him. One boy put at the head of his rather pedestrian *Allegro* the fiery superscription *Allegro con fuoco.* Looking at this creation, Schoenberg remarked dryly, " Vere are ze fire engines? " Another romantic lad one day brought in a sketch of about five measures, explaining, " Mr. Schoenberg, I thought of this *soaring melody,* but then after five measures I became *completely exhausted.*" Schoenberg's answer to this was short and to the point: " Don't be silly! "

Schoenberg gave great loyalty to his pupils in the sense of helping each one to develop his or her own personal capacities to the utmost. This meant not only attention to musical problems but also to those of character. " Talent without character is nothing," he used to say; and much of his extreme severity in teaching — for, in spite of the lighter moments that I have recorded above, he could be brutal in his rejection of a work or a person when it so pleased him — was motivated by his desire to build the student's character. If a student could not stand up under rough treatment, he felt, that person was probably unfit for professional competition in the dog-eat-dog musical world of today; on the other hand, if the student came through successfully, he was sure to be " ready for anything." That some gentler natures were driven from the field by such treatment is certain — that the self-confident ones were thereby strengthened in their determination to follow a path that might prove difficult is equally so.

No picture of Schoenberg would be complete without recollections of his home life in Brentwood, California. The big Spanish-type house, set in spacious enclosed grounds, was always a lively place to visit, what with three young children and assorted pets ranging from dogs, through Angora rabbits, to Easter chicks. A study crammed with books and scores, shut off from the rest of the house, was the scene of the composer's more meditative pursuits. Meditation, however, went by the board on Schoenberg's birthday on September 13. He, an ardent believer in numerology, always imagined that 13 was his unlucky number — but this did not keep him from celebrating the date in grand style. Never to be forgotten are his birthday parties with good food and drink, plenty of informal musicmaking, and the master of the house everywhere at once doing everything from playing tennis or ping-pong to singing (?) his own parody on " Wien, Wien, nur du allein . . ."

Lovable and humorous or bitter and exasperating — Arnold Schoenberg could be all of this, and much more as well. We should not expect to find his music, either, always " easy to take " or comfortable to live with. But even as long association with an often difficult man made one more and more aware of the lasting values of this personality that transcended the many superficial faults, a loving study of his music enabled one to cut through its prickly hull to the concentrated kernel of precious content. Is it any longer necessary to say that both the man and his music richly rewarded such effort?

THE COMPOSER SPEAKS

Arnold Schoenberg

IF a composer does not write from the heart, he simply cannot produce good music. I have never had a theory in my life. I get a musical idea for a composition, I try to develop a certain logical and beautiful conception, and I try to clothe it in a type of music that exudes from me naturally and inevitably. I do not consciously create a tonal or a polytonal or a polyplanal music. I write what I feel in my heart — and what finally comes on paper is what first coursed through every fiber of my body. It is for this reason I cannot tell anyone what the style of my next composition will be. For its style will be whatever I feel when I develop and elaborate my ideas.

I offer incontestable proof of the fact that in following the twelve-tone scale, a composer is neither less nor more bound, hindered, nor made independent. He may be as coldhearted and unmoved as an engineer, or, as laymen imagine, may conceive in sweet dreams — in inspiration.

What can be constructed with these twelve tones depends on one's inventive faculty. The basic tones will not invent for you. Expression is limited only by the composer's creativeness and his personality. He may be original or moving, with old or modern methods. Finally, success depends only on whether we are touched, excited, made happy, enthusiastic . . . or not.

The tempest raised about my music does not rest upon my ideas, but exists because of the dissonances. Dissonances are but consonances that appear later among the overtones.

There are relatively few persons who are able to understand music, merely from the purely musical point of view. The assumption that a musical piece must awaken images of some description or other, and that if it does not it has not been understood or is worthless, is as generally held as only the false and banal can be. On no other art is a similar demand made; one is satisfied with the effects of their substance, whereby, to be sure, the material of the represented object of itself meets the limited comprehensive grasp of the middle-class mentality halfway. Since music, as such, lacks a directly recognizable material, some seek pure formal beauty in its effects; others, poetic proceedings.

There is no such distinction as old and modern music, but only good music and bad. All music, in so far as it is the product of a truly creative mind, is *new*. Bach is just as *new* today as he ever was — a continual revelation. Truly good things are new. I warn you of the dangers lurking in the die-hard reaction against romanticism. The old romanticism is dead, long live the new! The composer of today without some trace of romanticism in his heart must be lacking in something fundamentally human. On the other hand, music consists essentially of ideas. Beethoven called himself a " brain proprietor." It is no use to rail at new music because it contains too many ideas. Music without ideas is unthinkable, and people who are not willing to use their brains to understand music that cannot be fully grasped at the first hearing are simply lazy-minded. Every true work of art to be understood has to be thought about; otherwise it has no inherent life. Style in music arises spontaneously out of the exigencies of form; it cannot be decreed. The solution of a problem in style is an end in itself. Therefore art remains for art's sake.

Beauty is intangible; for it is only present when one whose intuitive power is strong enough to produce it creates something by virtue of this intuitive power, and he creates something new every time he exercises that power. Beauty is the result of intuition; when the one ceases to be, the other ceases also. The other form of beauty that one can have, which consists of fixed rules and fixed forms, is merely the yearning of one who is unproductive. For the artist this is of secondary importance, as indeed is every accomplishment, since the artist is content with aspiration, whereas the mediocre must have beauty. And yet the artist attains beauty without willing it, for he is only striving after truthfulness.[1]

My music must be listened to in the very same way as is any other music — forget the theories, the twelve-tone method, the dissonances, etc., and may I add: if possible, try to forget the composer, too. I once said in a lecture: " A Chinese poet talks Chinese, but what does he *say?* " To this I add: it is my own private business to write in this or that style, to use one or another method — this should not be of interest to the listener. But I do want my mission to be understood and accepted.[2]

SCHOENBERG

Dika Newlin

WE in America may today view the work of Arnold Schoenberg in a new perspective, seeing it in closer relation to the Viennese classical and romantic traditions from which it sprang, and also appreciating the fruitfulness of his theories for those who came after him. It is now widely recognized that the " method of composition with twelve tones " first developed by Schoenberg is not a mere collection of mechanical devices of interest only to a small Central European intellectual clique, but, instead, is a way of writing that can be of help and value to every composer and that offers infinite room for a variety of personal expression. Even an Igor Stravinsky, once bitterly opposed to this so-called " serial technique," has now adopted it for his own. Also, the works of Schoenberg's most renowned disciples — Anton von Webern and Alban Berg — have won ever-increasing public acceptance. Typical

---

[1] The above statement is from the book *Schoenberg*, edited by Merle Armitage.
[2] The above statement is from a letter to Roger Sessions.

instances of this are the series of sold-out performances of Berg's
Wozzeck at the Metropolitan Opera House during the 1958–59
season; the choice, by the New York City Center, of von Webern's
orchestral music as the basis for a sensational ballet, *Episodes*
(choreographed by Martha Graham and George Balanchine),
which, in its first season, had to be scheduled for extra performances
by popular demand; and the unprecedented release by Columbia
Records of an album comprising *all* of von Webern's music. Finally,
the music of Schoenberg himself is far more available to a wide
listening public than it used to be. Whereas twenty years ago but a
handful of recordings of a few Schoenberg compositions were available, today we may choose from over twenty-five records of his
music, ranging from his romantic early songs to his monumental
unfinished opera, *Moses und Aron*.

Yet, to many, Schoenberg still looms as a forbidding figure, a
sort of " engineer of music " rather than an inspired composer.
Often, listeners who feel this way have been influenced by negative
criticisms (to which, in common with many of his great contemporaries, Schoenberg was inevitably prey throughout his life as
well as after his death) without having had the opportunity — or,
perhaps, taken the trouble — to familiarize themselves with the
music thus criticized. Of course, each listener must respond to a
given piece of music according to his own degree of personal preparation, of inner readiness for the work. No amount of description
can take the place of the music itself. But what every reader can
know is the evolution from which this music sprang — in the case
of Schoenberg, during the course of a career that seemed to fulfill
itself with inevitability at each stage of its unfolding, in spite of
all outward difficulties. Thus understanding, the listener may be
better prepared to enjoy each individual work of Schoenberg, not
only for its own special beauties but also for the part it plays in a
development that — it is no exaggeration to say — has changed
the face of music in our time.

The young Schoenberg, growing up in Vienna at the turn of
the century, had at his disposal the rich heritage of Viennese classical tradition. Brahms, Bruckner, and Wagner were still living
figures, centers of controversy. Mahler was soon to come upon the
scene, to blow the cobwebs out of the Vienna Court Opera and,
during ten unforgettable years, to give the pleasure-loving Viennese
public a new and oftentimes startling look at masterpieces like

Tristan und Isolde and *Don Giovanni*. Schoenberg benefited from all this wealth of tradition and activity while at the same time he often suffered from the innate conservatism of the Viennese public (still today, incidentally, a trait very much to be reckoned with). Even his earliest songs and his lushly romantic tone poem for string sextet (later for string orchestra), *Verklärte Nacht* (1899) — today one of his most popular works — were received, at their first hearings, with hostile demonstrations. Thus, it is not surprising that bitterness entered early into Schoenberg's soul. Luckily, however, this bitterness did not cause him either to stop creating or to compromise cynically with popular taste; rather, it made him all the more determined to go his own way without consideration of the material consequences.

The inherited tonal patterns of the classic era had undergone, to say the least, considerable stretching during the late nineteenth and early twentieth centuries. The many "wandering chords" (harmonies that are ambiguous in meaning and can belong to many, or even to all, tonalities) employed by Wagner and his successors hastened this process of expanding tonality to its utmost limits. Thus, the designation of a piece by its key signature as being, say, in G major or F minor eventually seemed to be a formality only. One might see this tonality on the written page, but it was scarcely perceptible to the ear any longer. Schoenberg, realizing this, took the bold step of formalizing in writing what had for some time been audible fact in his music — he abandoned the use of the written key signature. This he did for the first time in the Finale of his Second String Quartet, op. 10 (1907–08). Perhaps inspired by the example of Mahler's symphonic use of the human voice, he introduced a soprano into the last two movements of the quartet. The symbolic meaning of the words she sings after the mysterious, novel harmonies of the Finale's opening has often been pointed out by commentators. " Ich fühle Luft von anderen Planeten," she intones ("I feel an air from other planets blowing"). Indeed, Schoenberg, entering upon this new land of music, might well have felt as if he were breathing "an air from other planets."

The works Schoenberg composed between 1908 and 1920 have often been referred to as "atonal." The composer himself rejected this term, for he felt that its implications were too negative. He preferred the word "pantonal," which emphasizes the positive aspect of such music, its inclusion of all conceivable possibilities of combining the twelve tones of our tempered system. Now, composers could enjoy the consequences of the " emancipation of the dissonance." There were now no intervals that had to be used in a restricted fashion; none were forced to " resolve," that is, to move along prescribed harmonic and melodic paths, but all could be used with equal freedom. Nor was such music bound to a specific tonal center. Every note could be, in theory at least, as important as every other note.

Such freedom created great opportunities — but also great responsibilities and great problems. Classic large-scale forms such as the sonata form, the construction of which had depended upon the relationships within a specific tonality, had to disappear from Schoenberg's creation for the time being. Instead, he wrote very short pieces (e.g., *Six Small Pieces*, for piano, op. 19, 1911, which are not more than five minutes long in their entirety) or pieces utilizing sung or recited texts (e.g., the twenty-one " melodramas " of *Pierrot lunaire* for *Sprechstimme*, reciting voice, and chamber group), in which the poetic text would determine the form. In this manner Schoenberg achieved some of his most striking successes in the " expressionistic " vein — intense personal emotions were projected in concise, vivid form. At the same time, his experiments in painting and in literature were following expressionistic lines.

However, this way of writing could not satisfy the composer indefinitely. There had to be a method, he felt, whereby all the wealth of material opened up by the " emancipation of the dissonance " would be used in more organized, systematized fashion, just as the " church modes " and major-minor scales of the past had served to organize the materials available to Western composers of those centuries. Thus there came into being what Schoenberg called the " method of composition with twelve tones related only to one another," that is, not bound to a specific tonal center. This accurate, but lengthy, descriptive name has often been shortened, by writers on this subject, to " twelve-tone method." " Twelve-tone technique " or " twelve-tone system " are terms also used, but frowned upon by the composer himself, as he felt they implied an undesirable — and nonexistent — degree of academic rigidity in his approach. Of late, the somewhat cumbersome word " dodecaphony " has often been applied to the entire twelve-tone production of Schoenberg and others, while the terms " serialism " and " serial technique " may carry even broader implications of the extension of the idea of organized series in music to other elements than melody and harmony (e.g., rhythm).

Basic to the twelve-tone method is the twelve-tone row, series, or basic set, from which all melodic and harmonic contents of a given composition are derived. The twelve available tones of our tempered system may be arranged freely in any order selected by the composer: for example, E–F–G–D-flat–G-flat–E-flat, A-flat, D–B–C–A, B-flat (the row of Schoenberg's Suite for Piano, op. 25, 1924). This series may then be transposed up or down, played backward, inverted (its intervals reversed in direction), or inverted *and* played backward — a total, including all possible transpositions, of forty-eight different row forms. The tones in each of these row forms may be sounded successively in melodies, or simultaneously in harmonies; melody and harmony may be fashioned from tones of the same row form, or several different row forms may be sounded at once. In short, in the hands of a master of this method, the number of possibilities seems limited only by the skill and imagination of the composer. Contrary to what has been popularly supposed, the number of emotional shadings possible in such music is equally great. In Schoenberg's own twelve-tone compositions, for instance, the gamut runs from the cool crispness of the Wind Quintet (1924) to the heart-gripping drama of *A Survivor from Warsaw* (1947), a shattering account of a Nazi massacre in the Warsaw ghetto. Surely, it is this very universality that has led more and more composers to utilize the manifold possibilities of the twelve-tone method and thus to enrich the spiritual, emotional, and intellectual experience of the truly open-minded music listener.

In some of the works Schoenberg composed after coming to America in 1933, an interesting phenomenon, indicative of this universality, occurred. We find him often returning to definite tonalities (Suite for String Orchestra in G; *Theme and Variations*, for band, in G minor; *Variations on a Recitative*, for organ, with a clear tonal center of D, though without key signature). Also, within the framework of the twelve-tone method, he begins to use techniques (octave doublings, distinct cadence formations) that have definite tonal implications. Such instances may be seen in the *Ode to Napoleon* (1942), wherein E-flat major is made to symbolize the heroism and idealism of George Washington, as praised in Byron's poem, and in the Piano Concerto, op. 42 (1942), where the crashing chords with their octave doublings often suggest a latter-day adaptation of Liszt's or Brahms' piano techniques. Schoenberg's " returns " to the past have often been misunderstood and misinterpreted by critics. Some have thought they were " concessions to the American public." But this is a grave injustice both to the composer, who never made concessions to anyone, and to the public, which, at the level where it can appreciate the music of a Schoenberg at all, neither needs nor wants such concessions. Others proclaimed that, by returning to tonality, Schoenberg tacitly admitted the esthetic bankruptcy of the " twelve-tone system." The real truth is far otherwise. Actually, such fusions of twelve-tone and tonal techniques only strengthened the method, for they showed its power to include within itself the riches of the past as well as to develop new areas of sound. As Schoenberg himself once said in mildly chiding certain disciples for overorthodoxy, " My method is *inclusive*, not *exclusive!* "

The " disciples "! Ever an important part of Schoenberg's life, for, from his very early years onward, his teaching kept pace with his composing. True, teaching was a necessary means of making a living, as it has been for so many composers, but Schoenberg's attitude toward this task prevented it from ever degenerating into mere drudgery. Most truthfully, he wrote in the preface to his *Harmonielehre* (*Theory of Harmony*), first published in 1911 and still a valuable textbook in American universities, " This book I have learned from my pupils." That learning process continued in later years, too, for such exemplary textbooks as his *Structural Functions of Harmony*, *Models for Beginners in Composition,* and *Counterpoint* grew out of his experiences with his American university classes. In those classes, he dealt not only with the few who were destined to become composers of distinction, but also with the many average students preparing for more modest teaching careers. It could not always have been easy, yet he found the way to help these students, too, to hear and understand music more accurately than ever before and even to compose most acceptable little pieces. It should be stressed that, unlike some other composers of today, he made no effort to enforce imitation of his own personal style. On the contrary, he violently discouraged students from attempting twelve-tone composition until they had a thorough understanding of the basic principles of classic harmonies, counterpoint, and form. Any student who successfully completed Schoenberg's courses in these subjects, whatever his subsequent professional career, indeed, possessed a solid background and a training in disciplined thinking that would stand him in good stead throughout his lifetime.

A while back I used the word " spiritual." It is an important word here, for no verbal portrait of Schoenberg would be complete without at least a mention of the vital role that spiritual considerations played in Schoenberg's creative life (and not merely in those works of specifically Jewish subject matter, increasingly frequent in his later years). Someone has said: " To be an artist is a gift of God. To possess it is no merit of ours. Instead, it is an obligation not to misuse the gift." How well Schoenberg knew this! Always, he gave due credit to the role the " Supreme Commander " had played in his development as a composer. In the text for his incomplete oratorio *Die Jakobsleiter, Jacob's Ladder* (begun in 1915), the Angel Gabriel tells the aspiring souls, " Learn to pray." And the very last words Schoenberg set to music were those of his own " Modern Psalm ": " And yet I pray . . ." It is not too fanciful to suppose that so dedicated a teacher and inspirer of young composers would have found one of his prayers answered today, in the influence his lifework and the attitude of uncompromising integrity displayed therein are having upon the elite of young musicians. And so, the " consideration and reconsideration of Schoenberg's life and work " for which Paul Stefan called years ago will continue to have its beneficent effect for many generations to come.

(WILLIAM SCHUMAN)

1910-

BIOGRAPHY

WILLIAM HOWARD SCHUMAN was born in New York City on August 4, 1910. Music study began comparatively late, in his twentieth year, when he began lessons in harmony with Max Persin and soon thereafter in counterpoint with Charles Haubiel. During this period Schuman wrote popular songs and made arrangements for jazz band. After receiving his bachelor-of-science degree at Teachers College, Columbia University, in 1935, and attending the Mozarteum in Salzburg during that summer, he became instructor at Sarah Lawrence College, New York. Additional music study then took place with Roy Harris. Schuman achieved prominence as a serious composer between 1939 and 1941 with *An American Festival Overture* and the Third Symphony (each introduced by the Boston Symphony Orchestra under Koussevitzky) and the Third String Quartet. The first award presented by the New York Music Critics Circle went to Schuman in 1942 for his Third Symphony, and when, in 1943, a Pulitzer Prize was established for music, he became its first recipient for his secular cantata, *A Free Song*. From this time on, he rapidly rose to a dominating position among American composers. In 1939 and 1940 he received Guggenheim Fellowships. After leaving Sarah Lawrence College in 1945, he was appointed president of the Juilliard School of Music. He resigned from the Juilliard School in 1962 to become president of the Lincoln Center for the Performing Arts in New York.

PERSONAL NOTE

Flora Rheta Schreiber
and Vincent Persichetti

IN THE household of William and Frances Schuman in New Ro-
chelle any morning can be felt the excitement with which Schuman gets ready for a new day. Each day for him must somehow be
a " great " day exuberantly lived — each day must be all its hours.

This heightened sense of living, of getting things done, made
possible his achievements despite his late start as a composer. His
Faustian restlessness has always propelled him on. Time is a com-
modity to be hoarded, an enemy to be conquered, a friend to be
cultivated. Schuman himself is a personality seldom in repose.

The late start had another important influence. It meant that
the bedrock of Schuman's personality was firmly set before he ever
thought of himself as an artist. . . . For this reason he is free of two
of the most baffling problems confronting artists — a sense of isolation from average people and an ineptitude in the conduct of practical affairs. Once a " real boy," later a " regular guy," smooth, effective as an organizer, he is and always has been the reverse of the
popular picture of the artist as long-haired, gauche, living a life of
penury, beating ineffectual wings. Though musically he became a
radical, he clung to conservative manners. . . .

There are some writers who, more normally abnormal, resent
Schuman strongly. To them he seems *too* well adjusted to be an
artist at all. His integration strikes them as sterility, his ability to
get along with people of different types, as Philistinism. These artists
resent him for being acceptable and successful. He will admit that
his is a success story but not in the strict sense, insisting that it is
rather the story of artistic success urgently sought but of increasing
earnings coming unpredictably. " I'm glad I was never poor," he
says, " so I've never had any respect for wealth." On the whole he
takes a matter-of-fact view of his achievement, attributing this
achievement to hard work, to the right teachers, and above all to a
positive refusal to take " no " for an answer. He explains his career
as a musical administrator in equally realistic terms: there is a great

difficulty in filling administrative posts in music; many musicians are temperamentally unsuited to this kind of work; he, as it happens, is well suited to it.

He is sometimes surprisingly humble, as when, talking of outstanding men of affairs such as the Juilliard board of directors, he will say: " It is not given in the normal life of a musician to meet men of that caliber. Being president of Juilliard has meant the opportunity of knowing these men and men like them and I'm grateful." He is likely to be awed in the presence of an authority on a subject of which he has only a layman's knowledge.

Yet there are many subjects in which he qualifies as the intelligent layman. A regular reader of such publications as *Harper's*, *The New Republic*, and of England's *New Statesman and Nation*, a faithful reader of the *Times* and the *Herald Tribune*, reading real-estate page, financial figures, baseball scores, everything, he is conversant with contemporary events and opinion. These events he watches from a position in the middle of the road. To establish the exact position of that road one might describe his political and social philosophy as Rooseveltian. He has remained a consistent, if at times highly critical, admirer of the late president. Yet, at each election he gives the matter of voting for a Republican real consideration — as should be the habit of one who was named after William Howard Taft.

He reads a wide variety of books, biography, poetry — especially new poetry — economics, history, medicine, semantics, psychology, as the subject catches his fancy. He has time for novels only in the summer. When he reads fiction he gets so involved in the story that he can't put the book down. The only books that really bore him are routine musicological studies. He is fascinated by such works as Berlioz' *Memoirs*.

He goes to some sixty or seventy concerts a year — many of them Juilliard concerts. He was once a record collector, but stopped when he started teaching. Now he studies scores instead of buying records. He doesn't go to the opera often, but he has his favorites: *Carmen*, any opera by Mozart, Verdi's *Otello*. Nothing could induce him to sit through *Parsifal* although once he had his Wagner period.

He is in love with the theater. He loves it when it is high art and he loves it when it is out-and-out commercial. His most excited theater memories are of plays by Ibsen and Chekhov, *The Green*

Bay Tree, and the productions of the Group Theater, especially plays by Clifford Odets. In the theater and in literature he finds great emotional excitement, the same sort of excitement that he finds in music itself.

Movies are something else again. He likes to cry with the tortured and exult with the victorious. He expects nothing and always gets a lot, perhaps as much out of a bad picture as out of a good one if the picture is really bad enough.

He loves gadgets like meat slicers and ice-cream makers and is quite likely to insist on having a strawberry ice-cream soda on a freezing February night. He enjoys experimenting with startling combinations in food. Just to tease a Babbitt he will say: " Artistic people ought to be allowed to eat more than other people."

Yet there is also a severity about him, a refusal to tolerate people who play at music, or, for that matter, at any other art. Unrelenting is his contempt for a certain brand of intellectualism that he considers pretentious and arty. In his definition music becomes pretentious when it crosses the line between a direct expression of human emotion and a devious expression of an affected attitude toward life. The word " arty " from his lips has the same ring of disparagement as " atheist " would have from the mouth of a bishop.

He will listen to criticism and says that it is silly not to do so because through criticism he may learn something. He believes that talk of the content of instrumental music in terms of a direct, calculated extramusical expression is nonsense. He is unhappy when not writing music, and he writes it for the same reason that he once played baseball — because he finds it exciting.

When he writes, he shuts out everything else. If he is called to the phone he will come right back and pick up where he left off. Later, the return to the workaday world is quite easy. He works regularly — if pressed, on a strict schedule, after meticulously planning a chart of hours and faithfully punching a self-imposed time clock. People always ask him: " How can you be sure you'll accomplish anything when you work without inspiration? " He answers: " Of course you don't know whether you'll turn it out if you do work. But you can be sure you won't turn it out if you don't work."

And so each day is all its hours, and life seems good to him, so good that he is watching his calories because they say thin people live longer and he wants to live long, just as long as possible, because there are so many works he wants to write and there are so many projects he has in mind. More than fifty years are behind him, but there are years and years ahead — hours and hours to fill with work. This is the present, this time that is his. And as for the future — well, the future lives in the motion of the present.

THE COMPOSER SPEAKS

William Schuman [1]

You have asked me my credo as a composer. At the risk of over-simplification, I would like to state that the time-honored verities of artistic creation still seem to me basic. The *sine qua non* is an inner urge that knows no denying. A composition must have two fundamental ingredients — emotional validity and intellectual vigor.

Techniques constitute the objective working methods of art. In the mature artist, they are indistinguishable from the creative act. In our time, however, techniques are discussed at such length and with such partisanship that often they seem to be viewed as ends in themselves. The only test of a work of art is, of course, in the finished product and not in the process of its making. Furthermore, we know that adherence to a particular school of thought or esthetic predilection cannot, of itself, guarantee quality. Works of merit in our time, as in times past, have been composed through a variety of approaches and techniques encompassing the gamut of known devices, plus the invention of new ones.

Preoccupation with procedures has led to rather absurd lengths in categorizing composers. For myself, I am not much impressed with categories, but prefer rather to judge each work on its own terms. Over the years, my own music, for example, has been referred to as neoclassic, neoromantic, neobaroque, as well as strong, weak, ugly, beautiful, international, and American.

In sum, a composer's stated artistic credo does not tell us very much about the music itself. It can only report his views. Every

[1] This statement was written by the composer expressly for this book.

composer has read the history books and knows that his music will be evaluated in long time (or no time at all) through its inherent qualities. And these qualities can be found only in the hieroglyphics with which he fills his pages and which are revealed by performing musicians.

The composer's job is to be faithful to his gifts by composing the best music of which he is capable. No discussion of his work or championing of his esthetic in any way alters his final product. The continuing flow of the art of music through the centuries and the possibility, however modest, that his music may enter the stream is sufficient reward.

Finally, as with most American composers, I am involved in a variety of other professional activities. Functioning through the art of music in any capacity provides an avenue for expression of heart and mind. It does not matter whether this expression comes through the writing of music, the teaching of it, or administering its organizational aspects. Music is the core and, as such, is for me infinitely more than the exercise of the disciplines of an art or the means of a public career. And, since music is one of the glories of man, it is a deep satisfaction to be a living part of it.

SCHUMAN

Flora Rheta Schreiber and
Vincent Persichetti

IF THERE is more of one ingredient than another in the rich mixture of William Schuman's music it is the strong-fibered energy that generates a constant boil of movement. There is motion stirred by boldness and intensity, movement that pushes forward resourcefully and seriously, and beneath even the quietest pages a restless current that will eventually surface in a rush.

This youthful drive might well send the music catapulting over any real compositional problems. Sheer speed and quick changes of harmonic garb could carry it along, sidestepping direct solutions. In this most characteristic element of Schuman's music his kindest critics see potential weakness. Objectivity is often lost in music conceived in such passion, and many an earnest listener is swept on more by fury than by sound. A close study of Schuman's music and a real understanding of his creative approach will, we believe, reveal a solid composer with an original creative spirit.

Much of Schuman's music is linear, and its melodic contour forms huge arcs of sound. Lines without the usual phrase breaths move steadily through an entire section toward a goal well fixed in the composer's mind at the outset. The harmonies that result from this contrapuntal movement do not form a progression from chord to chord or bass note to bass note, but rather weave a pattern of similar chordal structures with matching textures suited to the mood and personality of the musical statement. And by the same token, when the problem is approached harmonically Schuman selects a unifying kind of harmony rather than a bass-regulated of chords.

The result is a forward-moving mass of sound in unorthodox treatment that is as unfamiliar to some ears as it is peculiar to the Schuman idiom. This music, without structural gaps and recurring cadences, can easily be mistaken for the misguided wanderings of a fundamentally conventional mode of writing. The surest path to the core of Schuman's music and to an understanding of his well-thought-out approach may be through a study of its melodic constituents and singing shape.

Enthusiasm, drive, and bite in a melodic frame give Schuman's music its power of projection. This huge-sounding music is made for billboard rather than newspapers. Boldness, freshness, and intensity of feeling are prominent; yet there is some grace and charm. Most of Schuman's music is about something big. Intimacy and delicacy appear as reflected images of the primary idea, and slip by easily. Only short periods of time are allowed for personal retrospection, and as contrast, the contemplative is overshadowed, or even swallowed, by surrounding passages. Long slow pages seem held in a firm masculine hand, yet sometimes bear the touch of gentleness, as in the Fourth String Quartet (1950), the first movement of which remains calm as the lines are led on unruffled by the serene second theme. When the even quieter opening theme is employed as a developing force this work virtually tiptoes. Except for three short agitated places, the closing section is soft and delicate to the end.

In early works Schuman lacked an objective approach. He was terribly anxious to write and loved his measures so fiercely that he was unable to evaluate them fairly. Inferior stuff was mixed with exciting, original material and carried by continuous drive to make the passage come off. Delighted with his ability to produce a variety of colors by combining fourths, he set out to build whole sections and sometimes pieces on these chords by fourths. The harmonic background became pale and the tension monotonous, so that there was a drain on his rhythmic and formal resources that sapped the quality of the output.

Schuman was quick to realize what was happening and began to demand that his abused harmonic formations take their place in the formal scheme. His structural thinking was imaginative and colorful, and required his harmonies to follow through in reciprocal relation. His palette widened, and progress in developing creative perspective was rapid. He was twenty-three years old when he completed his first published serious work, the *Four Canonic Choruses* (1932–33). One needs only to look at the Third String Quartet (1939) to find a maturer Schuman. The quartet ranks with the best of his output and begins a long line of remarkable compositions.

He does not seek aid from out-of-the-way experiments, those obvious attempts to lure the public to a work by way of an unheard-of combination of instruments or an extramusical association. The press is never able to hail or propagandize a coming Schuman event; they can only announce it. There is no parasiting on a prominent political event, nor are there self-eulogizing program notes at hand. One attends the performance and finds the excitement in the music.

Schuman's music springs from a single lexicon of thought. Its profile is strong and definite, and there is an over-all clarity. A conductor once dismissed his music with " but I want music with melodies." Schuman replied, " It is all melody. If you can't sing my music it is because you can't sing." This is our clue to the understanding of his music. Each idea pivots on the melodic. The rhythmic structure is implied in the thematic outlines, and the harmonies are suggested by the characteristic melodic skips and general textual feeling. Even form ideas are generated by the physical needs and implications of the primary melody. Ornamental tones in a slow theme will sooner or later be released in a fast section suggested by the embellishments. Or a melody may contain an interval that leaps upward. In development this characteristic skip will be expanded to help it in its reach, and a martial background of polychords might be punched out in assistance. A searching, lyric melody may establish a form in pursuing its winding course to the final cadence. Then again, a tune may have a stubborn tone as its low point, and an entire section may be built around this single tone. A nose-diving melody might suggest a background pattern of failing tones to support a new section that will be slow and singing. Melodic implication seems always at the source, and structural derivations of melodic character form Schuman's music.

He does a great deal of singing while composing. Speaking on a broadcast of his wordless *Choral Etude* (1937) Schuman hinted at the vocal approach. "Sounds can be sung on syllables uniquely suited to the nature of the music expressed. I feel we all do this subconsciously when we sing a tune without words and supply nonsense syllables. I simply listened to the way in which I sang my own choral music and recorded those sounds phonetically."

He works hard at his craft and knows his materials. Though a young man, he has, in a surprisingly short space of time, developed a personal style. His rhythmic and harmonic gestures are easily distinguished from those of his contemporaries, and his melodies contain unmistakable Schumanesque trade-marks. Even when he appropriated tunes from the eighteenth century, in the *William Billings Overture* (1943),[1] he took them so thoroughly through his own creative channels that they emerged good Schuman.

Schuman does not use tonality for structural purposes. Nevertheless, it is strongly felt in his music, even though there is no key signature. He does not restrict his thinking to major and minor dictates or to a set number of accidentals at the start of a piece. He covers the wide gamut of scales bestowed upon Occidental civilization, and needs the elbow room afforded by the freedom of shifting modes, "twelve-tone" melodies if he chooses, but always a tonality. Even though the first movement of the Fourth String Quartet is not glued fast to a prescribed key, tonality is felt. The "key" is a product of the opening viola tones in E-flat and D. These tones introduce the A theme at the beginning, and close the movement by sounding the top tones of the chords in the final cadence. Some of his harmony is misunderstood. The much-mentioned polytonality in Schuman is not polytonality but polyharmony. Triads of kindred tonalities joining to form one resonant five- or six-note chord result

[1] The composer has withdrawn this overture and used much of its material for the *New England Triptych* (1956).

in a harmony enriched by overtones and belonging to one key. He is fond of these chords and can manipulate them by adjusting the dissonant relationship of the chord members to acquire any texture he needs.

"Modernism" is usually associated with harmony. Many contemporary works that are generously supplied with dissonant chords are otherwise quite conventional and are not so new as they sound at first hearing. In Schuman, however, we have not only dissonance, but innovations in the rhythm, form, and melody. His modernism is distinctively individual and unique. In his song-plugging days he heard few of the serious works that were either grafted to jazz idioms or forced into a dissonant shell by experimentalists. He built his own path of dissonant thinking, and his ideas were already crystallized by the time he was fully exposed to new trends. He invariably found merit in techniques far removed from his own creative channels, but his personal conviction was such that atonality was rejected. He never became infatuated with the twelve-tone style. His music, however, has the melodic resources of twelve-tone technique without the atonal element. He approaches the problem through juxtaposition of modes, which often results in two sets of harmonies at once.

Schuman thinks in long-range terms, plotting the course of a large-scale work before the writing actually begins. Germinal ideas are chosen for their emotional power; then they are sorted and studied carefully for their potentialities and run a first-rate obstacle course, trying to break through his musical thought processes. The material selected takes form as a more or less complete organism before reaching paper. A thematic idea is seldom used unless a detailed plan of the entire work can be laid upon it. A picture of the future must be there. The possible sonorities of the medium are weighed and tested for properties in relation to the initial material. Occasionally, certain aspects of the music are sketched in the rough. A kind of "dummy" music is written to get the feel of the piece.

Schuman's faculty for self-criticism keeps him on the alert for bad spots. His ability to seek out beforehand the places where the music will falter, and either alter the original theme or nonchalantly throw it out, saves him many futile pages. Pieces do not have to be scrapped at the halfway mark because of irremovable defects. Hindsight has no place in the technique of composition.

It is during this process of blending form ideas beforehand that astoundingly original things happen. This panoramic view enables Schuman to contrive unique orchestral schemes. His Second Symphony (1937) [2] is a one-movement work integrated by a single predominating theme. The entire work is based on the single tone C. This tone is sounded or implied throughout the symphony. The freedom and energy that come from being able to compose mentally a passage leading to a coda for a piece that has not yet been written gives him a perspective, and consequently an architectural command, that is invaluable.

Schuman devotes himself to maintaining interest by not revealing his ultimate climactic point until the psychological moment for release comes. This suspense treatment precludes dangerous letdowns and carries even the uninitiated listener over strange and wildly imaginative passages with comparative ease.

The majority of works begin without introduction. Normally, introductions are used to establish a mood, to present material for further development, or to disclose a separate entity. These approaches hold little interest for Schuman. His initial ideas barge in intently and with impact. The *Symphony for Strings* (1943), for example, begins suddenly and noisily with all the violins in unison.

Up to about 1946, transitions gave Schuman trouble. They were either so important that they gave an impression of being independent sections or so short that they formed a bridge too weak to link the sections. He had better luck when he forgot about lacing his sections and kept them moving until they grew into each other. Schuman soon realized this. His later music moves in long lines and grows from one idea to the next without the customary transitions. Characteristic figures resulting from the development of one section's material generate the thematic constituents of the next. Therefore, all elements that make up a piece are related to each other and form a tight structure, free of loose ends.

This approach insures uniformity of design and accounts for the clear shape of his long works. It leaves no room for impressionistic scattering of ideas, or annoying breaks that let in fickle cadenzas. No vague harmonies are needed to glaze a page spattered with odds and ends of themes. Program music as so often diseased by impressionistic formulas of the twentieth century is alien to him. The few pieces that bear descriptive titles, with the sole exception of

[2] The composer has withdrawn his First and Second Symphonies, and the First String Quartet, pending revisions.

Newsreel (1941), are translations of psychological states into tonal language.

The absence of literal recapitulation is characteristic of Schuman's writing as well as that of most of his contemporaries. Once he makes a statement he cannot reiterate unless it has experienced alteration. In the first movement of the Piano Concerto (1942) the returning principal theme brings with it material that grew out of the development of the movement. The new ideas are interwoven among the elements of the returning theme, which, in itself, is drastically altered. Its dimensions, structural make-up, instrumentation, and texture have changed. Only the general feeling remains, though gaining in energy and precision.

In later works, themes are often introduced almost simultaneously. The first movement of the Fourth String Quartet is primed by the second theme, which enters before the first theme is fully stated. In the Sixth Symphony (1948) there are three outstanding themes: the *passacaglia*, which remains unaltered during four statements; the A theme, which begins in the seventh measure, before the *passacaglia* theme completes one statement; and B, which joins A, during the fourth *passacaglia* statement.

Ideas occur to Schuman in their inherent instrumental setting. A theme is never given the schoolmaster's instrumentation test of being put through the paces of all instruments beforehand, to see if it can be played by everyone. It may grow and take on changing shapes. Each player who gets a whack at it finds that his version is constructed in a manner best suited to his instrument, yet the most virtuoso fugue theme is played by every instrument, even though a player may have to share it with another member of his section.

Schuman is concerned with the possibilities rather than the limitations of his instruments. This is a healthy attitude. One never feels that the composer hesitates or is doubtful. He knows what instruments are just able to do and builds passages that exploit such extremes. Music of this kind is bold and sharp, and sometimes terrifying. He will take chances. The tremendous effect obtained from four agile trumpets in four independent parts, in the Third Symphony (1941), is that of an electric trumpet machine. By a clever manipulation of cross rhythms the fast runs keep up while the individual players have comfortable breathing spaces and well-spaced runs.

Schuman's orchestra shines, and full pages never sound

muddled. Each instrumental group is contrapuntally and harmonically integrated. He knows how to space the brass to make the most of the natural overtones of a resonant chord, and understands that reinforcing declamatory brass with woodwinds rubs off the luster. Instead of doubling the fugal horn passage in the Third Symphony with bassoons, clarinets, and arco strings as Richard Strauss might have done, Schuman gets more sound by preserving the horn luster. Pizzicato strings are added for punch.

Any device that will retain a musical idea in an easier form is worth consideration. Schuman is full of tricks that facilitate performance. He knows that it is safer to assume that his piece will be played with insufficient rehearsal. Difficult passages are divided between similar instruments whenever possible. Such division gives trumpets the freedom of an oboe and oboes the punch of a trumpet.

There are several marked characteristics in his orchestral coloring. Muted strings are not limited to soft and delicate playing. They sound like an additional string section when used as declaimers of intense passages. He can scramble strings and preserve their clarity by coupling. He is not afraid of backboning the orchestra by strings and is not afraid to use brasses for soft background. Schuman is fond of timpani solos, and of fast unison woodwind passages in continuous motion.

In some respects Schuman's vocal music is simpler than his instrumental because a great deal of it was written for amateur chorus. It is true that in writing for a chorus of girls from Sarah Lawrence he was constrained to the use of a simpler harmonic and contrapuntal technique, but he realized that he did not have to hold back rhythmically. He managed to cover a wide gamut of feeling within the physical limitations of this medium. On the printed page numerous passages look too difficult rhythmically for the amateur. These complexities are born of the natural rhythms of jazz, so much a part of the American people. With intelligent training, amateurs can sing rhythmically complicated music. These rhythms are second nature to the large percentage of the untrained population. It is on this score that Robert Shaw and his groups took off for heights seldom scaled by semiprofessional singers. It is on this premise that William Schuman set forth to write a choral literature challenging to the amateur and endearing to the professional, works that can well be treated as études in contemporary choral singing. They make a stilted small-town choral group supple, cut into the ice of a professionally stereotyped outfit, and widen the field for other composers.

Texts on democratic themes are preferred. The *Prelude for Voices* (1939), with words by Thomas Wolfe, is not typical of Schuman's choice of text. Introspection of the type represented by such a line as " Which of us is not forever a stranger and alone? " is seldom found in his choral works. Whitman or Whitmanesque lines of Genevieve Taggard are more usual. Lines on the destiny of American folk attract Schuman. He creates as one of the folk, yet avoids quotation; he can handle a patriotic theme without burlesque or nausea.

Schuman sets English to melody without falsifying the natural rhythm of the language. When music and words want to take different paths he usually gives in to the words. Form and melodic line are determined by the text, and the musical rhythm is guided by speech rhythm. The mood of the text strongly determines the harmonic texture and background patterns. Musical illustration is secondary to the verbal setting, yet the finished product entails no sacrifice of musical freedom. Schuman can twist voice parts unmercifully, and still they will " sound." Without a change of harmony he can create excitement solely from his rhythmic resources. His voices move freely in canonic passages, avoiding harmonic snags. He may content himself with no harmonic movement, but never with interrupted harmonic movement (the plague of canons). Schuman considers recitative less powerful than straight song, and avoids it. He must have power, even if he is compelled to use long unison passages or coupled two-part counterpoints to get it. The *a cappella* eight-part chorus, *Pioneers!* (1937), opens with a coupled two-part counterpoint using all voices. Later it spreads into rich eight-part writing.

None of his style traits are lost while writing for chorus. This music is less intricate than the symphonies but retains the essence of the larger works.

In his Sixth Symphony, *Judith* (1949), and the Fourth String Quartet one is no longer conscious of techniques or devices in Schuman. Here is music that gets under the notes and in the blood stream. It breathes lyric beauty, and stamps a vivid impression upon the listener. The pages of the score are complex, but the music that is projected from this complexity is clear and forceful. The control of emotional drive and the clarity of formal thinking bring the music directly within the reach of the listener. Logic is at no point outrun by invention and the architectural pattern is devoid of any feeling of experimentation.

Schuman has rid his harmonies of parallelism and shaken excess resonant sonorities from his tonal palette. Inner voices have become active, and sectionalism is no longer a stumbling block. His bass part has grown strong and now dictates harmonic progressions resulting in a new chromatic-melodic admixture. These recently acquired procedures mark clearly a growth in formal conception, harmonic imagination, and thematic scope in the later Schuman.

Each new piece brings forth more new harmonic elements, and Voyage (1953), a cycle of five piano pieces, for example, uncovers fantastic shapes and crevasses. There is less preoccupation with open confession and good health, as cringing gestures are veiled by complex harmonic textures that have been soaked in the chromatic liquor of the Fourth String Quartet. A touch of personal shyness is present in the late works while climactic points are approached cautiously and one section is never completely freed from the shadow of another. In the Sixth Symphony the fast music is under constant surveillance of the slow music, and in the light but straight serious opera, The Mighty Casey (1953), no one of the many short pieces ever completely rids itself of the contact made with the previous number. The elements of comedy and pathos rub so hard they fuse into a hot " freeze " — the tableaux of fans and players.

The heroic dualism caused by the resistance of the diatonic to the chromatic in the Sixth Symphony, the passion and violence of Voyage, and the spastic muscles bound tight by Judith's chromatic lines point to the new directions in Schuman's music. Though seeking new soils, this composer's musical personality never pales, for the foundation of his musical grammar remains based upon the principle of vocal harmony, and his musical rhetoric upon such phenomena as the emotional effect of top notes or guttural sounds in the human voice. The ability to deliver an entire sentence without interruption before taking apart its pregnant clauses has been his from the beginning. This sure technique enables Schuman to concentrate on a specific idea, regardless of new materials used, without digressing. The strength of his specific expressivity and dramatic conception will serve him well in his constant search for abstract perfection.

(DMITRI SHOSTAKOVICH)

1906 -

BIOGRAPHY

DMITRI SHOSTAKOVICH was born in St. Petersburg on September 25, 1906. He entered the Conservatory there in 1919, studying piano with Nikolaev and composition with Steinberg. His precocious talent was described by Glazunov, director of the Conservatory, at an examination in 1922 as " an outstanding and brilliant creative gift, abounding in imagination and inventiveness." Shostakovich composed his First Symphony as a graduation work at the age of nineteen; it was first performed in Leningrad in 1926 and became his most celebrated work. Soon Shostakovich acquired a world-wide reputation as the leading composer of the Soviet Union, but he met with difficulties when his satirical opera, *The Nose*, based on a tale by Gogol, was sharply criticized in the Soviet press as a product of " bourgeois modernism." He suffered an even more serious rebuke when his opera on a tragic subject by Leskov, *Lady Macbeth of Mtsensk*, produced in Leningrad in 1934 and later in Moscow, was denounced in a leading editorial in *Pravda* for its naturalistic vulgarity and decadence. This was followed shortly by another attack on his ballet on a Soviet theme, *The Limpid Stream*. Abandoning the stage for a time, Shostakovich returned to symphonic music and rehabilitated himself in the eyes of the Soviet critics with his Fifth Symphony, which was greatly praised as a truly representative work. His Seventh Symphony, written partly during the siege of Leningrad in 1941, and dedicated to the city's valiant defenders, was equally extolled and became tremendously popular in the Soviet Union and abroad.

In 1941, Shostakovich received the Stalin Prize for his Piano Quintet. He continued to compose prolifically, but in February, 1948, he was again placed under a cloud of official disapproval when, together with several other prominent Soviet composers, he was attacked in a Resolution of the Central Committee of the Communist Party as an adherent to formalistic methods of composition. Not until 1958 was this condemnation officially withdrawn.

In 1949, Shostakovich was one of the seven members of the Soviet delegation to the Cultural and Scientific Conference for World Peace held in New York. This was his first visit to the United States, but because of international tension he could not travel freely in this country. Much more successful was his second visit in November, 1959, as a member of the delegation of Soviet composers sent to the United States under the auspices of President Eisenhower's Special International Program for Cultural Presentations.

Shostakovich has received many honors. He was awarded the Stalin or Lenin Prize five times and the Order of Lenin twice. At the age of sixty he became the first musician to be given the title of Hero of Socialist Labor. In 1958 he was awarded an honorary doctor's degree by Oxford and the Sibelius Prize by Finland.

PERSONAL NOTE

Nicolas Slonimsky

WHEN Shostakovich visited the United States in 1959 as a member of the Soviet delegation of composers, American newspapers dwelt on the fact that he seemed uncomfortable at press conferences and was reluctant to speak. Some journalists even opined that Shostakovich had to keep silent, for fear of saying something out of keeping with Soviet policy. Nothing can be more unlikely. True, he had his ideological troubles in times past, but after the official nullification in 1958 of the notorious assault on Shostakovich and other Soviet composers a decade before, Shostakovich actually became a spokesman of the new Soviet line in the arts.

In private conversation Shostakovich speaks with considerable passion about things that preoccupy him most, the esthetic problems of music. When his cherished convictions are attacked, he turns against his opponent with great intellectual fury; but he reacts to personal criticism much more judiciously, and if he feels that such criticism is justified, he is almost eager to admit his failings. The latter attitude was taken by him in the face of sharp denunciation of his " naturalistic " tendencies in the 1930's. There can be no doubt, retrospectively, that he was completely sincere in admitting his faults; and having accepted ideological correctives, he incorporated them in his own artistic credo.

It is understandable, therefore, that he should bristle up when he is asked time and again about the fate of his two works that were under fire, the opera *Lady Macbeth* and the Fourth Symphony. He answers these questions quietly and factually: he revised the score of *Lady Macbeth* for a new production, but made no substantial changes in the vocal parts; he did eliminate an orchestral interlude that illustrated all too graphically the scene on the double bed and wrote a new one to replace it. The Fourth Symphony was never banned; he withdrew it voluntarily before performance. An arrangement for two pianos has been published.

I met Shostakovich for the first time in Leningrad when I visited there in the summer of 1935. He was twenty-eight years old, but was already famous. Bespectacled, scholarly-looking, attentive and responsive in conversation, he impressed me by his seriousness of purpose and his lack of selfish interest in his own successes. I also went to a concert of his works at which he was the pianist. The hall was only half full, which surprised me, but Shostakovich himself seemed to be quite unconcerned about it.

I brought him as a gift a copy of Stravinsky's *Symphony of Psalms*, and he mentioned the fact at our meeting in America twenty-four years later, adding that it is one of his favorite works.

I served as translator and moderator at a round-table discussion between the visiting Soviet delegation and a group of American composers and had ample opportunity to observe Shostakovich's reactions to various points. While I was translating into Russian, Shostakovich would quickly jot down thoughts that came to him. His mind worked incessantly: the preliminary tape recording that took nearly four hours did not affect his mental alertness.

With his Soviet colleagues, Shostakovich paid me a visit at my home in Boston. In my bland way I had made a little pile of Shostakovichiana on top of the piano — Soviet and American editions of his music, biographical materials, pictures, and so forth — but he ignored it. When my wife served refreshments, he showed particular appreciation for the preserved kumquats and kept coming back for more.

We began discussing some problems of modern harmony; Shostakovich went to the piano and played a few chords to demonstrate a point. Then we talked about the great Russian masters of the past, for whom Shostakovich has profound reverence. His eyes sparkled behind his thick glasses when I gave him a precious relic for the Soviet State Archives, a four-page letter from Glazunov to my late aunt, Isabelle Vengerova.

In his fifties, Shostakovich has enough physical strength and vitality to carry on his work as composer and teacher. His taciturnity, an air of withdrawal, and barely perceptible nervous movements give an impression of inner tension. He rarely laughs; an American news photographer claimed credit for the exclusive picture of Shostakovich with a smile on his face. But it takes much more than a flash bulb to illuminate the interior world of this extraordinary human being.

THE COMPOSER SPEAKS

Dmitri Shostakovich [1]

THERE can be no music without an ideology. The old composers, whether they knew it or not, were upholding a political theory. Most of them, of course, were bolstering the rule of the upper classes. Only Beethoven was a forerunner of the revolutionary movement. If you read his letters, you will see how often he wrote to his friends that he wished to give new ideas to the public and rouse it to revolt against its masters.

On the other hand, Wagner's biographers show that he began

[1] Shostakovich expressed this artistic mission in an interview published in *The New York Times.*

his career as a radical and ended it as a reactionary. His monarchistic patriotism had a bad effect on his mind. Perhaps it is a personal prejudice, but I do not consider Wagner an important composer. It is true that he is played rather frequently in Russia today; but we hear him in the same spirit with which we go to a museum to study the forms of the old regime. We can learn certain technical lessons from him, but we do not accept him.

We, as revolutionists, have a different conception of music. Lenin himself said that " music is a means of unifying broad masses of people." Not a leader of masses, perhaps, but certainly an organizing force! For music has the power of stirring specific emotions in those who listen to it. No one can deny that Tchaikovsky's Sixth Symphony produces a feeling of despair, while Beethoven's Third awakens us to the joy of struggle. Even the symphonic form, which appears more than any other to be divorced from literary elements, can be said to have a bearing on politics. Thus we regard Scriabin as our bitterest musical enemy, because Scriabin's music tends to an unhealthy eroticism, also to mysticism and passivity, and escape from the realities of life.

Not that the Soviets are always joyous, or supposed to be. But good music lifts and heartens and lightens people for work and effort. It may be tragic but it must be strong. It is no longer an end in itself but a vital weapon to the struggle. Because of this, Soviet music will probably develop along different lines from any the world has known. There must be a change! After all, we have entered a new epoch, and history has proved that every age creates its own language.

SHOSTAKOVICH

Nicolas Slonimsky

I AM not afraid of difficulties. It is perhaps easier, and certainly safer, to follow a beaten path, but it is also dull, uninteresting, futile." When Dmitri Shostakovich wrote these words in 1935, he little suspected that soon he would receive a painful demonstration of these difficulties. For, on January 28, 1936, the Moscow news-paper *Pravda* blazoned forth with an article denouncing Shostako-vich's opera *Lady Macbeth of Mtsensk* as a " leftist monstrosity " and an un-Soviet perversion of taste. " The listener is plunged into a mass of intentional discords," said *Pravda.* " Fragments of melody appear on the surface, are drowned, reappear, and are once more submerged in the general roar. . . . ' Love ' is smeared all over the plot in the most vulgar manner, and all ' problems ' are settled on the merchant's bed, which occupies the center of the stage." The writer added ominously that the reason *Lady Macbeth* was success-ful abroad lay in the fact that the music and the plot catered to the low instincts of the international *bourgeoisie.*

As if that were not enough, another article appeared in *Pravda,* this time taking Shostakovich severely to task for his ballet *The Limpid Stream.* The ballet depicted the life on a Soviet collective farm; the music was the very opposite of *Lady Macbeth* and was entirely devoid of all the " leftist monstrosities " that *Pravda* ex-coriated in the first article. Shostakovich was now accused of treating a Soviet theme lightly, not to say frivolously. This criticism started discussions on formalism and realism in music. Accounts of these discussions were featured in the Soviet press, under the headlines " Against Formalist Perversion of Art! " " Against Bourgeois Es-thetes and Formalists! " " For Music that Millions Need! " " Against the Advocates of Musical Perversion! " Summing up, the editorial of *The Worker and the Theater* said: " Shostakovich is the foremost representative of the two tendencies extremely dangerous to Soviet art: pathological naturalism, eroticism, and formalistic perversion, as demonstrated in *Lady Macbeth of Mtsensk,* and primitivistic schematicism, as in *The Limpid Stream.*"

The directional significance of the *Pravda* article was further emphasized by the pointed words of praise that Stalin, in a personal interview, addressed to Ivan Dzerzhinsky, the youthful composer of the opera *Quiet Flows the Don.* By an ironic coincidence, Dzerzhin-sky's opera was dedicated to Shostakovich.

That was a critical time for Shostakovich. His whole life was bound up with Soviet culture. He was only eleven years old at the time of the October Revolution. His allegiance to the Soviet way of life was undivided and absolute. He was sincerely convinced that his music was a Soviet music, accepted as such not only within the Soviet Union, but abroad. His works were popular, and his First

Symphony, written at the age of nineteen, had rapidly become a repertoire piece in the orchestras the world over. A brilliant pianist, Shostakovich was an authoritative interpreter of his own piano compositions. He wrote music for the films. He enjoyed fine health and was happily married. And now he had to improvise a decision that would remake his design for life and work as a Soviet musician and a Soviet citizen.

But although Shostakovich received a sharp rebuke, he continued to enjoy the privileges of a Soviet citizen; and Soviet musicians and composers expressed their faith in his ultimate rehabilitation. Shostakovich was encouraged to continue his creative work with undiminished energy. Leaving opera aside, he embarked on a symphony, which was his fourth. It was put into rehearsal by the Leningrad Philharmonic in December, 1936, but Shostakovich decided to withdraw it from performance after he found the orchestra members but little enthusiastic over the music. Undaunted, he set to work on a new symphony. The performance of this symphony, his fifth, took place in Leningrad on November 21, 1937, in the course of the festival of the twentieth anniversary of the Soviet Republic, and it was a success. The prime Soviet writer, Alexei Tolstoy, gave his impressions in the *Izvestia* in these words: " The powerful, rousing sounds of the Finale stirred the audience. All rose to their feet, infused with joy and happiness, streaming from the orchestra like a spring breeze. We cannot but trust the Soviet listener. His reaction to music is a just verdict. Our listener is organically unreceptive to decadent, gloomy, pessimistic art, but he responds enthusiastically to an art that is clear, bright, joyful, optimistic, viable." Such a sentiment was seconded by professional music critics. There was no question that the star of Shostakovich was once more in ascendance.

There is magic in numbers. Shostakovich has been singularly lucky with his odd-numbered symphonies, unlucky with the even-numbered ones. His First Symphony still remains the most popular. When Nicolai Malko conducted it for the first time at the concert of the Leningrad Philharmonic on May 12, 1926, Shostakovich was not yet twenty. The occasion was faintly reminiscent of the appearance, forty-four years before, of young Glazunov and the first performance in St. Petersburg of his youthful symphony. Glazunov's symphony was hailed then as a token of imperishable continuity of the national Russian school. Now Glazunov was director of the

Conservatory in a city that had since changed the name of Peter the Great to that of Lenin. Shostakovich was a product of the Leningrad Conservatory. His symphony, although by no means a revolutionary work, was nonetheless a thousand musical units distant from Glazunov in content and treatment of musical material. Rimsky-Korsakov had felt, in 1882, that he had found in Glazunov a musical heir who would carry on the torch. But there could be no handing over the torch from Glazunov to Shostakovich. He was the product of the new regime, in music as well as in social life.

The Second Symphony of Shostakovich was written on the occasion of the tenth anniversary of the October Revolution, and produced in Leningrad on November 6, 1927. It bore a subtitle, " To October," and had a choral finale. (It should be observed, in parentheses, that when an October symphony is performed in November, the fault is not with the tardiness of Soviet festivals, but with the vagaries of the Russian church calendar. The Soviet Revolution took place on October 25, 1917, according to the old Russian calendar, then still in force, and the reference to " October days " continued even after the change of calendar, which added thirteen days to the Old Style and pushed the October Revolution to November.)

The Second Symphony was not successful, and there were few further performances. The Third Symphony, written in 1929, and subtitled " May First," also had a choral finale. It had a better reception than the Second, but did not last long in the repertoire. We know already what happened to the Fourth Symphony. Then came the lucky Fifth. Encouraged by its success, Shostakovich announced plans for a new symphony dedicated to the memory of Lenin. This was a task involving great responsibility. Little was known about Lenin's tastes in music, except that he disliked "leftist art" in general and that in the early days of the Revolution he listened with pleasure to Beethoven's *Appassionata*. Shostakovich's Fifth Symphony opens, significantly, with flashes of Beethovenian lightning. For his new symphony Shostakovich planned to take a leaf from Beethoven's Ninth Symphony, and use chorus and soloists. For his " Hymn to Joy " he selected verses about Lenin by peasant poets that had an epical ring and an imprint of authentic self-expression. But something must have gone seriously wrong, for when the symphony was finally produced at Leningrad, on November 5, 1939, it was sans chorus, sans Lenin, sans everything.

The universal approbation that greeted the Fifth Symphony was singularly lacking at the performance of the Sixth. In the course of the Moscow Festival of November–December, 1939, several other works were performed — among them, three cantatas: Prokofiev's *Alexander Nevsky,* arranged from his music to the film of the same name; Shaporin's *On the Field of Kulikov;* and Koval's *Emelian Pugatchov.* All these cantatas drew their inspiration from the incidents of the remote past of Russian history. Alexander Nevsky was the Russian leader who routed the Teutonic Knights at the bloody Ice Battle on the frozen Peipus Lake on April 5, 1242. Shaporin's subject was the Russian victory over the Tartar chieftain Mamay in the year 1380. Koval selected the story of the rebel Emelian Pugatchov, executed by Catherine the Great on January 11, 1775. The cantatas of Prokofiev and Shaporin emphasized the national, and Koval's cantata the revolutionary, element. All three were extremely successful, and the press published long articles discussing their merits, while Shostakovich's Sixth Symphony was barely reported at all, and the technical analysis of the symphony, in the December, 1939, issue of *Sovietskaya Musica,* was definitely disparaging. The lesson was made fairly clear. What was needed at the present stage was the romanticization of Russia circa 1240, whereas Shostakovich had devoted his talents principally to satirizing Russia circa 1840. Apparently, Shostakovich felt that he was not equipped for tackling subjects of epical connotations. For a long time Shostakovich regarded himself as a satirist par excellence. On several occasions he explicitly stated his belief that satire presents the best material for original Soviet music. The dances in his *Golden Mountains* and *The Golden Age* (1930) are lampoons of the bourgeois, the parlor waltz and polka. The best of his twenty-four piano Preludes (1933) are brilliant grotesques. The Cello Sonata is pre-eminently a lyrical work, but there is an element of satire in the running passages suggesting Czerny at his industrious best. The Concerto for Piano, Trumpet, and String Orchestra (1933) is part Chopin, part blood-and-thunder band music. Shostakovich's early opera *The Nose* (1928) is a suite of musical witticisms. It is written to Gogol's story of an army major whose nose mysteriously vanishes from the surface of his face only to turn up in the uniform of a self-contained government official. There are orchestral sneezes and unusual vocal effects: for instance, the part of the reincarnated Nose was to be sung with nostrils closed. When the opera was produced in Leningrad, on January 12, 1930, it was cautiously billed as an " experimental spectacle." The Artistic Council of the Leningrad Little Theater, which produced the opera, found it expedient to give an explanation. Admitting that some proletarian listeners might be bewildered by the complexity and modernity of the musical idiom employed by Shostakovich, the Council went on to state its conviction that it is the purpose of Soviet art to create new forms and that Soviet opera should break with the tradition of its bourgeois predecessor to gain independence. *The Nose* was the last of Soviet operas of the constructivist period. In the thirties the drive toward classicism, tonality in music, and traditionalism in the theater assumed the proportion of a *Blitzkrieg*, not only in Russia, but everywhere else. Simultaneously, the art of satire went into eclipse. The grim decade demanded a more positive approach to art.

In his chamber music Shostakovich is less troubled by the problems of style. He has written seven string quartets, two piano trios, a string octet, a piano quintet, and a cello sonata. In all these works Shostakovich exhibits the familiar characteristics of his happy talent: a flowing melody with a modal, often plagal, cadential lilt; a brilliant technical display in rapid passages; a throbbing marchlike rhythm. Shostakovich has a knack for instrumental writing, and although his chamber music requires virtuoso playing, the natural limitations of the instruments are never violated.

Shostakovich is a professional pianist, and his piano compositions are particularly brilliant. His technique is not entirely novel; there is much in it that Prokofiev has used before, but Shostakovich adds enough spice to modern piano writing to produce the effect of novelty and ingenuity and arrive at a style of his own.

The Nazi invasion of Russia in 1941 aroused fervent patriotic spirit — World War II is known in Russia as the " Great Patriotic War " — and Shostakovich responded to it with all the might of his talent. He was at work on his Seventh Symphony when Leningrad was directly threatened by the German armies; he took part in its civil defense. The Seventh Symphony became the *Leningrad Symphony*. (Actually, there is no subtitle in the score, which is designated simply as op. 60.)

The opening theme of the symphony, the Leningrad theme proper, is conceived in epic tones and is contrasted with a mechanical marchlike second theme, descriptive of the Nazi war machine. In the development section, the Nazi theme sweeps through the entire orchestra, but the Leningrad melody emerges from the musical underground and overcomes the Nazi march, until only a pitifully muted trumpet, accompanied by a muffled military drum, remains from the proud Nazi march. The second movement is a scherzo; the slow third movement is a typical sample of Shostakovichian humor and wistful lyricism. The finale, completed on December 27, 1941, is designed in grandiose Russian style, and it ends in the glory of an anticipated triumph.

The Seventh Symphony was performed for the first time on March 5, 1942, in Kuibishev, on the Volga, a temporary capital set up during the Nazi offensive. The score was microfilmed, and rushed by air through Persia, west Africa, and Brazil to the United States, where a lively competition was already in progress among conductors for the right of first performance. The Seventh Symphony made a triumphant tour of American orchestras; *Life* magazine remarked ironically that it was almost unpatriotic, even for Americans, not to like the Seventh Symphony. There was a great clamor to have Shostakovich visit the United States, and Wendell Willkie, during his wartime trip to Russia, appealed to Stalin personally to allow Shostakovich to appear in America in concerts of his music. But the composer declined, explaining that his place during the war was in his own country. He did come to America much later, in March, 1949, as a delegate to the Cultural and Scientific Conference for World Peace. But in the meantime, Russo-American relations had deteriorated to the point of acknowledged ideological enmity. Far from being acclaimed and feted as he would have been a few short years before, Shostakovich was not allowed to travel outside of New York City, and his visa was limited to the duration of the conference. After a ten days' visit, and in an atmosphere charged with bitter controversy, he took the plane back to Russia.

After the Seventh Symphony, the Eighth was an anticlimax. It was inordinately long, and it failed to arouse great public interest when it was first performed in Moscow on November 4, 1943. But the name of Shostakovich still carried enough publicity value in America, and a sum of ten thousand dollars was paid by the New York Philharmonic for the right of first American performance of the Eighth Symphony, which took place in the spring of 1944.

Shostakovich's Ninth Symphony, written after the end of the war, is the briefest of his symphonic compositions, less than half as long as the Eighth. It was intended to reflect the joy of life after the end of a mortal struggle, and its music is characteristically facile, frivolous, and uninhibited. Performed for the first time in Leningrad on November 3, 1945, it was sharply criticized in the Soviet press for its lack of substance. A much greater blow was the inclusion of Shostakovich's name among the "formalist" Soviet composers attacked in the Resolution of the Communist Party of February 10, 1948. Like other Soviet composers, Shostakovich had to undergo the ordeal of accounting, in a public statement, for his errors.

The vindication came on May 28, 1958, when the Central Committee of the Communist Party issued a declaration repudiating the personal attacks on "the talented composers, comrades Shostakovich, Prokofiev, and others . . . indiscriminately described as representative of the formalist trend inimical to the people."

In the meantime Shostakovich never slacked the tempo of his work. His Tenth Symphony (1953) was performed in Leningrad on December 17, 1953. Its structure is typical of Shostakovich's symphonic style. There are four contrasing movements, of great inner variety of expression, lyric, dramatic, gay, somber, tragic, and jubilant. Aram Khatchaturian described the symphony as "a work of life-asserting idealism and of profound emotional and philosophical meaning."

Shostakovich completed his Eleventh Symphony in August, 1957, and it was brought out in Moscow on October 30, 1957, during the celebration of the fortieth anniversary of the Soviet Revolution. The score bears a subtitle, "1905," with reference to the year of the first revolutionary uprising against the czarist regime. The programmatic content of the Eleventh Symphony is determined by two thematic groups, one representing the nation in quest of freedom, and characterized by broad expansive melodies in the style of Russian folk songs, the other reflecting the dark oppression of the reactionary powers. For the first time in Shostakovich's symphonies, the movements themselves bear explicit programmatic titles: "The Palace Square"; "January Ninth" (the day of the massacre of workers who marched toward the Winter Palace to petition the czar); "Eternal Memory," a requiem for the martyrs; and "Alarm," in which revolutionary songs of the time are treated polyphonically, with church bells powerfully and ominously predicting the eventual victory of the Revolution.

The year 1960 saw the completion of Shostakovich's Twelfth Symphony. Its music is marked by the familiar qualities of "philosophical symphonism " that distinguishes most of its predecessors.

Despite the ideological storms that passed over Shostakovich during his spectacular career, he never strayed far from the fundamental principles of his style. From the First Symphony to the Twelfth, through thirty-five years, there is a continuity of development, without abrupt changes in the form and in the idiom. The harmonies may be more intricate and dissonant in one work than in another, the rhythms more aggressive, the melodies more independent from the basic tonality, but there is a Shostakovich stamp in every score he writes. Gaiety and contemplation, drama and lyric tenderness, these varied and contrasting moods alternate without creating an esthetic incongruity. Perhaps not since Mahler was there a composer who could reconcile as successfully as Shostakovich such conflicting materials, some derived from popular melodies and rhythms, others coming from the deepest " philosophical " sources, and build them into an integrated, forceful, and logically consistent style.

(JEAN SIBELIUS)

1865 - 1957

BIOGRAPHY

JEAN (JOHAN JULIUS CHRISTIAN) SIBELIUS was born in Tavastehus, Finland, on December 8, 1865. He studied music with Martin Wegelius and Ferruccio Busoni in Helsinki, Albert Becker in Berlin, and Robert Fuchs and Karl Goldmark in Vienna.

Shortly after his return to Finland, Sibelius was fired by a patriotic ardor then prevalent throughout the country as a result of the suppression of Finnish privileges by Russia. This patriotism gave direction to his creative work, which, up to then, had been without an identifying character. His first major work, *Kullervo*, was imbued with nationalistic spirit. *Kullervo* was followed by other works nationalistic in character, including *En Saga, Karelia, Four Legends*, and *Finlandia*.

Up to 1897, Sibelius earned his livelihood by teaching theory at the Helsinki Conservatory and at the orchestral school of the Philharmonic Society. In that year, however — following the performance of his *Four Legends*, one of which is the famous *Swan of Tuonela* — Sibelius received an annual government grant that made it possible for him to devote his time entirely to composition. He was the first Finnish composer ever to receive such a mark of recognition.

During the next seventeen years, Sibelius traveled frequently, visiting the leading European music capitals and coming into contact with their musical life. At the same time he produced a series of works, extraordinary in character and originality, including the Violin Concerto, the string quartet *Voces intimae,* and the first five symphonies. In 1914 Sibelius paid his only visit to the United States, when he participated at the Norfolk (Conn.) Festival of Music by conducting nine of his works.

When Sibelius' seventieth birthday was celebrated in December of 1935, his imperial position in the world of modern music was emphasized by celebrations everywhere. In Finland the day was a national holiday. In the leading cities of America and Europe there were commemorative programs of his major works. Festive celebrations throughout America and Finland also marked his seventy-fifth, eightieth, eighty-fifth, and ninetieth birthdays. Sibelius died in Järvenpää, Finland, on September 20, 1957.

PERSONAL NOTE

Ainö Sibelius

WE AT HOME knew that he lived constantly in the realm of tone. I generally never spoke to him in the morning until he addressed me. We did not want to trespass on his thoughts, interrupt the flow of his creative imaginings. When he did address me, we were likely to talk about everything under the sun, even about the weather.

Music irritated my husband more than anything else. Forced to hear a stray tune, a fragment of song, or someone whistling, he would throw his work overboard and wreck the inspiration. Afterward he must begin from the beginning. That is why at home one never heard music. No one ever sang. No one whistled. That is, unless my husband chose otherwise.

I remember an incident during some repair work at home. A certain painter liked to whistle at his job. It was my duty to tell him to desist, " since it bothers the professor." The fellow did not seem to understand. I tried to make my meaning graphic. " What would you say if someone came along with a broom just when you had finished painting that wall and swept a lot of dirt across it, and ruined the whole job? The professor feels the same way when anyone interrupts his thoughts by whistling." The painter understood.

Our children learned from earliest childhood to control their noisemaking. They never sang at home. Not even our grandchildren, toward whom he showed much more tolerance. Our children learned at an early age that their father was hard at work. He composed music. And when he made music, there must be peace. The family and home were consecrated to Father's art.

Time in the conventional sense meant nothing to him. All was a single instant, or infinity. Routine behavior dictated by clocks and calendars was foreign to his nature. Usually he did not have the least idea what day of the week it was. At nights, he resisted the necessity of going to sleep.

He was unbelievably energetic. He was just as fiery and enthusiastic in old age as he was in his youth. There was not the faintest hint of the peacefulness of old age about him. Often it struck me that he was still the youngster of infinite hope. In him one could always see a soaring aspirant. He lived at a terrific pace, intensely, boundlessly. His capacity for taking pains was unlimited. He worked tirelessly. He obeyed but one law, a merciless taskmaster — his conscience.

He did not have any hobbies. Work proved all in all for him — his hobby, too. Nevertheless, he did manage to keep an eye on the world about him. The range of his interests was incredible. He read much, always choosing his reading matter with discrimination. He followed current happenings all over the world with a watchfulness one would not expect in a composer. Only on special occasions did he attend concerts.

Because of his sensitive nature and his inclination for solitary contemplation, he attended very few social functions. Rarely did he even pay friendly visits. You could count upon the fingers of one hand the number of times he visited his own daughters. When he did make one of his rare visits to Helsinki it was on imperative business, immediately after which he hurried back to Järvenpää.

My husband liked to wander about alone. The country road near our home did not change appreciably with the years; but passing autos and bicycles chased him deeper into the woods. Our son-in-law cut a path for him in our own forest, and there he walked alone. Fortunately, our windows look out upon a landscape of many changing aspects, one of the most beautiful woodlands to be found in Finland.

In certain respects he changed his habits since youth. No longer did he suddenly dash off completed compositions. No longer

did he write pieces on the side, as of old, on order, and in the mad-
dest rush at time, to be finished for some special occasion. In olden
days he generally did not refuse to fill an order on request.

Our home centered about my husband. For the rest of us, his
lifework was all in all. I am glad I lived near him. It seemed that I
did not live in vain. I will not claim that it was always easy. Merciless self-discipline was always necessary. Yet, I consider myself a
fortunate person. My husband's music was like the word of God.
It sprang from a holy source, and near that source it was good to
live.

THE COMPOSER SPEAKS

Jean Sibelius [1]

COMPOSING has been the guiding line in my life, and it is still so.
My work has the same fascination for me as when I was young, a
fascination bound up with the difficulty of the task. Let no one
imagine that composing is easier for an old composer, if he takes his
art seriously. The demands one makes on himself have increased in
the course of years. Greater sureness makes one scorn solutions that
come too easily, that follow the line of least resistance, in a higher
degree than formerly. One is always faced with new problems. The
thing that has pleased me most is that I have been able to reject.
The greatest labor I have expended, perhaps, was on works that
have never been completed.

In my composition, I have never allied myself to any school of
music, or associated myself with any prevalent tendency. When you
have lived as long as I have and seen one tendency after another
being born, blossom, and die, you are inclined to take up a less decided position about them. You prefer to search for what is good,
wherever you can find it. In doing so you often discover that almost
every musical " school," even if it has on the whole aimed at a goal
of which you cannot approve, has, nevertheless, in some respect or
other had something good about it. If I were young again, but

---

[1] This statement is from Karl Ekman's biography, *Jean Sibelius.*

equipped with the experience life has given me, I think, for instance, that I should be considerably more appreciative of Wagner than I once was. My decided antagonism to Wagner in my youth was, I fancy, dictated to some extent by the fear of being subjected to an influence that I had seen taking possession of so many of my friends, both old and young. And yet I still place Verdi higher than Wagner. Opera after all is a conventional form of art and should be cultivated as such.

The composer for me above all others is Beethoven. I am affected as powerfully by the human side of him as by his music. He is a revelation to me. He was a Titan. Everything was against him, and yet he triumphed.

I believe that there is a kind of freemasonry among composers owing to things having been and being so difficult for us. All of us have to reckon with the critics and the public. For my part, thanks to the experience of a long lifetime, I have learned to accept disappointment and reverses with resignation. Scarcely one of my best works has met with the right comprehension when first performed. They took at least twenty years to succeed. With regard to immediate success I have long since been cured of all illusions.

I find much that is interesting in present-day music, although I cannot be in sympathy with all the tendencies that have been expressed within the last few decades. There has been too much experimenting, and unaffected feeling has not always been allowed to come into its own.

The error of our day has long been its faith in polyphony. It has seemed as if people imagined that the whole had become better by placing nonentities on top of each other. Polyphony, of course, is a force when there is a good reason for it, but for a long time it has almost seemed as if an illness had been raging among composers.

The instrumentation in many modern works has been too showy — " fire in your mouth and scare the children."

I have not been able to avoid the impression, too, that much, yes, too much, in present-day music has very little connection with life. The themes often seemed artificial, the elaboration mechanical.

At one time it appeared to me that many present-day composers lacked what Rydberg called joy in life. They made one think of court councilors composing, their works of doctors' dissertations.

That was then. Now that these gods have been cast down, I feel optimistic.

SIBELIUS

Cecil Gray

FEW, if indeed any, modern composers wrote such a vast quantity of music, in such a wide variety of forms and categories, as Sibelius. Apart from some fifty works in manuscript or without opus numbers, and also a large amount of music that has disappeared or been destroyed, the total of his numbered and published works stands at more than one hundred and twenty, comprising seven symphonies, about thirty large choral or orchestral works, and the same number of smaller ones, a hundred or so songs, and as many piano pieces, incidental music to a dozen or more plays, and innumerable miscellaneous compositions of every sort and description. Consequently, in the foregoing brief survey of his art we have been compelled to confine our attention to the more important and outstanding examples of it only; to have dealt at length and in detail with each separate work would have required a volume of well-nigh encyclopedic dimensions.

Fortunately, however, it was neither necessary nor desirable to do so. One does not as a rule need to be acquainted with everything a man has written in order to arrive at a reasonably accurate estimate of his artistic achievement as a whole, which is all that has been attempted here, and in such a large output as that of Sibelius in particular it goes without saying that there are many works of minor importance that can be conveniently ignored and even some that are completely negligible.

This immense fecundity, combined with a certain unevenness of quality, has always militated strongly against Sibelius in the eyes of many superior persons who are disposed to regard these characteristics of his with the same stern disapproval as that with which eugenists regard the unsystematic, uncontrolled proliferation of the lower classes. According to them, the artist should so control his creative urge as to permit nothing unworthy to escape into existence — he should either produce a masterpiece or else remain silent.

There is undoubtedly much that is sympathetic in this point of view, in theory at least. It is certainly better to produce one healthy and intelligent offspring than a large family of weaklings and mental defectives, and better to write one good composition than a vast horde of mediocre ones. In practice, however, it does not by any means work out as one might have expected, for in the same way that the best human specimens are generally members of large families, so the greatest works of art are as a rule the fruit of immense and frequently unequal productivity on the part of their creators. A certain reckless prodigality and effortless profusion is almost invariably, in fact, one of the distinguishing traits of the great artist, and the man of small and relatively perfect output is seldom in the first rank.

The exuberant fecundity of Sibelius, then, is a positive quality, even if some of its by-products are purely negative; it is a necessary condition of the highest creative achievements, and I do not think that the proportion of indifferent works to good ones is perceptibly greater with him than with any other composer of outstanding eminence, except possibly Bach.

"Granted," it may be said, "that the greatest masters are extremely prolific, and that their level of accomplishment may frequently be somewhat unequal, yet there are certain special features in connection with Sibelius' immense productivity that call for explanation. One accepts the fact that a composer cannot be expected to maintain the same high level consistently throughout such a large output, but one is surely at least entitled to expect that his aim and endeavor shall be consistently lofty; and the fact that Sibelius frequently condescends to write works of a frankly popular and even trivial character is exceedingly difficult to reconcile with the high claims that are put forward on his behalf. At the very least it must surely be admitted to constitute a serious failing, a weakness that reflects on his work as a whole."

This objection must be squarely faced, for there is no denying the fact that the sentiments above expressed represent the views of a considerable number of good people to whom this side of Sibelius' activities is a genuine stumbling block in the way of their understanding and appreciation of his work.

This popular side to the art of Sibelius, so far from being a fault, seems to me to be another positive virtue, like his immense fertility, and one of the signs of his true greatness. Most of the ills, indeed, to which modern music is subject are the outcome of oversophistication, the self-conscious fear of the banal and the commonplace, the inability to relax and to be spontaneous, simple, unaffected, straight-forward, unpretentious. Even many of those who are sufficiently in-telligent to be well aware of this are unable to escape from their in-hibitions. The desperate attempts, for example, of so many modern composers to write " popular " music — generally along the lines of jazz — are painfully labored, mannered, and unnatural, achieving cheapness without popularity, vulgarity without success, and ap-pealing only to the depraved palates of a sophisticated few. Sibe-lius, on the contrary, achieves genuine popularity and success with-out ever seeming to seek them. And if he is probably the most austere and inaccessible of living composers in some of his works, he is at the same time the most familiar and accessible in others, while between these two extremes there lie compositions of every con-ceivable gradation and variety of appeal.

This wide diversity of intellectual and emotional appeal is achieved by means of a style of quite remarkable breadth and catholicity; melodic writing that ranges from clear-cut symmetrical tunes of a comparatively obvious kind, on the one hand, to small incisive motifs of a few notes only, on the other; a harmonic idiom at times of the utmost simplicity and directness, and at others of great daring and singularity; rhythms now primitive, dynamic, insistent, now highly refined, sensitive, subtle; formal organizations compre-hending both the most elementary and straightforward, the most complex and intricate kinds; and an instrumental palette disposing of every shade of tone color from the darkest and most somber to the brightest and most luminous, sometimes employed with the utmost restraint and economy, and sometimes with the utmost lavishness and prodigality. At the same time, his command of these immense natural resources renders it unnecessary for him ever to go to violent extremes in any single direction. One does not find any-where in his music the melodic distortions, the harmonic excesses, the rhythmical obsessions, the formal complexities, the instrumen-tal perversities, that are, one or other, sometimes all, to be found in the work of most modern composers; his utterance is consistently natural, direct, unforced. Finally, and perhaps most important of all, behind this breadth of thought and catholicity of style one always feels a fundamental unity and the presence of a definite personality. Indeed, there is no music in the world more intensely personal than the music of Sibelius, yet none has fewer recognizable mannerisms than his. It is true that a close student of his work can point to certain stylistic peculiarities that are to be found in it — a constantly recurring triplet figuration in the melodic writing, a fondness for introducing a phrase with a held note beginning on an offbeat, a marked predilection for long, winding passages for strings alone, with repeated notes, *flautato*, a distinctively individual disposition of the woodwind ensemble, and so forth — but on the whole such idiosyncrasies are few and minute in comparison with those of most modern composers, and cannot alone be held responsible for the impression of a powerful personality that transpires through every bar in a way it is impossible to define in technical terms. Indeed, one often feels it most strongly in passages that, to all outward seeming, might have been written by anyone — in little fragments of scale passages, for example, or simple sequences of common chords. His originality, in fact, lies in the thought, not in the means employed; and whereas most of his eminent contemporaries achieve a personal utterance by means of selection and restriction of means, Sibelius achieves it through comprehensiveness and inclusion. The consequence is that, whereas most other modern composers can be — and are — easily imitated, Sibelius cannot be; his individuality is independent of formulas and methods of procedure.

Despite the fact that it is at first sight somewhat difficult to distinguish any definite or consistent line of development and progress from first to last in Sibelius' chronological catalogue, his work nevertheless, on close study, like that of so many other artists, reveals three distinct phases, or, more accurately perhaps, personalities: the first of which one may call the romantic or national, the second the eclectic and cosmopolitan, and the third the classic and universal. The first is primarily characterized by symphonic poems and choral works based upon, or related to in some way, episodes in the *Kalevala* or Finnish mythology in general, the last by the symphonies, and the intermediate one by miscellaneous compositions of every kind.

The most significant feature of the music of the first phase or personality consists in the fact that with it the North becomes fully articulate for the first time in the history of music. Up till then, largely as a result of the predominating role played by the Mediterranean countries, and particularly Italy, in the development of forms and idioms, music had always been overwhelmingly Latin in character, even in the work of such strongly Teutonic masters as Bach and Beethoven. Such things as *Kullervo*, op. 7 (1892) and

En Saga, op. 9 (1892), however, could not possibly have been written by a composer of any Southern race, or even by one of other than Baltic provenance; with these works, in fact, a whole world of infinite possibilities is opened up to musical exploitation — a vein of melody, of harmony, of rhythm, of orchestration, not so much new, perhaps, as neglected hitherto by composers. For the first time the potentialities of what may be called the lower end of the tonal spectrum are thoroughly explored. Until then the aim in scoring had always been, and was for some time to remain, in the direction of ever-greater brilliance and sonority; the more garish the scoring the greater was the orchestrator's reputation. Brahms, indeed, is perhaps the only composer of eminence before Sibelius deliberately and consciously to have recourse to half shades and subdued color schemes, and he has always been violently abused for doing so, but his experiments in this direction were timid and tentative in comparison with those of Sibelius. And though it would certainly be a mistake to imagine that Sibelius confines himself entirely to such dark and somber effects of tone color, or even that they noticeably predominate in his music viewed as a whole, it is nevertheless true that his innovations in this respect constitute the element of primary value and importance in the work of his first period.

This Northern and largely national phase of Sibelius' creative activity is in the ascendant until about the turn of the century. It never entirely disappears, however, and at least one of the best works of his middle period, *Luonnotar*, op. 70 (1913), and one of the best of his later period, *Tapiola*, op. 112 (1925), belong essentially to this category. The fact remains that the decade 1900–10 presents on the whole a very different aspect of physiognomy from the preceding one, as a study of his chronological catalogue clearly shows, consisting in a conspicuous decrease in the number and importance of the more predominantly nationalistic and Nordic works, and a corresponding increase in the number and importance of those which I have loosely designated as cosmopolitan and eclectic — loosely, because there is a sense in which such works can also be considered national, though in a different way from those of the first category, as representing, in fact, the Swedish side of the composer's personality. Cosmopolitanism and eclecticism, indeed, have always, paradoxically enough, been a racial characteristic of the Scandinavian people. The Latins in general, it may be observed, do not readily assimilate themselves to alien surroundings; wherever they go they take their national habits and language with them, as may be seen in America or in the French and Italian colonies in London. The Northerner, on the other hand, generally becomes entirely denationalized, and quickly identifies himself with his surroundings.

This characteristically assimilative propensity is, of course, a source of weakness in many ways; it is the chief fault of much Swedish art and of practically all Swedish music in particular, and it is true that in the works of Sibelius that belong to this category one occasionally feels a certain colorless neutrality and eclecticism that are in curiously striking contrast to the originality and sturdy independence of outlook that one finds in the rest of the music. At the same time this characteristic can also be a source of strength. In the same way that the transfusion of Northern blood has frequently, in the history of the past, given a fresh lease of life and energy to the rest of Europe, so we find much the same thing happening in the domain of art. Modern European drama owes whatever vitality it possesses to two Northerners, Ibsen and Strindberg — the fathers of realism and expressionism respectively — and from the North also has come the finest, indeed the only, architecture of modern times, of which the fruitful and stimulating influence is to be seen at work in every country. And just as the primary quality of the magnificent Town Hall at Stockholm of Ragnar Otsberg consists in its eclecticism of style, its triumphant revivification and revitalization of Southern European architectural motifs, so in such works as the Violin Concerto, op. 47 (1903), the String Quartet, op. 56 (1909), the *In Memoriam*, op. 59 (1909), of Sibelius one finds a similar rejuvenation of languishing classical motifs, an infusion of fresh life and vigor into effete traditions, which is primarily attributable to his strain of Northern adaptability and Swedish eclecticism.

But in spite of the greatness of his achievement in these two diametrically opposite directions — that of romantic Finnish nationalism on the one hand, of cosmopolitan Swedish traditionalism on the other — there can be little doubt that, everything considered, Sibelius' greatest achievement lies in his symphonies, which constitute the most outstanding landmarks in the third phase of his productivity. In the other two categories it is conceivable that he may be occasionally equaled by other modern composers — although *Luonnotar* and *Tapiola* in the first, and the Violin Concerto and the String Quartet in the second, seem to me, in their different ways, to be unsurpassed in contemporary music — but there is nothing in modern symphonic literature that can be placed by the side of Sibelius' achievement in this direction.

The first thing that strikes one about Sibelius' symphonies viewed as a whole is their astonishing range and diversity. Each one is sharply differentiated from all others; each has a definite character of its own. Similarly, within each individual symphony one finds the same strong contrast between constituent movements. They bear a spiritual relationship to each other, but they are always formally independent, self-sufficient entities, capable of standing alone by themselves. This is largely in consequence of the composer's consistent avoidance of thematic interconnection between the movements. It is true that in the First Symphony we find the theme of the introduction to the first movement recurring at the beginning of the last, but one can hardly say that the two movements are thematically connected, for the melody in question plays no part in the subsequent proceedings in the first movement, and only a very small one in the last. Still, it is significant to note that, after toying tentatively with this device in his First Symphony, op. 39 (1898–9), he then resolutely discarded it and henceforth uncompromisingly maintained the structural integrity of all the separate movements. One partial exception only may be found in the Fourth Symphony, op. 63 (1911), where a phrase that occurs near the end of the third movement bears a definite, though possibly accidental, resemblance to that with which the last movement begins; but as it only appears the once in each movement, and plays no thematic role in either, one cannot say that there is any real relation between the two movements.

Another striking feature of the series taken as a whole is that, starting with the full modern orchestra, complete with bass tuba and harp, Sibelius subsequently reduces his instrumental forces down practically to the level of the old classical orchestra. In this progression the Sixth, op. 104 (1923), provides an exception, but the momentary relaxation that this represents was not maintained in its successor. In any case, an inspection of the full score and a careful study of the way in which the accessory instruments — namely, bass clarinet and harp — are written for show that this seeming augmentation of resources is largely illusory. That is to say, they are employed in order to fulfill a humble function with regard to the whole and not on account of their instrumental personalities, so to

speak. Apart from a brief phrase of a single bar in the first movement, anticipating the return of the principal subject, the part for
the bass clarinet consists entirely in a doubling and reinforcement
of the other bass instruments and in holding unobtrusive pedal
notes. Similarly the harp part is of the utmost reticence and discretion, consisting almost entirely of the simplest kinds of chords and
arpeggios. In other words, these two intruders into the orchestral
symposium of the classical symphonic orchestra are only tolerated
on the strict condition that they lay aside their personalities and
subordinate themselves to the demands of the texture as a whole.

Again, from the First Symphony to the last one finds a steady,
consistent diminution in the use of contrapuntal devices, culminating in the Seventh, op. 105 (1924), in which no trace of *fugato* and
singularly little polyphony even of the freest kind are to be found.
Finally, the whole sequence shows a progressive disinclination to
employ large-scale symmetrical melodies as his thematic material,
and an ever-increasing tendency to build the movements out of short
and fragmentary subject matter.

In each successive symphony, in short, one finds Sibelius continually approximating ever more closely in one respect or another,
sometimes in several, and sometimes in all, to the ideal symphonic
style: characterized by the thematic independence of the movements, sobriety and restraint in the use of the orchestra, the absence of contrapuntal devices, and terseness and brevity of thematic
material — but above and beyond all, by the protean versatility, the
consummate breadth of style, the wide range of thought and emotion, the unique capacity to excel in every type of formal construction. It is in the combination of all these qualities in varying degrees that the greatness of Sibelius as symphonist primarily resides.

There is, indeed, only one partial shortcoming, one gap in his
otherwise all-round creative capacity, that prevents one from ranking
his finest symphonies with those, say, of Brahms. In his songs,
Sibelius, apart from occasional happy inspirations, is not a great
lyricist; and in his symphonies one feels a lack of that very quality in
which lies the greatest and indeed the only strength of his German
rivals. It is significant to note that he seldom attempts to write a
typical " slow movement." There is none in the accepted sense of
the words in either the Third, op. 52 (1904–7), Fifth, op. 82
(1914–15), Sixth, or Seventh symphonies; the second movement of
the First is the only one in the others that could properly be said to

be lyrical, and despite its undeniable beauty, it must be accounted the weakest in the work. It is certainly the least original, the least personal, and on the whole it is true to say of practically all his more lyrical moments that they verge perilously on the commonplace and the conventional. (An exception should, however, be made in favor of the lovely slow movements of the Violin Concerto and the String Quartet.)

One may freely concede, then, that there is a certain lack of warmth, of humanity, in the music of Sibelius; one will search in vain in it for anything to compare with the deep, heart-searching, slow movements of the later Beethoven, which seem to bear within them the very secret of the universe, and go far to justify the ways of God to man. Apart from this one qualification, I do not hesitate to express my considered opinion, for what it is worth, with all due consciousness of its implications, that in no other respect can he be regarded at all inferior even to Beethoven himself as a symphonist.

For this reason, quite apart from its intrinsic value, the later work of Sibelius is a highly significant symptom and a historical event of the first importance. Generally speaking, the whole history of music during the last hundred years or so has been one of idiomatic development and expansion, a progressive enrichment of every kind of tonal resource — melodic, harmonic, rhythmic, coloristic — accompanied by a corresponding weakness and impoverishment on the formal and intellectual side of art. The beginnings of this tendency are to be seen in the music of Bellini, Chopin, Weber, and Berlioz as clearly as its end in that of Strauss, Schoenberg, Bartók, and Stravinsky. In other words, the art of these latter composers, despite its factitious appearance of novelty, is in reality nothing more than the continuation and final phase of the romantic movement, the end of the old rather than the beginning of the new as it is commonly represented to be. That it is impossible to go any farther in the direction of idiomatic innovation can be almost mathematically proved; all notes of the chromatic scale have now been sounded together harmonically, every species of melodic progression, involving the widest imaginable leaps and the most unfamiliar and exotic intervals, has been employed, every conceivable instrumental combination and every possible device for the attainment of a novel shade of tone color have been systematically exploited. The ultimate confines of musical language have been reached, and its remotest possibilities have been explored. There is obviously nothing

further to be done in the direction of idiomatic expansion, short of
the adoption of third or quarter tones, and there is no reason to believe that any fruitful development of this kind will take place in our
day, if ever.

On the óther hand, however, there is nothing in the music of
the last hundred years that can be compared with that of Bach,
Mozart, or Beethoven, as regards depth of intellectual content or
formal subtlety and complexity; and while most modern composers
still continue desperately seeking for some hitherto unexploited
resource, some thrill or sensation not previously experienced, Sibelius, almost alone among them, has gone in the opposite direction.
In all his later work one finds a deliberate avoidance of anything in
the nature of idiomatic novelty or experiment for its own sake, together with a refinement and intricacy of form that are only paral-
leled in the art of the great classics.

The chief significance, then, of Sibelius' course of development,
viewed in broad outline, is that beginning as a romantic with more
or less pronounced national leanings, and passing through a transition period of eclectic cosmopolitanism, he ends up a supporter of
the classical tradition; after being a pioneer, an explorer of new paths
in the works of his first period, he comes back in the end to the great
highroad of musical art. In his early work, the emotional, the
colorist, the expressive elements predominate, and the formal and
intellectual ones are in comparative abeyance. With the growth and
development of his individuality, however, his style gradually under-
goes a complete change; the rich and elaborate orchestration of the
early works is replaced by an extreme sobriety and restraint in the
use of instrumental means, the massive, rough-hewn harmonies are
clarified and attenuated, the sharply defined and immediately arresting themes give way to melodic fragments, sometimes the merest
wisps of scale passages and sequences, unimportant in themselves,
which only acquire significance as a result of the treatment to which
they are subjected and of the general context and surroundings in
which they are placed. In the music of his later period, there are
absolutely no individual stylistic features whatsoever, yet no music
is more profoundly individual, and this is the essence of classicism.

Together with this sobriety and restraint of idiom, this imper-
sonality of style, we find a refinement and complexity of form that
have no parallel in modern music, and can only be compared to
those of the posthumous quartets and the last piano sonatas of Bee-

thoven. There is, indeed, a more than superficial resemblance between the later works of Beethoven and those of Sibelius, for the
latter's discarding in his later symphonies of the old formal conventions of two main themes or groups of themes out of which the
movement is constructed is to a great extent only the application to
symphonic writing of the revolutionary formal innovations introduced by Beethoven in his last quartets and sonatas, but which he
did not live long enough to apply to large-scale orchestral compositions.

In a purely technical sense, therefore — from the point of view
of formal structure — it is true to say that in his later work Sibelius
takes up music where Beethoven laid it down. Even in his early
work, however, it is important to note that, romantic in spirit though
it is, it bears no trace whatever of the influence of the great romantic composers themselves — the art of Weber, of Berlioz, of
Chopin, of Liszt has had no effect, no repercussion on that of Sibelius. His entire art, in fact, follows on straight from that of Beethoven without any intermediary influence of any kind; one can pass
from one to the other without feeling that there is an intervening
gap of a century. Indeed, there is less feeling of strangeness in passing from Beethoven to Sibelius than from Beethoven to Berlioz.
The latter opens up a new world, the former recognizably belongs
to the same one.

It is this fact that gives the peculiar quality to all his work; it is
as if the last hundred years had not existed, as if the entire romantic
movement so called were only a vast parenthesis containing much
of value and interest that is nevertheless essentially irrelevant in respect of the history of music as a whole — a bypath or a sidetrack
in which may be found much that is admirable in itself, but which
leads nowhere save into the morass in which most modern composers are still floundering. Above all, however, it is significant
that Sibelius would seem to be practically the only modern composer — certainly the only one of his generation — who has neither
been influenced by Wagner nor, what amounts to the very same
thing, reacted violently against him. The ferocious anti-Wagnerian-
ism of Debussy, for example, is in itself highly suspicious, and a most
eloquent tribute to the potent wizardry of the master of Bayreuth.
Sibelius, on the contrary, does not detest Wagner, for the very good
reason that he has never loved him. Not even when, as a young man,
he visited Bayreuth during the height of the Wagnerian cult in the

early nineties did Wagner mean anything to him at all, one way or the other; and the proof of this is to be found in the fact that it is impossible to lay one's finger on a single phrase in his entire work that one could attribute to the influence of Wagner, or one that would not have been exactly the same even if Wagner had never lived. I doubt very much whether there is any other composer of the last seventy years or so of whom this could be said, and it can be no mere coincidence that the one modern composer who has thus entirely escaped the influence of Bayreuth should be the one whose achievement, I firmly believe, will prove to have been the greatest of modern times. For whatever one's own personal reaction to the music of Wagner may be, it cannot, I think, be denied that his influence on other composers and on music in general has been wholly disastrous.

The influence of Sibelius, on the contrary, which is now gradually beginning to make itself felt, whatever may be the intrinsic esthetic value of his achievement, can only be salutary and beneficial, for his art is based upon the same fundamental, immutable, and ever-fruitful principles that have inspired the great art of the past and are equally destined to inspire that of the future. Sibelius has triumphantly disproved the belief that the idioms and methods of procedure that has served so many generations of composers have now become exhausted; almost alone at the present time he has conclusively shown, what most people had legitimately begun to doubt, that it is still just as possible as it ever was to say something absolutely new, vital, and original, without having to invent a new syntax, a new vocabulary, a new language, in order to do so. Sibelius, in fact, reveals a fresh and unsuspected beauty in the old, whereas most modern composers seek to discover a familiar beauty in the new.

There are many great artists, differing from each other widely in other ways, who are alike in this, that by virtue of the very unsurpassable perfection of their achievements they are apt to engender in their successors a feeling of profound discouragement and finality. One feels that they have exhausted all the possibilities they had opened up, and that there is nothing left for those who come after them. Such are Bach, Mozart, Wagner, Chopin, Delius. Others there are, however, such as Beethoven, Berlioz, Liszt, Mussorgsky, who suggest and inspire as much as they themselves actually achieve. And Sibelius is of this number. Over and above his actual tangible donation he gave us a sense of liberation, fresh hopes, and new energies with which to realize them. He cut a path through the *selva oscura* wherein most modern musicians have gone so hopelessly astray. Curiously applicable to Sibelius, indeed, are the words of his compatriot, the nameless Finnish poet of ancient days who composed the lines with which the great national epic, the *Kalevala*, concludes:

> *I have shown the way to singers,*
> *Showed the way, and broke the treetops,*
> *Cut the branches, shown the pathways.*
> *This way therefore leads the pathway,*
> *Here the path lies newly opened,*
> *Widely open for the singers,*
> *For the young, who now are growing,*
> *For the rising generation.*

(RICHARD STRAUSS)

1864 - 1949

BIOGRAPHY

RICHARD STRAUSS was born in Munich on June 11, 1864. His teachers in music included Tombo, Benno Walter, and F. W. Meyer, while his academic study took place at the Gymnasium and the University of Munich.

In 1885, Strauss became Hans von Bülow's assistant with the Meiningen Orchestra, rising to the post of principal conductor upon von Bülow's retirement. It was during this period that Strauss met and befriended Alexander Ritter, whose philosophical conversations with Strauss were powerful factors in inspiring Strauss to write program music in the vein of Liszt and Wagner and to adopt the plastic form of the Liszt tone poem.

The first work Strauss wrote in the new style came in 1886, *Aus Italien*. At its first performance it was greeted with hisses and cat-calls. But Strauss was not discouraged from the new path he had selected for himself. During the next few years he produced his remarkable set of tone poems, beginning with *Macbeth*, which established him as the champion of the modern school of music at the time.

Not until 1905 did Strauss assume that imposing position in the world of opera that he had acquired in orchestral music. In that year he presented *Salome*, based upon the play of Oscar Wilde. Again Strauss became the object of abuse — this time at the hands of censors and puritans. But a more important consideration than that it aroused antagonism was the fact that *Salome* was Strauss' first major operatic achievement. *Elektra* followed *Salome* by four years and inaugurated the fruitful collaboration of Strauss and the Austrian poet and dramatist Hugo von Hofmannsthal, which was to persist for almost twenty-five years and to produce such well-known operas as *Der Rosenkavalier* and *Ariadne auf Naxos.*

When, in 1933, the Nazi government came into power in Germany, Strauss was appointed president of the *Kulturkammer.* Eventually, Strauss came into conflict with his political superiors. During World War II he lived partly in Garmisch and partly in Switzerland where, his royalties impounded, he was virtually destitute. He emerged from this retirement on October 19, 1947, to conduct his first concert in nine years — in London during a week-long Strauss festival. His eighty-fifth birthday in 1949 was celebrated by an official celebration in Munich, a festival of his music in Paris, and commemorative concerts in other major music centers. He died soon thereafter, on September 8, 1949, at his home in Garmisch-Partenkirchen, Bavaria.

PERSONAL NOTE

William Leon Smyser

As I see him walking among the trees and past his little lakes, Strauss is an old man, yet extraordinarily tall. His thin topcoat sags in perpendicular lines to accommodate the hands he has thrust deep into his side pockets. His shoulders stoop together and he seems cadaverously, deceptively lean. The heavy head, square and shaggy as a mastiff's, comes as a surprise. It is in proportion to his height, yet not in proportion with the frame that has sunken and narrowed with the years. Dressed all in black, Strauss never fails to suggest a weird impression, as he moves slowly along, sauntering, slanting down the rows, like some giant bloom suddenly cut loose to become peripatetic and cruise about with its great head bowing on inadequate stalk.

Musicians often have high bulging foreheads. Strauss' forehead is more massive, more dominant under its light curling patch of hair than even that of Beethoven, who is familiar to us through his bust. In Strauss' youth, this Jovelike front almost overweighted the dreaming peasant's face beneath. It absorbed into itself the imperceptible blond eyebrows and lashes. It shadowed the great dark, round, almost bovine eyes. It rendered ridiculous the nose that tilted up into a diminutive bulb at the end, and made a caricature of the manly strivings after a bushy, dapper mustache. Strauss' face in his twenties reflected the Strauss of that day: a mind long since matured and self-expressive, a will and a character yet undecided.

Today, the Nietzschean principles, the Wagnerian thunderings to which Strauss has often vibrated, have put purpose into the eyes. Age has broadened the jaw. Instead of being top-heavy, the face is now pendulous and balanced. There is a certain humor in the lips, above which the mustache has become a close-cropped stubble, stoutly aggressive, where it was once tentative and flaxen.

Strauss has acquired the air of a man who wins his arguments in life. He is, indeed, like George Bernard Shaw, a notoriously good businessman. Both have had, as rebels and innovators, their callow apple-cart period. Both have developed into a Michelangelo-like modesty.

Strauss is like Stravinsky in that he insists upon the absolute, literal, point for point, mathematical reading of his scores. " I demand precision in the rendering of my own works, and try to achieve it in my own interpretation of others." He is a thorough German in his pedantry. " But I do not consider myself narrowly German. Music is a province largely international."

Frau Strauss must enter into any discussion of her husband's music. She not only aids in its making. She has been Strauss' muse and model in the *Sinfonia domestica* and *Intermezzo*. All the droll episodes at which Strauss hints in words and harmony she has suggested. She has even been known to hold up one of his dinner parties in order to search for the place cards that she must have somewhere " saved from the last time." Too categorical a hostess to think of letting her guests go in to table without having it set properly for them, she is at the same time too good a manager to make new favors when old ones are just under her hand, " just tucked away."

And so, Frau Strauss has been the efficient manager of his genius. It is she who has brought into Strauss' dreamy life an element of order almost fanatic in its absolutism and tyranny. It is she who has dictated the purification of all guests before his door; it is she who has kept him in form as if he were a boxer.

There was a party one night at the Kaiser Bar. " Come on, Maestro, you must dance with us! " cried one of the youngest, prettiest matrons of the party. " I'd love to . . . I want to . . . but I don't dare." Richard Strauss half glanced in the direction of his trainer. " I'm not allowed." And the great master's huge block cheeks flamed red with embarrassment. He may rebel, but he is too sane a creator long to think of disregarding his rules. As he grows older, they can be relaxed, yet they are always there, controlling even his hours of recreation. There has certainly been more Richard Strauss written because of the existence of Frau Strauss than ever there would have been without her. " Richard," she is reported to have said to him when the mood is backward and he wanders absently about in everybody's way, " Richard, jetzt gehst komponieren! " And this order to compose, though it may at times have forced and thinned his inspiration, has been beyond measure productive.[1]

THE COMPOSER SPEAKS

Richard Strauss [2]

CHERRIES do not blossom in the winter, nor do musical ideas come readily when nature is bleak and cold. I am a great lover of nature. Hence it is natural that I do my best creative work in the Bavarian highlands during the spring and summer. In fact, I usually compose from spring to autumn and then write out and polish the detailed scores in the winter.

Musical ideas, like young wine, should be put in storage and taken up again only after they have been allowed to ferment and ripen. I often jot down a motif or a melody and then tuck it away for a year. Then when I take it up again I find that, quite unconsciously, something within me — the imagination — has been at work on it.

. . .

[1] This was written while Strauss was still alive.
[2] From news items and interviews published in American newspapers and English journals concerning his *modus operandi*.

I compose everywhere, walking or driving, eating or drinking, at home or abroad, in noisy hotels, in my garden, in railway carriages. My sketchbook never leaves me, and as soon as a motif strikes me I jot it down. One of the most important melodies from my opera *Der Rosenkavalier* struck me while I was playing a Bavarian card game. But before I improvise even the smallest sketch for an opera, I allow the texts to permeate my thoughts and mature in me at least six months or so, that the situation and characters may be thoroughly assimilated. Then only do I let musical thoughts enter my mind. The subsketches then become sketches. They are copied out, worked out, arranged for the piano, and rearranged as often as four times. This is the hard part of the work. The score I write in my study, straightway, without troubling, working at it twelve hours a day.

I have long since learned that in my composition I am unable to write without a program to guide me.

It simply is not true that one can set " everything " to music, in so far as by " setting to music " the transference of a sensory or emotional experience into the symbolic language of music is understood. At the same time it is of course equally true that it is possible to paint with sounds and combinations of sound, in particular certain motifs relating to the movement, but the danger is always near of entrusting too much to music and relapsing into a barren imitation of nature. Be it contrived with never so much spirit and technical ability, such music will nevertheless remain second-class.

It is my conviction that in the future the only decisive factor of dramatic effectiveness will prove to be the orchestra of smaller dimensions, which does not suppress the singing voice as does the full orchestra. Many of the younger composers already understand this in part, namely, that the opera orchestra of the future is the chamber orchestra, which, by virtue of its clear, crystalline underlining of what is happening on the stage, is alone in a position to interpret and reflect the intentions of the composer in respect of the voices. And moreover, it is not entirely without importance that the public should not only be aware of the sounds and voices, but should also be able to follow the texts accurately.

Perhaps it is in the nature of the times that our successors, our " younger generation," can no longer accept my dramatic and sym-

phonic works as a valid expression of what I put into them, both as
a musician and a human being. But the musical and artistic problem
is settled as far as I am concerned, while for the " younger generation " it is just beginning. We are, all of us, children of our time
and can never jump over its shadows.

STRAUSS

Karl Geiringer

RECENTLY I read a letter in an American music journal that Richard
Strauss had written to a friend: " I am well. I have finished the
score of a new opera and have completed the piano sketch of another." This letter was apparently written in the spring of 1941.
Strauss might just as well have written it five or ten years earlier.
After the composer celebrated his fiftieth birthday, he completed a
dozen works for the stage. The tempo of his productivity almost increased in the course of years up to the very year of his death. While
the master of execution always remained equal, his creative power,
however, decidedly declined.

In his last years, Strauss was virtually a living monument to his
own great past. He was the greatest representative of German music
of the period of Wilhelm II. Just as the luster of the empire departed, so did the art of Strauss decline. The composer lived on the
honor given to his great past. Only a very restricted circle gave actual
acclaim to the works of the last twenty years.

Nonetheless, we must not forget that in his younger years
Strauss wrote works that were rightfully ranked among the best of
the period. Many of his earlier works can today be regarded as
classics. This also permits us today to consider the master's compositions historically. Their author is no longer our contemporary, no
longer standing in the field of conflicting opinions, but a figure who
belongs to the past, even if it be only the immediate past.

We can assign three periods to his creative power. The first em-
braces the apprentice works and those of his youth up to 1887, when
he was twenty-three years old. To this group, together with various

unpublished works, belong his compositions op. 1 to op. 19, and the *Burleske* for piano and orchestra, which appeared without opus number. The second period covers more than twenty-three years, up to 1910, and comprises Strauss' maturity, in which were included compositions from op. 20 to op. 58. The third period begins with the opera *Der Rosenkavalier*, op. 59, presented in 1911.

Classical and early romantic tendencies are characteristic of the works of Strauss' first period. Beethoven and Schumann are the immediate patterns for the young composer, while Brahms' influence makes itself felt only gradually. Strauss cultivated the most varied forms: piano pieces, the *Lied*, chamber music, concerto, symphony, and choral music. He is perfectly at ease in each of these; already the twenty-year-old composer shows an amazing technical dexterity. Characteristic of these early compositions is a wealth of inventiveness and power. Granted, there is also a certain dryness, as well as a lack of deeper feeling. The slow movements are usually the weakest parts of the compositions. This does not prevent many of these pieces — such as the *Serenade*, for wind instruments, op. 7 (1881), the Symphony, op. 12 (1884), the six-part chorus, *Wanderers Sturmlied*, op. 14 (1884), the Violin Sonata, op. 18 (1887), and the *Burleske* (1885) — from being of interest today.

Aus Italien, op. 16, which appeared in 1887, marks the transition to the second period, that of full maturity. It is a work of absolute music in which, however, the poetic titles of the individual movements prophetically indicate Strauss' future development. A truly new picture presents itself for the first time with *Macbeth*, op. 23 (1886–90), and *Don Juan*, op. 20 (1888–9). Here Strauss is no longer a disciple of Schmann or Brahms. The young man, who only a few years previously was counted among the most passionate opponents of Richard Wagner, suddenly became an enthusiastic disciple of the master of Bayreuth and his spiritual relations, Liszt and Berlioz. Strauss himself has said that this change is, for the most part, to be ascribed to the influence of his friend, the poet and composer, Alexander Ritter. It was Ritter " who urged him on to the development of the poetic, and expressive, in music." *Macbeth* and *Don Juan*, as well as all the ensuing works of Strauss, have this in common: a poetic program forms their basis, just as in the tone poems of Franz Liszt. In *Macbeth* it is the Shakespearian drama. In *Till Eulenspiegel*, op. 28 (1895), it is the well-known German folk tale. In *Ein Heldenleben*, op. 40 (1898–9), and *Sinfonia domestica,* op. 53 (1902–03), autobiographical themes. In the *Alpensinfonie*, op. 64 (1915),[1] a journey through the Alps. In none of these works does Strauss adhere strictly to the forms of absolute music. He is able, however, to find a form for his compositions that shows a certain relationship with traditional structures. In *Macbeth*, *Don Juan*, and *Tod und Verklärung*, op. 24 (1889–90), the sonata-allegro form provides the formal pattern, although in the last-named work the treatment is particularly free. *Till Eulenspiegel* was described by its composer as a rondo, while he gives to *Don Quixote*, op. 35 (1897–8), the subtitle of " Introduction, Theme with Variations, and Finale." *Also sprach Zarathustra*, op. 30 (1896), *Ein Heldenleben*, *Sinfonia domestica*, and *Alpensinfonie* are symphonic fantasies, which, despite the interweaving of their various parts into an uninterrupted whole, reveal clearly the groundwork of the old symphony, consisting of several different movements. Tone painting and realistic setting of the poetic program are certainly no rarities in Strauss' tone poems. The master, however, is constantly striving to plan his compositions in such a way that they can be enjoyed as pure music, even without a knowledge of their poetic programs.

The thematic material of the tone poems is characterized by marked *élan*. The themes are frequently diatonic in construction, built upon triads; a preference for wide intervals is characteristic. Inexhaustible is Strauss' fancy for developing and transforming his themes. He is particularly capable in his harmonic construction. In the chromatic alteration of chords and their free resolution, as well as in his daring use of dissonance, he goes far beyond Liszt and Wagner. In spite of all his boldness in modulation, the framework of his tonality is never completely abandoned. The composer is a consummate contrapuntalist, as is particularly disclosed by the masterly use of a combination of themes. In his instrumentation, Strauss discovered altogether new resources. His orchestration stands out not only because of its enormous dimensions (for the *Sinfonia domestica* the composer himself called for twenty-two woodwinds, sixteen brass instruments, and nine percussion, together with sixty-four strings) but also because of its extraordinary richness of color. Fantasy and daring realism, which do not recoil even from blatant effects (recall the bleating of the sheep in *Don Quixote* or Jochanaan's death rattle in *Salome!*), mark Strauss' orchestral effects.

---

[1] Although it was written during Strauss' third period, it is here mentioned because of its pertinence.

That, at the same time, the technical demands on the performer have been increased goes without saying.

From poetic-dramatic orchestral composition, Strauss was led naturally and inevitably toward music drama itself. The first work in this group, the music drama *Guntram*, op. 25 (1892–93), follows closely the example of the Bayreuth master. Like Wagner, Strauss is here his own librettist; he handles a legendary story from the German past in which the motive of redemption plays an important role. From a musical point of view the work is also too much a copy of Wagner to be able to claim any interest. On a higher plane stands the one-act opera *Feuersnot*, op. 50 (1900–01), with libretto by Ernst von Wolzogen. This work shows Strauss' feeling for gay persiflage. Characteristic of Strauss, also, is the splendid coloring and the soaring passages of the erotic lyrical scenes. Unfortunately, the composer made himself the hero of the opera, and his self-pity and self-aggrandizement in the text offend good taste too strongly to permit a wider popularity for the opera.

It is altogether different with the one-act music drama *Salome*, op. 54 (1904–05). Here Strauss adorned a coldly gleaming, decadent text by Oscar Wilde with music full of glowing passion. It is an unusually hectic work, holding the listener spellbound for almost two hours. Whether he despises it or admires it, he cannot help being gripped to the depths of his being. The chromaticism is of great importance in this score. The orchestra is handled independently in a symphonic manner, and in this Wagner's leitmotiv technique plays an important part. It far surpasses anything preceding it in realistic tone painting and wealth of sonority. The climax is a sort of symphonic interlude: Salome's Dance. Scenes built in definite musical forms occur also in other places of the score so that the powerful drama presents a clear-cut structure.

In *Elektra*, op. 58 (1906–08), the text for which was written by Hugo von Hofmannsthal after the drama of Sophocles, Strauss goes a step further than in *Salome*. The orchestra reaches enormous proportions (each group of woodwinds consists of four to eight varieties, while the strings are trebled). At times, the instruments are used to describe coarse realism and at other times to represent effects of supreme majesty. The harmonic structure is more complicated than in preceding works and the tonality is not infrequently forsaken. The voices are handled as though they were instruments and seldom assume the shape of actual song. The atmosphere in

Elektra is — if possible — even tense and more hysterical than in *Salome*. However, where in *Salome* pervese sensuality forms the essence of the drama, here it is the love of a daughter for her father.

Elektra represents the pinnacle and the conclusion of Strauss' productivity in the field of music drama proper. A further development, or even a continuation of his former principles, seemed impossible to the master. His next work for the stage, *Der Rosenkavalier*, op. 59 (1909–10), is once again a true opera of the style prevalent before Wagner. In Strauss' third creative period, which commences with *Der Rosenkavalier*, we find a completely changed picture, a return to simplicity and tradition. Elements of Strauss' retrospective first period come once more into play, although the modern development of the middle period is also recognizable. Perhaps it is owing to the Viennese Hugo von Hofmannsthal, who became Strauss' permanent librettist after *Elektra*, that the influence of Austrian music on Strauss' style prevailed so strongly in *Der Rosenkavalier*. Mozart and the waltz king Johann Strauss are the godfathers of this opera. Harmony, color, and melody lose their feverish modern character and become simpler and more natural. The somewhat forced one-act form of the earlier music drama makes way for the unconstrained and traditional three-act form. Once again we find in *Der Rosenkavalier* an overture, duets, trios, and finales in the style of the baroque opera. Although the work takes place in the rococo period, Strauss does not hesitate to give free play to the waltz, which found its full expression in the nineteenth century. We can only be grateful to him for this anachronism, since the waltzes of *Der Rosenkavalier* are among the most charming portions of the score.

In the succeeding stage work, *Ariadne auf Naxos*, op. 60 (1911–12), the tendency of the composer to revert to earlier styles is further marked. In this work, which originally served as an interpolation for Molière's *Le Bourgeois Gentilhomme*, and received its final form only after two revisions, Strauss mingles elements of the old *opera buffa* and the *opera seria*. Strongly stylized polyphonic passages alternate with homophonic passages. An important innovation in this opera, which looks backward and forward at the same time, is that in this work the composer found it sufficient to use a chamber orchestra of only thirty-seven men. Strauss, who, during his lifetime, had worked with the largest orchestral masses, is able to evoke from this small group tonal effects of extraordinary richness.

Salome, Elektra, Der Rosenkavalier, and *Ariadne* may be considered Strauss' masterpieces for the theater. *Die Frau ohne Schatten,* op. 65 (1914–17), a fairy-tale opera, forms a continuation of the archaic tendencies of *Ariadne.* Unfortunately, the exquisite chamber-music style of the older work was not sustained. The customary large Strauss orchestra is once more used in this opera, and in doing so his adherence to the tendencies of the postwar period, which began so promisingly, was discontinued despite the success of *Ariadne.*

In *Intermezzo,* op. 72 (1922–23), Strauss is once more his own librettist. This work belongs, with *Ein Heldenleben, Feuersnot,* and *Sinfonia domestica,* to the less felicitous group of Strauss' autobiographical compositions. The composer himself and his wife appear in this opera as characters. The voice parts are almost exclusively recitatives, while the orchestra presents symphonic interludes that have nothing to do with the dramatic treatment. This original stylistic experiment might have aroused interest if the text and the music were somewhat more inspired.

Die ägyptische Helena, op. 75 (1924–27), resumes the tendencies of *Die Frau ohne Schatten.* The deterioration in the inventiveness of the master is here very clearly perceptible, and in later works even more strongly so. *Arabella,* op. 79 (1930–32), is the last work he produced in collaboration with Hofmannsthal. In content and style it is similar to *Der Rosenkavalier.* After Hofmannsthal's death, Strauss found a competent librettist in Stefan Zweig. Together with him, he wrote the comic opera *Die schweigsame Frau,* op. 80 (1934–35). The fact that Zweig was " non-Aryan " and that his works could not be produced in Germany forced Strauss to change his librettist once more. Again he chose an Austrian, the director of the Theater Collection of the Vienna National Library, Joseph Gregor. The fruits of their collaboration were *Friedenstag* (1935–36), *Daphne* (1937), and *Die Liebe der Danae* (1938–40). The libretto of Strauss' last opera, *Capriccio* (1940–41) was by Clemens Krauss.

Apart from compositions for orchestra, and the operas, Strauss cultivated only the *Lied* assiduously. He wrote about a hundred and forty works in this *genre.* In the manner of Wagner and Hugo Wolf he placed the principal emphasis on the particularly expressive treatment of the accompaniment. And yet the voice part is often characterized by an unusually expansive range. Many of his songs

are technical masterpieces of great *élan* and imagination. The *Lie-*
der of his second period have become the most famous, among
which are to be found " Cäcilie," " Heimliche Aufforderung,"
" Morgen," " Traum durch die Dämmerung," " Ich trage meine
Minne," " Frühlingsfeier." In addition, " Allerseelen," from op. 10,
and " Ständchen," from op. 17, rightfully enjoy the greatest popularity.

In conclusion it can be said: Strauss was not a true revolutionary. He introduced no cataclysmic innovations. There was also lacking in him an inexorable self-criticism, which is the essential attribute to the truly great artist. His contribution was that he built
upon the revolutionary structure of others, above all that of Wagner
and Liszt following their achievements to their logical conclusion.
Strauss, with his rich imagination, his immense craftsmanship, his
flair for humor and satire, and his strong impassioned personality,
succeeded in producing a small number of masterpieces within
those limits mentioned above, masterpieces that are played throughout the world as practically the only products of Germanic music
since Brahms.

$\big($IGOR STRAVINSKY$\big)$

1882 -

BIOGRAPHY

IGOR STRAVINSKY was born in Oranienbaum, a suburb of
St. Petersburg, on June 17, 1882. In 1907 he began formal study
with Rimsky-Korsakov, the first fruits of which were a symphony
and a suite for voice and orchestra, *Le Faune et la bergère*, both performed successfully in St. Petersburg in 1908. Diaghilev, impresario
of the then newly founded Ballet Russe became impressed by Stravinsky's talent upon hearing the composer's *Scherzo fantastique* in
1909 and asked him to associate himself with the Ballet. Stravinsky's first assignment was the orchestration of some Chopin music.
This was followed by an original score for a ballet on the legend of
the firebird, *L'Oiseau de feu*, given its première at the Paris Opéra
in 1910 with immediate success. From that time on the collaboration of Diaghilev and Stravinsky produced a series of masterpieces
that placed Stravinsky in the front rank of living composers and at
the same time made him one of the most provocative figures in the
world of modern culture. *Petrouchka* came in 1911. *Le Sacre du
printemps*, which followed in 1913, created a world-famous scandal. The last of the famous works in this period of Stravinsky's career were *Le Chant du rossignol* (converted by the composer into a
ballet from an earlier opera) and *Les Noces*.

During World War I, Stravinsky lived in Switzerland. In 1919
he settled in France, becoming a French citizen. He changed his
nationality; but some time before this he had changed his artistic
domain as well. A radical metamorphosis had come over his style
beginning with *L'Histoire du soldat* (1918), in which he abandoned

his former role as a fiery rebel peering into the future and assumed that of a neoclassicist, turning to the past for his idiom and style.

In 1925, Stravinsky visited the United States for the first time. He returned to this country several times before making it his permanent home and becoming an American citizen in 1945. In many of his major works since 1955, Stravinsky once again changed his basic style of writing, this time by adopting a serial technique modeled after the twelve-tone idiom of Anton von Webern.

PERSONAL NOTE

Janet Flanner

OUTSIDE of his music, Stravinsky is equally extraordinary. He is an agitated little man with the will of a giant, fine formal gestures, and a cyclonic temperament. He is an inventive, contradictory, complicated mentality bent on comprehending everything immediately and from the ground up. Like many composers, he is social, and is a wit in two languages besides his own — German and French. He loves to talk, has the drawing-room charm of the verbal virtuoso, and when he listens gives the perfect attention of a clockmaker hearkening to a new movement. In an argument he always takes sides and, since he ignores concession in any form, always thinks his side is right. He hates to be alone, is always at the boiling point of gaiety or despair, has a tremendous capacity for *joie de vivre*, smokes forty cigarettes a day, is a connoisseur of claret, which he used to buy in the barrel at Bordeaux and have bottled for his special use, sensually enjoys fine brandy, champagne, and foods when he is not involved with conscience or diet, occasionally overeats, invariably keeps all church festivals. He is a hypochondriac who worries about his health, his family's health, everybody's health. " How are you feeling, I'm not feeling very well," he began a letter to a friend. He hurries back and forth between homeopathy, allopathy, and symptoms. For years he has taken daily gymnastic exercises before an open window and has the pride of the small male in his magnificent muscles. He is an energetic land traveler, terrified of the sea; he has a passion for shopping in capital cities, an alarming taste for luxury in silk pajamas, and a weakness for leather goods, masculine gadgets, and debonair clothes. When fully dressed, he has a great deal on even in mild weather — scarf to his ears, spats, sweater, tweeds, stick, cigarette lighter, *étui*, wrist watch, complicated double lenses for his myopic eyes, sacred medals and fetishes pinned to his underwear — for he is superstitious — and, over all, for fear of drafts, often two coats, one of fur. His friend Chanel once made and gave him a tremendous astrakhan-collared traveling coat and cap he became partial to.

He has an almost Oriental capacity for the domestic relations, was devoted to his first wife, who he used to say was his oldest friend (being cousins, they were acquainted since they were three), is despotically attached to his four children. Feodor, the eldest, is a painter; the second son, Sviatoslav (Soulima), is a pianist; the girls, both pretty, are Ludmilla, who is a textile artist, and Milena, who sings. All the children were brought up in French Switzerland, were for a long time officially French and domestically Russian in tongue, speak German, and had instruction in English. Stravinsky is a kind of cult for his family; his children have the loyalty for their father that offspring usually reserve for their own generation.

Stravinsky's genius is organized; he composes three hours every morning, spring and summer only. His working desk is bureaucratically neat; his manuscripts, which used to be in colors, like liturgies, are now in mere black and white, but museum pieces for meticulousness. After all, he was trained to be a lawyer.

Before 1939 the Stravinskys used to live in a flat in Paris in the rue de faubourg Saint-Honoré by the President's palace; before that, they lived modestly in furnished or borrowed dwellings in Switzerland, Italy, and France. More recently, Stravinsky established his home in Hollywood, California. His second wife was the widow of the painter Soudeikine.

The most famous of the many portraits done of him was the line drawing by Picasso, made in Rome during World War I and prevented from leaving the country by Italian border police who thought it was the plan of a fortification. It looks exactly like Stravinsky. He has a strange, prehistoric face — lean, bony, thicklipped, with that mysterious look of change in it which marked the profile of rare early animals, selected for survival in a different, nobler form.

THE COMPOSER SPEAKS

Igor Stravinsky [1]

FOR me, as a creative musician, composition is a daily function that I am compelled to discharge. I compose because I am made for that and cannot do otherwise. Just as any organ atrophies unless kept in a state of constant activity, so the faculty of composition becomes enfeebled and dulled unless kept up by practice and effort. The uninitiated imagine that one must await inspiration in order to create. That is a mistake. I am far from saying that there is no such thing as inspiration; quite the opposite. It is found as a driving force in every kind of human activity, and is in no wise peculiar to artists. But that force is only brought into action by an effort, and that effort is work. Just as appetite comes by eating, so work brings inspiration, if inspiration is not discernible at the beginning. But it is not simply inspiration that counts; it is the result of inspiration — that is, the composition.

At the beginning of my career as a composer I was a good deal spoiled by the public. Even such things as were at first received with hostility were soon afterward acclaimed. But I have a very distinct feeling that in the course of . . . years my written work has estranged me from the great mass of my listeners. They expected something different from me. Liking the music of *L'Oiseau de feu*, *Petrouchka*, *Le Sacre du printemps*, *Les Noces*, and being accustomed to the language of those works, they are astonished to hear me speaking in another idiom. They cannot and will not follow me in the progress of my musical thought. What moves and delights me leaves them indifferent, and what still continues to interest them holds no further attraction for me. For that matter, I believe that there was seldom any real communion of spirit between us. If it happened — and it still happens — that we liked the same things, I very much doubt whether it was for the same reasons. Yet art postulates communion, and the artist has an imperative need to make others share the joy he experiences himself. But, in spite of that

---

[1] This statement is from *Stravinsky: An Autobiography*.

need, he prefers direct and frank opposition to apparent agreement that is based on misunderstanding.

Unfortunately, perfect communion is rare, and the more the personality of the author is revealed the rarer that communion becomes. The more he eliminates all that is extraneous, all that is not his own or " in him," the greater is his risk of conflicting with the expectations of the bulk of the public, who always receive a shock when confronted by something to which they are not accustomed.

The author's need for communion is all-embracing, but unfortunately that is only an unattainable ideal, so that he is compelled to content himself with something less. In my own case, I find that while the general public no longer gives me the enthusiastic reception of earlier days, that does not in any way prevent a large number of listeners, mainly of the younger generation, from acclaiming my work with all the old ardor. I wonder whether, after all, it is simply a matter of generation?

It is very doubtful whether Rimsky-Korsakov would ever have accepted *Le Sacre* or even *Petrouchka*. Is it any wonder, then, that the hypercritics of today should be dumfounded by a language in which all the characteristics of their esthetic seem to be violated? What, however, is less justifiable is that they nearly always blame the author for what is in fact due to their own lack of comprehension, a lack made all the more conspicuous because in their inability to state their grievance clearly they cautiously try to conceal their incompetence in the looseness and vagueness of their phraseology.

Their attitude certainly cannot make me deviate from my path. I shall assuredly not sacrifice my predilections and my aspirations to the demands of those who, in their blindness, do not realize that they are simply asking me to go backward. It should be obvious that what they wish for has become obsolete for me, and that I could not follow them without doing violence to myself. But, on the other hand, it would be a great mistake to regard me as an adherent of *Zukunftsmusik* — the music of the future. Nothing could be more ridiculous. I live neither in the past nor in the future. I am in the present. I cannot know what tomorrow will bring forth. I can know only what the truth is for me today. That is what I am called upon to serve, and I serve it in all lucidity.

STRAVINSKY

Eric Walter White

STRAVINSKY's apprentice works belong to the years 1905–09. During the earlier part of this period he was taking tuition in harmony, counterpoint, and instrumentation from various private teachers in St. Petersburg, including Rimsky-Korsakov, and his compositions were academically correct but derivative. The Symphony in E flat (1905–07) is cast in a style of classicism popularized by Glazunov; *Le Faune et la bergère,* cycle for voice and orchestra (1905–06), and the *Scherzo fantastique* for orchestra (1908) show an awareness of Wagner and Tchaikovsky and of some contemporary French composers such as Dukas. Though these early works lacked personality, they showed definite technical ability; but his full powers as a composer did not become apparent until, after accepting a commission from Diaghilev to write a special score for the 1910 season of the Russian Ballet company in Paris he produced *L'Oiseau de feu,* or *The Firebird* (1910), to a scenario by Fokine. Here his musical idiom showed affinities with that of his master, Rimsky-Korsakov (who had died in 1908); and it was perhaps to Stravinsky's advantage that at that date the exotic chromaticism of *Le Coq d'or* was unknown outside Russia, otherwise *L'Oiseau de feu* might not have made so strong an impression of originality in western Europe as it actually did. Despite its debt to Rimsky-Korsakov, however, the score displayed magnificent powers of formal organization, which showed that in Stravinsky a composer of the first rank had arrived, and also contained the germ of certain polytonal processes that were soon to prove capable of much wider development.

Despite the success of *L'Oiseau de feu* with audiences in western Europe, it was not Stravinsky's immediate intention to continue writing ballet scores. While working on the instrumentation of *L'Oiseau de feu,* he had conceived the idea of composing a kind of pagan symphony (which was ultimately to become *Le Sacre du printemps,* or *The Rite of Spring*). Its composition, however, was temporarily shelved because in the summer of 1910 immediately after the Paris season of the Russian Ballet, a more urgent idea claimed priority. This Stravinsky intended should be a concerted piece for piano and orchestra, a kind of *Burlesque* or *Konzertstück* in three movements, in which (in Stravinsky's own words) the piano would represent "a puppet suddenly endowed with life, exasperating the orchestra with diabolical cascades of arpeggios, and the orchestra replying with menacing fanfares." When Diaghilev heard the rough sketches, he immediately perceived the dramatic possibilities of the work and persuaded Stravinsky to incorporate the movements of the concerto into a ballet score, the scenario of which was drawn up with the help of Alexandre Benois. This was the genesis of *Petrouchka* (1911), in which Stravinsky used polytonality as a means to further the dramatic action and showed a remarkable talent for organizing popular music within a symphonic framework.

Le *Sacre du printemps* (1913) followed; and here polytonality was used to shattering effect by setting large blocks of opposing chords against each other. Of even greater importance in this score was Stravinsky's attitude to rhythm and meter. So far his movements had been written in regular meters (time signatures) to a *tempo giusto*, which meant that the music's pulse was not to be vitiated by rubato playing. This was particularly noticeable in the case of fast movements, such as *Fireworks* (1908), the Allegro and Scherzo movements in *L'Oiseau de feu* (especially the "Infernal Dance of the Subjects of Kashchei"), and the "Russian Dance" in *Petrouchka*. But now, in his desire to avoid developing his musical material in the traditional way, he decided to break it down by varying the note values and changing the meters from regular to irregular patterns while maintaining a regular fundamental beat or pulse. In *Le Sacre du printemps* this procedure resulted in a nervous, almost hysterical, tension, which was emphasized by the extremely large orchestra employed, with its important percussion section. Perhaps it was not altogether surprising that at its first performance in Paris on May 29, 1913, *Le Sacre du printemps* provoked not only amazement and misunderstanding, but also ridicule and open hostility.

The polytonality of *Le Sacre du printemps* had led a considerable way from the diatonicism of classical tonality; and the chromatic implications of Stravinsky's latest manner were used to almost transcendental effect in a short cantata for male voice choir and orchestra entitled *The King of the Stars* (1911). In the *Three*

Japanese Lyrics (1912–13), for voice and nine instruments, there
was a sudden thinning of texture, and the third of these songs
("Tsaraiuki") displayed an unexpected and perhaps prophetic
tendency toward atonality.

Stravinsky's chromatic researches were also used to good effect
when he came to finish his three-act opera, *Le Rossignol*, or *The
Nightingale*, the first act of which had been written in 1908–09,
when he was still under the influence of Rimsky-Korsakov, Debussy,
and Scriabin. The subsequent two acts (written five years later) used
chromaticism partly to portray the fantastic baroque extravagance
of the court of the emperor of China in Act II, and partly in a more
attenuated form to deal with the rarer atmosphere of the scene between the sick Emperor, Death, and the Nightingale in Act III.

The outbreak of World War I caught Stravinsky outside Russia, and he elected to remain for the period of 1914–19 in exile in
Switzerland. As war conditions had severely curtailed the engagements of the Russian Ballet and cut him off from his home and
property in Russia, his activities as a composer took a new turn.

To begin with, his mind was filled with a wealth of Russian
folklore, and some of the tunes (whether authentic or of his own
composition) were used as the raw material for works for small ensembles. There are numerous groups of songs belonging to this period: *Pribaoutki* (1914), *Cat's Cradle Songs* (1915–16), *Three
Tales for Children* (1915–17), *Saucers* (1914–17), and *Four Russian Songs* (1918). But of greater importance were *Renard* (1916)
and *Les Noces* (1914–17), in which Stravinsky succeeded in weld-
ing this fragmentary, short-winded material into two magnificent
musical structures. In *Renard* he exploited the vein for burlesque he
had already opened up in *Petrouchka*; but this time the characters
were animals instead of puppets and the setting was a farmyard instead of a fairground. As for *Les Noces*, this vast cantata, a solid
block of almost unbroken singing for solo voices and chorus, is one
of Stravinsky's masterpieces. Its rich modal polyphony proliferates
from a single diatonic theme, and its different episodes are cun-
ningly geared together by simple time differentials. The vocal part
of the composition was completed by 1917; but it took Stravinsky
another six years before he was able to find the right instrumental
accompaniment. After various false starts, he ultimately chose four
pianos and a large body of percussion divided into two groups con-

sisting of instruments with and without pitch; and the score was finally completed at Monaco in April, 1923.

At the same time as these compositions in which his interest in Russian folk song was so marked, he embarked on a number of works that showed a more eclectic approach to musical material. In the *Eight Easy Pieces* for piano duet (1915–17) he treated a number of traditional dance forms (e.g., waltz, polka, galop, and so forth) in a light, humorous style; and in *L'Histoire du soldat*, or *The Soldier's Tale* (1918), he extended his interest to Spanish *paso doble* and tango and American ragtime. This tendency coincided with a radical change of direction in his life, for the termination of the war did not mean that he could resume his prewar life where he had left it off. The Russian Revolution of 1917 had cut him off from his native land; his property had been confiscated; and as an exile he had reached a point of no return. From this moment, the native Russian element in his melos, which had been so predominant in works like *Le Sacre du printemps* and *Les Noces*, began to wither, and he showed himself increasingly conscious of western European musical traditions and anxious to subject his own compositions to the rule of order. As he himself expressed it in his lectures on the *Poetics of Music* at Harvard University (1939–40), " the clear integration of a work of art and its crystallization demand that all the Dionysiac elements that stimulate a composer and set in motion the rising sap of his imagination be adequately controlled before we succumb to their fever, and ultimately subordinated to discipline: such is Apollo's command."

If the *Symphony of Wind Instruments* (1920) was the last of Stravinsky's works in which the Russian melos made a forceful appearance, *L'Histoire du soldat* and *Pulcinella* (1919) displayed clear signs of the new order. In *L'Histoire du soldat* this is manifest, not so much in the idiom as in the brilliant economy of the instrumentation (for seven players) and the plastic use of tone color. In *Pulcinella* Stravinsky deliberately set himself to work within certain historical conventions by adopting some of Pergolesi's music as the basis for this ballet score. Thereafter it became quite customary for him to exploit stylistic references to the music of other ages. Nevertheless, whatever material or idiom he might adopt, the process of composition was always complete, and the resulting work original and stamped with his powerful personality.

Early in the 1920's Stravinsky decided that he would like to embark on a subsidiary career as a concert pianist, and, in addition to writing two important works for piano solo — the Sonata (1924) and the *Serenade* in A (1925) — produced various piano concertos, of which he retained for himself the exclusive performing rights over a period of years. The Concerto for Piano and Wind Orchestra (1923–24) was followed by the *Capriccio* for piano and orchestra (1929) and the Concerto for Two Solo Pianos (1935). A friendship with the violinist Samuel Dushkin led to the Violin Concerto in D (1931) and the *Duo concertant* for violin and piano (1932). Similarly, the *Movements* for piano and orchestra (1959) was specially written for Margrit Weber.

His preoccupation with concerto writing coincided with a change in his manner of instrumentation. It was probably about 1917, when he was turning the last two acts of his opera *Le Rossignol* into a symphonic poem called *Le Chant du rossignol*, or *The Song of the Nightingale*, that he first realized the importance of carefully combining instruments in different groups (often like small chamber-music ensembles) so as to obtain special effects of color, plasticity, and tension. The *concertante* style of writing became a hallmark of most of his later scores; and the *concertante* method of construction is at the basis of works like the *Dumbarton Oaks Concerto* for chamber orchestra (1938), the *Danses concertantes* (1942), the *Ebony Concerto* for jazz band (1945), the Concerto in D for String Orchestra (1946), and the ballet *Orpheus* (1947).

Interest in concerto form led to interest in symphonic form. The Octet for Wind Instruments of 1922–23 was a precursor of symphonies to come. The *Symphony of Psalms* (1930), for mixed voices and orchestra, is a wonderfully successful solution of the problem of the choral symphony. The Symphony in C (1940) has the full stature of a classical symphony in the Haydn-Beethoven tradition; and the Symphony in Three Movements (1945) is of special interest because it shows a fusion of the characteristic features of symphony and concerto, the piano and harp playing particularly important *concertante* roles.

Although Stravinsky did not collaborate closely with Diaghilev during the last years of the Russian Ballet, he nevertheless retained a close interest in the theater. Commissions for ballet scores came from Elizabeth Sprague Coolidge (*Apollon Musagète*, 1927–28),

Ida Rubinstein (*Le Baiser de la fée*, 1928), the American Ballet
(*Jeux de cartes*, or A *Card Game*, 1936), the Ballet Society of New
York (*Orpheus*), and the New York City Ballet (*Agon*, 1954–57).
After *Le Rossignol* he wrote three more operas: *Mavra* (1922),
Oedipus Rex (1927), and *The Rake's Progress* (1951), which are
all based on the use of various classical procedures. *Mavra* is a
lighthearted *opera buffa*. *Oedipus Rex*, which is a setting of a brilliantly concise libretto by Jean Cocteau, is of truly tragic stature.
The Rake's Progress is longer than either of these (three acts instead of one) and makes a less intense, though more varied, impression, since the action (libretto by W. H. Auden and Chester
Kallman) runs the gamut of comedy, farce, and drama, as well as
tragedy.

Immediately after *The Rake's Progress* a fundamental change
of direction occurred in Stravinsky's idiom. His interest in the
music of Anton von Webern had been aroused by his friend Robert
Craft, and his composition began to show an increasing preoccupation with serial technique. To begin with, he was content to
exploit a limited series of different notes — e.g., eight in the *gigue*
of the Septet (1952) and five in the *In Memoriam Dylan Thomas*
(1954) — but in *Threni* (1958), the *Movements* for piano and
orchestra and *Epitaphium* (1959) the series became completely
dodecaphonal, and the tonal implications of earlier, partly serial
works like *Canticum sacrum* (1955) and *Agon* disappeared.

Nearly a hundred different works of Stravinsky's have been
published and performed during his lifetime. Never has he been
content to rest on the laurels he won in Paris in the years immediately preceding World War I or merely to exploit a vein of
established success. His enquiring mind has led him to explore new
directions, new instrumental combinations, new tone colors, new
musical material, new processes of construction. His example has
been a stimulus and a challenge to musicians and music lovers
everywhere in the world.

(RALPH VAUGHAN WILLIAMS)

1872 - 1958

BIOGRAPHY

RALPH VAUGHAN WILLIAMS was born in Down Ampney, in Gloucestershire, on October 12, 1872. His schooling took place at the Charterhouse School and at the Royal College of Music, in London, after which he entered Trinity College, Cambridge. Following this, he returned to the Royal College to become a pupil of Hubert Parry and Charles Stanford. After a period of travel in Germany, where he studied with Max Bruch, he took courses in music at Cambridge, where he received his doctorate in 1901. At the same time, he held several minor positions as organist and lecturer in London and Oxford.

While he was still a student, several examples of early Tudor music directed his interest toward the unexplored regions of old English music. The charm of this music inspired him to make a deeper study of this neglected field. He became a member of the English Folk-song Society and was instrumental in unearthing from obscurity many wonderful examples of early English music and in reconstructing some of these by giving them modern harmonizations or richer lines of counterpoint. His interest in English folk music influenced his style as a composer. The *First Norfolk Rhapsody*, composed in 1906, was based upon folk music native to King's Lynn, Norfolk. But this work, and others that followed, dissatisfied Vaughan Williams. He decided he was in need of further study. In 1909 he went to Paris and became a pupil of Maurice Ravel. After eight months he returned to England, surer of himself as a craftsman.

He composed his first major works following his trip to Paris, most notably the *Fantasia on a Theme by Thomas Tallis* and *A London Symphony.* In 1914, he served in France and Macedonia with the Territorial Royal Army Military Corps. After the war, he joined the faculty of the Royal College of Music and became a conductor of the Bach Choir. He continued to write music with fertility, producing such major compositions as the *Pastoral Symphony, The Shepherds of the Delectable Mountains, Sancta Civitas, Sir John in Love,* and *Hugh the Drover.* Later works include six additional symphonies, the opera *Pilgrim's Progress,* various concertos and choral works, and a second string quartet.

In 1922 Vaughan Williams visited the United States to conduct his *Pastoral Symphony* at the Norfolk Festival in Connecticut. He revisited the United States in 1932 to lecture at Bryn Mawr College and in 1954 to lecture at Yale and Cornell. In 1935 he received the Order of Merit from King George V. Vaughan Williams died in London on August 26, 1958.

PERSONAL NOTE

David Ewen

WHEN you tried to speak to Vaughan Williams about his own work he became as diffident as a schoolboy. He evaded questions about himself as though he had not heard them. He seemed to dislike intensely to discuss what he had done, or why he did it. Once I happened to remark to him that his F minor Symphony puzzled me since it was so different from the works that preceded it. His only answer was a slight shrug of the shoulders and a casual remark that there is no explaining a composer's style. A true composer wrote what he felt, and that was that; he does not sit down and theorize before putting down his feelings on paper. He, himself, did not know many times why he had chosen a certain idiom or manner. When I asked him, on another occasion, about his latest works and their nature, the answer, when it came, was not from his own lips but from those of his wife. " He will never talk about himself," she said. " It is useless to try to make him do it."

His attitude seemed to be, though he did not say so in so many words, that he was a composer because he felt the necessity to write music. Composing was a part of his daily life, as eating and breathing were. Vaughan Williams composed continually because he had to. Why speak about one's musical activities any more than about one's respiratory or digestive system? Some of his works were good in his eyes, others were not. But to talk about them at all embarrassed him, almost as though creation was too much of a personal function for him to discuss it openly.

Yet when he spoke about the music of other composers he became as effusive as he had previously been shy and retiring. With a true generosity of spirit he spoke about the music he admired. Generally speaking, he did not at the time seem to be sympathetic with experimental music, though a few scattered works in that vein by Alban Berg and Hindemith interested him. " There are some modern works that remind me I'm old-fashioned and make me grateful for it," he said to me softly. " Other modern works also remind me I'm old-fashioned but make me ashamed of myself."

There are many modern composers whose work he esteems highly — such fellow Englishmen as Bax, Lambert, Walton, for example. He has the greatest of admiration for Sibelius, whom he places with the greatest of our time. Stravinsky's *Symphony of Psalms* is one of his favorite modern works. In his entire conversation about music, and our talk traversed not only modern music but old music as well, he seemed to me to have magically retained the vitality, exuberance, and freshness of youth; there was certainly nothing effete about him.

It is this vitality and freshness of spirit that compelled him to continue at his post as teacher of composition at the Royal College of Music once each week. He did not like teaching particularly. But (as he once told me) he felt it is indispensable for an older composer to keep in constant touch with younger men, to know what they are thinking, to understand how they feel, to study their reactions. Constant contact with youth, he felt, keeps an old composer from becoming set in his thinking and creative habits. It keeps an older composer questioning himself about the standards he has set for himself; and to question oneself, from time to time, is always a healthy condition.

Vaughan Williams was a big man, tall, heavy-set, somewhat flabby. His head was large and had magnificent dignity and strength. His jaw was square and his lips thin. As he spoke, in his soft and well-modulated voice, his eyes blinked frequently, for they were bloodshot, and he seemed troubled by them. They were sad and contemplative eyes. To the casual observer he appeared to be the composer of storybook reputation. His reflectiveness gave him the air of being absent-minded. When he strolled in the streets, sometimes in the rain, absorbed with his thoughts, he was oblivious to everyone and everything. Besides, he had the sublime indifference to dress that tradition has so long established as a trait of the great composer. His coat was usually too large for him, his trousers were baggy. He often wore an old bowler hat.

In one of the rare moments in which he was tempted to speak about his creative work, he said to me: " I am a composer," which is to say he accepted his work as a tailor or an architect accepts his. " I always try to do my very best. But whether my music is good or bad, it is always honest, and by that I mean that I could not put down on paper a line that I did not first feel in every part of me."

THE COMPOSER SPEAKS

Ralph Vaughan Williams [1]

THE GREATEST artist belongs inevitably to his country as much as the humblest singer in a remote village — they and all those who come between them are links in the same chain, manifestations on their different levels of the same desire for artistic expression, and, moreover, the same nature of artistic expression.

I am quite prepared for the objection that nationalism limits the scope of art, that what we want is the best, from wherever it comes. My objectors will probably quote Tennyson and tell me that " we needs must love the highest when we see it " and that we should educate the young to appreciate this mysterious " highest " from the beginning. Or perhaps they will tell me with Rossini

[1] This statement is from Vaughan Williams' book *Music and Nationalism*.

that they know only two kinds of music, good and bad. So perhaps we had better digress here for a few moments and try to find out what good music is, and whether there is such a thing as absolute good music; or, even if there is such an absolute good, whether it must not take different forms for different hearers. Myself, I doubt if there is this absolute standard of goodness. I think it will vary with the occasion on which it is performed, with the period at which it is composed, and with the nationality of those who listen to it. Let us take examples of each of these — firstly, with regard to the occasion. The Venusberg music from *Tannhäuser* is good music when it comes at the right dramatic moment in the opera, but it is bad music when it is played on an organ in church. A waltz of Johann Strauss is good music in its proper place as an accompaniment to dancing and festivity, but it would be bad music if it were interpolated in the middle of the *St. Matthew Passion*. And may we not even say that Bach's B minor Mass would be bad music if it were played in a restaurant as an accompaniment to eating and drinking?

Secondly, does not the standard of goodness vary with time? What was good for the fifteenth century is not necessarily good for the twentieth. Surely each new generation requires something different to satisfy its different ideals. Of course there is some music that seems to defy the ravages of time and to speak a new message to each successive generation. But even the greatest music is not eternal. We can still appreciate Bach and Handel or even Palestrina, but Dufay and Dunstable have little more than historical interest for us now. But they were great men in their day, and perhaps the time will come when Bach, Handel, Beethoven, and Wagner will drop out and have no message left for us.

Then there is the question of place. Is music that is good music for one country or one community necessarily good for another? It is true that the great monuments of music, the *Missa Papae Marcelli*, or the *St. Matthew Passion*, or the Ninth Symphony, or *Die Meistersinger*, have a world-wide appeal, but first they must appeal to the people, and in the circumstances where they were created. It is because Palestrina and Verdi are essentially Italian and because Bach, Beethoven, and Wagner are essentially German that their message transcends their frontiers. And even so, the *St. Matthew Passion*, much as it is loved and admired in other countries, must mean much more to the German, who recognizes in it the consummation of all that he learned from childhood in the great traditional chorales that are his special inheritance. Beethoven has a universal meaning, but to the German, who finds in it that same spirit exemplified in its more homely form in those *Volkslieder* which he learned in his childhood, he must also have a specialized meaning.

Every composer cannot expect to have a world-wide message, but he may reasonably expect to have a special message for his own people, and many young composers make the mistake of imagining they can be universal without at first having been local. Is it not reasonable to suppose that those who share our life, our history, our customs, our climate, even our food, should have some secret to impart to us that the foreign composer, though he be perhaps more imaginative, more powerful, more technically equipped, is not able to give us? This is the secret of the national composer, the secret to which he only has the key, which no foreigner can share with him, and which he alone is able to tell to his fellow country-men. But is he prepared with his secret? Must he not limit himself to a certain extent so as to give his message its full force? For after all it is the millstream forcing its way through narrow channels that gathers strength to turn the water wheel. As long as composers persist in serving up at second hand the externals of the music of other nations, they must not be surprised if audiences prefer the real Brahms, the real Wagner, the real Debussy, or the real Stravinsky to their pale reflections.

What a composer has to do is to find out the real message he has to convey to the community and say it directly and without equivocation. I know there is a temptation each time a new star appears on the musical horizon to say: " What a fine fellow this is, let us try and do something like this at home," quite forgetting that the result will not sound at all the same when transplanted from its natural soil. It is all very well to catch at the prophet's robe, but the mantle of Elijah is apt, like all secondhand clothing, to prove the worst of misfits. How is the composer to find himself? How is he to stimulate his imagination in a way that will lead him to voicing himself and his fellows? I think that the composers are much too fond of going to concerts — I am speaking now, of course, of the technically equipped composer. At the concert we hear the finished product. What the artist should be concerned with is the raw ma-terial. Have we not all about us forms of musical expression that we can take and purify and raise to the level of great art? Have we not all around us occasions crying out for music? Do not all our great pageants of human beings require music for their full expression? We must cultivate a sense of musical citizenship. Why should not the musician be the servant of the state and build national monuments like the painter, the writer, or the architect?

Art for art's sake has never flourished among the English-speaking nations. We are often called inartistic because our art is unconscious. Our drama and poetry have evolved by accident while we thought we were doing something else, and so it will be with our music. The composer must not shut himself up and think about art; he must live with his fellows and make his art an expression of the whole life of the community. If we seek for art we shall not find it. There are very few great composers, but there can be many sincere composers. There is nothing in the world worse than sham good music. There is no form of insincerity more subtle than that which is coupled with great earnestness of purpose and determination to do only the best and highest, the unconscious insincerity that leads us to build up great designs that we cannot fill and to simulate emotions that we can only experience vicariously. But, you may say, are we to learn nothing from the great masters? Where are our models to come from? Of course we can learn everything from the great masters, and one of the great things we can learn from them is their sureness of purpose. When we are sure of our purpose we can safely follow the advice of St. Paul " to prove all things and to hold to that which is good." But it is dangerous to go about " proving all things " until you have made up your mind what is good for you.

First, then, see your direction clear and then by all means go to Paris, or Berlin, or Peking, if you like, and study and learn everything that will help you to carry out that purpose.

We have in England today a certain number of composers who have achieved fame. There are several others who thought that their country was not good enough for them and went off in the early stages to become little Germans or little Frenchmen; this latter class is unknown even to its fellow countrymen.

I am told that when grapevines were first cultivated in California the vineyard masters used to try the experiment of importing plants from France or Italy and setting them in their own soil. The result was that the grapes acquired a peculiar individual flavor, so strong was the influence of the soil in which they were planted. I think I need hardly draw the moral of this, namely, that if the roots of your art are firmly planted in your own soil and that soil has anything individual to give you, you may still gain the whole world and not lose your own soul.

VAUGHAN WILLIAMS

Oliver Neighbour

THE EARLIER years of this century were inimical to musical eclecticism. The gradual divergence of national schools during the nineteenth century became increasingly marked as tonality weakened, and it is hard to imagine a Tchaikovsky flourishing in the new situation that emerged. Of course, something that does not happen is not necessarily an impossibility, but it is noticeable that even such major figures as Bartók and Berg handled the eclectic streak in their musical thought with difficulty. Artists are sometimes said to have been born at the wrong time for their full development. No doubt this begs a number of questions, but one is tempted to see in Vaughan Williams a composer born at the only time in which he could have made his mark. From all accounts he was as a student quite exceptionally unreceptive of the principles even of decent academic composition, and the easy acceptance of the forms or vocabulary of the composers he admired was quite beyond him. There is no need to suppose such accounts exaggerated; the earliest compositions to reach publication, written when he was about thirty, bear them out. Such a mentality can only find salvation, if at all, in cultivating its own garden. History did nothing to help Vaughan Williams, but she refrained from hindering.

The crucial works in Vaughan Williams' output are those written immediately after World War I, when he was already fifty. The experience of the war, so disastrous to Elgar, turned Vaughan Williams away from the amiable bluster of his early symphonies toward the world of the *Fantasia on a Theme by Tallis* (1910) and the song cycles. At the same time the years of enforced silence seem to have obliged him to think theoretically about his music. One has the impression that previously he had preferred to do his hard thinking empirically over the compositional problems presented by work in progress. In the Mass (1922), the *Pastoral Symphony* (1922), and *The Shepherds of the Delectable Mountains* (1922) he clearly made a conscious effort to isolate and master the technical discoveries of his earlier work, as well as the spiritual ones. Alone among English composers he attempted to uncover, examine, and test the foundations of his art, and his courage was rewarded.

The works of the postwar group show two preoccupations. First, the vocabulary. The melody is modal, the harmony very largely restricted to major and minor triads, often in parallel motion. There are, of course, plenty of passages in the *Mystical Songs* (1911) and the *London Symphony* (1914) that display similar characteristics, and still more in the *Four Hymns* (1914), in which the modality is sometimes a little forced. But here the academic basis, upon which modality had first of all been grafted as a decoration, still serves as a framework. It only disappears in the postwar works, along with such chromatic features as had been used up till then. Vaughan Williams' extremely circumscribed idiom at this time is usually said to have arisen from his studies of English folk song. It may be so in part, but the main features that I have described are to be found in most nationalist schools from the Russian onward, and it was, no doubt, of this that Schoenberg was thinking when he remarked that the more nationalists tried to be different the more they sounded the same. Similar means were seized on by French and Italian composers, from Debussy down, not as a concomitant of folk song, for they had no need to establish national identity, but purely to inhibit tonal fluidity and oppose the invasion of chromaticism. This negative aim was no less important to nationalist composers, and it is probable that Vaughan Williams needed the break with German tradition quite as urgently as allegiance to English folk song. For I do not think that the highly personal quality of his use of mode and triad is to be explained with reference to English folk music. A few of his typical melodic turns may derive from forms particularly favored in England, but the great majority of them can be related equally well to other western European traditions, many to the common pentatonic source. In the *Pastoral Symphony* the melodies rarely resemble folk songs. The inflections of folk song go to make a melodic style inseparably bound up with a harmony in which the parallel triads create tonal balances of great subtlety, though over relatively short spans. Many other composers had discovered similar types of triadic harmony before, but none had found in it a complete language. Vaughan Williams discovered it anew for himself, used it with unique invention and flexibility, and saw in it a basis for further development.

In the *Pastoral Symphony* the composer is very much concerned not only with vocabulary but with the nature of his musical thought in a wider sense. The problem was really that of form, or should have been, but it presented itself in a rather different guise. I think the basis of Vaughan Williams' understanding of music, both as listener and creator, lay in the eloquence of the simple stanza melody, whether folk song, hymn tune, or any other kind. This is true of all of us, but one feels that to him the expressive force of a tune was something quite unusually precise and definite; a change of a few notes could alter its meaning as radically as a few words might change the meaning of a sentence. This is very well brought out in his essay on Beethoven's Ninth Symphony and in program notes to his own works, where he makes light of the connection between related themes that *feel* different to him. He even refers to the return of the first subject in the coda to the first movement of the Beethoven as a " new theme " because there is a change in the fourth bar that alters the balance of the phrase. Unlike much else in the essay the point is well made and touches a difficult truth about our response to music, as well as throwing light on his own musical sensibility. Musical continuity is thus seen as a kind of reasoned discourse in which " it is the duty of the composer to find the *mot juste*." When a composition nears completion " the composer wants to have the opportunity . . . to remember emotion in tranquillity, to sit down quietly and make sure that he has achieved the *mot juste* at every point." Occasionally in Holst's earlier music, " the *mot juste* fails him for the moment and he falls back on the common stock of musical device." Instances of dangerous stock devices would, I suspect, include most forms of passage work. Vaughan Williams does not often use anything of the kind himself, and, although the tonal formal aspect of his forms was in any case too weak to encompass it, his overriding objection would have been that it did not speak in the direct way he required.

It is curious that a composer whose mentality so strongly suggests the miniaturist should have done most of his best work in large forms. In structure as in vocabulary the *Pastoral Symphony* isolates and builds upon the personal methods of the best sections of the *London*. The music progresses in terms of a melodic discourse. In order to work this idea out fully, Vaughan Williams temporarily abandons strong contrasts, so that the work has sometimes been taken for a backwater in his progress, instead of the landmark it is. Except in the Scherzo there are no stanza melodies. These disappear for good from his sonata thinking after the *London Symphony*. The melodic lines have the direct quality of tunes sung to words, expanding as such tunes cannot, yet retaining the same character. Thus they scarcely use sequences or diminution of note values to heighten tension, but evolve eventually, now motivically, now more freely, each stage clinched with astonishing rhythmic resource. This process can build its own kind of tension, but as the melodies develop they give rise to countersubjects of kindred expression and direct imitations that intensify and do not diversify. They furnish the chief means of shaping a passage or movement. This is the pattern of thought that underlies all of Vaughan Williams' finest structures. Indeed, they stand or fall by it, for although he learned to make good use of tonalities, his modal thinking assigned a secondary role to them. To work outward toward a large form in this way is clearly very difficult. It is not surprising that he did not find the *mot juste* to bridge every gap; in some cases no such word could have existed. Such faults are so obvious that no one can miss them, and his amateurishness is a byword. The extraordinary intelligence that framed the paragraphs between should not be forgotten.

I have emphasized the element of retrenchment in the postwar works, but they break new ground in at least one important respect. A very personal factor in the use of parallel triads in the Mass is the strict adherence to modal inflection, so that false relations often occur. (The influence of the rather frequent use of false relations by English composers at certain periods may perhaps be present, though it is doubtful whether this has much bearing on what is felt to be the national character of Vaughan Williams' music.) When in the *Pastoral Symphony* and *The Shepherds of the Delectable Mountains* some of the contrapuntal strands are represented by rows of triads or partial triads, the modality quickly induces a chromatic situation that might loosely be termed bitonal. The chromaticism that invades the works of the next decade is rooted in this procedure, just as the marvelous diatonic counterpoint so typical of the composer's serene pastoral manner derives from diatonic chordal streams. This is apparent even where each part is only a single line, for it affects their highly characteristic movement in relation to one another and the frequent bichordal nature of their vertical coincidence. One has only to remember the chromatic excursions in certain early works, and the rather more attractive diatonic suspensions of *Easter* or the first movement of the *Sea Symphony* (1910), to realize how stylistic transformation has deepened inspiration.

In his essay on Holst, Vaughan Williams remarks that " idiom is a part of inspiration "; in other words, style in some degree generates idea. However that may be, it is certain that his works were never more varied in conception or vigorous in invention than during this period of stylistic expansion. The necessary technical means at last at his command, his genius burst out in new directions with each work. Perhaps *Sancta Civitas* (1926) was too ambitious a first step to be taken without some backward glances, but it initiates a remarkable series of works that includes *Flos Campi* (1925), *Concerto accademico* (1925), *Job* (1930), the *Magnificat* (1932), the Piano Concerto (1932), and culminates in the F minor Symphony (1935). It is perhaps the richest period of his career.

A contributory factor to these developments is to be found in Vaughan Williams' interest in the Continental scene, which began to present more sympathetic aspects to him than it had done before the war. Both he and Holst suddenly found themselves more in tune with events abroad than their juniors who had taken Strauss and Debussy as their models. Their swift development of chromaticism was certainly prompted by the keen interest they took in foreign contemporaries. Each wrote a neoclassical concerto, and Vaughan Williams at least learned a good deal from experience.

The only direct audience Vaughan Williams ever allowed himself was that of Holst. Imogen Holst has warned us that it is difficult to be certain whether her father or Vaughan Williams began any development that they shared, because publication dates were often delayed and each saw the other's work from the beginning.

All the same, I suspect that Holst, with his more analytical and adaptable mind, was usually in the lead, and it was plain that Vaughan Williams imitated him from time to time, not always with understanding. At this period he probably profited from his friend's view of contemporary events, though, as his later years show, he was not dependent on his mediation. Yet in a more real sense Vaughan Williams always held the lead. Holst's gifts were very different. His ear for sonorities and his harmonic sense were more refined in a limited context, but his style had no unified basis. He lacked Vaughan Williams' melodic invention and contrapuntal flair to carry on from his initial *trouvailles*. Every major step in a composition was perilous.

This, as I have already suggested, was also the point that gave Vaughan Williams most difficulty. *Flos Campi* and *Job*, for example, lack unity, but even so the vigor of the sections goes far to mitigate the defect. Except in the slow movement, the Piano Concerto succeeds better, and in the Fourth Symphony and the ensuing works such weaknesses are relatively unimportant. Unfortunately, fluency brought dangers as well as advantages. " Jane Scroop " from the *Tudor Portraits* (1936) is a wonderful piece, which Vaughan Williams could never have sustained at an earlier date, but in " Elinor Rumming " he finds music all too easily for a lengthy text that he is unwilling to sacrifice. He could only write his best music when he was intensely concerned with the eloquence of each phrase.

From this and all other points of view the Fourth Symphony, in F minor, and the Fifth Symphony (1943) are undoubtedly his crowning achievements. They contain the most perfect and the most ambitious expression of everything he had established in the *Pastoral Symphony* and developed subsequently. The two works are directly opposed in mood, but in each movement, except perhaps in the Scherzo of the Fourth, there are episodes or subtle undercurrents suggesting the world of the other symphony, so that both represent the composer's whole vision. A comparison of the slow or even the first movement of the F minor Symphony with the first or third of the Fifth Symphony, in D major, shows how completely the thought is of a piece. The derivation of the Fifth Symphony from the earlier parts of *Pilgrim's Progress* is most illuminating. Vaughan Williams never succeeded with full-scale opera as he did with choral and instrumental music. He had one

rare gift for the task — he could write good tunes in many
veins. . . .

Nearly all the major symphonies of the late nineteenth and
early twentieth centuries were post-Wagnerians in the sense that
they tried to make their symphonies a vehicle for the kind of
spiritual adventure and aspiration that his operas dealt with.
Vaughan Williams, who was deeply affected by Wagner, was perhaps the last of them. All his symphonies, except the Eighth
(1956), are Odysseys of the soul, programmatic but without defin-
able program. In none is this more striking than in the Sixth (1948),
which made a tremendous impact when it was first heard. It certainly contains great inspirations, but for the first time the program
is not part and parcel of the thought. It is imposed from without
upon a style in which the minor triad too often replaces subtler
harmonic thinking, and too much is demanded of its expressive
possibilities. The strongest movement, the second, is a tour de
force; the epilogue is extended for dramatic reasons beyond the
length required by the material. Neither can show the rich musical
content of the slow movement of the Fourth Symphony, with
which they invite comparison. The first movement has an un-
accountably weak center, and the main part of the Scherzo shows
a lack of judgment that was to reappear from time to time in later
works.

Most of the smaller works of the last ten years of Vaughan
Williams' life suffer in comparison with those of the best period
because their greater fluency cannot disguise the lower level of
thematic and harmonic invention. Even the Oboe Concerto
(1944), written before the Sixth Symphony, falls far short of the
similarly small-scale Violin Concerto of twenty years earlier, though
the A minor Quartet (1945), of the same period, is a much better
work, with a marvelous slow movement that would not disgrace
the Fifth Symphony. Many of the late works were written for
amateurs or special occasions and perhaps do not attempt very
much. In others the composer seizes on some extraneous idea, such
as pitting a speaker, a piano and chorus, a mouth organ, or a bass
tuba against the orchestra. This tends to create difficulties instead
of lending interest, though there are some fine things here and there
— for instance, the beautiful slow movement of the Tuba Concerto
(1954) and parts of the *Oxford Elegy* (1950). Very few of the
better passages in *The Pilgrim's Progress* belong to this time. The

attempts to enlarge vocabulary in the *Sinfonia antartica* (1952) do
not arise from the musical thought but are imposed upon it and
stifle it.

Only in his last three major works did Vaughan Williams
learn to make full use of the special capacities that old age and
long experience had left him. Seldom had he handled his hard-won
and well-known language with such inspired grace and precision
as in the songs from *This Day* (1954), which, despite the disappointing choruses at the end, is probably his finest choral work.
It has been greatly underrated, like the symphony that followed it,
the Eighth. Here each of the four movements is an excellent piece
of work, not least the very original Toccata. The disparity of mood
between them, and between the variations that form the first movement, is balanced by the almost monothematic structure. It is
neither so light nor so jolly a work as is often said. If its more
relaxed manner prevents its equalling the best things in the Sixth
Symphony, it maintains a more consistent level of musical interest
and can stand beside both the Sixth and the *Pastoral*. The Ninth
(1958) perhaps falls a little short of them, though the attempt to
construct the outer movements on more purely contrapuntal principles than ever before is impressive. The first movement is the
more successful formally, the discursive finale less well in focus
but very beautiful at times. The trios of the middle movements are
raised above their heavy-handed surroundings by a strange, melancholy quality that returns at the beginning of the finale, when a
last pilgrimage is made to the delectable mountains. The shepherds'
pipes still play, but the clear sunlight is hidden by gray mist. None
of the composer's earlier visions of desolation is so moving.

There are many views of Vaughan Williams' music, but it is
usually agreed that he and Holst made it in some way easier for
English composers to find themselves, though the evidence for this
may seem rather slender. It is certainly observable that national
traditions in composition are helpful, though less easy to see how
they arise. Vaughan Williams himself thought that, however little
younger composers cared for the folk-song movement, they tended
to show the influence of national melody as their elders had not.
There may be some truth in this as far as it goes, but his advice to
them that they should learn their craft at home before widening
their horizons seems to presuppose rather than point the way toward the tradition it was designed to foster.

In point of fact this warning is only concerned with nationalism as an extension of something more personal and fundamental. " What shall it profit a man if he gain the whole world and lose his own soul? " His quotation in this connection recalls Stravinsky's recent remark that composers must know what they love, and Schoenberg's reminder, " of course a soul you have to have." Not even these composers have a greater right to speak of idealism than Vaughan Williams. I am not only thinking of the courage required to sustain so many years of initial failure and active discouragement, then so long and difficult a pilgrimage toward the expression of his genius, and finally the late acclaim behind which he would discern a world to which he was a stranger. His late setting of Matthew Arnold was surely prompted by his sympathy for the poet's doubt; it was Holst's voice that he tried to hear in Clough's imagined words of reassurance, " Why faintest thou? I wandered till I died. Roam on! the light we sought is shining still."

More important still was an element of doubt at the core of Vaughan Williams' idealism, which Schoenberg's Moses might have understood. He believed that the " media that artists . . . use are symbols . . . of what lies beyond sense and knowledge." " The object of art is to stretch out to the ultimate realities through the medium of beauty." " All art is the imperfect human half-realization of that which is spiritually perfect." Art is a means, not an end; art for art's sake a heresy. For " the mass of people " realize that art is not " a mere luxury, but a necessity of the spiritual if not of the physical life." There is an intolerable contradiction in the necessity of remaining of the people and assuming the priest's role of interpreter. Hence the composer's abiding affection for the earliest and weakest of his seven real symphonies, the *London*, in which he speaks to the people with least risk of setting himself up, of claiming spiritual authority; hence, too, the occasional quixotic disclaimers that break in upon some of his later works. Art itself may fall under suspicion, since a means may be hired to various ends. In the *Sinfonia antartica* man is represented by music that thinks and speaks, the inanimate world by static music emptied of expression or aspiration. Complete artistic failure is inevitable because inherent in the idea of the work. In the third movement, which is purely a landscape, there is a horrifying moment when the organ enters fortissimo and shatters the music's orchestral framework. It is an act of astonishing violence, as though the composer wished to destroy music itself for its capacity to be false to its spiritual purpose. His troubled idealism is that of the English Puritan tradition. Its tensions give his greatest works their depth and power, inspiring intense sympathy in some listeners, but at the same time limiting his appeal.

We hear much of Vaughan Williams' simplicity and directness. He certainly possessed these qualities, but a complex musical personality underlies them. He wore the influence of folk song more lightly than almost any other eminent nationalist composer. He took a wider interest in the world around him than many who thought him provincial, his nationalism being an aspect of his positive and creative mentality. His obvious faults occur in a context of powerful and individual musical thinking. His most important service to English music lies quite simply in the quality of his music. In England his place is beside Elgar. No composer in that country less than forty years his junior can approach him.

(HEITOR VILLA-LOBOS)

1887 - 1959

BIOGRAPHY

Heitor VILLA-LOBOS was born in Rio de Janeiro on March 5, 1887. His early music study took place with his father, an amateur cellist, after which he attended the National Institute of Music, a student of Francisco Braga and Agnelo França. For a period, Villa-Lobos toured Brazil as a concert pianist. In 1912 he went on a scientific expedition into the interior of Brazil for the study of Brazilian folklore, his fourth and most ambitious of such exploratory trips. A lifelong preoccupation with Brazilian folk music inevitably influenced his own creative work greatly, his style assimilating many of the melodic and rhythmic characteristics of this art. In 1915, in Rio de Janeiro, there took place the first concert devoted to his works, which made a profound impression. From then on he grew in importance until he was generally accepted as the most important musical figure in Brazil. A government stipend enabled him to go to Europe in 1923, and, for a few years, he lived in Paris and visited several major European capitals. After returning to Brazil he became a leading figure in music education, revolutionizing the method of teaching music in schools. In 1930 he was appointed director of music education for the public schools of São Paulo and in 1932 of Rio de Janeiro. In 1945 he founded the Brazilian Academy of Music in the latter city.

Villa-Lobos was one of the most prolific composers of all time, having produced over two thousand works in every possible form. He evolved a new form, which he called the *chôros*, and which exploited some of the characteristics of popular Brazilian music.

He also created compositions combining Brazilian rhythms with Bachlike counterpoint, the *Bachianas brasileiras*.

His first visit to the United States took place in the winter of 1944, when the League of Composers arranged the celebration of a Villa-Lobos Week throughout the country. After that he made several tours of the United States and Europe. He died in Rio de Janeiro on November 17, 1959.

PERSONAL NOTE

Burle Marx

BECAUSE of his prodigious capacity to work and his small need for sleep (four hours of sleep was all he usually required) Villa-Lobos was able to create incessantly and overnight. Take, for instance, the very original sixteen *Cirandas*, for piano, and twelve of the fourteen *Serestas*, written in 1926 in less than a month. His maxim was always " Better bad of mine than good of others," and he lived by this. He even went so far as to try to avoid copying himself.

When you visited Villa-Lobos you may have gotten an electric-shock handshake, or a rubber chocolate to eat, or who knows what? His enjoyment of jokes came through in his music, too. When he wrote his *Suite sugestiva No. 1*, during his Paris sojourn, one of its numbers was for soprano, three metronomes, with the orchestra entering only in the last bars. There is no sound he was unable to reproduce with musical instruments. He even explained to you how he could reproduce the roar of the MGM lion.

Villa-Lobos, having always surrounded himself by people, was able to concentrate and work in the midst of commotion. In 1932 I remember going to his house to remind him of the orchestral work he had promised me for my Youth Concerts. It was 7 P.M., two days before the scheduled performance. He had just finished dinner, and the table was being cleared for his manuscripts. He assured me the work would be ready. While he was orchestrating, writing direct with ink, a friend of his was playing the piano reduction of the *Amazon as Symphonic Tone Poem*. From time to time Villa-Lobos

was correcting him by calling out, " G-flat in the bass," sometimes
getting up to show him how to interpret. I expressed my wonder at
his ability to work under these conditions. He said, " Just let me
finish this new page and I'll show you how it sounds on the piano."
The fact is we had the first performance of *The Magic Window*.
Villa-Lobos never rested, it seemed. People were always coming in
and out. Even business transactions were done while he composed.

Once, on arriving in New York, he had no India ink. He called
me up in the country. I arranged for a friend in New York to deliver
it to him within an hour. He had to orchestrate nearly 250 pages for
a ballet for La Scala in Milan. He was sending bunches of pages by
air mail to Brazil to be reproduced. Several copyists were to extract
the orchestral parts. The ballet was delivered in Milan, even before
the date line, with complete orchestration. Early one morning in
his office in Rio he wrote the now famous aria from *Bachiana
brasileira No. 5*, and called his assistants. " Let's all hum this
melody. How do you like it? " Twenty-four hours later he had it
ready with orchestration for eight cellos. In 1930, soon after the
Vargas revolution, Villa-Lobos was touring with seven other musicians through the state of São Paulo. One day on the train he composed the *Little Train of Caipira*, which is today the last movement
of his *Bachiana brasileira No. 2*. It was originally written for cello
and piano. He played it on the cello that same evening.

Villa-Lobos was an excellent billiard player, and he would play
once a week. He was a passionate kite builder. In the middle of
playing chamber music he would stop (" The weather is too good to
miss ") and go kite-flying in Paris. He even has a tone poem
Papagaio de moleque (*Kite of a Street Urchin*), written in 1932.

Villa-Lobos could not sit quietly. Everything had to be movement. Many of his children's piano pieces are full of the movement
of the games themselves. Someone said that if he were younger he
would be playing center in soccer and devising a fugue in four parts
at the same time. The third *Prole do bebé* is dedicated to sports —
among others, ring games, marbles, diabolo, *peteca*, soccer, and
capoeiragem (a sort of Brazilian jiujitsu).

Villa-Lobos loved to make music on any instrument whatsoever. If he was with a group of sympathetic people, he would sit at
the piano and improvise. Sometimes he decided to paint portraits of
people present, and it became a game to guess the subject. His
improvisations did not follow a routine pattern. He concentrated a

little, then created. When he was writing his Second Piano Concerto, someone asked him, " Do you have the thematic material for it already? " " Oh, no," he answered. " But if I squeeze a little bit it comes out."

The truth is that it was almost a physiological necessity for him to compose. Once when ill and being prepared for surgery, his only question to the doctor was, " When can I work again? " Still in great pain, he tried soon after but could not. Twenty-four hours later he started his Twelfth String Quartet. His surgeon wanted to present him to a group of fifty physicians as a medical phenomenon. Villa-Lobos replied that they had first to hear at least a dozen of his recorded works in order to understand better his " insides."

THE COMPOSER SPEAKS

Heitor Villa-Lobos [1]

I LIKE Vittoria, and I like Beethoven, because they went ahead from where their predecessors left off. I do not care for Schumann or Brahms, for the reason that they kept on employing methods that were known before their time.

I only ask that the maker of a piece of music be original. As for the epoch in which he works, I don't concern myself with it, except historically.

I do not walk in company with routine. I do not, for that matter, take any interest in composers who are modern on the mere ground that they belong to our day.

I compose in the folk style. I utilize thematic idioms in my own way, and subject to my own development. An artist must do this. He must select and transmit the material given him by his people. To make a potpourri of folk melody and think that in this way music has been created is hopeless. But it is only nature and humanity that can lead an artist to the truth. Do you think that as a composer I spend my time in technical exercises? I study the his-

[1] Heitor Villa-Lobos made these statements in interviews appearing in *The Christian Science Monitor* and *The New York Times*.

tory, the country, the speech, the customs, the background of the people. I have always done this, and it is from these sources, spiritual as well as practical, that I have drawn my art.

I am a nationalist, but not a patrioteer. The distinction is most important. Patriotism in music, and capitalizing upon it, is very dangerous. You cannot produce great music in that way. You will have instead propaganda. But nationalism — power of the earth, the geographic and ethnographic influences that a composer cannot escape; the musical idioms and sentiment of people and environment — these origins, in my opinion, are indispensable to a vital and genuine art.

So I say that race and environment must inhere in a composer's expression. Only if you can trust your ear can you possibly become a real musician and composer; you must be able to express yourself instinctively in the language of music. The rest follows.

VILLA-LOBOS

Herbert Weinstock

BRAZIL is a country of continental size and heedless lavishness. Everything about it abounds, formless with bulging vitality. Larger than the United States, it is watered for thousands of miles by the tributaries and parent flood of the earth's mightiest river. It stretches across forty degrees of longitude and almost as many of latitude, straddles the equator and the Tropic of Capricorn. In addition to every sort of climate but a cold one, it enjoys every sort of cultural, racial, and national influence: Portuguese and Indian first, and then French and African and German and Italian and Spanish and Hispano-American and Yankee. It is conglomerate, swiftly evolving, indeterminate, and frighteningly prolific in every direction. One quality unmistakably projects above and beyond everything else about it: vitality.

Only by thinking of Heitor Villa-Lobos as a Brazilian intensely native to his country is it possible to understand Brazil's foremost modern artist. True, this composer, all-round musician,

pedagogue, and polemicist lived in Paris, heard Falla and Stravinsky and Ravel. He knew Bach and Wagner and Schoenberg. He
traveled in the United States, was aware of New York and California. But he remained pure Brazilian in his energy, Amazonian in his
fecundity, tropical, hybrid, and evolving — always advancing
and seldom consolidating — in his profusion of styles. It is said
that his opus numbers, if they could ever be set down accurately,
would run beyond two thousand. He composed operas, ballets,
quantities of chamber music, piano pieces, a whole repertoire for
orchestra, concertos, Masses, an oratorio, many songs — even a
musical comedy. He wrote countless articles on Brazilian folklore.
He conducted. He educated. His activity, like Brazil's, was continental.

No one but Villa-Lobos himself could have heard all his music.
Nor could even those who lived near him in Rio de Janeiro pretend
to familiarity with more than a cross section of his representative
work. In the United States, it was only during the last fifteen years
of his life that we came to recognize him, to hear enough of him in
concert, via radio, and on records to know what was unmistakable
in his voice. Faced with the fascinating, impossible task of analyzing and judging Villa-Lobos, a critic can hope only to find in a
relative few of his compositions enough particulars to make preliminary generalization possible. To winnow and docket the immense, mind-numbing corpus of his work is a task too big for any
critic but time.

The most obvious fact about Villa-Lobos is that his production varied more widely in quality than that of any other recent
composer of importance but Sibelius. He allowed the publication
under his name of second-rate, trivial, and downright bad music,
not once or half a dozen times, but very often. It is possible to make
a bad start among his pieces and wander for hours through pages of
musicmaking that are commonplace and wearying, whole Mato
Grossos of facile, formless stuff. He lacked self-criticism to a damaging degree. It is impossible not to feel, after a tussle with much of
this evasive, half-living matter that, though it may be the plasm of
music, it is not music itself. In it, Villa-Lobos left his task unfinished. He neither set high enough standards for himself nor
rejected enough first thoughts.

Neither the art of music nor Villa-Lobos' reputation would
have suffered the smallest deprivation if he had refused to publish,

or allow performance of, a good half of his output. An admixture of that desire for perfection which has forced (for example) Carlos Chávez and Aaron Copland to weed and prune and manipulate themes and harmonies, timbres and rhythms and forms, would have made Villa-Lobos a composer whose unfamiliar works we could face with some certainty of encountering memorable, incisive utterance.

Predominantly, Villa-Lobos' music is evocative. He composed a *Nonetto* (1923) that purported to summon up a panorama of Brazil's geography, a mammoth piano piece called *Rudepoema* (1921–26) that is a psychograph of Artur Rubinstein, an orchestral poem named *Erosion, or The Origin of the Amazon River* (1951), a myriad small and large works esthetically descended from Albéniz' *Iberia*. But just as Portuguese is more guttural and throaty than Spanish, less decisive in rhythm, less clear in outline, so Villa-Lobos' regional, civic, and national evocations are less satisfactory in form than the Spaniard's. They drift toward the amorphous and end by being rhythmically invertebrate and harmonically vague. In the midst of color washed upon color, unmitigated popular tunes of irreverent banality serve only to make the environing texture sound pretentious.

And then, just when the listener unwillingly finds himself forced to decide that Villa-Lobos lacked, besides taste, any but the most rudimentary compositional talent, there comes an opportunity to hear his *Bachiana brasileira No. 1* (1930), *Chôros*, Nos. 6, 7, or 10 (1926, 1924, 1925), or the best of his fifteen string quartets, perhaps especially the Fifth (1931), to name a few from many possible examples. And here we find the very qualities for lack of which Villa-Lobos had seemed damned. In relief, the temptation is great to place these compositions high among the finest that our century has produced. For they are distinguished music, vital, defined by a powerful and well-knit personality, joyfully craftsmanlike, not at all plethoric, slipshod, or amorphous. Perhaps all of this is not truly Brazilian music (French and Spanish influences are constant and strong), but we shall in the near future be likely to judge other composers' work as more or less Brazilian by their degree of resemblance to it.

Chôros No. 7 is a brilliant exemplar of lush material justified by temperance of treatment, unyielding control, superb timing. Listened to carelessly, it is a virtuoso orchestral poem in one movement, an exotic outburst of barking sounds, ribbons of screaming glissandi, acrid harmonies, and nerve-racking pizzicati. But even such careless listening reveals the satisfaction brought by a self-created, exactly just form. Perhaps a hint or two was borrowed from *Le Sacre du printemps*: the complexities of the thudding rhythms suggest the Stravinsky of an earlier day. But *Chôros No. 7* is nonetheless an original creation. It unfolds, sends forth shoots, sinks tentacles like a living organism. It has an inception, a climax, and an outcome. Its plangent harmonies and jungle sounds constantly add to something, to what at last is found to be the creation of a work of art.

Or turn to the Fifth (*Brazilian*) Quartet. It too is virtuoso music. It was made, that is, not exclusively of so many melodies plus so many formal arrangements, rhythms, and harmonies, but as well of the capabilities of four instruments, out of what string timbres can be made to do, out of the commonest and least common reaches of their range. Rhythmic, dancelike melodies are set against long-breathed themes indicating a particular aspect of melancholy that seems at once climactic and Negro. In its bustle and strength, this music is not afraid of being impolite. The instruments wander far apart in pitch: the violins shimmer at a rarefied altitude above a sinuous cello accompaniment. Or — and here it is self-justifying — a popular dance tune is presented without comment. Motion is constant: the music really develops, has pace and direction. At times its humor is triumphant and gay; at times all is lost and nostalgic. But here, as in *Chôros No. 7*, every detail is purposeful, something added to a unified effect. The quartet satisfied because Villa-Lobos found a way to make his material fill the space he allotted to it. This is more than attractive, more than competent, string-quartet craftsmanship. In its spontaneity, or seeming spontaneity, it shows perhaps the best results of Villa-Lobos' incessant composing. Clearly, it was an utterance motivated by something in his mind, something to be said. It is as long as it is because what was to be said demanded that amount of time, without verbiage or excessive flourishes.

Although patently products of a greatly talented composer, the *Chôros No. 7* and the Fifth String Quartet are, perhaps, not in themselves major musical events. The *Bachiana brasileira No. 1*, however, is a sign of more important mastery. The composer believed that the spirit of Johann Sebastian Bach has remained universal. But in honoring that spirit he did not fall into mimicry. He wrote music that Bach, once having adjusted himself to modernities of idiom, might well have enjoyed. For the *Bachiana brasileira No. 1* has largeness of scope, persistence of motion, baroque abundance of ornament, that would have delighted the *Thomascantor*. He would have appreciated Villa-Lobos' way of exploiting the sonority of eight cellos until, in doing precisely what they can do best, they achieve rare variety and magnificence. The suite consists of three movements (Introduction, Prelude, and Fugue), of which the second reaches toward a grandeur scarce in twentieth-century music. The third movement reveals again what a richness of potentialities lies locked in fugue for a true composer. With this exceedingly attractive, unashamedly beautiful, and perfectly original music, Villa-Lobos honored not only Bach, but also himself, Brazil, and America as well.

Not so happy were the results of Villa-Lobos' wrongheaded attempts to construct symphonies by a mélange of old and new procedures. His imagination, not working in the symphonic direction, was not helped by his intelligence and intellect, both active enough, but not in that direction either. Enclosed in the pages of his twelve symphonies (the last dating from 1958) lie fragments of great interest and power. But they remain potential only, because badly placed. The same strictures are not so much invited as demanded by the concertos — for piano (1946), for harp (1955), and several for the cello (the last composed in 1955).

But it is as futile in Villa-Lobos' case as in all cases to judge a creative artist by failures, however numerous, to match his best. Not only must this Brazilian source of musical energy not be estimated by such unrefined ore as the *Nonetto* or *Rudepoema*. He must not be ignored because of the banalities of that not-quite operetta, the musical comedy *Magdalena* (1947). He must not be judged by the dazzling cleverness of *Prole do bebé* (1918), those Debussyan miniatures that Guiomar Novaes and Artur Rubinstein delighted in playing. For he was something better and less usual than they promise. At his full, he was a truly original composer. From our point of view, it may have been artistically wasteful for him to have spent so many of his seventy-two years evoking Brazil's jungles and torrents, exploring the interiors of dolls and men. He earned our gratitude, however, when from time to time he turned to the making of a kind of music that, at his best and most

serious, he alone knew how to make. For then Villa-Lobos provided
the musical sustenance it is in the power of relatively few men in
each century to create, the joy of the art of sound handled with
reverence and high justice by an original, inclusive, and loftly
imagination.

$\big($SIR WILLIAM WALTON$\big)$

1902 -

BIOGRAPHY

SIR WILLIAM TURNER WALTON was born in Oldham, Lancashire, on March 29, 1902. After matriculating from Christ Church College, he studied under Hugh Allen in Oxford. He subsequently was strongly influenced by the advice and criticism of such eminent musicians as Edward J. Dent, Busoni, and Ernest Ansermet. His first major work, a Piano Quartet composed in 1919, was published by the Carnegie Trust in 1924, while one year earlier a String Quartet was performed at the International Society of Contemporary Music festival in Salzburg. Recognition came in 1923, with the performance of *Façade*, a brilliant musical setting, for declamation and chamber orchestra, of a set of satirical poems by Edith Sitwell. From this time on, his rise to a position of major importance in English music became rapid, particularly with such striking works as *Portsmouth Point*, the Concerto for Viola and Orchestra (introduced by Paul Hindemith), *Belshazzar's Feast*, and the Symphony. *Façade*, the Viola Concerto, and *Belshazzar's Feast* were successfully performed at festivals of the International Society of Contemporary Music in 1928, 1929, and 1933, respectively.

In the spring of 1939 Walton visited the United States, bringing with him the manuscript of his Violin Concerto, which he had written on a commission from Jascha Heifetz. He had planned to revisit the United States that same winter for the première of his Violin Concerto in Cleveland, but the outbreak of the war frustrated this undertaking. Instead, he enlisted in the British Army and was assigned to the Ambulance Corps in London. His compositions at this time were mostly incidental music for stage and radio, and, especially, for films.

Walton's film music occupies an important place in his work. As early as 1934 he composed the score for *Escape Me Never*, and two years later he produced the first of his " Shakespeare " scores, *As You Like It*. Both of these starred Elisabeth Bergner. More significant was his association with Laurence Olivier, for all of whose Shakespeare films — *Henry V* (1944), *Hamlet* (1947), and *Richard III* (1954) — he composed music that contributed an important dimension to the effect. Other film scores include *Stolen Life* (1939), Shaw's *Major Barbara* (1941), and the wartime propaganda films *Next of Kin* (1941), *The First of the Few* (1942), and *Went the Day Well* (1942).

In 1945 Walton, at the request of the British Council, made the first of a number of tours as a conductor of his own music. These have taken him as far afield as Australia; he has several times visited the United States. During one such visit to Argentina in 1948 he married Señorita Susana Gil.

After the war Walton made his home on the island of Ischia, near Naples. There he produced a somewhat accelerated stream of works, notably the opera *Troilus and Cressida*, with libretto by Christopher Hassall, based on Chaucer. Originally commissioned by the BBC, it was produced in London in 1954, in San Francisco and New York in 1955, and in Milan in 1956.

Other commissions of the postwar period include the *Johannesburg Festival Overture* (1955, for the 70th anniversary of that city); the Violoncello Concerto (1956, for Gregor Piatigorsky); the *Partita* for orchestra (1958, for the 40th anniversary of the Cleveland Orchestra); the Second Symphony (1960, for the 750th anniversary of *the city of Liverpool*); and the *Variations on a Theme of Hindemith* (1963, for the 150th anniversary of the Royal Philharmonic Society of London).

The Coronation of Queen Elizabeth II in 1953 produced a Te Deum and the march *Orb and Sceptre*. In 1947 Walton wrote a string quartet, and in 1949 a violin sonata, dedicated to "Mrs. Yehudi Menuhin and Mrs. Louis Kentner " (they are sisters). In 1942 his own University of Oxford (where he had failed to get past his first examinations) conferred on him the honorary degree of Doctor of Music. In 1951 he joined the company of England's musical knights, and became Sir William.

PERSONAL NOTE

Dallas Bower

THERE are, I think, three distinct facets that contribute to the over-all make-up of William Walton's personality. The quintessential man lies in the deeply sensitive, acutely discriminating lyrical artist that his music reveals him to be, a man quite incapable of tolerating the second-rate, whose values are profoundly aristocratic in the strictly classical meaning of the word. Kindness, compassion, and consideration for others are among the finer qualities of such a nature, and these Walton has in no uncertain terms, although to those who do not know him well the qualities are not immediately apparent. There is the tough, shrewd, north-country Englishman gifted with a sardonic wit and at times a Rabelaisian humor that superficially mask the inner self. And, although seemingly at variance with these, as his friend and fellow musician Spike Hughes has said of him, there is something Augustan about Walton. The cool, impassive objectivity in his approach to affairs, the rather slow-moving and dignified, but never pompous, manner of his bearing, give an impression that Walton would have made a success in any walk of life he had cared to follow. Thus, it may seem a somewhat complex character emerges with sides of his nature in conflict.

The truth is that Walton's ebullient sense of humor and sophistication take a Puckish delight in consciously tending to hide his essential simplicity and humility, qualities that are the prerogatives of a true artist. The romanticism of the man, strictly disciplined by a wholly classical approach to his art — the nearest parallel is Berlioz — may certainly give credence to the supposition that the young Octavious conceivably looked like the young Walton and that both were of similar manner on the one hand and of like mentality on the other.

Walton has few interests outside the arts. If he had not been a born musician he might have become a doctor of medicine. Indeed, in personal appearance, particularly with regard to his clothes and the general effect of spruceness and good grooming, he could be mistaken for a fashionable surgeon, let us say, or chairman of some large and prosperous industrial enterprise. He reads widely, is devoted to Shakespeare, and has a good, if modest, collection of modern paintings. Walton has no interest in sport, but enjoys walking and swimming; his one material weakness, if it can be said to be such, is a liking for large, fast, and very expensive motorcars.

He has always found work a slow process, not enlightened in that respect by rigid self-criticism. A lover of Italy and her people, since becoming a resident on the Italian island of Ischia, where he lives with his charming and devoted wife, of latter years he has found peace of a kind that enables him to work faster, with, accordingly, a much increased output.

WALTON

Dyneley Hussey

BEFORE the two World Wars, there were still heads of Oxford colleges who cultivated, outside their scholastic and administrative duties, a wide and civilized existence, which also comprehended a lively appreciation and even practice of music. There was, for example, Dr. Thomas Case, the president of Corpus — a redoutable personality who styled himself in politics a Palmerstonian Liberal and who seriously held the opinion that music went to the dogs after the *Eroica Symphony*. Tommy Case, who was the son-in-law of Sterndale Bennett, and so made an exception in favor of Mendelssohn in his condemnation of all post-Beethoven music, was, none the less, a fine musician who tested the quality of young undergraduates by their reactions to Mozart and good vintage port. And there was Dr. Thomas Strong, dean of Christ Church and later bishop of Oxford. More liberal, in the accepted sense, than his colleague at Corpus, he could be seen at concerts of contemporary music as well as heard playing the classics.

Dr. Strong was, therefore, greatly interested when his organist, Henry Ley, drew his attention to the musical precocity of one of his choir boys who spent much of his spare time on the composition of music. The dean was sufficiently impressed by these untutored efforts to engage the interest of Dr. H. P. Allen, then professor of music at Oxford and always a willing helper of deserving youth. From him William Walton received his only professional training.

Dr. Strong further befriended the boy by securing his entry into Christ Church, as an undergraduate below the normal age, when his voice broke and he had to leave the choir. This was toward the end of World War I, when the comparative emptiness of the colleges made such a relaxation of the rules easier to obtain. During his residence at Oxford, Walton continued to compose, and among the works of this period is the First String Quartet (1919), which was to bring his name to the notice of an international audience at the first Festival of Contemporary Music at Salzburg in 1923.

Among Walton's contemporaries at Oxford was Sacheverell Sitwell, who came to know him and introduced him to his elder brother, Osbert. From this time Walton became an intimate associate of the Sitwells and their sister, Edith, all poets of unusual, though at that time unrecognized, stature.

In his autobiography Sir Osbert Sitwell has drawn a portrait of the young composer as he was in 1919. He had been invited with his brother to take tea with Walton in his rooms at Christ Church. " Our host," he writes, " not quite seventeen years of age, we found to be a rather tall, slight figure, of typically northern coloring, with pale skin, straight, fair hair, like that of a young Norwegian or Dane. The refinement of his rather long, narrow, delicately shaped head, and of his birdlike profile showing so plainly above the brow the so-called bar or mound of Michelangelo that phrenologists claim to be the distinguishing mark of the artist — especially the musician — even his prominent, well-cut nose, scarcely gave a true impression of his robust mental qualities or the strength of his physique. Sensitiveness rather than toughness was the quality at first most apparent in him." And so it has remained, in my experience, though the toughness must be there: for without it such works as *Belshazzar's Feast* (1931) and the First Symphony (1935) could hardly have been created. As to the physical strength of that deceptively delicate frame, Sir Osbert records that somehow Walton managed unaided, and without any special tackle, to conjure a large grand piano up a narrow staircase to his room after the removals men had abandoned it on the floor below. This incident, as recorded in *Laughter in the Next Room*, gives an impression of a physical strength worthy of Hercules coupled with the mechanical ingenuity of Leonardo. All he would vouchsafe in explanation of this feat was " I did it with a bit of string."

The friendship with the Sitwells soon ripened into an intimate association, so that he became the inseparable companion of the two brothers and sister, their " adopted or elected brother," as Sir Osbert puts it. The chief musical outcome of this association during its first years was *Façade* (1922). This was a novel kind of entertainment, consisting of the reading, or rather rhythmical declamation, of a series of poems by Edith Sitwell to the accompaniment of music composed by Walton for a small chamber orchestra. The orchestra was hidden behind a painted curtain designed by Frank Dobson, on which there was a huge face with open mouth, through which the poet spoke. The first performance was given privately in the drawing room of the Sitwells' house in Chelsea. It was repeated in public at the Aeolian Hall on June 12, 1923, when its novelty provoked a good deal of ill-informed discussion in the press.

There were sixteen poems in the original program. Walton provided for them an overture, accompaniments based rhythmically upon the meter of the various poems, and an interlude. The music was often allusive, referring by quotation to some of the ideas mentioned in the poems, sometimes used idioms from the popular music of the day or of the Victorian music hall, and was always consistently witty and brilliant. It was, indeed, a highly original and accomplished composition for a young man of twenty to produce. The mastery of instrumental effect was remarkable even in an age when orchestration seemed to be an open book to every student.

Some five years later Walton arranged five numbers of the *Façade* music — " Polka," " Valse," " Swiss Yodeling Song," " Tango-Pasodoble," and " Tarantella sevillana " — for a larger orchestra, and this Suite was played as an interlude during one of the Diaghilev company's performances at the Lyceum Theater in the summer of 1927. The Suite rapidly gained a wide popularity, and it was actually made into a ballet in Germany two years before Frederick Ashton's production in 1931.

The success achieved by *Façade* as a ballet brought Walton's name to the notice of a larger public than the devotees of Contemporary Music festivals. He was no longer one of the unintelligible sect of advanced composers. But if one misconception of his character as a musician was displaced, another was established in its stead. *Façade* and the overture *Portsmouth Point* (1925), based upon a drawing by Thomas Rowlandson, seemed to mark Walton out as the English counterpart of the Parisian playboys of the 1920's. But when the comparison is examined, it is evident at once that there is a greater substance and solidity even in the most frivolous of the Sitwell-Walton pieces than there is in anything that came from the school of Cocteau and " Les Six." Consider, for example, *Les Biches*, with its decadent atmosphere and its music as thin in substance as the colors of Marie Laurencin, who painted the *décor*. There is, certainly, nothing decadent about *Façade*. It might, in its original form, have seemed extravagant, even outrageous in its unexpectedness, but it could never be justly charged with triviality.

Nevertheless, these works — *Façade* and *Portsmouth Point* — are not fully representative of their composer, as we now know him. They were products of the effect upon him of that particular period, the "post-armstice period," when the relaxation of strain produced a reaction against serious-mindedness. The fashion was for caps over windmills, and Walton threw his with the rest. But there was so much real musicianship underlying what he wrote that his music transcended the mood of the moment and has taken its place among the light classics of our time. There was in it, too, a touch of bitterness, reflecting the mood of Dr. Sitwell's satire, that gave *Façade* a palatable astringency.

Whether at this early stage Walton was already master of his craft in all its aspects may, perhaps, be doubted in the light of an anecdote told by Osbert Sitwell. When *Façade* was in rehearsal for its first private performance, the clarinetist inquired whether the composer had ever received some injury from a clarinet player, as he appeared to bear a grudge against the whole tribe! I am, of course, unable to say whether this particular passage only seemed difficult to play on account of its novelty, as may often happen in the music of an original composer, or whether it was technically impracticable for the instrument, which is more than possible in a composer of Walton's inexperience. In the latter event the offending passage was presumably amended in the light of expert criticism. Much later in his career Walton acknowledged his indebtedness to Jascha Heifetz for the technical revision of the solo part in his Violin Concerto (1939). Ever since Mendelssohn's day it has been common form for composers to take specialist advice on such matters. When composing his concerto Mendelssohn corresponded with the violinist David at great length on every point in the solo; Brahms submitted his concerto to Joachim for comment, and Kreisler revised the solo part in Elgar's. There is, indeed, nothing but common sense in the arrangement.

In the meantime, before *Façade* made its appearance as a ballet, Walton had given evidence of his stature as a composer in *Sinfonia concertante* for piano and orchestra (1928). Even in this work, which is in three movements, each headed with a dedication to one of the three Sitwells, there was a certain air of defiant brightness that at first blinded the eye to the more solid qualities of the composition. That criticism on this score was not wholly unjust has been recognized by the composer, who revised the work in

1943, curbing some of the more willful extravagances and angularities of the original. In particular, the beauty of the slow movement, dedicated to Edith Sitwell, has been greatly enhanced by the revision, which here has amounted to a radical refashioning of the fabric of this music.

In 1929, another work was produced that marked its composer's arrival at mature mastery. No one could say that the Viola Concerto, which remains Walton's most beautiful poetic utterance, was either frivolous or trivial. Unlike the pianist in the *Sinfonia concertante*, whose part (as the title suggests) is treated as " the first among equals," the violist is given the prominence of the romantic concerto soloist. I well remember that first performance of this lovely work. It was directed by Walton himself, whose conducting had in those days a kind of nervous reticence that did not, perhaps, produce a perfect performance. The soloist was Paul Hindemith, then distinguished as much for his viola playing as for his compositions. The work made a deep impression, and we in the audience were not to know of the hectic preliminaries behind the scenes, which Bernard Shore, leading violist in Henry Wood's orchestra at that time, has described. The artist's room full of copyists up to the last minute, Walton anxiously supervising the corrections, Hindemith complaining of insufficient rehearsal, and Wood himself grumbling about the invasion of his sanctum by this agitated throng! Perhaps the performance was not impeccable, but the work made its effect and was chosen for inclusion at the International Society for Contemporary Music Festival at Liège in the following year. On that occasion it was played by Lionel Tertis, who has since been closely associated with the concerto.

Perhaps it was the Viola Concerto, rather than the *Façade* Suite, which was played at the Leeds Festival in 1928, that suggested to the Festival Committee the idea of commissioning Walton to write an oratorio for the Festival of 1931. Even so, the committee can hardly have reckoned that they would receive a work so powerfully dramatic and original as *Belshazzar's Feast*. In the composition of this work Walton had the collaboration of Osbert Sitwell, who, after the method, though not after the manner, of Charles Jennens, constructed a libretto from various passages in the Book of Daniel and the Psalms. The result was, indeed, so far unlike in spirit to Jennens' libretto for *Messiah* that the committee of the Three Choirs' Festival decided in the following year that the work was unsuitable for performance in a cathedral. Sitwell treated the downfall of Belshazzar with the utmost dramatic forcefulness, and Walton fitted the text with music of extraordinary nervous power. The final chorus of Jews exulting over the downfall of their enemies has a savage ferocity that matches the malignant rejoicing of the Hebrew poet at the destruction of Babylon. Yet finer than the sensational pagan choruses in praise of the Chaldean gods and that triumphant last chorus, and finer, too, than the eerie music accompanying the Writing on the Wall, is the beautiful setting of the penitential psalm, " By the Waters of Babylon, There We Sat Down and Wept." This deeply moving music, which is on the technical side the fruit of Walton's experience in the Christ Church Cathedral Choir, has a dignity and passion that match the psalmist's words. *Belshazzar's Feast* marks the culmination of the first phase of Walton's development. Those who experienced the tremendous impact of its first performance had full justification for feeling that a great composer had arisen in our land, a composer to whose potentialities it was impossible to set any limits.

The success of *Belshazzar's Feast* placed its composer at the top of his generation in the musical world. Even abroad, where his fame has hitherto been confined to the somewhat restricted circle of the Contemporary Music Society, a wider public began to be acquainted with his music. It was obvious that only one thing was now needed to confirm his position — the production of a symphony. And a symphony was produced, not without difficulty, during the years 1932–35. Walton has never been, despite his great powers of invention and his sure command of technique, a facile composer; everything he writes is hammered out with much mental labor. Latterly his larger compositions have been widely spaced in time. So the first performance of the First Symphony was delayed beyond the date originally announced, and when it was eventually given, under Sir Hamilton Harty's direction in December, 1934, the finale was still unwritten. The first complete performance took place just eleven months later. The strenuous mood and nervous energy that were evident in *Belshazzar's Feast* persist in the Symphony, which shows no signs of being labored, despite the toll it evidently exacted from the composer's resources.

Since Hamilton Harty's death Walton has been the finest interpreter of his First Symphony. He is not a great conductor in the virtuoso sense and never conducts any music but his own, but he is capable of communicating his wishes to the players efficiently, and of charging them with the intense electric energy that so surprisingly emanates from his apparently shy and self-effacing personality.

From about the date of the First Symphony Walton lived mostly in the country and less than ever was seen of him in London musical life, into which he had never entered fully. This was a period of rest after the great effort of the symphony. Coronation year, 1937, was marked by the composition of the *Crown Imperial* march, which proved that Walton was capable of wearing Elgar's laureate's cloak, and a new cantata for Leeds, *In Honour of the City of London*, which has never won the success of *Belshazzar's Feast* — perhaps because its merits are of a less dramatic kind. Nevertheless, it too reflects the festive mood of that time.

Next came a commission to write a Violin Concerto for Jascha Heifetz, and in the spring of 1939 Walton visited America to discuss the details of the solo part with the violinist. The score was completed in June, and the composer returned home and so was prevented by the outbreak of the war from attending the first performance at Cleveland, Ohio, in the autumn. It proved to be a work in the great virtuoso tradition. The influence of Elgar is noticeable again in some of the writing for the solo, which is of the utmost brilliance and sometimes seems to strain virtuosity almost too far.

The war years were occupied mainly in the composition of music for films. He had already in 1934 written music for the production of *Escape Me Never*. The wartime films *The First of the Few, Next of Kin*, and Laurence Olivier's production of *Henry V* evoked some excellent incidental music, much of which has been preserved beyond the ephemeral life of the films in concert suites. The only purely orchestral work of the war years is the *Scapino* overture (1940), which harks back to the style of *Portsmouth Point*, composed fifteen years earlier. Both these comedy overtures are based upon pictures, the one a drawing by Rowlandson, the other by Jacques Callot of one of the characters in the *commedia dell' arte* — a rascally valet, whom we know better under the names of Leporello and Figaro. Walton succeeded better with this Latin personality than with Rowlandson's rumbustious sailors and their wenches.

The most important product of this period, however, is the

ballet *The Quest* (1943). Three years before, he had orchestrated
the music by J. S. Bach used in Ashton's *The Wise Virgins*. Now for
the first time he composed music expressly for a ballet, *Façade*
having been adapted from the music of the Sitwellian " entertainment." The ballet was derived from Spenser's *Faerie Queene* and
had choreography by Ashton and *décor* by John Piper. The high
purpose of St. George's quest and the religious atmosphere of the
ballet chimed with the serious time at which it was produced.
Owing to wartime difficulties — Ashton had to arrange the dances
while serving in the RAF — some of the choreography, notably the
dances of the Seven Deadly Sins, was ineffective. But the ballet
certainly ought to be revived in a revised edition, for Walton's
music is much too good to lose and the idea of the ballet is admirable. Only its original translation into terms of spectacle and dance
was not, owing largely to the conditions under which it was produced, entirely successful.

After the war Walton produced a major work in the String
Quartet in A minor (1947), his first chamber music since his early
days and one of his finest compositions. To this he soon added a
Violin Sonata (1949), which was given its first performance by
Yehudi Menuhin and Louis Kentner in January, 1950; in 1953 he
contributed another march, *Orb and Scepter*, and a magnificent
setting on a large scale of the *Te Deum* for the coronation music of
Queen Elizabeth II. In the meantime the composer had received
the honor of knighthood in the New Year's Honors List of 1951.

Among his subsequent works are the *Johannesburg Festival
Overture* (1956), the Cello Concerto (1957), the *Partita* for orchestra (1958), and the Second Symphony (1959). But probably
most outstanding of all his recent larger works is the opera *Troilus
and Cressida*, with an excellent libretto by Christopher Karsall
based on Chaucer's poem. Produced at Covent Garden on December 3, 1954, it was found to be a romantic grand opera, full of fine
vocal melody and exhibiting a sure understanding of dramatic
composition. The part of Pandarus afforded opportunities for
characteristic touches of satire, and the main theme of the opera —
the betrayal of fine ideals by human frailty — provided the composer with a subject that he has handled with mastery.

APPENDICES

ACKNOWLEDGMENTS

&

INDEX

APPENDIX I

Principal Works of Modern Composers

SAMUEL BARBER

BALLETS: *Medea (Cave of the Heart,* or *The Serpent Heart;* 1946, revised 1947); *Souvenirs* (1952).

CHAMBER MUSIC: Cello Sonata (1932); String Quartet (1936); *Summer Music,* for woodwind quintet (1956).

CHORAL MUSIC: *Reincarnations* (1940); *A Stopwatch and an Ordnance Map* (1940).

OPERAS: *Vanessa* (1957); *Antony and Cleopatra* (1966).

ORCHESTRAL MUSIC: 2 *Essays* (1937, 1942); 2 Symphonies (1936, revised 1942; 1944, revised 1947); *Overture to The School for Scandal* (1933); *Music for a Scene from Shelley* (1933); *Adagio for Strings,* arranged from the Adagio of the String Quartet (1937); Violin Concerto (1940); Cello Concerto (1945); *Knoxville: Summer of 1915,* for voice and orchestra (1947); *Souvenirs* (1952); *Prayers of Kierkegaard,* for chorus, soprano, and orchestra (1954); *Medea's Meditation and Dance of Vengeance,* based on material from the ballet *Medea* (1956); *Toccata festiva* (1960); *Dei natali* (1960); Piano Concerto (1962); *Andromache's Farewell* (1962).

PIANO MUSIC: *Excursions* (1944); Sonata in E-flat minor (1949).

VOCAL MUSIC: *Dover Beach,* for voice and string quartet (1931); *Three Songs,* to poems by James Joyce (1936); *Mélodies passagères* (1951); *Hermit Songs* (1953).

BÉLA BARTÓK

BALLETS: *The Wooden Prince* (1914–16); *The Miraculous Mandarin* (1919).

CHAMBER MUSIC: 6 String Quartets (1907, 1917, 1927, 1928, 1934, 1939); 2 Violin Sonatas (1921, 1922); *Contrasts,* for violin, clarinet, and piano (1938); Sonata for Solo Violin (1944).

CHORAL MUSIC: *Cantata profana* (1930).

OPERA: *Duke Bluebeard's Castle* (1911).

ORCHESTRAL MUSIC: 3 Piano Concertos (1926, 1931, 1945); 2 Violin Concertos (1907–8) ; 2 Rhapsodies for Violin and Orchestra (1928), also for violin and piano; *Two Portraits* (1907–8); *Dance Suite* (1923); *Music for Strings, Percussion, and Celesta* (1936); *Divertimento,* for strings (1939); Two-Piano Concerto (1940); *Concerto for Orchestra* (1943); Viola Concerto (unfinished).

PIANO MUSIC: *Two Rumanian Dances* (1909); *Allegro barbaro* (1911); Sonata (1926); *Mikrokosmos* (1926–39); Sonata, for two pianos and percussion (1937).

ALBAN BERG

CHAMBER MUSIC: String Quartet (1910); *Four Pieces,* for clarinet and piano (1913); *Chamber Concerto,* for piano, violin, and 13 wind instruments (1925); *Lyric Suite,* for string quartet (1926), three movements also for string orchestra (1928).

OPERAS: *Wozzeck* (1921); *Lulu* (unfinished).

ORCHESTRAL MUSIC: *Five Orchestral Songs* (1912); *Three Orchestral Pieces* (1915); *Der Wein,* concert aria for soprano and orchestra (1929); Violin Concerto (1935).

PIANO MUSIC: Sonata (1908).

VOCAL MUSIC: *Four Songs* (1909).

ERNEST BLOCH

CHAMBER MUSIC: 5 String Quartets (1916, 1945, 1951, 1953, 1955); 2 Piano Quintets (1923, 1957); 2 Violin Sonatas (1920, 1924); Suite, for viola and piano (1919), also for viola and orchestra; *Baal Shem,* for violin and piano (1923); *Quartet Pieces* (1924); 2 Suites for Solo Violin (1958); 3 Suites for Solo Cello (1958).

CHORAL MUSIC: *Sacred Service* (1933).

OPERA: *Macbeth* (1909).

Orchestral Music: 2 *Concerti grossi*, for strings (1925, 1952); Symphony in C-sharp minor (1901); *Hiver-Printemps* (1905); *Trois poèmes juifs* (1913); *Two Psalms*, for soprano and orchestra (1914); *Psalm 22*, for baritone and orchestra (1914); *Schelomo*, for cello obbligato and orchestra (1916); *Israel Symphony* (1916); *America* (1927); *Helvetia* (1928); A *Voice in the Wilderness*, for cello obbligato and orchestra (1936); *Evocations* (1937); Violin Concerto (1938); *Suite Symphonique* (1944); *Concerto symphonique*, for piano and orchestra (1949); *Suite hebraïque*, for viola and orchestra (1952); *Sinfonia breve* (1953); Symphony, for trombone solo and orchestra (1954); Symphony in E-flat (1955); *Proclamation*, for trumpet and orchestra (1955); *Suite modale*, for flute solo and strings (1957).
Piano Music: Sonata (1935).

BENJAMIN BRITTEN

Ballet: *The Prince of Pagodas* (1956).
Chamber Music: 2 String Quartets (1941, 1945); *Sinfonietta*, for 10 instruments (1932); *Fantasy Quartet* (1932); Suite, for violin and piano (1934); *Lacrymae*, for viola and piano (1950); *Six Metamorphoses after Ovid*, for solo oboe (1951); Cello Sonata (1961); Suite, for solo cello (1964); *Gemini Variations*, for piano duet, flute, and violin (1964).
Choral Music: *Ballad of Heroes* (1939); *Hymn to St. Cecilia* (1942); A *Ceremony of Carols* (1942); *Rejoice in the Lamb* (1943); *Saint Nicolas* (1948); *Spring Symphony* (1949); *Missa Brevis* in D (1959); *Cantata academica* (1959); A *War Requiem* (1962); *Cantata misericordium* (1963); *Voices of Today* (1965).
Operas: *Peter Grimes* (1944); *The Rape of Lucretia* (1946); *Albert Herring* (1947); *Billy Budd* (1951); *Gloriana* (1953); *The Turn of the Screw* (1954); *Noye's Fludde* (1958); A *Midsummer Night's Dream* (1960); *Curlew River* (1964); *Crossing the River* (1965); *The Burning Fiery Furnace* (1966); *The Golden Vanity* (1966).
Orchestral Music: *Simple Symphony* (1925, revised 1934); *Our Hunting Fathers*, for soprano and orchestra (1936); *Variations on a Theme by Frank Bridge*, for strings (1937, revised 1946); Piano Concerto (1938); Violin Concerto in D minor (1939, revised 1950); *Les Illuminations*, for high voice and string orchestra (1939); *Sinfonia da Requiem* (1940); *Diversions*, for piano, left hand, and orchestra (1940, revised 1951); *Scottish Ballad*, for two pianos and orchestra (1941); *Prelude and Fugue*, for eighteen-part string orchestra (1943); *Serenade*, for tenor, horn, and string orchestra

(1943); *The Young Person's Guide to the Orchestra* (1945); *Divertimento*, for chamber orchestra (1952); *Symphony for Cello and Orchestra* (1963).

VOCAL MUSIC: Songs, song cycles, canticles, including *Seven Sonnets of Michelangelo* (1940), *Holy Sonnets of John Donne* (1945), *Winter Words* (1953), *Six Hölderlin Fragments* (1958), *Songs from the Chinese* (1958), *Nocturne* (1958), and *Songs and Proverbs of Blake* (1965).

MARIO CASTELNUOVO-TEDESCO

BALLETS: *The Birthday of the Infanta* (1942); *The Octoroon Ball* (1947); *Naomi and Ruth* (1947).

CHAMBER MUSIC: 2 Piano Quintets (1932, 1951); 2 String Quartets (1929, 1948); 2 Piano Trios (1928, 1932); Cello Sonata (1928); *Sonata quasi una fantasia*, for violin and piano (1929); *The Lark*, for violin and piano (1930); *Concertino*, for harp and seven instruments (1937); *Divertimento*, for two flutes (1943); Sonata for Viola and Violin (1945); Clarinet Sonata (1945); Quintet for Guitar and Strings (1950).

CHORAL MUSIC: *Sacred Service* (1943); *Liberty, Mother of Exiles* (1944); *The Book of Ruth* (1948); *The Book of Jonah* (1951); *The Song of Songs* (1955).

OPERAS: *La Mandragola* (1923); *Bacco in Toscana* (1926); *Aucassin et Nicolette*, puppet show with voices and instruments (1938); *The Merchant of Venice* (1958); *All's Well That Ends Well* (1959); *Saul* (1960); *The Importance of Being Earnest* (1962).

ORCHESTRAL MUSIC: 3 Violin Concertos (*Italiano*, 1924; *The Prophets*, 1933; 1939); 2 Piano Concertos (1927, 1937); 2 Guitar Concertos (1939, 1953); *Symphonic Variations*, for violin and orchestra (1928); *The Taming of the Shrew*, overture (1930); *The Merchant of Venice*, overture (1933); *Twelfth Night*, overture (1933); *Julius Caesar*, overture (1934); *The Winter's Tale*, overture (1934); Cello Concerto (1938); *A Midsummer Night's Dream*, overture (1940); *King John*, overture (1940); *Poem*, for violin and orchestra (1942); *Serenade*, for guitar and chamber orchestra (1943); *Indian Songs and Dances* (1943); *Humoresques on Foster's Themes* (1943); *An American Rhapsody* (1943); *Princess on the Pea*, overture for narrator and orchestra (1943); *Noah's Ark* (1944); *Antony and Cleopatra*, overture (1947); *Coriolanus*, overture (1947); *Romancero gitano*, for guitar and small orchestra (1953); Two-Guitar Concerto (1962).

PIANO MUSIC: *Alt Wien* (1923); *Le Danze del re David* (1925); 3

Poemi campestri (1926); *3 Corali su melodie ebraiche* (1926);
Sonata (1928); *Candide* (1944); *6 Canons* (1950).

CARLOS CHÁVEZ

BALLETS: *Los Cuatro Soles,* or *The Four Suns* (1926); *HP* (1927);
Antígona (1940); *La Hija de Cólquide,* or *The Daughter of
Colchis,* performed in the United States as *The Dark Meadow*
(1944).
CHAMBER MUSIC: 3 String Quartets (1921, 1932, 1944); Violin Sonatina
(1924).
CHORAL MUSIC: *La Paloma azul* (1940); *Canto a la tierra* (1946).
OPERA: *El Amor propiciado, Love Propitiated,* or *Panfilo and Lauretta*
(1957).
ORCHESTRAL MUSIC: 7 symphonies (*Antígona,* 1933; *Proletaria,* 1934;
India, 1935; 1951; *Romántica,* 1953; 1963; 1965); *Obertura republi-
cana* (1935); Harp Concerto (1938); *Xochipili-Macuilxochitl,* for
primitive Indian instruments (1940); Piano Concerto (1940); Toc-
cata, for percussion instruments (1942); Violin Concerto (1950);
Resonancias (1964).
PIANO MUSIC: Sonatina (1924); *36* (1925); *Solo, Blues, and Fox*
(1928); Third Piano Sonata (1928); *10 Preludes* (1937); *3 Etudes*
(1950); *Invención* (1958).
VOCAL MUSIC: Songs, including *Exágonos* (1923).

AARON COPLAND

BALLETS: *Billy the Kid* (1938); *Rodeo* (1942); *Appalachian Spring*
(1944); *Dance Panels* (1963).
CHAMBER MUSIC: *Vitebsk,* piano trio (1929); Sextet (1933); Violin
Sonata (1943); Piano Quartet (1950); Nonet, for three violins,
three violas, three cellos (1960).
CHORAL MUSIC: *In the Beginning,* for mezzo-soprano and chorus
(1947).
OPERAS: *The Second Hurricane,* a play-opera for children (1937); *The
Tender Land* (1954, revised 1955).
ORCHESTRAL MUSIC: 3 Symphonies (1923, 1933, 1946); *Music for the
Theater* (1925); Piano Concerto (1926); *Symphonic Ode* (1929);
Statements (1935); *El Salón México* (1936); *Lincoln Portrait,* for
narrator and orchestra (1942); *Danzón Cubano* (1944); *The Red
Pony,* suite (1948); Clarinet Concerto (1948); *Orchestral Varia-
tions,* adaptation of *Piano Variations* (1957); *Connotations* (1962);
Music for a Great City (1964).

PIANO MUSIC: *Piano Variations* (1930); Sonata (1941); *Piano Fantasy* (1957).
VOCAL MUSIC: *Twelve Poems of Emily Dickinson* (1950).

FREDERICK DELIUS

CHAMBER MUSIC: 3 Violin Sonatas (1915, 1924, 1930); Second String Quartet (1917); Cello Sonata (1917).
CHORAL MUSIC: *Sea Drift* (1903); *A Mass of Life* (1905); *Songs of Sunset* (1907); *Wanderer's Song* (1908); *A Song of the High Hills* (1911); *Requiem* (1919); *Songs of Farewell* (1932).
OPERAS: *Koanga* (1897); *A Village Romeo and Juliet* (1901); *Fennimore and Gerda* (1910).
ORCHESTRAL MUSIC: 2 *Dance Rhapsodies* (1908, 1916); *Florida* (1886); *Over the Hills and Far Away* (1895); *Paris: the Song of a Great City* (1899); *Appalachia*, with chorus (1902); Piano Concerto in C minor (1906); *Brigg Fair* (1907); *In a Summer Garden* (1908); *Summer Night on the River* (1912); *On Hearing the First Cuckoo in Spring* (1912); Concerto for Violin, Cello, and Orchestra (1916); *Violin Concerto* (1916); *Eventyr* (1917); *A Song Before Sunrise* (1918); Cello Concerto (1921); *A Song of Summer* (1930).
PIANO MUSIC: *Five Pieces* (1921); *Three Preludes* (1923).

SIR EDWARD ELGAR

CHAMBER MUSIC: Violin Sonata in E minor (1918); String Quartet in E minor (1918; Piano Quintet in A minor (1918).
CHORAL MUSIC: *The Black Knight* (1893); *The Light of Life* (1896); *Caractacus* (1898); *The Dream of Gerontius* (1900); *The Apostles* (1903); *The Kingdom* (1906).
ORCHESTRAL MUSIC: 2 Symphonies (1908, 1910); *Enigma Variations* (1899); *Pomp and Circumstance*, marches (1901–30); *Cockaigne* (1901); *In the South* (*Alassio*), overture (1903); *Introduction and Allegro*, for string quartet and orchestra (1905); *Elegy*, for strings (1909); Violin Concerto in B minor (1910); *Falstaff* (1913); Cello Concerto in E minor (1919); *Nursery Suite* (1931); *Severn Suite* (1932).

MANUEL DE FALLA

BALLETS: *El Amor brujo* (1915); *El Sombrero de tres picos*, or *The Three-Cornered Hat* (1919).

CHAMBER MUSIC: Concerto for harpsichord, flute, oboe, clarinet, violin, and cello (1926).
CHORAL MUSIC: *Balada de Mallorca* (1934); *La Atlántida* (unfinished)
OPERAS: *La Vida breve* (1905); *El Retablo de Maese Pedro*, or *Master Peter's Puppet Show*, for marionettes and singers (1919).
ORCHESTRAL MUSIC: *Noches en los jardines de España*, or *Nights in the Gardens of Spain*, for piano and orchestra (1915); *Homenajes*, or *Homages* (1920–39).
PIANO MUSIC: *4 Pièces espagnoles* (1908); *Fantasia Betica* (1919).
VOCAL MUSIC: *7 Canciones populares españolas* (1914).

GEORGE GERSHWIN

OPERA: *Porgy and Bess* (1935).
ORCHESTRAL MUSIC: *Rhapsody in Blue*, for piano and orchestra (1924); Piano Concerto in F (1925); *An American in Paris* (1928); *Second Rhapsody* (1931); *Cuban Overture* (1932); *Variations on I Got Rhythm*, for piano and orchestra (1934).
PIANO MUSIC: *Three Preludes* (1926).

ROY HARRIS

CHAMBER MUSIC: 3 String Quartets (1929, 1937, 1938); Concerto for piano, clarinet, and string quartet (1927); String Sextet (1932); *Fantasy*, for piano, flute, oboe, clarinet, horn, and bassoon (1932); *Three Variations on a Theme*, for string quartet (1933); Piano Trio (1934); Piano Quintet (1937); *Soliloquy and Dance*, for viola and piano (1939); String Quintet (1939); Violin Sonata (1941); *Duo*, for cello and piano (1964).
CHORAL MUSIC: *A Song for Occupations* (1934); *Symphony for Voices* (1936); *Service* (1946); Mass, for men's voices and organ (1948); *Jubilation* (1964).
ORCHESTRAL MUSIC: 10 Symphonies (1933; 1936; 1938; *Folk-Song*, 1939; 1942; *Gettysburg Address*, 1944; 1955; 1961; 1962; *Abraham Lincoln*, 1965); *Chorale*, for string orchestra (1933); *When Johnny Comes Marching Home* (1934); *Prelude and Fugue*, for string orchestra (1936); Violin Concerto (1938); Two-Piano Concerto (1946); *Elegy and Paean*, for viola and orchestra (1948); *Kentucky Spring* (1949); *Cumberland Concerto* (1951); Piano Concerto (1953); *Abraham Lincoln Walks at Midnight*, for soprano, piano, and orchestra (1952); *Fantasy*, for piano and orchestra (1954); *Give Me the Splendid Sun*, cantata for baritone and orchestra (1960); *Canticle to the Sun*, for soprano and chamber orchestra

(1961); *Horn of Plenty* (1964); *Rhythms and Spaces*, for string orchestra (1965).

PIANO MUSIC: Sonata (1928); *Little Suite* (1938); *American Ballads* (1942); *Toccata* (1949).

PAUL HINDEMITH

BALLET: *Noblissima Visione*, or *Saint Francis* (1938).

CHAMBER MUSIC: 7 String Quartets (?, 1919, 1922, 1922, 1924, 1944, 1945); 3 Violin Sonatas (1935, 1938, 1939); 2 String Trios (1924, 1934); *Kammermusik* Nos. 1–7 (1922; for piano and 12 instruments, 1925; for cello and 10 instruments, 1925; for violin and small ensemble, 1925; for solo viola and small ensemble, 1927; for viola d'amore and chamber ensemble, 1928; for organ and chamber ensemble, 1928); *Kleine Kammermusik* (1922); Clarinet Quintet (1923); 2 Sonatas for Unaccompanied Violin (1924); Flute Sonata (1936); Oboe Sonata (1938); Bassoon Sonata (1938); Viola Sonata (1939); Clarinet Sonata (1939); Horn Sonata (1939); Trumpet Sonata (1939); Harp Sonata (1939); English Horn Sonata (1941); Trombone Sonata (1941); Cello Sonata (1948).

CHORAL MUSIC: *Das Unaufhörliche* (1931); *When Lilacs Last in the Dooryard Bloom'd*, requiem (1945); *Apparebit repentina dies* (1947); Mass (1963).

OPERAS: *Cardillac* (1926, revised 1952); *Neues vom Tage* (1929); *Mathis der Maler* (1934); *Die Harmonie der Welt* (1950); *The Long Christmas Dinner* (1961).

ORCHESTRAL MUSIC: 2 Piano Concertos (1924, 1945); 2 Cello Concertos (1940, 1945); *Concerto for Orchestra* (1925); *Konzertmusik*, for strings and brass (1930); *Philharmonic Concerto* (1932); *Der Schwanendreher*, for viola and strings (1935); *Symphonic Dances* (1937); *Noblissima Visione*, suite (1938); Violin Concerto (1939); Symphony in E-flat (1940); *Theme and Variations According to the Four Temperaments*, for piano and orchestra (1940); *Symphonic Metamorphosis of Themes by Weber* (1943); *Symphonia Serena* (1946); Clarinet Concerto (1947); Concerto for Trumpet, Bassoon, and String Orchestra (1948, revised 1953); Concerto for Woodwinds, Harp, and Orchestra (1949); *Sinfonietta* (1950); Horn Concerto (1950); *Die Harmonie der Welt*, symphony (1951).

PIANO MUSIC: Sonata (1917); 3 Sonatas (1936); Two-Piano Sonata (1942); *Ludus tonalis* (1943).

VOCAL MUSIC: *Die junge Magd*, for contralto, flute, clarinet, and string quartet (1922); *Die Serenaden,* for soprano, oboe, viola, and cello (1925); *Das Marienleben,* song cycle (1923, revised 1941).

ARTHUR HONEGGER

BALLETS: *Skating Rink* (1921); *Sémiramis,* ballet-pantomime (1931); *Le Cantique des cantiques* (1937); *L'Appel de la montagne* (1945); *De la musique* (1950).

CHAMBER MUSIC: 3 String Quartets (1917, 1934–6, 1936); 2 Violin Sonatas (1916–18, 1919); Viola Sonata (1920); Sonatina, for two violins (1920); Cello Sonata (1920); Sonatina, for violin and cello (1932); Sonata, for solo violin (1940).

CHORAL MUSIC: *Le Roi David* (1921, revised 1922); *Cris du monde* (1931); *Jeanne d'Arc au bûcher* (1935); *La Danse des morts* (1938); *Nicolas de Flue* (1939); *Cantate de Noël* (1953).

OPERAS: *Judith* (1925); *Antigone* (1927); *Amphion* (1931).

ORCHESTRAL MUSIC: 5 Symphonies (1930; for strings, 1941; *Liturgique,* 1946; *Deliciae basilienses,* 1946; *Di tre re,* 1950); *Pastorale d'été* (1921); *Horace victorieux* (1921); *Chant de joie* (1923); *Pacific 231* (1923); Piano Concertino (1924); *Rugby* (1928); Cello Concerto (1929); *Mouvement symphonique No. 3* (1933); *Concerto da camera,* for flute, English horn, and strings (1949); *Suite archaïque* (1951); *Monopartita* (1951).

PIANO MUSIC: *Le Cahier romand* (1923); *Prelude, arioso et fughetta sur le nom de Bach* (1932); *Souvenir de Chopin* (1947).

VOCAL MUSIC: Songs, including *Poesies de Jean Cocteau* (1923), *5 Mélodies-minute* (1941), *Trois Psaumes* (1941).

BOHUSLAV MARTINU

BALLETS: *Špaliček* (1931); *The Judgment of Paris* (1935); *The Strangler* (1948).

CHAMBER MUSIC: 6 String Quartets (1921, 1926, 1931, 1936, 1938, 1947); 3 Violin Sonatas (1930, 1931, 1948); 2 Cello Sonatas (1940, 1941); String Quintet (1928); Piano Trio (1930); String Sextet (1932); Piano Quintet (1933); Piano Quartet (1942); *Madrigal Sonata,* for flute, violin, and piano (1942); *Madrigal Stanzas,* for violin and piano (1943); *Three Madrigals,* for violin and piano (1947); Quartet, for oboe, violin, cello, and piano (1949).

CHORAL MUSIC: *Czech Rhapsody* (1918); *Madrigals* (1938); *Prophecy of Isaiah* (1959).

OPERAS: *The Soldier and the Dancer* (1927); *The Miracle of Our Lady* (1933); *Comedy on a Bridge* (1936); *Julietta* (1938); *The Marriage* (1953); *What Men Live By* (1953); *La Locandiera* (1954); *Greek Passion* (1956); *Ariane* (1958); *Mirandolina* (1958); *Alexander bis*, opéra bouffe (1959).

ORCHESTRAL MUSIC: 6 Symphonies (1942; 1943; 1944; 1945; 1948; *Fantaisies symphoniques*, 1955); 3 Piano Concertos (1925, 1934, 1948); *La Bagarre* (1927); *Partita*, for string orchestra (1931); Cello Concerto (1931); Concerto for String Quartet and Orchestra (1931); Harpsichord Concerto (1935); *Suite concertante*, for violin and orchestra (1937, revised 1943); *Concerto grosso* (1937); *Three Ricercari*, for chamber orchestra (1938); *Double Concerto* (1938); *Sonata da camera*, for cello and chamber orchestra (1940); *Sinfonietta giocosa*, for piano and chamber orchestra (1941); Concerto for Violin, String Orchestra, and Percussion (1941); *Memorial to Lidice* (1943); *Toccata a due Canzone*, for piano and chamber orchestra (1946); *Concerto for Orchestra* (1947); *Sinfonia concertante*, for solo instruments, strings, and piano (1948); *Rhapsody Concerto*, for viola and orchestra (1952); *Incantation*, for piano and orchestra (1955); *The Frescoes of Piero della Francesca* (1956); *Variations on a Slovenian Theme* (1958); *Fantasia concertante*, for piano and orchestra (1958); *Estampes*, suite (1958); *Parables* (1958).

GIAN CARLO MENOTTI

BALLET: *Sebastian* (1944); *The Unicorn, the Gorgon, and the Manticore* (1956).

CHORAL MUSIC: *The Death of the Bishop of Brindisi*, cantata (1963).

OPERAS: *Amelia Goes to the Ball* (1936); *The Old Maid and the Thief* (1939); *The Island God* (1941); *The Medium* (1945); *The Telephone* (1946); *The Consul* (1949); *Amahl and the Night Visitors* (1951); *The Saint of Bleecker Street* (1954); *Maria Golovin* (1958); *The Labyrinth* (1963); *The Last Savage* (1963); *Martin's Lie* (1964).

ORCHESTRAL MUSIC: Piano Concerto (1945); *Apocalypse* (1951); Violin Concerto (1952).

DARIUS MILHAUD

BALLETS: *L'Homme et son désir* (1918); *Le Boeuf sur le toit* (1919); *La Création du monde* (1923); *Salade* (1924); *Le Train bleu* (1924); *Jeux de printemps* (1944); *The Bells* (1945); *'adame*

Miroir (1948); *La Cueillette de citrons* (1950); *L'Anneau de pourpre* (1952).

CHAMBER MUSIC: 19 String Quartets (1912, 1915, 1916, 1918, 1920, 1922, 1925, 1932, 1935, 1940, 1942, 1945, 1946, 1948, 1949, 1950, 1950, 1950, 1964, Fourteenth and Fifteenth Quartets capable of being played together as an octet); 2 Violin Sonatas (1917, 1935); *Pastorale,* for oboe, clarinet, and bassoon; Suite, for piano, violin, and clarinet (1936); *Sonatine,* for two violins (1940); *Sonatine,* for violin and viola (1941); Sonata for Violin and Harpsichord (1945); String Trio (1947); *Concertino d'automne,* for two pianos and eight instruments (1950); Piano Quintet (1950); Quintet, for two violins, viola, cello, and double bass (1952); String Septet (1964).

CHORAL MUSIC: *Cantique du Rhône* (1936); *Incantations* (1939); *Sabbath Morning Service* (1947); *La Naissance de Vénus* (1949); *Barba Garibo* (1950); *Cantate des proverbes* (1950); *Les Miracles de la foi* (1951); *Pacem in terris* (1963).

OPERAS: *Oresteia: Agamemnon* (1913–14), *Les Choëphores* (1915), and *Les Euménides* (1917–22); *Les Malheurs d'Orphée* (1924); *Le Pauvre Matelot* (1926); *Christophe Colomb* (1928); *Maximilien* (1930); *Médée* (1938); *Bolivar* (1943); *David* (1952); *The Guilty Mother* (1963).

ORCHESTRAL MUSIC: 12 Symphonies (1939; 1944; *Hymnus Abrosianus,* 1946; 1818, 1947; 1953; 1955; 1955; 1957; 1959; 1960; 1961; 1961, *Rural,* 1961); 5 Piano Concertos (1933, 1941, 1946, 1949, 1962); 2 Violin Concertos (1927, 1946); 2 Cello Concertos (1934, 1945); *Protée,* suite (1919); *Ballade,* for piano and orchestra (1920); *Saudades do Brasil* (1920); *Le Carnaval d'Aix,* for piano and orchestra (1926); Viola Concerto (1929); *Concertino de printemps,* for violin and orchestra (1934); *Suite provençale* (1936); Concerto, for flute, violin, and orchestra (1938–9); Two-Piano Concerto (1941); Clarinet Concerto (1941); *Concertino d'ete,* for viola and chamber orchestra (1951); *Concerto d'hiver,* for trombone and strings (1953); *Symphoniette,* for strings (1957); *Symphonie concertante,* for trumpet, bassoon, double bassoon, and chamber orchestra (1959); *Ouverture philharmonique* (1962); *Murder of a Great Chief of State* (1963).

PIANO MUSIC: 2 Sonatas (1916, 1949); *Saudades do Brasil* (1920), also for orchestra; *Quatre Romances sans paroles* (1933); *Scaramouche,* for two pianos (1937); *La Muse ménagère* (1944), also for orchestra; *Paris,* for four pianos (1948); *Jeu* (1950).

VOCAL MUSIC: Songs, song cycles, psalms, including *Trois Poèmes de Jean Cocteau* (1920), *6 Chants populaires hebraïques* (1925), *Le*

Cygne (1935), *Chanson du capitaine* (1937), *Trois Elégies* (1939), *Le Voyage d'été* (1940), *Quatre Chansons de Ronsard* (1941), *Rêves* (1942), *Ballade-Nocturne* (1949),

ILDEBRANDO PIZZETTI

CHAMBER MUSIC: 2 String Quartets (1906, 1933); Violin Sonata in A (1919); Cello Sonata in F (1921); Piano Trio in A (1925).

CHORAL MUSIC: *Lamento* (1920); *Requiem* (1922); *De profundis* (1938); *Epithalamium* (1939); *Cantico di gloria* (1948).

OPERAS: *Fedra* (1912); *Debora e Jaele* (1921); *Lo Staniero* (1925); *Fra Gherardo* (1927); *Orsèolo* (1935); *L'Oro* (1942); *Vanna Lupa* (1949); *Ifigenia* (1950); *Cagliostro* (1953); *La Figlia di Jorio* (1954); *Assassinio nella cattedrale* (1958); *Il Calzare d'argento,* sacred play (1960); *Clitennestra* (1964).

ORCHESTRAL MUSIC: *Concerto dell' estate* (1928); *Rondo veneziano* (1929); Cello Concerto (1934); Symphony in A (1940); Violin Concerto (1944); *Canzone dei beni perduti* (1949); *Preludio a un altro giorno* (1951).

PIANO MUSIC: *Sonata 1942* (1942).

VOCAL MUSIC: Songs, song cycles, including I *Pastori* (1908), *Tre Sonetti di Petrarca* (1922), *E il mio dolore io canto* (1947).

FRANCIS POULENC

BALLETS: *Les Biches* (1923); *Pastourelle* (1927); *Les Animaux modèles* (1942); *Allégresse* (1944).

CHAMBER MUSIC: *Rapsodie nègre,* for baritone, piano, string quartet, flute, and clarinet (1919); Sonata, for clarinet and bassoon (1922); Sonata, for horn, trumpet, and trombone (1922); Trio, for piano, oboe, and bassoon (1926); Sextet, for piano, flute, oboe, clarinet, bassoon, and horn (1932, revised 1940); Violin Sonata (1943); Flute Sonata (1947); Cello Sonata (1948).

CHORAL MUSIC: *Chanson à boire* (1922); *Sept Chansons* (1936); *Litanies à la vierge noire* (1937); Mass in G major (1937); *Sécheresses* (1937); *Figure humaine* (1943); *Chansons françaises* (1945); *Stabat Mater* (1950); *Ave Verum* (1952); *Gloria* (1960).

OPERAS: *Les Mamelles de Tirésias* (1944); *Les Dialogues des Carmélites* (1956); *La Voix humaine* (1959).

ORCHESTRAL MUSIC: *Concert champêtre,* for harpsichord and orchestra (1929); *Aubade,* choreographic concerto for piano and 18 instruments (1929); Concerto in D minor, for two pianos and orchestra (1932); *Suite française,* for chamber orchestra (1935); Concerto in G minor, for organ, orchestra, and timpani (1938); *Sinfonietta* (1947); Piano Concerto (1949); Viola Concerto (1960); *Sept répons des ténèbres* (1962).

PIANO MUSIC: *Trois Mouvements perpétuels* (1918); Suite in C (1920); *Promenades* (1924); *Pastourelle* (1927); *Deux Nouvellettes* (1928); *Trois Pièces: Pastorale, Toccata, Hymne* (1928); *Douze Improvisations* (1932–42).

VOCAL MUSIC: Songs, song cycles, and vocal compositions with orchestra, including *Le Bestiaire* (1919), *Le Bal masqué* (1932), *Cinq Poèmes* (1935), *Banalités* (1940), *La Fraîcheur et le feu* (1951), *Le Travail du peintre* (1956).

SERGE PROKOFIEV

BALLETS: *Chout* (1920); *Le Pas d'acier* (1924); *L'Enfant prodigue* (1928); *Romeo and Juliet* (1936); *Cinderella* (1944); *Tale of the Stone Flower* (1950).

CHAMBER MUSIC: 2 String Quartets (1930, 1941); 2 Violin Sonatas (1938, 1944); *Humorous Scherzo,* for four bassoons (1912); *Overture on Hebrew Themes* (1919); Flute Sonata in D major (1943); Sonata for Solo Violin (1947); Cello Sonata in C major (1949).

CHORAL MUSIC: *Seven, They Are Seven* (1917); *Alexander Nevsky* (1938); *Ballad of a Boy Who Remained Unknown* (1943); *Winter Bonfire* (1950); *On Guard for Peace* (1950).

OPERAS: *The Gambler* (1916); *The Love for Three Oranges* (1919); *The Flaming Angel* (1922–5); *Simeon Kotko* (1939); *The Convent Wedding,* or *The Duenna* (1940); *Tale of a Real Man* (1948); *War and Peace* (1952).

ORCHESTRAL MUSIC: 7 symphonies (*Classical,* 1917; 1924; 1928; 1930; 1944; 1947; 1952); 5 Piano Concertos (1911; 1913; 1921; for the left hand, 1931; 1932); 2 Violin Concertos (1917, 1935); 2 Cello Concertos (1938, 1952); *Scythian Suite* (1914); *Lieutenant Kije,* suite (1934); *Peter and the Wolf,* for narrator and orchestra (1936); *Romeo and Juliet,* three suites (1936–46).

PIANO MUSIC: 9 Sonatas (1909, 1910, 1917, 1917, 1923, 1940, 1942, 1944, 1947); *Toccata* (1912); *Sarcasms* (1914); *Visions fugitives* (1917); *Four Pieces* (1918); *Things in Themselves* (1928); *Six Pieces* (1930–1); *Children's Music* (1935).

VOCAL MUSIC: *The Ugly Duckling* (1914); *Five Songs,* to words by Anna Akhmatova (1916); *Five Songs Without Words* (1920).

SERGEI RACHMANINOFF

CHAMBER MUSIC: *Trio élégiaque* (1893); Cello Sonata in C minor (1901).

CHORAL MUSIC: *The Bells* (1910); *Vesper Mass* (1915).

OPERAS: *Aleko* (1892); *The Miserly Knight* (1904); *Francesca da Rimini* (1904).

ORCHESTRAL MUSIC: 4 Piano Concertos (1891, revised 1917; 1901; 1909; 1927); 2 Symphonies (1897, 1907); *The Isle of the Dead* (1907); *Rhapsody on a Theme by Paganini,* for piano and orchestra (1934); *Symphonic Dances* (1941).

PIANO MUSIC: Prelude in C-sharp minor (1892); *Polichinelle* (1892); 6 *Moments musicaux* (1896); First Suite, for two pianos (1893); Second Suite, for two pianos (1901); 10 *Preludes,* op. 23, including the famous *Prelude* in G minor (1903); First Piano Sonata, in D minor (1907); 13 *Preludes,* op. 32 (1910); 6 *Études-Tableaux,* op. 33 (1911); Second Piano Sonata, in B-flat minor (1913, revised 1931); 9 *Études-Tableaux,* op. 39 (1917); *Variations on a Theme by Corelli* (1932).

VOCAL MUSIC: Numerous songs, including "In the Silent Night" (1889), "The Little Island" (1896), "Fate" (1900), "The Lilacs" (1902), "Vocalise" (1912).

MAURICE RAVEL

BALLET: *Daphnis et Chloé* (1909–12).

CHAMBER MUSIC: String Quartet in F (1903); *Introduction and Allegro,* for harp, string quartet, flute, and clarinet (1906); Piano Trio in A minor (1914); Sonata, for violin and cello (1922); *Tzigane,* for violin and piano, also for violin and orchestra (1924); Violin Sonata (1927).

OPERAS: *L'Heure espagnole,* one-act opera (1907); *L'Enfant et les sortilèges,* one-act fantasy (1925).

ORCHESTRAL MUSIC: *Shéhérazade,* for voice and orchestra (1903); *Alborada del gracioso,* also for piano solo (1905); *Rapsodie espagnole* (1907); *La Valse* (1920); *Bolero* (1928); Piano Concerto in G major (1931); Piano Concerto in D major, for left hand (1931).

PIANO MUSIC: *Pavane pour une Infante défunte* (1899); *Jeux d'eau* (1901); Sonatina (1905); *Miroirs* (1905); *Gaspard de la nuit* (1908); *Mother Goose,* for piano four hands (1908, orchestrated in 1912); *Valses nobles et sentimentales* (1911); *Le Tombeau de Couperin* (1917).

VOCAL MUSIC: Songs, song cycles, including *Histoires naturelles* (1906), *Cinq Mélodies populaires grecques* (1907), *Chants populaires* (1910), *Trois Poèmes de Mallarmé* (1913), *Deux Mélodies hébraïques* (1914), *Ronsard à son âme* (1924), *Chansons madécasses* (1926), *Rêves* (1927).

ARNOLD SCHOENBERG

CHAMBER MUSIC: 4 String Quartets (op. 7, 1904; op. 10, with voice, 1908; op. 30, 1927; op. 37, 1936); *Verklaerte Nacht*, op. 4, for string sextet (1899, revised for string orchestra in 1917, revised again in 1943); *Serenade*, op. 24, for clarinet, bass clarinet, mandolin, guitar, violin, viola, and cello, with baritone voice (1923); Quintet, op. 26, for flute, oboe, clarinet, horn, and bassoon (1924); Suite, op. 29, for two clarinets, bass clarinet, violin, viola, cello, and piano (1927); *Ode to Napoleon*, op. 41, for speaker, strings, and piano (1942); String Trio, op. 45 (1946); *Fantasia*, op. 47, for violin and piano (1949).

CHORAL MUSIC: *Friede auf Erden* (1907); *Gurre-Lieder* (1901–11); *Kol Nidrei* (1938); *A Survivor from Warsaw* (1947); *De profundis* (1950); *Die Jacobsleiter* (unfinished).

OPERAS: *Erwartung*, monodrama (1909); *Die glückliche Hand*, drama with music (1913); *Von Heute auf Morgen*, one-act opera (1928); *Moses und Aron* (first two acts 1932, resumed in 1951 but never completed).

ORCHESTRAL MUSIC: *Pelleas und Melisande* (1903); *Kammersymphonie* (for 15 instruments, 1906, for large orchestra, 1935); *Five Pieces*, op. 16 (1909, revised 1949); *Variations* (1928); *Accompaniment Music to a Cinematographic Scene*, op. 34 (1930); Suite in G, for strings (1934); Violin Concerto (1936); Chamber Symphony No. 2 (1940); Piano Concerto (1942); *Theme and Variations* (1943).

PIANO MUSIC: 3 *Klavierstücke*, op. 11 (1909); 6 *kleine Klavierstücke*, op. 19 (1911); 5 *Klavierstücke* (1923); Suite, op. 25 (1921); *Klavierstück*, op. 33a (1928); *Klavierstück*, op. 33b (1932).

VOCAL MUSIC: *Pierrot lunaire*, for Sprechstimme, piano, flute, clarinet, violin, and cello (1912). Songs, including 15 poems from *Das Buch der hängenden Gärten*, op. 15 (1909).

WILLIAM SCHUMAN

BALLETS: *Undertow*, choreographic episodes (1945); *Night Journey* (1947); *Judith*, choreographic poem (1949); *The Witch of Endor* (1963).

CHAMBER MUSIC: 4 String Quartets (1936, 1937, 1939, 1950); *Amaryllis*, for string trio (1964).
CHORAL MUSIC: *Four Canonic Choruses* (1933); *Pioneers!* (1937); *This Is Our Time* (1940); *Holiday Song* (1942); *Te Deum* (1944); *Four Rounds on Famous Words* (1956); *The Lord Has a Child* (1957); *Carols of Death* (1958).
ORCHESTRAL MUSIC: 8 Symphonies (1935; 1937; 1941; 1941; for strings, 1943; 1948; 1960; 1962); *American Festival Overture* (1939); Concerto for Piano and Small Orchestra (1942); *Credendum* (1955); *New England Triptych* (1956); Violin Concerto (1959); *Song of Orpheus*, for cello and orchestra (1961).
PIANO MUSIC: *Three-Score Set* (1943); *Voyage* (1953); *Three Piano Moods* (1958).

DMITRI SHOSTAKOVICH

BALLETS: *The Golden Age* (1930); *Bolt* (1931); *The Limpid Stream* (1935).
CHAMBER MUSIC: 10 String Quartets (1938, 1944, 1946, 1949, 1952, 1956, 1960, 1962, 1963, 1964); 2 Piano Trios (1923, 1944); *Two Pieces*, for string octet (1924); Cello Sonata (1934); Piano Quintet (1940).
CHORAL MUSIC: *Leningrad* (1942); *Song of the Forests* (1949); *The Execution of Stenka Razin* (1964).
OPERAS: *The Nose* (1928); *Lady Macbeth of Mtsensk* (1932, revised in 1960 and renamed *Katerina Ismailova*); *Moskva Tcheremushki*, light opera (1958).
ORCHESTRAL MUSIC: 13 Symphonies (1925; *October*, 1927; *May First*, 1929; 1936; 1937; 1939; *Leningrad*, 1941; 1943; 1945; 1953; *1905*, 1957; *Lenin*, 1960; *Babi Yar*, 1962); 2 Piano Concertos (1933, 1957); 2 Cello Concertos (1959, 1963); *Suite for Jazz Orchestra* (1938); Violin Concerto (1955).
PIANO MUSIC: 2 Piano Sonatas (1926, 1943); *24 Preludes and Fugues* (1933); Concertino for Two Pianos (1954).
VOCAL MUSIC: 4 Songs to texts by Pushkin (1936); *From Jewish Folk Poetry* (1948).

JEAN SIBELIUS

CHAMBER MUSIC: *Voces intimae*, string quartet (1909).
CHORAL MUSIC: *The Origin of Fire* (1902); *The Captive Queen* (1906).
ORCHESTRAL MUSIC: 7 Symphonies (1899, 1901, 1907, 1911, 1915, 1923, 1924); *Kullervo* (1892); *En Saga* (1892, revised 1901); *Karelia*,

suite (1893); *Four Legends from the Kalevala: Lemminkäinen and the Maidens, Lemminkäinen in Tuonela, The Swan of Tuonela, The Return of Lemminkäinen* (1895); *King Christian II*, suite (1898); *Finlandia* (1899); *Valse triste* (1903); *Pelléas and Mélisande*, suite (1905); Violin Concerto in D minor (1903, revised 1905); *Pohjola's Daughter* (1906); *Night Ride and Sunrise* (1909); *The Oceanides* (1914); *Tapiola* (1925).

PIANO MUSIC: Sonata (1893); numerous pieces.

RICHARD STRAUSS

BALLETS: *Josephslegende* (1914); *Schlagobers* (1921).

CHAMBER MUSIC: String Quartet in A minor (1880); *Serenade,* for 13 wind instruments (1881); Cello Sonata in F major (1883); Suite, for 13 wind instruments (1884); Piano Quartet in C minor (1884); Violin Sonata in E-flat major (1887); *Metamorphosen,* for 23 solo string instruments (1945).

OPERAS: Guntram (1893, revised 1940); *Feuersnot* (1901); *Salome* (1905); *Elektra* (1908); *Der Rosenkavalier* (1910); *Ariadne auf Naxos* (1912); *Die Frau ohne Schatten* (1917); *Intermezzo* (1923); *Die ägyptische Helena* (1927, revised 1933); *Arabella* (1932); *Die schweigsame Frau* (1935); *Friedenstag* (1936); *Daphne* (1937); *Die Liebe der Danae* (1940); *Capriccio* (1941).

ORCHESTRAL MUSIC: 2 Horn Concertos (1883, 1942); Violin Concerto in D minor (1882); *Burleske,* for piano and orchestra (1885); *Aus Italien* (1886); *Don Juan* (1889); *Macbeth* (1890); *Tod und Verklärung* (1890); *Till Eulenspiegels lustige Streiche* (1895); *Also sprach Zarathustra* (1896); *Don Quixote* (1898); *Ein Heldenleben* (1899); *Symphonia domestica* (1903); *Eine Alpensinfonie* (1915); *Le Bourgeois gentilhomme*, suite (1918); *Divertimento,* or *Dance Suite,* for small orchestra, based on harpsichord music of Couperin (1941); Oboe Concerto (1946); *Duet Concertino,* for clarinet, bassoon, strings, and harp (1947).

VOCAL MUSIC: 26 albums of songs for voice and piano, including "Zueignung" (1883), "Allerseelen" (1883), "Ständchen" (1886), "Cäcilie" (1894), "Heimliche Aufforderung" (1894), "Morgen" (1894), and "Traum durch die Dämmerung" (1895); songs for voice and orchestra, including *Vier letzte Lieder* (1948).

IGOR STRAVINSKY

BALLETS: *L'Oiseau de feu,* or *The Firebird* (1910); *Petrouchka* (1911); *Le Sacre du printemps,* or *The Rite of Spring* (1913): *Les Noces,* or *The Wedding* (1917); *L'Histoire du soldat*, or *A Soldier's Tale* (1918); *Pulcinella*, based on music by Pergolesi (1919); *Le Chant du rossignol*, or *The Song of the Nightingale* (1920); *Apollon Musagète* (1928); *Le Baiser de la fée*, or *The Fairy's Kiss*, based on music by Tchaikovsky (1928); *Jeux de cartes*, or *The Card Party* (1936); *Orpheus* (1947); *Agon* (1957); *Noah and the Flood* (1961).

CHAMBER MUSIC: *Ragtime*, for 11 instruments (1918); *Concertino,* for string quartet (1920); Octet, for wind instruments (1923); *Duo Concertant*, for violin and piano (1932); *Suite italienne*, for cello and piano (1933); *Elegy*, for viola solo (1944); Septet (1952).

CHORAL MUSIC: *Symphony of Psalms* (1930); *Credo* (1932); *Ave Maria* (1934); Mass (1948); *Cantata on English Texts* (1952); *Canticum sacrum ad honorem sancti Marci nominis* (1955); *Threni* (1958); *Gesualdo Monumentum* (1960); *A Sermon, a Narrative and a Prayer*, for narrator, alto, chorus, and orchestra (1961); *Requiem Canticles* (1966).

OPERAS: *Le Rossignol* (1914); *Renard*, burlesque chamber opera (1916); *Mavra*, comic opera (1922); *Oedipus Rex*, opera-oratorio (1927); *The Rake's Progress* (1951).

ORCHESTRAL MUSIC: Symphony in E-flat major (1907); *Le Chant du rossignol* (1917); Symphonies for Wind Instruments (1920); Piano Concerto (1924); *Capriccio*, for piano and orchestra (1929); Violin Concerto (1931); *Divertimento* (1934); *Dumbarton Oaks Concerto*, for chamber orchestra (1938); Symphony in C major (1940); *Danses concertantes* (1942); *Four Norwegian Moods* (1942); *Ode* (1943); *Scènes de ballet* (1944); *Scherzo à la russe* (1944); Symphony in Three Movements (1945); Concerto in D, for strings (1946); *Movements*, for piano and orchestra (1959); *Abraham and Isaac*, sacred ballad for baritone and chamber orchestra (1963); *Variations* (1965).

PIANO MUSIC: *Piano Rag Music* (1920); *Serenade* in A (1925); Concerto, for two solo pianos (1935); Two-Piano Sonata (1944).

VOCAL MUSIC: *Three Songs from William Shakespeare*, for mezzo-soprano, flute, clarinet, and viola (1954); *In Memoriam Dylan Thomas*, for tenor, string quartet, and four trombones (1954).

RALPH VAUGHAN WILLIAMS

BALLETS: *Old King Cole* (1923); *On Christmas Night* (1926); *Job*, a masque for dancing (1930).

CHAMBER MUSIC: 2 String Quartets (1908, revised 1921; 1945); *Fantasy Quintet*, for strings (1910); *Six Studies in English Folk-song*, for cello and piano (1927); *Household Music: Three Preludes on Welsh Hymn Tunes*, for string quartet (1942).

Choral Music: *Toward the Unknown Region* (1905, revised 1918); *The Wasps*, incidental music (1909); *Five Mystical Songs* (1911); *Fantasia on Christmas Carols* (1912); Mass in G minor (1922); *Flos Campi* (1925); *Sancta Civitas* (1926); *Te Deum* (1928); *Magnificat* (1932); *Five Tudor Portraits* (1936); *Serenade to Music* (1938); *Epithalamion* (1953); *This Day* (1954); *A Vision of Aeroplanes* (1956).

Operas: *Hugh the Drover*, ballad opera (1914); *The Shepherds of the Delectable Mountains*, pastoral episode (1922); *Sir John in Love* (1929); *The Poisoned Kiss*, a romantic extravaganza (1936); *Riders to the Sea* (1937); *The Pilgrims' Progress*, a morality (1949).

Orchestral Music: 9 Symphonies (*Sea*, 1910; *London*, 1914, revised 1920; *Pastoral*, 1922; 1935; 1943; 1948; *Sinfonia antartica*, 1952; 1956; 1958); *Norfolk Rhapsody in E minor* (1906); *Fantasia on a Theme by Thomas Tallis*, for strings (1910); *The Lark Ascending*, romance for violin and orchestra (1914); *Concerto accademico* in D minor, for violin and orchestra (1925); Piano Concerto (1932); Suite for Viola and Orchestra (1934); *Fantasia on Greensleeves* (1934); Concerto for Oboe and Strings (1944); Bass-Tuba Concerto (1954).

HEITOR VILLA-LOBOS

Ballets: *Uirapurú* (1917); *Dança da terra* (1939).

Chamber Music: 15 String Quartets (1915; 1915; 1916; 1917; *Brazilian Quartet No. 1*, 1931; *Brazilian Quartet No. 2*, 1938; 1942; 1944; 1945; 1946; 1948; 1950; 1952; 1955; 1958); 4 Sonatas-Fantasias, for violin and piano (1912, 1914, 1915, 1918); 3 Piano Trios (1911, 1916, 1918); 2 Cello Sonatas (1915, 1916); Piano Quintet (1916); *Sexteto místico* (1917); Quartet, for harp, celesta, flute, and saxophone, with women's chorus (1921); Trio, for oboe, clarinet, and bassoon (1922); *Chôros No. 2*, for flute and clarinet (1921); *Nonetto* (1923); *Chôros No. 7*, for flute, oboe, clarinet, saxophone, bassoon, violin, and cello (1924); *Chôros No. 4*, for three horns and trombone (1926); Quintet, for flute, oboe, English horn, clarinet, and bassoon (1928); *Bachiana brasileira No. 1*, for eight cellos (1930); *Bachiana brasileira No. 5*, for voice and eight cellos (1938); *Bachiana brasileira No. 6*, for flute and bassoon (1938).

Choral Music: *Chôros No. 3*, for male chorus and seven wind instruments (1925); *Chôros No. 10, Rasga o coração* (1925); *Chôros No. 14*, for chorus, band and orchestra (1928); *Vida pura* (1934);

Descobrimento do Brasil, four suites for chorus and orchestra (1937).

OPERAS: Zoé (1919); *Malazarte* (1921); *Magdalena,* light opera (1947).

ORCHESTRAL MUSIC: 12 Symphonies (*Imprevisto,* 1916; *Ascenção,* 1917; *Guerra,* 1919; *Vitória,* 1920; *Paz,* 1921; *Montanhas do Brasil,* 1944; *America,* 1945; 1950; 1952; 1954; 1956; 1958); 2 Cello Concertos (1915, 1955); *Danças africanas* (1917); Chôros No. 8, for orchestra and two pianos (1925); Chôros No. 6 (1926); Chôros No. 11, for piano and orchestra (1928); Chôros No. 12 (1929); Chôros No. 9 (1929); Chôros No. 13, for two orchestras and band (1929); *Momo precoce* (1929); *Bachiana brasileira* No. 2, including *The Little Train of Caipira* (1930); *Bachiana brasileira No. 3,* for piano and orchestra (1938); *Rudepoema,* also for piano (1942); *Bachiana brasileira No. 4* (1944); Piano Concerto (1946); *Mandú-Carará* (1948); *Erosion, or The Origin of the Amazon River* (1951); *Dawn in a Tropical Forest* (1953); *Odyssey of a Race* (1954); Harp Concerto (1955).

PIANO MUSIC: *Prole do bebé,* two suites (1918, 1921); *História da carochinha* (1919); *Lenda do caboclo* (1920); *Dança infernal* (1920); *Cirandinha* (1925); Chôros No. 5, *Alma brasileira* (1926); *Saudades das selvas brasileiras* (1927); *Francette et Pià* (1929); *Ciclo brasileiro* (1936); *As três Marias* (1939); *Poema singelo* (1942).

SIR WILLIAM WALTON

BALLETS: *The Wise Virgins,* based on music by J. S. Bach (1940); *The Quest* (1943).

CHAMBER MUSIC: 2 String Quartets (1919, 1947); *Toccata,* for violin and piano (1923); *Façade,* an entertainment for narrator and instruments (1922–6, revised 1942); Violin Sonata (1949).

CHORAL MUSIC: *Belshazzar's Feast* (1931); *Te Deum* (1953).

OPERA: *Troilus and Cressida* (1954).

ORCHESTRAL MUSIC: 2 Symphonies (1935, 1960); *Façade,* two suites (1926, 1938); *Portsmouth Point* (1925); *Sinfonia concertante,* for piano and orchestra (1927); Viola Concerto (1929); Violin Concerto (1939); *Scapino,* comedy overture (1940); Cello Concerto (1956); *Partita* (1957); *Variations on a Theme by Hindemith* (1963).

APPENDIX II

Bibliography

GENERAL

Abraham, Gerald: *Eight Soviet Composers*. London: Oxford University Press; 1943.

———: *This Modern Stuff*. New York: W. W. Norton; 1952.

Austin, William W.: *Music in the 20th Century*. New York: W. W. Norton; 1966.

Bacharach, A. L., ed.: *British Music of Our Time*. London: Pelican Books; 1946.

———: *The Twentieth Century*. London: Pelican Books; 1957.

Bakst, James: *A History of Russian-Soviet Music*. New York: Dodd, Mead; 1966.

Cardus, Neville: *A Composers Eleven*. London: Jonathan Cape; 1958.

Chase, Gilbert: *America's Music. Rev. edn*. New York: McGraw Hill; 1966.

———: *The Music of Spain*. New York: Dover; 1959.

———, ed.: *The American Composer Speaks*. Baton Rouge: Louisiana State University Press; 1966.

Cohn, Arthur: *The Collector's 20th-Century Music in the Western Hemisphere*. New York: J. B. Lippincott; 1961.

———: *20th Century Music in Western Europe*. New York: J. B. Lippincott; 1965.

Collaer, Paul: *A History of Modern Music*. New York: Grosset and Dunlap; 1961.

Cooper, Martin: *French Music*. London: Oxford University Press; 1951.

Copland, Aaron: *Our New Music*. New York: Whittlesey House; 1941.

Cowell, Henry, ed.: *American Composers on American Music*. Stanford: Stanford University Press; 1933.

Demuth, Norman: *Musical Trends in the 20th Century*. London: Rockcliff; 1952.

Ewen, David: *American Composers Today*. New York: H. W. Wilson Co.; 1949.

————: *David Ewen Introduces Modern Music*. Philadelphia: Chilton; 1962.

————: *The Complete Book of 20th Century Music*. Rev. edn. New York: Prentice-Hall; 1961.

————: *European Composers Today*. New York: H. W. Wilson Co.; 1954.

Foulds, John H.: *Music Today*. London: Ivor Nicholson and Watson; 1934.

Goss, Madeleine: *Modern Music Makers*. New York: E. P. Dutton; 1952.

Graf, Max: *Modern Music*. New York: Philosophical Library; 1946.

Gray, Cecil: *A Survey of Contemporary Music*. London: Oxford University Press; 1924.

Hansen, Peter S.: *An Introduction to 20th Century Music*. Boston: Allyn and Bacon; 1961.

Hartog, Howard, ed.: *European Music in the 20th Century*. New York: Frederick A. Praeger; 1957.

Hodeir, André: *Since Debussy: A View of Contemporary Music*. New York: Grove; 1961.

Howard, John T.: *Our American Music*. 3rd edn. New York: Thos. Y. Crowell, 1946.

Howard, John T., and Lyons, James: *Modern Music*. New York: Mentor Books; 1958.

Lambert, Constant: *Music Ho!* New York: Charles Scribner's Sons; 1934.

Lang, Paul Henry, and Broder, Nathan, eds.: *Contemporary Music in Europe: A Comprehensive Survey*. New York: G. Schirmer; 1965.

Leonard, Richard Anthony: *A History of Russian Music*. New York: Macmillan; 1957.

Machlis, Joseph: *Introduction to Contemporary Music*. New York: W. W. Norton; 1961.

Mellers, W. H.: *Music in a New Found Land*. New York: Alfred A. Knopf; 1965.

————: *Romanticism and the 20th Century*. London: Rockcliff; 1957.

————: *Studies in Contemporary Music*. London: Dennis Dobson; 1947.

Mitchell, Donald: *The Language of Modern Music*. London: Faber and Faber; 1966.

Pannain, Guido: *Modern Composers*. New York: E. P. Dutton; 1933.

Reis, Claire, ed.: *Composers in America*. New York: Macmillan; 1947.

Rosenfeld, Paul: *Discoveries of a Music Critic*. New York: Harcourt, Brace; 1936.

Salazar, Adolfo: *Music in Our Time*. New York: W. W. Norton; 1946.

Salzman, Eric: *20th Century Music: An Introduction*. New York: Prentice-Hall; 1967.

Saminsky, Lazare: *Living Music of the Americas*. New York: Crown Publishers; 1949.

————: *Music of Our Day*. 2nd edn. New York: Thos. Y. Crowell; 1939.

Slonimsky, Nicolas: *Music of Latin America*. New York: Thos. Y. Crowell; 1945.

————: *Music Since 1900*. 3rd edn. New York: Coleman-Ross; 1949.

Thompson, Oscar, ed.: *Great Modern Composers*. New York: Dodd, Mead; 1941.

Yates, Peter: *Twentieth Century Music*. New York: Pantheon; 1967.

Individual Biographies

SAMUEL BARBER

Broder, Nathan: *Samuel Barber*. New York: G. Schirmer; 1953.

BÉLA BARTÓK

Fassett, Agatha: *The Naked Face of Genius: Bartók's American Years*. Boston: Houghton Mifflin; 1958.

Haraszti, Emil: *Béla Bartók: His Life and Works*. Paris: The Lyrebird Press; 1938.

Moreux, Serge: *Béla Bartók*. London: Harvill Press; 1953.

Petzoldt, Richard: *Béla Bartók: sein Leben in Bildern*. Leipzig: Verlag Enzyklopädie; 1958.

Stevens, Halsey: *Bartók*. Rev. edn. New York: Oxford University Press; 1964.

Szabolcsi, Bence: *Bartók: sa vie et son œuvre*. Budapest: Coruna; 1956.

ALBAN BERG

Redlich, H. F.: *Alban Berg*. New York: Abelard-Schuman; 1957.
Reich, Willi: *Alban Berg*. London: Dennis Dobson; 1954.
Vogelsang, Konrad: *Alban Berg*. Berlin: Max Hesses Verlag; 1959.

ERNEST BLOCH

Tibaldi Chiesa, Mary: *Ernest Bloch*. Turin: G. B. Paravia; 1933.

BENJAMIN BRITTEN

Mitchell, Donald, and Keller, Hans, eds.: *Benjamin Britten*. New York: Philosophical Library; 1952.
White, Eric Walter: *Benjamin Britten*. Rev. edn. London: Boosey and Hawkes; 1954.

CARLOS CHÁVEZ

Carlos Chávez: North American Press, 1936–1950. Mexico City: Ediciones Mexicanas de Música, 1951.
García Morillo, Roberto: *Carlos Chávez: Vida y Obra*. Mexico-Buenos Aires: Fondo de Cultura Económica; 1960.

AARON COPLAND

Berger, Arthur: *Aaron Copland*. New York: Oxford University Press; 1953.
Copland, Aaron: *Copland on Music*. New York: Doubleday; 1960.
Smith, Julia: *Aaron Copland*. New York: E. P. Dutton; 1955.

FREDERICK DELIUS

Beecham, Sir Thomas: *Delius*. New York: Alfred A. Knopf; 1960.
Fenby, Eric: *Delius as I Knew Him*. London: Quality Press; 1948.
Heseltine, Philip (Warlock Peter): *Frederick Delius*. London: Bodley Head; 1952.
Hutchings, Arthur: *Delius: a Critical Biography*. New York: Macmillan; 1948.

SIR EDWARD ELGAR

Anderson, William Robert: *Introduction to the Music of Elgar*. London: Dennis Dobson; 1949.

Chambers, George B.: *Edward Elgar: Centenary Sketches*. London: Novello; 1957.

Dunhill, Thomas Frederick: *Sir Edward Elgar*. London: Blackie; 1938.

Maine, Basil: *Elgar: His Life and Works*. London: G. Bell; 1933.

McVeagh, Diana M.: *Edward Elgar: His Life and Music*. London: Dent; 1955.

Porte, John F.: *Elgar and His Music*. London: I. Pitman; 1933.

Reed, William Henry: *Elgar*. New York: Pellegrini and Cudahy; 1949.

———: *Elgar as I Knew Him*. London: Victor Gollancz; 1936.

Young, Percy M.: *Elgar*. London: Collins; 1955.

MANUEL DE FALLA

Pahissa, Jaime: *Manuel de Falla*. London: Museum Press; 1954.

Pahlen, Kurt: *Manuel de Falla und die Musik in Spanien*. Olten: O. Walter; 1953.

Trend, John B.: *Manuel de Falla and Spanish Music*. New York: Alfred A. Knopf; 1929.

GEORGE GERSHWIN

Armitage, Merle: *George Gershwin, Man and Legend*. New York: Duell, Sloan and Pearce; 1958.

———, ed.: *George Gershwin*. New York: Longmans, Green; 1938.

Chalupt, René: *George Gershwin*. Paris: Amiot-Dumont; 1948.

Ewen, David: *A Journey to Greatness: The Life and Music of George Gershwin*. New York: Henry Holt; 1956.

Goldberg, Isaac: *George Gershwin*. New edn. with supplementary material by Edith Garson. New York: Frederick Ungar; 1958.

Jablonski, Edward, and Stewart, Lawrence: *The Gershwin Years*. New York: Doubleday; 1958.

PAUL HINDEMITH

Paul Hindemith: Zeugnis in Bildern. Mainz: B. Schott; 1955.

Strobel, Heinrich: *Paul Hindemith*. New edn. Mainz: B. Schott; 1948.

ARTHUR HONEGGER

Bruyr, José: *Honegger et son œuvre*. Paris: Corrêa; 1947.

Delannoy, Marcel: *Honegger*. Paris: B. Horay; 1953.

Gauthier, André: *Arthur Honegger*. Lyon: Éditions et imprimeries du Sudest; 1957.

Gérard, Claude: *Arthur Honegger*. Brussels: Éditeurs de la nouvelle Revue belgique; 1945.

Honegger, Arthur: *I Am a Composer*. New York: St. Martin's Press; 1966.

Landowski, Marcel: *Honegger*. Paris: Éditions du Seuil; 1957.

Matter, Jean: *Honegger*. Lausanne: Foetisch Frères; 1956.

Tappolet, Willy: *Arthur Honegger*. Zurich: Atlantis Verlag; 1954.

BOHUSLAV MARTINU

Šafránek, Miloš: *Bohuslav Martinu: The Man and His Music*. New York: Alfred A. Knopf; 1944.

DARIUS MILHAUD

Collaer, Paul: *Darius Milhaud*. Antwerp: Nederlandsche Boekhandel; 1947.

Milhaud, Darius: *Notes Without Music*. New York: Alfred A. Knopf; 1953.

ILDEBRANDO PIZZETTI

Gavazzeni, Gianandrea: *Tre studi su Pizzetti*. Como: E. Cavalleri; 1937.

Gatti, Guido M.: *Ildebrando Pizzetti*. London: Dennis Dobson; 1951.

FRANCIS POULENC

Hell, Henri: *Francis Poulenc*. New York: Grove Press; 1959.

SERGE PROKOFIEV

Hanson, Lawrence and Elisabeth: *Prokofiev*. New York: Random House; 1964.

Nestyev, Israel: *Serge Prokofiev: His Musical Life*. Stanford: Stanford University Press; 1960.

Samuel, Claude: *Prokofiev*. London: Calder and Calder; 1966.

SERGEI RACHMANINOFF

Bertenson, S., and Leyda, J.: *Rachmaninoff*. New York: New York University Press; 1956.

Culshaw, John: *Rachmaninoff: the Man and His Music*. New York: Oxford University Press; 1956.

Lyle, Watson: *Rachmaninoff*. London: W. Reeves; 1939.

Seroff, Victor: *Rachmaninoff*. New York: Simon and Schuster; 1950.

MAURICE RAVEL

Ackere, Jules van: *Maurice Ravel*. Brussels: Elsevier; 1957.

Bruyr, José: *Maurice Ravel*. Paris: Plon; 1950.

Demuth, Norman: *Ravel*. London: Dent; 1947.

Goss, Madeleine: *Bolero: the Life of Maurice Ravel*. New York: Henry Holt; 1940.

Jankelevitch, Vladimir: *Ravel*. New York: Grove; 1959.

Manuel, Roland. *Maurice Ravel*. London: Dennis Dobson, 1941.

Maurice Ravel, par quelques-uns de ses familiers. Paris: Éditions du Tambourinaire; 1939.

Myers, Rollo H.: *Ravel, Life and Works*. New York: Thos. Yoseloff; 1960.

Onnen, Frank: *Maurice Ravel*. Stockholm: Continental Book Co.; 1947.

Seroff, Victor: *Ravel*. New York: Henry Holt; 1953.

ARNOLD SCHOENBERG

Armitage, Merle, ed.: *Schoenberg*. New York: G. Schirmer; 1937.

Leibowitz, René: *Schoenberg and His School*. New York: Philosophical Library; 1949.

Newlin, Dika: *Bruckner, Mahler, Schoenberg*. New York: King's Crown Press; 1947.

Stuckenschmidt, H. H.: *Schoenberg*. New York: Grove Press; 1959.

WILLIAM SCHUMAN

Schreiber, Flora Rheta, and Persichetti, Vincent: *William Schuman*. New York: G. Schirmer; 1954.

DMITRI SHOSTAKOVICH

Martinov, Ivan: *Shostakovich*. New York: Philosophical Library; 1947.

Seroff, Victor: *Dmitri Shostakovich*. New York: Alfred A. Knopf; 1943.

JEAN SIBELIUS

Abraham, Gerald, ed.: *The Music of Sibelius*. New York: W. W. Norton; 1947.

Ekman, Karl: *Jean Sibelius*. New York: Tudor; 1945.

Gray, Cecil: *Sibelius*. Rev. edn. London: Oxford University Press; 1945.

Hannikainen, Ilmari: *Sibelius and the Development of Finnish Music*. London: Hinrichsen Editions; 1948.

Johnson, Harold E.: *Jean Sibelius*. New York: Alfred A. Knopf; 1959.

Ringbom, Nils-Eric: *Sibelius*. Norman: University of Oklahoma Press; 1954.

Törne, Bengt de: *Sibelius: a Close-up*. Boston: Houghton Mifflin; 1938.

Westerlund, Cy: *The Works of Sibelius*. Helsinki: Westerlund Publishers; 1955.

RICHARD STRAUSS

Brandl, Willy: *Richard Strauss*. Wiesbaden: Breitkopf und Härtel; 1949.

Del Mar, Norman: *Richard Strauss*, Vol I. New York: The Macmillan Company; 1962.

Erhardt, Otto: *Richard Strauss*. Olten: O. Walter; 1953.

Krause, Ernst: *Richard Strauss*. London: Collet; 1965.

Mann, William: *Richard Strauss: A Critical Study of His Operas*. New York: Oxford University Press; 1966.

Marek, George R. *Richard Strauss: The Life of a Non-Hero*. New York: Simon and Schuster, 1967.

Trenner, F., ed.: *Richard Strauss: Dokumente seines Lebens und Schaffens*. Munich: C. H. Beck; 1954.

Strauss, Richard, and Hofmannsthal, Hugo von: *Correspondence Between Richard Strauss and Hugo von Hofmannsthal*. New York: Alfred A. Knopf; 1927.

IGOR STRAVINSKY

Armitage, Merle, ed.: *Igor Stravinsky*. New York: G. Schirmer; 1936.

Corle, Edwin, ed.: *Igor Stravinsky*. New York: Duell, Sloan and Pearce; 1949.

Onnen, Frank: *Stravinsky*. New York: Macmillan; 1950.

Stravinsky, Igor: *Stravinsky: an Autobiography*. New York: Steuer; 1958.

————, and Craft, Robert: *Conversations with Igor Stravinsky*, 1959; *Memories and Commentaries*, 1960; *Expositions and Developments*, 1962; *Dialogues and a Diary*, 1963. All New York: Doubleday & Company. *Themes and Episodes*. New York: Alfred A. Knopf; 1966.

Strobel, Heinrich: *Stravinsky*. New York: Merlin Press; 1955.

Tansman, Alexander: *Igor Stravinsky*. New York: G. P. Putnam's Sons; 1949.

Vlad, Roman: *Stravinsky*. New York: Oxford University Press; 1960.

White, Eric Walter. *Stravinsky*. Berkeley: University of California Press; 1966.

RALPH VAUGHAN WILLIAMS

Dickinson, A. E.: *Ralph Vaughan Williams*. London: Faber and Faber; 1963.

Foss, Hubert: *Ralph Vaughan Williams: a Study*. London: Oxford University Press; 1950.

Howes, Frank: *The Music of Ralph Vaughan Williams*. London: Oxford University Press; 1954.

Kennedy, Michael: *The Works of Ralph Vaughan Williams*. London: Oxford University Press; 1964.

Pakenham, S.: *Ralph Vaughan Williams*. London: Macmillan; 1957.

Vaughan Williams, Ursula: *R.V.W.* London: Oxford University Press; 1964.

Young, Percy M.: *Vaughan Williams*. London: Dennis Dobson; 1953.

HEITOR VILLA-LOBOS

Barros, C.: *O Romance de Villa-Lobos*. Rio de Janeiro: Editora a Notte; 1951.

SIR WILLIAM WALTON

Howes, Frank: *The Music of William Walton*. London: Oxford University Press; 1965.

APPENDIX III

CONTRIBUTORS

WALTER ARLEN is a music critic of the *Los Angeles Times* and vice-president of the National Association for American Composers and Conductors.

ERNO BALOGH — concert pianist, teacher, composer — was an intimate friend of Béla Bartók.

MARION BAUER, well-known American composer and authority on modern American music, was the author of *Twentieth Century Music*.

DALLAS BOWER is a producer of motion pictures and television shows in London, in which capacity he has on several occasions worked with Sir William Walton.

SUZANNE BLOCH, daughter of the famous composer, is a celebrated performer on the lute and other old instruments.

NATHAN BRODER, musicologist, is an associate editor of *Musical Quarterly* and the author of a biography of Samuel Barber.

GILBERT CHASE is the author of *The Music of Spain* and *America's Music*. For several years he was a member of the State Department as cultural attaché in Lima and Buenos Aires.

ISRAEL CITKOWITZ, American composer, was a pupil of Aaron Copland, and for many years a teacher at the Dalcroze School of Music in New York.

NORMAN DEL MAR is the conductor of the Chelsea Symphony in London. He has written articles on contemporary composers for various magazines and anthologies.

BERNARD VAN DIEREN was a well-known Dutch composer and music critic, the author of *Down Among the Dead Men*.

NORMAN DEMUTH, professor of composition at the Royal Academy of Music in London, is a composer, and the author of biographies of César Franck, Albert Roussel, and Paul Dukas.

Eric Fenby was amanuensis for Delius during the last years of that composer's life, and has written a book about these experiences.

Janet Flanner is the Paris correspondent of *The New Yorker*.

Guido M. Gatti is one of Italy's most renowned music critics, the editor of *La Rassegna musicale*, and author of several notable books on music.

Karl Geiringer is a professor of history and theory of music at Boston University and the author of distinguished biographies of Haydn and Brahms.

Miriam Gideon, one of America's leading women composers, is on the music faculty of the Cantor's Institute of the Jewish Theological Seminary in New York.

Madeleine Goss is the author of a biography of Ravel, among other books.

Cecil Gray was the author of A *History of Music,* A *Survey of Contemporary Music,* and biographies of Gesualdo and Sibelius.

Johana Harris, wife of the composer, has distinguished herself as a pianist in performances of Roy Harris' music.

Everett Helm is a composer and musicologist who is a representative in Germany of *Musical America.*

Henri Hell is the author of a biography of Poulenc.

Dyneley Hussey is a distinguished English music critic whose writings have appeared in outstanding English journals and anthologies. He is the author of books on Haydn, Mozart, and Verdi.

Lincoln Kirstein is general director of the New York City Ballet.

John Krueger, a former pupil of Roy Harris, is conductor of the Youngstown Symphony and a member of the music faculty at the University of Indiana, in Bloomington.

Robert Lawrence was for several years a music critic of the *New York Herald Tribune* and has subsequently distinguished himself as a conductor.

Hugo Leichtentritt was lecturer on music history at Harvard University from 1933 to 1940. A distinguished musicologist, he was the author of many books, including biographies of Handel and Koussevitzky and *Music, History, and Ideas.*

Richard Anthony Leonard is the author of *The Stream of Music* and A *History of Russian Music.*

Edward Lockspeiser is the author of biographies of Debussy, Berlioz, and Bizet, and is the translator into English of Hell's biography of Poulenc.

Basil Maine, former music critic on English dailies, is the author of biographies of Elgar and Chopin and several other volumes.

Burle Marx is a distinguished conductor and teacher who has contributed many articles on South American music and musicians to various journals.

OLIVER NEIGHBOUR is head of the music division of the British Museum and contributor of essays on English composers to journals.

PAUL NETTL is a member of the music faculty at the University of Indiana, in Bloomington, and the author of many books on music.

DIKA NEWLIN, a member of the music faculty at Drew University, in Madison, New Jersey, is the author of *Bruckner, Mahler, Schoenberg*, and translator into English of Schoenberg's *Style and Idea*.

GUIDO PANNAIN was a teacher of musicology in Naples and the author of *Modern Composers*.

VINCENT PERSICHETTI is an American composer who is on the faculty of the Juilliard School of Music. He is coauthor of a biography of William Schuman.

PAUL A. PISK is a composer, and professor of music at the University of Texas, in Austin.

WILLIAM H. REED, a close friend of Elgar, was for many years concertmaster of the Royal Philharmonic Orchestra of London and a member of the faculty of the Royal College of Music.

ROBERT SABIN is the editor of *Musical America*.

MILOŠ ŠAFRÁNEK is the author of a biography of Bohuslav Martinu.

WINTHROP SARGEANT is music critic of *The New Yorker* and the author of *Geniuses, Goddesses, and People* and *Listening to Music*.

FLORA RHETA SCHREIBER is a frequent contributor to leading magazines and coauthor of a biography of William Schuman.

AINÖ SIBELIUS is the wife of the composer.

NICOLAS SLONIMSKY — author of *Music Since 1900* and *Music of Latin America*, among other books — has distinguished himself as a musicologist, encyclopedist, teacher, lecturer, and conductor.

WILLIAM LEON SMYSER is an English journalist who has frequently contributed articles to the English journals.

H. H. STUCKENSCHMIDT is one of the foremost music critics of Western Germany. He was a director of the Berlin radio station RIAS and is the author of several books on music, including a biography of Schoenberg.

ROLAND VON WEBER has contributed articles on contemporary Italian music and musicians to leading magazines.

HERBERT WEINSTOCK is coauthor of *Men of Music* and *The Opera*, and the author of biographies of Chopin, Handel, and Tchaikovsky.

ERIC WALTER WHITE is a member of the Arts Council of Great Britain and the author of biographies of Stravinsky and Britten.

ACKNOWLEDGMENTS

FOR PERMISSION to reprint material first published elsewhere, the editor wishes to express his gratitude to the following:

Alfred A. Knopf, Inc., for a personal portrait of Martinu, from Miloš Šafránek's *Bohuslav Martinu*, New York, 1944.

Associated Music Publishers, for Hindemith's artistic statement, from the Introduction to the new version of *Das Marienleben*, Schott & Co., Ltd., London, 1948, translated by Arthur Mendel.

The Bodley Head, London, Ltd., for Britten's artistic statement, which appeared in the Introduction of the Sadler's Wells libretto of *Peter Grimes*.

Boosey and Hawkes, for the personal note on Britten, which appeared in *Benjamin Britten*, by Eric Walter White, London, 1954, reprinted by permission.

Boston Symphony Program Notes, for several paragraphs by Nicolas Slonimsky, which Mr. Slonimsky incorporated into his essay on Shostakovich.

Cassell & Co., Ltd., for the essay on Walton by Dyneley Hussey, which appeared in *The Twentieth Century*, edited by A. L. Bacharach, London, 1954.

Coward-McCann, for a paragraph from *Revolt in the Arts*, edited by Oliver M. Saylor, New York, 1933, used in Gershwin's artistic statement.

E. P. Dutton & Co., for the critical essay on Ravel by Guido Pannain from *Modern Composers*, New York, 1933.

Etude, for the personal note on Sibelius by his wife, which appeared in an interview secured by Paul Sjöblom; for the artistic statement of Ravel, which appeared in an interview secured by David Ewen; for the artistic statement of Béla Bartók, which appeared in an interview secured by Friede F. Rothe.

Frederick A. Praeger, for the critical essay on Hindemith by Norman Del Mar, which appeared in *European Music in the Twentieth Century*, edited by Howard Hartog, New York, 1957.

G. Bell & Sons, Ltd., for the personal note on Delius, from *Delius As I Knew Him*, by Eric Fenby, London, 1938.

G. Schirmer, Inc., for the personal note and the critical essay on Samuel Barber, from *Samuel Barber*, by Nathan Broder, copyright 1954, reprinted by permission; also for the personal note and the critical essay on William Schuman, from *William Schuman*, by Flora R. Schreiber and Vincent Persichetti, copyright 1954, reprinted by permission.

Grove Press, for the personal note on Francis Poulenc, from *Poulenc*, by Henri Hell, translated from the French and introduced by Edward Lockspeiser, copyright 1959, John Calder Publishers, Ltd., London.

Harvard University Press, for Aaron Copland's artistic statement, from *Music and the Imagination*, Cambridge, 1958.

Holgar Schildts Förlag (also Alfred A. Knopf, Inc.), for the artistic statement by Sibelius, from *Jean Sibelius*, by Karl Ekman, Helsinki, 1935.

Holt, Rinehart and Winston, for the personal note and the critical essay on George Gershwin, from *A Journey to Greatness: the Life and Music of George Gershwin*, by David Ewen, New York, 1956; also for the personal note on Ravel, from *Bolero: the Life of Maurice Ravel*, by Madeleine Goss, New York, 1940.

Life Magazine, for the personal note on Gian Carlo Menotti, from an article on Menotti by Winthrop Sargeant.

Macmillan and Co., for the critical essay on Rachmaninoff, from *A History of Russian Music*, by Richard Anthony Leonard, New York, 1957.

Music and Letters, for the personal note on Richard Strauss, from an article by William Leon Smyser (also to the *New York Herald Tribune*, which republished it).

Musical Courier, for the personal note on Heitor Villa-Lobos, from an article by Burle Marx.

Musical Quarterly, for the artistic statement by Pizzetti, from an article on opera by Pizzetti.

Musical Times (London), for the critical essay on Delius by Bernard van Dieren.

The New Yorker, for the personal note on Stravinsky by Janet Flanner, a condensation of a " profile."

New York Herald Tribune, for the personal note on Manuel de Falla by Lincoln Kirstein.

The New York Times, for the artistic statement by Prokofiev, from an interview with Olin Downes; for a quotation for Poulenc's artistic statement, from an interview with Olin Downes; for Shostakovich's artistic statement, from an interview with Rose Lee; for Gian Carlo Menotti's artistic statement, from an article in the Magazine section.

Oxford University Press, for the critical essay on Sibelius by Cecil Gray, from *Sibelius*, London, 1931; for Vaughan Williams' artistic statement, from *Music and Nationalism*, by Vaughan Williams, New York, 1924.

Pantheon, for the artistic statement of Manuel de Falla from *Composers on Music*, edited by Sam Morgenstern, New York, 1956.

The Score (London), for the critical essay on Vaughan Williams by Oliver Neighbour.

Simon and Schuster, for the artistic statement by Stravinsky, from *Stravinsky: an Autobiography*, New York, 1936.

Stanford University Press, for Gershwin's artistic statement, from *American Composers on American Music*, edited by Henry Cowell, Stanford, 1933.

Victor Gollancz, Ltd., for the personal note on Elgar by William H. Reed, from *Elgar as I Knew Him*, London, 1936.

W. W. Norton & Co., for Carlos Chávez' artistic statement, from his book, *Toward a New Music*, New York, 1937.

The personal note on Hindemith by H. H. Stuckenschmidt was translated from the German by Dr. Frederic Ewen. The personal note and critical essay on Pizzetti by Guido M. Gatti were translated from the Italian by S. Hazzard.

INDEX

A NOTE ON THE TYPE

THIS BOOK is set in ELECTRA, a Linotype face designed by the late W. A. Dwiggins (1880–1956). This face cannot be classified as either modern or old-style. It is not based on any historical model, nor does it echo any particular period or style. It avoids the extreme contrasts between thick and thin elements that mark most modern faces, and attempts to give a feeling of fluidity, power, and speed.

Typography and binding based on designs by
W. A. DWIGGINS

47760